Why Do You Need This New Edition?

Whatever your major or interest, the seventh edition of *Reading Culture* offers you a chance to explore how culture organizes everyday social experience and how written and visual texts represent the world and shape our identities as individuals.

- **Over half the readings and images are new** and have been carefully chosen for the insights they provide, for the lively class discussions they can inspire, and for the rich array of topics for writing that they offer. Included are provocative texts like Henry Jenkins' "Why Heather Can't Write," David Itzkoff's "The Shootout over Hidden Meanings in Video Games," Inderpal Gerwal's "Traveling Barbie," and "A More Perfect Union," a speech by Barack Obama.

- **A new opening chapter, "Analyzing Literacy Events,"** with virtually all new readings, offers an opportunity for you to think critically about the writing you have done in the past, in and out of school, and to analyze the range of purposes reading and writing enact.

- Chapter 1's new case study also provides **instruction on how to read critically** by underlining, annotation, exploratory writing, and synthesizing sources, and includes two examples of student papers—a personal essay and an academic essay—that demonstrate how the results of your research on literacy events might be represented.

- **An extensively revised last chapter, "Living in a Transnational World,"** emphasizes the transnational character of contemporary social and cultural life, with readings and images designed to help you make sense of the networks that connect people to multiple communities and identities.

- **"Making Connections,"** a new feature, groups two or three readings together under topics like Geek Culture, Urban Legends, and Off-Shoring the American Dream, and includes study questions that encourage you to think of the readings as a conversation—and to find your own place within that conversation.

- **Redesigned assignments** throughout now include Exploratory Writing to help you come to terms with the readings and images; Class Activities to allow you to work with classmates and deepen your investigation; and three Writing Assignments to offer more flexibility.

- **The Writing Assignments** have been written (or rewritten) to emphasize how to work with the readings as sources for your own writing projects.

Reading Culture

CONTEXTS FOR CRITICAL
READING AND WRITING

Seventh Edition

Diana George
Virginia Tech

John Trimbur
Emerson College

Longman

New York   San Francisco   Boston
London   Toronto   Sydney   Tokyo   Singapore   Madrid
Mexico City   Munich   Paris   Cape Town   Hong Kong   Montreal

Executive Editor: Lynn M. Huddon
Senior Development Editor: Katharine Glynn
Senior Marketing Manager: Sandra McGuire
Senior Supplements Editor: Donna Campion
Production Manager: Ellen MacElree
Project Coordination, Text Design, and Electronic Page Makeup: Electronic Publishing Services Inc., NYC
Cover Designer/Manager: Nancy Danahy
Photo Researcher: Linda Sykes
Manufacturing Buyer: Roy Pickering
Printer and Binder: Courier/Kendallville
Cover Printer: Coral Graphic Services, Inc.

Cover Image: "Outdoor Dining, Bonneville Salt Flats, Utah," © Richard Misrach.
Richard Misrach is an American photographer best known for his pictures of the Southwest in works
such as the *Desert Cantos*. Misrach combines landscape and social-documentary traditions in photographs
that explore the natural beauty of the region and the effects of human intervention.

For permission to use copyrighted material, grateful acknowledgment is made to the copyright holders
on pp. 567–570, which are hereby made part of this copyright page.

Library of Congress Cataloging-in-Publication Data
Reading culture : contexts for critical reading and writing / [edited by] Diana George,
John Trimbur. — 7th ed.
    p. cm.
  Includes bibliographical references and index.
  ISBN-13: 978-0-205-68807-4
  ISBN-10: 0-205-68807-1
  1. College readers. 2. English language—Rhetoric—Problems, exercises, etc. 3. Critical
thinking—Problems, exercises, etc. 4. Academic writing—Problems, exercises, etc. I.
George, Diana, 1948- II. Trimbur, John.
PE1417.R38 2009
808'.0427—dc22   2009015552

Longman
is an imprint of

www.pearsonhighered.com

ISBN-13: 978-0-205-68807-4
ISBN-10:   0-205-68807-1

1 2 3 4 5 6 7 8 9 10—CRK—12 11 10 9

Contents

Generations 48

Schooling   114

Images   194

Style   246

Public Space   280

Storytelling   327

Living in a Transnational World   513

Visual Resources

Alternate Contents

Preface

Every edition of *Reading Culture* has opened with these words from Raymond Williams: "Culture is ordinary; that is where we must start." We start, then, with the world that surrounds us and the experience of everyday life. In *Reading Culture,* we ask students to look at culture as a way of life that organizes social experience and shapes the identities of individuals and groups. We will be using the term *culture* in this textbook to talk about how people make sense of their worlds and about the values, beliefs, and practices in which they invest their energies and allegiances. We want to provide students with reading and writing assignments so they can understand how their familiar ways of life fit into the diverse, mass-mediated, multicultural realities of contemporary America.

Reading Culture assumes that students are already immersed in a wealth of cultural information and that their experiences of everyday life can usefully be brought to attention as material for reflection and deliberation. The reading and writing assignments in *Reading Culture* are designed to promote a critical distancing so that students can begin to observe and evaluate as well as participate in contemporary America. To this end, *Reading Culture* asks students to read in two ways. First we ask students to read carefully and critically the range of writing about culture we have assembled here. We ask them to identify the purposes and assumptions writers bring to the study of culture and the rhetorical patterns they use to enact their aims. Second, we ask students to read the social world around them, to identify the patterns of meaning in the commonplace, and to put into words the familiar experiences of everyday life that often go without saying.

Reading Culture is organized into ten chapters. The first chapter, "Analyzing Literacy Events," introduces students to the study of culture by looking at the way reading and writing are embedded in cultural life and the uses ordinary people make of literacy. The chapter includes readings on literacy, examples of how researchers analyze literacy events, and a sequence of reading and writing activities culminating with an assignment that engages students in analysis.

The chapters that form the main part of *Reading Culture,* as in past editions, are arranged under several broad topics. "Generations" and "Schooling" explore the personal experience of growing up and going to school. "Images," "Style," and "Public Space" emphasize the visual dimension of culture—in the popular media, in design and packaging, and in the way public space is planned, legislated, and used. The next three chapters, "Storytelling," "Work," and "History," investigate narratives Americans tell themselves, the experience of the workplace, and the meaning of the past in contemporary America. The final chapter, "Living in a Transnational World," examines the movement of people, cultures, and languages in an era of globalization.

In each chapter, a Visual Culture section presents strategies for analyzing and interpreting films, photographs, television shows, ads, public health messages, page design, signs in public places, and other forms of visual communication. Many chapters also include Visual Essays that offer students further opportunities to examine visual communication. Most chapters include a Fieldwork section that provides ways of studying culture through interviews, participant observation, questionnaires, oral histories, and other forms of on-site research. Many chapters include as well a Mining the Archives feature that shows how archival research can be integrated into a course that uses *Reading Culture*.

Reading Culture is designed to be used flexibly and creatively. Instructors may wish to ask students to work on the chapters in *Reading Culture* as they are arranged, but this is only one possible order.

New to the Seventh Edition

This seventh edition includes new and expanded features to help students investigate contemporary and past cultures. These additions come in large part from discussions we've had with writing teachers who have used previous editions of *Reading Culture*.

- **New Opening Chapter:** "Analyzing Literacy Events." *Reading Culture* has always opened with a case study, and in response to teacher's interests, we have redesigned the case study to focus in this edition on the examination of reading and writing in students' and others' lives. This chapter provides a way for students to think critically about the writing they have done in the past, in and out of school, and to analyze the range of purposes reading and writing enact. The case study includes instruction on underlining, annotation, exploratory writing, and synthesizing sources, along with two examples of student papers—a personal essay and an academic essay—that demonstrate how the results of students' research on literacy events might be represented.

- **Revised Final Chapter:** "Life in a Transnational World." Chapter 10 has been revised—and accordingly renamed—to emphasize the transnational character of contemporary social and cultural life in an era of globalization. The chapter provides students with opportunities to make sense of how transnational networks connect people to multiple communities and identities and how crossings in music, art, writing, visual style, and ordinary speech have created hybrid forms of expression and new social solidarities.

- **New Making Connections Feature:** This new feature groups two or three readings together and includes an Assignment Sequence that calls on students to work with readings to stage a conversation and to find their own place within it. Each sequence typically asks students to do exploratory writing, to synthesize the readings, and to write a culminating essay.

- **Redesigned Writing Assignments.** The assignments that follow each reading have been redesigned in two ways. First, they have been sequenced to enhance their pedagogical value by beginning with an Exploratory Writing prompt, then setting up a Class Activity; and finally presenting Writing Assignments that give students and teachers choices. Second, the Writing Assignments have been structured to emphasize how students might work with the writings as sources to incorporate into their own writing projects.

The seventh edition of *Reading Culture* offers opportunities extending across chapters to work with visual communication, literacy events, and microethnography. The work you do with this text will, however, depend on your needs and your students' interests. We think that with this edition, *Reading Culture* has become a more flexible resource for teaching writing and critical reading and for asking students to write about, and in the culture of, contemporary America.

Additional Teaching Resources

- **The Instructor's Manual** (0-205-68810-1) for *Reading Culture* provides a wealth of resources for instructors wishing to extend their students' investigations on any of the chapter topics or individual readings.

- **The MyCompLab Website** integrates the market-leading instruction, multimedia tutorials, and exercises for writing, grammar, and research that users have come to identify with the program with a new online composing space and new assessment tools. The result is a revolutionary application that offers a seamless and flexible teaching and learning environment built specifically for writers. Created after years of extensive research and in partnership with composition faculty and students across the country, the new MyCompLab provides help for writers in the context of their writing, enables instructor and peer commenting, and includes proven tutorials and exercises for writing, grammar, and research. Other features are an e-portfolio, an assignment-builder, a bibliography tool, tutoring services, and a gradebook and course management organization created specifically for writing classes. MyCompLab can be packaged with this textbook at no additional cost. Visit www.mycomplab.com for more information.

Acknowledgments

There are a number of people we want to thank for their insight and advice. Lynn Huddon and Katharine Glynn provided the editorial support for this edition. We appreciate as well the careful readings we received by reviewers of this book: Lena Ampadu, Towson University; David Bordelon, Ocean County College; Stephanie L. Dowdle, Salt Lake Community College; Africa Fine, Palm Beach Community College; Tim Giles, Georgia Southern University; Janele D. Johnson, Pikes Peak Community College; Karissa McCoy, Georgia Institute of Technology; and Marie Trevino, Lansing Community College.

We want to thank the teachers who have used the first six editions of *Reading Culture*. The feedback, suggestions, and insights they have offered us over the years have enabled us to see the book in new ways and to plan the seventh edition with their ideas in mind. Lauren Goldstein provided invaluable research assistance. We thank the students at Virginia Tech and Emerson College who have used *Reading Culture* and the graduate students and instructors who have worked with it, designing assignments, activities, and projects. In *Reading Culture,* they recognized themselves, their peers, and the rich challenge of what it means to live in the United States. This is the best confirmation of our intentions that we could possibly receive, and it lets us know that the cultural resources we are seeking to tap are vitally important to students and teachers in contemporary America.

We dedicate this book to the late Jim Berlin, whose work challenged a generation of teachers and students to turn their attention to the small things of everyday life—those ways of living and communicating that constitute a culture.

Diana George

John Trimbur

Introduction

culture: education, enrichment, erudition, learning, wisdom, breeding, gentility, civilization, colony, community, crowd, folks, group, settlement, society, staff, tribe, background, development, environment, experience, past, schooling, training, upbringing, customs, habits, mores, traditions.

Culture is ordinary; that is where we must start.

—Raymond Williams

The British cultural historian Raymond Williams has written that culture "is one of the two or three most complicated words in the English language." This is so, Williams explains, because the term *culture* has acquired new meanings over time without losing the older meanings along the way. Therefore, writers sometimes use the term *culture* in quite different and incompatible ways. Even a simple list of synonyms, such as the one that opens this chapter, can illustrate the truth of Williams's observation.

For some, culture refers to great art in the European tradition—Beethoven's symphonies, Shakespeare's plays, Picasso's paintings, or Jane Austen's novels. *Culture* in that tradition refers to something that you read; something that you see in a museum, art gallery, or theater; or something that you hear in a concert hall. It is often called "high culture" and is closely linked to the idea of *becoming* cultured—of cultivating good taste and discriminating judgment. A cultured person, according to this sense of the term, is someone who has achieved a certain level of refinement and class.

Those who equate culture with high art would most likely think, for example, that rock musicians like Jimi Hendrix and Nirvana or pop stars like Marilyn Monroe or Madonna do not belong in the domain of culture. They would not include popular entertainment like *The Daily Show, The Dark Knight,* the latest graphic novel, or NASCAR stock car racing in that category either. In making a distinction between high and low art, this view of culture is largely interested in the classics and in holding what might be considered "serious" art separate from popular culture.

Others, however, take an alternative approach to the study of culture. Instead of separating high from low art, they think of culture in more inclusive terms. For them, culture refers not only to the literary and artistic works that critics have called masterpieces but also to the way of life that characterizes a particular group of people at a particular time. Developed since the turn of the twentieth century by anthropologists, though it has now spread into common use, this approach to culture offers a way to think about how individuals and groups organize and make sense of their social experience—at home, in school, at work, and at play.

Culture in this broader view includes all the social institutions, patterns of behavior, systems of belief, and kinds of popular entertainment that create the social world we live in. Taken this way, *culture* means not simply masterpieces of art, music, and literature, but lived experience—what goes on in the everyday lives of individuals and groups.

Reading Culture explores the interpretation of contemporary culture and how cultural ideas and ideals are communicated. When we use the term *culture* in this book, we are using a definition that is much closer to the second definition than to the first. The distinction between high and low art is indeed an important one but not because high art is necessarily better or more "cultured" than popular entertainment. What interests us, instead, is how the two terms are used in an ongoing debate about the meaning of contemporary culture in the United States—about, say, what languages should be taught in the schools, about the way media interpret daily events, or about the quality of popular tastes. We will ask you to explore these issues in the following chapters to see how arguments over media or schooling or national identity tell stories of contemporary U.S. culture.

In short, the purpose of this book is not to bring you culture or to make you cultured but to invite you to become more aware of the culture you are already living. According to the way we will be using the term, culture is not something you can go out and get. Rather, culture means all the familiar pursuits and pleasures that shape people's identities and that enable and constrain what they do and what they might become. Our idea is to treat contemporary American culture as a research project—to understand its ways of life from the inside as we live and observe them.

The following chapters offer opportunities to read, research, and write about contemporary culture. The reading selections present writers who have explored central facets of culture and who offer information and ideas for you to draw on as you do your own work of reading and writing about culture. Each chapter raises a series of questions about how culture organizes social experience and how individuals understand the meaning and purpose of their daily lives.

In these chapters, we will be asking you to think about how the writers find patterns in culture and how they position themselves in relation to contemporary cultural realities. We will be asking you to read not only to understand what the writers are saying but also to identify what assumptions they are making about cultural issues such as schooling, the media, or national identity. We also will be asking you to do another kind of reading, where the text is not the printed word but the experience of everyday life. We will be asking you to read culture—to read the social world around you, at home and in classrooms, at work and at play, in visual images and public places.

Reading a culture means finding patterns in the familiar. In many respects, of course, you are already a skilled reader of culture. Think of all the reading that you do in the course of a day. You read not only the textbooks assigned in your courses or the books and magazines you turn to for pleasure. You probably read a variety of other "texts" without thinking about what you are actually reading. You read the logos on clothes people wear, the cars they drive, and the houses they live in. As you read these texts, you might make guesses about people's social status or about how you will relate to them. You read the way social experience is organized on your campus to determine who your friends will be, who the jocks are, where the geeks hang out.

You read all kinds of visual images in the media not only for the products advertised or the entertainment offered but for the lifestyles that are proposed as attractive and desirable. Most of your reading takes place as you move through the day, and it often takes place below the threshold of consciousness. Often, people just take this kind of reading for granted.

To read culture means *not* taking that reading for granted. Reading culture means bringing forward for analysis and reflection those commonplace aspects of everyday life that people normally think of as simply being there, a part of the natural order of things. Most likely you do some of that kind of reading when you stop to think through an ad or a history lesson or anything that makes you connect what you are seeing or reading with other ideas coming your way every day. Very likely, you do not accept without question all that you see and read. You probably turn a skeptical eye to much of it. Still, to read culture you will have to be more consistent as you learn to bring the familiar back into view so that you can begin to understand how people organize and make sense of their lives. To read the world in this way is to see that culture is not simply passed down from generation to generation in a fixed form but rather is a way of life through which individuals and groups are constantly making their own meanings in the contemporary world.

We are all influenced by what cultural critics call mainstream culture, whether we feel part of it or not. Everyone in the United States, to one extent or another (and whether they embrace or reject America's tenets), is shaped by what is sometimes called the "American way of life" and the value that it claims to place on hard work, fair play, individual success, romantic love, family ties, and patriotism. This is, undoubtedly, the most mass-mediated culture in human history, and it is virtually impossible to avoid the dominant images of America past and present—whether of the Pilgrims gathered at that mythic scene of the first Thanksgiving or of retired pro football players in a Miller Lite commercial.

Yet for all the power of the "American way of life" as it is presented by schools, the mass media, and the culture industry, U.S. culture is hardly monolithic or homogeneous. The culture in which Americans live is a diverse one, divided along the lines of race, class, gender, language, ethnicity, age, occupation, region, politics, economics, religion, and more. Ours is a multicultural society, and in part because of that diversity, contemporary culture is constantly changing, constantly in flux. To read culture, therefore, is to see not only how its dominant cultural expressions shape people but also how individuals and groups shape culture—how their responses to and interpretations of contemporary life rewrite its meanings according to their own purposes, interests, and aspirations.

Getting Started

In what follows, we have gathered a number of what might be considered key statements about and definitions of culture. As you can see from these brief selections, the concept of culture is a contested one.

EXPLORATORY WRITING

Begin your investigations of culture by reading through the passages reprinted here. When you have finished reading, write for 10 minutes about what, according to these writers, the term *culture* means. Use the following questions to help direct this initial exploratory writing:

- What does each individual statement claim about culture?
- How do they differ?

- What do they have in common?
- Which of these statements or definitions comes closest to your own understanding of culture? Why?

MATTHEW ARNOLD, FROM *CULTURE AND ANARCHY* (1869)

But there is of culture another view, in which not solely the scientific passion, the sheer desire to see things as they are, natural and proper in an intelligent being, appears as the ground of it. There is a view in which all the love of our neighbour, the impulses towards action, help, and beneficence, the desire for removing human error, clearing human confusion, and diminishing human misery, the noble aspiration to leave the world better and happier than we found it,—motives eminently such as are called social,—come in as part of the grounds of culture, and the main and pre-eminent part. Culture is then properly described not as having its origin in curiosity, but as having its origin in the love of perfection; it is a study of perfection. It moves by the force, not merely or primarily of the scientific passion for pure knowledge, but also of the moral and social passion for doing good. As, in the first view of it, we took for its worthy motto Montesquieu's words: "To render an intelligent being yet more intelligent!" so, in the second view of it, there is no better motto which it can have than these words of Bishop Wilson: "To make reason and the will of God prevail!"

MATTHEW ARNOLD, FROM THE PREFACE TO *LITERATURE AND DOGMA* (1873)

Culture is to know the best that has been said and thought in the world.

RAYMOND WILLIAMS, FROM "CULTURE IS ORDINARY" (1958)

Culture is ordinary: that is the first fact. Every human society has its own shape, its own purposes, its own meanings. Every human society expresses these, in institutions, and in arts and learning. The making of a society is the finding of common meanings and directions, and its growth is an active debate and amendment under the pressures of experience, contact, and discovery, writing themselves into the land. The growing society is there, yet it is also made and remade in every individual mind. . . . A culture has two aspects: the known meanings and directions, which its members are trained to; the new observations and meanings, which are offered and tested. These are the ordinary processes of human societies and human minds, and we see through them the nature of a culture: that it is always both traditional and creative; that it is both the most ordinary common meanings and the finest individual meanings. We use the word culture in these two senses: to mean a whole way of life—the common meanings; to mean the arts and learning—the special processes of discovery and creative effort. Some writers reserve the word for one or other of these senses; I insist on both, and on the significance of their conjunction. . . . Culture is ordinary, in every society and in every mind.

AIMÉ CÉSAIR, MARTINIQUE WRITER SPEAKING TO THE WORLD CONGRESS OF BLACK WRITERS AND ARTISTS IN PARIS (1959)

Culture is everything. Culture is the way we dress, the way we carry our heads, the way we walk, the way we tie our ties—it is not only the fact of writing books or building houses.

CLIFFORD GEERTZ, FROM *INTERPRETATION OF CULTURE* (1973)

The concept of culture I espouse . . . is essentially a semiotic one. Believing, with Max Weber, that man is an animal suspended in webs of significance he himself has spun, I take culture to be those webs, and the analysis of it to be therefore not an experimental science in search of law but an interpretative one in search of meaning.

E. D. HIRSCH, FROM *THE DICTIONARY OF CULTURAL LITERACY* (2002)

[C]ultural literacy is not knowledge of current events, although it can help us understand those events as they occur. To become part of cultural literacy, an item must have lasting significance. . . . This rule of lasting significance tended to eliminate certain fields altogether, or nearly so. For example, our collective memory of most of the people and events in the fields of sports and entertainment is too ephemeral to take a permanent place in our cultural heritage.

ANDREI CODRESCU, FROM "WHAT IS CULTURE?" (BESTOFNEWORLEANS.COM, APRIL 3, 2007)

The purpose of the word "culture" these days is to express something large and unwieldy that nonetheless has some common features. It's shorthand for atmosphere, only instead of vapor and clouds, it's made of thoughts, ideas, people and operating procedures. . . .

The word "culture" has either a positive or negative sense depending on what you already think about the thing it qualifies. The "culture of New Orleans" generally means good things: music, food, easy-going people, street festivals. It is invoked to bring business and tourists to the city. There is, no doubt, a real culture at the origin of this bloated gumbo, but that culture is not so easily described. For one thing, culture is poverty: the expression of people who can't afford the ready-made. Most Americans appreciate such a thing only if it comes packaged as a ready-made. Live culture, in New Orleans or anywhere else, is difficult to package because it is an evolving artistic activity whose purpose is to undo such generalities as the "culture of . . ." In other words, most of what marketers, journalists and academics call "culture" is not.

SUGGESTED ASSIGNMENT

Work together with a group of classmates. Share the exploratory writing you each did in response to these passages about culture. As a group, first discuss how these statements differ, what they have in common, and what each adds to the others.

When you have completed your discussion, write your own statement on what culture is and what it means to be "cultured" today. In your statement, draw on any or all of the statements reprinted here to identify which statements come closest to your own understanding and which you and your group members would take issue with.

A Guide to Visual Analysis: Images, Film, and Web Sites

Throughout *Reading Culture,* you will be asked to analyze visual texts of all sorts. The following brief guide is designed to introduce some of the questions you can begin with. It will also help you locate various tools of visual analysis that appear in *Reading Culture*.

Reading Images

Most of the images you will be asked to examine are still images—photographs, advertisements, logos, graphic novels, comics, and so on. As with the 1936 Dorothea Lange documentary photograph of Florence Thompson (often called *Migrant Madonna*) reprinted here, the way you analyze a still image depends very much on the questions you ask.

Dorothea Lange, "Florence Thompson, 1936."

- What do you see in the photo? What details do you notice first? Who are these people?

- What does the photograph seem to be about?

- How do you respond to the image? Does it remind you of anything you have seen before?

- What is the medium (photography, digital image, painting, drawing, etc.)?

- What kind (*genre*) of image is it (documentary photo, publicity photo, family snapshot, news photo, etc.)?

- Who took the photo and for what purpose? Where can you find out about the photographer and her career?

- When was it made? What do you know about the historical background?

- Who is the intended audience for the image?

- How are the people in the image arranged and what relationships are indicated by the arrangement?

- What is the relationship between the people in the photograph and the viewer? How would that relationship change if the woman were looking at the camera instead of away from it?

◼ How would the meaning change if you saw the photograph in the following settings:

A family album?

A history book?

A poster about hunger in America?

A news story?

An advertisement for antidepressants?

Resources for Reading Images

Visual analysis is the process of explaining how an image works, so it is important to keep in mind the tools useful for performing that analysis. While Chapter 4, Images, offers a good introduction to visual analysis—especially to reading print advertisements—you will find resources for analyzing the visual throughout *Reading Culture*.

Composition

Visual composition usually refers to how elements of an image are arranged within the space or frame and how that visual design conveys meaning and sets up a relationship with the viewer or reader.

◼ *page layout*—arrangement of elements on the page; this includes attention to the text-to-graphics ratio, use of color, choice of font size and style (in Chapter 1, see the section "Words, Images, and the Design of the Page," p. 21).

◼ *vectors*—arrangement of subjects or elements that set up or complete a story or action and establish relationships among elements in the image (in Chapter 3, see the section "Picturing Schooldays," pp. 181–185).

◼ *perspective*—angle of vision; also, a technique for representing three-dimensional objects and depth relationships in a two-dimensional space to give the appearance of depth; how camera angle establishes a point of view (in Chapter 3, see the section "Picturing Schooldays," pp. 181–185).

◼ *the gaze*—the direction in which a subject looks at or away from the viewer, creating either an *offer* (offering the subject to the viewer to be looked at) or a *demand* (engaging the viewer in a direct way); common term in visual analysis of gender (in Chapter 4, see "Reading the Gaze: Gender Roles in Advertising," pp. 220–224).

Genre Analysis

Genres are familiar acts of communication that take place across a broad range of media. Genre analysis examines a visual in terms of how it conforms to or breaks with various genres of visual representation. Documentary photography, news photos, and landscape paintings, for example, are different visual types or genres that carry with them the expectations and forms of their type. Genres featured in *Reading Culture* for visual analysis include,

◼ *documentary photography*—see "Photographic Icons," pp. 230–236 (Chapter 4); "Camera of Dirt," pp. 421–427 (Chapter 8); "American Photographs," pp. 452–456 (Chapter 9).

- *news photography*—see "Representations of War," p. 501 (Chapter 9).
- *landscape photography*—see "The Troubled Landscape," p. 316 (Chapter 6).
- *glamour photography/publicity shots*—see "Hollywood Stars: Brando, Dean, and Monroe," pp. 104–106 (Chapter 2).
- *print advertising*—see Chapter 4, especially "Suggestions for Reading Advertising," pp. 206–207.
- *publicity campaign posters*—see "Literacy Campaign Posters," p. 17 (Chapter 1); "Public Health Messages," pp. 225–227 (Chapter 4); "Transnational Solidarity," p. 560 (Chapter 10).
- *graphic narrative/comics*—see "The Veil," an autobiographical graphic novel, p. 370 (Chapter 7).
- *performance art*—see Coco Fusco and Guillermo Gómez-Peña, p. 549 (Chapter 10).
- *charts and diagrams/information design*—see "Talk is the thing," p. 31 (Chapter 1); "Classroom Observation," p. 187 (Chapter 3); "Geek Love," p. 268 (Chapter 5); "Reconstructing the Network of a Workplace," p. 428 (Chapter 8).
- *page design*—"Words, Images, and the Design of the Page," p. 21 (Chapter 1).
- *college viewbooks*—see "Analyzing College Viewbooks," p. 136 (Chapter 3).
- *logos*—see "Graphic Design in Rock Culture," p. 251; and "Race and Branding," p. 278 (Chapter 5).
- *product design*—see "The Aura," p. 272 (Chapter 5).
- *packaging*—see "Reading Labels, Selling Water," p. 274 (Chapter 5).

Analyzing Visual Representations

In visual theory, *representation* is a term that refers to how cultural ideas, ideals, and attitudes are popularized and presented visually. See "Representations of Youth Culture in Movies," p. 98 (Chapter 2), for a good brief overview of cultural representation in visual media.

- *images of gender*—an examination of how women and men are treated visually. See "Reading the Gaze: Gender Roles in Advertising," pp. 220–227 (Chapter 4); "When You Meet Estella Smart, You Been Met!" pp. 201–206 (Chapter 4); "Advertising Through the Ages," p. 245 (Chapter 4); "The Veil," p. 370 (Chapter 7).
- *images of difference*—an examination of how difference—racial, ethnic, economic, etc.—is treated visually; sometimes called the process of "othering." See "Race and Branding," p. 278 (Chapter 5); Warren Neidich, Contra Curtis: Early American Cover-Ups," p. 473 (Chapter 9); Coco Fusco and Guillermo Gómez-Peña, p. 549 (Chapter 10); Samuel Fosso, "Le chef qui a vendu l'Afrique aux colons," p. 550 (Chapter 10); "Nineteenth-Century Orientalism," p. 564 (Chapter 10).

Historical Analysis

Though historical analysis can refer to the history of the image itself or to the history of the technology that is used to create an image (glass plate, film, and digital technology are all a part of the history of photography), in *Reading Culture,* historical analysis refers to an examination of the relation of an image to historical events (what the image can tell viewers about those events as well as the role it might have played in events) and to public memory of the past (how images are selected to represent the past and what this selection can tell us about the present).

- See "Lewis Hine and the Social Uses of Photography," p. 435 (Chapter 8), a discussion of documentary photography and its relationship to social movements.
- See "Contra Curtis: Early American Cover-Ups," p. 473 (Chapter 9), rereading history by using original photographs and photographic technology as the basis for telling a different story; "reinventing" history.
- See "Reading American Photographs," p. 451 (Chapter 9), an examination of the role of photography in establishing a collective memory of history; making meaning from the "uncoded message" that is the photographic image; how readers create historical accounts from the photographic image.

Visual Parody/Satire

Visual parody and satire overturns or overwrites the original image as a commentary on the original message or the politics of the image. Parody begins with analysis—to understand what the original is saying and how it conveys that message in order to rewrite or satirize the original message.

- See "Rewriting the Image," pp. 237–241 (Chapter 4), rewriting advertising; visual parody.
- See "Contra Curtis: Early American Cover-Ups," p. 473 (Chapter 9), rewriting/reinventing history using original technology—platinum prints—to bring to mind the original images and reveal the politics unspoken in those original prints.
- See Coco Fusco and Guillermo Gómez-Peña, "Two Undiscovered Amerindians Visit the West," p. 549 (Chapter 10), performance art that uses references to stereotypes and mainstream history as political commentary.

Reading Film

Film adds elements of movement, camera work, lighting, design, storyline, and sound to visual. Notice, however, that many of the questions you will begin with are similar to those you would ask about still images.

- What is your first impression of the film?
- What is it about? (What is the storyline? Who are the characters?)
- Who are the actors? Do they influence your response? Did they influence whether you wanted to see the film or not?

- Is it a Hollywood movie or an independent production? Is it a network or cable production?
- Who directed the film? Do you know of other films by this director? Is this one similar to those others?
- When was the film made? If it is an older film, what do you know about that period?
- What kind (genre) of film or program is it (documentary, drama, comedy, action/adventure, fantasy, feature-length animation, etc.)? How do you know?
- How does lighting contribute to the way you read this film? Is it brightly lit? Dark and grainy? Idealistic? Brooding?
- What do you notice about camera work? Does the camera move like a handheld camera might, to give the impression of walking or running with a character? Does the camera stay at a distance? When do you see close-ups? What characters or objects are at the center or in the foreground of the camera frame?
- How does costuming and makeup contribute to the way you read this film or respond to the characters?
- How would you describe the set design? Does it look like a town, city, or landscape you recognize? Is it a fantasy setting?
- Is the film a remake of a novel, play, short story, graphic novel, or video game that you know well? How does your knowledge of the original influence your reading of the film?

You will find a good introduction to writing about film (reviews, history, and criticism) in "Film Clip: Reading and Writing About Film," p. 186 (Chapter 3). For a list of terms useful for writing about film, see "Camera Work and Editing: Some Useful Terms," p. 243 (Chapter 4). Additional resources on film (as well as television) analysis are listed below:

Resources for Film and Television Analysis

Camera Work and Editing

A focus on camera work and editing means examining how a film is shot, how the camera is used, and the way those shots are then assembled and sequenced to create a storyline.

- See "Camera Work: Screening the Gaze," pp. 241–242 (Chapter 4);
- "Camera Work and Editing: Some Useful Terms," p. 243 (Chapter 4)

Genres

As with still images, films can be grouped into genres that have characteristic features and recognizable conventions.

- See "The Gangster as Tragic Hero," p. 360 (Chapter 7), an analysis of the gangster film genre as a story of outlaw heroes.
- See "Documentary Film and the Narrator," p. 427 (Chapter 8), a discussion of point of view and the convention of the voice-over narrative in film documentary.

- See "Film Genres: The Western," p. 506 (Chapter 9), an examination of the formula western as an expression of the mythology of westward expansion and the cowboy hero.
- See "Bollywood," p. 560 (Chapter 10), a discussion of the film industry in India and the extravaganza productions of Bollywood.

Film Representations

Film representation analysis is an examination of the way film representations are filtered through cultural codes and ideals.

- See "Representations of Youth Culture in Movies," pp. 99–104 (Chapter 2), an examination of the ways youth, especially juvenile delinquency, has been represented in film.
- See "Hollywood Stars: Brando, Dean, and Monroe," pp. 104–106 (Chapter 2), an exploration of the iconic power of Hollywood stars.

Design

Design analysis is an examination of elements that give a film or television program a specific look.

- See "Makeup and Costumes: Monsters and the Middle Ages," p. 277 (Chapter 5), an examination of how makeup and costuming account for the look of a film, with a focus on monster movies and period films.
- See "Analyzing Set Design: Cities in Decay," p. 321 (Chapter 6), an examination of the film set design as a crucial component in conveying meaning, tone, and symbol, with a focus on dystopia.

The Script

The script is the text used for making a film. An analysis of script can lead to content and audience analysis or to an examination of how the script translates or interprets an original text.

- See "The Art of Adaptation," p. 379 (Chapter 7), a discussion of the film adaptation as an interpretation of other genres like novels, short stories, graphic novels, and video games.

Reading Web Sites

One of the attractions of the World Wide Web is that anyone with an Internet connection and some technical knowledge can put up a site. There is little question that, despite the growing commercialization of the Web, it still provides broad access to the means of communication and a new forum for discussion and debate. At the same time, it is also important to understand that the information and perspectives that show up on the Web are largely unregulated—they can range from the thoroughly reliable to the utterly crackpot. That's part of the creative and chaotic anarchy of the Web that makes it so interesting and so much fun. But it also means that

Web users need to learn to read in a new way, so they can assess the various sites they visit—to identify who put up a site, what its purposes are, and what can be expected from it in terms of the reliability of the information and ideas it contains.

What to Look For on a Web Site

Though there is great variation among Web site designs, several standard features have emerged that users come to expect when they get to a site:

URL

The header at the top of your screen gives you the Web page address, or URL (Uniform Resource Locator). You can find out a good deal about a Web site from the URL alone. Take, for example, the URL for Journalism.org, from the Columbia School of Journalism Graduate School's Project for Excellence in Journalism and the Pew Charitable Trust: http://www.journalism.org.

The URL of the main page offers the host name www.journalism.org, which identifies where the page is located (Web), the name of the organization that owns the site (Journalism.org), and the domain (org).

Domain names identify the kinds of organizations that sponsor Web sites: ".edu" refers to educational institutions, ".org" to nonprofit organizations, ".gov" to government agencies, ".mil" to the military, and ".com" and ".net" to commercial enterprises.

If you click on a story link at the Journalism.org site, you will get an address that looks like this:

http://www.journalism.org/resources/briefing/default.asp

The second half of that address (resources/briefing/default.asp) identifies the file path—the path that takes you to the page you want to read. In this case, the path leads first to the Resources page and from there to the Daily Briefing page.

Organizational Logo and Title

Web pages often feature an organization's logo or a common header at the top of each page. This feature helps to unify a Web site visually and to identify the sponsoring organization from page to page. It is often more difficult to locate where you are on a site that does not repeat the logo or header on each page.

Links

Links appear as text or graphics to help you navigate from place to place, both within a particular Web site and to Web pages at other sites. They may appear at the top or bottom of the page or both places. Wherever they appear, links offer clues about the purpose of the site—they indicate the range and type of information and opinion the Web site considers relevant.

Signature and Credits

Signatures give the name and often the e-mail address of the person who maintains the Web page, information on when the Web page was established, when it was last updated, those who have contributed to it, and sometimes a postal address and phone number for the person or organization responsible for the site. Often this information is on the home page.

Advertising

As the Web becomes increasingly commercialized, more and more advertising appears. The type of products and services advertised can help give you a sense of the kind of Web site you are visiting, much as you can draw some inferences about how magazines see themselves and their readers from their ads. The absence of advertising can also offer you information on how the organization or institution wants to relate to its readers.

What Can You Do at the Site?

The possibilities that a Web site offers readers can give you further information to assess the site. Some, such as journalism.org, offer a number of reports, links to other sites covering media issues, and information about the organizations responsible for the site. Some sites invite you to sign a guest book, send e-mail, fill out surveys, enter contests, watch animation and videos, listen to music, or take part in message-board discussions. Commercial sites, of course, want you to buy something. Consider whether the Web site you are visiting provides you with choices about where you can go and whether it invites you to participate interactively. What purpose do these possibilities serve? What kind of relationship does the site seem to want to establish with people who visit it?

Analyzing Literacy Events

A literacy event is any occasion in which
a piece of writing is integral to the nature
of participants' interactions and their
interpretive processes.

—Shirley Brice Heath

Photo courtesy the Library of Congress.

*R*eading Culture always begins with a case study. In this edition, the opening
chapter "Analyzing Literacy Events" involves research and analysis of how
people use reading and writing and the purposes literacy serves in their lives.
The chapter is meant to raise questions for you to investigate by reading what others have written about the uses of literacy and by examining your own experience.

You'll be asked to identify situations in which reading and writing take place—in your own and others' lives—and to think about the forms that literacy takes, the role it plays in social interactions, and the cultural meanings given to it.

One place reading and writing happens, of course, is in the classroom. But we don't want to limit the meaning of literacy to just a school subject. We want to look as well at those occasions outside of educational settings, where people use reading and writing for their own reasons—whether to communicate with friends and family, organize work and play, influence public life, or create new group and individual identities. Accordingly, this chapter asks you to consider the various and wide-ranging forms literacy can take, such as text messaging your roommate, keeping a "to do" list, filling out a job application, reading a safety manual, signing a petition, making a poster, writing a blog, spray painting graffiti, and so forth.

In the opening section, we put this investigation of literacy in context by looking at some of the meanings that have accumulated around the term *literacy* and at the much heralded shift that's currently taking place from "page to screen"—from the print culture of the past 500 years to the age of digital media that's emerged in the last twenty years.

With this as background, we turn to the central work of the chapter: identifying and analyzing acts of reading and writing and what they can tell us about the nature of cultural experience. You'll be asked to recall, think, and write about your own experiences with reading and writing, not so much as the acquisition of skills but as cultural moments whose meanings you can unlock. And in this sense, like the case studies in previous editions of *Reading Culture,* "Analyzing Literacy Events" is meant to serve as an introduction to the investigation of culture.

What Is Literacy?

There are too many layers of meaning, deposited over time by changes in how writing is produced and used, for the term *literacy* to have a single definition that captures its true essence. That's why, as you'll see in these excerpts from her article "Literacy in Three Metaphors," which appeared in the *American Journal of Education* in 1984, Sylvia Scribner turns to metaphor to examine, in her words, "differing points of view about the central meaning of literacy" and their enabling assumptions.

LITERACY IN THREE METAPHORS

██— *Sylvia Scribner*

Sylvia Scribner (1923–1991) was a psychologist and literacy researcher at the City University of New York. Her works include *The Psychology of Literacy* (1981), with Michael Cole as coauthor.

SUGGESTION FOR READING Before reading, write for 5 minutes in response to the question "What is literacy?" When you're finished reading, consider how what you've written fits (or doesn't) with Scribner's three metaphors of literacy.

LITERACY AS ADAPTATION

1 This metaphor is designed to capture concepts of literacy that emphasize its survival or pragmatic value. When the term "functional literacy" was originally introduced during World War I, it specified the literacy skills required to meet the tasks of modern soldiering. Today, functional literacy is conceived broadly as the level of proficiency necessary for effective performance in a range of settings and customary activities.

This concept has a strong commonsense appeal. The necessity for literacy skills in daily life is obvious: on the job, riding around town, shopping for groceries, we all encounter situations requiring us to read or produce written symbols. No justification is needed to insist that schools are obligated to equip children with literacy skills that will enable them to fulfill these mundane situational demands. And basic educational programs have a similar obligation to equip adults with the skills they must have to secure jobs or advance to better ones, receive the training and benefits to which they are entitled, and assume their civic and political responsibilities. Within the United States, as in other nations, literacy programs with these practical aims are considered efforts at human resource development and, as such, contributors to economic growth and stability.

LITERACY AS POWER

While functional literacy stresses the importance of literacy to the adaptation of the individual, the literacy-as-power metaphor emphasizes a relationship between literacy and group or community advancement.

Historically, literacy has been a potent tool in maintaining the hegemony of elites and dominant classes in certain societies, while laying the basis for increased social and political participation in others. In a contemporary framework, expansion of literacy skills is often viewed as a means for poor and politically powerless groups to claim their place in the world. The International Symposium for Literacy, meeting in Persepolis, Iran (1976), appealed to national governments to consider literacy as an instrument for human liberation and social change. Paolo Freire bases his influential theory of literacy education on the need to make literacy a resource for fundamental social transformation. Effective literacy education, in his view, creates a critical consciousness through which a community can analyze its conditions of social existence and engage in effective action for a just society. Not to be literate is a state of victimization.

LITERACY AS A STATE OF GRACE

5 Now we come to the third metaphor. I have variously called it literacy as salvation and literacy as a state of grace. Both labels are unsatisfactory because they give a specific religious interpretation to the broad phenomenon I want to depict—that is, the tendency in many societies to endow the literate person with special virtues. A concern with preserving and understanding scripture is at the core of many religious traditions. As studies by Resnick and Resnick have shown, the literacy-as-salvation metaphor had an almost literal interpretation in the practice of post-Luther Protestant groups to require of the faithful the ability to read and remember the Bible and other religious material. Older religious traditions—Hebraic and Islamic—have also traditionally invested the written word with great power and respect. "This is a perfect book. There is no doubt in it," reads a passage from the Qur'an. Memorizing the Qur'an—literally taking its words into you and making them part of yourself—is simultaneously a process of becoming both literate and holy.

The attribution of special powers to those who are literate has its ancient secular roots as well. Plato and Aristotle strove to distinguish the man of letters from the poet of the oral tradition. In the perspective of Western humanism, literateness has come to be considered synonymous with being "cultured," using the term in the old-fashioned sense to refer to a person who is knowledgeable about the content and techniques of the sciences, arts, and humanities as they have evolved historically. The term sounds elitist and archaic, but the notion that participation in a literate—that is, bookish—tradition enlarges and develops a person's essential self is pervasive and still undergirds the concept of a liberal education. In the literacy-as-state-of-grace con-

cept, the power and functionality of literacy is not bounded by political or economic perameters but in a sense transcends them; the literate individual's life derives its meaning and significance from intellectual, aesthetic, and spiritual participation in the accumulated creations and knowledge of humankind, made available through the written word.

TALKING ABOUT THE READING

Come to class with one instance of reading or writing that you think fits each of Sylvia Scribner's three metaphors. Work in a group of three or four. Share the examples of each metaphor. Consider how they illustrate what Scribner is trying to capture about literacy in her metaphors. Pick one example for each metaphor to present to class. Compare your results with other groups. What do Scribner's metaphors bring to light about the examples? Do the metaphors sometimes overlap? Are there things about literacy in the examples that the metaphors don't account for?

VISUAL ESSAY   Literacy Campaign Posters

At least 2,000 posters were made by graphic designers during Franklin Delano Roosevelt's New Deal, 1936–1943, under the Works Progress Administration (WPA), a federal project to put unemployed Americans, including artists, writers, and musicians, back to work. WPA poster makers used silkscreen, lithograph, and woodcut to promote health and safety, travel and tourism, cultural events, community activities, and educational programs.

The three posters in this chapter come from literacy campaigns and library programs in New York and Chicago. The poster "Books Are Weapons" at the beginning of the chapter, designed for WPA War Services, 1941–1943, publicizes the holdings of the Schomberg Collection in the New York Public Library and encourages people to learn more about African and African American history and culture. The first of the two posters shown here, "Free Classes in English," which uses Yiddish and the Star of David to promote English language programs geared to non-English-speaking Jews, was created for the New York City Board of Education's Adult Education Program. The second, "Read the Books You've Always Meant to Read," was created by WPA artists in Chicago for a statewide library program.

TALKING ABOUT LITERACY POSTERS

What social meanings are given to literacy in the posters on the next page? What uses of literacy do the posters emphasize? What are the posters trying to sell about literacy? Do you see evidence in the poster of Scribner's three metaphors? How do these posters and the messages they convey compare to other literacy campaign or reading posters you've seen?

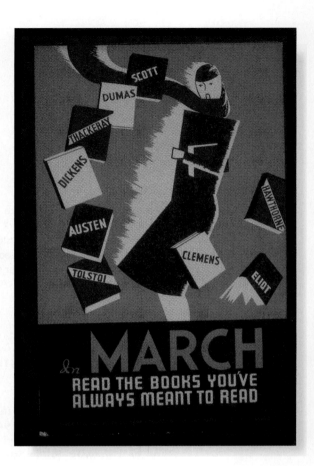

— WPA Literacy Posters.

CLASS ACTIVITY: RESEARCH ON LITERACY POSTERS

Work in a group of three to do some research on literacy campaigns and reading posters. There are more literacy posters at the Library of Congress Web site, "By the People, For the People: Posters from the WPA, 1936–1943." Visit the site memory.loc.gov/ammem/wpaposters/wpahome.html. Use "read" or "reading" as a keyword to search the collection. That will take you to links for twenty-one WPA posters, including the three here. You can find other examples of literacy campaigns and reading posters by doing a regular Google search and a Google Images search. (You'll find, for example, posters from Soviet, Cuban, and Nicaraguan literacy campaigns, from the National Literacy Trust in Britain featuring soccer stars and pro wrestlers, the Oklahoma statewide "Ya'll Read" program with country-western singer Carrie Underwood, and campaigns sponsored by corporations, foundations, and libraries.) Pick two or three posters that take contrasting approaches to promoting literacy. Present these to class in a report that explains what you see as the main differences in how the posters represent the meaning of literacy and its uses.

Page to Screen: Print Culture and Digital Media

Decried by some as the end of the book, celebrated by others as the start of an exciting new cyber-age, the shift from page to screen as the dominant medium of communication has certainly brought about changes in the way people produce and use reading and writing. As many have noted, these are not just changes in how information and knowledge are stored and presented. There are also significant changes in the dynamics of communication. Here are some of the most striking features of digital media:

- Digital media have an *immediacy* unimaginable in print culture—the time lapse between sending and receiving messages is reduced to nearly zero.
- Digital media promote *connectivity*—individuals feel wired into networks of people and information technology which make the world seem immediately present.
- Digital media possess *interactivity*—the capacity to respond is built directly into the technology itself, which is evident in the difference between reading a book page by page in sequential order and surfing the Web, where people make decisions about their own reading paths.

As the following reading suggests, we are just beginning to grapple conceptually with the scope and consequences of these changes in the nature of literacy. What is clear, however, is that any investigation of reading and writing in contemporary culture must take into account text messaging, e-mail, instant messaging, blogs, social networking, Web design, desktop publishing, and so on.

FROM LITERACY IN THE NEW MEDIA AGE

◼— *Gunther Kress*

Gunther Kress is a professor of education at the University of London and the author of many books on language and literacy, including *Literacy in the New Media Age* (2003). This reading consists of two brief excerpts from its opening chapter, where Kress explains the project of his book.

SUGGESTION FOR READING   As you read, notice how Kress, in the first two paragraphs, presents a sweeping view of the shift from page to screen and its social and cultural effects. Then, in the five paragraphs that follow, Kress responds to possible objections to the way he has characterized this shift. Consider how these responses complicate the shift from page to screen you find in the opening two paragraphs.

1 It is no longer possible to think about literacy in isolation from a vast array of social, technological and economic factors. Two distinct yet related factors deserve to be particularly highlighted. These are, on the one hand, the broad move from the now centuries-long dominance of writing to the new dominance of the image and, on the other hand, the move from the dominance of the medium of the book to the dominance of the medium of the screen. These two together are producing a revolution in the uses and effects of literacy and of associated means for representing and communicating at every level and in every domain. Together they raise two questions: what

is the likely future of literacy, and what are the likely larger-level social and cultural effects of that change?

One might say the following with some confidence. Language-as-speech will remain the major mode of communication; language-as-writing will increasingly be displaced by image in many domains of public communication, though writing will remain the preferred mode of the political and cultural elites. The combined effects on writing of the dominance of the mode of image and of the medium of the screen will produce deep changes in the forms and functions of writing. This in turn will have profound effects on human, cognitive/affective, cultural and bodily engagement with the world, and on the forms and shapes of knowledge. *The world told* is a different world to *the world shown*. The effects of the move to the screen as the major medium of communication will produce far-reaching shifts in relations of power, and not just in the sphere of communication. Where significant changes to distribution of power threaten, there will be fierce resistance by those who presently hold power, so that predictions about the democratic potentials and effects of the new information and communication technologies have to be seen in the light of inevitable struggles over power yet to come. It is already clear that the effects of the two changes taken together will have the widest imaginable political, economic, social, cultural, conceptual/cognitive and epistemological consequences.

. . .

It may be as well to try and answer here and now three objections that will be made. One is that more books are published now than ever before; the second is, that there is more writing than ever before, including writing on the screen. The third, the most serious, takes the form of a question: what do we lose if many of the forms of writing that we know disappear?

To the first objection I say: the books that are published now are in very many cases books which are already influenced by the new logic of the screen, and in many cases they are not "books" as that word would have been understood thirty or forty years ago. I am thinking here particularly of textbooks, which then were expositions of coherent "bodies of knowledge" presented in the mode of writing. The move from chapter to chapter was a stately and orderly progression through the unfolding matter of the book. The contemporary textbook—since the late 1970s for lower years of secondary school and by now for all the years of secondary school—is often a collection of "worksheets," organised around the issues of the curriculum, and put between more or less solid covers. This is still called a book. But there are no chapters, there is none of that sense of a reader engaging with and absorbing a coherent exposition of a body of knowledge, authoritatively presented. Instead there is a sense that the issue now is to involve students in action around topics, of learning by doing. Above all, the matter is presented through image more than through writing—and writing and image are given different representational and communicational functions.

5   These are still called "book," though I think we need to be wary of being fooled by the seeming stability of the word. These are not books that can be "read," for instance, in anything like that older sense of the word "read." These are books for working with, for acting on. So yes, there are more "books" published now than ever before, but in many cases the "books" of now are not the "books" of then. And I am not just thinking of factual, information books but of books of all kinds.

And yes, there is more writing than ever before. Let me make two points. The first is, who is writing more? Who is filling the pages of websites with writing? Is it the young? Or is it those who grew up in the era when writing was clearly the dominant mode? The second point goes to the question of the future of writing. Image has coexisted with writing, as of course has speech. In the era of the dominance of writing, when the logic of writing organised the page, image appeared on the page subject to the logic of writing. In simple terms, it fitted in how, where and when the logic of the written text and of the page suggested. In the era of the dominance of the screen, writing appears on the screen subject to the logic of the image. Writing fits in how, where and when the logic of the image-space suggests. The effects on writing, as is already "visible" in any number of ways, tiny at times, larger at others, will be inescapable.

That leaves the third objection. It cannot be dealt with quickly. It requires a large project, much debate, and an uncommon generosity of view. On one level the issue is one of gains and losses; on another level it will require from us a different kind of reflection on what writing is, what forms of imagination it fosters. It asks questions of a profounder kind, about human potentials, wishes, desires—questions which go beyond immediate issues of utility for social or economic needs.

TALKING ABOUT THE READING

Consider Kress's responses to the three objections. How do these responses clarify what Kress means by the shift from page to screen? In what sense has the emergence of the screen influenced the composition of pages and what we mean when we call something a book? What future for writing does Kress foresee? What are the "gains and losses" he refers to in the final paragraph?

Words, Images, and the Design of the Page

Kress says that in the older print culture, images fit into the way that the "logic of writing" organized the page, mainly as illustrations of written text. In the new media age, however, it is increasingly the case that writing fits into the "logic of the image." This can be seen not just in terms of Web design on the screen but also in terms of how writing is integrated into the visual design of magazines, books, textbooks, and other print materials—in two-page spreads, infographics, sidebars, and other forms of information design. The move here, as Kress describes it, is from *narrating* information, with the primary emphasis on continuous writing, to *displaying* information, where chunks of writing appear in the "image space" of the page.

CHAOS IN THE CRESCENT CITY

The two-page spread on the next two pages appeared as part of the "Special Report: After Katrina" in *Newsweek* on September 12, 2005. The combination of words and images presented here is representative of the style of information design you'll find in current magazines such as *Newsweek, Time, Scientific American,* and *Esquire.*

SUGGESTION FOR READING

As you read, pay attention to how you navigate the page. Where do your eyes go? Where you do you stop and look at an image or read a chunk of text?

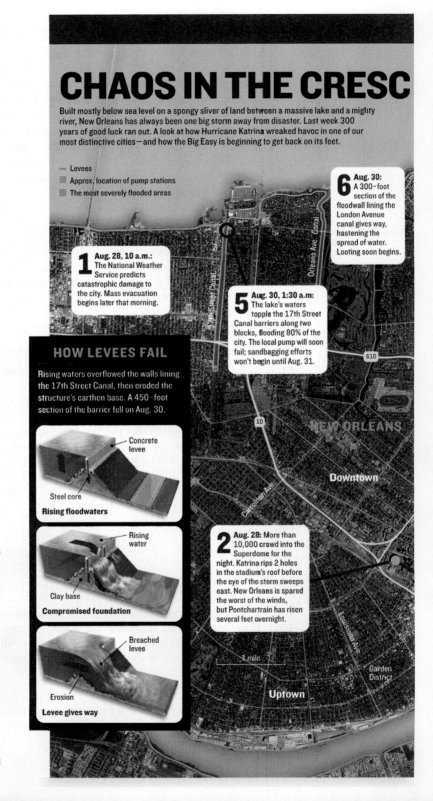

CHAOS IN THE CRESC

Built mostly below sea level on a spongy sliver of land between a massive lake and a mighty river, New Orleans has always been one big storm away from disaster. Last week 300 years of good luck ran out. A look at how Hurricane Katrina wreaked havoc in one of our most distinctive cities—and how the Big Easy is beginning to get back on its feet.

— Levees
▨ Approx. location of pump stations
▨ The most severely flooded areas

1 Aug. 28, 10 a.m.: The National Weather Service predicts catastrophic damage to the city. Mass evacuation begins later that morning.

5 Aug. 30, 1:30 a.m: The lake's waters topple the 17th Street Canal barriers along two blocks, flooding 80% of the city. The local pump will soon fail; sandbagging efforts won't begin until Aug. 31.

6 Aug. 30: A 300-foot section of the floodwall lining the London Avenue canal gives way, hastening the spread of water. Looting soon begins.

2 Aug. 28: More than 10,000 crowd into the Superdome for the night. Katrina rips 2 holes in the stadium's roof before the eye of the storm sweeps east. New Orleans is spared the worst of the winds, but Pontchartrain has risen several feet overnight.

HOW LEVEES FAIL

Rising waters overflowed the walls lining the 17th Street Canal, then eroded the structure's earthen base. A 450-foot section of the barrier fell on Aug. 30.

Concrete levee
Steel core
Rising floodwaters

Rising water
Clay base
Compromised foundation

Breached levee
Erosion
Levee gives way

NEW ORLEANS
Downtown
Uptown
Garden District
1 mile

— Notice how the two-page spread "Chaos in the Crescent City" superimposes diagrams and information boxes on an aerial map of New Orleans. The combination of words and images enables readers to locate events in time and space and to visualize the topography of the city, the process of flooding, and the intervention of engineers to deal with the flood.

Newsweek. Research and Text by Andrew Romano. Illustrations by Kevin Hand. Sources: Army Corps of Engineers, Rockland District. Map courtesy of Digital Globe.

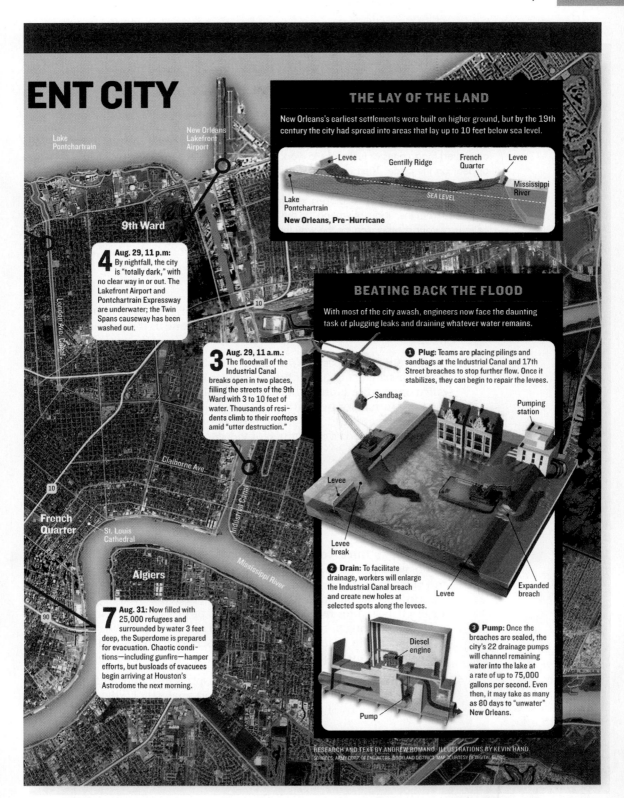

ENT CITY

Lake Pontchartrain

New Orleans Lakefront Airport

9th Ward

4 **Aug. 29, 11 p.m.:** By nightfall, the city is "totally dark," with no clear way in or out. The Lakefront Airport and Pontchartrain Expressway are underwater; the Twin Spans causeway has been washed out.

London Ave. Canal

3 **Aug. 29, 11 a.m.:** The floodwall of the Industrial Canal breaks open in two places, filling the streets of the 9th Ward with 3 to 10 feet of water. Thousands of residents climb to their rooftops amid "utter destruction."

Claiborne Ave.

Industrial Canal

French Quarter

St. Louis Cathedral

Algiers

Mississippi River

7 **Aug. 31:** Now filled with 25,000 refugees and surrounded by water 3 feet deep, the Superdome is prepared for evacuation. Chaotic conditions—including gunfire—hamper efforts, but busloads of evacuees begin arriving at Houston's Astrodome the next morning.

THE LAY OF THE LAND

New Orleans's earliest settlements were built on higher ground, but by the 19th century the city had spread into areas that lay up to 10 feet below sea level.

Levee — Gentilly Ridge — French Quarter — Levee

Mississippi River

Lake Pontchartrain

SEA LEVEL

New Orleans, Pre-Hurricane

BEATING BACK THE FLOOD

With most of the city awash, engineers now face the daunting task of plugging leaks and draining whatever water remains.

1 **Plug:** Teams are placing pilings and sandbags at the Industrial Canal and 17th Street breaches to stop further flow. Once it stabilizes, they can begin to repair the levees.

Sandbag

Pumping station

Levee

Levee break

2 **Drain:** To facilitate drainage, workers will enlarge the Industrial Canal breach and create new holes at selected spots along the levees.

Levee

Expanded breach

Diesel engine

3 **Pump:** Once the breaches are sealed, the city's 22 drainage pumps will channel remaining water into the lake at a rate of up to 75,000 gallons per second. Even then, it may take as many as 80 days to "unwater" New Orleans.

Pump

RESEARCH AND TEXT BY ANDREW ROMANO. ILLUSTRATIONS BY KEVIN HAND. SOURCES: ARMY CORP OF ENGINEERS, ROOKLAND DISTRICT; MAP COURTESY OF DIGITAL GLOBE

TALKING ABOUT THE READING

Compare the ways that you and classmates read this page. What reading paths did people follow? How can you explain the differences? To what extent is this a matter of differences in individual interests? How are multiple reading paths facilitated by the page design?

PAGE DESIGN, PAST AND PRESENT

Work in a group of three. Compare the past and present visual design either of *Time* or *Newsweek* or of high school or college textbooks. Find copies of recent and past (from the 1960s or earlier) magazines or textbooks to work with. First notice patterns in how writing and images appear on the page. Then choose a page (or two-page spread) from each for more detailed comparison. Prepare a report that explains the main differences (and similarities) in the way the pages integrate word and image. To what extent do your pages exemplify the shift Kress describes from the "logic of writing" to the "logic of the image"? What do you see as the implications of your comparison for the way that people read and use magazines and textbooks?

WRITING INVENTORY: IN AND OUT OF SCHOOL

To begin researching the role that reading and writing has played in your life, create an inventory of the types of writing you've done in the past, in and out of school.

1. List the different types of writing you've done in school. Think back to grammar school and junior high as well as high school. Were you ever called on to write as an act of punishment? Did teachers assign creative writing, journals, or freewriting? Were you assigned essays, reports, and research papers? Did you make posters or other displays? Did you design Web sites or write scripts for videos?

2. List the different types of writing you've done outside school. Think of keeping a diary or lists of favorite movie stars; creative writing, including comics, songs, and raps; writing you did on the job, from a resume and job application to work reports; and writing for community, political, church, or other groups, such as newsletters, flyers, petitions, posters, and so on.

3. In a group of three, compare your findings. Do in-school and out-of-school writing separately at first, to get a sense of the variety of writing and range of purposes. Then compare in-school and out-of school writing. How do the purposes vary? What's the difference between writing for teachers and for readers outside school or just yourself? How does the tone of writing differ (or overlap) in and out of school? What is your own relationship to in-school and out-of-school writing—in terms of personal investment, pleasure, what you've learned, and so on.

4. Write a brief report on your findings that displays in-school and out-of-school writing in tables and provides a short analysis of what you see as the implications of their differences and similarities.

Literacy Narratives

Literacy narrative is a term we'll use to describe stories of how people encounter and make sense of reading and writing. These stories often appear as passages in a memoir or autobiography, as in the selections below from Eudora Welty and Malcolm X, where writers narrate their formative experiences with literacy as part of their unfolding life histories. Or a literacy narrative might appear in a personal essay, as in Conor Boyland's "Confessions of an Instant Messenger." It's unlikely, of course, that any of the three writers said to himself or herself, "I'm going to write a literacy narrative today." The term is an analytical one that's useful for our purposes—to apply to the telling fact that so many writers have written about their experiences with literacy and to see what patterns we can find in these writings.

FROM ONE WRITER'S BEGINNINGS

— *Eudora Welty*

Eudora Welty (1909–2001) was a photographer, novelist, and short story writer. Her novel *The Optimist's Daughter* won the Pulitzer Prize in 1973. This is a passage from her memoir *One Writer's Beginnings* (1983) about her childhood in Jackson, Mississippi, in the early twentieth century.

1   Jackson's Carnegie Library was on the same street where our house was, on the other side of the State Capitol. "Through the Capitol" was the way to go to the Library. You could glide through it on your bicycle or even coast through on roller skates, though without family permission.

I never knew anyone who'd grown up in Jackson without being afraid of Mrs. Calloway, our librarian. She ran the Library absolutely by herself, from the desk where she sat with her back to the books and facing the stairs, her dragon eye on the front door, where who knew what kind of person might come in from the public? SILENCE in big black letters was on signs tacked up everywhere. She herself spoke in her normally commanding voice; every word could be heard all over the Library above a steady seething sound coming from her electric fan; it was the only fan in the Library and stood on her desk, turned directly onto her streaming face.

As you came in from the bright outside, if you were a girl, she sent her strong eyes down the stairway to test you; if she could see through your skirt she sent you straight back home; you could just put on another petticoat if you wanted a book that badly from the public library. I was willing; I would do anything to read.

My mother was not afraid of Mrs. Calloway. She wished me to have my own library card to check out books for myself. She took me in to introduce me and I saw I had met a witch. "Eudora is nine years old and has my permission to read any book she wants from the shelves, children or adult," Mother said. "With the exception of *Elsie Dinsmore*," she added. Later she explained to me that she'd made this rule because Elsie the heroine, being made by her father to practice too long and hard at the piano, fainted and fell off the piano stool. "You're too impressionable, dear," she told me. "You'd read that and the very first thing you'd do, you'd fall off the piano stool." "Impressionable" was a new word. I never hear it yet without the image that comes with it of falling straight off the piano stool.

5   Mrs. Calloway made her own rules about books. You could not take back a book to the Library on the same day you'd taken it out; it made no difference to her that you'd read every word in it and needed another to start. You could take out two books at a time and two only; this applied as long as you were a child and also for the rest of your life, to my mother as severely as to me. So, two by two, I read library books as fast as I could go, rushing them home in the bas-ket of my bicycle. From the minute I reached our house, I started to read. Every book I seized on, from *Bunny Brown and His Sister Sue at Camp Rest-a-While* to *Twenty Thousand Leagues under the Sea,* stood for the devouring wish to read being instantly granted. I knew this was bliss, I knew it at the time. Taste isn't nearly so impor-tant; it comes in its own time. I wanted to read *immediately.* The only fear was that of books coming to an end.

TALKING ABOUT THE READING

What insights does Eudora Welty gain from getting a library card and access to library books? How do each of the main characters—Eudora, her mother, and Mrs. Calloway—make sense of Eudora's encounter with literacy? What role, if any, does gender play in this episode?

Exploratory Writing

Exploratory writing is a way to work with the ideas in a reading that is more tenta-tive and preliminary than a finished piece of writing you'd turn in to be graded. You'll be asked to do exploratory writing throughout *Reading Culture,* so this is a good opportunity to get started. In exploratory writings, you don't need to worry about organization or correctness (or even being consistent). You follow a prompt from *Reading Culture* or your teacher and see where it takes you. Here is a sample of exploratory writing based on the "Talking about the Reading" section that follows the excerpt from Eudora Welty's *One Writer's Beginnings.*

SAMPLE EXPLORATORY WRITING OF *ONE WRITER'S BEGINNINGS*

It looks to me like the main characters are connected to each other in a power struggle over what Eudora is allowed to read. Mrs. Calloway is a scary guardian of the library with her own rules about who can read what, how many books you can take out, and so on. She's basically the villain in the drama. Eudora's mother acts on behalf of Eudora, to get her past Mrs. Calloway. She's like the intermediary or fairy godmother. But even her mother has her own rules—or one rule about the book *Elsie Dinsmore.* Books are magical. They are so powerful they can make Eudora fall off a piano stool. Eudora just wants to read. What's interesting is that she's willing to be a proper young girl and wear a petticoat to get into the library, another of Mrs. Calloway's weird rules. There's a connection here between femininity and reading.

Now it's your turn. Do a page or two of exploratory writing in response to the "Talking about the Reading" section following the reading selection by either Malcolm X or Conor Boyland.

FROM THE AUTOBIOGRAPHY OF MALCOLM X

— Malcolm X

> Malcolm X (1925–1965) was a revolutionary activist whose calls for black power and the international solidarity of people of color against Western racism made him one of the most influential African American leaders in the twentieth century. The following excerpts, taken from *The Autobiography of Malcolm X* (1964), which he wrote with Alex Haley, describe his political awakening in prison.

1 Many who today hear me somewhere in person, or on television, or those who read something I've said, will think I went to school far beyond the eighth grade. This impression is due entirely to my prison studies.

It had really begun back in the Charlestown Prison, when Bimbi first made me feel envy of his stock of knowledge. Bimbi had always taken charge of any conversation he was in, and I had tried to emulate him. But every book I picked up had few sentences which didn't contain anywhere from one to nearly all of the words that might as well have been in Chinese. When I just skipped those words, of course, I really ended up with little idea of what the book said. So I had come to the Norfolk Prison Colony still going through only book-reading motions. Pretty soon, I would have quit even these motions, unless I had received the motivation that I did.

I saw that the best thing I could do was get hold of a dictionary—to study, to learn some words. I was lucky enough to reason also that I should try to improve my penmanship. It was sad. I couldn't even write in a straight line. It was both ideas together that moved me to request a dictionary along with some tablets and pencils from the Norfolk Prison Colony school.

I spent two days just riffling uncertainly through the dictionary's pages. I'd never realized so many words existed! I didn't know *which* words I needed to learn. Finally, just to start some kind of action, I began copying.

5 In my slow, painstaking, ragged handwriting, I copied into my tablet everything printed on that first page, down to the punctuation marks.

I believe it took me a day. Then, aloud, I read back, to myself, everything I'd written on the tablet. Over and over, aloud, to myself, I read my own handwriting.

I woke up the next morning, thinking about those words—immensely proud to realize that not only had I written so much at one time, but I'd written words that I never knew were in the world. Moreover, with a little effort, I also could remember what many of these words meant. I reviewed the words whose meanings I didn't remember. Funny thing, from the dictionary first page right now, that "aardvark" springs to my mind. The dictionary had a picture of it, a long-tailed, long-eared, burrowing African mammal, which lives off termites caught by sticking out its tongue as an anteater does for ants.

I was so fascinated that I went on—I copied the dictionary's next page. And the same experience came when I studied that. With every succeeding page, I also learned of people and places and events from history. Actually the dictionary is like a miniature encyclopedia. Finally the dictionary's A section had filled a whole tablet—and I went on into the B's. That was the way I started copying what eventually became the entire dictionary. It went a lot faster after so much practice helped me to pick up handwriting speed. Between what I wrote in my tablet, and writing letters, during the rest of my time in prison I would guess I wrote a million words.

I suppose it was inevitable that as my word-base broadened, I could for the first time pick up a book and read and now begin to understand what the book was saying. Anyone who has read a great deal can imagine the new world that opened. Let me tell you something: from then until I left that prison, in every free moment I had, if I was not reading in the library, I was reading on my bunk. You couldn't have gotten me out of books with a wedge. Between Mr. Muhammad's teachings, my correspondence, my visitors—usually Ella and Reginald—and my reading of books, months passed without my even thinking about being imprisoned. In fact, up to then, I never had been so truly free in my life.

. . .

10   I never will forget how shocked I was when I began reading about slavery's total horror. It made such an impact upon me that it later became one of my favorite subjects when I became a minister of Mr. Muhammad's. The world's most monstrous crime, the sin and the blood on the white man's hands, are almost impossible to believe. Books like the one by Frederick Olmstead opened my eyes to the horrors suffered when the slave was landed in the United States. The European woman, Fannie Kimball, who had married a Southern white slaveowner, described how human beings were degraded. Of course I read *Uncle Tom's Cabin*. In fact, I believe that's the only novel I have ever read since I started serious reading.

Parkhurst's collection also contained some bound pamphlets of the Abolitionist Anti-Slavery Society of New England. I read descriptions of atrocities, saw those illustrations of black slave women tied up and flogged with whips; of black mothers watching their babies being dragged off, never to be seen by their mothers again; of dogs after slaves, and of the fugitive slave catchers, evil white men with whips and clubs and chains and guns. I read about the slave preacher Nat Turner, who put the fear of God into the white slavemaster. Nat Turner wasn't going around preaching pie-in-the-sky and "non-violent" freedom for the black man. There in Virginia one night in 1831, Nat and seven other slaves started out at his master's home and through the night they went from one plantation "big house" to the next, killing,

until by the next morning 57 white people were dead and Nat had about 70 slaves following him. White people, terrified for their lives, fled from their homes, locked themselves up in public buildings, hid in the woods, and some even left the state. A small army of soldiers took two months to catch and hang Nat Turner. Somewhere I have read where Nat Turner's example is said to have inspired John Brown to invade Virginia and attack Harper's Ferry nearly thirty years later, with thirteen white men and five Negroes.

I read Herodotus, "the father of History," or, rather, I read about him. And I read the histories of various nations, which opened my eyes gradually, then wider and wider, to how the whole world's white men had indeed acted like devils, pillaging and raping and bleeding and draining the whole world's non-white people. I remember, for instance, books such as Will Durant's story of Oriental civilization, and Mahatma Gandhi's accounts of the struggle to drive the British out of India.

Book after book showed me how the white man had brought upon the world's black, brown, red, and yellow peoples every variety of the sufferings of exploitation. I saw how since the sixteenth century, the so-called "Christian trader" white man began to ply the seas in his lust for Asian and African empires, and plunder, and power. I read, I saw, how the white man never has gone among the non-white peoples bearing the Cross in the true manner and spirit of Christ's teachings—meek, humble, and Christ-like.

I perceived, as I read, how the collective white man had been actually nothing but a piratical opportunist who used Faustian machinations to make his own Christianity his initial wedge in criminal conquests. First, always "religiously," he branded "heathen" and "pagan" labels upon ancient non-white cultures and civilizations. The stage thus set, he then turned upon his non-white victims his weapons of war.

15   I read how, entering India—half a *billion* deeply religious brown people—the British white man, by 1759, through promises, trickery and manipulations, controlled much of India through

Great Britain's East India Company. The parasitical British administration kept tentacling out to half of the sub-continent. In 1857, some of the desperate people of India finally mutinied—and, excepting the African slave trade, nowhere has history recorded any more unnecessary bestial and ruthless human carnage than the British suppression of the non-white Indian people.

Over 115 million African blacks—close to the 1930's population of the United States—were murdered or enslaved during the slave trade. And I read how when the slave market was glutted,

the cannibalistic white powers of Europe next carved up, as their colonies, the richest areas of the black continent. And Europe's chancelleries for the next century played a chess game of naked exploitation and power from Cape Horn to Cairo.

Ten guards and the warden couldn't have torn me out of those books. Not even Elijah Muhammad could have been more eloquent than those books were in providing indisputable proof that the collective white man had acted like a devil in virtually every contact he had with the world's collective non-white man.

TALKING ABOUT THE READING

Malcolm X says that he had never "been so truly free in my life" until he began his "prison studies." What was so liberating for him? In what sense does Malcolm X's reading involve a new identity and a new relationship to the dominant white culture?

CONFESSIONS OF AN INSTANT MESSENGER

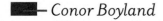— *Conor Boyland*

Conor Boyland was a sophomore at Northeastern University when "Confessions of an Instant Messenger" appeared in the *Boston Globe* in 2005.

1   I was sitting at my computer, and I realized something: I spend way too much time sitting at my computer. Granted, I'm a college student, and my options on where to sit in my room are limited, but that just makes it easier to justify the time I waste every day online, mostly instant messaging. Admit it, you do it too. We all do, to different degrees. It's just one of the most commonly accepted things to do when you have a computer; "I think, therefore IM."

It seems fairly harmless, but it snowballs, and before you know it, you can't stop or you'll go into withdrawal. When you get to the point where you can't take a shower without putting up that witty away message that says, "I'm all hot and steamy," you're officially addicted—welcome to the club. You're also really sick.

One of the lamest aspects of addiction to AIM, America Online's instant messaging system, is that

even if you have people on your buddy list you haven't talked to in years, you can still keep up on their day-to-day activities by checking their away messages when you're bored. Or when you're doing homework. Or when you're supposed to be in class. The funny thing is, some of them are probably doing it to you too, but it doesn't matter. Next thing you know, you're fiending for recent pictures of them, who they're dating, where they're living, and what their favorite movies are.

Enter: The facebook. If AIM is a gateway drug, the facebook is Internet crack. If you're in college, you know the deal: upload your picture, add in some interests, list every single band you've ever listened to, girls write down your favorite "I love shopping and my best friends" quote from "Sex and the City," and guys write down that you like "Scarface" and "The Da Vinci Code." Then you browse through different profiles and compile a list of friends, some of which you know and some of which you've (maybe) met once but never talked to after that. You can even hunt down people from your hometown that now go to other colleges. That way you can ignore over the Internet the same people you used to ignore in high school!

5   If you're one of those people who like to stay up on the latest trends, like striped shirts and quoting Napoleon Dynamite, you're probably thinking, "Idiot! Facebook is so last semester, gosh!" Well, there's a new friend-making site for you folks called Catch27, which is basically the facebook with attitude. You actually trade friends here based on how hot they are, and if you can't get hot friends on your own you can even pay money for them. "99 ¢ for a Wax Pack of 3: just like real life, only cheaper," writes the site's creator, E. Jean Carroll, who is either really desperate for friends or is laughing all the way to the bank. Now, don't get me wrong here, if you want to spend money to create an online list of "friends" you've never actually met, that's your own business. Just remember (and I quote my roommate on this one), "FBI agents make the sexiest cyber babes."

I don't have a problem with gimmicky websites, but I do take issue with the rapidly growing trend of communicating online rather than in person. I hate it, but I find the temptation increasingly hard to resist. When it comes down to it, reading someone's profile is so much easier than actually talking to them, and it carries no risk of them not liking you. Therein lies the problem: Online directories like the facebook make it possible to find out quite a lot about a person without ever speaking to them, which not only appeals to stalkers but ruins your social skills as

well. Actually, I shouldn't speak for anybody else, but I admit that mine have certainly suffered.

On top of that, browsing the facebook can quickly go from being fun to becoming a compulsion, just like with AIM. It's not that we don't know this compulsive behavior is unhealthy; it's just another one of those guilty pleasures you know is bad for you but that you don't care enough about to stop doing. The Internet is so addicting that in many ways it has now become the most popular way to contact new people. A friend of mine met a cute girl at a party recently, and as he was leaving he told her to look him up on the facebook, no joke. I waited until he left and then got her *phone number*.

If drug addiction damages your mental capacities, then Internet addiction damages your social ones (Do you really think my friend has any chance with that girl?), and as with any addiction, admitting that you have a problem is only the first step. I'm just as guilty as the next guy, so I'm not going to say something preachy like "seize the day," or "get out and live life to the fullest," but I will say this: We need to sign off AIM and facebook and get up off our asses a little more often. Go run around outside, read a book, or—God forbid—talk to a stranger. Practice the dying art of conversation.

Communicating online is convenient, but no amount of smileys or pokes can substitute for real human connection, which is far more worthy of our time than anonymous facebook connections (of which I have 2,137 by the way). As for the compulsive behavior, I'm quitting cold turkey. I just have to put one more witty away message up, one last fix, and then I'm done. TTYL.

TALKING ABOUT THE READING

Conor Boyland frames this literacy narrative as a confession that uses an addiction metaphor. Like any metaphor, the notion of addiction brings certain things to light while ignoring or suppressing others. What does the addiction metaphor allow Boyland to show? What does it leave out? His confession, in Gunther Kress's terms, emphasizes the "losses" of such digital media as IM and Facebook. Are there also "gains" you could point to?

WRITE YOUR OWN LITERACY NARRATIVE

Use the readings in the "Literacy Narratives" section as models to think about the role reading and/or writing has played in your life. Focus on a particular instance, like Eudora Welty trying to get a library card or Malcolm X copying the dictionary, or on a particular use of reading and writing, like IM or Facebook. Tell the story in as much detail as you can, paying attention to setting and other characters involved, as well as your own and others' motivations and feelings. Think of this literacy narrative as a mini-research project—to provide you with data you might use later in a more formal analytical paper.

Analyzing Literacy Events

According to Shirley Brice Heath, a literacy event "is any occasion in which a piece of writing is integral to the nature of the participants' interactions and their interpretive practices." A literacy event, as Heath explains it, is a "conceptual tool" to examine how people use reading and writing and how they make sense of the social interactions that revolve around "pieces of writing." For our purposes in this case study, the notion of a literacy event is a way of moving from *telling* stories about situations in which reading or writing played an important part, as in the three literacy narratives above, to *analyzing* the social interactions of the people involved and the cultural meanings assigned to literacy.

The two readings that follow offer examples of how literacy researchers identify and analyze literacy events. Looking at the way they write about literacy events will help you sharpen your own sense of how to work with the term and apply it to examine your own experience with reading and writing.

Underline/Highlight, Annotate, Summarize

Most students underline or highlight when they read to catch key points they can return to later to study for a test or write a paper. Annotation is a good complement to highlighting because it provides readers with a way of keeping track of what the writer is saying and doing at various points in the text (e.g. "states main point," "key supporting evidence," "refutes opposing views," etc.). Summary takes reading one step further by putting what you've read into your own words and quoting selected words and phrases to make sense of the writer's purpose and the key concepts he or she is working with. We have highlighted and annotated "Talk is the thing." The summary that follows the reading, as you will see, is focused on coming to grips with the aims and implications of the research Heath reports.

"TALK IS THE THING"

▬▬—*Shirley Brice Heath*

Shirley Brice Heath is a well-known linguistic anthropologist who taught for many years at Stanford and is now in the education department at Brown University. This reading is a passage from her *Ways with Words: Life, Language, and Work in Communities and Classrooms* (1983), a groundbreaking study of reading and writing in two working-class communities in North Carolina. Trackton is an African American community of textile mill workers and their families.

"TALK IS THE THING"

1   In almost every situation in Trackton in which a piece of writing is integral to the nature of the participants' interactions and their interpretations of meaning, talk is a necessary component. Knowing which box of cereal is Kellogg's raisin bran does little good without announcing that choice to older brothers and sisters helping pour the cereal. Knowing the kind of bicycle tire and tube on one's old bike is translated into action only at Mr. Green's bicycle shop or with a friend who has an old bike he is not using. Certain types of talk describe, repeat, reinforce, frame, expand, and even contradict written materials, and children in Trackton learn not only how to read print, but also when and how to surround the print in their lives with appropriate talk. For them there are far more occasions in the community which call for appropriate knowledge of forms and uses of talk around or about writing, than there are actual occasions for reading and writing extended connected discourse.

Defines literacy event

Connects talk to reading

For Trackton adults, reading is a social activity; when something is read in Trackton, it almost always provokes narratives, jokes, sidetracking talk, and active negotiation of the meaning of written texts among the listeners. Authority in the written word does not rest in the words themselves, but in the meanings which are negotiated through the experiences of the group. The evening newspaper is read on the front porch for most months of the year. The obituaries on the back page are usually read first, followed by employment listings, advertisements for grocery and department store sales, and captions beneath pictures and headlines. An obituary is read for some trace of acquaintance with either the deceased, his relatives, place of birth, church, or school; active discussion follows about who the individual was and who he might have known. Circulars or letters to individuals regarding the neighborhood center and its recreational or medical services are read aloud and their meanings jointly negotiated by those who have had experience with such activities or know about the forms to be filled out to be eligible for such services. Neighbors share stories of what they did or what happened to them in similar circumstances. One day when Lillie Mae had received a letter about a daycare program, several neighbors were sitting on porches, working on cars nearby, or sweeping their front yards. Lillie Mae came out on her front porch, read the first paragraph of a letter, and announced:

Examples of talk about printed texts

TRACKTON TEXT X

Lillie Mae:	You hear this, it says Lem [then two years old] might can get into Ridgeway [a local neighborhood center daycare program], but I hafta have the papers ready and apply by next Friday.

Sample of Trackton talk

Visiting friend:	You ever been to Kent to get his birth certificate? [friend is mother of three children already in school]
Mattie Crawford:	But what hours that program gonna be? You may not can get him there.
Lillie Mae:	They want the birth certificate? I got his vaccination papers.
Annie Mae:	Sometimes they take that, 'cause they can 'bout tell the age from those early shots.
Visiting friend:	But you better get it, 'cause you gotta have it when he go to school anyway.
Lillie Mae:	But it says here they don't know what hours yet. How am I gonna get over to Kent? How much does it cost? Lemme see if the program costs anything. (She reads aloud part of the letter.)

Conversation on various parts of the letter continued for nearly an hour, while neighbors and Lillie Mae pooled their knowledge of the pros and cons of such programs. They discussed ways of getting rides to Kent, the county seat thirty miles away, to which all mothers had to go to get their children's birth certificates to prove their age at school entrance. The question "What does this mean?" was answered not only from the information in print, but from the group's joint bringing of experience to the text. Lillie Mae, reading aloud, decoded the written text, but her friends and neighbors interpreted the text's meaning through their own experiences. The experience of any one individual had to become common to the group, however, and that was done through the recounting of members' experience. Such recounting re-created scenes, embellished the truth, illustrated the character of the individuals involved, and to the greatest extent possible brought the audience into the experience itself. Beyond these recountings of episodes (such as one mother's efforts to get her doctor to give her "papers" to verify her son's age), there was a reintegration of these now commonly shared experiences with the text itself. After the reading episode, Lillie Mae had to relate the text's meaning to the experiences she had heard shared, and she checked out this final synthesis of meaning for her with some of the group. Some members did not care about this final synthesis and had wandered off, satisfied to have told their stories, but others commented that they thought her chosen course of action the right one, and her understanding of the letter to fit their interpretations.

Analyzes conversation

About the only material not delivered for group negotiation is that which involves private finances or information which members feel might somehow give them an opportunity their neighbors do not have. A postcard from a local mill announcing days on which the mill will be accepting new employment applications will not be shared aloud, but kept secret because of the competition for jobs. On

Notes an exception

Table 1 *Types of uses of reading in Trackton*

INSTRUMENTAL:	Reading to accomplish practical goals of daily life (price tags, checks, bills, telephone dials, clocks, street signs, house numbers).
SOCIAL-INTERACTIONAL/ RECREATIONAL:	Reading to maintain social relationships, make plans, and introduce topics for discussion and story-telling (greeting cards, cartoons, letters, newspaper features, political flyers, announcements of community meetings).
NEWS-RELATED:	Reading to learn about third parties or distant events (local news items, circulars from the community center or school).
CONFIRMATIONAL:	Reading to gain support for attitudes or beliefs already held (Bible, brochures on cars, loan notes, bills).

Note. Listed in relative order of frequency of occasions when time on these types of tasks exceeded five minutes per day.

the other hand, a newspaper story about the expansion of the mill will be read aloud, and all will pool information in general terms.

5   Tables 1 and 2 show that the uses of writing and reading in the community are multiple, though there are few occasions for reading of extended connected discourse and almost no occasions for writing such material, except by those school children who diligently try to complete their homework assignments. Foremost among the types of uses of reading and writing are those which are *instrumental.* Adults and children read what they have to read to solve practical problems of daily life: price tags, traffic signs, house numbers, bills, checks. Other uses are perhaps not as critical to problem-solving, but *social-interactional* uses give information relevant to social relations and contacts with persons not in Trackton's primary group. Some write letters; many send greeting cards; almost all read bumper stickers, newspaper obituaries and features, and church news bulletins. Other types of reading and writing are *news-related.* From the local newspaper, political flyers, memos from the city offices, and circulars from the neighborhood center, Trackton residents learn information about local and distant events. They rarely read much more than headlines about distant events, since the evening news programs on television give them the same national or metropolitan news. Stories about the local towns are, however, read, because there is often no other source of information on happenings there. Some individuals in Trackton read for *confirmation*—to seek support for beliefs or ideas they already hold. Miss Lula reads the Bible. When the mayor maintains that one kind of car gets better mileage than another, and others disagree, he has to produce a brochure from a car dealer to prove his point. Children who become involved in boasts often called

Uses of reading on Table 1

Table 2 *Types of uses of writing in Trackton*

MEMORY AIDS: (primarily used by women)	Writing to serve as a reminder for the writer and, only occasionally, others (telephone numbers, notes on calendars).
SUBSTITUTES FOR ORAL MESSAGES: (primarily used by women)	Writing used when direct oral communication was not possible or would prove embarrassing (notes for tardiness or absence from school, greeting cards, letters).
FINANCIAL:	Writing to record numerals and to write out amounts and accompanying notes (signatures on checks and public forms, figures and notes for income tax preparation).
PUBLIC RECORDS: (church only)	Writing to announce the order of the church services and forthcoming events and to record financial and policy decisions (church bulletins, reports of the church building fund committee).

Note. Listed in relative order of frequency of occasions when time on these types of tasks exceeded five minutes per day.

on written proof to confirm their lofty accounts of themselves or others. Every home has some permanent records—loan notes, tax forms, birth certificates—which families keep, but can rarely find when they are needed. However, if they can be found and are read, they can confirm an oral statement.

The most frequent occasions for writing are those when Trackton family members say they cannot trust their memory (*memory-supportive*), or they have to write to *substitute for an oral message*. Beside the telephone, women write frequently called numbers and addresses; they tack calendars on the kitchen wall and add notes reminding them of dates for their children's vaccinations and the school holidays, etc. Some few women in the community write letters. Lillie Mae often writes relatives up-North to invite them to come home and to thank them for bringing presents. Women sometimes have to write notes to school about children's absences or tardiness or to request a local merchant to extend credit a few weeks longer. Men almost never write except to sign their paychecks, public forms, and to collect information for income tax preparation. One exception in Trackton is the mayor who meets once a month with a group of other church members to prepare Sunday church bulletins as well as to handle business related to the building fund or to plan for revival meetings. These written materials are negotiated cooperatively at the meetings; no individual takes sole responsibility.

Community literacy activities are public and social. Written information almost never stands alone in Trackton. It is reshaped and reworded into an oral mode by adults and children who incorporate

Uses of writing on Table 2

Sums up research findings

chunks of the written text in their talk. They often reflect their own awareness that print imposes a different kind of organization on written materials than talk does. Literacy events in Trackton which bring the written word into a central focus in interactions and interpretations have their rules of occurrence and appropriateness, just as talking junk, fussing, or performing a playsong do. The group activities of reading the newspaper across porches, debating the power of a new car, or discussing the city's plans to bring in earthmoving equipment to clear lots behind the community, produce more speaking than reading, more group than individual effort. There are repeated metaphors, comparisons, and fast-paced, overlapping language as Trackton residents move from print to what it means in their lives. On some occasions, they attend to the text itself; on others, they use it only as a starting point for wide-ranging talk. On all occasions, they bring in knowledge related to the text and interpret beyond the text for their own context; in so doing, they achieve a new synthesis of information from the text and the joint experiences of community members.

SAMPLE SUMMARY OF "TALK IS THE THING"

In "Talk is the Thing," Shirley Brice Heath examines literacy events in Trackton, with an emphasis on how "talk is a necessary component" of the reading and writing that takes place in this community. To illustrate this point, Heath presents a transcript of a conversation that revolves around a letter about a daycare program, as a group of neighbors draw on their knowledge and experiences to make sense of the letter. Heath goes on to make up tables for reading and writing, where she classifies the different types of reading and writing that people do in Trackton. This shows the wide variety and different purposes of literacy in Trackton. By the end of this reading, it becomes clear that for the Trackton community "literacy activities are public and social." As "Trackton residents move from print to what it means in their lives," they add their own knowledge and, as Heath says, "achieve a new synthesis" that integrates information from print material with the knowledge and experience of people who live in Trackton.

KEEPING A LITERACY LOG

Keep a literacy log for at least 8 hours. Carry with you a notebook and pen so that you can record every time you read or write something. Note where the literacy event takes place and what kind of text is involved. Bring your literacy log to class and work in a group of three. Your task here is to create two tables, one for "Types of Uses of Reading" and one for "Types of Uses of Writing," using Heath's tables in "Talk is the thing" as a model. You will need to create categories for the examples of reading and writing, just as Heath did, to group types of reading and writing together and to give them a label (e.g., "instrumental," "social-interactional/recreational," as in Heath's Table 1). Use Heath's categories to the extent they are applicable, but note that Trackton residents did not often read or write the "extended connected discourse" which is typical of academic settings. Present your tables to the class and compare them to those of other groups.

NOTE-PASSING: STRUGGLES FOR STATUS

■—*Margaret J. Finders*

Margaret J. Finders is associate dean and director of the School of Education at the University of Wisconsin, La Crosse. The following selection is taken from *Just Girls: Hidden Literacies and Life in Junior High* (1997), where Finders studied a group of popular junior high girls (the "social queens") and how they used literacy outside the official school curriculum—signing yearbooks, passing notes, writing bathroom graffiti, and reading teen 'zines.

WRITING A SUMMARY   Underline or highlight, annotate, and then write a summary of this reading selection, using "Talk is the thing" as a model. In the summary, focus on Finders's research—what is she examining, what are her findings, how does she interpret these findings? Integrate key words or phrases from "Note-Passing" in your summary.

1   Note-writing as a genre did not allow for much individual expression or originality. The girls all protested indignantly whenever I suggested such a notion: "You can write whatever you want." Yet the following notes illustrate the standards required for the genre of note-writing.

Lauren,

Yo! What's up? Not much here. I'm in math and it is BORING. Did you know that I like Nate a lot. But he'd probably never go out with me caz I'm too ugly. AND FAT. Oh, well though. I'm still going to try and get him to go with me caz I like him. I hope he goes with me before the football game Friday. I want to be going with him at the game. Are you and Ricky going to the game? I want to go somewhere after that. Maybe you could come over or I could come to your house. Don't show this to anyone. W-B [Write Back] Maggie

Lauren,

Hey. What's up? You don't need to ask Bill for me cause he won't go and he's just that way I guess. You can try but I know he's not going to go. Well I'm almost positive. I'm in social studies and I just got busted caz I had none of my homework done. Fun. My handwriting majorly Sucks. I hate it. Go to *Body Guard* at the mall and I'll say you need a ride home. Then you can spend the night at my house. Call me tonight. I will be at my mom's. S.S. [Stay Sweet or Stay Sexy] Carrie.

Notes regularly began with a common salutation, "Hey, what's up?" followed by a reference to where the note was written—"I'm in math." "I'm in social studies." Because notes were always written in school, this move positioned the queen in opposition to the institutional power by boldly announcing an act of defiance during one particular class and then adding a condemning judgment such as, "It's so boring." In this move, queens perceived themselves as powerful by defying authority. Yet that power was somewhat diffused as they often embedded in the body of the note a reference to themselves as inadequate: too fat, too ugly, my handwriting sucks. Often in notes, messages closed with "Sorry So Sloppy," which were sometimes shortened to S.S.S. For the most part, extreme care was taken to write neatly, at times dotting the i's with circles or hearts.

The content of notes was generally about making social arrangements for after-school activities and for requesting help in making romantic contacts. The notes carried highly coded messages such as N.M.H. (not much here) that limited the readership to those who were inside the circle of friends. The closing, as well, was most often highly coded—B.F.F. (best friends forever) W-B (write back)—to provide an insider quality to those who knew the codes. Britton (1970), noting the "with-it" language of adolescents, argues for the necessity of "drawing together members of a group or the set, and keeping outsiders out" (p. 235). The meaning behind S.S.S. evolved over time. At first it meant "Sorry So Sloppy," but over the course of the seventh-grade year, it came to carry a completely different meaning: "Stay Sweet and Sexy." The evolution of this one code illustrates the demands embedded within shifting social roles from girl to adolescent.

Although notes generally followed a standard format, a few did contain important unknown information such as the appropriate time to receive a call, an apology for flirting with a boyfriend, or guarded information about family problems. The queens attempted to control the circulation of their notes and regularly added to their messages, "Don't show this to anyone." For the most part, notes created boundaries around a group of friends. By creating a tangible document, girls created proof of their memberships.

5   As stated previously, girls all voiced the opinion that "you just write whatever you want," yet when someone outside the intimate circle of friends wrote a note to one of the most popular girls, she was criticized. As one girl described it, "Look at that. She doesn't even know how to write right." These teens were criticized for not recognizing or following the rules and rituals on note-writing, a primary rule being that notes could be passed only to friends of equal social status. The unstated rules of adhering to established social hierarchies were clearly enforced. If, for example, a girl did not know her place in the social hierarchy and wrote a note to a more popular girl, she became the object of ridicule and laughter within the higher circle.

This need for social sorting at the junior high was visible to teachers. Debra Zmoleck described the practice in this way:

I think part of the way junior high kids feel good about themselves is they've got to have that ego, you know, it's a pecking order. They've got to have somebody that's down there that all the other chickens peck at, you know. And I don't know why, I guess it's just part of junior high.

The "pecking order" to which Debra referred was often documented in literate practices. Literacy was a tool used to document and maintain social position. In private interviews, Angie and Lauren both made statements in accord with Tiffany's own self-assessment.

I don't write notes much so now I don't get 'em. Lauren gets the most because she writes the most. She's the most popular. Me, not so much.

Tiffany lost status because she didn't write as many notes as other girls and slowly over time received fewer and fewer, marking her as less popular. On the other hand, Lauren was perceived to be the most popular girl among her network of friends because "she has the most notes." She also received more notes from boys, which further served to document her high status among her friends.

In the fall of seventh grade, the number of notes passed increased until mid-November when a plateau was reached; January saw a sharp decline. When asked about this decline, the queens all relayed the fact that there just wasn't as much to write about; yet the events that they had written about all year—social arrangements, sports, and boys—had not decreased in their interest or in their activity. I contend that note-passing had served its purpose—to sort and select a hierarchy among the queens who had just entered a new arena in the fall. Arriving from different sixth-grade classrooms, the queens used literacies in the new school context to negotiate entry into new friendship networks. Through print sources, they maintained familiar ties in this strange new world, connecting at first with old sixth-grade friends and then negotiating their ways into other social groups. By January, new social positions were securely established, and note-passing decreased because jockeying for position was no longer an option for gaining status or entry into the social queens' network.

10   Note-passing was clearly a gendered activity. It functioned to control male voices and to try

out women's voices. Circulation of notes was controlled exclusively by girls. Girls decided who was entitled to see, receive, or write a note. Boys did not write notes to boys, and they wrote to girls only when they were invited or instructed to do so by a girl directly or through a channeling system, where one girl wrote to another girl who would then write to a boy, thereby granting him permission to write to the first girl. This act of literacy bestowed power and control of romantic interactions exclusively to females. The hierarchical arrangement placed power firmly in the hands of the social queens, who controlled and regulated which boys wrote or received notes.

To guard the circulation of messages, the queens informed me that learning to fold a note properly was vital to ensure that it would not open if it were dropped. Notes were folded into small triangles or squares with edges tucked in, serving as a lock to protect messages from unauthorized eyes. Such skill in intricate folding was also used to gain status within the inner circle. One's knowledge of elaborate folds signaled one as a member in good standing. Again, literacy served to document status within the circle of friends. If one queen learned a new and extremely complex fold, she received high praise and then attained the honored position of teacher, instructing others in how to fold.

Note-folding was a crucial skill because passing the note was a fine game that required a small, streamlined object. A note could have no rough edges to catch in a pocket lining, and it must be easily manipulated in the palm of one hand in order to avoid detection as it slipped from hand to hand boldly under the nose of a teacher. Passing notes from one of the social queens to another under the sharp scrutiny of a teacher was seen by these girls as an act of defiance and a behavior to be admired. Girls wrote, circulated, and responded to notes while reading aloud, participating in classroom discussions, and completing written work. A girl, for instance, could participate in a large-group dis-

cussion while writing and then passing notes without skipping a beat as she actively engaged in the classroom discussion. Designed to fool the teacher into thinking one was paying attention, such a game documented allegiance to peers. Ironically, a queen had to pay extremely close attention to keep the game going in her favor, yet this game was played to make the teacher appear foolish and the teen powerful.

Whenever the risk became heightened by a teacher's reprimands or threats of posting notes on classroom walls, notes became a greater avenue of status-building. When the risks were greatest, girls began lacing their texts with obscene language to up the ante, for to have one such note confiscated would mean not only a disruption at school but disruption at home as well.

More often than not, the content of the note was inconsequential; meaning was conveyed in the passing of the note rather than within the text itself. The act of passing the note during class relayed the message, an act of defiance of adult authority. The message was modified not through words but through the creative manipulation of the passing. The closer one was to the teacher physically when the note was written or delivered, the more powerful the message. By mid-November, after the girls had grown to trust me, they would often dig into their pockets and notebooks and hand me unopened notes. They did not need to read the notes because the message was implicit in the process of passing: in clues such as who sent, who received, who was present during the passing, and how the note was transported.

15 After I examined note-passing as a ritualized event, several themes emerged: (1) Writing is a social event; (2) special status is ascribed to the girl who received the most notes, especially from boys; and (3) meaning often resides in the act of passing a note. Note-passing was a tool used to document and maintain social position. For the most part, notes were used to bestow power and patrol boundaries around a group of friends.

COMPARING SUMMARIES

Compare with classmates the summaries you wrote, noting differences and similarities, including words and phrases quoted from "Note-Passing." How would you account for these differences and similarities? Don't assume one person's summary is necessarily better or more accurate. Instead, try to identify the principle of selection each student used. Discuss how others' summaries add to or change your understanding of Finders's research project, her results, and the conclusions she draws.

Making Connections: Staging a Conversation Between Readings

At times in *Reading Culture*—in some of the "Exploratory Writing" prompts and writing assignments after individual readings, and in the assignment sequences you will be asked to make connections between the readings, to see how each offers a particular perspective or takes a particular approach to whatever issue is at hand. Putting readings in relation to each other this way is often called a synthesis— a way of positioning the readings in relation to each other as though they were in a conversation.

After reading Shirley Brice Heath's "Talk is the thing" and Margaret J. Finders's "Note-Passing: Struggles for Status," for example, you might put the two selections— and how they go about researching and analyzing literacy events—into conversation with each other this way in a piece of exploratory writing:

SAMPLE SYNTHESIS OF "TALK IS THE THING" AND "NOTE-PASSING"

Both Heath and Finders are interested in "literacy events," which they think of as the social interactions that take place around written texts. Before reading about their research, I had always thought of literacy in terms of skills, as measured in school on standardized tests that tell you your grade level in reading or writing. To me, literacy just meant whether you could communicate properly. Heath and Finders, on the other hand, emphasize the social functions reading and writing perform and the meanings that various uses of literacy have for people. In "Talk is the thing," Heath researched how people in a black working-class community used reading and writing in very pragmatic and sociable ways that fit into their everyday lives, like reading and talking about newspaper stories or letters about daycare services. It's like neighbors worked together to make sense of the printed material they encountered. In contrast, the "social queens" who passed notes in junior high, in Finders's research study, were involved in very competitive behavior to gain social status in relation to peers and to determine who was or wasn't in the "in-group."

TURNING LITERACY NARRATIVES INTO LITERACY EVENTS

Turning a literacy narrative into a literacy event involves a move from *telling* to *analyzing* what happened. Working in groups of four or five, return to the literacy narratives by Eudora Welty, Malcolm X, and Conor Boyland that occur earlier in this chapter. Reread these narratives in terms of how a "piece of writing is integral to the nature of participants' interactions and their interpretive processes." Consider how Shirley Brice Heath and Margaret J. Finders might analyze and interpret these narratives.

The Assignment: Writing an Analysis of a Literacy Event

The culminating assignment in this chapter calls on you to identify and analyze a literacy event that you took part in directly, observed, or heard or read about. Your task is to explain how a "piece of writing" was centrally involved in people's interactions and how the participants made sense of things.

Consider the writing you've done so far in this chapter—the Writing Inventory, Literacy Narrative, Exploratory Writing, and so forth. Think of these pieces as data—the findings that have resulted from your research on the role reading and writing has played in your experience. The next step is to identify a particularly good example of a literacy event to analyze. In many respects, your paper will depend on how interesting your literacy event is and what it enables you to bring to light.

CHOOSING A LITERACY EVENT

Bring to class a paragraph or two that describes the literacy event you're considering for this writing assignment. Work in a group of three. Take turns. Read aloud what you've written. Then discuss with other group members:

- What social interaction takes place?
- How is a written text or an act of reading and/or writing involved in the interaction?
- How do the participants make sense of the literacy event?
- Is this a good example of a literacy event to use for this assignment?

CONSIDERATIONS FOR ANALYZING LITERACY EVENTS

Once you've decided on a literacy event, take these considerations into account to develop your analysis. This is not a checklist to do in order from start to finish but a list that isolates factors that can only be understood in relation to each other.

- **Context.** What is the social situation in which the literacy event takes place? What is the setting? Where does it happen—school, family, neighborhood, work, library, peer group, some combination? What is the moment? What led up to the literacy event? Why does it happen when it does?
- **Text.** What form or forms of writing are involved? Why these particular forms? Are these "official" or "unofficial" forms of writing?
- **Participants.** Who is involved? What are their relationships to each other? How are these relationships played out through the literacy event? How and why do the participants interact as they do? What identities do they express through reading and/or writing?

- **Event.** What happens? How is an act of writing and/or reading integral to the event? What role exactly does it play? What are the consequences or results?
- **Participants' interpretive processes.** How do the participants understand the event? What account or explanations would each give?

Sample Student Essays

The two student essays that follow offer different ways of addressing this writing assignment. The first, Russell Kim's "Petitioning the Powers," uses the genre of the personal essay to analyze a literacy event, while the second, Valery Sheridan's "'Please, order whatever you want. I insist': Ordering Meals at the Burning Spear Country Club as a Literacy Event," is an academic essay. As you read, notice the different writing strategies that are employed—differences that are evident in terms of the writer's voice and stance toward readers, the level of formality or informality, how the writer uses (or doesn't) work by literacy researchers to frame the investigation and draw out implications, and whether the analysis is presented explicitly or embedded in a narrative of the literacy event.

Kim 1

Russell Kim

Professor Batts

Eng 1102

November 12, 2008

Petitioning the Powers

I think I really started to understand something about how writing actually works in the world when I was in the eighth grade. If you can remember what eighth grade is like, you might recall what hot shits kids think they are at that age. They've left childhood and are briefly at the top of the world before they go to high school and begin all over again as freshmen. That's how we were. And one of the things we got into was knowing our rights. This was a combination of what we heard on Clash and Rage Against the Machine albums and what we learned in American history.

We knew that grownups couldn't just walk all over us. We knew we had rights and could petition the powers that be to change things.

Along with my friend Mike, I was a member of our junior high chorus. This was a big deal because the chorus director, Mr. DeSouza, was a legendary figure in our community. Every year for the past fifteen years or so, he took the chorus on a trip to an international competition, held in places like San Francisco, Toronto, Miami, and once in London. Every year the chorus won a gold medal. But Mike and I thought Mr. DeSouza was getting out of step with the times and that our repertoire of songs needed some updating. We mentioned this to him but he was not responsive. So, naturally, knowing our rights, we took the logical next step.

We went over to Mike's house after school and wrote a petition that asked Mr. DeSouza to add a few contemporary songs to the chorus's repertoire. We printed the petition and circulated it the next day among chorus members and other students as well to sign, figuring the chorus belonged to the school and the added names would make us look good.

We thought that Mr. DeSouza would see the numbers and meet right away to negotiate a settlement. We weren't asking for all that much, so we didn't think it would be a hassle. Wrong. The day after we left the petition in Mr. DeSouza's box, Mike and I got called into the principal's office. Mr. Boisvert, the principal, said we had a big problem. Mr. DeSouza was totally offended and insulted by the petition and had threatened to quit as chorus director, which would be a disaster because he was one of the most successful chorus directors in the country. And it was all our fault. We had "gone too far this time." When Mike and I said it was our right—and the American way—to petition for change peacefully, Mr. Boisvert looked right through us and said we weren't being fair to Mr. DeSouza, to the chorus, or to the school. We could write petitions later, when we were adults and could "accept responsibility for our actions" (whatever that meant). We had a choice: we could either apologize and stay on the chorus or quit. No deals.

Kim 3

The fact that Mike and I quit, missing a great trip the chorus took that year to Puerto Rico, isn't exactly the point of this literacy tale. Looking back on it, I'm interested in how writing a petition created such a crisis. Neither Mike nor I had imagined that Mr. DeSouza would react as he did. We certainly didn't intend to hurt his feelings or insult him. We thought we were just acting on our rights. But more important, the principal showed us that in fact we didn't have any rights. To him, we were still little kids and while we were expected to learn all about the Declaration of Independence and the Bill of Rights, we were really dependents. Knowing your rights, he said, was "for later."

Sheridan 1

Valery Sheridan

Professor Wheeler

WR101

October 6, 2008

"Please, order whatever you want. I insist":

Ordering Meals at the Burning Spear Country Club as a Literacy Event

Literacy events are often so embedded in everyday social life that they are hidden from plain sight, even when they happen right in front of us. A good example of this is how members of the Burning Spear Country Club order meals when they are hosting guests. At first glance, it may be hard to see how reading or writing is involved. But if we think of a "literacy event," in Shirley Brice Heath's words, as "any occasion in which a piece of writing is integral to the nature of the participants' interactions and their interpretive processes" ("Protean Shapes" 93), then the literacy involved in ordering meals starts to come into view. The "piece of writing" in this case is the menu. In my experience as a waitress at the Burning Spear Country Club for the last two years, I have witnessed literally hundreds of instances of members and their guests reading the menu, making their choices, and ordering meals. Heath puts particular emphasis on talk as a "necessary component" in analyzing literacy events (*Ways with Words* 196). In this paper, I will examine the talk between members and guests that takes place once the menu appears and what these social interactions reveal about relationships and identities.

When taking guests to dinner at Burning Spear, the club member is often concerned that guests will make an entree choice based on price as a courtesy to their host rather than on their actual preference. In order to deter this from happening, at Burning Spear, as well as at other country clubs where I've waitressed, two different menus are used. The menus look identical, including the supposedly elegant embossed cover, the tacky gold tassel peeking out of the menu's binding, and the typical restaurant prose (e.g., "hand-torn lettuce," "our chef's secret demi-glaze"). The difference is that the member menu lists the prices while the guest menu does not. Many hosts apparently feel, however, that even hiding the price is not enough. I've heard it happen so many times, after a dinner party has been seated and served cocktails, as guests are starting to read the menu, the host will say, "Please, order whatever you want. I insist."

Such statements are often followed by further talk on the part of the member host, addressed to guests, about their dinner order:

"No, don't get the baked haddock. It's usually not fresh here."
"The Catch of the Week was excellent. I had it last night."
"Get an appetizer, too."
"You're going to get a salad, right?"

As talk that revolves around a "piece of writing," the menu, the member's statements serve a number of purposes, establishing his identity

Sheridan 3

as a discriminating food connoisseur and a generous host for whom the prices on the menu are of no concern. And such statements also reinforce his standing and sense of belongingness, as an insider, at Burning Spear Country Club, in comparison to his guests who are identified, in turn, as visitors invited by the host member.

As the moment of ordering approaches, I've often overheard conversations like this one:

GUEST: "Ooh, the chicken piccata sounds good . . . but I don't care for capers."

MEMBER: "Oh! Well, they can make it any way you want!"

Members often encourage guests not just to order what they want but to feel free to include alterations and special orders. If guests seem reluctant to make a special order, members will typically say something like:

MEMBER: "Don't worry. I have special orders made for me all the time."

What the member is asserting here is that having "special orders made for me all the time" means the member is a special person, to whom the restaurant staff extends special courtesies and considerations. It enhances the member's social status, in relation to other members who don't get "special orders" and underlines the member's personal relationship to the restaurant staff, who supposedly want to take good care of him and pamper him with "special orders." Of course, this is amusing to us, as staff, because the reality is that all the members act similarly, requesting special orders, and all are accommodated by the kitchen.

In conclusion, we see that the talk in ordering meals by member hosts at Burning Spear functions similarly to the note-passing of the "social queens" in Margaret J. Finders's study of hidden literacies in junior high— "to document and maintain social position." Like the notes, this talk serves "to bestow power" on the host and "patrol boundaries" between members and guests (69).

Sheridan 4

Works Cited

Finders, Margaret J. *Just Girls: Hidden Literacies and Life in Junior High*.
New York: Teachers College P., 1997. Print.

Heath, Shirley Brice. "Protean Shapes in Literacy Events: Ever-Shifting Oral
and Literate Traditions." *Spoken and Written Language: Exploring
Orality and Literacy*. Ed. Deborah Tannen. Norwood, NJ: Ablex, 1982.
91-117. Print.

———. *Ways with Words: Language, Life, and Work in Communities and
Classrooms*. Cambridge: Cambridge UP, 1983. Print.

Looking Ahead

What you have been doing in the assignments in this chapter amounts to a cultural analysis of literacy events. Throughout the chapters that follow, we will be presenting further opportunities to do this kind of cultural investigation and analysis—to read and write your way into some of the meanings of contemporary U.S. culture. The work you do will be informed by what others have written, but it will also rely on your own knowledge of the culture you live in and on the observations you make in doing research into cultural practices, modes of expression, and patterns of meaning.

CHAPTER TWO

Generations

Children are always episodes in someone else's narratives.

— Carolyn Steedman

Photo courtesy Big Cheese Photo/Index Stock Imagery, Inc.

The United States is a nation of immigrants, and it is common to distinguish between first and second generations—between those who first came to the United States (voluntarily and involuntarily, from Europe, Asia, Africa, and Latin America) and their children who were born here. The two generations are biologically related to each other as well as to older generations as far back as people can trace their ancestry. Yet first-generation and second-generation Americans often differ in the way they live their lives, in the hopes they have for themselves and their children, and in the ties they feel to the traditions and customs of their places of ancestry. People are also members of a historical generation that is formed by a common history and common experiences shared by others their age. To be a member of a generation in cultural terms, then, is to belong both to a family you are related to biologically and to a group of people you are related to historically.

In this chapter, you will be asked to read, think, and write about what it means to be a member of and a participant in your historical generation. Whether you are straight out of high school or returning to college, it can be valuable for you to consider how your own personal experience has been shaped by growing up at a particular moment in a particular historical generation.

Each generation produces its own way of speaking and its own forms of cultural expression. Cultural historian Raymond Williams says that "no generation speaks quite the same language as its predecessor." Young people, for example, use their own slang to recognize friends, to distinguish between insiders and outsiders, to position themselves in relation to the older generation. Whether you say "whatever," "sweet," or "far out"; the kind of music you listen to; the way you dance; your style of dress; where you go to hang out—all of these reveal something about you and your relation to the constantly changing styles of youth culture in the contemporary United States.

How a generation looks at itself is inevitably entangled in the decisive historical events, geopolitical changes, and popular entertainment of its day. Events such as the Great Depression, World War II, the Vietnam War, the Reagan years, the dot.com boom and bust of the 1990s, the attacks on 9/11, and the invasion and occupation of Iraq have influenced a generation profoundly. To understand what it means to belong to your generation, you will need to locate your experience growing up as a member of your generation in its historical times—to see how your generation has made sense of its place in American history and its relation to past generations.

From the invention of the American teenager and juvenile delinquency in movies such as *Rebel Without a Cause* and *The Wild One* in the 1950s, American media have been fascinated by each new generation of young people. Each generation seems to have its own characteristic mood or identity that the media try to capture in a label: the "lost" generation of the Jazz Age in the 1920s, the "silent" generation of the Eisenhower years in the 1950s (traditionalists), the "baby boomers" of the 1960s, the "yuppies" of the 1980s, the Generation X "slackers" of the 1990s, and the "millennials" (or "nexters") of the 2000s. When people use these labels, they are not only referring to particular groups of people but are also calling up a set of values, styles, and images, a collective feeling in the air. When thinking about your generation, look at how the media have represented it and how these media representations have entered into your generation's conception of itself.

Of course, no generation is a monolithic thing. Not all thirty-somethings think alike or value the same things. Every generation is divided along the same lines of race, class, gender, and ethnicity that divide the wider society. But a generation is not simply a composite of individuals either. To think about the mood of your generation—the sensibility that suffuses its lived experience—you will need to consider how the character of your generation distinguishes it from generations of the past, even if that character is contradictory or inconsistent.

GEN (FILL IN THE BLANK): COMING OF AGE, SEEKING AN IDENTITY

—Arlie Russell Hochschild

Arlie Russell Hochschild is a professor of sociology at the University of California, Berkeley, where she codirects the Center for Working Families; she is also the author of such sociological studies as *The Time Bind: When Work Becomes Home and Home Becomes Work* (2001) and *The Managed Heart: Commercialization of Human Feelings* (1985). This article appeared in a special section of the *New York Times* on "Generations" on March 8, 2000.

SUGGESTION FOR READING Arlie Russell Hochschild offers a definition of the idea of a generation based on sociologist Karl Mannheim's 1927 essay "The Problem of Generations." As Hochschild notes, according to Mannheim, "a generation is a cohort of people who feel the impact of a powerful historical event and develop a shared consciousness about it." As you read, pay attention to how Hochschild uses this definition to analyze the generation of twenty- and thirty-year-olds and how she finds, in the absence of a large historical crisis in the life of this generation before September 11, 2001, an underlying trend.

1 "I'm not part of the 1960's generation," said Sandy de Lissovoy. "I don't feel part of Gen X or Gen Y. I'm sure not part of the 'Me Generation.' Who made up that term? I hate it. What's really in front of me is my computer, but even with it, I'm between the generation that barely tolerates computers and the one that treats them like a member of the family."

Mr. de Lissovoy, a 29-year-old graphic designer in San Francisco, was expressing as well as anyone the feelings that, as a sociology professor, I frequently hear during office hours. At this moment he was having a hard time defining his generation. He raised his eyebrows quizzically, smiled and said, "Call me the @ Generation One and a Half."

Can we make up our generation, as Mr. de Lissovoy playfully did, or is it imposed upon us, like it or not?

These are questions that the German sociologist Karl Mannheim took up in his classic 1927 essay, "The Problem of Generations." Is a generation a collection of people born in the same span of years? No, he thought, that is a cohort, and many cohorts are born, come of age and die without becoming generations. For Mannheim, a generation is a cohort of people who feel the impact of a powerful historical event and develop a shared consciousness about it. Not all members of a generation may see the event the same way, and some may articulate its defining features better than others. But what makes a generation is its connection to history.

5 Americans who came of age in the 1930's, 40's and 60's have been branded by large events—the Great Depression, World War II, Vietnam—and the collective moods they aroused. But from the 70's through the 90's, history's signal events happened elsewhere. Communism collapsed, but not in the United States. Wars raged in Rwanda, the Balkans and elsewhere, but they had little effect here. The forces in the United States have been social and economic, and they have shifted the focus to personal issues—matters of lifestyle that are shaped by consumerism, the mass media and an increasing sense of impermanence in family and work.

"There is no overarching crisis or cause for our generation," Mr. de Lissovoy said. "It's more a confusing, ambiguous flow of events. There's a slow, individual sorting out to do."

But underneath this confusing, ambiguous flow of events is a trend toward a more loosely jointed, limited-liability society, the privatizing influence of that trend and the crash-boom-bang of the market, which, in the absence of other voices, is defining generations left and right.

People in their 20's and early 30's are often called Gen X'ers, a term derived from a novel by Douglas Coupland. The book, *Generation X,* was followed by a film, *Slacker,* directed by Richard Linklater, about a group of overeducated, under-employed oddballs who drop to the margins of society. But for Jim Kreines, a 32-year-old grad-uate student of philosophy at the University of Chicago, the label fit loosely, if at all.

When I asked him what generation he belonged to, Mr. Kreines replied, "I'm not sure I care enough to argue about this." He had read the Coupland book and seen the film. But did the Gen X'er label apply to him? He was not sure it mattered.

10   Many Gen X'ers may be trying to sort out a certain cultural sleight of hand. They feel luck-ier than previous generations because they enjoy many more options. In the 50's, said Charles Sellers, a 28-year-old urban planner in Portland, Ore., there was only one choice. "If you were a woman you were a housewife," he said. "If you were a man you married and supported your family. Today, except for the Mormons, Americans have a long cultural menu to choose from. If you're a woman, you can be a single woman, a career woman, a lesbian, a single mom by choice, a live-in lover, a married-for-now wife, a married-forever wife. And the same for work: I'm on my third career."

But the wider menu of identities comes with a decreasing assurance that any particular iden-tity will last. This is because a culture of dereg-ulation has slipped from our economic life into our cultural life. Gen X'ers, at least in the middle class, can be more picky in finding "just the right mate" and "just the right career." But once you've found them, you begin to wonder if you can keep them.

In his book *The New Insecurity,* Jerald Wallulis, a philosopher at the University of South Carolina, observed that in the last 30 years, peo-ple have shifted the way they base their identity: from marriage and employment to marriageabil-ity and employability. Old anchors no longer hold, and a sense of history is lost. For the gen-erations of the 80's and 90's, this rootlessness is their World War II, their Vietnam. And it pres-ents a more difficult challenge than the one faced by the 60's generation.

Mr. de Lissovoy's parents divorced when he was a baby and now live on opposite coasts. Consider, too, the shifting family ties of a 27-year-old computer programmer in Silicon Valley, who asked that her name be withheld. "My mother divorced four times and is living on uncertain terms with her fifth," she said, "so I'm not sure if she'll stay with him either. I haven't gotten attached to any of my stepdads. My dad remar-ried four times, too, only now he's married to a woman I like."

When her parents divorced, she spent every other weekend with her father. "My dad was glad to see me, but I'd have to remind him of the name of my best friends," she said. "He didn't know what mattered to me. After a while it just got to be dinner and a video, and after that, I didn't feel much like going to his apartment."

15   Talking about her love life, she said: "If I meet someone I really like, I become shy and tied up in knots. I can't talk about anything personal." It was as if she did not dare to begin a relationship for fear of ending it.

After the parents of another young woman divorced, her father married a woman as young as his daughter, and is very involved with his new, young children who are the same age as his grandchildren. Now, when his daughter tries to arrange a visit between her father and his grand-children, he is often too pinched for time to see them. His daughter feels hurt and angry—first to miss out on a father, then a grandfather.

Reflecting on these generational jumbles, Mr. de Lissovoy commented: "Today's hype is that 'You can get it if you really want it'—a mate, career and love still sells a lot of tickets. We're the Generation of Individual Choice. Which? Which? Which? But the bottom can fall out from some of those choices. And in the end, we're orphans. We're supposed to take care of ourselves. That's our only choice."

Not every young person I have talked with has felt so adrift. The 20-somethings of the 90's have more material resources than their predecessors—ample job opportunities, for example.

Still, Mr. de Lissovoy's feelings reflect something true about America these days. Despite the recent economic miracle, we are experiencing a care deficit. Social services have been cut; hospitals release patients 24 hours after surgery to recover at home. But who is home to do the caring? Two-thirds of mothers are working. One-quarter of households are headed by single mothers; they need help, too. Paradoxically, American individualism and pride in self-sufficiency lead us to absorb rather than resist this deficit: "Care? Who needs care? I can handle it," thus adding one problem to another.

20 If in previous decades large historic events drew people together and oriented them to action, the recent double trend toward more choice but less security leads the young to see their lives in more individual terms. Big events collectivize, little events atomize. So with people facing important but private problems, and thinking in individual, not collective, terms, the coast became clear in the 80's and 90's for the marketplace to stalk into this cultural void and introduce generation-defining clothes, music and videos.

Generations X and Y function as market gimmicks nowadays. The market dominates not just economic life, as the economist Robert Kuttner argues in "Everything for Sale," but our cultural life as well. It tells us what a generation is—a Pepsi generation, a Mac generation, an Internet generation. And a magazine about shoot-'em-up computer games calls itself *NextGen*.

Advertisers are appealing to children over the heads of their parents. Juliet B. Schor, an economics lecturer at Harvard, suggests that the younger generation is the cutting edge of a full-blown market culture. More than $2 billion is spent on advertising directed at them, 20 times the amount spent a decade ago. Most of the advertising is transmitted through television; it is estimated that youngsters increased their viewing time one hour a day between 1970 and 1990. Three out of five children ages 12 to 17 now have a TV in their bedroom. Advertisers are trying to enlist children against their parents' better judgment, Dr. Schor said recently, and overworked parents sometimes give in and go along. If Dr. Schor is correct, Generation Y might be defined even more than Generation X by what its members buy than by what they do or who they are.

Marketing strategists, meanwhile, are turning over all the generations faster, slicing and dicing the life cycle into thinner strips. In the computer industry, an advertising generation is nine months; in the clothing industry, a season. In department stores, between the displays for girls in their preteens and teens, is a new age, "tweens." The identity promised by a style or a brand name for one generation is marked off from an increasing number of others. And the styles continually replace old with new.

This creates a certain consumer logic. Older consumers buy what makes them feel young, while young consumers, up to a point, buy what makes them feel older. So the preteenager will buy the tween thing while the teenager will buy the 20-something jacket, and the 40-year-old will browse in the racks for 30-year-olds.

25 To be sure, every American decade has fashion marketeers define generational looks and sounds, but probably never before have they so totally hijacked a generation's cultural expression. Allison Pugh, a 33-year-old married mother of two and a graduate student in sociology at the University of California at Berkeley, said: "I definitely feel like people just two or three years younger than me are the beginning of another generation. But I can only say why by pointing

to superficial things, like how many pierces they have, how high their shoes are and what kind of music they listen to. I roomed with a girl just two years younger and she listened to Smashing Pumpkins, Nirvana and Hole. I was 'old'—as in out of it—even just a few years out of college. I started to sound like my mother: 'That's not music; what is that noise?'"

Like Ms. Pugh, Mr. de Lissovoy is considered old to the generation at his heels. He is wired, but feels ambivalent about it. "What I don't like is disposability, hyperspeed, consumption," he said. "I'd like to reduce these. What I want more of is face-to-face interaction, a value on repair, families living nearby each other. I'd love to live in a multigenerational, multiracial cohousing project. And a more leisurely pace of life. I want some pretty old-fashioned things."

The 60's generation is hitting 60, and with some computer nerds striking it rich, 60's-era protests are not defining the new generation. But that era's flame is not dead. In front of a large gathering at the Pauley ballroom on the Berkeley campus a few months ago, the Mario Savio Young Activist Award for 1999—named after the leader of the 1964 Free Speech Movement—was given to Nikki Bas, a 31-year-old American of Filipino descent who coordinates Sweatshop Watch, a campaign against the poor pay and working conditions of third-world workers who make football uniforms and other clothing sold on American college campuses. Mr. de Lissovoy remembers hearing about Mr. Savio from his 60's activist mother, but he does not know Nikki Bas, is no longer a student and is under time pressure at work. So he is not signing up.

Still, from a distance he watched the protests in Seattle against the World Trade Organization late last year, and they kindled a sense of the importance of history that he feels the market is driving out. "I hated the mindless anarchists who broke shop windows," he said. "But the other protesters who went there to speak up against mega-corporations running the show, and for the family farm, local communities, monarch butterflies and sea turtles—they are taking the long view of the planet. We usually think it's the older generation that wants to preserve the past, and it's the young who don't mind tearing things up. In Seattle, the young environmentalists had their eye on history, and it was the old who had an eye on their pocketbooks."

Ultimately, market generations are generations of things, and they can make us forget generations of people. "My generation doesn't know how globalization will turn out," Mr. de Lissovoy said. "But we won't see how globalization is messing us up if we've forgotten how the world used to be. Whichever way, we don't see that what we are doing is forgetting the past. And we're nobodies without a sense of history."

He recalled how baseball caps with X's became popular with teenagers, especially in Detroit, after Spike Lee's film on Malcolm X came out. "When a TV interviewer asked a kid about the X on his cap, he didn't know who Malcolm X was," Mr. de Lissovoy said. "He didn't even know he was a person. We need to appreciate the work it takes to get us where we are. Otherwise we aren't anywhere."

30

EXPLORATORY WRITING

Looking for a defining feature of the generation of young people at the beginning of the twenty-first century, Arlie Russell Hochschild suggests that there "is a trend toward a more loosely jointed, limited-liability society, the privatizing influence of that trend and the crash-boom-bang of the market." In a 2–3 page exploratory writing, explain what exactly she means by this trend. In what sense does it help explain the collective mood of a generation?

TALKING ABOUT THE READING

Hochschild cites the sociologist Karl Mannheim's idea that a "generation is a cohort of people who feel the impact of powerful historical events and develop a shared consciousness about it." "Gen (Fill in the Blank)" was written before 9/11, the "war on terrorism," and the invasion and occupation of Iraq. With a group of your classmates, consider how or if these more recent events might define a generation in the way that the Great Depression, World War II, and Vietnam defined the generations coming of age in the 1930s, 1940s, and 1960s. This article was published in 2000. If Hochschild were writing the article today, how would she have to revise her description of a generation informed by events since then?

WRITING ASSIGNMENTS

1. Neither Hochschild nor any of the people she interviews offer a term to "fill in the blank" and characterize the current generation of young people. In a 3–5 page essay, write about what it means to describe an entire generation using a label. Consider, for example, the terms used to characterize earlier generations: the greatest generation of World War II, the Beat generation, baby boomers, the Me generation, Generation X, slackers, and so on. What do such terms say about the generations they are meant to define? What do they leave out? In your essay, suggest the qualities of your own generation you would like to see in any term that might be used to define it.

2. Consider Hochschild's claim that the "market dominates not just economic life . . . but our cultural life as well." Write a 3–5 page essay that applies the statement to your generation. You'll want to take into account, of course, how individual identities are shaped by what people buy and consume—whether styles of clothes or music or digital technology. But consider also how the market permeates people's thinking, their relationships with others, and their capacity to experience the world.

3. Assume that Hochschild has hired you to help her update her article. Write a memo to her that first explains to what extent her findings remain valid and why. Then provide an explanation of what she would need to add or revise in order to update the article.

GOTHS IN TOMORROWLAND

— *Thomas Hine*

Thomas Hine is well known for his writing about architecture and design. He is the author of *Populuxe* (1987), a book on American design in the 1950s and 1960s, and *The Total Package* (1995), a study of brand names and packaging. The following selection comes from his book *The Rise and Fall of the American Teenager* (1999). Hine explores the diversity of teen culture and its relation to adult society.

SUGGESTION FOR READING   Hine begins with an anecdote about the goth "invasion" of Disneyland in 1997 and the "zero tolerance" policy adopted by Disney's security forces. Notice that Hine wants to do more than just tell his story. He sees in it a larger issue about how the "mere presence of teenagers threatens us." As you read, keep in mind this general theme of the alienation of teenagers from adult society, how adults enforce it, and how teenagers maintain it.

I feel stupid and contagious.

—*Kurt Cobain, "Smells Like Teen Spirit" (1991)*

1 In the summer of 1997, the security forces at Disneyland and the police in surrounding Anaheim, California, announced a "zero tolerance" policy to fend off a new threat.

Hordes of pale, mascaraed goths—one of the many tribes of teendom—were invading. It was an odd onslaught. Unlike their barbarian namesakes, they weren't storming the gates of the walled Magic Kingdom. They had yearly passes, purchased for $99 apiece. Many of them had not even been goths when their parents dropped them off at the edge of the parking lot. Rather, they changed into their black sometimes gender-bending garments, applied their white makeup accented with black eyeliner and gray blush-on. The punkier among them accessorized with safety pins and other aggressively ugly, uncomfortable-looking pierceables. And most important of all, they reminded themselves to look really glum. Once inside, they headed for Tomorrowland, Disneyland's most unsettled neighborhood, and hogged all the benches.

It was a sacrilege. Disneyland, said those who wrote letters to the editor, is supposed to be "the happiest place on earth," and these young people with their long faces clearly didn't belong. The presence of sullen clusters of costumed teens showed, some argued, that Disney had given up its commitment to family values. It was no longer possible to feel safe in Disneyland, came the complaints, and that was about the last safe place left.

Actually, the safety of Disneyland was part of the attraction for the goth teens. They told reporters that their parents bought them season passes because the theme park's tight security would assure nothing bad would happen to them. In the vast sprawl of Orange County, California, there are very few safe places where teens are welcome, and Disneyland has always been one of them.

5 Those who complained spoke of the goths as if they were some sort of an alien force, not just white suburban California teenagers. Only a few years earlier, they had been kids who were delighted to go with their parents to meet Mickey. And only a few years from now, they will be young adults—teaching our children, cleaning our teeth, installing our cable television. But now they insist on gloom. And the adult world could not find a place for them—even in Tomorrowland.

Unlike Minnesota's Mall of America—which became a battleground for gang warfare transplanted from Minneapolis and which eventually barred unescorted teenagers from visiting at night—the perceived threat to Disneyland was handled in a low-key way. Teenagers were arrested for even the tiniest infractions outside the park and forced by security guards to follow Disneyland's quite restrictive rules of decorum within the park. After all, the theme park's administrators had an option not available to government; they could revoke the yearly passes. While Disneyland doesn't enforce a dress code for its visitors, it can keep a tight rein on their behavior.

Yet, despite its lack of drama, I think the situation is significant because it vividly raises many of the issues that haunt teenagers' lives at the end of the twentieth century. It is about the alienation of teenagers from adult society, and equally about the alienation of that society from its teenagers. The mere presence of teenagers threatens us.

It is also a story about space. How, in an environment devoid of civic spaces, do we expect people to learn how to behave as members of a community? And it is about the future. Is a meaningful tomorrow so far away that young people can find nothing better to do than engage in faux-morbid posturing? (Even Disney's theme parks are losing track of the future; they are converting their Tomorrowlands into nostalgic explorations of how people used to think about the future a century and more ago.)

And even its resolution—a stance of uneasy tolerance backed by coercion and force—seems symptomatic of the way Americans deal with young people now.

10   Inevitably, a lack of perspective bedevils efforts to recount the recent past, but the problem is more than that. The last quarter of the twentieth century has, in a sense, been about fragmentation. Identity politics has led to a sharpening of distinctions among the groups in the society, and a suspicion of apparent majorities. Postmodern literary theory warns us to mistrust narratives. Even advertising and television, which once united the country in a common belief in consumption, now sell to a welter of micromarkets. Thus we are left without either a common myth, or even the virtual common ground of *The Ed Sullivan Show*.

It seems crude now to speak of teenagers and think of the white middle-class, heterosexual young people that the word "teenager" was originally coined to describe. The "echo" generation of teenagers, whose first members are now entering high school, is about 67 percent non-Hispanic white, 15 percent black, 14 percent Hispanic, and 5 percent Asian or American Indian. The proportion of Hispanic teens will grow each year, and the Census Bureau also reports significantly greater numbers of mixed-race teens and adoptees who are racially different from their parents.

Even the word "Hispanic" is a catch-all that conceals an enormous range of cultural difference between Mexicans, Cubans, Puerto Ricans, Dominicans, and other groups whose immigration to the United States has increased tremendously during the last quarter century. Urban school systems routinely enroll student populations that speak dozens of different languages at home.

Differences among youth do not simply involve differences of culture, race, income, and class—potent as these are. We now acknowledge differences in sexual orientation among young people. Today's students are also tagged with bureaucratic or medical assessments of their abilities and disabilities that also become part of their identities.

There are so many differences among the students at a high school in Brooklyn, Los Angeles, or suburban Montgomery County, Maryland, that one wonders whether the word "teenager" is sufficient to encompass them all. Indeed, the terms "adolescent" and "teenager" have always had a middle-class bias. In the past, though, working-class youths in their teens were already working and part of a separate culture. Now that the work of the working class has disappeared, their children have little choice but to be teenagers. But they are inevitably different from those of the postwar and baby boomer eras because they are growing up in a more heterogeneous and contentious society.

15   What follows, then, is not a single unified narrative but, rather, a sort of jigsaw puzzle. Many pieces fit together nicely. Others seem to be missing. It's easier to solve such a puzzle if you know what picture is going to emerge, but if I were confident of that, I wouldn't be putting you, or myself, to such trouble.

These discussions do have an underlying theme: the difficulty of forging the sort of meaningful identity that Erik Erikson described at midcentury. But if we look for a picture of the late-twentieth-century teenager in these fragments, we won't find it. That's because we're expecting to find something that isn't there.

The goths who invaded Tomorrowland are examples of another kind of diversity—or perhaps pseudo-diversity—that has emerged gaudily during the last two decades. These are the tribes of youth. The typical suburban high school is occupied by groups of teens who express themselves through music, dress, tattoos and piercing, obsessive hobbies, consumption patterns, extracurricular activities, drug habits, and sex practices. These tribes hang out in different parts of the school, go to different parts of town. Once it was possible to speak of a youth culture, but now there is a range of youth subcultures, and clans, coteries, and cliques within those.

In 1996 a high school student asked fellow readers of an Internet bulletin board what groups were found in their high schools. Nearly every school reported the presence of "skaters," "geeks," "jocks," "sluts," "freaks," "druggies," "nerds," and those with "other-colored hair," presumably third-generation punks. There were also, some students reported, "paper people," "snobs," "band geeks," "drama club types" (or "drama queens"), "soccer players" (who aren't counted as jocks, the informant noted), "Satanists," "Jesus freaks," "industrial preps," "techno-goths," and "computer dweebs." Several took note of racial and class segregation, listing "blacks," "Latinos," "white trash," and "wannabe blacks." There were "preppies," who, as one writer, possibly a preppie herself, noted, "dress like the snobs but aren't as snobbish." "Don't forget about the druggie preps," another writer fired back.

This clearly wasn't an exhaustive list. Terms vary from school to school and fashions vary from moment to moment. New technologies emerge, in-line skates or electronic pagers for instance, and they immediately generate their own dress, style, language, and culture.

20   The connotations of the technologies can change very quickly. Only a few years ago, pagers were associated mostly with drug dealers, but now they've entered the mainstream. Pagers became respectable once busy mothers realized that they could use them to get messages to their peripatetic offspring. Young pager users have developed elaborate codes for flirtation, endearment, assignation, and insults. They know that if 90210 comes up on their pager, someone's calling them a snob, and if it's 1776, they're revolting, while if it's 07734, they should turn the pager upside down and read "hELLO."

Most of the youth tribes have roots that go back twenty years or more, though most are more visible and elaborate than they once were. Many of these tribes are defined by the music they like, and young people devote a lot of energy to distinguishing the true exemplars of heavy metal, techno, alternative, or hip-hop from the mere poseurs. Hybrid and evolutionary versions of these cultures, such as speed metal, thrash, or gangsta rap make things far more confusing.

One thing that many of these subcultures have in common is what has come to be known as modern primitivism. This includes tattooing, the piercing of body parts, and physically expressive and dangerous rituals, such as the mosh pits that are part of many rock concerts. Young people use piercing and tattoos to assert their maturity and sovereignty over their bodies.

"Can this be child abuse?" Sally Dietrich, a suburban Washington mother, asked the police when her thirteen-year-old son appeared with a bulldog tattooed on his chest. "I said, 'What about destruction of property?' He's my kid." Her son was, very likely, trying to signal otherwise. Nevertheless, Dietrich mounted a successful campaign to bar tattooing without permission in the state of Maryland, one of many such restrictions passed during the 1990s.

It may be a mistake to confuse visible assertions of sexual power with the fact of it. For example, heavy-metal concerts and mosh pits are notoriously male-dominated affairs. And the joke of MTV's *Beavis and Butt-head* is that these two purported metalheads don't have a clue about how to relate to the opposite sex. Those whose costumes indicate that they have less to prove are just as likely to be sexually active.

25   In fact, visitors to Disneyland probably don't need to be too worried about the goths, a tribe which, like many of the youth culture groups, has its roots in English aestheticism. As some goths freely admit, they're pretentious, and their morbid attitudes are as much a part of the dress-up games as the black clothes themselves.

The goth pose provides a convenient cover. For some males, it gives an opportunity to try out an androgynous look. The costumes, which emphasize the face and make the body disappear, may also provide an escape for young women and men who fear that they're overweight or not fit. Black clothes are slimming, and darkness even more so. "Until I got in with goths, I hadn't met other people who are depressed like I am and that I could really talk to," said one young woman on an Internet bulletin board. Another said being a goth allowed her relaxation from life as a straight-A student and a perfect daughter.

Although young people recognize an immense number of distinctions among the tribes and clans of youth culture and are contemptuous of those they regard as bogus, most adults cannot tell them apart. They confuse thrashers with metalheads and goths because they all wear black. Then they assume that they're all taking drugs and worshipping Satan.

The adult gaze is powerful. It classes them all as teenagers, whether they like it or not. The body alterations that young people use to assert that they are no longer children successfully frighten grown-ups, but they also convince them these weird creatures are well short of being adults. The ring through the lip or the nipple merely seems to demonstrate that they are not ready for adult responsibility. What they provoke is not respect but restrictions.

Tribes are about a yearning to belong to a group—or perhaps to escape into a disguise. They combine a certain gregariousness with what seems to be its opposite: a feeling of estrangement. The imagery of being alone in the world is not quite so gaudy as that of modern primitivism, yet it pervades contemporary youth culture.

30 While youthful exploration of the 1920s, 1940s, 1950s, or 1960s often took the form of wild dancing, more recently it has been about solitary posing. This phenomenon is reflected, and perhaps encouraged, by MTV, which went on the air in 1981. In contrast with the rudimentary format of *American Bandstand*, in which the viewer seemed simply to be looking in on young people having fun dancing with one another, MTV videos tend to be more about brooding than participation. They are highly subjective, like dreams or psychodramas. They connect the viewer with a feeling, rather than with other people.

And while the writhing, leaping, and ecstatic movement of the mosh pit seems to be an extreme form of *American Bandstand*-style

participation, it embodies a rather scary kind of community. One's own motions have little relationship to those of others. And there's substantial risk of injury. The society implied by the dance is not harmonious and made up of couples. Rather, it is violent and composed of isolated individuals who are, nevertheless, both seeking and repulsing contact with others. If this sounds like a vision of American society as a whole, that's not surprising. Figuring out what things are really like is one of the tasks of youth. Then they frighten their elders by acting it out.

When a multinational company that sells to the young asked marketing psychologist Stan Gross to study teenagers around the country, he concluded after hundreds of interviews and exercises that the majority of young people embraced an extreme if inchoate individualism. Most believe that just about every institution they come in contact with is stupid. When asked to choose an ideal image for themselves, the majority selected a picture that depicted what might be described as confident alienation. The figure sits, comfortably apart from everything, his eyes gazing out of the image at something unknown and distant.

Such studies are done, of course, not to reform the young but to sell to them. And the collective impact of such knowledge of the young has been the proliferation of advertising that encourages young people not to believe anything—even advertising—and to express their superiority by purchasing the product that's willing to admit its own spuriousness.

The distance between spontaneous expression and large-scale commercial exploitation has never been shorter. Creators of youth fashion, such as Nike, go so far as to send scouts to the ghetto to take pictures of what young people are wearing on the streets and writing on the walls. Nike seeks to reflect the latest sensibilities, both in its products and its advertising. The company feeds the imagery right back to those who created it, offering them something they cannot afford as a way of affirming themselves.

35   One result of this quick feedback is that visual symbols become detached from their traditional associations and become attached to something else. Rappers, having made droopy pants stylish in the suburbs, began to wear preppie sportswear, and brand names like Tommy Hilfiger and Nautica became badges of both WASP and hip-hop sensibilities. Thus, even when the fashions don't change, their meaning does. Such unexpected shifts in the meaning of material goods cannot be entirely manipulated by adults. But marketers have learned that they must be vigilant in order to profit from the changes when they come.

More overtly than in the past, many of today's young are looking for extreme forms of expression. This quest is just as apparent in sports, for example, as in rock culture. The 1996 Atlanta Olympics began with an exhibition of extreme cycling and extreme skating. These and other extreme sports, categorized collectively as "X-Games," have become a cable television fixture because they draw teenage males, an otherwise elusive audience. "Extreme" was one of the catchwords of the 1990s, and it became, by 1996, the most common word in newly registered trade names, attached either to products aimed at youth or which sought to embody youthfulness.

Young people are caught in a paradox. They drive themselves to extremes to create space in which to be themselves. Yet the commercial machine they think they're escaping is always on their back, ready to sell them something new.

EXPLORATORY WRITING

Thomas Hine uses the opening anecdote about goth teens and Disneyland to announce the theme of this piece. In an exploratory writing, explain what this story is meant to represent about the relations between teenagers and adults. What further examples and evidence does Hine offer in the rest of the selection to support his point?

TALKING ABOUT THE READING

In a 10-minute writing, describe what "tribes" are represented in your high school or college. Share that writing with a group of your classmates. After you have read each other's descriptions, together develop a classification of the various groups. What do you see as the leading ways in which groups of young people define themselves? What are the meanings of the identities they take on? What are the relationships among the various groups? What are the various groups' relationship to adult society?

WRITING ASSIGNMENTS

1. As a follow-up to your class discussion, write an essay that classifies the various groups (or "tribes") of youth culture at the high school you attended or at your college. Describe the leading groups, their styles, behaviors, values, and attitudes. After providing an overview of the groups, explain their relationship to each other and to the adult society that surrounds them.

2. Notice how Hine's perspective differs from Arlie Russell Hochschild's in the previous reading selection. Hochschild is interested in characterizing the collective mood of a generation, while Hine sees instead diverse "tribes of youth" defined by different styles of dress, music, body ornamentation, extracurricular activity, drug use, and sexual practices, as well as racial and ethnic markers. Write an essay in which you compare the two perspectives. What does each bring to the surface in their discussions of young people? What does each neglect?

3. At the end of this selection, Hine says that young people are "caught in a paradox": no matter how much they rebel against adult society to create a space for themselves, the "commercial machine" they're trying to escape from reincorporates their cultural styles in the form of new products and merchandise. Do you think this is a reasonable assessment? Why or why not? Write an essay that explains your answer—and whether you think young people can establish their own way of doing things, independent of the market and the workings of adult society.

A PORTRAIT OF "GENERATION NEXT": HOW YOUNG PEOPLE VIEW THEIR LIVES, FUTURES, AND POLITICS

— Pew Research Center for the People and the Press

The Pew Research Center for the People and the Press describes itself as "independent opinion research group that studies attitudes toward the press, politics and public policy issues." A division of the Pew Research Center, the Center for the People and the Press, issues an annual report on the state of the media detailing publishing and broadcasting trends, audience demographics, and which media outlets the public considers most trustworthy. On January 9, 2007, the center published the following summary of its survey on young people's attitudes.

SUGGESTION FOR READING The *Generation Next* study, aimed at understanding the lives and opinions of young people today, is based on special surveys conducted in September and October 2006. These survey results were then placed in the context of twenty years of survey and polling results aimed at understanding young peoples' attitudes toward politics and cultural issues. The summary of findings that appears here is taken from the Pew site at http://people-press.org. The entire report (as a pdf file) is available to download from the site. If you would like a fuller context for these findings, visit the site and read through the survey questions available for download.

SUMMARY OF FINDINGS

1 A new generation has come of age, shaped by an unprecedented revolution in technology and dramatic events both at home and abroad. They are Generation Next, the cohort of young adults who have grown up with personal computers, cell phones and the internet and are now taking their place in a world where the only constant is rapid change.

In reassuring ways, the generation that came of age in the shadow of Sept. 11 shares the characteristics of other generations of young adults. They are generally happy with their lives and optimistic about their futures. Moreover, Gen Nexters feel that educational and job opportunities are better for them today than for the previous generation. At the same time, many of their attitudes and priorities reflect a limited set of life experiences. Marriage, children and an established career remain in the future for most of those in Generation Next.

More than two-thirds see their generation as unique and distinct, yet not all self-evaluations are positive. A majority says that "getting rich" is the main goal of most people in their age group, and large majorities believe that casual sex, binge drinking, illegal drug use and violence are more prevalent among young people today than was the case 20 years ago.

In their political outlook, they are the most tolerant of any generation on social issues such as immigration, race and homosexuality. They are also much more likely to identify with the Democratic Party than was the preceding generation of young people, which could reshape politics in the years ahead. Yet the evidence is mixed as to whether the current generation of young Americans will be any more engaged in the nation's civic life than were young people in the past, potentially blunting their political impact.

5   This report takes stock of this new generation. It explores their outlook, their lifestyle and their politics. Because the boundaries that separate generations are indistinct, the definition of Generation Next and other generational groups mentioned in this report are necessarily approximate. For analysis purposes, Generation Next includes those Americans between the ages of 18 and 25 years old.

MEET GENERATION NEXT:

- They use technology and the internet to connect with people in new and distinctive ways. Text messaging, instant messaging and email keep them in constant contact with friends. About half say they sent or received a text message over the phone in the past day, approximately double the proportion of those ages 26–40.

- They are the "Look at Me" generation. Social networking sites like Facebook, MySpace and My Yearbook allow individuals to post a personal profile complete with photos and descriptions of interests and hobbies. A majority of Gen Nexters have used one of these social networking sites, and more than four-in-ten have created a personal profile.

- Their embrace of new technology has made them uniquely aware of its advantages and disadvantages. They are more likely than older adults to say these cyber-tools make it easier for them to make new friends and help them to stay close to old friends and family. But more than eight-in-ten also acknowledge that these tools "make people lazier."

- About half of Gen Nexters say the growing number of immigrants to the U.S. strengthens the country more than any generation. And they also lead the way in their support for gay marriage and acceptance of interracial dating.

- Beyond these social issues, their views defy easy categorization. For example, Generation Next is less critical of government regulation of business but also less critical of business itself. And they are the most likely of any generation to support privatization of the Social Security system.

- They maintain close contact with parents and family. Roughly eight-in-ten say they talked to their parents in the past day. Nearly three-in-four see their parents at least once a week, and half say they see their parents daily. One reason: money. About three-quarters of Gen Nexters say their parents have helped them financially in the past year.

- Their parents may not always be pleased by what they see on those visits home: About half of Gen Nexters say they have either gotten a tattoo, dyed their hair an untraditional color, or had a body piercing in a place other than their ear lobe. The most popular are tattoos, which decorate the bodies of more than a third of these young adults.

- One-in-five members of Generation Next say they have no religious affiliation or are atheist or agnostic, nearly double the proportion of young people who said that in the late 1980s. And just 4% of Gen Nexters say people in their generation view becoming more spiritual as their most important goal in life.

- They are somewhat more interested in keeping up with politics and national affairs than were young people a generation ago. Still, only a third say they follow what's going on in government and public affairs "most of the time."

- In Pew surveys in 2006, nearly half of young people (48%) identified more with the Democratic Party, while just 35% affiliated

Generation Next

		Age 18–25
		%
Think your generation is unique and distinct?	Yes	68
	No	31
	DK	1
		100
Compared with 20 years ago young adults today have		%
Better educational opportunities		84
Access to higher paying jobs		72
Live in more exciting times		64
Compared with 20 years ago young adults today		%
Have more casual sex		75
Resort to violence more		70
Binge drink more		69
Use more illegal drugs		63
Vote less often		49

	······ Age ······	
	18–25	26+
2004 presidential vote*	%	%
John Kerry	56	47
George W. Bush	43	52
Other/Didn't vote	1	1
	100	100
Homosexuality should be		
Accepted	58	50
Discouraged	32	39
Mixed/DK	10	11
	100	100
Impact of immigration		
Strengthens nation	52	39
A burden	38	42
Mixed/DK	10	19
	100	100

Based on 2006 Gen Next Survey.

*2004 NEP Exit Polls, 18–24 year-old voters.

more with the GOP. This makes Generation Next the least Republican generation.

■ Voter turnout among young people increased significantly between 2000 and 2004, interrupting a decades-long decline in turnout among the young. Nonetheless, most members of Generation Next feel removed from the political process. Only about four-in-ten agree with the statement: "It's my duty as a citizen to always vote."

- They are significantly less cynical about government and political leaders than are other Americans or the previous generation of young people. A majority of Americans agree with the statement: "When something is run by the government, it is usually inefficient and wasteful," but most Generation Nexters reject this idea.

- Their heroes are close and familiar. When asked to name someone they admire, they are twice as likely as older Americans to name a family member, teacher, or mentor. Moreover, roughly twice as many young people say they most admire an entertainer rather than a political leader.

- They are more comfortable with globalization and new ways of doing work. They are the most likely of any age group to say that automation, the outsourcing of jobs, and the growing number of immigrants have helped and not hurt American workers.

- Asked about the life goals of those in their age group, most Gen Nexters say their generation's top goals are fortune and fame. Roughly eight-in-ten say people in their generation think getting rich is either the most important, or second most important, goal in their lives. About half say that becoming famous also is valued highly by fellow Gen Nexters.

This report is drawn from a broad array of Pew Research Center polling data. The main survey was conducted Sept. 6–Oct. 2, 2006 among 1,501 adults including 579 people ages 18–25. In addition, the report includes extensive generational analysis of Pew Research Center surveys dating back to 1987.

Much of the analysis deals with comparisons among the four existing adult generations. For purposes of this report, **Generation Next** is made up of 18–25 year-olds (born between 1981 and 1988). **Generation X** was born between 1966 and 1980 and ranges in age from 26–40. The **Baby Boom** generation, born between 1946 and 1964, ranges in age from 41–60. Finally, those over age 60 (born before 1946) are called the **Seniors**. These generational breaks are somewhat arbitrary but are roughly comparable to those used by other scholars and researchers.

The report is divided into four main sections: (1) Outlook and World View, (2) Technology and Lifestyle, (3) Politics and Policy, and (4) Values and Social Issues.

EXPLORATORY WRITING

The Pew researchers have called this report a "portrait" of Generation Next. Reread the summary, especially the list of findings labeled "Meet Generation Next." In an exploratory piece of writing, describe your impression of the people this survey calls Generation Next.

TALKING ABOUT THE READING

As we noted in the introduction to this chapter, to characterize a generation is not to say everyone in that generation thinks alike or even has the same experiences. With a group of your classmates, go through the summary list included in this report and place each item in one of two categories: (1) those clearly quantifiable (e.g., an increase in young people voting); and (2) those that are not quantifiable (e.g., "They are the 'Look at Me' generation"). What overall portrait do those nonquantifiable items present of this generation? How well do you recognize that description of your generation?

WRITING ASSIGNMENTS

1. Write an essay in which you write your own summary description of Generation Next using the bulleted list of "findings" offered in the Pew report. In your essay, discuss which characteristics from these findings you recognize in yourself and others in your generation. Which of these characteristics would you take issue with? Why?

2. In a March 3, 2007, feature article for the *New York Times Sunday Magazine*, reporter Ann Hulbert notes that one of the most distinctive findings of this study is that their social views are significantly different from those of previous generations ("Beyond the Pleasure Principle"). She writes, "Young Americans, it turns out, are unexpectedly conservative on abortion but notably liberal on gay marriage. Given that 18- to 25-year-olds are the least Republican generation (35 percent) and less religious than their elders (with 20 percent of them professing no religion or atheism or agnosticism), it is curious that on abortion they are slightly to the right of the general public. Roughly a third of Gen Nexters endorse making abortion generally available, half support limits and 15 percent favor an outright ban. By contrast, 35 percent of 50- to 64-year-olds support readily available abortions." Without arguing whether or not abortion should be available or how others should respond to gay rights issues, write an essay in which you account for these findings among members of your generation. What influences—such as television, music, politics, changing demographics, education—might account for these findings?

3. In their summary list, Pew researchers call Generation Next the "Look at Me Generation" primarily because of their use of social networking sites like MySpace, Facebook, and MyYearbook. Write an essay in which you explain to what extent that characterization represents the uses of social networking sites. Are they solely about wanting to be noticed, or do they serve other functions? What are those other functions? You might also include sites like YouTube and blogging sites in your discussion of this characterization of Generation Next.

MY SATIRICAL SELF: HOW MAKING FUN OF ABSOLUTELY EVERYTHING IS DEFINING A GENERATION

—*Wyatt Mason*

Wyatt Mason is an award-winning essayist and critic whose writing has appeared in such publications as *the New Yorker, London Review of Books, New Republic, Nation,* and *New York Times Sunday Magazine,* where the selection here first appeared on September 17, 2006. He currently serves as a contributing editor to *Harper's Magazine* and writes the *Harper's* blog "Sentences."

SUGGESTION FOR READING   Mason begins by contrasting his response to the politics of the day with that of his father. His father's anger, Mason tells us, is fueled by op-eds that echo his frustration with the way things are today. Satire and ridicule are the forms Mason's generation turns to in response to the same frustrating news. As you read, notice that the article does at least two things: It defines a generation by its response to the news of the day. As well, it examines the playfulness, the promise, and the limits of satire as an adequate response to absurdity or tragedy. Keep track—with annotations, highlighting, or note-taking—of those two threads.

1   Lately, my father has been angry. Seventy-nine, a veteran of the U.S. Navy, a lifelong dues-paying member of three labor unions and now a collector of Social Security, my father, temperamentally a gentle person, is often filled with rage. The news does this to him, not so much the stories of tsunamis or hurricanes or any instances of environmental malice that lawyers call "acts of God." No, acts of God fill my godless, liberal father with melancholy, if not sorrow, over the inequity of the world, whereas it is the iniquity of the world, what you might call "acts of man," that are, these days, driving him to distraction. My father's solution to such furies, dependable as the daily newspaper, to the anger that sets upon him when he learns of the latest folly in the corridors of power, is to turn to the op-ed pages. For our purposes here, it hardly matters who is writing, though, naturally, he has his favorites. What matters to him is that every day, in those well-reasoned column inches, he finds a mirror for his rage.

Whereas, over the same period, his son has managed not to be angry, not in the least. Thirty-seven, a veteran of nothing, a subscription-paying reader of two magazines, a person whose Social Security pay-in, so far, is a sad little sum, I am, just as often as my father is furious, filled with mirth. Yes, I am aware of the disasters of the world, and they affect me no less deeply than they do him. What's more, my father and I are of one mind about the inveterate folly, craven hypocrisy, unchecked greed, rampant abuse of office, ugly abuse of trust, vile abuse of language and galloping display of ignorance that has become a daily standard. And yes, I should admit that when I happen to think about such matters—when, say, my father phones me to chew over some morsel of maddening news—I find myself overtaken by a most unpleasant feeling. I imagine it is not unlike what must be suffered by a man who returns home after a long day's work to find, in his absence, that his lovely house has been looted. And whereas my father, standing, as it were, at the front door of that plundered house, has come to find temporary shelter nearby, in reason—the arguments marshaled by those whose views he shares—I have found no relief in such reading, which lately I have forgone.

In its stead, though, I have found a way not to be angry at all.

I have taken shelter in the ridiculous.

5   Imagine, for example, another warm morning in August 2005. The national atmosphere that summer was humid with talk of intelligent design, the evangelical putsch—in Pennsylvania, in Kansas, in America—to see pseudoscience imparted to our keen young scholars in place of the theory of evolution. My father, I knew, would be calling on such a day (and did) to rail thereupon. "Did you read Paul Krugman?" my father asked.

"Of course," I replied, "I did not read Paul Krugman."

What did I read? A newspaper I keep bookmarked on my computer browser and which, among many destinations, I visit every morning. Here, in part, is what it read:

Evangelical Scientists Refute Gravity With New "Intelligent Falling" Theory

Aug. 17, 2005 | Issue 41.33

Kansas City, KS—As the debate over the teaching of evolution in public schools continues, a new controversy over the science curriculum arose Monday in this embattled Midwestern state. Scientists from the Evangelical Center for Faith-Based Reasoning are now asserting that the long-held "theory of gravity" is flawed, and they have responded to it with a new theory of Intelligent Falling.

"Things fall not because they are acted upon by some gravitational force, but because a higher intelligence, 'God' if you will, is pushing them down," said Gabriel Burdett, who holds degrees in education, applied Scripture and physics from Oral Roberts University.

Should N.S.A. satellite footage surface of me reading the above report—which appeared in The Onion: America's Finest News Source—you would witness me nodding with pleasure, shaking with delight and laughing aloud (or, more accurately, snorting un-self-consciously). Why is this man snorting? I am doing so with relief, saved, as I was, from having to endure another reasonable argument in unreasonable times. This is, after all, a country where anyone is free to believe that the fingerprints of the Creator, however small, are discernible on even the tiniest microorganism (just as I am free to hold my sober conviction that chocolate rainbows pave the way to a heaven made of fudge). And yet, to my uncaffeinated morning self, intelligent design seemed as brusque a turn of the American evangelical screw as I had encountered—a crude, anticonstitutional crack at marrying church to state. It was just too ridiculous! How ridiculous was it? Pretty perfectly on par, I'd have to say, with the refutation, along evangelical lines, of gravity.

That comedic turn, that comedic tone—a smart blend of parody and hyperbole and mockery—provided, that day, a remedy for my rage: it got channeled smoothly into ridicule. And that channel—a broadband of joco-serious rebuke—has been eating up the major part of my personal market share. As much as caffeine has become a matutinal necessity, a means of brokering, yet again, an uneasy truce with daylight, the kind of laughter—a well-aimed dart—induced by the larky bulletin above has become a no less necessary stimulant. How I hunger for that knowing tone! Like our little friend the lab rat at his lever—all a-jitter from another marching-powder marathon—I have acquired a taste for an addictive brand of fun.

10   Which means, of course, that I'm in luck: for that tone has been resonating through every echelon of American culture, a shift affecting and informing every storytelling medium, whether factual or fictional. The Onion, of course, is only where my day gets cooking. Other browser bookmarks send me to half a dozen sites where I hope to extract similarly intemperate snorts. The best of these, for sure, I forward along to friends—fellow traffickers in yuks—who, young and old, unfailingly send me links found during their own morning frolics. These I follow no less intrepidly than Theseus did Ariadne's thread, leading me, once again, out of my labyrinth of rage to that happier place: YouTube. There, with a dependability that would make a demographer pump his fist and an advertiser lose his shirt, I watch segments from "The Daily Show" and its spinoff, "The Colbert Report" (programs that, funnily enough, poached The Onion's top writers). In such shows, then, I find that tone—so knowing, so over it, so smart, so asinine. And given the choice, these days, between a smartass and, well, a dumb ass, even the Academy Awards, that most treacle-toned of evenings, picked this year's host from that clever category.

And picking the smartass, it seems, is what we've been doing, across the televised board. We've been tuning in to "The Simpsons" (in its 18th season, the longest-running sitcom in television history), which pokes tirelessly away at the idea of the American family, not to say America. We've been turning on "South Park" (in its 10th season, the longest-running sitcom in cable-television history), with its bile-tongued children probing every asininity (and which made a successful trip to the big screen in "South Park: Bigger, Longer and Uncut"). We've been ordering in "Chappelle's Show" (the top-selling DVD of a television series in, well . . . DVD history), with its now-embittered impresario, who, erewhile, was acid-tongued as he chewed up (and out) another cracker, whistling all the way. We've been showing up at "The Office," in branches on either side of the Atlantic, each of which, with regionally adjusted inflections, paws away at its constricting white collar (not to say its creator's later "Extras"—another kind of office, a celebrity waiting room with sexier furniture). Like the soulless producer in the Coen brothers' "Barton Fink," our Hollywood executives have been courting the equivalent of That Barton Fink Feeling: that ubiquitous tone—so "young," so "hip," so "edgy." Like the lava lamp of yore, it has been tucked into the hot corner of every room, whether "Da Ali G Show," "Curb Your Enthusiasm," "Boondocks," "American Dad!," "King of the Hill," "The Thick of It" or, on the big screen, the no less knowing "Dawns"—and Shaun—"of the Dead," "American Dreamz" and "Thank You for Smoking."

But if we were to think that that tone—so sarcastic, so ironic, so sardonic—were trapped within entertainments trundled onto screens, we would be wrong. It has pervaded literary fiction for decades, from Joseph Heller's "Catch-22" to Philip Roth's "Our Gang" to David Foster Wallace's "Infinite Jest." No surprise, then, that it should feature in the work of our most heralded young authors of the past year, whether Gary Shteyngart's unbridled "Absurdistan," Colson Whitehead's mocking "Apex Hides the Hurt," Marisha Pessl's madcap "Special Topics in Calamity Physics," not to mention books by our more seasoned storytellers—"In Persuasion Nation," by George Saunders; "The Diviners," by Rick Moody; "Little Children," by Tom Perotta; and "A Changed Man," by Francine Prose.

All of these varied entertainments—human emanations on the Web, on television, at the movies and between hardcovers (whatever their differences in ambition, conception and achievement)—are attuned to the ridiculous in modern life. They are all, in other words, satirical: they revel in, and trade on, knowingness. And if we seem to be enjoying a sort of golden age of the satirical, that invites the question How successfully does satire serve our culture? That there is so much might seem proof of its expediency. After all, what could be wrong with a mode of expression that orients a critical, comical eye to flaws in the contemporary weave? And yet, you might wonder, as well, whether a culture can have too much of that knowing tone and, if so, just what that "too much" might mean.

The ancient Romans provide the beginnings of an answer, in large measure because that's where satire has its beginnings. Just as Americans like to claim jazz as "our art form," the Romans claimed satire as theirs. Gaius Lucilius (second century B.C.) was the first satirist, a writer vocal about the negative virtues of his fellow citizens—mostly the tendency to imitate their Greek neighbors in everything. As boastful as a modern-day rapper, Lucilius pointed to himself as the original Roman—not some Helleno-wannabe—as much because of what he lampooned (things Greek) as the fact that he lampooned at all. I am Roman, his writings say, hear me mock. And indeed, it was how such criticism was delivered that made satire different—and differently effective—from, say, a sermon. "A cultivated wit," wrote Horace, a later Roman satirist, "one that badgers less, can persuade all the more. Artful ridicule can address contentious issues more competently and vigorously than can severity alone." Sounding like the always-fulminating Lewis Black of "The Daily Show," Rome's Juvenal tells us: "It is harder not to write satire. For who could endure this monstrous city, however callous at heart, and swallow his wrath? . . . Today, every vice has reached its ruinous zenith. So, satirist, hoist your sails." The idiot wind, blowing every time Rome's hypocrites moved their mouths, drove her satirists, in their artful way, to bluster back, setting a course pursued by writers living in turbulent eras ever since.

15   When, in 1729, the Tory politician Jonathan Swift (1667–1745) published his satirical "A Modest Proposal"—which, in the straight-faced language of a sermon, advocated solving the problem of poverty by selling Irish children as meat—his mode was perfectly ironic. Swift did not wish to see his countrymen's children ground into shepherd's pies. Rather, he wanted to level an attack on political opponents who were devouring the Irish people. Swift, then, was approaching a troubling question upside down and intimating a sarcastic answer. (As such, Stephen Colbert, in parodying Bill O'Reilly's extreme rhetoric, is fully Swiftian: "The Colbert

Report" works to convince us of the opposite of its host's every misguided opinion.) For Swift's part, he believed that satire was a way of "prompting men of genius and virtue to mend the world as far as they are able." His fellow Augustan Alexander Pope wrote, "When truth or virtue an affront endures, the affront is mine, my friend, and should be yours." And although satire could not be a remedy in and of itself, it was doing a good deal, Pope assured, when it could "deter, if not reform."

Indeed, this elegant, not to say defiant, means of addressing "affronts" to truth has proved a liberating mode of expression for authors across the ages, from Chaucer to Cervantes to Voltaire. Most comprehensible of all, perhaps, is the attraction that so insubordinate a brand of comedy, a very free kind of speech, held for writers in a country formed through insubordination—our own. Prerevolutionary America was rife with satirical pamphleteers, and even Benjamin Franklin, in his "Rules by Which a Great Empire May Be Reduced to a Small One," lampooned the misadministration of the colonies. And yet, when readers today experience the best satires of our past, editorial points that once took center stage now shuffle toward the wings. Whether in the rueful parody of Mark Twain's "War Prayer" ("It was a time of great and exalting excitement"), the wicked ironies of Ambrose Bierce's "Devil's Dictionary" ("Conversation, n. A fair for the display of the minor mental commodities, each exhibitor being too intent upon the arrangement of his own wares to observe those of his neighbor") or even the mordant sarcasm of Dorothy Parker's "Comment"—

> Oh, life is a glorious cycle of song,
>
> A medley of extemporanea;
>
> And love is a thing that can never go wrong;
>
> And I am Marie of Roumania.

—we are responding, not so much to the underlying "point" each author makes as to the virtuosity of its execution, the satirist's fine ear for language, the pleasurable spectacle of seeing words used originally, used well. Yes, as it happens, Parker, Bierce and Twain are making timeless points: love, often unlovely; conversation, frequently dull; war, not exalting. No one, though, would needlepoint these revelations onto pillows—they're old news. In the hands of an adept satirist, however, the old news satire brings becomes a special report. It reads, in part, that human civilization is not so wonderful: look, satire testifies, at the latest, artless shenanigans we've gotten ourselves into. But the report also shows that human civilization can be wonderful: look, satire says, at how artful we can be.

Satire, then, signals both the sickness and health of a society in equal measure: it showcases the vigor of the satirist and the debility of the satiree. As such, we might conclude, in America, that its abundance suggests a normal balance of destructive yin and creative yang, a human need to view the most vexing frailties of a culture through the liberating prism of lampoon.

An episode of "South Park" from last year, "Best Friends Forever," was shown on the eve of Terri Schiavo's final day, inspired by the grim battle among family members. Their private tragedy, we know well, became a series of loggerheaded squabbles in which efforts to reach consensus on what we mean by "human life" rapidly devolved. The creators of "South Park" addressed this rhetorical erosion with no small insight and freakish speed. (Like all their episodes, this one was produced in less than a week.) Kenny, the accident-prone child, is killed by an ice cream truck while playing his Sony PSP—the portable game console that, last year, was the grail of children everywhere. At the reading of Kenny's will, Cartman, the obese, morally repugnant child who, on another episode, ate the parents of a kid he disliked, is left the PSP. Alas for Cartman, Kenny, dead for almost 24 hours, is belatedly revived. Now on a feeding tube and, as his doctor explains, in "a persistive vegetative state . . . like a tomato," Kenny is, by law, alive. Kenny's possessions, therefore, revert to him. As Cartman goes to the Colorado Supreme Court to seek the removal of Kenny's feeding tube (so he can get the PSP), Kenny's more altruistic friends, Kyle and Stan, court the media: "We'll make everyone in the country know that they're killing Kenny."

20   The national uproar that ensued on this cartoon was, in temper, not a great deal more cartoonish than the one that was playing out that evening in Schiavo's real America. The episode, however distorted by crudity, mirrored the polarizing rage of our citizenry, recalling nothing so much as Ambrose Bierce's satirical definition of conversation. The genius of "South Park," scatologically over the top though it tends to be (Oprah, this season, was kidnapped at gunpoint by her vagina), is how it nonetheless manages, with glee, to go after everyone, artfully sketching our society's inability to make sense of itself, to itself.

Another target that our satirists have been skewering is our confusion about the responsibility that corporations, governments or, indeed, parents, have to tell the truth. Released in the spring of 2005, "Thank You for Smoking" (adapted from Christopher Buckley's very funny novel) featured the charismatic tobacco-industry lobbyist Nick Naylor, a villain with a hero's face and a salesman's mouth. As one senator puts it, "The man shills . . . for a living," a profession about which Nick's son is curious. Joey, 12, understands that his father makes arguments on behalf of corporations, but given that the corporation in question manufactures death, he wonders what happens when his father's arguments are wrong:

Nick: Joey, I'm never wrong.
Joey: But you can't always be right.
Nick: Well, if it's your job to be right, then you're never wrong.
Joey: But what if you are wrong?
Nick: O.K. Let's say that you're defending chocolate, and I'm defending vanilla. Now, if I were to say to you, "Vanilla is the best flavor ice cream," you'd say . . .

Joey: No, chocolate is.
Nick: Exactly. But you can't win that argument. So, I'll ask you, "So you think chocolate is the end all and be all of ice cream, do you?"
Joey: It's the best ice cream. I wouldn't order any other.
Nick: Oh, so it's all chocolate for you, is it?
Joey: Yes, chocolate is all I need.
Nick: Well, I need more than chocolate. And for that matter, I need more than vanilla. I believe that we need freedom, and choice when it comes to our ice cream, and that, Joey Naylor, that is the definition of liberty.
Joey: But that's not what we're talking about.
Nick: Ah. But that's what I'm talking about.
Joey: But . . . you didn't prove that vanilla's the best.
Nick: I didn't have to. I proved that you're wrong, and if you're wrong, I'm right.
Joey: But you still didn't convince me.
Nick: I'm not after you. I'm after them.

Nick's "them" are the people beyond the table where they sit, the wider world he would have believe that smoking is an expression of freedom. For Nick, "liberty" is merely rhetorical: it is, as he says, what he's "talking about." He doesn't mean a word of it: he only means to win. The truth is not his—or, we are to understand, perhaps no longer our—business.

The business of scoring this frustratingly debased game of contemporary conversation has been the main focus of "The Daily Show." Stewart et al. have built careers as liberal foils to conservative talk radio. Where the Limbaughosphere thrives on a muscular, hectoring rhetoric, the mode of "The Daily Show" has been a lampooning of such bullying. Although "The Daily Show" can revel in the same kind of posturing, even if the stance is far more liberal, the best of its work is restrained in the Horatian manner. The show's "artful ridicule" is at its most scrupulous when attentive to, critical of and vocal about abuses of language. When James Frey, author of the fraudulent memoir "A Million Little Pieces," was being torn apart by an array of talking heads indignant over his distortions, Stewart offered a deadpan summation that spoke to the perfervid journalistic outrage. Pundits were upset with Frey, Stewart explained, "because he misled us . . . into a book we had no business getting into." Armed with scrupulous syntax alone, Stewart ironically evoked two infamies that rhymed with Frey's: the claim that the Bush administration had misled us into war and the observation that the media, so severe in its judgments of Frey's lie-world, had remained less dogged before the administration's possible untruths.

This is artful indeed, but a high point both for "The Daily Show" and contemporary satire more generally came shortly after The New Yorker published Seymour Hersh's 2004 exposé, "Torture at Abu Ghraib." There was genuine shock, both here and abroad, that a prison taken from a dictator who had used it to torture Iraqi dissidents had in turn served as a forum for the torture of Iraqis by their American "liberators." Much of our high-flown rhetoric, billowing grandly over Operation Iraqi Freedom, collapsed on the mast. The irony—uncomplicatedly galling—seemed obvious enough, but its precise grade was measured nowhere more finely than in an exchange between Stewart and Rob Corddry, a player who has since departed. As Corddry explained to Stewart, his voice that of a schoolteacher instructing an uncommonly simple-minded child:

Jon, there's no question what took place in that prison was horrible, but the Arab world has to realize that the U.S. shouldn't be judged on the actions of a . . . well, that we shouldn't be judged on actions. It's our principles that matter; our inspiring, abstract notions. Remember, Jon, just because torturing prisoners is something we did doesn't mean it's something we would do.

25 This is not, as it is sometimes called, "fake news"; rather, blunt satire. Co-opting the patronizing, abstraction-rich rhetoric of the administration of which "The Daily Show" has often been critical, Corddry shined a bright light on an empty set of bromides. All too clearly, words can prove seductive—but only to a point: the point where such seductions become fundamentally ridiculous.

Of recent examples of American satire, though, most remarkable may be Stephen Colbert's appearance this spring at the White House Correspondents' Association Dinner. For anyone familiar with Colbert's lampoonery on "The Daily Show," not to say his rise to headlining "The Colbert Report," it was something to see him following in the footsteps of Cedric the Entertainer, Jay Leno and Drew Carey—comedians who most recently tummled at the pleasure of the president. Whatever your tastes, we can agree that they are creatures of the mainstream. Whereas Colbert is nothing if not a critic of that mainstream, one traveling its trashy wake. Consider, then, his straight-faced, pseudoconservative patter, as he expressed, that night, his parodic support of a president sitting a few feet away:

I stand by this man. I stand by this man because he stands for things. Not only for things, he stands on things. Things like aircraft carriers and rubble and recently flooded city squares. And that sends a strong message: that no matter what happens to America, she will always rebound—with the most powerfully staged photo ops in the world.

Or how he "defended" the administration's apparently chaotic profile:

Everybody asks for personnel changes. So, the White House has personnel changes. And then you write, "Oh, they're just rearranging the deck chairs on the Titanic." First of all, that is a terrible metaphor. This administration is not sinking. This administration is soaring. If anything, they are rearranging the deck chairs on the Hindenburg!

And how he reproached the "liberal press that's destroying America" for its lack of professionalism:

> Let's review the rules. Here's how it works: the president makes decisions. He's the Decider. The press secretary announces those decisions, and you people of the press type those decisions down. Make, announce, type. Just put 'em through a spell-check and go home. Get to know your family again. Make love to your wife. Write that novel you got kicking around in your head. You know, the one about the intrepid Washington reporter with the courage to stand up to the administration. You know—fiction!

To go by the media swirl that followed, Colbert's speech that night represents in our culture a culmination of what satire does well or, rather, cannot but do: when it bends to kiss a hand, it bites. Such Lucilian ferocity drew the intended attention. By a great many journalists, Colbert's "antics" were deemed abusive, discourteous, tasteless. And yet, by a great many citizens, Colbert's appearance was a moment of hallelujah: he made many people—most poignantly the press—uncomfortable. Colbert stood in their midst, yes, but stood apart, just as the first Roman satirists stood apart, initially from things Greek and then from the corruption that flooded the mainstream. Whatever its latest stance, satire always finds its footing high above the polluted river of a culture, a vantage point from which it taunts. From Juvenal to Swift, from Franklin to Twain: each stood above his era's lies and, from such a lofty perspective, named the truths of his time.

30   The appeal of such a mode of discourse to any vice-blighted age is understandable: it provides another means to editorial ends. And yet, more than merely editorializing, it also demonstrates a capacity for better behavior in human beings—our creativity, our subtlety, our panache. That so many people are responding to satire in the public square, and, indeed, that so much satire is thriving at a center usually held by more anodyne entertainments, suggests our hunger for the better—the better articulated, the better said, the better thought, the better done.

At the outset, I said I had taken shelter in the ridiculous. Upon reflection, the ridiculous may not be the most well shielded of retreats. Can you take shelter in the ridiculous if everywhere becomes ridiculous? For the tools of satire, the sharp knives of sarcasm and the pointy shivs of irony and the toy hammer of lampoon are being wielded with widespread enthusiasm, and not merely by cunning builders of satirical speeches and stories. Rather, they are being lent to us all, to enable every possible construction. Did you hear, for example, the news conference President Bush gave in Germany over the summer? "I'm looking forward to the feast you're going to have tonight," he said to the German chancellor in a moment of folksy charm, "and I understand that I may have the honor of slicing the pig." This drew laughs, and when his remarks wound down, the president repeated, "I'm looking forward to that pig tonight." This before fielding the following from a reporter:

> "Does it concern you," the man asked, stuttering, "that the Beirut airport has been bombed, and do you see a risk of triggering a wider war? And on Iran, they've so far refused to respond. Is it now past the deadline, or do they still have more time to respond?"
>
> "I thought," Bush replied, "you were going to ask about the pig."

Try to ignore, if you can, the image of the carcass of a pig, Bush poised, knife in hand, ready to carve. Consider instead that when asked on an international stage about real carnage—about spreading violence in the Middle East, about a constellation of worries suggesting a world at the brink of war—the president's reply did not take the questioner's inquiry seriously but, rather, sarcastically. His rhetoric sounded less like that of a steward of state—one addressing serious matters with sobriety—than that of a smartass. And this was not Juvenal's sarcasm, or Twain's, or even Colbert's: it was not elegantly tuned to a point nor artfully part of a formal design. It was, instead, almost perfectly inappropriate and, of course, not unindicative of the president's normal rhetorical mode. For it is not, I think, as is so often said, that the president is as much inarticulate as he is too clearly articulate, in a way: his tone, consistently condescending, betrays his sense of being, like a satirist, above those he calls down to. And that tone—carelessly sarcastic, thoughtlessly ironic, indiscriminately sardonic—that is the very one you now find everywhere. Bush is us; Bush is me: his is the same sarcasm I employ when I tell my father, once again, that of course I didn't read today's op-ed.

It makes me wonder what happens when the language of argument and the language of ridicule become the same, when the address of a potentate is voiced no more soberly than the goofings of some rube. Perhaps that leveling of language merely passes, the rhetorical registers recalibrated by nothing so much as an unfolding of the days. Or perhaps there's another way of putting it, one voiced by President Bush himself. After Colbert, after Germany, just before Labor Day, there was yet another news conference, one that found the president asking the press corps—who so lately protested their mistreatment at satirical hands—how long they were to be stationed in a temporary briefing room across from their typical quarters. "The decision will be made by commanders on the ground," cracked one. "There's no timetable," went another. "What do you think this is," quipped the president, "the correspondents' dinner or something?"

That, it seems to me, is an excellent question.

CORRECTION: OCT. 1, 2006

An article on Sept. 17 about the abundance of satire in American culture referred incorrectly to an episode of "South Park." In it, the character Cartman tricks another child into eating his own parents in a bowl of chili; Cartman himself does not eat them.

EXPLORATORY WRITING

In an exploratory writing, lay out the two primary threads of discussion this article follows (see our Suggestion for Reading). Describe, first, what Mason is saying about his father's generation's response to news that is hard to take. Then, explain what Mason is saying about the uses of satire both to define his generation's response to the same news and as a form of rhetoric both powerful and powerless.

TALKING ABOUT THE READING

With a group of your classmates, use your exploratory writings to sort out what Mason is saying about his father's generation, his own generation, and the possibility of satire as both provoking change and avoiding the real issues.

WRITING ASSIGNMENTS

1. This article might be broken down into three parts. In the first, Mason posits generational differences. In the second, he provides both a short history and a definition of satire. In the third, he questions the effectiveness of satire. Drawing on your notes, your exploratory writing, and your class discussions, write a summary of this article that clarifies those three parts. What, in the end, is Mason saying about his generation, about satire, and about appropriate or useful responses to hard issues? What is he saying with the anecdote, at the end of his article, about President Bush? What does he mean when he writes, "Bush is us; Bush is me: his is the same sarcasm I employ when I tell my father,

once again, that of course I didn't read today's op-ed"? What is he suggesting with the statement, "It makes me wonder what happens when the language of argument and the language of ridicule become the same, when the address of a potentate is voiced no more soberly than the goofings of some rube"?

2. Choose a satirical news source like *TheOnion.com, The Daily Show,* or *The Colbert Report* and watch or read very carefully the stories and commentary offered there. (*The Onion* is online. Currently, both *The Daily Show* and *The Colbert Report* offer free full episodes at thedailyshow.com. Or choose another contemporary news satire for your analysis.) Write an essay in which you analyze the source as a voice for a particular generation. What, in the source, suggests who the audience is? To what extent is the source providing social satire meant to, as Mason quotes Swift saying, "prompt men of genius and virtue to mend the world as far as they are able." To what extent is the source not useful in that way at all but, instead, as Mason suggests it can be, "carelessly sarcastic, thoughtlessly ironic, indiscriminately sardonic"?

3. In March 2004, the Pew Research Center for the People and the Press reported that 21 percent of Americans age 18–29 get most of their news from *The Daily Show* and *Saturday Night Live.*

   For this project, form a group with 3–4 of your classmates. Each group member should use the questions in the survey below to interview 5–10 people in different age groups about where they get their news. Use written questions so that people can answer on paper or via e-mail, or ask the questions in person and record answers in a notebook. You don't need to take anyone's name for this survey, but you should get a general age range for each person.

   You might wish to preview this exercise by first interviewing each other in class; then make plans to interview people who are not your classmates.

   Where do you get most of your news or information about what is going on in the world?

   Radio Talk Shows? If yes, which ones?

   Network television?

   Cable news?

   The Daily Show

   The Colbert Report

   Internet? (Which sites?)

   Newspapers? (The front page? Op-ed columns?)

   Age:

   __ 16–23   __ 35–45   __ 45–60   __ over 60

When you have completed your survey, meet with your group to summarize the findings of your interviews. Tally how many people were interviewed and note their ages. Where do the people you interviewed get their news—television, radio, newspapers, news magazines, the Internet? How many turn to news satire programs regularly?

   Report your findings in class. Compare them with the findings of other groups. What, if anything, do you see as the significance of these findings in terms of generational differences?

MAKING CONNECTIONS   Where Generations Meet

As much of this chapter illustrates, each generation seems to want to establish itself as distinct. We like to think we have moved past the generations before, and in some ways that is exactly what each generation does. Still, the character of any generation is always informed by generations that came before it. We tend to overlap rather than become entirely separate from one another. As individuals, that generational awareness often comes the moment we see our parents' generation in ourselves—in the ways we talk, the things we like to do, or the habits of mind we've established.

In the two selections that follow, E. B. White (writing in 1941) and Gloria Naylor (writing nearly forty years later, in 1980) take us to those moments when our lives, our thoughts, our memories are barely separable from those of our parents.

ONCE MORE TO THE LAKE

— E. B. White

E. B. White (1899–1985) was one of the best-known and admired American writers of his time. For many years, he wrote a regular column ("One Man's Meat") for *Harper's Magazine*, where this essay originally appeared in October 1941. Today, he is still remembered for his children's books, especially *Stuart Little* (1945), *Charlotte's Web* (1952), and *The Trumpet and the Swan* (1970). In 1955, he edited and updated William Strunk's popular writer's handbook *The Elements of Style* (first published in 1918), which ultimately became known by the shorthand *Strunk and White* and is still used in some classrooms today. The essay we have reprinted here is perhaps one of the most commonly anthologized essays for college writing courses. White is remembered especially for his elegant and easy style, something "Once More to the Lake" illustrates beautifully.

SUGGESTION FOR READING White's is a narrative essay—an essay that uses story to make a point. The story itself may be intriguing or well crafted, but the story is not at all the point of the essay. Read this essay through quickly. Then reread. In your rereading, notice where White is simply telling a story or describing a place and where he is making a comment or getting to the real point of telling the story. Highlight or underline those places where that happens. Pay special attention to those places where White comments on days past, his father's generation, and what he calls the sustained illusion that his son was White when he was a boy and White had become his father.

1 One summer, along about 1904, my father rented a camp on a lake in Maine and took us all there for the month of August. We all got ringworm from some kittens and had to rub Pond's Extract on our arms and legs night and morning, and my father rolled over in a canoe with all his clothes on; but outside of that the vacation was a success and from then on none of us ever thought there was any place in the world like that lake in Maine. We returned summer after summer—always on August 1st for one month. I have since become a salt-water man, but sometimes in summer there are days when the restlessness of the tides and the fearful cold of the sea water and the incessant wind which blows across the afternoon and into the evening make me wish for the

placidity of a lake in the woods. A few weeks ago this feeling got so strong I bought myself a couple of bass hooks and a spinner and returned to the lake where we used to go, for a week's fishing and to revisit old haunts.

I took along my son, who had never had any fresh water up his nose and who had seen lily pads only from train windows. On the journey over to the lake I began to wonder what it would be like. I wondered how time would have marred this unique, this holy spot—the coves and streams, the hills that the sun set behind, the camps and the paths behind the camps. I was sure that the tarred road would have found it out and I wondered in what other ways it would be desolated. It is strange how much you can remember about places like that once you allow your mind to return into the grooves which lead back. You remember one thing, and that suddenly reminds you of another thing. I guess I remembered clearest of all the early mornings, when the lake was cool and motionless, remembered how the bedroom smelled of the lumber it was made of and of the wet woods whose scent entered through the screen. The partitions in the camp were thin and did not extend clear to the top of the rooms, and as I was always the first up I would dress softly so as not to wake the others, and sneak out into the sweet outdoors and start out in the canoe, keeping close along the shore in the long shadows of the pines. I remembered being very careful never to rub my paddle against the gunwale for fear of disturbing the stillness of the cathedral.

The lake had never been what you would call a wild lake. There were cottages sprinkled around the shores, and it was in farming although the shores of the lake were quite heavily wooded. Some of the cottages were owned by nearby farmers, and you would live at the shore and eat your meals at the farmhouse. That's what our family did. But although it wasn't wild, it was a fairly large and undisturbed lake and there were places in it which, to a child at least, seemed infinitely remote and primeval.

I was right about the tar: it led to within half a mile of the shore. But when I got back there, with my boy, and we settled into a camp near a farmhouse and into the kind of summertime I had known, I could tell that it was going to be pretty much the same as it had been before—I knew it, lying in bed the first morning, smelling the bedroom, and hearing the boy sneak quietly out and go off along the shore in a boat. I began to sustain the illusion that he was I, and therefore, by simple transposition, that I was my father. This sensation persisted, kept cropping up all the time we were there. It was not an entirely new feeling, but in this setting it grew much stronger. I seemed to be living a dual existence. I would be in the middle of some simple act, I would be picking up a bait box or laying down a table fork, or I would be saying something, and suddenly it would be not I but my father who was saying the words or making the gesture. It gave me a creepy sensation.

5   We went fishing the first morning. I felt the same damp moss covering the worms in the bait can, and saw the dragonfly alight on the tip of my rod as it hovered a few inches from the surface of the water. It was the arrival of this fly that convinced me beyond any doubt that everything was as it always had been, that the years were a mirage and there had been no years. The small waves were the same, chucking the rowboat under the chin as we fished at anchor, and the boat was the same boat, the same color green and the ribs broken in the same places, and under the floor-boards the same freshwater leavings and debris—the dead helgramite, the wisps of moss, the rusty discarded fishhook, the dried blood from yesterday's catch. We stared silently at the tips of our rods, at the dragonflies that came and wells. I lowered the tip of mine into the water, tentatively, pensively dislodging the fly, which darted two feet away, poised, darted two feet back, and came to rest again a little farther up the rod. There had been no years between the ducking of this dragonfly and the other one—the one that was part of memory.

I looked at the boy, who was silently watching his fly, and it was my hands that held his rod, my eyes watching. I felt dizzy and didn't know which rod I was at the end of.

We caught two bass, hauling them in briskly as though they were mackerel, pulling them over the side of the boat in a businesslike manner without any landing net, and stunning them with a blow on the back of the head. When we got back for a swim before lunch, the lake was exactly where we had left it, the same number of inches from the dock, and there was only the merest suggestion of a breeze. This seemed an utterly enchanted sea, this lake you could leave to its own devices for a few hours and come back to, and find that it had not stirred, this constant and trustworthy body of water. In the shallows, the dark, water-soaked sticks and twigs, smooth and old, were undulating in clusters on the bottom against the clean ribbed sand, and the track of the mussel was plain. A school of minnows swam by, each minnow with its small, individual shadow, doubling the attendance, so clear and sharp in the sunlight. Some of the other campers were in swimming, along the shore, one of them with a cake of soap, and the water felt thin and clear and insubstantial. Over the years there had been this person with the cake of soap, this cultist, and here he was. There had been no years.

Up to the farmhouse to dinner through the teeming, dusty field, the road under our sneakers was only a two-track road. The middle track was missing, the one with the marks of the hooves and the splotches of dried, flaky manure. There had always been three tracks to choose from in choosing which track to walk in; now the choice was narrowed down to two. For a moment I missed terribly the middle alternative. But the way led past the tennis court, and something about the way it lay there in the sun reassured me; the tape had loosened along the backline, the alleys were green with plantains and other weeds, and the net (installed in June and removed in September) sagged in the dry noon, and the whole place steamed with midday heat and hunger and emptiness. There was a choice of pie for dessert, and one was blueberry and one was apple, and the waitresses were the same country girls, there having been no passage of time, only the illusion of it as in a dropped curtain—the waitresses were still fifteen; their hair had been washed, that was the only difference—they had been to the movies and seen the pretty girls with the clean hair.

Summertime, oh summertime, pattern of life indelible, the fade proof lake, the woods unshatterable, the pasture with the sweet fern and the juniper forever and ever, summer without end; this was the background, and the life along the shore was the design, the cottages with their innocent and tranquil design, their tiny docks with the flagpole and the American flag floating against the white clouds in the blue sky, the little paths over the roots of the trees leading from camp to camp and the paths leading back to the outhouses and the can of lime for sprinkling, and at the souvenir counters at the store the miniature birch-bark canoes and the post cards that showed things looking a little better than they looked. This was the American family at play, escaping the city heat, wondering whether the newcomers at the camp at the head of the cove were "common" or "nice," wondering whether it was true that the people who drove up for Sunday dinner at the farmhouse were turned away because there wasn't enough chicken.

It seemed to me, as I kept remembering all this, that those times and those summers had been infinitely precious and worth saving. There had been jollity and peace and goodness. The arriving (at the beginning of August) had been so big a business in itself, at the railway station the farm wagon drawn up, the first smell of the pine-laden air, the first glimpse of the smiling farmer, and the great importance of the trunks and your father's enormous authority in such matters, and the feel of the wagon under you for the long ten-mile haul, and at the top of the last long hill catching the first view of the lake after eleven months of not seeing this cherished body of water. The shouts and cries of the other campers when they saw you, and the trunks to be unpacked, to give up their rich burden. (Arriving was less exciting nowadays, when you sneaked up in your car and parked it under a tree near the camp and took out the bags and in five minutes it was all over, no fuss, no loud wonderful fuss about trunks.)

10   Peace and goodness and jollity. The only thing that was wrong now, really, was the sound of the place, an unfamiliar nervous sound of the outboard motors. This was the note that jarred, the one thing that would sometimes break the illusion and set the years moving. In those other summertimes, all motors were inboard; and when they were at a little distance, the noise they made was a sedative, an ingredient of summer sleep. They were one-cylinder and two-cylinder engines, and some were make-and-break and some were jump-spark, but they all made a sleepy sound across the lake. The one-lungers throbbed and fluttered, and the twin-cylinder ones purred and purred, and that was a quiet sound too. But now the campers all had outboards. In the daytime, in the hot mornings, these motors made a petulant, irritable sound; at night, in the still evening when the afterglow lit the water, they whined about one's ears like mosquitoes. My boy loved our rented outboard, and his great desire was to achieve single-handed mastery over it, and authority, and he soon learned the trick of choking it a little (but not too much), and the adjustment of the needle valve. Watching him I would remember the things you could do with the old one-cylinder engine with the heavy flywheel, how you could have it eating out of your hand if you got really close to it spiritually. Motor boats in those days didn't have clutches, and you would make a landing by shutting off the motor at the proper time and coasting in with a dead rudder. But there was a way of reversing them, if you learned the trick, by cutting the switch and putting it on again exactly on the final dying revolution of the

flywheel, so that it would kick back against compression and begin reversing. Approaching a dock in a strong following breeze, it was difficult to slow up sufficiently by the ordinary coasting method, and if a boy felt he had complete mastery over his motor, he was tempted to keep it running beyond its time and then reverse it a few feet from the dock. It took a cool nerve, because if you threw the switch a twentieth of a second too soon you would catch the flywheel when it still had speed enough to go up past center, and the boat would leap ahead, charging bull-fashion at the dock.

We had a good week at the camp. The bass were biting well and the sun shone endlessly, day after day. We would be tired at night and lie down in the accumulated heat of the little bedrooms after the long hot day and the breeze would stir almost imperceptibly outside and the smell of the swamp drift in through the rusty screens. Sleep would come easily and in the morning the red squirrel would be on the roof, tapping out his gay routine. I kept remembering everything, lying in bed in the mornings—the small steamboat that had a long rounded stern like the lip of a Ubangi, and how quietly she ran on the moonlight sails, when the older boys played their mandolins and the girls sang and we ate doughnuts dipped in sugar, and how sweet the music was on the water in the shining night, and what it had felt like to think about girls then. After breakfast we would go up to the store and the things were in the same place—the minnows in a bottle, the plugs and spinners disarranged and pawed over by the youngsters from the boys' camp, the fig newtons and the Beeman's gum. Outside, the road was tarred and cars stood in front of the store. Inside, all was just as it had always been, except there was more Coca Cola and not so much Moxie and root beer and birch beer and sarsaparilla. We would walk out with a bottle of pop apiece and sometimes the pop would backfire up our noses and hurt. We explored the streams, quietly, where the turtles slid off the sunny logs and dug their way into the soft bottom; and we lay on the town wharf and fed worms to the tame bass. Everywhere we went I had trouble making out which was I, the one walking at my side, the one walking in my pants.

One afternoon while we were there at that lake a thunderstorm came up. It was like the revival of an old melodrama that I had seen long ago with childish awe. The second-act climax of the drama of the electrical disturbance over a lake in America had not changed in any important respect. This was the big scene, still the big scene. The whole thing was so familiar, the first feeling of oppression and heat and a general air around camp of not wanting to go very far away. In mid-afternoon (it was all the same) a curious darkening of the sky, and a lull in everything that had made life tick; and then the way the boats suddenly swung the other way at their moorings with the coming of a breeze out of the new quarter, and the premonitory rumble. Then the kettle drum, then the snare, then the bass drum and cymbals, then crackling light against the dark, and the gods grinning and licking their chops in the hills. Afterward the calm, the rain steadily rustling in the calm lake, the return of light and hope and spirits, and the campers running out in joy and relief to go swimming in the rain, their bright cries perpetuating the deathless joke about how they were getting simply drenched, and the children screaming with delight at the new sensation of bathing in the rain, and the joke about getting drenched linking the generations in a strong indestructible chain. And the comedian who waded in carrying an umbrella.

When the others went swimming my son said he was going in too. He pulled his dripping trunks from the line where they had hung all through the shower, and wrung them out. Languidly, and with no thought of going in, I watched him, his hard little body, skinny and bare, saw him wince slightly as he pulled up around his vitals the small, soggy, icy garment. As he buckled the swollen belt suddenly my groin felt the chill of death.

EXPLORATORY WRITING

Look back over the places you have marked that indicate where the story pauses and E. B. White's commentary or reflection takes over. In an exploratory piece of writing, explain what the story is all about—not the events but the point of telling the story. What does White want his readers to take from this story?

TALKING ABOUT THE READING

Share the exploratory writing you did with a group of classmates and discuss with each other why White wrote this narrative essay. What did he want to tell his reader—about himself, about the ways the world is changing and how it is not, about his relationship with his father and his son's relationship with him? How is this an essay about generations meeting and overlapping?

WRITING ASSIGNMENT

In his essay, White writes that, once he was at the lake with his son, "I began to sustain the illusion that he was I, and therefore, by simple transposition, that I was my father." Write an essay in which you explain what, in sustaining this illusion, White tells his readers about his father and the way the world was when White was a boy. In your essay, consider as well what he reveals about himself as a boy by imagining that his son is really White as a young boy. What is he saying about his connection to his father's generation?

KISWANA BROWNE

—Gloria Naylor

Gloria Naylor's highly acclaimed novel *The Women of Brewster Place* (1980) tells the stories of several African American women who live in a housing project in an unnamed city. "Kiswana Browne" presents a powerful account of the encounter between a mother and daughter that explores both their generational differences and the aspirations that they hold in common. Naylor's story reveals how the much-publicized generation gap of the 1960s is never simply a matter of differences in politics and lifestyle but rather is complicated by the intersecting forces of race, class, and gender. The cultural shift signified by Kiswana's change of name represents both a break with the past and, as Kiswana discovers, a continuation of her family's resistance to racial oppression.

SUGGESTION FOR READING As you read, highlight/underline and annotate the passages where the story establishes conflict between the two characters and where (or whether) it resolves the conflict.

1   From the window of her sixth-floor studio apartment, Kiswana could see over the wall at the end of the street to the busy avenue that lay just north of Brewster Place. The late-afternoon shoppers looked like brightly clad marionettes as they moved between the congested traffic, clutching their packages against their bodies to guard them from sudden bursts of the cold autumn wind. A portly mailman had abandoned his cart and was bumping into indignant window-shoppers as he puffed behind the cap that the wind had snatched from his head. Kiswana leaned over to see if he was going to be successful, but the edge of the building cut him off from her view.

A pigeon swept across her window, and she marveled at its liquid movements in the air waves. She placed her dreams on the back of the bird and fantasized that it would glide forever in transparent silver circles until it ascended to the center of the universe and was swallowed up. But the wind died down, and she watched with a sigh as the bird beat its wings in awkward, frantic movements to land on the corroded top of a fire escape on the opposite building. This brought her back to earth.

Humph, it's probably sitting over there crapping on those folks' fire escape, she thought. Now, that's a safety hazard . . . And her mind was busy again, creating flames and smoke and frustrated tenants whose escape was being hindered because they were slipping and sliding in pigeon shit. She watched their cussing, haphazard descent on the fire escapes until they had all reached the bottom. They were milling around, oblivious to their burning apartments, angrily planning to march on the mayor's office about the pigeons. She materialized placards and banners for them, and they had just reached the corner, boldly sidestepping fire hoses and broken glass, when they all vanished. A tall copper-skinned woman had met this phantom parade at the corner, and they had dissolved in front of her long, confident strides. She plowed through the remains of their faded mists, unconscious of the lingering wisps of their presence on her leather bag and black fur-trimmed coat. It took a few seconds for this transfer from one realm to another to reach Kiswana, but then suddenly she recognized the woman.

"Oh, God, it's Mama!" She looked down guiltily at the forgotten newspaper in her lap and hurriedly circled random job advertisements. By this time Mrs. Browne had reached the front of Kiswana's building and was checking the house number against a piece of paper in her hand. Before she went into the building she stood at the bottom of the stoop and carefully inspected the condition of the street and the adjoining property. Kiswana watched this meticulous inventory with growing annoyance but she involuntarily followed her mother's slowly rotating head, forcing herself to see her new neighborhood through the older woman's eyes. The brightness of the unclouded sky seemed to join forces with her mother as it high-lighted every broken stoop railing and missing brick. The afternoon sun glittered and cascaded across even the tiniest fragments of broken bottle, and at that very moment the wind chose to rise up again, sending unswept grime flying into the air, as a stray tin can left by careless garbage collectors went rolling noisily down the center of the street.

5   Kiswana noticed with relief that at least Ben wasn't sitting in his usual place on the old garbage can pushed against the far wall. He was just a harmless old wino, but Kiswana knew her mother only needed one wino or one teenager with a reefer within a twenty-block radius to decide that her daughter was living in a building seething with dope factories and hang-outs for derelicts. If she had seen Ben, nothing would have made her believe that practically every apartment contained a family, a Bible, and a dream that one day enough could be scraped from those meager Friday night paychecks to make Brewster Place a distant memory.

As she watched her mother's head disappear into the building, Kiswana gave silent thanks that the elevator was broken. That would give her at least five minutes' grace to straighten up the apartment. She rushed to the sofa bed and hastily closed it without smoothing the rumpled sheets and blanket or removing her nightgown. She felt that somehow the tangled bedcovers would give away the fact that she had not slept alone last night. She silently apologized to Abshu's memory as she heartlessly crushed his spirit between the steel springs of the couch. Lord, that man was sweet. Her toes curled involuntarily at the passing thought of his full lips moving slowly over her instep. Abshu was a foot man, and he always started his lovemaking from the bottom up. For that reason Kiswana changed the color of the polish on her toenails every week. During the course

of their relationship she had gone from shades of red to brown and was now into the purples. I'm gonna have to start mixing them soon, she thought aloud as she turned from the couch and raced into the bathroom to remove any traces of Abshu from there. She took up his shaving cream and razor and threw them into the bottom drawer of her dresser beside her diaphragm. Mama wouldn't dare pry into my drawers right in front of me, she thought as she slammed the drawer shut. Well, at least not the bottom drawer. She may come up with some sham excuse for opening the top drawer, but never the bottom one.

When she heard the first two short raps on the door, her eyes took a final flight over the small apartment, desperately seeking out any slight misdemeanor that might have to be defended. Well, there was nothing she could do about the crack in the wall over that table. She had been after the landlord to fix it for two months now. And there had been no time to sweep the rug, and everyone knew that off-gray always looked dirtier than it really was. And it was just too damn bad about the kitchen. How was she expected to be out job-hunting every day and still have time to keep a kitchen that looked like her mother's, who didn't even work and still had someone come in twice a month for general cleaning. And besides . . .

Her imaginary argument was abruptly interrupted by a second series of knocks, accompanied by a penetrating, "Melanie, Melanie, are you there?" Kiswana strode toward the door. She's starting before she even gets in here. She knows that's not my name anymore.

She swung the door open to face her slightly flushed mother. "Oh, hi, Mama. You know, I thought I heard a knock, but I figured it was for the people next door, since no one hardly ever calls me Melanie." Score one for me, she thought.

10   "Well, it's awfully strange you can forget a name you answered to for twenty-three years," Mrs. Browne said, as she moved past Kiswana into the apartment. "My, that was a long climb. How long has your elevator been out? Honey, how do you manage with your laundry and groceries up all those steps? But I guess you're

young, and it wouldn't bother you as much as it does me." This long string of questions told Kiswana that her mother had no intentions of beginning her visit with another argument about her new African name.

"You know I would have called before I came, but you don't have a phone yet. I didn't want you to feel that I was snooping. As a matter of fact, I didn't expect to find you home at all. I thought you'd be out looking for a job." Mrs. Browne had mentally covered the entire apartment while she was talking and taking off her coat.

"Well, I got up late this morning. I thought I'd buy the afternoon paper and start early tomorrow."

"That sounds like a good idea." Her mother moved toward the window and picked up the discarded paper and glanced over the hurriedly circled ads. "Since when do you have experience as a fork-lift operator?"

Kiswana caught her breath and silently cursed herself for her stupidity. "Oh, my hand slipped—I meant to circle file clerk." She quickly took the paper before her mother could see that she had also marked cutlery salesman and chauffeur.

15 "You're sure you weren't sitting here moping and day-dreaming again?" Amber specks of laughter flashed in the corner of Mrs. Browne's eyes.

Kiswana threw her shoulders back and unsuccessfully tried to disguise her embarrassment with indignation.

"Oh, God, Mama! I haven't done that in years—it's for kids. When are you going to realize that I'm a woman now?" She sought desperately for some womanly thing to do and settled for throwing herself on the couch and crossing her legs in what she hoped looked like a nonchalant arc.

"Please, have a seat," she said, attempting the same tones and gestures she'd seen Bette Davis use on the late movies.

Mrs. Browne, lowering her eyes to hide her amusement, accepted the invitation and sat at the window, also crossing her legs. Kiswana saw immediately how it should have been done. Her celluloid poise clashed loudly against her

mother's quiet dignity, and she quickly uncrossed her legs. Mrs. Browne turned her head toward the window and pretended not to notice.

20 "At least you have a halfway decent view from here. I was wondering what lay beyond that dreadful wall—it's the boulevard. Honey, did you know that you can see the trees in Linden Hills from here?"

Kiswana knew that very well, because there were many lonely days that she would sit in her gray apartment and stare at those trees and think of home, but she would rather have choked than admit that to her mother.

"Oh, really, I never noticed. So how is Daddy and things at home?"

"Just fine. We're thinking of redoing one of the extra bedrooms since you children have moved out, but Wilson insists that he can manage all that work alone. I told him that he doesn't really have the proper time or energy for all that. As it is, when he gets home from the office, he's so tired he can hardly move. But you know you can't tell your father anything. Whenever he starts complaining about how stubborn you are, I tell him the child came by it honestly. Oh, and your brother was by yesterday," she added, as if it had just occurred to her.

So that's it, thought Kiswana. That's why she's here.

25 Kiswana's brother, Wilson, had been to visit her two days ago, and she had borrowed twenty dollars from him to get her winter coat out of layaway. That son-of-a-bitch probably ran straight to Mama—and after he swore he wouldn't say anything. I should have known, he was always a snotty-nosed sneak, she thought.

"Was he?" she said aloud. "He came by to see me, too, earlier this week. And I borrowed some money from him because my unemployment checks hadn't cleared in the bank, but now they have and everything's just fine." There, I'll beat you to that one.

"Oh, I didn't know that," Mrs. Browne lied. "He never mentioned you. He had just heard that Beverly was expecting again, and he rushed over to tell us."

Damn. Kiswana could have strangled herself.

"So she's knocked up again, huh?" she said irritably.

30 Her mother started. "Why do you always have to be so crude?"

"Personally, I don't see how she can sleep with Willie. He's such a dishrag."

Kiswana still resented the stance her brother had taken in college. When everyone at school was discovering their blackness and protesting on campus, Wilson never took part; he had even refused to wear an Afro. This had outraged Kiswana because, unlike her, he was dark-skinned and had the type of hair that was thick and kinky enough for a good "Fro." Kiswana had still insisted on cutting her own hair, but it was so thin and fine-textured, it refused to thicken even after she washed it. So she had to brush it up and spray it with lacquer to keep it from lying flat. She never forgave Wilson for telling her that she didn't look African, she looked like an electrocuted chicken.

"Now that's some way to talk. I don't know why you have an attitude against your brother. He never gave me a restless night's sleep, and now he's settled with a family and a good job."

"He's an assistant to an assistant junior part-ner in a law firm. What's the big deal about that?"

35 "The job has a future, Melanie. And at least he finished school and went on for his law degree."

"In other words, not like me, huh?"

"Don't put words into my mouth, young lady. I'm perfectly capable of saying what I mean."

Amen, thought Kiswana.

"And I don't know why you've been trying to start up with me from the moment I walked in. I didn't come here to fight with you. This is your first place away from home, and I just wanted to see how you were living and if you're doing all right. And I must say, you've fixed this apartment up very nicely."

40 "Really, Mama?" She found herself softening in the light of her mother's approval.

"Well, considering what you had to work with." This time she scanned the apartment openly.

"Look, I know it's not Linden Hills, but a lot can be done with it. As soon as they come and paint, I'm going to hang my Ashanti print over the couch. And I thought a big Boston Fern would go well in that corner, what do you think?"

"That would be fine, baby. You always had a good eye for balance."

Kiswana was beginning to relax. There was little she did that attracted her mother's approval. It was like a rare bird, and she had to tread care-fully around it lest it fly away.

45 "Are you going to leave that statue out like that?"

"Why, what's wrong with it? Would it look better somewhere else?"

There was a small wooden reproduction of a Yoruba goddess with large protruding breasts on the coffee table.

"Well," Mrs. Browne was beginning to blush, "it's just that it's a bit suggestive, don't you think? Since you live alone now, and I know you'll be having male friends stop by, you wouldn't want to be giving them any ideas. I mean, uh, you know, there's no point in putting yourself in any unpleasant situations because they may get the wrong impressions and uh, you know, I mean, well . . ." Mrs. Browne stammered on miserably.

Kiswana loved it when her mother tried to talk about sex. It was the only time she was at a loss for words.

50 "Don't worry, Mama." Kiswana smiled. "That wouldn't bother the type of men I date. Now maybe if it had big feet . . ." And she got hysterical, thinking of Abshu.

Her mother looked at her sharply. "What sort of gibberish is that about feet? I'm being serious, Melanie."

"I'm sorry, Mama." She sobered up. "I'll put it away in the closet," she said, knowing that she wouldn't.

"Good," Mrs. Browne said, knowing that she wouldn't either. "I guess you think I'm too picky, but we worry about you over here. And you refuse to put in a phone so we can call and see about you."

"I haven't refused, Mama. They want seventy-five dollars for a deposit, and I can't swing that right now."

55   "Melanie, I can give you the money."

"I don't want you to be giving me money— I've told you that before. Please, let me make it by myself."

"Well, let me lend it to you, then."

"No!"

"Oh, so you can borrow money from your brother, but not from me."

60   Kiswana turned her head from the hurt in her mother's eyes. "Mama, when I borrow from Willie, he makes me pay him back. You never let me pay you back," she said into her hands.

"I don't care. I still think it's downright self-ish of you to be sitting over here with no phone, and sometimes we don't hear from you in two weeks—anything could happen—especially living among these people."

Kiswana snapped her head up. "What do you mean, these people. They're my people and yours, too, Mama—we're all black. But maybe you've forgotten that over in Linden Hills."

"That's not what I'm talking about, and you know it. These streets—this building—it's so shabby and rundown. Honey, you don't have to live like this."

"Well, this is how poor people live."

65   "Melanie, you're not poor."

"No, Mama, *you're* not poor. And what you have and I have are two totally different things. I don't have a husband in real estate with a five-figure income and a home in Linden Hills—*you* do. What I have is a weekly unemployment check and an overdrawn checking account at United Federal. So this studio on Brewster is all I can afford."

"Well, you could afford a lot better," Mrs. Browne snapped, "if you hadn't dropped out of college and had to resort to these dead-end clerical jobs."

"Uh-huh, I knew you'd get around to that before long." Kiswana could feel the rings of anger begin to tighten around her lower back-bone, and they sent her forward onto the couch.

"You'll never understand, will you? Those bourgie schools were counterrevolutionary. My place was in the streets with my people, fighting for equality and a better community."

"Counterrevolutionary!" Mrs. Browne was raising her voice. "Where's your revolution now, Melanie? Where are all those black revolutionar-ies who were shouting and demonstrating and kicking up a lot of dust with you on that campus? Huh? They're sitting in wood-paneled offices with their degrees in mahogany frames, and they won't even drive their cars past this street because the city doesn't fix potholes in this part of town."

70   "Mama," she said, shaking her head slowly in disbelief, "how can you—a black woman—sit there and tell me that what we fought for during the Movement wasn't important just because some people sold out?"

"Melanie, I'm not saying it wasn't important. It was damned important to stand up and say that you were proud of what you were and to get the vote and other social opportunities for every per-son in this country who had it due. But you kids thought you were going to turn the world upside down, and it just wasn't so. When all the smoke had cleared, you found yourself with a fistful of new federal laws and a country still full of obsta-cles for black people to fight their way over—just because they're black. There was no revolution, Melanie, and there will be no revolution."

"So what am I supposed to do, huh? Just throw up my hands and not care about what happens to my people? I'm not supposed to keep fighting to make things better?"

"Of course, you can. But you're going to have to fight within the system, because it and these so-called 'bourgie' schools are going to be here for a long time. And that means that you get smart like a lot of your old friends and get an important job where you can have some influ-ence. You don't have to sell out, as you say, and work for some corporation, but you could become an assemblywoman or a civil liberties lawyer or open a freedom school in this very neighborhood. That way you could really help the community. But what help are you going to be to these people on Brewster while you're living hand-to-mouth on file-clerk jobs waiting for a revolution? You're wasting your talents, child."

"Well, I don't think they're being wasted. At least I'm here in day-to-day contact with the problems of my people. What good would I be after four or five years of a lot of white brainwashing in some phony, prestige institution, huh? I'd be like you and Daddy and those other educated blacks sitting over there in Linden Hills with a terminal case of middle-class amnesia."

75 "You don't have to live in a slum to be concerned about social conditions, Melanie. Your father and I have been charter members of the NAACP for the last twenty-five years."

"Oh, God!" Kiswana threw her head back in exaggerated disgust. "That's being concerned? That middle-of-the-road, Uncle Tom dumping ground for black Republicans!"

"You can sneer all you want, young lady, but that organization has been working for black people since the turn of the century, and it's still working for them. Where are all those radical groups of yours that were going to put a Cadillac in every garage and Dick Gregory in the White House? I'll tell you where."

I knew you would, Kiswana thought angrily.

"They burned themselves out because they wanted too much too fast. Their goals weren't grounded in reality. And that's always been your problem."

80 "What do you mean, my problem? I know exactly what I'm about."

"No, you don't. You constantly live in a fantasy world—always going to extremes—turning butterflies into eagles, and life isn't about that. It's accepting what is and working from that. Lord, I remember how worried you had me, putting all that lacquered hair spray on your head. I thought you were going to get lung cancer—trying to be what you're not."

Kiswana jumped up from the couch. "Oh, God, I can't take this anymore. Trying to be something I'm not—trying to be something I'm not, Mama! Trying to be proud of my heritage

and the fact that I was of African descent. If that's being what I'm not, then I say fine. But I'd rather be dead than be like you—a white man's nigger who's ashamed of being black!"

Kiswana saw streaks of gold and ebony light follow her mother's flying body out of the chair. She was swung around by the shoulders and made to face the deadly stillness in the angry woman's eyes. She was too stunned to cry out from the pain of the long fingernails that dug into her shoulders, and she was brought so close to her mother's face that she saw her reflection, distorted and wavering, in the tears that stood in the older woman's eyes. And she listened in that stillness to a story she had heard from a child.

"My grandmother," Mrs. Browne began slowly in a whisper, "was a full-blooded Iroquois, and my grandfather a free black from a long line of journeymen who had lived in Connecticut since the establishment of the colonies. And my father was a Bajan who came to this country as a cabin boy on a merchant mariner."

85 "I know all that," Kiswana said, trying to keep her lips from trembling.

"Then, know this." And the nails dug deeper into her flesh. "I am alive because of the blood of proud people who never scraped or begged or apologized for what they were. They lived asking only one thing of this world—to be allowed to be. And I learned through the blood of these people that black isn't beautiful and it isn't ugly—black is! It's not kinky hair and it's not straight hair—it just is."

"It broke my heart when you changed your name. I gave you my grandmother's name, a woman who bore nine children and educated them all, who held off six white men with a shotgun when they tried to drag one of her sons to jail for 'not knowing his place.' Yet you needed to reach into an African dictionary to find a name to make you proud.

"When I brought my babies home from the hospital, my ebony son and my golden daughter, I swore before whatever gods would listen—those of my mother's people or those of my father's people—that I would use everything I had and could ever get to see that my children were prepared to meet this world on its own terms, so that no one could sell them short and make them ashamed of what they were or how they looked—whatever they were or however they looked. And Melanie, that's not being white or red or black—that's being a mother."

Kiswana followed her reflection in the two single tears that moved down her mother's cheeks until it blended with them into the woman's copper skin. There was nothing and then so much that she wanted to say, but her throat kept closing up every time she tried to speak. She kept her head down and her eyes closed, and thought, Oh, God, just let me die. How can I face her now?

90   Mrs. Browne lifted Kiswana's chin gently. "And the one lesson I wanted you to learn is not to be afraid to face anyone, not even a crafty old lady like me who can outtalk you." And she smiled and winked.

"Oh, Mama, I . . ." and she hugged the woman tightly.

"Yeah, baby." Mrs. Browne patted her back. "I know."

She kissed Kiswana on the forehead and cleared her throat. "Well, now, I better be moving on. It's getting late, there's dinner to be made, and I have to get off my feet—these new shoes are killing me."

Kiswana looked down at the beige leather pumps. "Those are really classy. They're English, aren't they?"

95   "Yes, but, Lord, do they cut me right across the instep." She removed the shoe and sat on the couch to massage her foot.

Bright red nail polish glared at Kiswana through the stockings. "Since when do you polish your toenails?" she gasped. "You never did that before."

"Well . . ." Mrs. Browne shrugged her shoulders, "your father sort of talked me into it, and, uh, you know, he likes it and all, so I thought, uh, you know, why not so . . ." And she gave Kiswana an embarrassed smile.

I'll be damned, the young woman thought, feeling her whole face tingle. Daddy into feet! And she looked at the blushing woman on her couch and suddenly realized that her mother had trod through the same universe that she herself was now traveling. Kiswana was breaking no new trails and would eventually end up just two feet away on that couch. She stared at the woman she had been and was to become.

"But I'll never be a Republican," she caught herself saying aloud.

100   "What are you mumbling about, Melanie?" Mrs. Browne slipped on her shoe and got up from the couch.

She went to get her mother's coat. "Nothing, Mama. It's really nice of you to come by. You should do it more often."

"Well, since it's not Sunday, I guess you're allowed at least one lie."

They both laughed.

After Kiswana had closed the door and turned around, she spotted an envelop sticking between the cushions of her couch. She went over and opened it up; there was seventy-five dollars in it.

105   "Oh, Mama, darn it!" She rushed to the window and started to call to the woman, who had just emerged from the building, but she suddenly changed her mind and sat down in the chair with a long sigh that caught in the upward draft of the autumn wind and disappeared over the top of the building.

EXPLORATORY WRITING

Near the end of this story, Naylor writes that Kiswana "suddenly realized that her mother had trod through the same universe that she was now traveling. Kiswana was breaking no new trails and would eventually end up just two feet away on that couch. She stared at the woman she had been and was to become." In an exploratory piece of writing, explain what Kiswana is trying to run away from and what brings her to this final discovery about her mother's generation and the generations before that.

TALKING ABOUT THE READING

As we mentioned earlier in this chapter, generations are defined by historical events, current cultural attitudes, a shared language, and more. These two stories were written nearly forty years apart, but both use language and reveal attitudes specific to their time and place. White, for example, describes a steamboat as having "a long rounded stern like the lip of a Ubangi." That isn't a simile that would be acceptable today and certainly would raise hackles for Kiswana Browne, her mother and many others, black and white. With a group of your classmates, go back through both selections to find language, descriptions, and attitudes that identify the generation that wrote each and the times in which they were written. What meanings do these generational details add to the stories?

WRITING ASSIGNMENT

For this essay, take the perspective of either Kiswana Browne or her mother and explain how the character you have chosen sees the other—first taking Kiswana's point of view, then taking her mother's point of view. How are generational differences between the two characters indicated in specific places in the story? Where do generations seem to overlap with the two?

WRITING SEQUENCE

1. Reread the exploratory writing you did in response to these two selections by White and Naylor. (If you did not do those assignments, complete them before you continue with this assignment.) In many ways, these two stories are very different, written in very different times, and they take place in very different settings. They do, however, share the theme of one generation recognizing itself in the one before or after it. Draw on the exploratory writings you did for each piece to create a new and longer piece of exploratory writing. In it, examine what each writer has to say about generational differences and the notion of meeting oneself in the generation that came before. What differences do you see in the two writers' relationships with their parents? What similarities?

2. In your writing so far, you have considered the relationships that are revealed as each story unfolds. One significant difference between these two pieces is the fact that the first is a father/son story. The second is a mother/daughter story. Revise your longer exploratory writing for an essay in which you explain how gender affects the way the characters relate to each other and, possibly, how each responds to generational differences. What in each of these stories indicates that gender is important?

3. On one level, "Kiswana Browne" seems to be concerned with a generation gap between Kiswana and her mother. By contrast, in "Once More to the Lake" White embraces the past and the generation that came before him and seems to blame progress or a rapidly changing world for losing some of those earlier ways and attitudes. One way to read White, in fact, is to think of his trip to the lake with his son as an attempt to recapture that past and the generation that made up that earlier time. For this culminating assignment, write an essay that explains what the central figure in each story learns about himself or herself as they confront their parents' generation. Are there suggestions that White does, to an extent, want to distinguish himself from his father's generation and from his son's? What of her mother's generation does Kiswana want to embrace?

This should be a finished piece of writing, approximately 4–6 pages in length (drafted, revised, and edited). Make sure you read over earlier writing you have done in response to the readings. Look back, as well, at places in each text you have marked as important.

THE PROBLEM WITH YOUTH ACTIVISM

—*Courtney E. Martin*

Courtney Martin is an award-winning writer and teacher whose most recent book is *Perfect Girls, Starving Daughters: The Frightening New Normalcy of Hating Your Body* (2007). She writes a regular column for *American Prospect Online,* where the selection here originally appeared on November 19, 2007. She has been honored with the Elie Wiesel Prize in Ethics, the Joan Cook Scholarship from the Journalism and Women's Symposium, the Setting the Message Straight Award from ChoiceUSA, a Books for a Better Life nomination, and a Clark Foundation fellowship.

SUGGESTION FOR READING   Before you begin reading, think about the term *youth activism*. Have you been involved in anything you consider activism? Community change projects? Social justice movements? Make a list of community or activist projects you and your friends or classmates have been a part of. Which were sponsored by institutions—school or church, for example? Which originated with a group of young people wanting to change things? Do you think young people today are interested in joining movements to advocate change? Why? Why not?

1 "Do you think this is the right color ribbon?" asked a petite brunette, her hair pulled back in a haphazard ponytail, her college sweatshirt engulfing her tiny frame. "And do you think these are the right length of sections I'm cutting? I don't want it to be all funky when we pin them on."

"Mmm . . . I'm not sure," said the guy next to her, sucking on a lollipop, his football-player physique totally evident in his tight band T-shirt.

"Looks good to me," his roommate said without even glancing over at the ribbon or the girl.

Meet the college anti-war movement.

5 I just got back from a two-week campus speaking tour during which I had the privilege of hanging out in a women's center at a Catholic college, eating bad Mexican food with Mennonite feminists, and chatting with aspiring writers and activists at a college in which half the students are the first in their families to experience higher education. I heard the stories of transgender youth in Kansas City, jocks with food addictions in Jacksonville, and student organizers who are too overwhelmed to address all the world's problems in Connecticut.

When my plane finally landed with a resounding bump at LaGuardia, I felt totally inspired by the earnest enthusiasm that beamed out of almost every student I encountered—and also terrified that the university system is sucking the life out of them. At the risk of biting the hand that feeds me (I am usually paid to speak, in part, by student organizations and women's centers), I have to attest that the institutionalization of activism on college campuses seems to be a key culprit in the absence of visible youth movements in this country.

The scene above illustrates just the kind of vibe you can find at an anti-war or nonviolence club on college campuses any day of the week. It is sweetly collaborative, mainly focused on raising awareness among students, very keyed in to particular dates (Love Your Body Day, Earth

Day, Black History Month), and most of all, safe. This is not terribly surprising considering that these clubs are sanctioned and funded (sometimes with upward of thousands of dollars a year) by the school administration through a formal application process. They are structured to legitimize but also to domesticate student passions and actions from the start.

And students do have passions, contrary to what some hippies-turned-well-paid-pundits argue. A survey conducted just this year by the National Association of Campus Activities (NACA) found that 98 percent of students at their annual meeting saw the war in Iraq as one of the issues most important to them. Erin Wilson, the director of communication for NACA, reports that student involvement in campus activities is increasing all the time and adds that among their 1,040 member schools, a yearly total of $150 million is spent on campus programming.

As great as it might seem that colleges and universities are supporting student causes, I actually believe that it has tamed the critical energy necessary to be young, outraged, and active. When you're being funded by a team of white-haired academics in suits, taking real risks—acts of civil disobedience like sit-ins, hunger strikes, boycotts—don't seem like such a smart idea. Students rightly wonder whether they will "ruin it" for the next class if they cross the line and lose the school leadership's support. Plus, it's so much easier to just eat the free pizza and cut the three-inch ribbons than to mastermind a rebellious and potentially dangerous student uprising.

10 The academy, in general, encourages specialization, intellectualization, civility—not exactly the key ingredients for effective social action. Students are surrounded by professors reminiscing about the glory days of youth activism, when groups like Students for a Democratic Society, the Weather Underground, and the Black Panther Party really ignited social change. But the professors don't seem to make the connection that none of these were school-sanctioned organizations.

Today's youth activism is largely enacted within the gated fortresses of higher learning.

Students are overwhelmingly and often motivated by applying to law school or resumé-building. (How do you think they got into these undergraduate institutions in the first place?) They funnel their outrage into weekly club meetings and awareness campaigns that look good on paper— activities that convey to future employers and institutions that they are socially involved and aware but not at odds with the system. Students seem to join sanctioned, existing clubs, rather than launch their own radical actions, without much resistance or critical questioning. Perhaps they've been socialized to accept the status quo, but even more, I believe they simply don't have the time or energy to start innovative revolutions from scratch because they are so busy taking standardized tests and building their resumés with internships and assistantships.

I watched a group of them sort through a brightly colored stack of anti-war quotations to make sure that every single one, literally, bore the stamp of approval from the college activities office so they could hang them around campus without getting in trouble. It made me cringe. This is where their energies were being diverted during the deadliest month yet in the Iraq War.

It made me reflect on my own undergraduate days—just about five years ago now. I wasn't a rah-rah student government officer, but I certainly did my share of club activities: school newspaper, writing fellows program, resident assistant, volunteering at a Harlem preschool, even the hip-hop club (talk about taming outrage). I remember feeling so busy, so responsible, so important. Now I realize that there was a real cost to that frenzy of school-sanctioned productivity. I rarely thought beyond the borders of folding tables that lined the student activities fairs. I rarely put my body or my future on the line. While I was tutoring fellow students in grammar and composition and making door tags for my residence halls, I missed the escalation of a bogus justification for a messy war in my name.

In one of the largest studies ever conducted of Generation Y, psychology professor Jean M. Twenge found that college students "increasingly believe that their lives are controlled by outside forces"—called "externality" in the psychology field. Twenge writes, "The average college student in 2002 had more external control beliefs than 80 percent of college students in the early 1960s."

15   Is it any wonder? We were raised to organize our adolescent lives in pursuit of external approval: church awards, athletic scholarships, and college admissions. More than any generation in history, we've been signed up, roped in, and overscheduled. When we get to college, many of us rush to join clubs in an attempt to recreate this safe feeling of sanctioned activity, of organized energies, of potential approval by authorities. Our innate passions and spontaneous actions have essentially been bred out of us.

The LearningWork Connection, a consulting firm on youth issues, reports that from September 2004 to September 2005, 79 percent of first-year males and 87 percent of first-year females described themselves as "volunteers." They add, however, that "Gen Y is less engaged with civic and political activities than they are with other causes."

Which prompts me to ask, what are "causes," really? The word stinks of bureaucracy and timidity, of the most educated, wanted generation in history sprawled across standard university furniture—not planning the next revolution, but eating free cookies and voting on whether buttons or ribbons will be less destructive to students' clothing.

I saw the surefire glimmer of pure passion in these students' eyes. I know they are capable of great and ingenious uprisings, a type of protest that is totally 21st century, a trademark Generation Y invention. Viruses in campus administrators' computers with pop-up windows demanding no more expansion into poor, local neighborhoods? Mock draft cards sent home to their parents? A dance party—1 million youth strong—on the Washington lawn? It all seems possible.

They need to stay out of the student center long enough to figure out what their version of outraged activism really is. Small as it may sound, big change would happen if college students today could protect their purest intentions from the pacifying force of free pizza and resumé kudos. Our generation needs to step into our raw power—the priceless power of being young and mad. We need to stay hungry long enough to get angry.

EXPLORATORY WRITING

In an exploratory writing, trace how Martin argues her claim that the "the institutionalism of activism on college campuses seems to be a key culprit in the absence of visible youth movements in this country."

TALKING ABOUT THE READING

With a group of your classmates, list examples of student activism that you know of. Which of these were school sponsored? Which were spontaneous with the students themselves? Do you agree that activism has been institutionalized on college campuses and, to an extent, in high schools in the United States?

WRITING ASSIGNMENTS

1. In many ways, the argument Martin makes is about generations. She writes, "Students are surrounded by professors reminiscing about the glory days of youth activism, when groups like Students for a Democratic Society, the Weather Underground, and the Black Panther Party really ignited social change. But the professors don't seem to make the connection that none of these were school-sanctioned organizations." Write an essay in

which you examine how Martin makes this argument. What is she saying (or suggesting) about each generation and its commitment to activism as well as its opportunity for activism? What is the problem with school-sponsored activism, according to Martin?

2. Martin seems, for the most part, to be sympathetic to young people and the dilemma she believes colleges and universities have put young people in by institutionalizing activism and social awareness. At times, however, she also seems to be portraying young people as shallow or simply resume builders. Write an essay in which you examine what her attitude toward young people is. What signals that attitude?

3. Martin's column appears in the *American Prospect Online,* which means that readers can respond publicly to the arguments she makes. Write your response to the arguments Martin is making about student activism. Are there no real youth movements? Is all youth activism institutionalized? In order to write a credible response, you will need to do research on youth movements today. Students Against Sweatshops, for example, is one movement that grew very quickly in the 1990s and, in some cases, was instrumental in forcing universities to cancel contracts with companies that used sweatshop labor. Use what you have found about youth activism to either counter or support Martin's central argument.

WE ARE ALL THIRD GENERATION

▬▬—*Margaret Mead*

Margaret Mead (1901–1978) was an anthropologist interested in the way culture influences the development of individual personality. Curator of ethnology at the American Museum of Natural History in New York City from 1926 to 1969, Mead produced a series of books, including *Coming of Age in Samoa* (1928), *Growing Up in New Guinea* (1930), *Sex and Temperament in Three Primitive Societies* (1935), and *Culture and Commitment* (1970). This selection comes from *And Keep Your Powder Dry: An Anthropologist Looks at America* (1942). As you will see, Mead believed the "American character" could be described and analyzed as "shared habits and view of the world." Of particular pertinence to the discussion of generations in this chapter is her view—now commonly held—that by the third generation, immigrants become fully "American."

SUGGESTION FOR READING As you read, keep in mind the title of this selection, "We Are All Third Generation." Notice how Margaret Mead traces the changes from one generation to the next. Consider how she sets up her line of analysis to explain how the "American character" reaches "its most complete expression in the third-generation American."

1 What then is this American character, this expression of American institutions and of American attitudes which is embodied in every American, in everyone born in this country and sometimes even in those who have come later to these shores? What is it that makes it possible to say of a group of people glimpsed from a hotel step in Soerabaja or strolling down the streets of Marseilles, "There go some Americans," whether they have come from Arkansas or Maine or Pennsylvania, whether they bear German or Swedish or Italian surnames? Not clothes alone, but the way they wear them, the way they walk along the street without awareness that anyone of higher status may be walking there also, the way their eyes rove as if by right over the façade of palaces and the rose windows of cathedrals, interested and unimpressed, referring what they see back to the Empire State building, the Chrysler tower, or a good-sized mountain in Montana.

Not the towns they come from—Sioux City, Poughkeepsie, San Diego, Scotsdale—but the tone of voice in which they say, "Why, I came from right near there. My home town was Evansville. Know anybody in Evansville?" And the apparently meaningless way in which the inhabitant of Uniontown warms to the inhabitant of Evansville as they name over a few names of people whom neither of them know well, about whom neither of them have thought for years, and about whom neither of them care in the least. And yet, the onlooker, taking note of the increased warmth in their voices, of the narrowing of the distance which had separated them when they first spoke, knows that something has happened, that a tie has been established[1] between two people who were lonely before, a tie which every American hopes he may be able to establish as he hopefully asks every stranger: "What's your home town?"

Americans establish these ties by finding common points on the road that all are expected to have traveled, after their forebears came from Europe one or two or three generations ago, or from one place to another in America, resting for long enough to establish for each generation a "home town" in which they grew up and which they leave to move on to a new town which will become the home town of their children. Whether they meet on the deck of an Atlantic steamer, in a hotel in Singapore, in New York or in San Francisco, the same expectation underlies their first contact—that both of them have moved on and are moving on and that potential intimacy lies in paths that have crossed. Europeans, even Old Americans whose pride lies not in the circumstance that their ancestors have moved often but rather in the fact that they have not moved for some time, find themselves eternally puzzled by this "home town business." Many Europeans fail to find out that in nine cases out of ten the "home town" is not where one lives but where one did live; they mistake the sentimental tone in which an American invokes Evansville and Centerville and Unionville for a desire to live there again; they miss entirely the symbolic significance of the question and answer which say

diagrammatically, "Are you the same kind of person I am? Good, how about a coke?"

Back of that query lies the remembrance and the purposeful forgetting of European ancestry. For a generation, they cluster together in the Little Italies, in the Czech section or around the Polish Church, new immigrants clinging together so as to be able to chatter in their own tongue and buy their own kind of red peppers, but later there is a scattering to the suburbs and the small towns, to an "American" way of life, and this is dramatized by an over acceptance of what looks, to any European, as the most meaningless sort of residence—on a numbered street in Chicago or the Bronx. No garden, no fruit trees, no ties to the earth, often no ties to the neighbors, just a number on a street, just a number of a house for which the rent is $10 more than the rent in the old foreign district from which they moved—how can it mean anything? But it does. . . .

If this then, this third-generation American, always moving on, always, in his hopes, moving up, leaving behind him all that was his past and greeting with enthusiasm any echo of that past when he meets it in the life of another, represents one typical theme of the American character structure, how is this theme reflected in the form of the family, in the upbringing of the American child? For to the family we must turn for an understanding of the American character structure. We may describe the adult American, and for descriptive purposes we may refer his behavior to the American scene, to the European past, to the state of American industry, to any other set of events which we wish; but to understand the regularity of this behavior we must investigate the family within which the child is reared. Only so can we learn how the newborn child, at birth potentially a Chinaman or an American, a Pole or an Irishman, becomes an American. By referring his character to the family we do not say that the family is the cause of his character and that the pace of American industry or the distribution of population in America are secondary effects, but merely that all the great configuration of American culture is mediated to the child by his parents, his siblings,[2] his near relatives, and his nurses. He meets American law first in the warning note of his mother's voice: "Stop digging, here comes a cop." He meets American economics when he finds his mother unimpressed by his offer to buy another copy of the wedding gift he has just smashed: "At the 5 and 10 cent store, can't we?" His first encounter with puritan standards may come through his mother's "If you don't eat your vegetables you can't have any dessert." He learns the paramount importance of distinguishing between vice and virtue; that it is only a matter of which comes first, the pleasure or the pain.[3] All his great lessons come through his mother's voice, through his father's laughter, or the tilt of his father's cigar when a business deal goes right. Just as one way of understanding a machine is to understand how it is made, so one way of understanding the typical character structure of a culture is to follow step by step the way in which it is built into the growing child. Our assumption when we look at the American family will be that each experience of early childhood is contributing to make the growing individual "all of a piece," is guiding him towards consistent and specifically American inconsistency in his habits and view of the world.

5   What kind of parents are these "third generation" Americans? These people who are always moving, always readjusting, always hoping to buy a better car and a better radio, and even in the years of Depression orienting their behavior to their "failure" to buy a better car or a better radio. Present or absent, the better car, the better house, the better radio are key points in family life. In the first place, the American parent expects his child to leave him, leave him physically, go to another town, another state; leave him in terms of occupation, embrace a different calling, learn a different skill; leave him socially, travel if possible with a different crowd. Even where a family has reached the top and actually stayed there for two or three generations, there are, for all but the very, very few, still larger cities or foreign courts to be stormed. Those American families which settle back to maintain a position

of having reached the top in most cases moulder there for lack of occupation, ladder-climbers gone stale from sitting too long on the top step, giving a poor imitation of the aristocracy of other lands. At the bottom, too, there are some without hope, but very few. Studies of modern youth dwell with anxiety upon the disproportion between the daydreams of the under-privileged young people and the actuality which confronts them in terms of job opportunities. In that very daydream the break is expressed. The daughter who says to her hard-working mother: "You don't know. I may be going to be a great writer," is playing upon a note in her mother's mind which accepts the possibility that even if her daughter does not become famous, she will at least go places that she, the mother, has never gone. . . .

With this orientation towards a different future for the child comes also the expectation that the child will pass beyond his parents and leave their standards behind him. Educators exclaim impatiently over the paradox that Americans believe in change, believe in progress and yet do their best—or so it seems—to retard their children, to bind them to parental ways, to inoculate them against the new ways to which they give lip service. But here is a point where the proof of the pudding lies in the eating. If the parents were really behaving as the impatient educators claim they are, really strangling and hobbling their children's attempts to embrace the changing fashions in manners or morals, we would not have the rapid social change which is so characteristic of our modern life. We would not go in twenty years from fig leaves on Greek statues to models of unborn babies in our public museums. It is necessary to distinguish between ritual and ceremonial resistances and real resistances. Among primitive peoples, we find those in which generation after generation there is a mock battle between the young men and the old men: generation after generation the old men lose. An observer from our society, with an unresolved conflict with his father on his mind, might watch that battle in terror, feeling the outcome was in doubt. But the members of the tribe who are fighting the mock battle consciously or unconsciously know the outcome and fight with no less display of zeal for the knowing of it. The mock battle is no less important because the issue is certain.

Similarly, on the island of Bali, it is unthinkable that a father or a brother should plan to give a daughter of the house to some outsider. Only when a marriage is arranged between cousins, both of whose fathers are members of the same paternal line, can consent be appropriately given. Yet there flourishes, and has flourished probably for hundreds of years, a notion among Balinese young people that it is more fun to marry someone who is not a cousin. So, generation after generation, young men carry off the daughters of other men, and these daughters, their consent given in advance, nevertheless shriek and protest noisily if there are witnesses by. It is a staged abduction, in which no one believes, neither the boy nor the girl nor their relatives. Once in a while, some neurotic youth misunderstands and tries to abduct a girl who has not given her consent, and as a result the whole society is plunged into endless confusion, recrimination, and litigation.

So it is in American society. American parents, to the extent that they are Americans, expect their children to live in a different world, to clothe their moral ideas in different trappings, to court in automobiles although their forebears courted, with an equal sense of excitement and moral trepidation, on horsehair sofas. As the parents' course was uncharted when they were young—for they too had gone a step beyond their parents and transgressed every day some boundary which their parents had temporarily accepted as absolute—so also the parents know that their children are sailing uncharted seas. And so it comes about that American parents lack the sure hand on the rudder which parents in other societies display, and that they go in for a great deal of conventional and superficial grumbling. To the traditional attitudes characteristic of all oldsters who find the young a deteriorated version of themselves, Americans add the mixture of hope and envy and anxiety which comes from knowing that their children are not deteriorated versions of themselves, but actually—very actually—manage

a car better than father ever did. This is trying; sometimes very trying. The neurotic father, like the neurotic lover in Bali, will misunderstand the license to grumble, and will make such a fuss over his son or daughter when they behave as all of their age are behaving, that the son or daughter has to be very unneurotic indeed not to take the fuss as something serious, not to believe that he or she is breaking father's heart. Similarly, a neurotic son or daughter will mistake the ceremonial grumbling for the real thing, and break their spirits in a futile attempt to live up to the voiced parental standards. To the average child the parents' resistance is a stimulus. . . .

By and large, the American father has an attitude towards his children which may be loosely classified as autumnal. They are his for a brief and passing season, and in a very short while they will be operating gadgets which he does not understand and cockily talking a language to which he has no clue. He does his best to keep ahead of his son, takes a superior tone as long as he can, and knows that in nine cases out of ten he will lose. If the boy goes into his father's profession, of course, it will take him a time to catch up. He finds out that the old man knows a trick or two; that experience counts as over against this newfangled nonsense. But the American boy solves that one very neatly: he typically does not go into his father's profession, nor take up land next to his father where his father can come over and criticize his plowing. He goes somewhere else, either in space or in occupation. And his father, who did the same thing and expects that his son will, is at heart terrifically disappointed if the son accedes to his ritual request that he docilely follow in his father's footsteps and secretly suspects the imitative son of being a milksop. He knows he is a milksop—so he thinks—because he himself would have been a milksop if he had wanted to do just what his father did.

10   This is an attitude which reaches its most complete expression in the third-generation American. His grandfather left home, rebelled against a parent who did not expect final rebellion, left a land where everyone expected him to

stay. Come to this country, his rebellious adventuring cooled off by success, he begins to relent a little, to think perhaps the strength of his ardor to leave home was overdone. When his sons grow up, he is torn between his desire to have them succeed in this new country—which means that they must be more American than he, must lose entirely their foreign names and every trace of allegiance to a foreign way of life—and his own guilt towards the parents and the fatherland which he has denied. So he puts on the heat, alternately punishing the child whose low marks in school suggest that he is not going to be a successful American and berating him for his American ways and his disrespect for his father and his father's friends from the old country. When that son leaves home, he throws himself with an intensity which his children will not know into the American way of life; he eats American, talks American, dresses American, he will be American or nothing. In making his way of life consistent, he inevitably makes it thin; the overtones of the family meal on which strange, delicious, rejected European dishes were set, and about which low words in a foreign tongue wove the atmosphere of home, must all be dropped out. His speech has a certain emptiness; he rejects the roots of words—roots lead back, and he is going forward—and comes to handle language in terms of surfaces and clichés. He rejects half of his life in order to make the other half self-consistent and complete. And by and large he succeeds. Almost miraculously, the sons of the Polish day laborer and the Italian fruit grower, the Finnish miner and the Russian garment worker become Americans.

Second generation—American-born of foreign-born parents—they set part of the tone of the American eagerness for their children to go onward. They have left their parents; left them in a way which requires more moral compensation than was necessary even for the parent generation who left Europe. The immigrant left his land, his parents, his fruit trees, and the little village street behind him. He cut the ties of military service; he flouted the king or the emperor; he built himself a new life in a new country. The father whom he left behind was strong, a part of something terribly strong, something to be feared and respected and fled from. Something so strong that the bravest man might boast of a successful flight. He left his parents, entrenched representatives of an order which he rejected. But not so his son. He leaves his father not a part of a strong other-way of life, but bewildered on the shores of the new world, having climbed only halfway up the beach. His father's ties to the old world, his mannerisms, his broken accent, his little foreign gestures are not part parcel of something strong and different; they are signs of his failure to embrace this new way of life. Does his mother wear a kerchief over her head? He cannot see the generations of women who have worn such kerchiefs. He sees only the American women who wear hats, and he pities and rejects his mother who has failed to become—an American. And so there enters into the attitude of the second-generation American—an attitude which again is woven through our folkways, our attitude towards other languages, towards anything foreign, towards anything European—a combination of contempt and avoidance, a fear of yielding, and a sense that to yield would be weakness. His father left a father who was the representative of a way of life which had endured for a thousand years. When he leaves his father, he leaves a partial failure; a hybrid, one who represents a step towards freedom, not freedom itself. His first-generation father chose between freedom and what he saw as slavery; but when the second-generation American looks at his European father, and through him, at Europe, he sees a choice between success and failure, between potency and ignominy. He passionately rejects the halting English, the half-measures of the immigrant. He rejects with what seems to him equally good reasons "European ties and entanglements." This second-generation attitude which has found enormous expression in our culture especially during the last fifty years, has sometimes come to dominate it—in those parts of the country which we speak of as "isolationist." Intolerant of foreign language, foreign ways, vigorously determined on being themselves, they are, in attitude if not in fact, second-generation Americans.

When the third-generation boy grows up, he comes up against a father who found the task of leaving his father a comparatively simple one. The second-generation parent lacks the intensity of the first, and his son in turn fails to reflect the struggles, the first against feared strength and the second against guiltily rejected failure, which have provided the plot for his father and grandfather's maturation. He is expected to succeed; he is expected to go further than his father went; and all this is taken for granted. He is furthermore expected to feel very little respect for the past. Somewhere in his grandfather's day there was an epic struggle for liberty and freedom. His picture of that epic grandfather is a little obscured, however, by the patent fact that his father does not really respect him; he may have been a noble character, but he had a foreign accent. The grandchild is told in school, in the press, over the radio, about the founding fathers, but they were not after all *his* founding fathers; they are, in ninety-nine cases out of a hundred, somebody else's ancestors. Any time one's own father, who in his own youth had pushed his father aside and made his own way, tries to get in one's way, one can invoke the founding fathers—those ancestors of the real Americans; the Americans who got here earlier—those Americans which father worked so very hard, so slavishly, in fact, to imitate. This is a point which the European observer misses. He hears an endless invocation of Washington and Lincoln, of Jefferson and Franklin. Obviously, Americans go in for ancestor worship, says the European. Obviously, Americans are longing for a strong father, say the psycho-analysts.[4] These observers miss the point that Washington is not the ancestor of the man who is doing the talking; Washington does not represent the past to which one belongs by birth, but the past to which one tries to belong by effort. Washington represents the thing for which grandfather left Europe at the risk of his life, and for which father rejected grandfather at the risk of his integrity. Washington is not that to

which Americans passionately cling but that to which they want to belong, and fear, in the bottom of their hearts, that they cannot and do not.

This odd blending of the future and the past, in which another man's great-grandfather becomes the symbol of one's grandson's future, is an essential part of American culture. "Americans are so conservative," say Europeans. They lack the revolutionary spirit. Why don't they rebel? Why did President Roosevelt's suggestion of altering the structure of the Supreme Court and the Third-Term argument raise such a storm of protest? Because, in education, in attitudes, most Americans are third generation, they have just really arrived. Their attitude towards this country is that of one who has just established membership, just been elected to an exclusive club, just been initiated into the rites of an exacting religion. Almost any one of them who inspects his own ancestry, even though it goes back many more generations than three, will find a gaping hole somewhere in the family tree. Campfire girls give an honor to the girl who can name all eight great-grandparents, including the maiden names of the four great-grandmothers. Most Americans cannot get this honor. And who was that missing great-grandmother? Probably, oh, most probably, not a grandniece of Martha Washington.

We have, of course, our compensatory mythology. People who live in a land torn by earthquakes have myths of a time when the land was steady, and those whose harvest are uncertain dream of a golden age when there was no drought. Likewise, people whose lives are humdrum and placid dream of an age of famine and rapine. We have our rituals of belonging, our DAR's and our Descendants of King Philip's Wars, our little blue book of the blue-blooded Hawaiian aristocracy descended from the first missionaries, and our *Mayflower,* which is only equaled in mythological importance by the twelve named canoes which brought the Maoris to New Zealand. The mythology keeps alive the doubt. The impressive president of a patriotic society knows that she is a member by virtue of only one of the some eight routes through which membership is possible.

Only one. The other seven? Well, three are lost altogether. Two ancestors were Tories. In some parts of the country she can boast of that; after all, Tories were people of substance, real "old families." But it doesn't quite fit. Of two of those possible lines, she has resolutely decided not to think. Tinkers and tailors and candlestick makers blend indistinctly with heaven knows what immigrants! She goes to a meeting and is very insistent about the way in which the Revolutionary War which only one-eighth of her ancestors helped to fight should be represented to the children of those whose eight ancestors were undoubtedly all somewhere else in 1776.

15   On top of this Old American mythology, another layer has been added, a kind of placatory offering, a gesture towards the Old World which Americans had left behind. As the fifth- and sixth- and seventh-generation Americans lost the zest which came with climbing got to the top of the pecking order[5] in their own town or city and sat, still uncertain, still knowing their credentials were shaky, on the top of the pile, the habit of wanting to belong—to really belong, to be accepted absolutely as something which one's ancestors had NOT been—became inverted. They turned towards Europe, especially towards England, towards presentation at Court, towards European feudal attitudes. And so we have had in America two reinforcements of the European class attitudes—those hold-overs of feudal caste attitudes, in the newlycome immigrant who carries class consciousness in every turn and bend of his neck, and the new feudalism, the "old family" who has finally toppled over backwards into the lap of all that their remote ancestors left behind them.

When I say that we are most of us—whatever our origins—third-generation in character structure, I mean that we have been reared in an atmosphere which is most like that which I have described for the third generation. Father is to be outdistanced and outmoded, but not because he is a strong representative of another culture, well entrenched, not because he is a weak and ineffectual attempt to imitate the new culture; he did very well in his way, but he is out of date. He, like us,

was moving forwards, moving away from something symbolized by his own ancestors, moving towards something symbolized by other people's ancestors. Father stands for the way things were done, for a direction which on the whole was a pretty good one, in its day. He was all right because he was on the right road. Therefore, we, his children, lack the mainsprings of rebellion. He was out of date; he drove an old model car which couldn't make it on the hills. Therefore it is not necessary to fight him, to knock him out of the race. It is much easier and quicker to pass him. And to pass him it is only necessary to keep on going and to see that one buys a new model every year. Only if one slackens, loses one's interest in the race towards success, does one slip back. Otherwise, it is onward and upward, *towards* the world of Washington and Lincoln; a world in which we don't fully belong, but which we feel, if we work at it, we some time may achieve.

NOTES

1. I owe my understanding of the significance of these chronological ties to discussions with Kurt Lewin and John G. Pilley.

2. Sibling is a coined word used by scientists for both brothers and sisters. The English language lacks such a word.

3. Cf. Samuel Butler's definition: That vice is when the pain follows the pleasure and virtue when the pleasure follows the pain.

4. I owe my classification of the American attitude towards the 'founding fathers' to a conversation with Dr. Ernst Kris, in which he was commenting on the way in which Americans, apparently, wanted a strong father, although, in actual fact, they always push their fathers aside.

5. Pecking order is a very convenient piece of jargon which social psychologists use to describe a group in which it is very clear to everybody in it just which bird can peck which, or which cow can butt which other cow away from the water trough. Among many living creatures these 'pecking orders' are fixed and when a newcomer enters the group he has to fight and scramble about until everybody is clear just where he belongs—below No. 8 chick, for instance, and above old No.9.

EXPLORATORY WRITING

In a piece of exploratory writing, explain what Margaret Mead means when she says that we are all "third generation." In your writing, describe how she answers the question "What is this American character?" Why do you think she has chosen to locate the formation of the American "character structure" in the dynamics of the American family? How does her analysis of the immigrant family from first to second to third generation work in this discussion?

TALKING ABOUT THE READING

With a group of your classmates, consider the ad "They knew they had to learn English to survive," reproduced here. To what extent does the ad draw on a representation of American immigrant generations that is similar to Mead's? What is the ad's purpose in comparing older waves of immigration to more recent immigration?

WRITING ASSIGNMENTS

1. Use Mead's idea that "we are all third generation" to analyze your own family. She offers a predictable sequence from first to second to third generation. Begin by describing this sequence and then show how it fits or fails to fit the experience of your family. What modifications, if any, would you want to make?

2. Mead wrote this chapter in 1942. Is it possible to update it—to identify a common "American character" today as confidently as Mead did sixty years ago? Is the notion of an "American character" useful at all? Explain your answers to these questions by either proposing an updated version or explaining why the notion doesn't work in contemporary America. (Consider also whether it ever worked.)

3. Consider Mary Gordon's sense of what it means to be an American in "More Than Just a Shrine: Paying Homage to the Ghosts of Ellis Island," in Chapter 9, and compare that with Mead's sense in "We Are All Third Generation." Pay particular attention to how each writer uses the notion of generation.

VISUAL CULTURE   Representations of Youth Culture in Movies

The identity of a generation takes shape in part through the movies. Since the 1950s, movies about teenagers and youth culture have explored generational identities and intergenerational conflicts. In *The Wild One, Blackboard Jungle,* and *Rebel Without a Cause* (the 1950s); *The Graduate* and *Easy Rider* (the 1960s); *Saturday Night Fever* and *American Graffiti* (the 1970s); *River's Edge, The Breakfast Club,* and *Fast Times at Ridgemont High* (the 1980s); *Do the Right Thing, Boyz 'n the Hood, Slackers,* and *Clerks* (the 1990s); and *Elephant* and *Dogtown and Z-Boys* (2000s), to name some of the best-known movies, Hollywood and independent filmmakers have fashioned influential representations of young people.

This section considers how movies represent various youth cultures and their relations to adult culture. Think about what the term *representation* means. A key term in cultural analysis, it is more complex than it appears. At first glance, it seems to mean simply showing what is there, reflecting life as it occurs. But the complexity comes in because the medium of representation—whether language or moving images—has its own codes and conventions that shape the way people see and understand what is being shown. By the same token, representation is not just the result of a writer's or filmmaker's intentions. Readers and viewers make sense of the codes and conventions of representation in different ways, depending on their interests and social position. So to think about the representation of youth cultures in films in a meaningful way, consider how the images of youth culture in film have been filtered through such conventions as the feature film, the Hollywood star system, and the available stock of characters and plots viewers will recognize and respond to.

JUVENILE DELINQUENCY FILMS

— *James Gilbert*

James Gilbert is an American historian at the University of Maryland. The following selection is taken from his book *A Cycle of Outrage: America's Reaction to Juvenile Delinquency in the 1950s* (1988). Here, Gilbert traces the emergence in the 1950s of juvenile delinquency films and popular responses to them. This selection consists of the opening paragraph of Gilbert's chapter "Juvenile Delinquency Movies" and his analysis of *The Wild One*, *The Blackboard Jungle*, and *Rebel Without a Cause*.

SUGGESTION FOR READING   Notice how Gilbert sets up his dominant theme in the opening paragraph, when he explains that widespread public concern with juvenile delinquency presents Hollywood with "dangerous but lucrative possibilities." Take note of how Gilbert defines these "possibilities" in the opening paragraph and then follow how he traces this theme through his discussion of the three films.

Whereas, shortly after the screening of this movie the local police had several cases in which the use of knives by young people were involved and at our own Indiana Joint High School two girls, while attending a high school dance, were cut by a knife wielded by a teen-age youth who by his own admission got the idea from watching *Rebel Without a Cause*.

Now Therefore Be It Resolved by the Board of Directors of Indiana Joint High School that said Board condemns and deplores the exhibition of pictures such as *Rebel Without a Cause* and any other pictures which depict abnormal or subnormal behavior by the youth of our country and which tend to deprave the morals of young people.

—*Indiana, Pennsylvania, Board of Education to the MPAA, January 9, 1956*

1 The enormous outpouring of concern over juvenile delinquency in the mid-1950s presented the movie industry with dangerous but lucrative possibilities. An aroused public of parents, service club members, youth-serving agencies, teachers, adolescents, and law enforcers constituted a huge potential audience for delinquency films at a time when general audiences for all films had declined. Yet this was a perilous subject to exploit, for public pressure on the film industry to set a wholesome example for youth remained unremitting. Moreover, the accusation that mass culture caused delinquency—especially the "new delinquency" of the postwar period—was the focus of much contemporary attention. If the film industry approached the issue of delinquency, it had to proceed cautiously. It could not present delinquency favorably; hence all stories would have to be set in the moral firmament of the movie Code. Yet to be successful, films had to evoke sympathy from young people who were increasingly intrigued by the growing youth culture of which delinquency seemed to be one variant.

Stanley Kramer's picture *The Wild One*, released in 1953, stands in transition from the somber realism of "film noir" pessimism and environmentalism to the newer stylized explorations of delinquent culture that characterized the mid-1950s. Shot in dark and realistic black and white, the film stars Marlon Brando and Lee Marvin as rival motorcycle gang leaders who invade a small California town. Brando's character is riven with ambiguity and potential violence—a prominent characteristic of later juvenile delinquency heroes. On the other hand, he is clearly not an adolescent, but not yet an adult either, belonging to a suspended age that seems alienated from any recognizable stage of development. He appears to be tough and brutal, but he is not, nor, ultimately, is he as attractive as he might have been. His character flaws are appealing, but unnerving. This is obvious in the key symbol of the film, the motorcycle trophy which he carries. He has not won it as the townspeople assume; he has stolen it from a motorcycle "scramble." Furthermore, he rejects anything more than a moment's tenderness with the girl he meets. In the end, he rides off alone, leaving her trapped in the small town that his presence has so disrupted and exposed. The empty road on which he travels leads to similar nameless towns; he cannot find whatever it is he is compelled to seek.

Brando's remarkable performance made this film a brilliant triumph. Its moral ambiguity, however, and the very attractiveness of the alienated hero, meant that the producers needed to invoke two film code strategies to protect themselves from controversy. The first of these was an initial disclaimer appearing after the titles: "This is a shocking story. It could never take place in most American towns—but it did in this one. It is a public challenge not to let it happen again." Framing the other end of the film was a speech by a strong moral voice of authority. A sheriff brought in to restore order to the town lectures Brando on the turmoil he has created and then, as a kind of punishment, casts him back onto the lonesome streets.

Aside from Brando's stunning portrayal of the misunderstood and inarticulate antihero, the film did not quite emerge from traditional modes of presenting crime and delinquency: the use of black and white; the musical score with its foreboding big-band sound; the relatively aged performers; and the vague suggestions that Brando and his gang were refugees from urban slums. Furthermore, the reception to the film was not, as some might have predicted, as controversial as what was to come. Of course, there were objections—for example, New Zealand banned

the film—but it did not provoke the outrage that the next group of juvenile delinquency films inspired.

5   The film that fundamentally shifted Hollywood's treatment of delinquency was *The Blackboard Jungle,* produced in 1955, and in which traditional elements remained as a backdrop for contemporary action. The movie was shot in black and white and played in a slum high school. But it clearly presented what was to become the driving premise of subsequent delinquency films—the division of American society into conflicting cultures made up of adolescents on one side and adults on the other. In this film the delinquent characters are portrayed as actual teenagers, as high school students. The crimes they commit are, with a few exceptions, crimes of behavior such as defying authority, status crimes, and so on. Of most symbolic importance is the transition in music that occurs in the film. Although it includes jazz numbers by Stan Kenton and Bix Beiderbecke, it is also the first film to feature rock and roll, specifically, "Rock Around the Clock" played by Bill Haley.

The story line follows an old formula of American novels and films. A teacher begins a job at a new school, where he encounters enormous hostility from the students. He stands up to the ringleader of the teenage rowdies, and finally wins over the majority of the students. In itself this is nothing controversial. But *Blackboard Jungle* also depicts the successful defiance of delinquents, who reject authority and terrorize an American high school. Their success and their power, and the ambiguous but attractive picture of their culture, aimed at the heart of the film Code and its commitment to uphold the dignity of figures and institutions of authority. . . .

Following swiftly on this commercial success was *Rebel Without a Cause,* a very different sort of film, and perhaps the most famous and influential of the 1950s juvenile delinquency endeavors. Departing from the somber working-class realism of *Blackboard Jungle, Rebel* splashed the problem of middle-class delinquency across America in full color. Moreover, its sympathy lay entirely with adolescents, played by actors James Dean, Natalie Wood, and Sal Mineo, who all live wholly inside the new youth culture. Indeed, this is the substantial message of the film: each parent and figure of authority is grievously at fault for ignoring or otherwise failing youth. The consequence is a rebellion with disastrous results.

Once the script had been developed, shooting began in the spring of 1955, during the height of the delinquency dispute and following fast on the heels of the box-office success of *Blackboard Jungle*. Warner Brothers approved a last minute budget hike to upgrade the film to color. In part this was a response to the box office appeal of the star, James Dean, whose *East of Eden* was released to acclaim in early April.

When it approved the film, the Code Authority issued two warnings. Geoffrey Shurlock wrote to Jack Warner in March 1955: "As you know, we have steadfastly maintained under the requirements of the Code that we should not approve stories of underage boys and girls indulging in either murder or illicit sex." He suggested that the violence in the picture be toned down. Furthermore, he noted: "It is of course vital that there be no inference of a questionable or homosexual relationship between Plato [Sal Mineo] and Jim [James Dean]." A follow-up commentary suggested the need for further changes in the area of violence. For example, Shurlock noted of the fight at the planetarium: "We suggest merely indicating that these high-school boys have tire chains, not showing them flaunting them."

10   Despite these cautions, the film, when it was released, contained substantial violence: the accidental death of one of the teenagers in a "chickie run"; the shooting of another teenager; and Plato's death at the hands of the police. Furthermore, there remained strong echoes of Plato's homosexual interest in Jim.

The film also took a curious, ambiguous position on juvenile delinquency. Overtly, it disapproved, demonstrating the terrible price paid for misbehavior. Yet the film, more than any other thus far, glorified the teenage life-styles it purported to reject. Adult culture is pictured as insecure, insensitive, and blind to the problems of youth. Teenagers, on the other hand, are portrayed as searching for genuine family life, warmth, and security. They choose delinquency in despair of rejection by their parents. Indeed, each of the three young heroes is condemned to search for the emotional fulfillment that adults deny: Dean for the courage his father lacks; Natalie Wood (as his girlfriend) for her father's love; and Plato for a family, which he finds momentarily in Dean and Wood. Instead of being securely set in adult society, each of these values must be constructed outside normal society and inside a new youth-created world. What in other films might have provided a reconciling finale—a voice of authority—becomes, itself, a symbol of alienation. A policeman who befriends Dean is absent at a decisive moment when he could have prevented the tragic ending. Thus no adults or institutions remain unscathed. The ending, in which adults recognize their own failings, is thus too sudden and contrived to be believable. It is as if the appearance of juvenile delinquency in such a middle-class setting is impossible to explain, too complex and too frightening to be understood in that context.

And also too attractive, for the film pictures delinquent culture as an intrusive, compelling, and dangerous force that invades middle-class homes and institutions. The producers carefully indicated that each family was middle class, although Plato's mother might well be considered wealthier than that. Teenage, delinquent culture, however, has obvious working-class origins, symbolized by souped-up jalopies, levis, and T-shirts that became the standard for youth culture. In fact, when Dean goes out for his fateful "chickie run," he changes into T-shirt and levis from his school clothes. Furthermore, the film presents this delinquent culture without judgment. There is no obvious line drawn between what is teenage culture and what is delinquency. Is delinquency really just misunderstood youth culture? The film never says, thus reflecting public confusion on the same issue.

A second tactic of the filmmakers posed a philosophic problem about youth culture and delinquency. This emerges around the symbol of the planetarium. In the first of two scenes there, Dean's new high school class visits for a lecture and a show. The lecturer ends his presentation abruptly with a frightening suggestion—the explosion of the world and the end of the universe. He concludes: "Man existing alone seems an episode of little consequence." This existential reference precedes the rumble in which Dean is forced to fight his new classmates after they puncture the tires of his car. The meaning is clear: Dean must act to establish an identity which his parents and society refuse to grant him. This is a remarkable translation of the basic premise of contemporary Beat poets, whose solitary search for meaning and self-expression tinged several of the other initial films in this genre also.

Another scene at the planetarium occurs at night, at the end of the film. The police have pursued Plato there after he shoots a member of the gang that has been harassing Dean. Dean follows him into the building, and, in a reprise of the earlier scene, turns on the machine that lights the stars and planets. The two boys discuss the end of the world. Dean empties Plato's gun, and the confused youth then walks out of the building. The police, mistaking his intent, gun him down. Once again tragedy follows a statement about the ultimate meaninglessness of life.

15   By using middle-class delinquency to explore questions of existence, this film undeniably contested the effectiveness of traditional family and community institutions. There is even the hint that Dean, Wood, and Mineo represent the possibility of a new sort of family; but this is only a fleeting suggestion. In the end it is family and community weakness that bring tragedy for which there can be no real solution. Without the strikingly sympathetic performances of Dean, Wood, and Mineo, this picture might have fallen under the weight of its bleak (and pretentious) message. As it was, however, *Rebel Without a Cause* was a box office smash, and Dean's short, but brilliant career was now assured.

As with *Blackboard Jungle,* the MPAA was the focus of furious reaction to the film. Accusations of copycat crimes, particularly for a stabbing in Indiana, Pennsylvania, brought condemnations and petitions against "pictures which depict abnormal or subnormal behavior by the youth of our country and which tend to deprave the morals of young people." The MPAA fought back against this accusation in early 1956 as Arthur DeBra urged an investigation to discover if the incident at the Indiana, Pennsylvania, high school had any relationship to the "juvenile delinquency situation in the school and community." As one writer for the *Christian Science Monitor* put it, "the new Warner Brothers picture will emerge into the growing nationwide concern about the effects on youth of comics, TV, and movies." This prediction was based upon actions already taken by local censors. The Chicago police had ordered cuts in the film, and the city of Milwaukee banned it outright.

On the other hand, much of the response was positive. As *Variety* noted in late 1955, fan letters had poured in to Hollywood "from teenagers who have identified themselves with the characters; from parents who have found the film conveyed a special meaning; and from sociologists and psychiatrists who have paid tribute to the manner in which child-parent misunderstanding is highlighted."

Quite clearly, the film became a milestone for the industry. It established youth culture as a fitting subject for films, and created some of the most pervasive stereotypes that were repeated in later films. These included the tortured, alienated, and misunderstood youth and intolerant parents and authority figures. It did not, however, lead to more subtle explorations of the connections between youth culture and delinquency. If anything, the opposite was true. For one thing, Dean was killed in an auto accident shortly after this enormous success. Furthermore, it was probably the seriousness of *Blackboard Jungle* and *Rebel* that provoked controversy, and the movie industry quickly learned that it could attract teenage audiences without risking the ire of adults if it reduced the dosage of realism. Thus the genre deteriorated into formula films about teenagers, made principally for drive-in audiences who were not particular about the features they saw.

SUGGESTIONS FOR DISCUSSION

1. Gilbert notes that *Rebel Without a Cause* became a "milestone" for the film industry, establishing youth culture as a fitting (and profitable) subject and creating stereotypes of alienated youth and intolerant adults that recurred in later movies. Consider to what extent these stereotypes continue to appear in movies. How would you update their appearance since the 1950s? List examples of movies that use the conventionalized figures of alienated youth and intolerant adults. What continuity do you see over time? In what ways have the portrayals changed?

2. Gilbert says that by "using middle-class delinquency to explore questions of existence," *Rebel Without a Cause* "contested the effectiveness of traditional family and community institutions." Explain what Gilbert means. Can you think of other films that "contest" family and community institutions?

3. Watch the three films Gilbert discusses—*The Wild One, The Blackboard Jungle,* and *Rebel Without a Cause.* Working together with a group of classmates, first summarize Gilbert's discussion of how each film handles the dilemma of evoking viewers' sympathy for young people while in no way presenting delinquency in a favorable light. Next, develop your own analysis of how (or whether) each film creates sympathy for young people in their confrontations with the adult world. To what extent do you agree with Gilbert's line of analysis? Where do you differ with or want to modify his analysis?

SUGGESTED ASSIGNMENT

Pick a film or group of films that in some way characterizes a generation of young people. For example, analyze how *The Graduate* captures something important about youth in the 1960s. Or look at how a cluster of three or four films portrays the "twentysomething" generation of the 1990s. Or put together a timeline that reveals some trend in youth films.

Write an analysis of how the film or films represent youth. Do not decide whether the portrayal is accurate, but analyze how it constructs a certain image of youth culture and what might be the significance of the representation.

Here are some suggestions to help you examine how a film represents youth culture:

■ *How does the film portray young people?* What in particular marks them as "youth"? Pay particular attention to the characters' clothing, hairstyles, body posture, and ways of speaking.

■ *How does the film mark young people generationally?* Are the characters part of a distinctive youth subculture? How would you characterize the group's collective identity?

What is the relation of the group to the adult world and its institutions? What intergenerational conflicts figure in the film?

■ *How does the film portray a particular historical moment or decade? What visual clues enable viewers to locate the era of the film? What historical events, if any, enter into the film?*

■ *How does the sound track contribute to the representation of youth culture that is projected by the film?*

■ *How do the stars of the film influence viewers' perceptions of youth culture? Do they enhance viewers' sympathies? Are the main characters cultural icons like James Dean or Marlon Brando?*

FILM CLIP　Hollywood Stars: Brando, Dean, and Monroe

Part of the appeal of Hollywood films is the star system. For movie-goers, the attraction of films is not just the story but the stars who are featured in the leading roles. The star system dates back to the Hollywood studios of the 1920s, 1930s, and 1940s that signed the most prominent actors of the time to exclusive contracts and then developed film projects as vehicles for Spencer Tracy, Katharine Hepburn, Clark Gable, Cary Grant, Humphrey Bogart, and Lana Turner among others. Movie fans began to identify with the actors as much as or more than with the films, and the star system became a crucial ingredient in the formation of Hollywood's entertainment industry. The Hollywood studios tightly controlled the public image of its stars, going so far as to arrange sham marriages for gay actors such as Rock Hudson. With the breakup of the Hollywood studios and the rise of American independent films in the 1960s, stars were no longer studio properties, and actors such as Tom Cruise, Julia Roberts, and Denzel Washington now have tremendous bargaining power.

We show here pictures of three of the most prominent Hollywood stars of the 1950s: Marlon Brando, James Dean, and Marilyn Monroe. Unlike actors such as Meryl Streep or Robert De Niro, who are famous for their ability to lose themselves in their roles, each of these stars brought a particular personality to the screen, radiating a sex appeal that seemed to challenge the buttoned-down conservatism of the United States in the 1950s. Monroe projected a vulnerable sexuality and a nearly childlike innocence that made her appear to be both a seductress and a "dumb blonde" in need of protection. Brando and Dean, on the other hand, embodied a moody masculinity that suggested rebellion and a cool alienation from mainstream society. In each case, these stars have taken on the status of icons whose images seem to capture something simmering just below the surface of America in the Eisenhower years.

Consider the 1950s films of one of these three stars. Think in particular of the types of roles in which Brando, Dean, or Monroe is cast. What do these roles have in common? What makes them a likely vehicle for the star? What does Brando, Dean, or Monroe bring to the role that seems uniquely their own personality? What is the appeal to film-goers. Here are some of the films you might use:

Marlon Brando: *The Wild One*; *A Streetcar Named Desire*; *On the Waterfront*.

James Dean: *Rebel Without a Cause*; *East of Eden*; *Giant*.

Marilyn Monroe: *Some Like It Hot*; *Bus Stop*; *Gentlemen Prefer Blondes*.

Consider, too, the stars of today and what they seem to embody about contemporary culture.

Marlon Brando in *The Wild One* (1953)

Marilyn Monroe in *The Seven Year Itch* (1955)

JAMES DEAN

The overnight sensation of 'East of Eden'

Warner Bros. put
all the force of
the screen
into a challenging
drama of today's
juvenile violence!

"REBEL WITHOUT A CAUSE"

CinemaScope
AND WarnerColor

ALSO STARRING
NATALIE WOOD · SAL MINEO · JIM BACKUS · ANN DORAN · COREY ALLEN · WILLIAM HOPPER · STEWART STERN

FIELDWORK   Ethnographic Interviews

Music is one of the keys to generational identities. Songs carry the emotional power to define for their listeners what it means to be alive at a particular moment. Singers and musicians evoke generations and decades: Frank Sinatra's emergence as a teen idol in the big band era of the 1940s; Elvis Presley, Little Richard, Buddy Holly, and early rock and roll in the 1950s; the Beatles, Rolling Stones, Bob Dylan, Motown, and the Memphis sound of Aretha Franklin and Otis Redding in the 1960s; the funk of Parliament and War, disco, and punk bands such as the Clash and Sex Pistols in the 1970s; megastars Bruce Springsteen, Madonna, and Michael Jackson, the rap of Public Enemy and NWA, alternative, and the grunge groups of the 1980s and 1990s.

One way to figure out how people experience their lives as part of a generation is to investigate what music means to them. The fieldwork project in this chapter investigates how people across generations use music daily to create, maintain, or subvert individual and collective identities. The method is the ethnographic interview, a nondirective approach that asks people to explain how they make sense of music in their lives. "Ethnographic" means literally graphing—getting down in the record—the values and practices of the ethnos, the tribe or group.

MY MUSIC

 Susan D. Craft, Daniel Cavicchi, and Charles Keil

The following two ethnographic interviews come from the Music in Daily Life Project in the American Studies program at the State University of New York at Buffalo. The project's goal was to use open-ended ethnographic interviews to find out what music means to people and how they integrate music into their lives and identities. Two undergraduate classes conducted the interviews and began with the question "What is music about for you?" (The classes settled on this question "so as not to prejudge the situation" and to give the respondents "room to define music of all kinds in their lives.") Then the interviews were edited, organized by age group, and published in the book *My Music* (1993).

SUGGESTION FOR READING Keep in mind that the interviews you are reading were not scripted but are the result of interviewers' on-the-spot decisions. As you read, notice how the interviewers ask questions and when they ask for more details or redirect the conversation.

EDWARDO

Edwardo is fifteen years old and is enrolled in an auto mechanics program at a vocational high school.

Q: What kind of music do you like to listen to?
A: Basically, I listen to anything. I prefer rap and regular . . . R and B and rock.

Q: What groups do you listen to when you get a choice?
A: When I'm by myself, I listen to rap like Eric B, MC Hammer, and KRS I. People like that. When I'm with my friends, I listen to Ozzie, and Pink Floyd, Iron Maiden, Metallica. You know, groups like that.

Q: Why do you listen to different stuff when you're by yourself? Different than when you're with your friends?

A: Usually when I'm over at their house they have control of the radio, and they don't like to listen to rap that much.

Q: What kind of things do you do when you are listening to music by yourself?

A: I lip-synch it in the mirror. I pretend I'm doing a movie. Kind of embarrassing, but I do that. And I listen to it while I'm in the shower. And . . . that's about all.

Q: Would you like to be a professional musician?

A: Kind of. Yeah.

Q: If you pictured yourself as a musician, how would you picture yourself? What kind of music would you play?

A: I'd probably rap. If I didn't, I'd like to play the saxophone.

Q: When you're walking along, do you ever have a song going through your head? Do you have specific songs that you listen to and, if not, do you ever make up songs?

A: Yes. I rap a lot to myself. I make up rhymes and have one of my friends give it a beat. Sometimes we put it on tape. Sometimes we don't.

Q: Could you give me an example of some of the stuff you have put together on your own?

A: I made up one that goes something like, "Now I have many mikes / stepped on many floors. / Shattered all the windows / knocked down all the doors." That's just a little part of it. This is hard for me. I'm nervous.

Q: So what kind of things do you try to put together in your songs? What kinds of things do you try to talk about in your songs?

A: I make up different stories. Like people running around. Sometimes I talk about drugs and drinking. Most of the time I just brag about myself.

Q: Do you have any brothers and sisters who listen to the same sort of stuff?

A: Yes. My older brother . . . he's the one who got me into rap. We're originally from the Bronx, in New York, and he doesn't listen to anything else.

My cousin, he listens to heavy metal but he's kind of switched to late-seventies, early-seventies rock. He listens to Pink Floyd and all them, so I listen with him sometimes. I listen with my friends. That's about all.

Q: How long have you been listening to rap?

A: For about seven or eight years.

Q: What kind of stuff were you listening to before that?

A: Actually, I don't remember. Oh yeah. We used to live in California and I was listening to oldies . . . like the Four Tops and all them. In California . . . the Mexicans down there, they only listen to the oldies and stuff like that.

Q: Why would you say you changed to rap?

A: When I came down here, everything changed. People were listening to different kinds of music and I was, you know, behind times. So I just had to switch to catch up.

Q: So you would say that your friends really influence you and the kind of music you listen to by yourself?

A: Yeah. I would say that.

Q: When you're listening to music by yourself, what kinds of things go through your mind? Are you concentrating on the words or what?

A: Sometimes I think about life, and all the problems I have. Sometimes I just dwell on the lyrics and just listen to the music.

Q: Do you ever use music as a way to change your mood? If you're really depressed, is there a record you put on?

A: No. Usually when I listen to music and it changes me is when I'm bored and I don't have anything to do or I just get that certain urge to listen to music.

STEVE

Steve is fifty-seven years old and works as a salesman. He was interviewed by his daughter.

Q: Dad, what does music do for you?

A: What does music do for me? Well, music relaxes me. In order for me to explain, I have to go back and give you an idea exactly how my whole life was affected by music. For example, when I was five or six years old, my mother and father had come from Poland, so naturally all music played at home was ethnic music. This established my ethnic heritage. I had a love for Polish music. Later on in life, like at Polish weddings, they played mostly Polish music . . . since we lived in Cheektowaga and there is mostly Polish people and a Polish parish. My love for Polish music gave me enjoyment when I was growing up and it carried on all these years to the present time.

But naturally as I got educated in the English language I started going to the movies. I was raised during the Depression and, at that time, the biggest form of escape was musicals . . . people like Dick Powell, Ruby Keeler, Eddie Cantor, Al Jolson, and Shirley Temple. These were big stars of their day and in order to relax and forget your troubles . . . we all went through hard times . . . everybody enjoyed musicals, they were the biggest thing at that time. A lot of musicals were shows from Broadway so, as I was growing up in the Depression and watching movie musicals, I was also getting acquainted with hit tunes that came from Broadway. In that era, Tin Pan Alley was an expression for the place where all these song writers used to write and compose music, and these songs became the hits in the musicals.

Later on these writers went to the movies and it seemed as if every month there was a new hit song that everyone was singing. Some of the writers, like Irving Berlin, Gershwin, Jerome Kern, Harry Warren, and Sammy Kahn . . . some of these songs are the prettiest songs that were ever written. Even though I never played a musical instrument or was a singer, I was like hundreds of thousands of people in my era who loved music. In fact, radio was very popular at that time, so you heard music constantly on the radio, in the musicals, and all my life I could sing a song all the way through, knowing the tune *and knowing the words*.

Later on in life, when we get to W.W. II, music used to inspire patriotism, and also to bring you closer to home when overseas. For example, one place that just meant music was the Stage Door Canteen in Hollywood. All the stars of the movies and musicals used to volunteer their services and entertain everybody. Later on, as these stars went overseas and performed for the G.I.s, I had a chance to see a lot of these stars in person—stars that I really enjoyed, seeing their movies and listening to their music. So it was like bringing home to overseas. Of course, there was a lot of patriotic songs that stirred us . . . we were young . . . say, the Air Force song like "Praise the Lord and Pass the Ammunition." There was sentimental songs like "There'll Be Blue Birds Over the White Cliffs of Dover," "I Heard a Nightingale Sing Over Berkeley Square." But it was actually music that helped you through tough times like W.W. II, the way music helped you feel better during the Depression . . . in days that I was younger.

When I came back from overseas . . . now I'm entering the romantic part of my life, in my early twenties . . . it was the era of the big bands. One of the greatest events in music history were bands like Glenn Miller and Benny Goodman, the Dorsey Brothers and Sammy Kaye . . . big bands were popular at the time you used to go to local Candy Kitchens and play the jukebox, and, just like some of the songs said, it was a wonderful time to be with your friends. Good clean entertainment; you listen to the jukebox, dance on the dance floor.

In the big band era, we get into the popular singers who used to sing with the big bands. They went on their own and the era of the ballads was born, and to me this was my favorite era of music in my life. I'll mention some of the big singers just to give you an idea of what I mean—singers like Bing Crosby, Frank Sinatra, Doris Day, Margaret Whiting, Jo Stafford, and Perry Como.

The time of your life when you meet the "girl of your dreams." I was fortunate that we had the Canadiana. It was just like the Love Boat of its time. They used to have a band, and you used to be able to dance on the dance floor. If they didn't have a dance band that night, they would play records, and you could listen to music riding on the lake at night under the stars and moon. It was unbelievable, that particular part of life. It's a shame the younger people of today couldn't experience, not only the boat, but a lot of the things we went through. We thought it was tough at that time, but it was the music that really made things a lot happier and the reason why it's so easy for someone like myself to hear a song and just place myself back in time, at exactly where I was. Was I in the Philippines, or Tokyo, or on the boat? What were the songs that were playing when I first met my wife, what were they playing when I was a young recruit in the Air Force? All I have to do is hear the songs and it'll just take me back in time and I will relive a lot of the parts of my life and, of course, you only remember the good parts! (laughing) You don't remember the bad.

Music to me is very important. One thought that I wanted to mention, about going back in time: when I was just five or six years old, my parents, because they were from the old country, played Polish music, so that when I did meet the girl I was going to marry . . . every couple has a favorite song and ours was one that was very popular at that time . . . it was a Polish song to which they put American lyrics. The song was "Tell Me Whose Girl You Are," and I think it was because my wife and I came from a Polish background that Polish music was still a very important part of our life.

Q: What music really did for you was to make you get through bad times and made you think of good things mostly, right?
A: Well, yes, and I would say that music became part of my personality. I use music to not only relax, I use it to relieve tension. About thirty percent of the time I am singing, and it has become part of my personality because it has given me a certain amount of assurance. Not only does it relax me but I think it also bolsters my confidence in being a salesman where you have to always be up. You can't be depressed. Otherwise, you're just going to waste a day. I think music to me is also something that bolsters my spirit.
Q: Does music amplify your mood or does it change your mood? For example, when you're in a depressed mood do you put on something slow or something happy to get you out of that mood?
A: Well, when I was single, if my love life wasn't going right, I used to play sad songs. Well, I guess like most young kids when their love life isn't going right they turn to sad music. I know that after I'm married and have children and more experience, if I get in a depressed mood then I switch to happier music to change the mood.

TALKING ABOUT THE READING

1. Edwardo's responses to the interviewer's questions are much shorter than Steve's. One senses the pressure that the interviewer must have felt to keep the conversation going. Steve's interview, in contrast, contains an extended statement that is followed by question and answer. Take a second look at the questions that the interviewer asked Steve. What do the purposes of those questions seem to be? Try to get a sense of how and why the interviewer decided to ask particular questions. What alternatives, if any, can you imagine?

2. Notice that the interviewees do not fall easily into one distinct musical subculture. Each talks about a range of music. How do Edwardo and Steve make sense of these various forms of musical expression?

3. Each of the interviewees relates his musical tastes to particular social groups or moments in time. How do they connect music to their relationship with others and/or their memories of the past?

FIELDWORK PROJECT

Work with two or three other students on this project. Each group member should interview three people of different ages to get a range of responses across generations. Use the opening question "What is music about for you?" from the Music in Daily Life Project. Tape and transcribe the interview.

As a group, assemble and edit a collection of the interviews and write an introduction that explains the purpose of the interviews and their significance. Refer to "A Note on Interviewing" below.

Editing

An edited interview is not simply the transcribed tape recording. It's important to capture the person's voice, but you also want the interview to be readable. Taped interviews can be filled with pauses, um's and ah's, incomplete or incoherent thoughts, and rambling associations. It is standard practice to "clean up" the interview, as long as doing so does not distort or change the subject's meanings. Cleaning up a transcript may include editing at the sentence level, but you may also leave out some of the taped material if it is irrelevant.

Writing an Introduction

In the introduction to the edited interviews, explain your purpose in asking people about the role that music plays in their lives. Follow this with some observations and interpretations of the results. Remember that the interviews have a limited authority. They don't "prove" anything about the role of music in daily life and the formation of individual or group identity. But they can be suggestive—and you will want to point out how and why.

The Music in Daily Life Project emphasizes the verbs you can use to describe people's relationship to music:

> Is this person *finding* music to explore and express an identity or being *invaded* by music to the point of identity diffusion, *using* music to solve personal problems, *consuming* music to fill a void and relieve alienation and boredom, *participating* in musical mysteries to feel fully human, *addicted* to music and evading reality, *orienting* via music to reality?

As you can see, each verb carries a different interpretation.

A NOTE ON INTERVIEWING

- *Choosing subjects.* Choose carefully. The three subjects you choose don't have to be big music buffs, but you will get your best interviews from people who are willing to talk about their likes, dislikes, memories, and associations.

- *Preparing your subject.* Make an appointment for the interview, and be on time. Tell your subject how long you will be spending and why you want this information.

- *Preparing yourself.* Before the interview, make a list of questions you want to ask. Most questions should be open ended—they should not lead to a yes or no response. Just keep in mind that your goal is to listen, so you'll want to give your subject plenty of time to talk.

■ *Conducting the interview*. Remember that in many respects, you control the agenda because you scheduled the interview and have determined the questions. The person you interview will be looking for guidance and direction. You are likely to have choices to make during the interview. The guidelines used by the Music in Daily Life Project note the following situation:

> Somebody says, "I really love Bruce Springsteen and his music, can't help it, I get weepy over 'Born in the USA,' you know? But sometimes I wonder if I haven't just swallowed the hype about his being a working-class hero from New Jersey with the symbolic black guy by his side, you know what I mean?" and then pauses, looking at you for some direction or an answer. A choice to make.

The choice concerns which thread in the conversation to follow—the person's love for Springsteen or his feeling of being hyped by the working-class hero image. You could do several things at this point in the interview. You could just wait for the person to explain, or you could say, "Tell me a little more about that," and hope the person will decide on which thread to elaborate. Or you could ask a direct question: "Why do you love Springsteen's music so much?" "What makes you weepy about 'Born in the USA'?" "Why do you think you're being hyped?" (Notice that each of these questions involves a choice that may take the interview in a different direction.)

The point here is that a good interviewer must listen carefully during the interview. The goal is not to dominate but to give the subject some help in developing his or her ideas. Your task as an interviewer is to keep the conversation going.

■ *Get permission*. If you plan to use the subject's name in class discussion or a paper, get permission and make arrangements to show your subject what you have written.

MINING THE ARCHIVE   Life Magazine

During the 1940s and 1950s, *Life* was the most popular general magazine in the United States, with an estimated readership of 20 million. Founded as a weekly in 1936, *Life* was the first American magazine to give a prominent place to the photoessay—visual narratives of the week's news as well as special features about American life and culture. If anything, *Life* taught generations of Americans what events in the world looked like, bringing them the work of such noted photographers as Robert Capa, Margaret

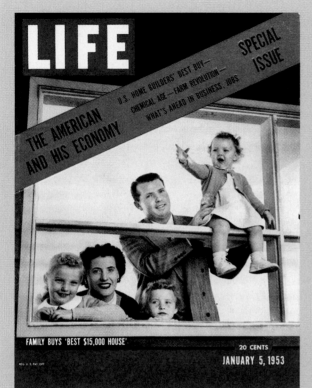

LIFE

SPECIAL ISSUE

THE AMERICAN AND HIS ECONOMY

U.S. HOME BUILDERS' BEST BUY— CHEMICAL AGE.—FARM REVOLUTION.— WHAT'S AHEAD IN BUSINESS, JOBS

FAMILY BUYS 'BEST $15,000 HOUSE'

20 CENTS

JANUARY 5, 1953

Bourke-White, and W. Eugene Smith in photo-journalistic accounts of the farm crisis and labor conflicts during the Great Depression and of battlefront situations during World War II.

In another sense, *Life* also taught Americans what the world should look like. After World War II, *Life* regularly featured families in postwar America, ordinary people in their new suburban homes, driving new cars on America's newly built freeway systems to work, school, and church. Perhaps no other source offers such a rich archive of what domestic life was supposed to be in the 1940s and 1950s in these pictorial representations of white, middle-class, nuclear families.

To get a sense of how *Life* pictured America in the early postwar period, look up the December 3, 1945, issue at your library and read the news story "U.S. Normalcy: Against the Backdrop of a Troubled World *Life* Inspects an American City at Peace." Published just four months after World War II ended, the article juxtaposed images of international instability (the beginnings of the Cold War, the Nuremburg Trials, and child refugees in war-torn Europe and China) and of domestic turmoil (industrial strikes and unemployment) with the concerns of people in Indianapolis returning "their minds and energies to work, football games, automobile trips, family reunions and all the pleasant trivia of the American way of life."

Most college and public libraries have *Life* in their collection. Take a look through several issues. You will find many family portraits. You could develop various projects from this photojournalistic archive about family values in the postwar period, the role of women as homemakers, representations of teenagers, and the relation of domestic life to the Cold War. Keep in mind that the photoessays on the American family not only provide slices of life from the 1940s and 1950s but they also codify Americans' understanding of the ideal family and the American dream. Remember too that audiences did not read these photoessays on the family in isolation from advertisements and other photoessays. You might want to consider the overall flow of *Life* and how its messages about the family are connected to other messages.

Finally, you might think about why there is no longer a general magazine such as *Life* that claims to picture the "American way of life." The magazine industry today is thriving by attracting specialized readerships based on such interests as computers, skateboarding, mountain biking, and indie rock. The era of such general national magazines as *Life, Look, Colliers,* and the *Saturday Evening Post* has clearly been replaced by niche marketing and subcultural 'zines. What does this proliferation of specialized magazines suggest to you about the current state of American culture?

Schooling

"A New York Elementary Classroom, 1942" *All The Children, Annual Report of the Superintendent of Schools, City of New York (1942–1943) #70,* 217. Courtesy of Teachers College, Columbia University.

I wish first that we should recognize that education is ordinary; that it is, before everything else, the process of giving to the ordinary members of society its full common meanings, and the skills that will enable them to amend these meanings, in the light of their personal and common experience.

—Raymond Williams, *Culture Is Ordinary*

By the time you read this chapter, you will likely have spent a considerable amount of time in school. From the moment people enter school, their personal development is intimately connected to going to school and learning to be a student. Much of growing up takes place in school, and schools are key agents of acculturation in America. One of the purposes of schooling is to transmit bodies of knowledge from one generation to the next, and classrooms are the place where this intergenerational communication occurs, from teacher to student.

Americans have always put a lot of faith in schools to educate the younger generation—to prepare them for the work of the future and to teach them what it means to be an American. But it is precisely because Americans put so much faith—and invest so many resources—in schooling that they worry and argue incessantly about what the schools are—or should be—accomplishing. For many, American education seems to be in a state of crisis, with declining test scores in science and mathematics compared to other countries, a loss of confidence in public education, skyrocketing college costs, controversy over the No Child Left Behind legislation and high-stakes testing, and the growing corporatization of American education.

As a student, you are at the center of much of this controversy, in a unique position to comment on schooling in your life and in the lives of others. The purpose of this chapter is to offer you opportunities to read, think, and write about the role of schooling today. You are invited to identify how it has influenced you as a student, a learner, and a person. You will be asked in the reading and writing assignments to recall classroom episodes from your past and observe classroom life in the present. You will work your way from examining the everyday practices of schooling to considering the mission and function of education.

One way to begin is to ask what sounds like a very simple question: what have you learned in school? On one hand, there is the formal curriculum, the subjects you have studied, the knowledge you have acquired, the tests and papers and projects. On the other hand, the experience of of going to school involves more than learning the content of the courses. It is a way of life that shapes students' sense of themselves and their life chances. The kind of knowledge students acquire when they learn to be students and go to school forms what educators call the "hidden curriculum," all the unspoken beliefs and procedures that regulate classroom life—the rules of the game no one writes down but that teachers and students have internalized in their expectations about each other.

Students begin to learn the hidden curriculum in the early grades, when they learn how to sit still, pay attention, raise their hands to be called on, follow directions, perform repetitive tasks, and complete work on time. Students learn what pleases teachers and what doesn't, what they can say and what they ought to keep to themselves.

Examining the hidden curriculum offers a useful way to look at classroom life, in part because it asks you to look at things that teachers and students often take for granted. Why, for example, do students sit in rows? Why do teachers ask questions when they already know the answer? Why is the high school day divided as it is, and what is the effect of moving from subject to subject in fifty-minute intervals? You will be asked in the reading and writing assignments to research questions such as these, to bring the hidden curriculum's unstated norms to light, and to assess their effects on students and on the role schooling plays in American culture.

WHAT HIGH SCHOOL IS

—Theodore R. Sizer

Theodore R. Sizer has been chair of the education department at Brown University; headmaster of Phillips Academy, Andover; and dean of the Graduate School of Education at Harvard. The following selection is the opening chapter from *Horace's Compromise,* Sizer's book-length study of American high schools. Sizer's book takes a critical look at high schools—at overworked teachers, undermotivated students, and the "assembly-line" educational practices that process people rather than educate them. Originally published in 1984, Sizer's study was one of a number of national reports that appeared in the 1980s and raised serious questions about the quality of American education. This reading selection looks at how the school day is organized and what it means to students to "take subjects."

SUGGESTION FOR READING   As you read, notice that Sizer gives a full account of Mark's day before stepping back to generalize about its significance. Underline and annotate this selection to indicate where Sizer begins to analyze the meaning of Mark's day and how Sizer goes on to develop a critical analysis of the typical high school day.

1   Mark, sixteen and a genial eleventh-grader, rides a bus to Franklin High School, arriving at 7:25. It is an Assembly Day, so the schedule is adapted to allow for a meeting of the entire school. He hangs out with his friends, first outside school and then inside, by his locker. He carries a pile of textbooks and notebooks; in all, it weighs eight and a half pounds.

From 7:30 to 8:19, with nineteen other students, he is in Room 304 for English class. The Shakespeare play being read this year by the eleventh grade is *Romeo and Juliet*. The teacher, Ms. Viola, has various students in turn take parts and read out loud. Periodically, she interrupts the (usually halting) recitations to ask whether the thread of the conversation in the play is clear. Mark is entertained by the stumbling readings of some of his classmates. He hopes he will not be asked to be Romeo, particularly if his current steady, Sally, is Juliet. There is a good deal of giggling in class, and much attention paid to who may be called on next. Ms. Viola reminds the class of a test on this part of the play to be given next week.

The bell rings at 8:19. Mark goes to the boys' room, where he sees a classmate who he thinks is a wimp but who constantly tries to be a buddy.

Mark avoids the leech by rushing off. On the way, he notices two boys engaged in some sort of transaction, probably over marijuana. He pays them no attention. 8:24. Typing class. The rows of desks that embrace big office machines are almost filled before the bell. Mark is uncomfortable here: typing class is girl country. The teacher constantly threatens what to Mark is a humiliatingly girl future: "Your employer won't like these erasures." The minutes during the period are spent copying a letter from a handbook onto business stationery. Mark struggles to keep from looking at his work; the teacher wants him to watch only the material from which he is copying. Mark is frustrated, uncomfortable, and scared that he will not complete his letter by the class's end, which would be embarrassing.

Nine tenths of the students present at school that day are assembled in the auditorium by the 9:18 bell. The dilatory tenth still stumble in, running down aisles. Annoyed class deans try to get the mob settled. The curtains part; the program is a concert by a student rock group. Their electronic gear flashes under the lights, and the five boys and one girl in the group work hard at being casual. Their movements on stage are studiously at three-quarter time, and they chat with one another as though the tumultuous screaming of their schoolmates were totally inaudible. The girl balances on a stool; the boys crank up the music. It is very soft rock, the sanitized lyrics surely cleared with the assistant principal. The girl sings, holding the mike close to her mouth, but can scarcely be heard. Her light voice is tentative, and the lyrics indecipherable. The guitars, amplified, are tuneful, however, and the drums are played with energy.

5 The students around Mark—all juniors, since they are seated by class—alternately slouch in their upholstered, hinged seats, talking to one another, or sit forward, leaning on the chair backs in front of them, watching the band. A boy near Mark shouts noisily at the microphone-fondling singer, "Bite it . . . ohhh," and the area around Mark explodes in vulgar male laughter, but quickly subsides. A teacher walks down the aisle. Songs continue, to great applause. Assembly is over at 9:46, two minutes early.

9:53 and biology class. Mark was at a different high school last year and did not take this course there as a tenth-grader. He is in it now, and all but one of his classmates are a year younger than he. He sits on the side, not taking part in the chatter that goes on after the bell. At 9:57, the public address system goes on, with the announcements of the day. After a few words from the principal ("Here's today's cheers and jeers . . ." with a cheer for the winning basketball team and a jeer for the spectators who made a ruckus at the gymnasium), the task is taken over by officers of ASB (Associated Student Bodies). There is an appeal for "bat bunnies." Carnations are for sale by the Girls' League. Miss Indian American is coming. Students are auctioning off their services (background catcalls are heard) to earn money for the prom. Nominees are needed for the ballot for school bachelor and school bachelorette. The announcements end with a "thought for the day. When you throw a little mud, you lose a little ground."

At 10:04 the biology class finally turns to science. The teacher, Mr. Robbins, has placed

one of several labeled laboratory specimens—some are pinned in frames, other swim in formaldehyde—on each of the classroom's eight laboratory tables. The three or so students whose chairs circle each of these benches are to study the specimen and make notes about it or drawings of it. After a few minutes each group of three will move to another table. The teacher points out that these specimens are of organisms already studied in previous classes. He says that the period-long test set for the following day will involve observing some of these specimens—then to be without labels—and writing an identifying paragraph on each. Mr. Robbins points out that some of the printed labels ascribe the specimens' names different from those given in the textbook. He explains that biologists often give several names to the same organism.

The class now falls to peering, writing, and quiet talking. Mr. Robbins comes over to Mark, and in whispered words asks him to carry a requisition form for science department materials to the business office. Mark, because of his "older" status, is usually chosen by Robbins for this kind of errand. Robbins gives Mark the form and a green hall pass to show to any teacher who might challenge him, on his way to the office, for being out of a classroom. The errand takes Mark four minutes. Meanwhile Mark's group is hard at work but gets to only three of the specimens before the bell rings at 10:42. As the students surge out, Robbins shouts a reminder about a "double" laboratory period on Thursday.

Between classes one of the seniors asks Mark whether he plans to be a candidate for schoolwide office next year. Mark says no. He starts to explain. The 10:47 bell rings, meaning that he is late for French class.

10 There are fifteen students in Monsieur Bates's language class. He hands out tests taken the day before: "*C'est bien fait, Etienne . . . c'est mieux, Marie . . . Tch, tch, Robert . . .*" Mark notes his C+ and peeks at the A- in front of Susanna, next to him. The class has been assigned seats by M. Bates; Mark resents sitting

next to prissy, brainy Susanna. Bates starts by asking a student to read a question and give the correct answer. *"James, question un."* James haltingly reads the question and gives an answer that Bates, now speaking English, says is incomplete. In due course: *"Mark, question cinq."* Mark does his bit, and the sequence goes on, the eight quiz questions and answers filling about twenty minutes of time.

"Turn to page forty-nine. *Maintenant, lisez après moi . . ."* and Bates reads a sentence and has the class echo it. Mark is embarrassed by this and mumbles with a barely audible sound. Others, like Susanna, keep the decibel count up, so Mark can hide. This I-say-you-repeat drill is interrupted once by the public address system, with an announcement about a meeting for the cheerleaders. Bates finishes class, almost precisely at the bell, with a homework assignment. The students are to review these sentences for a brief quiz the following day. Mark takes notes of the assignment, because he knows that tomorrow will be a day of busywork in French class. Much though he dislikes oral drills, they are better than the workbook stuff that Bates hands out. Write, write, write, for Bates to throw away, Mark thinks.

11:36. Down to the cafeteria, talking noisily, hanging out, munching. Getting to Room 104 by 12:17: U.S. history. The teacher is sitting cross-legged on his desk when Mark comes in, heatedly arguing with three students over the fracas that had followed the previous night's basketball game. The teacher, Mr. Suslovic, while agreeing that the spectators from their school certainly were provoked, argues that they should neither have been so obviously obscene in yelling at the opposing cheerleaders nor have allowed Coke cans to be rolled out on the floor. The three students keep saying that "it isn't fair." Apparently they and some others had been assigned "Saturday mornings" (detentions) by the principal for the ruckus.

At 12:34, the argument appears to subside. The uninvolved students, including Mark, are in their seats, chatting amiably. Mr. Suslovic climbs off his desk and starts talking: "We've almost finished this unit, chapters nine and ten . . ." The students stop chattering among themselves and turn toward Suslovic. Several slouch down in their chairs. Some open notebooks. Most have the five-pound textbook on their desks.

Suslovic lectures on the cattle drives, from north Texas to railroads west of St. Louis. He breaks up this narrative with questions ("Why were the railroad lines laid largely east to west?"), directed at nobody in particular and eventually answered by Suslovic himself. Some students take notes. Mark doesn't. A student walks in the open door, hands Mr. Suslovic a list, and starts whispering with him. Suslovic turns from the class and hears out this messenger. He then asks, "Does anyone know where Maggie Sharp is?" Someone answers, "Sick at home"; someone else says, "I thought I saw her at lunch." Genial consternation. Finally Suslovic tells the messenger, "Sorry, we can't help you," and returns to the class: "Now, where were we?" He goes on for some minutes. The bell rings. Suslovic forgets to give the homework assignment.

15   1:11 and Algebra II. There is a commotion in the hallway: someone's locker is rumored to have been opened by the assistant principal and a narcotics agent. In the five-minute passing time, Mark hears the story three times and three ways. A locker had been broken into by another student. It was Mr. Gregory and a narc. It was the cops, and they did it without Gregory's knowing. Mrs. Ames, the mathematics teacher, has not heard anything about it. Several of the nineteen students try to tell her and start arguing among themselves. "O.K., that's enough." She hands out the day's problem, one sheet to each student. Mark sees with dismay that it is a single, complicated "word" problem about some train that, while traveling at 84 mph, due west, passes a car that was going due east at 55 mph. Mark struggles: Is it $d = rt$ or $t = rd$? The class becomes quiet, writing, while Mrs. Ames writes some additional, short problems on the blackboard. "Time's up."

A sigh; most students still writing. A muffled "Shit." Mrs. Ames frowns. "Come on, now." She collects papers, but it takes four minutes for her to corral them all.

"Copy down the problems from the board." A minute passes. "William, try number one." William suggests an approach. Mrs. Ames corrects and cajoles, and William finally gets it right. Mark watches two kids to his right passing notes; he tries to read them but the handwriting is illegible from his distance. He hopes he is not called on, and he isn't. Only three students are asked to puzzle out an answer. The bell rings at 2:00. Mrs. Ames shouts a homework assignment over the resulting hubbub.

Mark leaves his books in his locker. He remembers that he has homework, but figures that he can do it during English class the next day. He knows that there will be an in-class presentation of one of the *Romeo and Juliet* scenes and that he will not be in it. The teacher will not notice his homework writing, or won't do anything about it if she does.

Mark passes various friends heading toward the gym, members of the basketball teams. Like most students, Mark isn't an active school athlete. However, he is associated with the yearbook staff. Although he is not taking "Yearbook" for credit as an English course, he is contributing photographs. Mark takes twenty minutes checking into the yearbook staff's headquarters (the classroom of its faculty adviser) and getting some assignments of pictures from his boss, the senior who is the photography editor. Mark knows that if he pleases his boss and the faculty adviser, he'll take that editor's post for the next year. He'll get English credit for his work then.

After gossiping a bit with the yearbook staff, Mark will leave school by 2:35 and go home. His grocery market bagger's job is from 4:45 to 8:00, the rush hour for the store. He'll have a snack at 4:30, and his mother will save him some supper to eat at 8:30. She will ask whether he has any homework, and he'll tell her no. Tomorrow, and virtually every other tomorrow, will be the same

for Mark, save for the lack of the assembly; each period then will be five minutes longer.

20   Most Americans have an uncomplicated vision of what secondary education should be. Their conception of high school is remarkably uniform across the country, a striking fact, given the size and diversity of the United States and the politically decentralized character of the schools. This uniformity is of several generations' standing. It has, however, two appearances, each quite different from the other, one of words and the other of practice, a world of political rhetoric and Mark's world.

A California high school's general goals, set out in 1979, could serve equally well most of America's high schools, public and private. This school had as its ends:

■ Fundamental scholastic achievement . . . to acquire knowledge and share in the traditionally accepted academic fundamentals . . . to develop the ability to make decisions, to solve problems, to reason independently, and to accept responsibility for self-evaluation and continuing self-improvement.

■ Career and economic competence

■ Citizenship and civil responsibility

■ Competence in human and social relations

■ Moral and ethical values

■ Self-realization and mental and physical health

■ Aesthetic awareness

■ Cultural diversity

In addition to its optimistic rhetoric, what distinguished this list is its comprehensiveness. The high school is to touch most aspects of an adolescent's existence—mind, body, morals, values, career. No one of these areas is given especial prominence. School people arrogate to themselves an obligation to all.

An example of the wide acceptability of these goals is found in the courts. Forced to present a detailed definition of "thorough and efficient education," elementary as well as secondary, a West

Virginia judge sampled the best of conventional wisdom and concluded that

> there are eight general elements of a thorough and efficient system of education: (a) Literacy, (b) The ability to add, subtract, multiply, and divide numbers, (c) Knowledge of government to the extent the child will be equipped as a citizen to make informed choices among persons and issues that affect his own governance, (d) Self-knowledge and knowledge of his or her total environment to allow the child to intelligently choose life work—to know his or her options, (e) Work-training and advanced academic training as the child may intelligently choose, (f) Recreational pursuits, (g) Interests in all creative arts such as music, theater, literature, and the visual arts, and (h) Social ethics, both behavioral and abstract, to facilitate compatibility with others in this society.

25   That these eight—now powerfully part of the debate over the purpose and practice of education in West Virginia—are reminiscent of the influential list, "The Seven Cardinal Principles of Secondary Education," promulgated in 1918 by the National Education Association, is no surprise. The rhetoric of high school purpose has been uniform and consistent for decades. Americans agree on the goals for their high schools.

That agreement is convenient, but it masks the fact that virtually all the words in these goal statements beg definition. Some schools have labored long to identify specific criteria beyond them; the result has been lists of daunting pseudospecificity and numbing earnestness. However, most leave the words undefined and let the momentum of traditional practice speak for itself. That is why analyzing how Mark spends his time is important: from watching him one uncovers the important purposes of education, the ones that shape practice. Mark's day is similar to that of other high school students across the country, as similar as the rhetoric of one goal statement to others'. Of course, there are variations, but the extent of consistency in the shape of school routine for a large and diverse adolescent population

is extraordinary, indicating more graphically than any rhetoric the measure of agreement in America about what one does in high school, and, by implication, what it is for.

The basic organizing structures in schools are familiar. Above all, students are grouped by age (that is, freshman, sophomore, junior, senior), and all are expected to take precisely the same time—around 720 school days over four years, to be precise—to meet the requirements for a diploma. When one is out of his grade level, he can feel odd, as Mark did in his biology class. The goals are the same for all, and the means to achieve them are also similar.

Young males and females are treated remarkably alike; the schools' goals are the same for each gender. In execution, there are differences, as those pressing sex discrimination suits have made educators intensely aware. The students in metalworking classes are mostly male; those in home economics, mostly female. But it is revealing how much less sex discrimination there is in high schools than in other American institutions. For many young women, the most liberated hours of their week are in school.

School is to be like a job: you start in the morning and end in the afternoon, five days a week. You don't get much of a lunch hour, so you go home early, unless you are an athlete or are involved in some special school or extracurricular activity. School is conceived of as the children's workplace, and it takes young people off parents' hands and out of the labor market during prime-time work hours. Not surprisingly, many students see going to school as little more than a dogged necessity. They perceive the day-to-day routine, a Minnesota study reports, as one of "boredom and lethargy." One of the students summarizes: School is "boring, restless, tiresome, puts ya to sleep, tedious monotonous, pain in the neck."

30   The school schedule is a series of units of time: the clock is king. The base time block is about fifty minutes in length. Some schools, on what they call modular scheduling, split that

fifty-minute block into two or even three pieces. Most schools have double periods for laboratory work, especially in the sciences, or four-hour units for small numbers of students involved in intensive vocational or other work-study programs. The flow of all school activity arises from or is blocked by these time units. "How much time do I have with my kids" is the teacher's key question.

Because there are many claims for those fifty-minute blocks, there is little time set aside for rest between them, usually no more than three to ten minutes, depending on how big the school is and, consequently, how far students and teachers have to walk from class to class. As a result, there is a frenetic quality to the school day, a sense of sustained restlessness. For the adolescents, there are frequent changes of room and fellow students, each change giving tempting opportunities for distraction, which are stoutly resisted by teachers. Some schools play soft music during these "passing times," to quiet the multitude, one principal told me.

Many teachers have a chance for a coffee break. Few students do. In some city schools where security is a problem, students must be in class for seven consecutive periods, interrupted by a heavily monitored twenty-minute lunch period for small groups, starting as early as 10:30 A.M. and running to after 1:00 P.M. A high premium is placed on punctuality and on "being where you're supposed to be." Obviously, a low premium is placed on reflection and repose. The student rushes from class to class to collect knowledge. Savoring it, it is implied, is not to be done much in school, nor is such meditation really much admired. The picture that these familial patterns yield is that of an academic supermarket. The purpose of going to school is to pick things up, in an organized and predictable way, the faster the better.

What is supposed to be picked up is remarkably consistent among all sorts of high schools. Most schools specifically mandate three out of every five courses a student selects. Nearly all of these mandates fall into five areas—English, social studies, mathematics, science, and physical education. On the average, English is required to be taken each year, social studies and physical education three out of the four high school years, and mathematics and science one or two years. Trends indicate that in the mid-eighties there is likely to be an increase in the time allocated to these last two subjects. Most students take classes in these four major academic areas beyond the minimum requirements, sometimes in such special areas as journalism and "yearbook," offshoots of English departments.

Press most adults about what high school is for, and you hear these subjects listed. *High school? That's where you learn English and math and that sort of thing.* Ask students, and you get the same answers. High school is to "teach" these "subjects."

What is often absent is any definition of these subjects or any rationale for them. They are just there, labels. Under those labels lie a multitude of things. A great deal of material is supposed to be "covered"; most of these courses are surveys, great sweeps of the stuff of their parent disciplines.

While there is often a sequence *within* subjects—algebra before trigonometry, "first-year" French before "second-year" French—there is rarely a coherent relationship or sequence *across* subjects. Even the most logically related matters—reading ability as a precondition for the reading of history books, and certain mathematical concepts or skills before the study of some physics—are only loosely coordinated, if at all. There is little demand for a synthesis of it all; English, mathematics, and the rest are discrete items, to be picked up individually. The incentive for picking them up is largely through tests and, with success at these, in credits earned.

Coverage within subjects is the key priority. If some imaginative teacher makes a proposal to force the marriage of, say, mathematics and physics or to require some culminating challenges to students to use several subjects in the solution of a complex problem, and if this proposal will take "time" away from other things, opposition is usually phrased in terms of what may be thus forgone. If we do that, we'll have to give up colonial history. We won't be able to get to programming. We'll not be able to read *Death of a Salesman*. There isn't time. The protesters usually win out.

The subjects come at a student like Mark in random order, a kaleidoscope of worlds: algebraic formulae to poetry to French verbs to Ping-Pong to the War of the Spanish Succession, all before lunch. Pupils are to pick up these things. Tests measure whether the picking up has been successful.

The lack of connection between stated goals, such as those of the California high school cited earlier, and the goals inherent in school practice is obvious and, curiously, tolerated. Most striking is the gap between statements about "self-realization and mental and physical growth" or "moral and ethical values"—common rhetoric in school documents—and practice. Most physical education programs have neither the time nor the focus really to ensure fitness. Mental health is rarely defined. Neither are ethical values, save at the negative extremes, such as opposition to assault or dishonesty. Nothing in the regimen of a day like Mark's signals direct or implicit teaching in this area. The "schoolboy code" (not ratting on a fellow student) protects the marijuana pusher, and a leechlike associate is shrugged off without concern. The issue of the locker search was pushed aside, as not appropriate for class time.

40 Most students, like Mark, go to class in groups of twenty to twenty-seven students. The expected attendance in some schools, particularly those in low-income areas, is usually higher, often thirty-five students per class, but high absentee rates push the actual numbers down. About twenty-five per class is an average figure for expected attendance, and the actual numbers are somewhat lower. There are remarkably few students who go to class in groups much larger or smaller than twenty-five.

A student such as Mark sees five or six teachers per day; their differing styles and expectations are part of his kaleidoscope. High school staffs are highly specialized; guidance counselors rarely teach mathematics, mathematics teachers rarely teach English, principals rarely do any classroom instruction. Mark, then, is known a little bit by a number of people, each of whom sees him in one specialized situation. No one may know him as a "whole person"— unless he becomes a special problem or has special needs.

Save in extracurricular or coaching situations, such as in athletics, drama, or shop classes, there is little opportunity for sustained conversation between student and teacher. The mode is a one-sentence or two-sentence exchange: *Mark, when was Grover Cleveland president? Let's see, was 1890 . . . or something . . . wasn't he the one . . . he was elected twice, wasn't he? . . . Yes . . . Gloria, can you get the dates right?* Dialogue is strikingly absent, and as a result the opportunity of teachers to challenge students' ideas in a systematic and logical way is limited. Given the rushed, full quality of the school day, it can seldom happen. One must infer that careful probing of students' thinking is not a high priority. How one gains (to quote the California school's statement of goals again) "the ability to make decisions, to solve problems, to reason independently, and to accept responsibility for self-evaluation and continuing self-improvement" without being challenged is difficult to imagine. One certainly doesn't learn these things merely from lectures and textbooks.

Most schools are nice places. Mark and his friends enjoy being in theirs. The adults who work in schools generally like adolescents. The academic pressures are limited, and the accommodations to students are substantial. For example, if many members of an English class have jobs after school, the English teacher's expectations for them are adjusted, downward. In a word, school is sensitively accommodating, as long as students are punctual, where they are supposed to be, and minimally dutiful about picking things up from the clutch of courses in which they enroll.

This characterization is not pretty, but it is accurate, and it serves to describe the vast majority of American secondary schools. "Taking subjects" in a systematized, conveyer-belt way is what one does in high school. That this process is, in substantial respects, not related to the rhetorical purposes of education is tolerated by most people, perhaps because they do not really either believe in those ill-defined goals or, in their heart of hearts, believe that schools can or should even try to achieve them. The students are happy taking subjects. The parents are happy, because that's what they did in high school. The rituals, the most important of which is graduation, remain intact. The adolescents are supervised, safely and constructively most of the time, during the morning and afternoon hours, and they are off the labor market. That is what high school is all about.

EXPLORATORY WRITING

Sizer says, "Press most adults about what high school is for, and you hear these subjects listed. *High school? That's where you learn English and math and that sort of thing.*" How does Sizer answer his question, what is high school for? How would you answer it? Explain how you would account for differences and similarities between Sizer's answer and your own.

TALKING ABOUT THE READING

The portrait of Mark that begins this selection, as Sizer notes, is a composite blending of several real students and real high schools—"somewhere," Sizer says, "between precise journalism and nonfiction fiction." Sizer's portrait of Mark's school day must appear to be typical and recognizable for it to be persuasive and credible. Does Sizer achieve the kind of typicality he is trying for? Work together in a group of three or four other students. Draw on your own experience and observations in high school to decide whether this is a reasonable portrait and what you would add or modify. Do these additions or modifications change the conclusions Sizer makes about "what high school is"?

WRITING ASSIGNMENTS

1. At the end of this selection, Sizer says, " 'Taking subjects' in a systematized, conveyer-belt way is what one does in high school." A few lines later he says, "students are happy taking subjects." Do you agree with Sizer? Are high school students, in your experience, happy "taking subjects," or do they feel something is missing? Write an essay that develops your own position. Begin by summarizing what Sizer views as "conveyer-belt" education. Then explain to what extent and why you agree or disagree with his sense that students are happy "taking subjects."

2. Sizer says, "Most schools are nice. . . . The academic pressures are limited, and the accommodations to students are substantial. For example, if many members of an English class have jobs after school, the English teacher's expectations for them are adjusted, downward." Write an essay that describes the expectations of teachers in the high school you attended and explains what influence those expectations have had on you as a student, a learner, and a person. Take into account whether teachers' expectations varied and whether they held the same expectations for all students.

3. Use Sizer's composite portrait of Mark's school day as a model to write a portrait of a typical day at the high school you attended or your college. You can draw on your own experience and memories, but keep in mind that Sizer's portrait is a made-up character, not a real person. Similarly, in this writing task, you'll need to invent your own typical student and his or her experience of the school day.

SOCIAL CLASS AND THE HIDDEN CURRICULUM OF WORK

— Jean Anyon

Jean Anyon teaches social and educational policy in the Ph.D. program in urban education at the City University of New York Graduate Center. "Social Class and the Hidden Curriculum of Work," which appeared in a 1980 issue of the *Journal of Education,* is a groundbreaking study that examined the work fifth-grade students did, their interactions with teachers, and how they were evaluated in five schools that reflected in different socioeconomic groups. As you will see, Anyon sees the differences in what students do in school as preparation for very different social outcomes.

SUGGESTION FOR READING In the second section "The Sample of Schools," Anyon identifies the social status of each school—working-class, middle-class, affluent professional, and executive elite. Use these categories to guide your reading, as Anyon presents her findings on each type of school, and to evaluate the conclusions Anyon draws at the end, based on her findings.

1 Scholars in political economy and the sociology of knowledge have recently argued that public schools in complex industrial societies like our own make available different types of educational experience and curriculum knowledge to students in different social classes. Bowles and Gintis for example, have argued that students in different social-class backgrounds are rewarded for classroom behaviors that correspond to personality traits allegedly rewarded in the different occupational strata—the working classes for docility and obedience, the managerial classes for initiative and personal assertiveness. Basil Bernstein, Pierre Bourdieu, and Michael W. Apple, focusing on school knowledge, have argued that knowledge and skills leading to social power and regard (medical, legal, managerial) are made available to the advantaged social groups but are withheld from the working classes to whom a more "practical" curriculum is offered (manual skills, clerical knowledge).

While there has been considerable argumentation of these points regarding education in England, France, and North America, there has been little or no attempt to investigate these ideas empirically in elementary or secondary schools and classrooms in this country.

This article offers tentative empirical support (and qualification) of the above arguments by providing illustrative examples of differences in student work in classrooms in contrasting social class communities. The examples were gathered as part of an ethnographical study of curricular, pedagogical, and pupil evaluation practices in five elementary schools. The article attempts a theoretical contribution as well and assesses student work in the light of a theoretical approach to social-class analysis. . . . It will be suggested that there is a "hidden curriculum" in schoolwork that has profound implications for the theory—and consequence—of everyday activity in education. . . .

THE SAMPLE OF SCHOOLS

. . . The social-class designation of each of the five schools will be identified, and the income, occupation, and other relevant available social characteristics of the students and their parents will be described. The first three schools are in a medium-sized city district in northern New Jersey, and the other two are in a nearby New Jersey suburb.

The first two schools I will call working-class schools. Most of the parents have blue-collar jobs. Less than a third of the fathers are skilled, while the majority are in unskilled or semiskilled jobs. During the period of the study (1978–1979), approximately 15 percent of the fathers were unemployed. The large majority (85 percent) of the families are white. The following occupations are typical: platform, storeroom, and stockroom workers; foundry-men, pipe welders, and boilermakers; semiskilled and unskilled assembly-line operatives; gas station attendants, auto mechanics, maintenance workers, and security guards. Less than 30 percent of the women work, some part-time and some full-time, on assembly lines, in storerooms and stockrooms, as waitresses, barmaids, or sales clerks. Of the fifth-grade parents, none of the wives of the skilled workers had jobs. Approximately 15 percent of the families in each school are at or below the federal "poverty" level; most of the rest of the family incomes are at or below $12,000, except some of the skilled workers whose incomes are higher. The incomes of the majority of the families in these two schools (at or below $12,000) are typical of 38.6 percent of the families in the United States.

5   The third school is called the middle-class school, although because of 5 neighborhood residence patterns, the population is a mixture of several social classes. The parents' occupations can he divided into three groups: a small group of blue-collar "rich," who are skilled, well-paid workers such as printers, carpenters, plumbers, and construction workers. The second group is composed of parents in working-class and middle-class white-collar jobs: women in office jobs, technicians, supervisors in industry, and parents employed by the city (such as firemen, policemen, and several of the school's teachers). The third group is composed of occupations such as personnel directors in local firms, accountants, "middle management," and a few small capitalists (owners of shops in the area). The children of several local doctors attend this school. Most family incomes are between $13,000 and $25,000, with a few higher. This income range is typical of 38.9 percent of the families in the United States.

The fourth school has a parent population that is at the upper income level of the upper middle class and is predominantly professional. This school will be called the affluent professional school. Typical jobs are: cardiologist, interior designer, corporate lawyer or engineer, executive in advertising or television. There are some families who are not as affluent as the majority (the family of the superintendent of the district's schools, and the one or two families in which the fathers are skilled workers). In addition, a few of the families are more affluent than the majority and can be classified in the capitalist class (a partner in a prestigious Wall Street stock brokerage firm). Approximately 90 percent of the children in this school are white. Most family incomes are between $40,000 and $80,000. This income span represents approximately 7 percent of the families in the United States.

In the fifth school the majority of the families belong to the capitalist class. This school will be called the executive elite school because most of the fathers are top executives (for example, presidents and vice-presidents) in major United States-based multinational corporations—for example, AT&T, RCA, Citibank, American Express, U.S. Steel. A sizable group of fathers are top executives in financial firms in Wall Street. There are also a number of fathers who list their occupations as "general counsel" to a particular corporation, and these corporations are also among the large multi-nationals. Many of the mothers do volunteer work in the Junior League, Junior Fortnightly, or other service groups; some are intricately involved in town politics; and some are themselves in well-paid occupations. There are no minority children in the school. Almost all the family incomes are over $100,000 with some in the $500,000 range. The incomes in this school represent less than 1 percent of the families in the United States.

Since each of the five schools is only one instance of elementary education in a particular social class context, I will not generalize beyond the sample. However, the examples of schoolwork which follow will suggest characteristics of education in each social setting that appear to have theoretical and social significance and to be worth investigation in a larger number of schools.

THE WORKING-CLASS SCHOOLS

In the two working-class schools, work is following the steps of a procedure. The procedure is usually mechanical, involving rote behavior and very little decision making or choice. The teachers rarely explain why the work is being assigned, how it might connect to other assignments, or what the idea is that lies behind the procedure or gives it coherence and perhaps meaning or significance. Available textbooks are not always used, and the teachers often prepare their own dittos or put work examples on the board. Most of the rules regarding work are designations of what the children are to do; the rules are steps to follow. These steps are told to the children by the teachers and are often written on the board. The children are usually told to copy the steps as notes. These notes are to be studied. Work is often evaluated not according to whether it is right or wrong but according to whether the children followed the right steps.

10   The following examples illustrate these points. In math, when two-digit division was introduced, the teacher in one school gave a four-minute lecture on what the terms are called (which number is the divisor, dividend, quotient,

and remainder). The children were told to copy these names in their notebooks. Then the teacher told them the steps to follow to do the problems, saying, "This is how you do them." The teacher listed the steps on the board, and they appeared several days later as a chart hung in the middle of the front wall: "Divide, Multiply, Subtract, Bring Down." The children often did examples of two-digit division. When the teacher went over the examples with them, he told them what the procedure was for each problem, rarely asking them to conceptualize or explain it themselves: "Three into twenty-two is seven; do your subtraction and one is left over." During the week that two-digit division was introduced (or at any other time), the investigator did not observe any discussion of the idea of grouping involved in division, any use of manipulables, or any attempt to relate two-digit division to any other mathematical process. Nor was there any attempt to relate the steps to an actual or possible thought process of the children. The observer did not hear the terms dividend, quotient, and so on, used again. The math teacher in the other working-class school followed similar procedures regarding two-digit division and at one point her class seemed confused. She said, "You're confusing yourselves. You're tensing up. Remember, when you do this, it's the same steps over and over again—and that's the way division always is." Several weeks later, after a test, a group of her children "still didn't get it," and she made no attempt to explain the concept of dividing things into groups or to give them manipulables for their own investigation. Rather, she went over the steps with them again and told them that they "needed more practice."

In other areas of math, work is also carrying out often unexplained fragmented procedures. For example, one of the teachers led the children through a series of steps to make a 1-inch grid on their paper without telling them that they were making a 1-inch grid or that it would be used to study scale. She said, "Take your ruler. Put it across the top. Make a mark at every number.

Then move your ruler down to the bottom. No, put it across the bottom. Now make a mark on top of every number. Now draw a line from . . ." At this point a girl said that she had a faster way to do it and the teacher said, "No, you don't; you don't even know what I'm making yet. Do it this way or it's wrong." After they had made the lines up and down and across, the teacher told them she wanted them to make a figure by connecting some dots and to measure that, using the scale of 1 inch equals 1 mile. Then they were to cut it out. She said, "Don't cut it until I check it."

In both working-class schools, work in language arts is mechanics of punctuation (commas, periods, question marks, exclamation points), capitalization, and the four kinds of sentences. One teacher explained to me, "Simple punctuation is all they'll ever use." Regarding punctuation, either a teacher or a ditto stated the rules for where, for example, to put commas. The investigator heard no classroom discussion of the aural context of punctuation (which, of course, is what gives each mark its meaning). Nor did the investigator hear any statement or inference that placing a punctuation mark could be a decision-making process, depending, for example, on one's intended meaning. Rather, the children were told to follow the rules. Language arts did not involve creative writing. There were several writing assignments throughout the year but in each instance the children were given a ditto, and they wrote answers to questions on the sheet. For example, they wrote their "autobiography" by answering such questions as "Where were you born?" "What is your favorite animal?" on a sheet entitled "All About Me."

In one of the working-class schools, the class had a science period several times a week. On the three occasions observed, the children were not called upon to set up experiments or to give explanations for facts or concepts. Rather, on each occasion the teacher told them in his own words what the book said. The children copied the teacher's sentences from the board. Each day that preceded the day they were to do a science experiment, the teacher told them to copy the directions from the book for the procedure they would carry out the next day and to study the list at home that night. The day after each experiment, the teacher went over what they had "found" (they did the experiments as a class, and each was actually a class demonstration led by the teacher). Then the teacher wrote what they "found" on the board, and the children copied that in their notebooks. Once or twice a year there are science projects. The project is chosen and assigned by the teacher from a box of 3-by-5-inch cards. On the card the teacher has written the question to be answered, the books to use, and how much to write. Explaining the cards to the observer, the teacher said, "It tells them exactly what to do, or they couldn't do it."

Social studies in the working-class schools is also largely mechanical, rote work that was given little explanation or connection to larger contexts. In one school, for example, although there was a book available, social studies work was to copy the teacher's notes from the board. Several times a week for a period of several months the children copied these notes. The fifth grades in the district were to study United States history. The teacher used a booklet she had purchased called "The Fabulous Fifty States." Each day she put information from the booklet in outline form on the board and the children copied it. The type of information did not vary: the name of the state, its abbreviation, state capital, nickname of the state, its main products, main business, and a "Fabulous Fact" ("Idaho grew twenty-seven billion potatoes in one year. That's enough potatoes for each man, woman, and . . .") As the children finished copying the sentences, the teacher erased them and wrote more. Children would occasionally go to the front to pull down the wall map in order to locate the states they were copying, and the teacher did not dissuade them. But the observer never saw her refer to the map; nor did the observer ever hear her make other than perfunctory remarks concerning the information the children were copying. Occasionally the children colored in a ditto and cut it out to make a stand-up figure (representing, for example, a man roping a cow in the Southwest). These were referred to by the teacher as their social studies "projects."

15   Rote behavior was often called for in classroom work. When going over 15 math and language art skills sheets, for example, as the teacher asked for the answer to each problem, he fired the questions rapidly, staccato, and the scene reminded the observer of a sergeant drilling recruits: above all, the questions demanded that you stay at attention: "The next one? What do I put here? . . . Here? Give us the next." Or "How many commas in this sentence? Where do I put them . . . The next one?"

The four fifth-grade teachers observed in the working-class schools attempted to control classroom time and space by making decisions without consulting the children and without explaining the basis for their decisions. The teacher's control thus often seemed capricious. Teachers, for instance, very often ignored the bells to switch classes—deciding among themselves to keep the children after the period was officially over to continue with the work or for disciplinary reasons or so they (the teachers) could stand in the hall and talk. There were no clocks in the rooms in either school, and the children often asked, "What period is this?" "When do we go to gym?" The children had no access to materials. These were handed out by teachers and closely guarded. Things in the room "belonged" to the teacher: "Bob, bring me my garbage can." The teachers continually gave the children orders. Only three times did the investigator hear a teacher in either working-class school preface a directive with an unsarcastic "please," or "let's" or "would you." Instead, the teachers said, "Shut up," "Shut your mouth," "Open your books," "Throw your gum away—if you want to rot your teeth, do it on your own time." Teachers made every effort to control the movement of the children, and often shouted, "'Why are you out of

your seat??!!" If the children got permission to leave the room, they had to take a written pass with the date and time. . . .

MIDDLE-CLASS SCHOOL

In the middle-class school, work is getting the right answer. If one accumulates enough right answers, one gets a good grade. One must follow the directions in order to get the right answers, but the directions often call for some figuring, some choice, some decision making. For example, the children must often figure out by themselves what the directions ask them to do and how to get the answer: what do you do first, second, and perhaps third? Answers are usually found in books or by listening to the teacher. Answers are usually words, sentences, numbers, or facts and dates; one writes them on paper, and one should be neat. Answers must be given in the right order, and one cannot make them up.

The following activities are illustrative. Math involves some choice: one may do two-digit division the long way or the short way, and there are some math problems that can be done "in your head." When the teacher explains how to do two-digit division, there is recognition that a cognitive process is involved; she gives you several ways and says, "I want to make sure you understand what you're doing—so you get it right"; and, when they go over the homework, she asks the children to tell how they did the problem and what answer they got.

In social studies the daily work is to read the assigned pages in the textbook and to answer the teacher's questions. The questions are almost always designed to check on whether the students have read the assignment and understood it: who did so-and-so; what happened after that; when did it happen, where, and sometimes, why did it happen? The answers are in the book and in one's understanding of the book; the teacher's hints when one doesn't know the answers are to "read it again" or to look at the picture or at the rest of the paragraph. One is to search for the answer in the "context," in what is given.

20   Language arts is "simple grammar, what they need for everyday life." The language arts teacher says, "They should learn to speak properly, to write business letters and thank-you letters, and to understand what nouns and verbs and simple subjects are." Here, as well, actual work is to choose the right answers, to understand what is given. The teacher often says, "Please read the next sentence and then I'll question you about it." One teacher said in some exasperation to a boy who was fooling around in class, "If you don't know the answers to the questions I ask, then you can't stay in this class! [pause] You never know the answers to the questions I ask, and it's not fair to me—and certainly not to you!"

Most lessons are based on the textbook. This does not involve a critical perspective on what is given there. For example, a critical perspective in social studies is perceived as dangerous by these teachers because it may lead to controversial topics; the parents might complain. The children, however, are often curious especially in social studies. Their questions are tolerated and usually answered perfunctorily. But after a few minutes the teacher will say, "All right, we're not going any farther. Please open your social studies workbook." While the teachers spend a lot of time explaining and expanding on what the textbooks say, there is little attempt to analyze how or why things happen, or to give thought to how pieces of a culture, or, say, a system of numbers or elements of a language fit together or can be analyzed. What has happened in the past and what exists now may not be equitable or fair, but (shrug) that is the way things are and one does not confront such matters in school. For example, in social studies after a child is called on to read a passage about the pilgrims, the teacher summarizes the paragraph and then says, "So you can see how strict they were about everything." A child asks, "Why?" "Well, because they felt that if you weren't busy you'd get into trouble." Another child asks, "Is it true that they burned women at the stake?"

The teacher says, "Yes, if a woman did anything strange, they hanged them. [sic] What would a woman do, do you think, to make them burn them? [sic] See if you can come up with better answers than my other [social studies] class." Several children offer suggestions, to which the teacher nods but does not comment. Then she says, "Okay, good," and calls on the next child to read.

Work tasks do not usually request creativity. Serious attention is rarely given in school work on how the children develop or express their own feelings and ideas, either linguistically or in graphic form. On the occasions when creativity or self-expression is requested, it is peripheral to the main activity or it is "enriched" or "for fun." During a lesson on what similes are, for example, the teacher explains what they are, puts several on the board, gives some other examples herself, and then asks the children if they can "make some up." She calls on three children who give similes, two of which are actually in the book they have open before them. The teacher does not comment on this and then asks several others to choose similes from the list of phrases in the book. Several do so correctly, and she says, "Oh good! You're picking them out! See how good we are?" Their homework is to pick out the rest of the similes from the list.

Creativity is not often requested in social studies and science projects, either. Social studies projects, for example, are given with directions to "find information on your topic" and write it up. The children are not supposed to copy but to "put it in your own words." Although a number of the projects subsequently went beyond the teacher's direction to find information and had quite expressive covers and inside illustrations, the teacher's evaluative comments had to do with the amount of information, whether they had "copied," and if their work was neat.

The style of control of the three fifth-grade teachers observed in this school varied from somewhat easygoing to strict, but in contrast to the working-class schools, the teachers' decisions were usually based on external rules and regulations—for example, on criteria that were known or available to the children. Thus, the teachers always honor the bells for changing classes, and they usually evaluate children's work by what is in the textbooks and answer booklets.

25 There is little excitement in schoolwork for the children, and the assignments are perceived as having little to do with their interests and feelings. As one child said, what you do is "store facts up in your head like cold storage—until you need it later for a test or your job." Thus, doing well is important because there are thought to be other likely rewards: a good job or college.

AFFLUENT PROFESSIONAL SCHOOL

In the affluent professional school, work is creative activity carried out independently. The students are continually asked to express and apply ideas and concepts. Work involves individual thought and expressiveness, expansion and illustration of ideas, and choice of appropriate method and material. (The class is not considered an open classroom, and the principal explained that because of the large number of discipline problems in the fifth grade this year they did not departmentalize. The teacher who agreed to take part in the study said she is "more structured this year than she usually is.) The products of work in this class are often written stories, editorials and essays, or representations of ideas in mural, graph, or craft form. The products of work should not be like anybody else's and should show individuality. They should exhibit good design, and (this is important) they must also fit empirical reality. The relatively few rules to be followed regarding work are usually criteria for, or limits on, individual activity. One's product is usually evaluated for the quality of its expression and for the appropriateness of its conception to the task. In many cases, one's own satisfaction with the product is an important criterion for its evaluation. When right answers are called for, as in commercial materials like SRA (Science Research Associates) and math, it is important that the children decide on an answer as a result of thinking about the idea involved in what they're being asked to do. Teacher's hints are to "think about it some more."

The following activities are illustrative. The class takes home a sheet requesting each child's parents to fill in the number of cars they have, the number of television sets, refrigerators, games, or rooms in the house, and so on. Each child is to figure the average number of a type of possession owned by the fifth grade. Each child must compile the "data" from all the sheets. A calculator is available in the classroom to do the mechanics of finding the average. Some children decide to send sheets to the fourth-grade families for comparison. Their work should be "verified" by a classmate before it is handed in.

Each child and his or her family has made a geoboard. The teacher asks the class to get their geoboards from the side cabinet, to take a handful of rubber bands, and then to listen to what she would like them to do. She says, "I would like you to design a figure and then find the perimeter and area. When you have it, check with your neighbor. After you've done that, please transfer it to graph paper and tomorrow I'll ask you to make up a question about it for someone. When you hand it in, please let me know whose it is and who verified it. Then I have something else for you to do that's really fun. [pause] Find the average number of chocolate chips in three cookies. I'll give you three cookies, and you'll have to eat your way through, I'm afraid!" Then she goes around the room and gives help, suggestions, praise, and admonitions that they are getting noisy. They work sitting, or standing up at their desks, at benches in the back, or on the floor. A child hands the teacher his paper and she comments, "I'm not accepting this paper. Do a better design." To another child she says, "That's fantastic! But you'll never find the area. Why don't you draw a figure inside [the big one] and subtract to get the area?"

The school district requires the fifth grade to study ancient civilization (in particular, Egypt, Athens, and Sumer). In this classroom, the emphasis is on illustrating and re-creating the culture of the people of ancient times. The following are typical activities: the children made an 8mm film on Egypt, which one of the parents edited. A girl in the class wrote the script, and the class acted it out. They put the sound on themselves. They read stories of those days. They wrote essays and stories depicting the lives of the people and the societal and occupational divisions. They chose from a list of projects, all of which involved graphical presentations of ideas: for example. "Make a mural depicting the division of labor in Egyptian society."

Each wrote and exchanged a letter in hieroglyphics with a fifth grader in another class, and they also exchanged stories they wrote in cuneiform. They made a scroll and singed the edges so it looked authentic. They each chose an occupation and made an Egyptian plaque representing that occupation, simulating the appropriate Egyptian design. They carved their design on a cylinder of wax, pressed the wax into clay, and then baked the clay. Although one girl did not choose an occupation but carved instead a series of gods and slaves, the teacher said, "That's all right, Amber, it's beautiful." As they were working the teacher said, "Don't cut into your clay until you're satisfied with your design."

30   Social studies also involves almost daily presentation by the children of some event from the news. The teacher's questions ask the children to expand what they say, to give more details, and to be more specific. Occasionally she adds some remarks to help them see connections between events.

The emphasis on expressing and illustrating ideas in social studies is accompanied in language arts by an emphasis on creative writing. Each child wrote a rebus story for a first grader whom they had interviewed to see what kind of story the child liked best. They wrote editorials on pending decisions by the school board and radio plays, some of which were read over the school intercom from the office and one of which was performed in the auditorium. There is no language arts textbook because, the teacher said, "The principal wants us to be creative." There is not much grammar, but there is punctuation. One morning when the observer arrived, the class was doing a punctuation ditto. The teacher later apologized for using the ditto. "It's just for review," she said. "I don't teach punctuation that way. We use their language." The ditto had three unambiguous rules for where to put commas in a sentence. As the teacher was going around to help the children with the ditto, she repeated several times, "where you put commas depends on how you say the sentence; it depends on the situation and what you want to say. Several weeks later the observer saw another punctuation activity. The teacher had printed a five-paragraph story on an oak tag and then cut it into phrases. She read the whole story to the class from the book, then passed out the phrases. The group had to decide how the phrases could best be put together again. (They arranged the phrases on the floor.) The point was not to replicate the story, although that was not irrelevant, but to "decide what you think the best way is." Punctuation marks on cardboard pieces were then handed out, and the children discussed and then decided what mark was best at each place they thought one was needed. At the end of each paragraph the teacher asked, "Are you satisfied with the way the paragraphs are now? Read it to yourself and see how it sounds." Then she read the original story again, and they compared the two.

Describing her goals in science to the investigator, the teacher said, "We use ESS (Elementary Science Study). It's very good because it gives a hands-on experience—so they can make sense out of it. It doesn't matter whether it [what they find] is right or wrong. I bring them together and there's value in discussing their ideas."

The products of work in this class are often highly valued by the children and the teacher. In fact, this was the only school in which the investigator was not allowed to take original pieces of the children's work for her files. If the work was small enough, however, and was on paper, the investigator could duplicate it on the copying machine in the office.

The teacher's attempt to control the class involves constant negotiation. She does not give direct orders unless she is angry because the children have been too noisy. Normally, she tries to get them to foresee the consequences of their actions and to decide accordingly. For example, lining them up to go see a play written by the sixth graders, she says, "I presume you're lined up by someone with whom you want to sit. I hope you're lined up by someone you won't get in trouble with." . . .

35   One of the few rules governing the children's movement is that no more than three children may be out of the room at once. There is a school rule that anyone can go to the library at any time to get a book. In the fifth grade I observed, they sign their name on the chalkboard and leave. There are no passes. Finally, the children have a fair amount of officially sanctioned say over what happens in the class. For example, they often negotiate what work is to be done. If the teacher wants to move on to the next subject, but the children say they are not ready, they want to work on their present projects some more, she very often lets them do it.

EXECUTIVE ELITE SCHOOL

In the executive elite school, work is developing one's analytical intellectual powers. Children are continually asked to reason through a problem, to produce intellectual products that are both logically sound and of top academic quality. A primary goal of thought is to conceptualize rules by which elements may fit together in systems and then to apply these rules in solving a problem. Schoolwork helps one to achieve, to excel, to prepare for life.

The following are illustrative. The math teacher teaches area and perimeter by having the children derive formulas for each. First she helps them, through discussion at the board, to arrive at $A = W \times L$ as a formula (not the formula) for area. After discussing several, she says, "Can anyone make up a formula for perimeter? Can you figure that out yourselves? [pause] Knowing what we know, can we think of a formula?" She works out three children's suggestions at the board, saying to two, "Yes, that's a good one," and then asks the class if they can think of any more. No one volunteers. To prod them, she says, "If you use rules and good reasoning, you get many ways. Chris, can you think up a formula?"

She discusses two-digit division with the children as a decision-making process. Presenting a new type of problem to them, she asks, "What's the first decision you'd make if presented with this kind of example? What is the first thing you'd think? Craig?" Craig says, "To find my first partial quotient." She responds, "Yes, that would be your first decision. How would you do that?" Craig explains, and then the teacher says, "OK, we'll see how that works for you." The class tries his way. Subsequently, she comments on the merits and shortcomings of several other children's decisions. Later, she tells the investigator that her goals in math are to develop their reasoning and mathematical thinking and that, unfortunately, "there's no time for manipulables."

While right answers are important in math, they are not "given" by the book or by the teacher but may be challenged by the children. Going over some problems in late September the teacher says, "Raise your hand if you do not agree." A child says, "I don't agree with sixty-four." The teacher responds, "OK, there's a question about sixty-four. [to class] Please check it. Owen, they're disagreeing with you. Kristen, they're checking yours." The teacher emphasized this repeatedly during September and October with statements like "Don't be afraid to say you disagree. In the last [math] class, somebody disagreed, and they were right. Before you disagree, check yours, and if you still think we're wrong, then we'll check it out." By Thanksgiving, the children did not often speak in terms of right and wrong math problems but of whether they agreed with the answer that had been given.

40　　There are complicated math mimeos with many word problems. Whenever they go over the examples, they discuss how each child has set up the problem. The children must explain it precisely. On one occasion the teacher said, "I'm more—just as interested in how you set up the problem as in what answer you find. If you set up a problem in a good way, the answer is easy to find.

Social studies work is most often reading and discussion of concepts and independent research. There are only occasional artistic, expressive, or illustrative projects. Ancient Athens and Sumer are, rather, societies to analyze. The following questions are typical of those that guide the children's independent research. "What mistakes did Pericles make after the war?" "What mistakes did the citizens of Athens make?" "What are the elements of a civilization?" "How did Greece build an economic empire?" "Compare the way Athens chose its leaders with the way we choose ours." Occasionally the children are asked to make up sample questions for their social studies tests. On an occasion when the investigator was present, the social studies teacher rejected a child's question by saying, "That's just fact. If I asked you that question on a test, you'd complain it was just memory! Good questions ask for concepts."

In social studies—but also in reading, science, and health—the teachers initiate classroom discussions of current social issues and problems. These discussions occurred on every one of the investigator's visits, and a teacher told me, "These children's opinions are important—it's important that they learn to reason things through." The classroom discussions always struck the observer as quite realistic and analytical, dealing with concrete social issues like the following: "Why do workers strike?" "Is that right or wrong?" "Why do we have inflation, and what

can be done to stop it?" "Why do companies put chemicals in food when the natural ingredients are available?" and so on. Usually the children did not have to be prodded to give their opinions. In fact, their statements and the interchanges between them struck the observer as quite sophisticated conceptually and verbally, and well-informed. Occasionally the teachers would prod with statements such as, "Even if you don't know [the answers], if you think logically about it, you can figure it out." And "I'm asking you [these] questions to help you think this through."

Language arts emphasizes language as a complex system, one that should be mastered. The children are asked to diagram sentences of complex grammatical construction, to memorize irregular verb conjugations (he lay, he has lain, and so on . . .), and to use the proper participles, conjunctions, and interjections in their speech. The teacher (the same one who teaches social studies) told them, "It is not enough to get these right on tests; you must use what you learn [in grammar classes] in your written and oral work. I will grade you on that."

Most writing assignments are either research reports and essays for social studies or experiment analyses and write-ups for science. There is only an occasional story or other "creative writing" assignment. On the occasion observed by the investigator (the writing of a Halloween story), the points the teacher stressed in preparing the children to write involved the structural aspects of a story rather than the expression of feelings or other ideas. The teacher showed them a filmstrip, "The Seven Parts of a Story," and lectured them on plot development, mood setting, character development, consistency, and the use of a logical or appropriate ending. The stories they subsequently wrote were, in fact, well-structured, but many were also personal and expressive. The teacher's evaluative comments, however, did not refer to the expressiveness or artistry but were all directed toward whether they had "developed" the story well.

45   Language arts work also involved a large amount of practice in presentation of the self and in managing situations where the child was expected to be in charge. For example, there was a series of assignments in which each child had to be a "student teacher." The child had to plan a lesson in grammar, outlining, punctuation, or other language arts topic and explain the concept to the class. Each child was to prepare a worksheet or game and a homework assignment as well. After each presentation, the teacher and other children gave a critical appraisal of the "student teacher's" performance. Their criteria were: whether the student spoke clearly, whether the lesson was interesting, whether the student made any mistakes, and whether he or she kept control of the class. On an occasion when a child did not maintain control, the teacher said, "When you're up there, you have authority and you have to use it. I'll back you up."

The executive elite school is the only school where bells do not demarcate the periods of time. The two fifth-grade teachers were very strict about changing classes on schedule, however, as specific plans for each session had been made. The teachers attempted to keep tight control over the children during lessons, and the children were sometimes flippant, boisterous, and occasionally rude. However, the children may be brought into line by reminding them that "It is up to you." "You must control yourself," "you are responsible for your work," you must "set your own priorities." One teacher told a child, "You are the only driver of your car—and only you can regulate your speed." A new teacher complained to the observer that she had thought "these children" would have more control.

While strict attention to the lesson at hand is required, the teachers make relatively little attempt to regulate the movement of the children at other times. For example, except for the kindergartners the children in this school do not have to wait for the bell to ring in the morning; they may go to their classroom when they arrive at school. Fifth graders often came early to read, to finish work, or to catch up. After the first two months of school, the fifth-grade teachers did not line the children up to change classes or to go to gym, and so on, but, when the children were ready and quiet, they were told they could go—sometimes without the teachers.

In the classroom, the children could get materials when they needed them and took what they needed from closets and from the teacher's desk. They were in charge of the office at lunchtime. During class they did not have to sign out or ask permission to leave the room; they just got up and left. Because of the pressure to get work done, however, they did not leave the room very often. The teachers were very polite to the children, and the investigator heard no sarcasm, no nasty remarks, and few direct orders. The teachers never called the children "honey" or "dear" but always called them by name. The teachers were expected to be available before school, after school, and for part of their lunchtime to provide extra help if needed.

The foregoing analysis of differences in schoolwork in contrasting social class contexts suggests the following conclusion: the "hidden curriculum" of schoolwork is tacit preparation for relating to the process of production in a particular way. Differing curricular, pedagogical, and pupil evaluation practices emphasize different cognitive and behavioral skills in each social setting and thus contribute to the development in the children of certain potential relationships to physical and symbolic capital, to authority, and to the process of work. School experience, in the sample of schools discussed here, differed qualitatively by social class. These differences may not only contribute to the development in the children in each social class of certain types of economically significant relationships and not others but would thereby help to reproduce this system of relations in society. In the contribution to the reproduction of unequal social relations lies a theoretical meaning and social consequence of classroom practice.

50   The identification of different emphases in classrooms in a sample of contrasting social class contexts implies that further research should be conducted in a large number of schools to investigate the types of work tasks and interactions in each to see if they differ in the ways discussed here and to see if similar potential relationships are uncovered. Such research could have as a product the further elucidation of complex but not readily apparent connections between everyday activity in schools and classrooms and the unequal structure of economic relationships in which we work and live.

EXPLORATORY WRITING

Write a quick sketch, in a paragraph or two, of each type of school Jean Anyon identifies—working class, middle class, affluent professional, and executive elite. In your sketch, explain how classroom practices give each type of school its class character. If it's helpful, use elementary or high schools where you grew up as examples.

TALKING ABOUT THE READING

Divide the class into four groups—one for each type of schools. The first task for each group is to compare the exploratory sketches you wrote of the type of school your group is considering. Note the differences and similarities in order to prepare a statement by your group on how classroom practices give that type of school its class character. Second, consider to what extent Anyon's findings might need to be updated from the time of her research in the 1970s. Use her framework of identifying types of schools to extend her analysis of the class character of schools into the present. Each group will present its findings in order to see what generalizations about schooling, the hidden curriculum, and social class can be made by reading Anyon's work from the perspective of the present.

WRITING ASSIGNMENTS

1. Use Anyon's approach to classroom practices and the formation of social classes to examine an elementary, junior high, or high school that you attended. Keep the focus on Anyon's method of looking at how the work students do, how they interact with teachers, and how they are evaluated influence their social futures. If her types of school do not fit the school you're examining, you may have to invent another category of schools based on class background.

2. Write an essay that examines the hidden curriculum of the writing assignments you were given in high school. You will need to recall as many assignments as possible. Make a list of all you can remember, not just in English classes but in all classes. Next, group the assignments into categories (book report, lab report, research paper, critical essays, responses to reading, etc.). Choose one or two for your paper. Your task here is to examine the skills, the attitudes toward authority, and the work habits the assignment was meant to inculcate. Using Anyon's approach to schoolwork and the hidden curriculum, consider the extent to which the assignments can be seen as preparation for a particular place in socioeconomic society.

3. Write an essay that extends Anyon's analysis of the hidden curriculum from elementary school to college. To what extent do colleges and universities have class characteristics? How would you group colleges and universities into types of schools, as Anyon does? How does each type of school lead to different social outcomes?

VISUAL ESSAY   Analyzing College Viewbooks

◼︎◼︎— University of Arizona's A has become an immediately recognizable brand.

College viewbooks have become a standard feature of applying to college on students' part and in recruiting students on the part of colleges. High school seniors rely on viewbooks to get a sense of a particular college or university, the kind of students who go there, the culture of the place, and whether it's a good match. Colleges, which compete with each other for the available pool of students, have increasingly adopted concepts from marketing to design their recruitment material. Viewbooks, along with college Web sites, are often part of a campaign to "brand" the college by using professional design firms to develop "identity packages" that project a particular image and set of values. We present here the covers and sample pages from two college viewbooks. You can get some idea of how this "branding" works from these examples, but to do the assignments below you will need to obtain copies of college viewbooks, including that of your own college or university.

SUGGESTION FOR READING   Obtain a viewbook from another college or university. In making your choice, consider the type of institution that the viewbook represents—community college, state college, state university, liberal arts college, selective private university, religious college, women's college, trade or technical college, and so on. Pick a type of institution that interests you. As you read the viewbook, consider how words and images go together to give the school an identity. What students, faculty, and college programs are featured in the viewbook? What do the design choices indicate about the identity the institution wants to project? (This assignment is a good one to do as a group project.)

◼︎◼︎— Russell Sage College combines illustrations and photos in this viewbook, designed by Robert Rytter & Associates as part of the women college's branding statement: "Women of Influence."

I am completely focused.

Russell Sage College

Virginia Tech's viewbook and its branding message "Energize Your Intellect" emphasize the range of challenges and opportunities at a large state university.

EXPLORATORY WRITING

Notice key words and phrases in the viewbook that project the values and identity of the college or university. What are the main emphases—being challenged academically, getting a good job, making a contribution to society, becoming a well-rounded person, having a good time in college, living in an interesting place? How do the key words and phrases combine with images to "brand" the college or university? In a phrase or sentence, describe what you see as the brand.

TALKING ABOUT THE VISUAL ESSAY

If you are doing this assignment as a group, use the exploratory writing you and other members of your group have done to develop an analysis of the viewbook and the brand it is trying to establish. If you are doing the assignment individually, work on this part of it in a group with three or four other students to compare the design strategies across viewbooks. What do they have in common? How do colleges and universities attempt to distinguish themselves from other colleges and universities?

WRITING ASSIGNMENTS

1. In a group or individual paper, write an analysis of the viewbook you've been examining. Consider the questions listed above in Exploratory Writing and Talking About the Visual Essay to determine how the viewbook addresses prospective students. What type of student does the viewbook seek to attract? What kind of college experience does it project? What are the underlying assumptions about the value of a college education?

2. How would you characterize the visual style of the viewbook? Focus on the cover or a page or two to analyze the visual meaning of the viewbook. How do the visuals on their own contribute to the identity the college wishes to project? How do the visuals combine with text to "brand" the college or university?

3. Consider the viewbook of your college or university. How would you rewrite and redesign it from a first-year student's point of view? Write a statement of purpose that includes a brief analysis of the viewbook in its current form and your reasons for redesigning it. Follow this with a design plan about the changes you would make and why. Design a few pages to illustrate your plan.

MAKING CONNECTIONS   Memories of Home and School

Going to school typically involves a realignment of relationships, to a larger or smaller degree, between students and their parents and teachers. The two essays that follow are remarkably dramatic accounts of this transition and how Richard Rodriguez and Min-Zhan Lu dealt with the tensions they experienced between home and school. As autobiographical accounts, the essays may seem at first glance to be highly personal and idiosyncratic. From another angle, however, the essays can be read as inquiries into the social dynamics of schooling in a more general sense, with a focus on issues of language and learning. As you will see, the social circumstances of each writer differ considerably. Richard Rodriguez is the son of Mexican immigrants who settled in Sacramento, California, while Min-Zhan Lu grew up in Shanghai, China. Despite (or maybe because of) these differences, their memoirs of going to school—and the conflicts between home and school that resulted—raise telling questions about the nature of schooling and the positions the two writers develop to make sense of their experience.

THE ACHIEVEMENT OF DESIRE

■— *Richard Rodriguez*

Richard Rodriguez has published a number of books, including *Brown: The Last Discovery of America* (2002), *Days of Obligation: An Argument with My Mexican Father* (1992), and *Hunger of Memory* (1981), from which this selection is taken. For Rodriguez, the transition from home to school is a difficult but necessary one that has led him to become an outspoken opponent of bilingual education on the grounds that it impedes integration into mainstream English-speaking society.

SUGGESTION FOR READING At the end of this essay, Rodriguez says, "I came to trust the silence of reading and the habit of abstracting from immediate experience—moving away from a life of closeness and immediacy I remembered with my parents, growing older—before I turned unafraid to desire the past, and thereby achieved what had eluded me for so long—the end of education." As you read, consider how Rodriguez makes the essay into a personal journey, from home to the wider world, and what he represents as the "end of education."

1 I stand in the ghetto classroom—"the guest speaker"—attempting to lecture on the mystery of the sounds of our words to rows of diffident students. "Don't you hear it? Listen! The music of our words. *'Sumer is icumen in . . .'* And songs on the car radio. We need Aretha Franklin's voice to fill plain words with music— her life." In the face of their empty stares, I try to create an enthusiasm. But the girls in the back row turn to watch some boy passing outside. There are flutters of smiles, waves. And someone's mouth elongates heavy, silent words through the barrier of glass. Silent words—the lips straining to shape each voiceless syllable: "*Meet meee late errr.*" By the door, the instructor smiles at me, apparently hoping that I will be able to spark some enthusiasm in the class. But only one student seems to be listening. A girl, maybe fourteen. In this gray room her eyes shine with ambition. She keeps nodding and nodding at all that I say; she even takes notes. And each time I ask a question, she jerks up and down in her desk like a marionette, while her hand waves over the bowed heads of her classmates. It is myself (as a boy) I see as she faces me now (a man in my thirties).

The boy who first entered a classroom barely able to speak English, twenty years later concluded his studies in the stately quiet of the reading room in the British Museum. Thus with one sentence I can summarize my academic career. It will be harder to summarize what sort of life connects the boy to the man.

With every award, each graduation from one level of education to the next, people I'd meet would congratulate me. Their refrain always the same: "Your parents must be very proud" Sometimes then they'd ask me how I managed it—my "success." (How?) After a while, I had several quick answers to give in reply. I'd admit, for one thing, that I went to an excellent grammar school. (My earliest teachers, the nuns, made my success their ambition.) And my brother and both my sisters were very good students. (They often brought home the shiny school trophies I came to want.) And my mother and father always encouraged me. (At every graduation they were behind the stunning flash of the camera when I turned to look at the crowd.)

As important as these factors were, however, they account inadequately for my academic advance. Nor do they suggest what an odd success I managed. For although I was a very good student, I was also a very bad student. I was a "scholarship boy," a certain kind of scholarship boy. Always successful, I was always unconfident.

Exhilarated by my progress. Sad. I became the prized students—anxious and eager to learn. Too eager, too anxious—an imitative and unoriginal pupil. My brother and two sisters enjoyed the advantages I did, and they grew to be as successful as I, but none of them ever seemed so anxious about their schooling. A second-grade student, I was the one who came home and corrected the "simple" grammatical mistakes of our parents. ("Two negatives make a positive.") Proudly I announced—to my family's startled silence—that a teacher had said I was losing all trace of a Spanish accent. I was oddly annoyed when I was unable to get parental help with a homework assignment. The night my father tried to help me with an arithmetic exercise, he kept reading the instructions, each time more deliberately, until I pried the textbook out of his hands, saying, "I'll try to figure it out some more by myself."

5   When I reached the third grade, I outgrew such behavior. I became more tactful, careful to keep separate the two very different worlds of my day. But then, with ever-increasing intensity, I devoted myself to my studies. I became bookish, puzzling to all my family. Ambition set me apart. When my brother saw me struggling home with stacks of library books, he would laugh, shouting: "Hey, Four Eyes!" My father opened a closet one day and was startled to find me inside, reading a novel. My mother would find me reading when I was supposed to be asleep or helping around the house or playing outside. In a voice angry or worried or just curious, she'd ask: "What do you see in your books?" It became the family's joke. When I was called and wouldn't reply, someone would say I must be hiding under my bed with a book.

(How did I manage my success?)

What I am about to say to you has taken me more than twenty years to admit: *A primary reason for my success in the classroom was that I couldn't forget that schooling was changing me and separating me from the life I enjoyed before becoming a student.* That simple realization! For years I never spoke to anyone about it. Never mentioned a thing to my family or my teachers or classmates. From a very early age, I understood enough, just enough about my classroom experiences to keep what I knew repressed, hidden beneath layers of embarrassment. Not until my last months as a graduate student, nearly thirty years old, was it possible for me to think much about the reasons for my academic success. Only then. At the end of my schooling, I needed to determine how far I had moved from my past. The adult finally confronted, and now must publicly say, what the child shuddered from knowing and could never admit to himself or to those many faces that smiled at his every success. ("Your parents must be very proud . . .")

I

At the end, in the British Museum (too distracted to finish my dissertation) for weeks I read, speed-read, books by modern educational theorists, only to find infrequent and slight mention of students like me. (Much more is written about the more typical case, the lower-class student who barely is helped by his schooling.) Then one day, leafing through Richard Hoggart's *The Uses of Literacy*, I found, in his description of the scholarship boy, myself. For the first time I realized that there were other students like me, and so I was able to frame the meaning of my academic success, its consequent price—the loss.

Hoggart's description is distinguished, at least initially, by deep understanding. What he grasps very well is that the scholarship boy must move between environments, his home and the classroom, which are at cultural extremes, opposed. With his family, the boy has the intense pleasure of intimacy, the family's consolation in feeling public alienation. Lavish emotions texture home life. *Then,* at school, the instruction bids him to trust lonely reason primarily. Immediate needs set the pace of his parents' lives. From his mother and father the boy learns to trust spontaneity and non-rational ways of knowing. *Then,* at school, there is mental calm. Teachers emphasize the value of a reflectiveness that opens a space between thinking and immediate action.

10   Years of schooling must pass before the boy will be able to sketch the cultural differences in his day as abstractly as this. But he senses those differences early. Perhaps as early as the night he brings home an assignment from school and finds the house too noisy for study.

> He has to be more and more alone, if he is going to "get on." He will have, probably unconsciously, to oppose the ethos of the hearth, the intense gregariousness of the working-class family group. Since everything centres upon the living-room, there is unlikely to be a room of his own; the bedrooms are cold and inhospitable, and to warm them or the front room, if there is one, would not only be expensive, but would require an imaginative leap—out of the tradition—which most families are not capable of making. There is a corner of the living-room table. On the other side Mother is ironing, the wireless is on, someone is singing a snatch of song or Father says intermittently whatever comes into his head. The boy has to cut himself off mentally, so as to do his homework, as well as he can.[1]

The next day, the lesson is as apparent at school. There are even rows of desks. Discussion is ordered. The boy must rehearse his thoughts and raise his hand before speaking out in a loud voice to an audience of classmates. And there is time enough, and silence, to think about ideas (big ideas) never considered at home by his parents.

Not for the working-class child alone is adjustment to the classroom difficult. Good schooling requires that any student alter early childhood habits. But the working-class child is usually least prepared for the change. And, unlike many middle-class children, he goes home and sees in his parents a way of life not only different but starkly opposed to that of the classroom. (He enters the house and hears his parents talking in ways his teachers discourage.)

Without extraordinary determination and the great assistance of others—at home and at school—there is little chance for success. Typically most working-class children are barely changed by the classroom. The exception succeeds. The relative few become scholarship students. Of these, Richard Hoggart estimates, most manage a fairly graceful transition. Somehow they learn to live in the two very different worlds of their day. There are some others, however, those Hoggart pejoratively terms "scholarship boys," for whom success comes with special anxiety. Scholarship boy: good student, troubled son. The child is "moderately endowed," intellectually mediocre, Hoggart supposes—though it may be more pertinent to note the special qualities of temperament in the child. High-strung child. Brooding. Sensitive. Haunted by the knowledge that one *chooses* to become a student. (Education is not an inevitable or natural step in growing up.) Here is a child who cannot forget that his academic success distances him from a life he loved, even from his own memory of himself.

Initially, he wavers, balances allegiance. ("The boy is himself [until he reaches, say, the upper forms] very much of *both* the worlds of home and school. He is enormously obedient to the dictates of the world of school, but emotionally still strongly wants to continue as part of the family circle.") Gradually, necessarily, the balance is lost. The boy needs to spend more and more time studying, each night enclosing himself in the silence permitted and required by intense concentration. He takes his first step toward academic success, away from his family.

From the very first days, through the years following, it will be with his parents—the figures of lost authority, the persons toward whom he feels deepest love—that the change will be most powerfully measured. A separation will unravel between them. Advancing in his studies, the boy notices that his mother and father have not changed as much as he. Rather, when he sees them, they often remind him of the person he once was and the life he earlier shared with them. He realizes what some Romantics also know when they praise the working class for the capacity for human closeness, qualities of passion and spontaneity, that the rest of us experience in like measure only in the earliest part of our youth. For the Romantic, this doesn't make working-class life childish. Working-class life challenges precisely because it is an *adult* way of life.

15   The scholarship boy reaches a different conclusion. He cannot afford to admire his parents. (How could he and still pursue such a contrary life?) He permits himself embarrassment at their lack of education. And to evade nostalgia for the life he has lost, he concentrates on the benefits education will bestow upon him. He becomes especially ambitious. Without the support of old certainties and consolations, almost mechanically, he assumes the procedures and doctrines of the classroom. The kind of allegiance the young student might have given his mother and father only days earlier, he transfers to the teacher, the new figure of authority. "[The scholarship boy] tends to make a father-figure of his form-master," Hoggart observes.

But Hoggart's calm prose only makes me recall the urgency with which I came to idolize my grammar school teachers. I began by imitating their accents, using their diction, trusting their every direction. The very first facts they dispensed, I grasped with awe. Any book they told me to read, I read—then waited for them to tell me which books I enjoyed. Their every casual opinion I came to adopt and to trumpet when I returned home. I stayed after school "to help"— to get my teacher's undivided attention. It was the nun's encouragement that mattered most to me. (She understood exactly what—my parents never seemed to appraise so well—all my achievements entailed.) Memory gently caressed each word of praise bestowed in the classroom so that compliments teachers paid me years ago come quickly to mind even today.

The enthusiasm I felt in second-grade classes I flaunted before both my parents. The docile, obedient student came home a shrill and precocious son who insisted on correcting and teaching his parents with the remark: "My teacher told us . . ."

I intended to hurt my mother and father. I was still angry at them for having encouraged me toward classroom English. But gradually this anger was exhausted, replaced by guilt as school grew more and more attractive to me. I grew increasingly successful, a talkative student. My hand was raised in the classroom; I yearned to answer any question. At home, life was less noisy than it had been. (I spoke to classmates and teachers more often each day than to family members.) Quiet at home, I sat with my papers for hours each night. I never forgot that schooling had irretrievably changed my family's life. That knowledge, however, did not weaken ambition. Instead, it strengthened resolve. Those times I remembered the loss of my past with regret, I quickly reminded myself of all the things my teachers could give me. (They could make me an educated man.) I tightened my grip on pencil and books. I evaded nostalgia. Tried hard to forget. But one does not forget by trying to forget. One only remembers. I remembered too well that education had changed my family's life. I would not have become a scholarship boy had I not so often remembered.

Once she was sure that her children knew English, my mother would tell us, "You should keep up your Spanish." Voices playfully groaned in response. "*¡Pochos!*" my mother would tease. I listened silently.

20   After a while, I grew more calm at home. I developed tact. A fourth-grade student, I was no longer the show-off in front of my parents. I became a conventionally dutiful son, politely affectionate, cheerful enough, even—for reasons beyond choosing—my father's favorite. And much about my family life was easy then, comfortable,

happy in the rhythm of our living together: hearing my father getting ready for work; eating the breakfast my mother had made me; looking up from a novel to hear my brother or one of my sisters playing with friends in the backyard; in winter, coming upon the house all lighted up after dark.

But withheld from my mother and father was any mention of what most mattered to me: the extraordinary experience of first-learning. Late afternoon: in the midst of preparing dinner, my mother would come up behind me while I was trying to read. Her head just over mine, her breath warmly scented with food. "What are you reading?" Or, "Tell me all about your new courses." I would barely respond, "Just the usual things, nothing special." (A half smile, then silence. Her head moving back in the silence. Silence! Instead of the flood of intimate sounds that had once flowed smoothly between us, there was this silence.) After dinner, I would rush to a bedroom with papers and books. As often as possible, I resisted parental pleas to "save lights" by coming to the kitchen to work. I kept so much, so often, to myself. Sad. Enthusiastic. Troubled by the excitement of coming upon new ideas. Eager. Fascinated by the promising texture of a brand-new book. I hoarded the pleasures of learning. Alone for hours. Enthralled. Nervous. I rarely looked away from my books—or back on my memories. Nights when relatives visited and the front rooms were warmed by Spanish sounds, I slipped quietly out of the house.

It mattered that education was changing me. It never ceased to matter. My brother and sisters would giggle at our mother's mispronounced words. They'd correct her gently. My mother laughed girlishly one night, trying not to pronounce *sheep* as *ship*. From a distance I listened sullenly. From that distance, pretending not to notice on another occasion, I saw my father looking at the title pages of my library books. That was the scene on my mind when I walked home with a fourth-grade companion and heard him say that his parents read to him every night. (A strange-sounding book—*Winnie the Pooh*.) Immediately, I wanted to know, "What is it like?" My companion, however, thought I wanted to know about the plot of the book. Another day, my mother surprised me by asking for a "nice" book to read. "Something not too hard you think I might like." Carefully I chose one, Willa Cather's *My Ántonia*. But when, several weeks later, I happened to see it next to her bed unread except for the first few pages, I was furious and suddenly wanted to cry. I grabbed up the book and took it back to my room and placed it in its place, alphabetically on my shelf.

"Your parents must be very proud of you." People began to say that to me about the time I was in sixth grade. To answer affirmatively, I'd smile. Shyly I'd smile, never betraying my sense of the irony: I was not proud of my mother and father. I was embarrassed by their lack of education. It was not that I ever thought they were stupid, though stupidly I took for granted their enormous native intelligence. Simply, what mattered to me was that they were not like my teachers.

But, "Why didn't you tell us about the award?" my mother demanded, her frown weakened by pride. At the grammar school ceremony several weeks after, her eyes were brighter than the trophy I'd won. Pushing back the hair from my forehead, she whispered that I had "shown" the *gringos*. A few minutes later, I heard my father speak to my teacher and felt ashamed of his labored, accented words. Then guilty for the shame. I felt such contrary feelings. (There is no simple road-map through the heart of the scholarship boy.) My teacher was so soft-spoken and her words were edged sharp and clean. I admired her until it seemed to me that she spoke too carefully. Sensing that she was condescending to them, I became nervous. Resentful. Protective. I tried to move my parents away. "You both must be very proud of Richard," the nun said. They responded quickly. (They were proud.) "We are proud of all our children." Then this after-thought: "They sure didn't get their brains from us." They all laughed. I smiled.

25 Tightening the irony into a knot was the knowl-edge that my parents were always behind me. They made success possible. They evened the path. They sent their children to parochial schools because the nuns "teach better." They paid a tuition they couldn't afford. They spoke English to us.

For their children my parents wanted chances they never had—an easier way. It sad-dened my mother to learn that some relatives forced their children to start working right after high school. To *her* children she would say, "Get all the education you can." In schooling she rec-ognized the key to job advancement. And with the remark she remembered her past.

As a girl new to America my mother had been awarded a high school diploma by teachers too careless or busy to notice that she hardly spoke English. On her own, she determined to learn how to type. That skill got her jobs typing envelopes in letter shops, and it encouraged in her an optimism about the possibility of advancement. (Each morning when her sisters put on uniforms, she chose a bright-colored dress.) The years of young womanhood passed, and her typing speed increased. She also became an excellent speller of words she mispronounced. "And I've never been to college," she'd say, smil-ing, when her children asked her to spell words they were too lazy to look up in a dictionary.

Typing, however, was dead-end work. Finally frustrating. When her youngest child started high school, my mother got a full-time office job once again. (Her paycheck combined with my father's to make us—in fact—what we had already become in our imagination of our-selves—middle class.) She worked then for the (California) state government in numbered civil service positions secured by examinations. The old ambition of her youth was rekindled. During the lunch hour, she consulted bulletin boards for announcements of openings. One day she saw mention of something called an "anti-poverty agency." A typing job. A glamorous job, part of the governor's staff. "A knowledge of Spanish required." Without hesitation she applied and became nervous only when the job was sud-denly hers.

"Everyone comes to work all dressed up," she reported at night. And didn't need to say more than that her co-workers wouldn't let her answer the phones. She was only a typist, after all, albeit a very fast typist. And an excellent speller. One morning there was a letter to be sent to a Washington cabinet officer. On the dictating tape, a voice referred to urban guerrillas. My mother typed (the wrong word, correctly): "gorillas." The mistake horrified the anti-poverty bureaucrats who shortly after arranged to have her returned to her previous position. She would go no further. So she willed her ambition to their children. "Get all the education you can; with an education you can do anything." (With a good education *she* could have done anything.)

30 When I was in high school, I admitted to my mother that I planned to become a teacher some-day. That seemed to please her. But I never tried to explain that it was not the occupation of teaching I yearned for as much as it was some-thing more elusive: I wanted to *be* like my teach-ers, to possess their knowledge, to assume their authority, their confidence, even to assume a teacher's persona.

In contrast to my mother, my father never verbally encouraged his children's academic suc-cess. Nor did he often praise us. My mother had to remind him to "say something" to one of his children who scored some academic success. But whereas my mother saw in education the oppor-tunity for job advancement, my father recog-nized that education provided an even more startling possibility: it could enable a person to escape from a life of mere labor.

In Mexico, orphaned when he was eight, my father left school to work as an "apprentice" for an uncle. Twelve years later, he left Mexico in frustration and arrived in America. He had great expectations then of becoming an engineer. ("Work for my hands and my head.") He knew a Catholic priest who promised to get him money enough to study full time for a high school diploma. But the promises came to nothing. Instead there was a dark succession of warehouse, cannery, and factory jobs. After work he went to night school along with my mother. A year, two passed. Nothing much changed, except that fatigue worked its way into the bone; then everything changed. He didn't talk anymore of becoming an engineer. He stayed outside on the steps of the school while my mother went inside to learn typing and shorthand.

By the time I was born, my father worked at "clean" jobs. For a time he was a janitor at a fancy department store. ("Easy work; the machines do it all.") Later he became a dental technician. ("Simple.") But by then he was pessimistic about the ultimate meaning of work and the possibility of ever escaping its claims. In some of my earliest memories of him, my father already seems aged by fatigue. (He has never really grown old like my mother.) From boyhood to manhood, I have remembered him in a single image: seated, asleep on the sofa, his head thrown back in a hideous corpselike grin, the evening newspaper spread out before him. "But look at all you've accomplished," his best friend said to him once. My father said nothing. Only smiled.

It was my father who laughed when I claimed to be tired by reading and writing. It was he who teased me for having soft hands. (He seemed to sense that some great achievement of leisure was implied by my papers and books.) It was my father who became angry while watching on television some woman at the Miss America contest tell the announcer that she was going to college. ("Majoring in fine arts.") "College!" he snarled. He despised the trivialization of higher education, the inflated grades and cheapened diplomas, the half education that so often passed as mass education in my generation.

35   It was my father again who wondered why I didn't display my awards on the wall of my bedroom. He said he liked to go to doctors' offices and see their certificates and degrees on the wall. ("Nice.") My citations from school got left in closets at home. The gleaming figure astride one of my trophies was broken, wingless, after hitting the ground. My medals were placed in a jar of loose change. And when I lost my high school diploma, my father found it as it was about to be thrown out with the trash. Without telling me, he put it away with his own things for safekeeping.

These memories slammed together at the instant of hearing that refrain familiar to all scholarship students: "Your parents must be proud . . ." Yes, my parents were proud. I knew it. But my parents regarded my progress with more than mere pride. They endured my early precocious behavior—but with what private anger and humiliation? As their children got older and would come home to challenge ideas both of them held, they argued before submitting to the force of logic or superior factual evidence with the disclaimer, "It's what we were taught in our time to believe." These discussions ended abruptly, though my mother remembered them on other occasions when she complained that our "big ideas" were going to our heads. More acute was her complaint that the family wasn't close anymore, like some others she knew. Why weren't we close, "more in the Mexican style"? Everyone is so private, she added. And she mimicked the yes and no answers she got in reply to her questions. Why didn't we talk more? (My father never asked.) I never said.

I was the first in my family who asked to leave home when it came time to go to college. I had been admitted to Stanford, one hundred miles away. My departure would only make physically apparent the separation that had occurred long before. But it was going too far. In the months preceding my leaving, I heard the question my mother never asked except indirectly. In the hot kitchen, tired at the end of her workday, she demanded to know, "Why aren't the colleges here in Sacramento good enough for you? They are for your brother and sister." In the middle of a car ride, not turning to face me, she wondered, "Why do you need to go so far away?" Late at night, ironing, she said with disgust, "Why do you have to put us through this big expense? You know your scholarship will never cover it all." But when September came there was a rush to get everything ready. In a bedroom that last night I packed the big brown valise, and my mother sat nearby sewing initials onto the clothes I would take. And she said no more about my leaving.

Months later, two weeks of Christmas vacation: the first hours home were the hardest. ("What's new?") My parents and I sat in the kitchen for a conversation. (But, lacking the same words to develop our sentences and to shape our interests, what was there to say? What could I tell them of the term paper I had just finished on the "universality of Shakespeare's appeal"?) I mentioned only small, obvious things: my dormitory life; weekend trips I had taken; random events. They responded with news of their own. (One was almost grateful for a family crisis about which there was much to discuss.) We tried to make our conversation seem like more than an interview.

II

From an early age I knew that my mother and father could read and write both Spanish and English. I had observed my father making his way through what, I now suppose, must have been income tax forms. On other occasions I waited apprehensively while my mother read onion-paper letters airmailed from Mexico with news of a relative's illness or death. For both my parents, however, reading was something done out of necessity and as quickly as possible. Never did I see either of them read an entire book. Nor did I see them read for pleasure. Their reading consisted of work manuals, prayer books, newspaper, recipes.

40   Richard Hoggart imagines how, at home,

> [the scholarship boy] sees strewn around, and reads regularly himself, magazines which are never mentioned at school, which seem not to belong to the world to which the school introduces him; at school he hears about and reads books never mentioned at home. When he brings those books into the house they do not take their place with other books which the family are reading, for often there are none or almost none; his books look, rather, like strange tools.

In our house each school year would begin with my mother's careful instruction: "Don't write in your books so we can sell them at the end of the year." The remark was echoed in public by my teachers, but only in part: "Boys and girls, don't write in your books. You must learn to treat them with great care and respect."

OPEN THE DOORS OF YOUR MIND WITH BOOKS, read the red and white poster over the nun's desk in early September. It soon was apparent to me that reading was the classroom's central activity. Each course had its own book. And the information gathered from a book was unquestioned. READ TO LEARN, the sign on the wall advised in December. I privately wondered: What was the connection between reading and learning? Did one learn something only by reading it? Was an idea only an idea if it could be written down? In June, CONSIDER BOOKS YOUR BEST FRIENDS, Friends? Reading was, at best, only a chore. I needed to look up whole paragraphs of words in a dictionary. Lines of type were dizzying, the eye having to move slowly across the page, then down, and across . . . The sentences of the first books I read were coolly impersonal. Toned hard. What most bothered me, however, was the isolation reading required. To console myself for the loneliness I'd feel when I read, I tried reading in a very soft voice. Until: "Who is doing all that talking to his neighbor?" Shortly after, remedial reading classes were arranged for me with a very old nun.

At the end of each school day, for nearly six months, I would meet with her in the tiny room that served as the school's library but was actually only a storeroom for used textbooks and a vast collection of *National Geographics.* Everything about our sessions pleased me: the smallness of the room; the noise of the janitor's broom hitting the edge of the long hallway outside the door; the green of the sun, lighting the wall; and the old woman's face blurred white with a beard. Most of the time we took turns. I began with my elementary text. Sentences of astonishing simplicity seemed to me lifeless and drab: "The boys ran from the rain . . . She wanted to sing . . . The kite rose in the blue." Then the old nun would read from her favorite books, usually biographies of early American presidents. Playfully she ran through complex sentences, calling the words alive with her voice, making it seem that the author somehow was speaking directly to me. I smiled just to listen to her. I sat there and sensed for the very first time some possibility of fellowship between a reader and a writer, a communication, never *intimate* like that I heard spoken words at home convey, but one nonetheless *personal.*

One day the nun concluded a session by asking me why I was so reluctant to read by myself. I tried to explain; said something about the way written words made me feel all alone—almost, I wanted to add but didn't, as when I spoke to myself in a room just emptied of furniture. She studied my face as I spoke; she seemed to be watching more than listening. In an uneventful voice she replied that I had nothing to fear. Didn't I realize that reading would open up whole new worlds? A book could open doors for me. It could introduce me to people and show me places I never imagined existed. She gestured toward the bookshelves. (Bare-breasted African women danced, and the shiny hubcaps of automobiles on the back covers of the *Geographic* gleamed in my mind.) I listened with respect. But her words were not very influential. I was thinking then of another consequence of literacy, one I was too shy to admit but nonetheless trusted. Books were going to make me "educated." *That* confidence enabled me, several months later, to overcome my fear of the silence.

In fourth grade I embarked upon a grandiose reading program. "Give me the names of important books," I would say to startled teachers. They soon found out that I had in mind "adult books." I ignored their suggestion of anything I suspected was written for children. (Not until I was in college, as a result, did I read *Huckleberry Finn* or *Alice's Adventures in Wonderland.)* Instead, I read *The Scarlet Letter* and Franklin's *Autobiography.* And whatever I read I read for extra credit. Each time I finished a book, I reported the achievement to a teacher and basked in the praise my effort earned. Despite my best efforts, however, there seemed to be more and more books I needed to read. At the library I would literally tremble as I came upon whole shelves of books I hadn't read. So I read and I read and I read: *Great Expectations;* all the short stories of Kipling; *The Babe Ruth Story;* the entire first volume of the *Encyclopedia Britannica* (A-ANSTEY); the *Iliad; Moby Dick; Gone with the Wind; The Good Earth; Ramona; Forever Amber; The Lives of the Saints; Crime and Punishment; The Pearl* . . . Librarians who initially frowned when I checked out the maximum ten books at a time started saving books they thought I might like. Teachers would say to the rest of the class, "I only wish the rest of you took reading as seriously as Richard obviously does."

45   But at home I would hear my mother wondering, "What do you see in your books?" (Was reading a hobby like her knitting? Was so much reading even healthy for a boy? Was it the sign of "brains"? Or was it just a convenient excuse for not helping about the house on Saturday mornings?) Always, "What do you see. . . ?"

What *did* I see in my books? I had the idea that they were crucial for my academic success, though I couldn't have said exactly how or why. In the sixth grade I simply concluded that what gave a book its value was some major idea or theme it contained. If that core essence could be mined and memorized, I would become learned like my teachers. I decided to record in a notebook the themes of the books that I read. After reading *Robinson Crusoe,* I wrote that its theme was "the value of learning to live by oneself." When I completed *Wuthering Heights,* I noted the danger of "letting emotions get out of control." Rereading these brief moralistic appraisals usually left me disheartened. I couldn't believe that they were really the source of reading's value. But for many more years, they constituted the only means I had of describing to myself the educational value of books.

In spite of my earnestness, I found reading a pleasurable activity. I came to enjoy the lonely good company of books. Early on weekday mornings, I'd read in my bed. I'd feel a mysterious comfort then, reading in the dawn quiet—the blue-gray silence interrupted by the occasional churning of the refrigerator motor a few rooms away or the more distant sounds of a city bus beginning its run. On weekends I'd go to the public library to read, surrounded by old men and women. Or, if the weather was fine, I would take my books to the park and read in the shade of a tree. A warm summer evening was my favorite reading time. Neighbors would leave for vacation and I would water their lawns. I would sit through the twilight on the front porches or in backyards, reading to the cool, whirling sounds of the sprinklers.

I also had favorite writers. But often those writers I enjoyed most I was least able to value. When I read William Saroyan's *The Human Comedy,* I was immediately pleased by the narrator's warmth and the charm of his story. But as quickly I became suspicious. A book so enjoyable to read couldn't be very "important." Another summer I determined to read all the novels of Dickens. Reading his fat novels, I loved the feeling I got—after the first hundred pages—of being at home in a fictional world where I knew the names of the characters and cared about what was going to happen to them. And it

bothered me that I was forced away at the conclusion, when the fiction closed tight, like a fortune-teller's fist—the futures of all the major characters neatly resolved. I never knew how to take such feelings seriously, however. Nor did I suspect that these experiences could be part of a novel's meaning. Still, there were pleasures to sustain me after I'd finish my books. Carrying a volume back to the library, I would be pleased by its weight. I'd run my fingers along the edge of the pages and marvel at the breadth of my achievement. Around my room, growing stacks of paperback books reenforced my assurance.

I entered high school having read hundreds of books. My habit of reading made me a confident speaker and writer of English. Reading also enabled me to sense something of the shape, the major concerns, of Western thought. (I was able to say something about Dante and Descartes and Engels and James Baldwin in my high school term papers.) In these various ways, books brought me academic success as I hoped that they would. But I was not a good reader. Merely bookish, I lacked a point of view when I read. Rather, I read in order to acquire a point of view. I vacuumed books for epigrams, scraps of information, ideas, themes—anything to fill the hollow within me and make me feel educated. When one of my teachers suggested to his drowsy tenth-grade English class that a person could not have a "complicated idea" until he had read at least two thousand books, I heard the remark without detecting either its irony or its very complicated truth. I merely determined to compile a list of all the books I had ever read. Harsh with myself, I included only once a title I might have read several times. (How, after all, could one read a book more than once?) And I included only those books over a hundred pages in length. (Could anything shorter be a book?)

50   There was yet another high school list I compiled. One day I came across a newspaper article about the retirement of an English professor at a nearby state college. The article was accompanied by a list of the "hundred most important

books of Western Civilization." "More than any-thing else in my life," the professor told the reporter with finality, "these books have made me all that I am." That was the kind of remark I couldn't ignore. I clipped out the list and kept it for the several months it took me to read all of the titles. Most books, of course, I barely understood. While reading Plato's *Republic,* for instance, I needed to keep looking at the book jacket comments to remind myself what the text was about. Nevertheless, with the special patience and superstition of a scholarship boy, I looked at every word of the text. And by the time I reached the last word, relieved, I convinced myself that I had read *The Republic.* In a cere-mony of great pride, I solemnly crossed Plato off my list.

III

The scholarship boy pleases most when he is young—the working-class child struggling for academic success. To his teachers, he offers great satisfaction; his success is their proudest achievement. Many other persons offer to help him. A businessman learns the boy's story and promises to underwrite part of the cost of his col-lege education. A woman leaves him her entire library of several hundred books when she moves. His progress is featured in a newspaper article. Many people seem happy for him. They marvel. "How did you manage so fast?" From all sides, there is lavish praise and encouragement.

In his grammar school classroom, however, the boy already makes students around him uneasy. They scorn his desire to succeed. They scorn him for constantly wanting the teacher's attention and praise. "Kiss Ass," they call him when his hand swings up in response to every question he hears. Later, when he makes it to college, no one will mock him aloud. But he detects annoyance on the faces of some students and even some teachers who watch him. It puz-zles him often. In college, then in graduate school, he behaves much as he always has. If anything is different about him it is that he dares

to anticipate the successful conclusion of his studies. At last he feels that he belongs in the classroom, and this is exactly the source of the dissatisfaction he causes. To many persons around him, he appears too much the academic. There may be some things about him that recall his beginnings—his shabby clothes; his persist-ent poverty; or his dark skin (in those cases when it symbolizes his parents' disadvantaged condition)—but they only make clear how far he has moved from his past. He has used education to remake himself.

It bothers his fellow academics to face this. They will not say why exactly. (They sneer.) But their expectations become obvious when they are disappointed. They expect—they want—a student less changed by his schooling. If the scholarship boy, from past so distant from the classroom, could remain in some basic way unchanged, he would be able to prove that it is possible for anyone to become educated without basically changing from the person one was.

Here is no fabulous hero, no idealized scholar-worker. The scholarship boy does not straddle, can-not reconcile, the two great opposing cultures of his life. His success is unromantic and plain. He sits in the classroom and offers those sitting beside him no calming reassurance about their own lives. He sits in the seminar room—a man with brown skin, the son of working-class Mexican immigrant par-ents. (Addressing the professor at the head of the table, his voice catches with nervousness.) There is no trace of his parents' in his speech. Instead he approximates the accents of teachers and class-mates. Coming from *him* those sounds seem sud-denly odd. Odd too is the effect produced when *he* uses academic jargon—bubbles at the tip of his tongue: "Topos . . . negative capability . . .vegeta-tion imagery in Shakespearean comedy." He lifts an opinion from Coleridge, takes something else from Frye or Empson or Leavis. He even repeats exactly his professor's earlier comment. All his ideas are clearly borrowed. He seems to have no thought of his own. He chatters while his listeners smile—their look one of disdain.

55   When he is older and thus when so little of the person he was survives, the scholarship boy makes only too apparent his profound lack of *self*-confidence. This is the conventional assessment that even Richard Hoggart repeats:

> [The scholarship boy] tends to over-stress the importance of examinations, of the piling-up of knowledge and of received opinions. He discovers a technique of apparent learning, of the acquiring of facts rather than of the handling and use of facts. He learns how to receive a purely literate education, one using only a small part of the personality and challenging only a limited area of his being. He begins to see life as a ladder, as permanent examination with some praise and some further exhortation at each stage. He becomes an expert imbiber and doler-out; his competence will vary, but will rarely be accompanied by genuine enthusiasms. He rarely feels the reality of knowledge, of other men's thoughts and imaginings, on his own pulses . . . He has something of the blinkered pony about him. . . .

But this is criticism more accurate than fair. The scholarship boy is a very bad student. He is the great mimic; a collector of thoughts, not a thinker; the very last person in class who ever feels obliged to have an opinion of his own. In large part, however, the reason he is such a bad student is because he realizes more often and more acutely than most other students—than Hoggart himself—that education requires radical self-reformation. As a very young boy, regarding his parents, as he struggles with an early homework assignment, he knows this too well. That is why he lacks self-assurance. He does not forget that the classroom is responsible for remaking him. He relies on his teacher, depends on all that he hears in the classroom and reads in his books. He becomes in every obvious way the worst student, a dummy mouthing the opinions of others. But he would not be so bad—nor would he become so successful, a *scholarship* boy—if he did not accurately perceive that the best synonym for primary "education" is "imitation."

Those who would take seriously the boy's success—and his failure—would be forced to realize how great is the change any academic undergoes, how far one must move from one's past. It is easiest to ignore such considerations. So little is said about the scholarship boy in pages and pages of educational literature. Nothing is said of the silence that comes to separate the boy from his parents. Instead, one hears proposals for increasing the self-esteem of students and encouraging early intellectual independence. Paragraphs glitter with a constellation of terms like *creativity* and *originality*. (Ignored altogether is the function of imitation in a student's life.) Radical educationalists meanwhile complain that ghetto schools "oppress" students by trying to mold them, stifling native characteristics. The truer critique would be just the reverse: not that schools change ghetto students too much, but that while they might promote the occasional scholarship student, they change most students barely at all.

From the story of the scholarship boy there is no specific pedagogy to glean. There is, however, a much larger lesson. His story makes clear that education is a long, unglamorous, even demeaning process—*a nurturing never natural to the person one was before one entered a classroom.* At once different from most other students, the scholarship boy is also the archetypal "good student." He exaggerates the difficulty of being a student, but his exaggeration reveals a general predicament. Others are changed by their schooling as much as he. They too must reform themselves. They must develop the skill of memory long before they become truly critical thinkers. And when they read Plato for the first several times, it will be with awe more than deep comprehension.

The impact of schooling on the scholarship boy is only more apparent to the boy himself and to others. Finally, although he may be laughable—a blinkered pony—the boy will not let his critics forget their own change. He ends up too much like them. When he speaks, they hear themselves echoed. In his pedantry, they trace their own. His ambitions are theirs. If his failure were singular, they might readily pity him. But he is more troubling than that. They would not scorn him if this were not so.

IV

Like me, Hoggart's imagined scholarship boy spends most of his years in the classroom afraid to long for his past. Only at the very end of his schooling does the boy-man become nostalgic. In this sudden change of heart, Richard Hoggart notes:

> He longs for the membership he lost, "he pines for some Nameless Eden where he never was." The nostalgia is the stronger and the more ambiguous because he is really "in quest of his own absconded self yet scared to find it." He both wants to go back and yet thinks he has gone beyond his class, feels himself weighted with knowledge of his own and their situation, which hereafter forbids him the simpler pleasures of his father and mother. . . .

According to Hoggart, the scholarship boy grows nostalgic because he remains the uncertain scholar, bright enough to have moved from his past, yet unable to feel easy, a part of a community of academics.

60   This analysis, however, only partially suggests what happened to me in my last year as a graduate student. When I traveled to London to write a dissertation on English Renaissance literature, I was finally confident of membership in a "community of scholars." But the pleasure that confidence gave me faded rapidly. After only two or three months in the reading room of the British Museum, it became clear that I had joined a lonely community. Around me each day were dour faces eclipsed by large piles of books. There were the regulars, like the old couple who arrived every morning, each holding a loop of the shopping bag which contained all their notes. And there was the historian who chattered madly to herself. ("Oh dear! Oh! Now, what's this? What? Oh, my!") There were also

the faces of young men and women worn by long study. And everywhere eyes turned away the moment our glance accidentally met. Some persons I sat beside day after day, yet we passed silently at the end of the day, strangers. Still, we were united by a common respect for the written word and for scholarship. We did form a union, though one in which we remained distant from one another.

More profound and unsettling was the bond I recognized with those writers whose books I consulted. Whenever I opened a text that hadn't been used for years, I realized that my special interests and skills united me to a mere handful of academics. We formed an exclusively— eccentric!—society, separated from others who would never care or be able to share our concerns. (The pages I turned were stiff like layers of dead skin.) I began to wonder: Who, beside my dissertation director and a few faculty members, would ever read what I wrote? And: Was my dissertation much more than an act of social withdrawal? These questions went unanswered in the silence of the Museum reading room. They remained to trouble me after I'd leave the library each afternoon and feel myself shy—unsteady, speaking simple sentences at the grocer's or the butcher's on my way back to my bed-sitter.

Meanwhile my file cards accumulated. A professional, I knew exactly how to search a book for pertinent information. I could quickly assess and summarize the usability of the many books I consulted. But whenever I started to write, I knew too much (and not enough) to be able to write anything but sentences that were overly cautious, timid, strained brittle under the heavy weight of footnotes and qualifications. I seemed unable to dare a passionate statement. I felt drawn by professionalism to the edge of sterility, capable of no more than pedantic, lifeless, unassailable prose.

Then nostalgia began.

After years spent unwilling to admit its attractions, I gestured nostalgically toward the past. I yearned for that time when I had not been so alone. I became impatient with books. I wanted experience more immediate. I feared the library's silence. I silently scorned the gray, timid faces around me. I grew to hate the growing pages of my dissertation on genre and Renaissance literature. (In my mind I heard relatives laughing as they tried to make sense of its title.) I wanted something—I couldn't say exactly what. I told myself that I wanted a more passionate life. And a life less thoughtful. And above all, I wanted to be less alone. One day I heard some Spanish academics whispering back and forth to each other, and their sounds seemed ghostly voices recalling my life. Yearning became preoccupation then. Boyhood memories beckoned, flooded my mind. (Laughing intimate voices. Bounding up the front steps of the porch. A sudden embrace inside the door.)

65   For weeks after, I turned to books by educational experts. I needed to learn how far I had moved from my past—to determine how fast I would be able to recover something of it once again. But I found little. Only a chapter in a book by Richard Hoggart. . . . I left the reading room and the circle of faces.

I came home. After the year in England, I spent three summer months living with my mother and father, relieved by how easy it was to be home. It no longer seemed very important to me that we had little to say. I felt easy sitting and eating and walking with them. I watched them, nevertheless, looking for evidence of those elastic, sturdy strands that bind generations in a web of inheritance. I thought as I watched my mother one night: of course a friend had been right when she told me that I gestured and laughed just like my mother. Another time I saw for myself: my father's eyes were much like my own, constantly watchful.

But after the early relief, this return, came suspicion, nagging until I realized that I had not neatly sidestepped the impact of schooling. My desire to do so was precisely the measure of how much I remained an academic. *Negatively* (for that is how this idea first occurred to me):

my need to think so much and so abstractly about my parents and our relationship was in itself an indication of my long education. My father and mother did not pass their time thinking about the cultural meanings of their experience. It was I who described their daily lives with airy ideas. And yet, *positively:* the ability to consider experience so abstractly allowed me to shape into desire what would otherwise have remained indefinite, meaningless longing in the British Museum. If, because of my schooling, I had grown culturally separated from my parents, my education finally had given me ways of speaking and caring about that fact.

My best teachers in college and graduate school, years before, had tried to prepare me for this conclusion, I think, when they discussed texts of aristocratic pastoral literature. Faithfully, I wrote down all that they said. I memorized it: "The praise of the unlettered by the highly educated is one of the primary themes of 'elitist' literature." But, "the importance of the praise given the unsolitary, richly passionate and spontaneous life is that it simultaneously reflects the value of a reflective life." I heard it all. But there was no way for any of it to mean very much to me. I was a scholarship boy at the time, busily laddering my way up the rungs of education. To pass an examination, I copied down exactly what my teachers told me. It would require many more years of schooling (an inevitable miseducation) in which I came to trust the silence of reading and the habit of abstracting from immediate experience—moving away from a life of closeness and immediacy I remembered with my parents, growing older—before I turned unafraid to desire the past, and thereby achieved what had eluded me for so long—the end of education.

NOTE

1. All quotations in this essay are from Richard Hoggart, *The Uses of Literacy* (London: Chatto and Windus, 1957), chapter 10. [Author's note]

EXPLORATORY WRITING

Much of this essay concerns the tension Rodriguez experiences between home and school. How, exactly, does he develop this conflict? How does he draw on Richard Hoggart's thoughts about the "scholarship boy" to deal with this conflict? What vantage point does Hoggart offer that Rodriguez finds clarifying? What does this perspective enable Rodriguez to see in his own experience?

TALKING ABOUT THE READING

In a class discussion, consider the "end of education" as Rodriguez poses it in the final words of the essay. Examine how Rodriquez gets to this final point. What are the steps he takes and the explanations he offers?

WRITING ASSIGNMENT

Rodriguez wants readers to understand his story as not simply personal but as one that has a more general applicability. Write an essay that draws on an experience in your life that is similar in some sense to the tensions Rodriguez feels between home, school, and the wider world. Set up your essay by explaining Rodriguez's situation and how he resolves it. Your situation will be different, of course. Your task is to use Rodriguez's approach—his way of posing questions about home and school—to analyze your own experience.

FROM SILENCE TO WORDS: WRITING AS STRUGGLE

▰▬ *Min-Zhan Lu*

Min-Zhan Lu teaches English at the University of Louisville. She has written many important articles about literacy and the teaching of writing as well as a memoir, *Shanghai Quartet* (2001). The article included here, "From Silence to Words: Writing as Struggle," appeared in the journal *College English* in 1987.

SUGGESTION FOR READING Like Richard Rodriguez in "The Achievement of Desire," Min-Zhan Lu uses autobiography to raise larger issues about the possible tensions between "home" and "school" languages. In a large part of the selection, Lu tells the story of her experience growing up in China. Sometimes, though, she steps back to make sense of what happened. As you read, note those passages where Lu explains what she sees as the significance of her struggle with writing.

Imagine that you enter a parlor. You come late. When you arrive, others have long preceded you, and they are engaged in a heated discussion. . . .You listen for a while, until you decide that you have caught the tenor of the argument; then you put in your oar. Someone answers; you answer him; another comes to your defense; another aligns himself against you, to either the embarrassment or gratification of your opponent, depending upon the quality of your ally's assistance. However, the discussion is interminable. The hour grows late, you must depart. And you do depart, with the discussion still vigorously in progress.

—*Kenneth Burke*, The Philosophy of Literary Form

Men are not built in silence, but in word, in
work, in action-reflection.

—*Paulo Freire,* Pedagogy of the Oppressed

1   My mother withdrew into silence two months
before she died. A few nights before she fell
silent, she told me she regretted the way she had
raised me and my sisters. I knew she was referring to the way we had been brought up in the
midst of two conflicting worlds—the world of
home, dominated by the ideology of the Western
humanistic tradition, and the world of a society
dominated by Mao Tse-tung's Marxism. My
mother had devoted her life to our education, an
education she knew had made us suffer political
persecution during the Cultural Revolution. I
wanted to find a way to convince her that, in
spite of the persecution, I had benefited from the
education she had worked so hard to give me.
But I was silent. My understanding of my education was so dominated by memories of confusion and frustration that I was unable to reflect
on what I could have gained from it.

This paper is my attempt to fill up that
silence with words, words I didn't have then,
words that I have since come to by reflecting on
my earlier experience as a student in China and
on my recent experience as a composition
teacher in the United States. For in spite of the
frustration and confusion I experienced growing
up caught between two conflicting worlds, the
conflict ultimately helped me to grow as a reader
and writer. Constantly having to switch back and
forth between the discourse of home and that of
school made me sensitive and self-conscious
about the struggle I experienced every time I
tried to read, write, or think in either discourse.
Eventually, it led me to search for constructive
uses for such struggle.

From early childhood, I had identified the
differences between home and the outside world
by the different languages I used in each. My
parents had wanted my sisters and me to get the
best education they could conceive of—
Cambridge. They had hired a live-in tutor, a Scot,

to make us bilingual. I learned to speak English
with my parents, my tutor, and my sisters. I was
allowed to speak Shanghai dialect only with the
servants. When I was four (the year after the
Communist Revolution of 1949), my parents sent
me to a local private school where I learned to
speak, read, and write in a new language—
Standard Chinese, the official written language
of New China.

In those days I moved from home to school,
from English to Standard Chinese to Shanghai
dialect, with no apparent friction. I spoke each
language with those who spoke the language. All
seemed quite "natural"—servants spoke only
Shanghai dialect because they were servants;
teachers spoke Standard Chinese because they
were teachers; languages had different words
because they were different languages. I thought
of English as my family language, comparable to
the many strange dialects I didn't speak but had
often heard some of my classmates speak with
their families. While I was happy to have a special family language, until second grade I didn't
feel that my family language was any different
than some of my classmates' family dialects.

5   My second grade homeroom teacher was a
young graduate from a missionary school. When
she found out I spoke English, she began to practice her English on me. One day she used English
when asking me to run an errand for her. As I
turned to close the door behind me, I noticed the
puzzled faces of my classmates. I had the same
sensation I had often experienced when some
stranger in a crowd would turn on hearing me
speak English. I was more intensely pleased on
this occasion, however, because suddenly I felt
that my family language had been singled out
from the family languages of my classmates. Since
we were not allowed to speak any dialect other
than Standard Chinese in the classroom, having
my teacher speak English to me in class made
English an official language of the classroom. I
began to take pride in my ability to speak it.

This incident confirmed in my mind what my
parents had always told me about the importance

of English to one's life. Time and again they had told me of how my paternal grandfather, who was well versed in classic Chinese, kept losing good-paying jobs because he couldn't speak English. My grandmother reminisced constantly about how she had slaved and saved to send my father to a first-rate missionary school. And we were made to understand that it was my father's fluent English that had opened the door to his success. Even though my family had always stressed the importance of English for my future, I used to complain bitterly about the extra English lessons we had to take after school. It was only after my homeroom teacher had "sanctified" English that I began to connect English with my education. I became a much more eager student in my tutorials.

What I learned from my tutorials seemed to enhance and reinforce what I was learning in my classroom. In those days each word had one meaning. One day I would be making a sentence at school: "The national flag of China is red." The next day I would recite at home, "My love is like a red, red rose." There seemed to be an agreement between the Chinese "red" and the English "red," and both corresponded to the patch of color printed next to the word. "Love" was my love for my mother at home and my love for my "motherland" at school; both "loves" meant how I felt about my mother. Having two loads of homework forced me to develop a quick memory for words and a sensitivity to form and style. What I learned in one language carried over to the other. I made sentences such as, "I saw a red, red rose among the green leaves," with both the English lyric and the classic Chinese lyric—red flower among green leaves—running through my mind, and I was praised by both teacher and tutor for being a good student.

Although my elementary schooling took place during the fifties, I was almost oblivious to the great political and social changes happening around me. Years later, I read in my history and political philosophy textbooks that the fifties were a time when "China was making a transition from a semi-feudal, semi-capitalist, and semi-colonial country into a socialist country," a period in which "the Proletarians were breaking into the educational territory dominated by Bourgeois Intellectuals." While people all over the country were being officially classified into Proletarians, Petty-bourgeois, National-bourgeois, Poor-peasants, and Intellectuals, and were trying to adjust to their new social identities, my parents were allowed to continue the upper middle-class life they had established before the 1949 Revolution because of my father's affiliation with British firms. I had always felt that my family was different from the families of my classmates, but I didn't perceive society's view of my family until the summer vacation before I entered high school.

First, my aunt was caught by her colleagues talking to her husband over the phone in English. Because of it, she was criticized and almost labeled a Rightist. (This was the year of the Anti-Rightist movement, a movement in which the Intellectuals became the target of the "socialist class-struggle.") I had heard others telling my mother that she was foolish to teach us English when Russian had replaced English as the "official" foreign language. I had also learned at school that the American and British Imperialists were the arch-enemies of New China. Yet I had made no connection between the arch-enemies and the English our family spoke. What happened to my aunt forced the connection on me. I began to see my parents' choice of a family language as an anti-Revolutionary act and was alarmed that I had participated in such an act. From then on, I took care not to use English outside home and to conceal my knowledge of English from my new classmates.

10   Certain words began to play important roles in my new life at the junior high. On the first day of school, we were handed forms to fill out with our parents' class, job, and income. Being one of the few people not employed by the government, my father had never been officially classified. Since he was a medical doctor, he told me to put

him down as an Intellectual. My homeroom teacher called me into the office a couple of days afterwards and told me that my father couldn't be an Intellectual if his income far exceeded that of a Capitalist. He also told me that since my father worked for Foreign Imperialists, my father should be classified as an Imperialist Lackey. The teacher looked nonplussed when I told him that my father couldn't be an Imperialist Lackey because he was a medical doctor. But I could tell from the way he took notes on my form that my father's job had put me in an unfavorable position in his eyes.

The Standard Chinese term "class" was not a new word for me. Since first grade, I had been taught sentences such as, "The Working class are the masters of New China." I had always known that it was good to be a worker, but until then, I had never felt threatened for not being one. That fall, "class" began to take on a new meaning for me. I noticed a group of Working-class students and teachers at school. I was made to understand that because of my class background, I was excluded from that group.

Another word that became important was "consciousness." One of the slogans posted in the school building read, "Turn our students into future Proletarians with socialist consciousness and education!" For several weeks we studied this slogan in our political philosophy course, a subject I had never had in elementary school. I still remember the definition of "socialist consciousness" that we were repeatedly tested on through the years: "Socialist consciousness is a person's political soul. It is the consciousness of the Proletarians represented by Marxist Mao Tse-tung's thought. It takes expression in one's action, language, and lifestyle. It is the task of every Chinese student to grow up into a Proletarian with a socialist consciousness so that he can serve the people and the motherland." To make the abstract concept accessible to us, our teacher pointed out that the immediate task for students from Working-class families was to strengthen their socialist consciousnesses. For

those of us who were from other class backgrounds, the task was to turn ourselves into Workers with socialist consciousnesses. The teacher never explained exactly how we were supposed to "turn" into Workers. Instead, we were given samples of the ritualistic annual plans we had to write at the beginning of each term. In these plans, we performed "self-criticism" on our consciousnesses and made vows to turn ourselves into Workers with socialist consciousnesses. The teacher's division between those who did and those who didn't have a socialist consciousness led me to reify the notion of "consciousness" into a thing one possesses. I equated this intangible "thing" with a concrete way of dressing, speaking, and writing. For instance, I never doubted that my political philosophy teacher had a socialist consciousness because she was from a steelworker's family (she announced this the first day of class) and was a Party member who wore grey cadre suits and talked like a philosophy textbook. I noticed other things about her. She had beautiful eyes and spoke Standard Chinese with such a pure accent that I thought she should be a film star. But I was embarrassed that I had noticed things that ought not to have been associated with her. I blamed my observation on my Bourgeois consciousness.

At the same time, the way reading and writing were taught through memorization and imitation also encouraged me to reduce concepts and ideas to simple definitions. In literature and political philosophy classes, we were taught a large number of quotations from Marx, Lenin, and Mao Tse-tung. Each concept that appeared in these quotations came with a definition. We were required to memorize the definitions of the words along with the quotations. Every time I memorized a definition, I felt I had learned a word: "The national red flag symbolizes the blood shed by Revolutionary ancestors for our socialist cause"; "New China rises like a red sun over the eastern horizon." As I memorized these sentences, I reduced their metaphors to dictionary meanings: "red" meant "Revolution" and "red sun" meant "New China" in the "language" of the Working class. I learned mechanically but eagerly. I soon became quite fluent in this new language.

As school began to define me as a political subject, my parents tried to build up my resistance to the "communist poisoning" by exposing me to the "great books"—novels by Charles Dickens, Nathaniel Hawthorne, Emily Brontë, Jane Austen, and writers from around the turn of the century. My parents implied that these writers represented how I, their child, should read and write. My parents replaced the word "Bourgeois" with the word "cultured." They reminded me that I was in school only to learn math and science. I needed to pass the other courses to stay in school, but I was not to let the "Red doctrines" corrupt my mind. Gone were the days when I could innocently write, "I saw the red, red rose among the green leaves," collapsing, as I did, English and Chinese cultural traditions. "Red" came to mean Revolution at school, "the Commies" at home, and adultery in *The Scarlet Letter*. Since I took these symbols and metaphors as meanings natural to people of the same class, I abandoned my earlier definitions of English and Standard Chinese as the language of home and the language of school. I now defined English as the language of the Bourgeois and Standard Chinese as the language of the Working class. I thought of the language of the Working class as someone else's language and the language of the Bourgeois as my language. But I also believed that, although the language of the Bourgeois was my real language, I could and would adopt the language of the Working class when I was at school. I began to put on and take off my Working class language in the same way I put on and took off my school clothes to avoid being criticized for wearing Bourgeois clothes.

15 In my literature classes, I learned the Working-class formula for reading. Each work in the textbook had a short "Author's Biography": "X X X, born in 19- in the province of X X, is from a Worker's family. He joined the Revolution in 19-. He is a Revolutionary realist with a passionate love for the Party and Chinese Revolution. His work expresses the thoughts and emotions of the masses and sings praise to the prosperous socialist construction on all fronts of China." The teacher used the "Author's Biography" as a yardstick to measure the texts. We were taught to locate details in the texts that illustrated these summaries, such as words that expressed Workers' thoughts and emotions or events that illustrated the Workers' lives.

I learned a formula for Working-class writing in the composition classes. We were given sample essays and told to imitate them. The theme was always about how the collective taught the individual a lesson. I would write papers about labor-learning experiences or school-cleaning days, depending on the occasion of the collective activity closest to the assignment. To make each paper look different, I dressed it up with details about the date, the weather, the environment, or the appearance of the Master-worker who had taught me "the lesson." But as I became more and more fluent in the generic voice of the Working-class Student, I also became more and more self-conscious about the language we used at home.

For instance, in senior high we began to have English classes ("to study English for the Revolution," as the slogan on the cover of the textbook said), and I was given my first Chinese–English dictionary. There I discovered the English version of the term "class-struggle." (The Chinese characters for a school "class" and for a social "class" are different.) I had often used the English word "class" at home in sentences such as, "So and so has class," but I had not connected this sense of "class" with "class-struggle." Once the connection was made, I heard a second layer of meaning every time someone at home said a person had "class." The expression began to mean the person had the style and sophistication characteristic of the Bourgeoisie. The word lost its innocence. I was uneasy about hearing that second layer of meaning because I was sure my parents did not hear the word that way. I felt that therefore I should not be hearing it that way either. Hearing the second layer of meaning made me wonder if I was losing my English.

My suspicion deepened when I noticed myself unconsciously merging and switching between the "reading" of home and the "reading" of school. Once I had to write a report on *The Revolutionary Family,* a book about an illiterate woman's awakening and growth as a Revolutionary through the deaths of her husband and all her children for the cause of the Revolution. In one scene the woman deliberated over whether or not she should encourage her youngest son to join the Revolution. Her memory of her husband's death made her afraid to encourage her son. Yet she also remembered her earlier married life and the first time her husband tried to explain the meaning of the Revolution to her. These memories made her feel she should encourage her son to continue the cause his father had begun.

I was moved by this scene. "Moved" was a word my mother and sisters used a lot when we discussed books. Our favorite moments in novels were moments of what I would now call internal conflict, moments which we said "moved" us. I remember that we were "moved" by Jane Eyre when she was torn between her sense of ethics, which compelled her to leave the man she loved, and her impulse to stay with the only man who had ever loved her. We were also moved by Agnes in *David Copperfield* because of the way she restrained her love for David so that he could live happily with the woman he loved. My standard method of doing a book report was to model it on the review by the Publishing Bureau and to dress it up with detailed quotations from the book. The review of *The Revolutionary Family* emphasized the woman's Revolutionary spirit. I decided to use the scene that had moved me to illustrate this point. I wrote the report the night before it was due.

When I had finished, I realized I couldn't possibly hand it in. Instead of illustrating her Revolutionary spirit, I had dwelled on her internal conflict, which could be seen as a moment of weak sentimentality that I should never have emphasized in a Revolutionary heroine. I wrote another report, taking care to illustrate the grandeur of her Revolutionary spirit by expanding on a quotation in which she decided that if the life of her son could change the lives of millions of sons, she should not begrudge his life for the cause of Revolution. I handed in my second version but kept the first in my desk.

20   I never showed it to anyone. I could never show it to people outside my family, because it had deviated so much from the reading enacted by the jacket review. Neither could I show it to my mother or sisters, because I was ashamed to have been so moved by such a "Revolutionary" book. My parents would have been shocked to learn that I could like such a book in the same way they liked Dickens. Writing this book report increased my fear that I was losing the command over both the "language of home" and the "language of school" that I had worked so hard to gain. I tried to remind myself that, if I could still tell when my reading or writing sounded incorrect, then I had retained my command over both languages. Yet I could no longer be confident of my command over either language because I had discovered that when I was not careful—or even when I was—my reading and writing often surprised me with its impurity. To prevent such impurity, I became very suspicious of my thoughts when I read or wrote. I was always asking myself why I was using this word, how I was using it, always afraid that I wasn't reading or writing correctly. What confused and frustrated me most was that I could not figure out why I was no longer able to read or write correctly without such painful deliberation.

I continued to read only because reading allowed me to keep my thoughts and confusion private. I hoped that somehow, if I watched myself carefully, I would figure out from the way

I read whether I had really mastered the "languages." But writing became a dreadful chore. When I tried to keep a diary, I was so afraid that the voice of school might slip in that I could only list my daily activities. When I wrote for school, I worried that my Bourgeois sensibilities would betray me.

The more suspicious I became about the way I read and wrote, the more guilty I felt for losing the spontaneity with which I had learned to "use" these "languages." Writing the book report made me feel that my reading and writing in the "language" of either home or school could not be free of the interference of the other. But I was unable to acknowledge, grasp, or grapple with what I was experiencing, for both my parents and my teachers had suggested that, if I were a good student, such interference would and should not take place. I assumed that once I had "acquired" a discourse, I could simply switch it on and off every time I read and wrote as I would some electronic tool. Furthermore, I expected my readings and writings to come out in their correct forms whenever I switched the proper discourse on. I still regarded the discourse of home as natural and the discourse of school alien, but I never had doubted before that I could acquire both and switch them on and off according to the occasion.

When my experience in writing conflicted with what I thought should happen when I used each discourse, I rejected my experience because it contradicted what my parents and teachers had taught me. I shied away from writing to avoid what I assumed I should not experience. But trying to avoid what should not happen did not keep it from recurring whenever I had to write. Eventually my confusion and frustration over these recurring experiences compelled me to search for an explanation: how and why had I failed to learn what my parents and teachers had worked so hard to teach me?

I now think of the internal scene for my reading and writing about *The Revolutionary Family* as a heated discussion between myself,

the voices of home, and those of school. The review on the back of the book, the sample student papers I came across in my composition classes, my philosophy teacher—these I heard as voices of one group. My parents and my home readings were the voices of an opposing group. But the conversation between these opposing voices in the internal scene of my writing was not as polite and respectful as the parlor scene Kenneth Burke has portrayed (see epigraph). Rather, these voices struggled to dominate the discussion, constantly incorporating, dismissing, or suppressing the arguments of each other, like the battles between the hegemonic and counter-hegemonic forces described in Raymond Williams's *Marxism and Literature* (108–14).

25   When I read *The Revolutionary Family* and wrote the first version of my report, I began with a quotation from the review. The voices of both home and school answered, clamoring to be heard. I tried to listen to one group and turn a deaf ear to the other. Both persisted. I negotiated my way through these conflicting voices, now agreeing with one, now agreeing with the other. I formed a reading out of my interaction with both. Yet I was afraid to have done so because both home and school had implied that I should speak in unison with only one of these groups and stand away from the discussion rather than participate in it.

My teachers and parents had persistently called my attention to the intensity of the discussion taking place on the external social scene. The story of my grandfather's failure and my father's success had from my early childhood made me aware of the conflict between Western and traditional Chinese cultures. My political education at school added another dimension to the conflict: the war of Marxist-Maoism against them both. Yet when my parents and teachers called my attention to the conflict, they stressed the anxiety of having to live through China's transformation from a semi-feudal, semi-capitalist, and semi-colonial society to a socialist one. Acquiring the discourse of the dominant group was, to them, a means of seeking alliance with that group and thus of surviving the whirlpool of cultural currents around them. As a result, they modeled their pedagogical practices on this utilitarian view of language. Being the eager student, I adopted this view of language as a tool for survival. It came to dominate my understanding of the discussion on the social and historical scene and to restrict my ability to participate in that discussion.

To begin with, the metaphor of language as a tool for survival led me to be passive in my use of discourse, to be a bystander in the discussion. In Burke's "parlor," everyone is involved in the discussion. As it goes on through history, what we call "communal discourses"—arguments specific to particular political, social, economic, ethnic, sexual, and family groups—form, re-form and transform. To use a discourse in such a scene is to participate in the argument and to contribute to the formation of the discourse. But when I was growing up, I could not take on the burden of such an active role in the discussion. For both home and school presented the existent conventions of the discourse each taught me as absolute laws for my action. They turned verbal action into a tool, a set of conventions produced and shaped prior to and outside of my own verbal acts. Because I saw language as a tool, I separated the process of producing the tool from the process of using it. The tool was made by someone else and was then acquired and used by me. How the others made it before I acquired it determined and guaranteed what it produced when I used it. I imagined that the more experienced and powerful members of the community were the ones responsible for making the tool. They were the ones who participated in the discussion and fought with opponents. When I used what they made, their labor and accomplishments would ensure the quality of my reading and writing. By using it, I could survive the heated discussion. When my immediate experience in writing the book report suggested that knowing the conventions of school did not guarantee the

form and content of my report, when it suggested that I had to write the report with the work and responsibility I had assigned to those who wrote book reviews in the Publishing Bureau, I thought I had lost the tool I had earlier acquired.

Another reason I could not take up an active role in the argument was that my parents and teachers contrived to provide a scene free of conflict for practicing my various languages. It was as if their experience had made them aware of the conflict between their discourse and other discourses and of the struggle involved in reproducing the conventions of any discourse on a scene where more than one discourse exists. They seemed convinced that such conflict and struggle would overwhelm someone still learning the discourse. Home and school each contrived a purified space where only one discourse was spoken and heard. In their choice of textbooks, in the way they spoke, and in the way they required me to speak, each jealously silenced any voice that threatened to break the unison of the scene. The homogeneity of home and of school implied that only one discourse could and should be relevant in each place. It led me to believe I should leave behind, turn a deaf ear to, or forget the discourse of the other when I crossed the boundary dividing them. I expected myself to set down one discourse whenever I took up another just as I would take off or put on a particular set of clothes for school or home.

Despite my parents' and teachers' attempts to keep home and school discrete, the internal conflict between the two discourses continued whenever I read or wrote. Although I tried to suppress the voice of one discourse in the name of the other, having to speak aloud in the voice I had just silenced each time I crossed the boundary kept both voices active in my mind. Every "I think . . ." from the voice of home or school brought forth a "However . . ." or a "But . . ." from the voice of the opponents. To identify with the voice of home or school, I had to negotiate through the conflicting voices of both by restating, taking back, qualifying my thoughts. I was unconsciously doing so when I did my book report. But I could not use the interaction comfortably and constructively. Both my parents and my teachers had implied that my job was to prevent that interaction from happening. My sense of having failed to accomplish what they had taught silenced me.

30   To use the interaction between the discourses of home and school constructively, I would have to have seen reading or writing as a process in which I worked my way towards a stance through a dialectical process of identification and division. To identify with an ally, I would have to have grasped the distance between where he or she stood and where I was positioning myself. In taking a stance against an opponent, I would have to have grasped where my stance identified with the stance of my allies. Teetering along the "wavering line of pressure and counter-pressure" from both allies and opponents, I might have worked my way towards a stance of my own (Burke, *A Rhetoric of Motives* 23). Moreover, I would have to have understood that the voices in my mind, like the participants in the parlor scene, were in constant flux. As I came into contact with new and different groups of people or read different books, voices entered and left. Each time I read or wrote, the stance I negotiated out of these voices would always be at some distance from the stances I worked out in my previous and my later readings or writings.

I could not conceive such a form of action for myself because I saw reading and writing as an expression of an established stance. In delineating the conventions of a discourse, my parents and teachers had synthesized the stance they saw as typical for a representative member of the community. Burke calls this the stance of a "god" or the "prototype"; Williams calls it the "official" or "possible" stance of the community. Through the metaphor of the survival tool, my parents and teachers had led me to assume I could automatically reproduce the official stance of the discourse

I used. Therefore, when I did my book report on *The Revolutionary Family*, I expected my knowledge of the official stance set by the book review to ensure the actual stance of my report. As it happened, I began by trying to take the official stance of the review. Other voices interrupted. I answered back. In the process, I worked out a stance approximate but not identical to the official stance I began with. Yet the experience of having to labor to realize my knowledge of the official stance or to prevent myself from wandering away from it frustrated and confused me. For even though I had been actually reading and writing in a Burkean scene, I was afraid to participate actively in the discussion. I assumed it was my role to survive by staying out of it.

Not long ago, my daughter told me that it bothered her to hear her friend "talk wrong." Having come to the United States from China with little English, my daughter has become sensitive to the way English, as spoken by her teachers, operates. As a result, she has amazed her teachers with her success in picking up the language and in adapting to life at school. Her concern to speak the English taught in the classroom "correctly" makes her uncomfortable when she hears people using "ain't" or double negatives, which her teacher considers "improper." I see in her the me that had eagerly learned and used the discourse of the Working class at school. Yet while I was torn between the two conflicting worlds of school and home, she moves with seeming ease from the conversations she hears over the dinner table to her teacher's words in the classroom. My husband and I are proud of the good work she does at school. We are glad she is spared the kinds of conflict between home and school I experienced at her age. Yet as we watch her becoming more and more fluent in the language of the classroom, we wonder if, by enabling her to "survive" school, her very fluency will silence her when the scene of her reading and writing expands beyond that of the composition classroom.

For when I listen to my daughter, to students, and to some composition teachers talking about the teaching and learning of writing, I am often alarmed by the degree to which the metaphor of a survival tool dominates their understanding of language as it once dominated my own. I am especially concerned with the way some composition classes focus on turning the classroom into a monological scene for the students' reading and writing. Most of our students live in a world similar to my daughter's, somewhere between the purified world of the classroom and the complex world of my adolescence. When composition classes encourage these students to ignore those voices that seem irrelevant to the purified world of the classroom, most students are often able to do so without much struggle. Some of them are so adept at doing it that the whole process has for them become automatic.

However, beyond the classroom and beyond the limited range of these students' immediate lives lies a much more complex and dynamic social and historical scene. To help these students become actors in such a scene, perhaps we need to call their attention to voices that may seem irrelevant to the discourse we teach rather than encourage them to shut them out. For example, we might intentionally complicate the classroom scene by bringing into it discourses that stand at varying distances from the one we teach. We might encourage students to explore ways of practicing the conventions of the discourse they are learning by negotiating through these conflicting voices. We could also encourage them to see themselves as responsible for forming or transforming as well as preserving the discourse they are learning.

35   As I think about what we might do to complicate the external and internal scenes of our students' writing, I hear my parents and teachers saying: "Not now. Keep them from the wrangle of the marketplace until they have acquired the discourse and are skilled at using it." And I answer: "Don't teach them to 'survive' the whirlpool of crosscurrents by avoiding it. Use the classroom to moderate the currents. Moderate the currents, but teach them from the beginning to struggle." When I think of the ways in which the teaching of reading and writing as classroom activities can frustrate the development of students, I am almost grateful for the overwhelming complexity of the circumstances in which I grew up. For it was this complexity that kept me from losing sight of the effort and choice involved in reading or writing with and through a discourse.

WORKS CITED

Burke, Kenneth. *The Philosophy of Literary Form: Studies in Symbolic Action.* 2nd ed. Baton Rouge: Louisiana State UP, 1967.

——— *A Rhetoric of Motives.* Berkeley: U of California P, 1969.

Freire, Paulo. *Pedagogy of the Oppressed.* Trans. M. B. Ramos. New York: Continuum, 1970.

Williams, Raymond. *Marxism and Literature.* New York: Oxford UP, 1977.

EXPLORATORY WRITING

In the opening paragraph, Lu notes that her understanding of education was "so dominated by memories of confusion and frustration" that she was unable to speak about them to her dying mother. How does Lu go on to explain what rendered her confused, frustrated, and silent? How does she generalize her silence as something embedded in the nature of schooling that affects many people?

TALKING ABOUT THE READING

Lu says that part of her problem was that she had adopted a view of language as a "tool for survival." In class discussion, explain what she means by the term "tool for survival" and why she thinks it caused her to be passive and unable to participate in public discussions. In place of the metaphor of language as a "tool for survival," Lu wants to substitute a metaphor of multiple "voices in my mind" contending for her allegiance and attention. Explain what Lu means by these contending voices. Consider how she analyzes writing a book report on *The Revolutionary Family* "as a heated discussion between myself, the voices of home, and those of school." How was this an instance of "contending voices"? How did Lu deal with these voices at the time? What does she see in retrospect?

WRITING ASSIGNMENT

Use Min-Zhan Lu's essay as a model to think about how you became aware of the type of reading that is valued in literature classes. Your experience will differ from Lu's, but all students in some fashion or another come to grips with English teachers' expectations about what they should find in the assigned reading. Write an essay that explains your own understanding of what English teachers are looking for when you read literature, whether poems, plays, short stories, or novels. What are you supposed to notice and admire? What kinds of analyses are you supposed to perform when you read literary texts? Consider how this type of schooled reading fits with the way you read literature on your own. To what extent do you read for the same purposes that are called for when you are assigned literary works in school? How would you explain the differences and similarities?

WRITING SEQUENCE

1. Reread your Rodriguez and Lu Exploratory Writing and any other writing you have done the so far (if you haven't done the suggested Exploratory Writing, write for 10 minutes on each at this point). Reread Rodriguez and Lu with the purpose of explaining how they represent the conflict between home and school in their essays. Begin a new exploratory writing that explains how each poses this conflict and how their accounts differ and are similar. As differences and similarities come to light, consider the underlying assumptions each is making and how those assumptions affect their examination of home and school.

2. In place of the metaphor of language as a "tool for survival," Lu substitutes the metaphor of multiple "voices in my mind," from which she must negotiate her own stance. Write a 2-page essay that explains how the view of language as "voices in my mind" enabled Lu to move from being a passive performer in school to imagining a place for herself as an active participant. Compare Lu's resolution of the conflicts between home and school to the resolution Rodriguez achieves.

3. As a culminating assignment, write a longer finished essay (drafted, revised, and edited) that locates your own experience in relation to that of Rodriguez and Lu. Use their writing to set up a context of issues about relations and possible conflicts between home and school. Then explain how your experience fits into this set of issues. As you write, keep in mind the terms and ways of thinking in Rodriguez's and Lu's writings and how you can draw on them to clarify your experience.

CREDENTIALING VS. EDUCATING

■■■—*Jane Jacobs*

Jane Jacobs (1916–2006) is best known for her influential books on urban studies, including the seminal *The Death and Life of Great American Cities* (1961), *The Economy of Cities* (1969), and *Cities and the Wealth of Nations* (1984). In "Credentialing vs. Educating," which appeared as an essay in the *Virginia Quarterly Review* and as a chapter in *Dark Age Ahead* (2004), Jacobs turns her attention to how higher education reflects, in her words, "American culture's gloss on the purpose of life."

SUGGESTION Notice how Jacobs first establishes the trend toward credentialing as the aim of higher edu-
FOR READING cation and then explains the phenomenon of credentialing as an "indirect legacy of the Great Depression of the 1930s." As you read, pay attention to how she develops an analysis of the roots of credentialing.

1 In addition to their other major expenses, some North American nuclear families bear the cost of a four-year college or university degree for the family's child or children. The cost has become as necessary as the cost of a car, and for a similar reason: without it, access to a remunerative job is difficult or even impossible. It has long been recognized that getting an education is effective for bettering oneself and one's chances in the world. But a degree and an education are not necessarily synonymous. Credentialing, not educating, has become the primary business of North American universities. This is not in the interest of employers in the long run. But in the short run, it is beneficial for corporations' departments of human resources, the current name for personnel departments. People with the task of selecting successful job applicants want them to have desirable qualities such as persistence, ambition, and the ability to cooperate and conform, to be a "team player." At a minimum, achieving a four-year university or college degree, no matter in what subject, seems to promise these traits. From the viewpoint of a government agency's or corporation's department of human resources, the institution of higher learning has done the tedious first winnowing or screening of applicants. For the applicant, this means that a résumé without one or more degrees from a respected institution will not be taken seriously enough even to be considered, no matter how able or informed the applicant may be. The credential is not a passport to a job, as naive graduates sometimes suppose. It is more basic and necessary: a passport to consideration for a job. A degree can also be a passport out of an underclass, or a safety strap to prevent its holder from sinking into an underclass. Without it, as North American high school students are forever being warned, they will be doomed to a work life of "flipping hamburgers." With it, all manner of opportunities may be accessible.

University credentialing thus efficiently combines the services to employers that in simpler and more frugal days were provided by First Class or Eagle rank in the Boy Scouts, and the services to aspiring climbers that in olden days were provided by a College of Heralds with its monopoly on granting the coats of arms that separated their possessors from the underclass. A coat of arms didn't really certify that its possessor could wield a bow or a battle-ax. That wasn't the point. Students themselves understand perfectly well what they are buying with four years of their youth and associated tuition and living costs. While a degree in some subject has become indispensable, one in a field with a currently promising job market and good pay is thought to be even better; thus student enrollment statistics have become an unofficial appendix to stock market performance. In the summer of 2002, when Internet and other high-tech stocks had gone into the doldrums, the *Washington Post* surveyed enrollment figures in undergraduate computer science departments in the Washington, D.C., area; it reported:

At Virginia Tech, enrollment of undergraduates in the computer science department will drop 25 percent this year to 300. At George Washington University, the number of incoming freshmen who plan to study computer science fell by more than half this year. . . . In 1997, schools with Ph.D. programs in computer science and computer engineering granted 8,063 degrees. . . . [T]he numbers rose through 2001 when 17,048 [Ph.D.] degrees were awarded. . . . Nine hundred of the 2,000 plus undergraduates studying information technology and engineering at George Mason University were computer science majors last year. This year the enrollment in that major is down to 800, although a newly created and more general information technology major has attracted 200 students. . . . "Having it ease off for a while is a bit of a relief," said a [George Mason] dean. "Particularly with the field as it has been, they don't want to spend four years on something and then not get a job."

The two students whose comments were included in the newspaper's report, apparently as representative of student thinking, advanced somewhat different reasons for shifts from earlier plans. One, who was switching to an unspecified engineering major, said he wanted to do something "more social and more interesting than working with computers. . . . Besides, you can't get the chicks with that anymore." The other, who was switching to business marketing, said, "Technology comes natural to people my age. It's not fascinating anymore." In the meantime, the *Post* reported, the U.S. Department of Labor was contradictorily projecting that "software engineering will be the fastest growing occupation between 2000 and 2010 with other computer-related industries trailing close behind."

All universities possess their own subcultures, and so do departments within universities, varying to the point of being indifferent or even antagonistic to one another, so a generalization cannot describe all accurately. But it is safe to say that credentialing as the primary business of institutions of higher learning got under way in the 1960s. Students were the first to notice the change. In the unrest and turbulence of that decade, one thread of complaint came from students who claimed they were shortchanged in education. They had expected more personal rapport with teachers, who had become only remote figures in large, impersonal lecture halls. The students were protesting attempts to transmit culture that omitted acquaintance with personal examples and failed to place them on speaking terms with wisdom. In another decade, however, students dropped that cause, apparently taking it for granted that credentialing is the normal primary business of institutions of higher learning and that its cost is an unavoidable fee for initiation into acceptable adulthood. If a student takes out a loan to meet the expense, he or she may reach early middle age by the time the loan is paid off. The guarantee behind the loan is the valuable credential itself. "College degree worth millions, survey finds," my morning paper tells me in July 2002. Every summer for years readers have been given similar tidings, buttressed by statistics, sometimes from government, sometimes from universities themselves. The survey in this case had been made by the U.S. Census Bureau, which reported, the paper said, that "someone whose education does not go beyond high school and who works full time can expect to earn about $1.2 million between ages 25 and 64. . . . Graduating from college and earning advanced degrees translate into higher lifetime earnings: an estimated $4.4 million for doctors, lawyers and others with professional degrees; $2.5 million for college graduates," that is, those with a bachelor's degree.

5   At this point in the news report, a policy analyst (presumably with a degree to validate

the title) working for the American Council on Education, identified as "a higher education advocacy group," chimed in with the moral: "Not all students look at college as an investment, but I'm sure their parents do. The challenge is to convince those high school students on the margins that it is really worth their time to go to college." The survey found that men with professional degrees may expect to earn almost $2 million more than "women with the same level of education," a difference attributed to the time out that women take to bear and rear children. The trends in the United States have followed in Canada, with the usual time lag. A forum panelist in Toronto, asked by a troubled parent, "When did we decide to change the way we thought about public education?" replied in an essay published in 2003: "Today's youngsters have had it drummed into their heads that a post-secondary education is the key to a good job. . . . [It] is no longer considered as an investment that society makes in the next generation; it is seen as an investment that students make in themselves." The panelist/essayist assigned the start of the Canadian change to the late 1980s, tracing it as a decline then and through the 1990s in public funding to universities and colleges while their enrollments were growing from 15 percent of high school graduates in 1975 to 20 percent in 2001, with educators and legislators expecting that it will reach 25 percent in the near future.

Expansion of first-rate faculty—memorable teachers of the kind the 1960s student protesters were mourning—has not kept pace with expansion of enrollments and courses offered; professors lack the time and energy they could once devote to personal contact with students. Slack has been taken up by what became known as "gypsy faculty," lecturers hoping for permanent appointments as they move from university to university, and by graduate students as part of their apprenticeships. So many papers to mark, relative to numbers and qualities of mentors to mark them, changed the nature of test papers.

Some came to consist of "True or false?" and "Which of the following is correct?" types of questions fit for robots to answer and to rate, rather than stimulants and assessments of critical thinking and depth of understanding.

In the meantime, rejoicing that university education has become a growth industry, administrators and legislators seek increasingly to control problems of scale by applying lessons from profit-making enterprises that turn expanded markets to advantage by cutting costs. Increased output of product can be measured more easily as numbers of credentialed graduates than as numbers of educated graduates. Quantity trumps quality.

Community colleges that grant two-year diplomas in applied arts and sciences represent a midstation in life, like a second-class ticket in the traditional European transportation arrangement of first and second classes and third class or steerage. Two-year community colleges supply the economy with technicians of many kinds for hospitals and clinics, draftsmen for architectural and engineering firms, designers of graphics, lighting, and costumes for television shows, expositions, and plays, and many, many other skilled workers and craftsmen. Community colleges have typically maintained an admirably close connection between education and training and the diploma credential. But this, too, is now on the verge of a transformation into credentialing disconnected from education. In my home province of Ontario, Canada, a few community colleges have already promoted themselves into "an elite level" by gaining government licenses to grant four-year degrees that will upstage diplomas. The push for this change came from community college administrators, although they were divided about its desirability. Some feared it would "compromise access." One, who applauded it, argued that his institution needed a degree-granting license "in order for our college to compete in a sophisticated economy where a degree is the currency of the realm."

To put it crassly, first-class, elite-level tickets cost more than second-class tickets. "Undergrad Tuition Fees up 135% over 11 Years," shouts a headline over a 2002 analysis by Statistics Canada, the country's census bureau. Cuts in government funding have caused budgets to fall far behind fifteen years of compounded inflation, despite cost cutting. Appended to the newspaper report of the cost increases was a comment by the chair of a national student federation, who noted, "It's no longer just the poorest of the poor who are denied. It's creeping up the income ladder." As currency of the realm, credentials are attractive to counterfeiters. So it is not surprising to learn that "experts" (credentials unspecified) estimate that 30 percent of job applicants concoct false résumés, or that a former mayor of San Francisco, when told that his chief of police had lied about his college degrees, pooh-poohed the revelation with the comment, "I don't know who doesn't lie on their résumés." It is surprising, however, to learn that captains of industry give in to the temptation. After an unsuccessful career as an executive at General Motors, the successful chief executive of Bausch & Lomb, a venerable and respected maker of lenses and eye-care products, was shown not to possess a master of business administration degree, as claimed in his biographical materials. His competence was affirmed by his corporation's board, and neither he nor the company suffered from the revelation, except for a sharp but temporary drop in the company's stock. Other executives have been less fortunate. The chief executive of Veritas Software was fired for falsely claiming an MBA from Stanford University, and others have been publicly embarrassed. One told the press, "At some point I probably felt insecure and it perpetuated itself." The Bausch & Lomb president, standing on his dignity, wins the arm's-length prize: "I'm embarrassed," he told the press, "that some of this incorrect information appeared in some of our published materials on my background. Clearly, it's my obligation to proofread such things carefully and ensure their accuracy."

10   Credentialing is an indirect legacy of the Great Depression of the 1930s. Along with much else in North American culture, credentialing's origins and appeal cannot be understood without harking back to the Depression years. The physical and financial hardships of America in the years 1930–39 were mild in comparison with hardships endured in the 20th century by societies that suffered famine, genocide, ethnic cleansing, oppression, bombing raids, or defeat in war. The Depression, however, exerted a lasting influence on Americans, out of all proportion to its short duration and relatively mild ordeals. Nobody understood what was happening when jobs and savings vanished and stagnation settled on the United States and Canada. Even now, some seventy years later, economists continue to dispute the Depression's causes. Mass unemployment was the single greatest disaster. At its worst, it idled some 25 percent of workers in the United States and Canada, and higher percentages in hard-hit localities. When one considers all the others who directly and indirectly depended on those workers, unemployment or its effects touched almost everyone other than the exceptionally rich or sheltered. Government make-work and semiwelfare programs, some of them admirably ingenious and constructive, helped but did not cure, and they had their own insecurities and humiliations.

Some people spent most of the Depression years standing in lines for a chance at a temporary job, for delayed pay from bankrupt companies, for lost savings in failed banks, for bowls of soup or loaves of day-old bread. One sees the anxious rows of pinched faces in photographs of the time. Also in photographs one sees rallies of protesters with their signs, quailing before mounted police and raised billy clubs. Often with incredible bravery, and always with incalculable expenditures of time, scrimped savings, and hopes, protesters devoted themselves to political activities that they had convinced themselves would be beneficial. Quieter involvement with intellectual schemes, like technocracy, social credit, and EPIC (End Poverty in California, the platform of Upton Sinclair's unsuccessful campaign for election as that state's governor), was a comfort to many. Others busied themselves politically with combat against those who espoused Marxism, Trotskyism, or other radical politics. Some of these, too, and their opponents turn up in photographs of sessions of the U.S. House of Representatives Committee on Un-American Activities.

However, most attempts at living through the Depression are not documented in photographs at all; they were only very lightly touched on in films, and almost as lightly in music. People who weren't used to being idle and unwanted tried to keep busy somehow; but even jobs at no pay, valued for learning and experience, were hard to get. Architects made jigsaw puzzles and renderings of ghastly, inhuman utopian cities and sold them if customers could be found. I got a job without pay, for a year, on the Scranton, Pennsylvania, morning paper. It was my journalism school.

For individuals, the worst side effect of unemployment was repeated rejection with its burden of shame and failure. Many quietly despaired that the world had a place for them. This hopelessness, at the time, seemed endless. Would life always be like this? Something unfathomable, without visible cause, had engulfed everyone's expectations and plans. For someone in her teens or early twenties, as I was during this time, it wasn't really so bad. My friends and I could make stories out of our rejections and frugalities and the strange people we met up with in our futile searches, and could bask in the gasps or laughs we generated. It was harder for people in their thirties, who had gotten launched (they thought) in careers that so soon came to nothing. For people in their forties or fifties, rejections and idleness could be devastating. The parents of some of my friends never recovered ease with themselves, their families, or society after this demoralizing break in their lives. It was harder on men who had been family breadwinners than on women who devoted themselves to homemaking and child-rearing, as most did after marriage.

My father, a doctor, worked long hours, seven days a week, and in spite of weariness, he stayed in good spirits because he was needed and, especially, because his work interested him. But like everyone else, he worried about getting by. In our little city of Scranton, where the chief industry was mining expensive, high-grade anthracite coal, the Great Depression was intensified because, in effect, it had started four years early with a long and bitter coal strike and subsequent loss of markets.

15   Few of my father's patients were able to pay him as the effects of mass unemployment spread. He told me one Saturday evening in 1936 that he had to earn $48 a day merely to pay for his office rent, his subscriptions to medical journals, office supplies, and the salary of his assisting nurse. To me that seemed an incomprehensibly formidable sum; I was earning $12 a week in New York as a stenographer in a candy manufacturing company that soon went into bankruptcy. He expressed relief as he told me about the $48; that day, he had broken even, thanks to twelve hours of hard, concentrated work in his office and the hospitals where he was a visiting physician and surgeon. He was not unique. Countless Americans who thought of themselves as the backbone of the country kept doing their work, regardless of the struggle, and helped hold things together.

When the stagnation lifted, at first tentatively in 1938–39 as the armament economy clicked in, and then in full force in 1942 after America entered the war, the change was miraculous. It was too late for my father, who had died in 1937. Everyone knew it was ghoulish to delight in jobs and prosperity at the price of war; nevertheless, everyone I knew was grateful that suddenly good jobs and pay raises showered like rain after a drought. It seemed that the world did need us, and had places for us.

After the war was over, during the euphoria of victory and the minor booms of the Marshall

Plan and the Korean War, a consensus formed and hardened across North America. If it had been voiced, it would have gone something like this: We can endure meaningful trials and overcome them. But never again—never, never—will we suffer the meaningless disaster of mass unemployment. Cultures take purposes for themselves, cling tenaciously to them, and exalt them into the purposes and meanings of life itself. For instance, in ancient Rome the ideal of service to the state was the overriding cultural purpose. After the republic was succeeded by the empire, Virgil added a slightly new spin, in a passage of the *Aeneid* cited with reverence by the emperor Augustus: "Your task, Roman, is this: to rule the peoples. This is your special genius: to enforce the habits of peace, to spare the conquered, to subdue the proud." In medieval Western Europe and in early colonial Puritan America, the purpose of life, which had been reshaped during the Dark Age, became the salvation of souls, one's own and others', for the Christian Kingdom of Heaven.

From the 1950s on, American culture's gloss on the purpose of life became assurance of full employment: jobs. Arguably, this has remained the American purpose of life, in spite of competition from the Cold War with the Soviet Union, and maybe even from the War on Terrorism, in which postwar reconstruction is being linked with contracts for American companies and hence jobs for Americans.

Whether jobs have been succeeded by the War on Terrorism as the American purpose of life is still unclear. The swift surrender of entitlement to a speedy trial, protection against being held without legal counsel or charges, and privacy and, in the case of captured combatants, the abrogation of the Geneva Conventions on treatment of prisoners of war, argue that the exigencies of outmaneuvering putative terrorists have overridden other values, including economic prudence. As Margaret Atwood has pointed out, the surrender of civil rights is "a recipe for widespread business theft . . . and fraud." Perhaps we

must wait for new arrangements for control of Middle Eastern oil and reconstruction of Afghanistan and Iraq to learn whether the purpose of American life has actually switched from providing jobs and earning profits.

20   It has been truly said that the past lives on in the present. This is true of credentialism's origins. It emerged partly out of America's humiliation and worry when the Soviet Union, with its *Sputnik,* had beaten America into space, and partly from the still-fresh dread of the Depression. Credentialism emerged, mostly in California at first, in the late 1950s, when it dawned upon university administrators there that modern economic development, whether in the conquest of space or any other field, depended on a population's funds of knowledge—a resource that later came to be known as human capital. It followed that development's most culturally valuable product—jobs—also depended on knowledge. The administrators were quite right, and it was brainy of them to reason that the more of this crucial resource their institutions could nurture and certify, the better for all concerned.

Initially there was no conflict between this aim and the quality of the education that administrators expected their institutions to supply. That conflict began to arise in the 1960s, partly out of universities' attempts to take on many new tasks at once as they engaged with the communities that supported them. Under the civic banner of the "multiversity," they aimed at furthering every good thing they set their abundant intellects to. Far from elevating credentialing above educating, they were sweepingly enlarging the idea of educating to embrace whatever skills seemed needed, from cost-benefit analysis to marketing. Administrators surely did not recognize how much these enlarged ambitions, coupled with the promise of riches to society from credentialed graduates, would change universities themselves.

As always in a culture, everything that happened connected with everything else. In this case, multiversity educational expansion had connections with a constructive U.S. government program for war veterans.

After World War II and then the Korean War, the government provided tuition and encouragement for veterans who had the desire and qualifications to attend universities or colleges. Tens of thousands of former GIs, many from families in which nobody had ever before been given a chance at higher education, took advantage of this opportunity. On the whole, the veterans were noted for applying themselves more seriously than students just out of high school. They also swelled student enrollments. When the stream of GI students ran dry, their hunger for education was missed in university communities, along with their government-guaranteed tuitions. Credentialing emerged as a growth industry in the 1960s, just when universities needed it to address problems of their own.

The more successful credentialing became as a growth industry, the more it dominated education, from the viewpoints of both teachers and students. Teachers could not help despairing of classes whose members seemed less interested in learning than in doing the minimum work required to get by and get out. Enthusiastic students could not help despairing of institutions that seemed to think of them as raw material to process as efficiently as possible rather than as human beings with burning questions and confusions about the world and doubts about why they were sinking time and money into this prelude to their working lives.

25   Students who are passionate about learning, or could become so, do exist. Faculty members who love their subjects passionately and are eager to teach what they know and to plumb its depths further also exist. But institutions devoted to respecting and fulfilling these needs as their first purposes have become rare, under pressure of different necessities. Similar trends in Britain have begun to worry some educators there. My impression is that university-educated parents and grandparents of students presently in university do not realize how much the experience has changed since their own student days, nor do the students themselves, since they have not experienced anything else. Only faculty who have lived through the loss realize what has been lost.

EXPLORATORY WRITING

Jane Jacobs says that a college "degree and an education are not necessarily synonymous" but doesn't really develop the distinction or the possible overlap between the two terms. What sense do you make of the title of her essay, "Credentialing vs. Educating"?

TALKING ABOUT THE READING

Do some informal research to test Jacobs's assertion that "Credentialing, not educating, has become the primary business of North American universities" from the perspective of students. As a class, develop a short open-ended questionnaire. Two or three questions are enough, such as "What's your purpose in coming to college?" or "What does a college degree mean to you?" Work in groups of three, with each member interviewing five undergraduates. Try to get respondents from all four years. Compile the results and identify patterns in the responses. Design a report on your findings to present in class and to compare to other groups' findings. (This is a good assignment in which to use PowerPoint.)

WRITING ASSIGNMENT

1. Write a personal essay on your reasons for coming to college. Use Jacobs's distinction between credentialing and educating to explain your motivations. Consider to what extent they are not identical and to what extent they overlap.

2. How do the aims of higher education reflect the larger purposes of American culture? To answer this question, consider Jacobs's argument that credentialing is "an indirect legacy of the Great Depression of the 1930s." Explain her line of reasoning, and add other considerations that you think should be taken into account.

3. Write a report with your group on the findings of your research. Begin by explaining the significance of the issues you have investigated, drawing on Jacobs's essay to help you define your research questions. Then explain how your questionnaire was designed to answer these questions and who constituted your student sample. Next, present the findings by identifying common themes in the responses to the questionnaire. Finally, offer an interpretation of the findings, keeping in mind the limited scope of the research and the tentativeness of the conclusions you reach.

NOBODY MEAN MORE TO ME THAN YOU AND THE FUTURE LIFE OF WILLIE JORDAN

███─ *June Jordan*

June Jordan (1936–2002) was a poet, playwright, essayist, and professor of English at the University of California, Berkley. The following selection, "Nobody Mean More to Me Than You and the Future Life of Willie Jordan," opens *On Call,* a collection of Jordan's political essays published in 1985. In this essay, Jordan weaves two stories together, one concerning a class she taught on Black English and the other concerning Willie Jordan, a young black student in the class trying to come to terms with injustice in South Africa while facing the death of his brother through police brutality at home in Brooklyn. Jordan's story of how her students discovered the communicative power and clarity of Black English forms the backdrop for Willie Jordan's struggle to articulate his own understanding of oppressive power.

SUGGESTION FOR READING Notice that there are many voices speaking in this essay—not just June Jordan the essayist and teacher but also Alice Walker in *The Color Purple,* Jordan's students studying and translating Black English, and Willie Jordan in the essay that closes the selection. Underline and annotate passages to indicate who is speaking and where the voice shifts.

1 Black English is not exactly a linguistic buffalo; as children, most of the thirty-five million Afro-Americans living here depend on this language for our discovery of the world. But then we approach our maturity inside a larger social body that will not support our efforts to become anything other than the clones of those who are neither our mothers nor our fathers. We begin to grow up in a house where every true mirror shows us the face of somebody who does not belong there, whose walk and whose talk will never look or sound "right," because that house was meant to shelter a family that is alien and hostile to us. As we learn our way around this environment, either we hide our original word habits, or we completely surrender our own voice, hoping to please those who will never respect anyone different from themselves: Black English is not exactly a linguistic buffalo, but we should understand its status as an endangered species, as a perishing, irreplaceable system of community intelligence, or we should expect its extinction, and, along with that, the extinguishing of much that constitutes our own proud, and singular, identity.

What we casually call "English," less and less defers to England and its "gentlemen." "English" is no longer a specific matter of geography or an element of class privilege; more than thirty-three countries use this tool as a means of "intranational communication."[1] Countries as disparate as Zimbabwe and Malaysia, or Israel and Uganda, use it as their non-native currency of convenience. Obviously, this tool, this "English," cannot function inside thirty-three discrete societies on the basis of rules and values absolutely determined somewhere else, in a thirty-fourth other country, for example.

In addition to that staggering congeries of non-native users of English, there are five countries, or 333,746,000 people, for whom this thing called "English" serves as a native tongue.[2] Approximately 10 percent of these native speakers of "English" are Afro-American citizens of the U.S.A. I cite these numbers and varieties of human beings dependent on "English" in order, quickly, to suggest how strange and how tenuous is any concept of "Standard English." Obviously, numerous forms of English now operate inside a natural, an uncontrollable, continuum of development. I would suppose "the standard" for English in Malaysia is not the same as "the standard" in Zimbabwe. I know that standard forms of English for Black people in this country do not copy that of Whites. And, in fact, the structural differences between these two kinds of English have intensified, becoming more Black, or less White, despite the expected homogenizing effects of television[3] and other mass media.

Nonetheless, White standards of English persist, supreme and unquestioned, in these United States. Despite our multi-lingual population, and despite the deepening Black and White cleavage within that conglomerate, White standards control our official and popular judgments of verbal proficiency and correct, or incorrect, language skills, including speech. In contrast to India, where at least fourteen languages co-exist as legitimate Indian languages, in contrast to Nicaragua, where all citizens are legally entitled to formal school instruction in their regional or tribal languages, compulsory education in America compels accommodation to exclusively White forms of "English." White English, in America, is "Standard English."

5   This story begins two years ago. I was teaching a new course, "In Search of the Invisible Black Woman," and my rather large class seemed evenly divided among young Black women and men. Five or six White students also sat in attendance. With unexpected speed and enthusiasm we had moved through historical narration of the 19th century to literature by and about Black women, in the 20th. I then assigned the first forty pages of Alice Walker's *The Color Purple,* and I came, eagerly, to class that morning:

"So!" I exclaimed, aloud. "What did you think?" How did you like it?"

The students studied their hands, or the floor. There was no response. The tense, resistant feeling in the room fairly astounded me.

At last, one student, a young woman still not meeting my eyes, muttered something in my direction:

"What did you say?" I prompted her.

10   "Why she have them talk so funny. It don't sound right."

"You mean the language?"

Another student lifted his head: "It don't look right, neither. I couldn't hardly read it."

At this, several students dumped on the book. Just about unanimously, their criticisms targeted the language. I listened to what they wanted to say and silently marvelled at the similarities between their casual speech patterns and Alice Walker's written version of Black English.

But I decided against pointing to these identical traits of syntax, I wanted not to make them self-conscious about their own spoken language—not while they clearly felt it was "wrong." Instead I decided to swallow my astonishment. Here was a negative Black reaction to a prize-winning accomplishment of Black literature that White readers across the country had selected as a best seller. Black rejection was aimed at the one irreducibly Black element of Walker's work: the language—Celie's Black

English. I wrote the opening lines of *The Color Purple* on the blackboard and asked the students to help me translate these sentences into Standard English:

You better not never tell nobody but God. It'd kill your mommy.

> Dear God,
>
> I am fourteen years old. I have always been a good girl. Maybe you can give me a sign letting me know what is happening to me.
>
> Last spring after Little Lucious come I heard them fussing. He was pulling on her arm. She say it too soon, Fonso. I aint well. Finally he leave her alone. A week go by, he pulling on her arm again. She say, Naw, I ain't gonna. Can't you see I'm already half dead, an all of the children.[4]

15   Our process of translation exploded with hilarity and even hysterical, shocked laughter: The Black writer, Alice Walker, knew what she was doing! If rudimentary criteria for good fiction include the manipulation of language so that the syntax and diction of sentences will tell you the identity of speakers, the probable age and sex and class of speakers, and even the locale—urban/rural/southern/western—then Walker had written, perfectly. This is the translation into Standard English that our class produced:

Absolutely, one should never confide in anybody besides God. Your secrets could prove devastating to your mother.

> Dear God,
>
> I am fourteen years old. I have always been good. But now, could you help me to understand what is happening to me?
>
> Last spring, after my little brother, Lucious, was born, I heard my parents fighting. My father kept pulling at my mother's arm. But she told him, "It's too soon for sex, Alfonso. I am still not feeling well." Finally, my father left her alone. A week went by, and then he began bothering my mother, again: pulling her arm. She told him, "No, I won't! Can't you see I'm already exhausted from all of these children?"

(Our favorite line was "It's too soon for sex, Alfonso.")

Once we could stop laughing, once we could stop our exponentially wild improvisations on the theme of Translated Black English, the students pushed to explain their own negative first reactions to their spoken language on the printed page. I thought it was probably akin to the shock of seeing yourself in a photograph for the first time. Most of the students had never before seen a written facsimile of the way they talk. None of the students had ever learned how to read and write their own verbal system of communication: Black English. Alternatively, this fact began to baffle or else bemuse and then infuriate my students. Why not? Was it too late? Could they learn how to do it, now? And, ultimately, the final test question, the one testing my sincerity: Could I teach them? Because I had never taught anyone Black English and, as far as I knew, no one, anywhere in the United States, had ever offered such a course, the best I could say was "I'll try."

He looked like a wrestler.

He sat dead center in the packed room and, every time our eyes met, he quickly nodded his head as though anxious to reassure, and encourage me.

20   Short, with strikingly broad shoulders and long arms, he spoke with a surprisingly high, soft voice that matched the soft bright movement of his eyes. His name was Willie Jordan. He would have seemed even more unlikely in the context of Contemporary Women's Poetry, except that ten or twelve other Black men were taking the course, as well. Still, Willie was conspicuous. His extreme fitness, the muscular density of his presence underscored the riveted, gentle attention that he gave to anything anyone said. Generally, he did not join the loud and rowdy dialogue flying back and forth, but there could be no doubt about his interest in our discussions. And, when he stood to present an argument he'd prepared, overnight, that nervous

smile of his vanished and an irregular stammering replaced it, as he spoke with visceral sincerity, word by word.

That was how I met Willie Jordan. It was in between "In Search of the Invisible Black Women" and "The Art of Black English." I was waiting for departmental approval and I supposed that Willie might be, so to speak, killing time until he, too, could study Black English. But Willie really did want to explore contemporary women's poetry and, to that end, volunteered for extra research and never missed a class.

Towards the end of that semester, Willie approached me for an independent study project on South Africa. It would commence the next semester. I thought Willie's writing needed the kind of improvement only intense practice will yield. I knew his intelligence was outstanding. But he'd wholeheartedly opted for "Standard English" at a rather late age, and the results were stilted and frequently polysyllabic, simply for the sake of having more syllables. Willie's unnatural formality of language seemed to me consistent with the formality of his research into South African apartheid. As he projected his studies, he would have little time, indeed, for newspapers. Instead, more than 90 percent of his research would mean saturation in strictly historical, if not archival, material. I was certainly interested. It would be tricky to guide him into a more confident and spontaneous relationship both with language and apartheid. It was going to be wonderful to see what happened when he could catch up with himself, entirely, and talk back to the world.

September, 1984: Breezy fall weather and much excitement! My class, "The Art of Black English," was full to the limit of the fire laws. And in Independent Study, Willie Jordan showed up weekly, fifteen minutes early for each of our sessions. I was pretty happy to be teaching, altogether!

I remember an early class when a young brother, replete with his ever-present porkpie hat, raised his hand and then told us that most of what he'd heard was "all right" except it was "too clean." "The brothers on the street," he continued, "they mix it up more. Like 'fuck' and 'motherfuck.' Or like 'shit.'" He waited. I waited. Then all of us laughed a good while, and we got into a brawl about "correct" and "realistic" Black English that led to Rule 1.

25   Rule 1: *Black English is about a whole lot more than mothafuckin.*

As a criterion, we decided, "realistic" could take you anywhere you want to go. Artful places. Angry places. Eloquent and sweetalkin places. Polemical places. Church. And the local Bar & Grill. We were checking out a language, not a mood or a scene or one guy's forgettable mouthing off.

It was hard. For most of the students, learning Black English required a fallback to patterns and rhythms of speech that many of their parents had beaten out of them. I mean beaten. And, in a majority of cases, correct Black English could be achieved only by striving for incorrect Standard English, something they were still pushing at, quite uncertainly. This state of affairs led to Rule 2.

Rule 2: *If it's wrong in Standard English it's probably right in Black English, or, at least, you're hot.*

It was hard. Roommates and family members ridiculed their studies, or remained incredulous, "You studying that shit? At school?" But we were beginning to feel the companionship of pioneers. And we decided that we needed another rule that would establish each one of us as equally important to our success. This was Rule 3.

30   Rule 3: *If it don't sound like something that come out somebody mouth then it don't sound right. If it don't sound right then it ain't hardly right. Period.*

This rule produced two weeks of compositions in which the students agonizingly tried to spell the sound of the Black English sentence they wanted to convey. But Black English is, preeminently, an oral/spoken means of communication. And spelling don't talk. So we needed Rule 4.

Rule 4: *Forget about the spelling. Let the syntax carry you.*

Once we arrived at Rule 4 we started to fly, because syntax, the structure of an idea, leads you to the world view of the speaker and reveals her values. The syntax of a sentence equals the structure of your consciousness. If we insisted that the language of Black English adheres to a distinctive Black syntax, then we were postulating a profound difference between White and Black people, per se. Was it a difference to prize or to obliterate?

There are three qualities of Black English—the presence of life, voice, and clarity—that intensify to a distinctive Black value system that we became excited about and self-consciously tried to maintain.

1. *Black English has been produced by a pre-technocratic, if not anti-technological, culture:* More, our culture has been constantly threatened by annihilation or, at least, the swallowed blurring of assimilation. Therefore, our language is a system constructed by people constantly needing to insist that we exist, that we are present. Our language devolves from a culture that abhors all abstraction, or anything tending to obscure or delete the fact of the human being who is here and now/the truth of the person who is speaking or listening. Consequently, there is no passive voice construction possible in Black English. For example, you cannot say, "Black English is being eliminated." You must say, instead, "White people eliminating Black English." The assumption of the presence of life governs all of Black English. Therefore, overwhelmingly, all action takes place in the language of the present indicative. And every sentence assumes the living and active participation of at least two human beings, the speaker and the listener.

2. *A primary consequence of the person-centered values of Black English is the delivery of voice:* If you speak or write Black English, your ideas will necessarily possess that otherwise elusive attribute, voice.

3. *One main benefit following from the person-centered values of Black English is that of clarity:*

If your idea, your sentence, assumes the presence of at least two living and active people, you will make it understandable, because the motivation behind every sentence is the wish to say something real to somebody real.

35   As the weeks piled up, translation from Standard English into Black English or vice versa occupied a hefty part of our course work.

Standard English (hereafter S.E.): "In considering the idea of studying Black English those questioned suggested—"

(What's the subject? Where's the person? Is anybody alive in here, in that idea?)

Black English (hereafter B.E.): "I been asking people what you think about somebody studying Black English and they answer me like this:"

But there were interesting limits. You cannot "translate" instances of Standard English preoccupied with abstraction or with nothing/nobody evidently alive, into Black English. That would warp the language into uses antithetical to the guiding perspective of its community of users. Rather you must first change those Standard English sentences, themselves, into ideas consistent with the person-centered assumptions of Black English.

GUIDELINES FOR BLACK ENGLISH

1. Minimal number of words for every idea: This is the source for the aphoristic and/or poetic force of the language; eliminate every possible word.

2. *Clarity:* If the sentence is not clear it's not Black English.

3. *Eliminate use of the verb* to be *whenever possible:* This leads to the deployment of more descriptive and, therefore, more precise verbs.

4. *Use* be *or* been *only when you want to describe a chronic, ongoing state of things.*

   He *be* at the office, by 9: (He is always at the office by 9.)

   He *been* with her since forever.

5. *Zero copula:* Always eliminate the verb *to be* whenever it would combine with another verb, in Standard English.

S.E.: She is going out with him.

B.E.: She going out with him.

6. *Eliminate* do *as in:*

S.E.: What do you think? What do you want?

B.E.: What you think? What you want?

7. Rules number 3, 4, 5, and 6 provide for the use of the minimal number of verbs per idea and, therefore, greater accuracy in the choice of verb.

8. *In general, if you wish to say something really positive, try to formulate the idea using emphatic negative structure.*

S.E.: He's fabulous.

B.E.: He bad.

9. *Use double or triple negatives for dramatic emphasis.*

S.E.: Tina Turner sings out of this world.

B.E.: Ain nobody sing like Tina.

10. *Never use the* ed *suffix to indicate the past tense of a verb.*

S.E.: She closed the door.

B.E.: She close the door. Or, she have close the door.

11. *Regardless of intentional verb time, only use the third person singular, present indicative, for use of the verb* to have, *as an auxiliary.*

S.E.: He had his wallet then he lost it.

B.E.: He have him wallet then he lose it.

S.E.: We had seen that movie.

B.E.: We seen that movie. Or, we have see that movie.

12. *Observe a minimal inflection of verbs:* Particularly, never change from the first person singular forms to the third person singular.

S.E.: Present Tense Forms: He goes to the store.

B.E.: He go to the store.

S.E.: Past Tense Forms: He went to the store.

B.E.: He go to the store. Or, he gone to the store. Or, he been to the store.

13. *The possessive case scarcely ever appears in Black English:* Never use an apostrophe ('s) construction. If you wander into a possessive case component of an idea, then keep logically consistent: ours, his, theirs, mines. But, most likely, if you bump into such a component, you have wandered outside the underlying world view of Black English.

S.E.: He will take their car tomorrow.

B.E.: He taking they car tomorrow.

14. *Plurality:* Logical consistency, continued: If the modifier indicates plurality then the noun remains in the singular case.

S.E.: He ate twelve doughnuts.

B.E.: He eat twelve doughnut.

S.E.: She has many books.

B.E.: She have many book.

15. *Listen for, or invent, special Black English forms of the past tense, such as:* "He losted it. That what she felted." If they are clear and readily understood, then use them.

16. *Do not hesitate to play with words, sometimes inventing them:* e.g. "astropotomous" means huge like a hippo plus astronomical and, therefore, signifies real big.

17. *In Black English, unless you keenly want to underscore the past tense nature of an action, stay in the present tense and rely on the overall context of your ideas for the conveyance of time and sequence.*

18. *Never use the suffix* -ly *form of an adverb in Black English.*

S.E.: The rain came down rather quickly.

B.E.: The rain come down pretty quick.

19. *Never use the indefinite article* an *in Black English.*

S.E.: He wanted to ride an elephant.

B.E.: He wanted to ride him a elephant.

20. *Invariant syntax:* in correct Black English it is possible to formulate an imperative, an interrogative, and a simple declarative idea with the same syntax:

B.E.: You going to the store?

You going to the store.

You going to the store!

40   Where was Willie Jordan? We'd reached the mid-term of the semester. Students had formulated Black English guidelines, by consensus, and they were now writing with remarkable beauty, purpose, and enjoyment:

I ain hardly speakin for everybody but myself so understan that.

Kim Parks

Samples from student writings:

Janie have a great big ole hole inside her. Tea Cake the only thing that fit that hole. . . .

That pear tree beautiful to Janie, especial when bees fiddlin with the blossomin pear there growin large and lovely. But personal speakin, the love she get from starin at that tree ain the love what starin back at her in them relationship. (Monica Morris)

Love a big theme in, *They Eye Was Watching God.* Love show people new corners inside theyself. It pull out good stuff and stuff back bad stuff. . . . Joe worship the doing uh his own hand and need other people to worship him too. But he ain't think about Janie that she a person and ought to live like anybody common do. Queen life not for Janie. (Monica Morris)

In both life and writin, Black womens have varietous experience of love that be cold like a iceberg or fiery like a inferno. Passion got for the other partner involve, man or women, seem as shallow, ankle-deep water or the most profoundest abyss. (Constance Evans)

Family love another bond that ain't never break under no pressure. (Constance Evans)

You know it really cold/When the friend you/Always get out the fire/Act like they don't know you/When you in the heat. (Constance Evans)

Big classroom discussion bout love at this time. I never take no class where us have any long arguin for and against for two or three day. New to me and great. I find the class time talkin a million time more interestin than detail bout the book. (Kathy Esseks)

As these examples suggest, Black English no longer limited the students, in any way. In fact, one of them, Philip Garfield, would shortly "translate" a pivotal scene from Ibsen's *A Doll's House,* as his final term paper.

Nora: I didn't gived no shit. I thinked you a asshole back then, too, you make it so hard for me save mines husband life.

Krogstad: Girl, it clear you ain't any idea what you done. You done exact what I once done, and I losed my reputation over it.

Nora: You asks me believe you once act brave save you wife life?

Krogstad: Law care less why you done it.

Nora: Law must suck.

Krogstad: Suck or no, if I wants, judge screw you wid dis paper.

Nora: No way, man. (Philip Garfield)

But where was Willie? Compulsively punctual, and always thoroughly prepared with neat typed compositions, he had disappeared. He failed to show up for our regularly scheduled conference, and I received neither a note nor a phone call of explanation. A whole week went by. I wondered if Willie had finally been captured by the extremely current happenings in South Africa: passage of a new constitution that did not enfranchise the Black majority, and militant Black South African reaction to that affront. I wondered if he'd been hurt, somewhere. I wondered if the serious workload of weekly readings and writings had overwhelmed him and changed his mind about independent study. Where was Willie Jordan?

One week after the first conference that Willie missed, he called: "Hello, Professor Jordan? This is Willie. I'm sorry I wasn't there last week. But something has come up and I'm pretty upset. I'm sorry but I really can't deal right now."

45   I asked Willie to drop by my office and just let me see that he was okay. He agreed to do that. When I saw him I knew something hideous had happened. Something had hurt him and scared him to the marrow. He was all agitated and stammering and terse and incoherent. At last, his sadly jumbled account let me surmise, as follows: Brooklyn police had murdered his unarmed, twenty-five-year-old brother, Reggie Jordan. Neither Willie nor his elderly parents knew what to do about it. Nobody from the press was interested. His folks had no money. Police ran his family around and around, to no point. And Reggie was really dead. And Willie wanted to fight, but he felt helpless.

With Willie's permission I began to try to secure legal counsel for the Jordan family. Unfortunately, Black victims of police violence are truly numerous, while the resources available to prosecute their killers are truly scarce. A friend of mine at the Center for Constitutional Rights estimated that just the preparatory costs for bringing the cops into court normally approaches $180,000. Unless the execution of Reggie Jordan became a major community cause for organizing and protest, his murder would simply become a statistical item.

Again, with Willie's permission, I contacted every newspaper and media person I could think of. But the Bastone feature article in *The Village Voice* was the only result from that canvassing.

Again, with Willie's permission, I presented the case to my class in Black English. We had talked about the politics of language. We had talked about love and sex and child abuse and men and women. But the murder of Reggie Jordan broke like a hurricane across the room.

There are few "issues" as endemic to Black life as police violence. Most of the students knew and respected and liked Jordan. Many of them came from the very neighborhood where the murder had occurred. All of the students had known somebody close to them who had been killed by police, or had known frightening moments of gratuitous confrontation with the cops. They wanted to do everything at once to avenge death. Number One: They decided to compose a personal statement of condolence to Willie Jordan and his family, written in Black English. Number Two: They decided to compose individual messages to the police, in Black English. These should be prefaced by an explanatory paragraph composed by the entire group. Number Three: These individual messages, with their lead paragraph, should be sent to *Newsday*.

50   The morning after we agreed on these objectives, one of the young women students appeared with an unidentified visitor, who sat through the class, smiling in a peculiar, comfortable way.

Now we had to make more tactical decisions. Because we wanted the messages published, and because we thought it imperative that our outrage be known by the police, the tactical question was this: Should the opening, group paragraph be written in Black English or Standard English?

I have seldom been privy to a discussion with so much heart at the dead beat of it. I will never forget the eloquence, the sudden haltings of speech, the fierce struggle against tears, the furious throwaway, and useless explosions that this question elicited.

That one question contained several others, each of them extraordinarily painful to even contemplate. How best to serve the memory of Reggie Jordan? Should we use the language of the killer—Standard English—in order to make our ideas acceptable to those controlling the killers? But wouldn't what we had to say be rejected, summarily, if we said it in our own language, the language of the victim, Reggie Jordan? But if we sought to express ourselves by abandoning our language wouldn't that mean our suicide on top of Reggie's murder? But if we expressed ourselves in our own language wouldn't that be suicidal to the wish to communicate with those who, evidently, did not give a damn about us/Reggie/police violence in the Black community?

At the end of one of the longest, most difficult hours of my own life, the students voted, unanimously, to preface their individual messages with a paragraph composed in the language of Reggie Jordan. *"At least we don't give up nothing else. At least we stick to the truth: Be who we been. And stay all the way with Reggie."*

55   It was heartbreaking to proceed, from that point. Everyone in the room realized that our decision in favor of Black English had doomed our writings, even as the distinctive reality of our Black lives always has doomed our efforts to "be who we been" in this country.

I went to the blackboard and took down this paragraph dictated by the class:

You Cops!

We the brother and sister of Willie Jordan, a fellow Stony Brook student who the brother of the dead Reggie Jordan. Reggie, like many brother and sister, he a victim of brutal racist police, October 25, 1984. Us appall, fed up, because that another senseless death what occur in our community. This what we feel, this, from our heart, for we ain't stayin' silent no more.

With the completion of this introduction, nobody said anything. I asked for comments. At this invitation, the unidentified visitor, a young Black man, ceaselessly smiling, raised his hand. He was, it so happens, a rookie cop. He had just joined the force in September and, he said, he thought he should clarify a few things. So he came forward and sprawled easily into a posture of barroom, or fire-side, nostalgia:

"See," Officer Charles enlightened us, "most times when you out on the street and something come down you do one of two things. Over-react or under-react. Now, if you under-react then you can get yourself kilt. And if you over-react then maybe you kill somebody. Fortunately it's about nine times out of ten and you will over-react. So the brother got kilt. And I'm sorry about that, believe me. But what you have to understand is what kilt him: Over-reaction. That's all. Now you talk about Black people and White police but see, now, I'm a cop myself. And (big smile) I'm Black. And just a couple months ago I was on the other side. But it's the same for me. You a cop, you the ultimate authority: the Ultimate Authority. And you on the street, most of the time you can only do one of two things: over-react or under-react. That's all it is with the brother. Over-reaction. Didn't have nothing to do with race."

That morning Officer Charles had the good fortune to escape without being boiled alive. But barely. And I remember the pride of his smile when I read about the fate of Black policemen and other collaborators in South Africa. I remember him, and I remember the shock and palpable feeling of shame that filled the room. It was as though that foolish, and deadly, young man had just relieved himself of his foolish, and deadly, explanation, face to face with the grief of

Reggie Jordan's father and Reggie Jordan's mother. Class ended quietly. I copied the paragraph from the blackboard, collected the individual messages and left to type them up.

60 *Newsday* rejected the piece.

The Village Voice could not find room in their "Letters" section to print the individual messages from the students to the police.

None of the TV news reporters picked up the story.

Nobody raised $180,000 to prosecute the murder of Reggie Jordan.

Reggie Jordan is really dead.

65 I asked Willie Jordan to write an essay pulling together everything important to him from that semester. He was still deeply beside himself with frustration and amazement and loss. This is what he wrote, unedited, and in its entirety:

Throughout the course of this semester I have been researching the effects of oppression and exploitation along racial lines in South Africa and its neighboring countries. I have become aware of South African police brutalization of native Africans beyond the extent of the law, even though the laws themselves are catalyst affliction upon Black men, women and children. Many Africans die each year as a result of the deliberate use of police force to protect the white power structure.

Social control agents in South Africa, such as policemen, are also used to force compliance among citizens through both overt and covert tactics. It is not uncommon to find bold-faced coercion and cold-blooded killings of Blacks by South African police for undetermined and/or inadequate reasons. Perhaps the truth is that the only reasons for this heinous treatment of Blacks rests in racial differences. We should also understand that what is conveyed through the media is not always accurate and may sometimes be construed as the tip of the iceberg at best.

I recently received a painful reminder that racism, poverty, and the abuse of power are global problems which are by no means unique to South Africa. On October 25, 1984 at approximately 3:00 p.m. my brother, Mr. Reginald Jordan, was shot and killed by two

New York City policemen from the 75th precinct in the East New York section of Brooklyn. His life ended at the age of twenty-five. Even up to this current point in time the Police Department has failed to provide my family, which consists of five brothers, eight sisters, and two parents, with a plausible reason for Reggie's death. Out of the many stories that were given to my family by the Police Department, not one of them seems to hold water. In fact, I honestly believe that the Police Department's assessment of my brother's murder is nothing short of ABSOLUTE BULLSHIT, and thus far no evidence had been produced to alter perception of the situation.

Furthermore, I believe that one of three cases may have occurred in this incident. First, Reggie's death may have been the desired outcome of the police officer's action, in which case the killing was premeditated. Or, it was a case of mistaken identity, which clarifies the fact that the two officers who killed my brother and their commanding parties are all grossly incompetent. Or, both of the above cases are correct, i.e., Reggie's murderers intended to kill him and the Police Department behaved insubordinately.

Part of the argument of the officers who shot Reggie was that he had attacked one of them and took his gun. This was their major claim. They also said that only one of them had actually shot Reggie. The facts, however, speak for themselves. According to the Death Certificate and autopsy report, Reggie was shot eight times from point-blank range. The Doctor who performed the autopsy told me himself that two bullets entered the side of my brother's head, four bullets were sprayed into his back, and two bullets struck him in the back of his legs. It is obvious that unnecessary force was used by the police and that it is extremely difficult to shoot someone in his back when he is attacking or approaching you.

After experiencing a situation like this and researching South Africa I believe that to a large degree, justice may only exist as rhetoric. I find it difficult to talk of true justice when the oppression of my people both at home and abroad attests to the fact that inequality and injustice are serious problems whereby Blacks and Third World people are perpetually short-changed by society. Something has to be done about the way in which this world is set up. Although it is a difficult task, we do have the power to make a change.

Willie J. Jordan Jr.

EGL 487, Section 58, November 14, 1984

It is my privilege to dedicate this book to the future life of Willie J. Jordan Jr., August 8, 1985.

NOTES

1. *English Is Spreading, But What Is English?* A presentation by Prof. S. N. Sridhar, Department of Linguistics, SUNY, Stony Brook, April 9, 1985: Dean's Convocation Among the Disciplines.

2. Ibid.

3. *New York Times,* March 15, 1985, Section One, p. 14: Report on Study by Linguists at the University of Pennsylvania.

4. Alice Walker, *The Color Purple* (New York: Harcourt Brace Jovanovich, 1982), p. 11.

EXPLORATORY WRITING

How does June Jordan intertwine the story of her class on Black English and the story of Willie Jordan? Would these stories have the same impact if they were presented separately? What does Jordan accomplish by weaving them together?

TALKING ABOUT THE READING

What are the advantages and disadvantages of Jordan's students' decision to write the preface to their individual messages to the police in Black English? In considering this question, take into account how Jordan's exploration of Black English in the early sections of the essay set up the difficulty of the decision.

WRITING ASSIGNMENTS

1. Write an essay that explains the point June Jordan is making about the relationship between Black English and Standard English and what she thinks ought to be taught in school and why. What are the underlying assumptions Jordan is making about the relation between language and identity?

2. Write an essay that explains what you see as the advantages and disadvantages of Jordan's students' decision to compose the introduction to their letters to the police in Black English. Arrive at your own evaluation of their decision, but before you do, explain how and in what sense the decision they had to make was a difficult one.

3. Choose a passage of dialogue in a novel or play you know well in which the speakers are speaking Standard English. Using Phil Garfield's Black English translation of a scene from *A Doll's House* as a model, translate the passage into some form of non-Standard English—whether the spoken language of your neighborhood, the vernacular of youth culture, or the dialect of a region.

VISUAL CULTURE   Picturing Schooldays

Visual images of teachers and children can be found in many places and put to many uses. A photograph of a one-room schoolhouse, for example, recaptures the early days of American schooling and summons up nostalgia for tight-knit communities of the past. By the same token, Norman Rockwell's paintings of school scenes summon up pictures of lost innocence—a time when students were well behaved and learned the three R's from strict but benevolent teachers. More recently, images of school have been used to illustrate the plight of American education, to argue for uniforms or dress codes, and to advertise new educational products.

Viewing images of schooling releases fond and not-so-fond emotional associations. Nearly everyone can remember what it was like to be in school and what their relationships were like with teachers and peers. The way people make sense of images of schooling, however, depends on more than just their personal experience. The composition of the images also provides cues about how to respond to them.

This section investigates the composition of photographs of school—to see how the pictures represent teachers and students and to examine their relationship to each other and to the institution of schooling. In particular, the section looks at how the composition of photographs uses *vectors* to establish relationships among the people in a photograph and *perspective* to establish the viewer's attitude toward what the photo represents.

Vectors

When viewers look at visual images of schooling, such as the photographs assembled below, they turn these images into a story about what the people are doing and what their relationship is to each other. Because the photograph itself is a still shot, it can't record action that occurs over time. Accordingly, viewers have to fill in the story themselves based on their familiarity with the scene pictured and the cues they take from the photograph.

To see how the composition of a photograph enables the viewer to fill in the story, look at how the people and things in the photo are connected by vectors, or the diagonal lines a viewer's eyes follow from one element of the photograph to another.

Take, for example, the first photograph—Francis Benjamin Johnston's picture of schoolchildren at the Hampton Institute saluting the American flag. The viewer recognizes the flag salute right away because it is such a familiar part of schooling and civic life. What may be puzzling is why the students' arms are outstretched in salute. The outstretched arm—or Roman salute—was the conventional way of saluting the flag until World War II, when it was changed because it reminded people of the Nazi salute to Hitler. But the photograph also contains visual cues that enable the viewer to recognize this familiar gesture. Notice in the schematic drawing how the outstretched arms and eyelines of the schoolchildren create a vector that connects them to the image of the flag and cues viewers to the interaction taking place.

Francis Benjamin Johnston, "Pledging Allegiance."

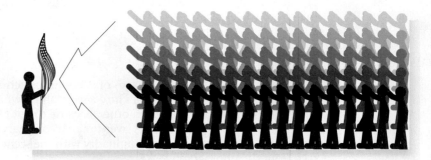

Vectors in "Pledging Allegiance."

— Wallace Kirkland, "Jane Addams Reading at Hull House, Chicago, 1930s."

Perspective

Perspective is the angle of sight—or point of view—that a photograph offers a viewer. Viewers' attitudes toward what is represented in a photograph will vary depending on perspective.

1. **Frontal** angle promotes a high level of involvement and the sense that viewers are directly engaged with the image.

2. **Oblique** angle gives viewers a sense of detachment, as though they are simply looking on as a bystander.

3. **High** angle, in which the camera looks down on the people in the photo, gives the viewer a sense of power.

4. **Low** angle, in which the camera looks up, makes the people in the photo seem powerful.

SUGGESTIONS FOR DISCUSSION

1. Francis Benjamin Johnston's photograph of the schoolchildren saluting the flag at Hampton Institute can be an unsettling one that may provoke mixed feelings. How is the viewer to respond to the photo? How do the outstretched arms, and their now unavoidable association with the Hitler salute, influence the viewer's attitude to the photograph?

Make sense of our times.

The New York Times

Expect the World®
nytimes.com

Is the viewer being asked to admire the students' patriotism and the sense of order depicted, or does the image cast the students as victims of an authoritarian system? Could both, in some sense, be true? How does the fact that the students are African Americans at an all-black school in the time of segregated education enter into your response?

2. Notice how the children are grouped in the photo "Jane Addams Reading at Hull House." What do these groupings suggest about the children's relationship to each other and to the teacher? Follow the eyelines in the photo. What vectors connect the participants, and what story do they tell? Compare the vectors in this photo to the classroom photo at the opening of the chapter. Notice too how the frontal perspective in the photo of Jane Addams compares to the oblique angle in the classroom photo. What effects on viewers' attitudes and involvement are these differing angles like to have?

3. The ad from the November 9, 2001, *New York Times* updates Norman Rockwell's fondly nostalgic painting of an idealized American classroom by overlaying a map of Afghanistan on a blackboard of birthday messages the children have written to their teacher Miss Jones. The *New York Times* designer uses this combination of Rockwell's innocent American past and the breaking news of the U.S. invasion of Afghanistan as the visual counterpoint to the ad's message "Makes sense of our times. Expect the World." Consider how the low angle of Rockwell's painting positions viewers to look up at the teacher. Notice how this compares to the high angle of the photo in the chapter's opening that looks down into the classroom.

SUGGESTED ASSIGNMENT

What photographic image could tell the story of your classroom and the prevailing relationships among the students and between the teacher and the students? For this project, work in a group with two or three other students to take a photograph of your classroom.

When composing a photographic image, consider the following questions. How would students and the teacher be distributed and grouped in space? What vectors, or eyelines, would connect them? How would you want to position the viewer in relation to the classroom? How would you frame a shot that creates the point of view and angle of sight that you want for the viewer?

When you have decided on the shot you want, take the picture. This may involve posing students and the teacher in particular ways or asking them to do certain things. Everyone in class needs to cooperate on this project—whether you are taking the picture or being its subject.

When all the groups have developed the photos, bring them to class and discuss to what extent they portray different and similar stories. Identify the main vectors in each and how they establish the key relationships among the participants. Consider, too, how the photos create points of view and degrees of involvement on the viewer's part.

Reading and Writing About Film: Reviews, History, Criticism

Understanding films involves more than just watching movies. For film buffs, fans, academics, and people in the entertainment industry, there is a wealth of material to read—from the movie reviews that appear in daily newspapers to industry information in *Variety* and other publications to popular books on the Hollywood history and academic articles in film studies. Given the sheer volume of writing about film, it can be helpful to sort these writings into categories, to look at the various genres of writing about film in order to identify the purposes they embody and the interests they serve. Here we consider three common genres of writing about film:

- **Reviews**. Reviews offer description and evaluation of recently released films. Most newspapers and many magazines have film reviewers on staff. The reviews of a film create what is called its critical reception. Sometime reviewers agree about the merits of a film but often they are divided in their views. Of course, the reviewers' opinions may or may not match the popularity of a particular film, and in some cases films that have come to be considered "classics" received negative or lukewarm reviews.

- **Histories**. Film histories enable readers to see the evolution of the media—whether they trace the Hollywood studios, postwar Italian cinema, or such genres as westerns, musicals, or thrillers. Histories can lead you to watch older films, to see the role they played in the development of film. They are particularly valuable in research projects to analyze, say, how film noir reflected the anxieties of the Cold War of the 1950s (which is discussed in Jon Tuska's *Dark Cinema: American Film Noir in Cultural Perspective*) or how independent filmmakers challenged the Hollywood studios in the 1970s (described in Gene Biskind's *Easy Riders, Raging Bulls*).

- **Criticism**. Film criticism offers more specialized analyses of particular aspects of filmmaking. Typically, film criticism begins with a sense of an issue: the contribution of a particular director, how viewers watch films, how films represent particular groups of people, how films reflect social understandings of sexuality. You can find studies of individual directors, such as Alfred Hitchcock or Stanley Kubrick or Orson Welles. There are also studies of how films position their viewers, such as Laura Mulvey's classic essay "Visual Pleasure and Narrative Cinema," and bell hooks's writings about how films represent African Americans, in *Black Looks*. To get a sense of the range of issues and topics film critics write about, browse through leading film journals such as *Film Quarterly, Sight and Sound*, and *Screen*.

FIELDWORK   Classroom Observation

Most students know that being successful in school means understanding what teachers value and what they expect from students. This is sometimes called "psyching out" a teacher, and students learn to be good at it. They do this by evaluating the formal requirements of the course (e.g., reading assignments, labs, homework, tests, papers), by observing what takes place in the classroom (e.g., lectures, discussion, films, group work), and by learning the teacher's personality and eccentricities.

The purpose of this project is to investigate what it takes to be successful in a course in which you are enrolled and to draw some conclusions about the nature of teaching and learning. The method used is participant/observation. You are asked, in effect, to observe yourself, your teacher, and other students and to take detailed notes on what you do in and out of class.

Several weeks will be needed for this project so that you can accumulate a sufficient amount of entries in your field log to make your observations reliable and conclusions possible.

FIELD LOG

As a participant-observer, you need to keep a field log on the classes, reading assignments, papers, exams, sections or labs if pertinent, study groups, and informal conversations outside class.

Background

When you start this project, write a statement that summarizes what you know about the course at this time. Ask yourself the following questions:

1. *Why are you taking the class?* To fulfill a requirement, for personal interest, for some other motivation?

2. *Read the syllabus:* How does it describe the content of the course and what you will learn? What are the assignments? How will the course grade be determined?

3. *Describe the format of the class:* What size is the class? In what kind of room does it meet? Does it look like it will be mostly lecture, discussion, a combination of the two, something else? Keep track of attendance patterns. Note where students sit to see if patterns develop.

4. *From what you can tell so far, what will you need to do to get the grade you want?*

Field Notes

Field notes consist of the observations you record during and outside class. Use these questions:

1. *Where do you sit in class?* Why?

2. *How do you actually spend your time in class?* Taking notes, doodling, engaging in class discussion, looking around, writing notes to other students, daydreaming,

talking to other students, working on something for another class, reading a newspaper or magazine?

3. *What does the teacher do in class?* Is it the same thing every day or does it change? How does the teacher run the class? Do individual class meetings have a routine format? Is there a set schedule (e.g., lecture Monday, discussion Wednesday, film Friday)? Who talks?

4. *What do other students do?*

5. *What do you do outside class?* Keep track of the time devoted to various activities: reading assignments, reviewing or rewriting notes, studying for tests (alone or with others), attending lab sessions or section meetings, doing research, writing papers, meeting with the teacher or assistant, talking informally with other students about the class, and so on.

Analysis

Review your notes and look for patterns and key points. Here are some questions to consider:

1. *Compare what you know now about the course with what you wrote earlier on in your field log:* Have your responses changed? Does the course syllabus give an accurate forecast of what to expect, or have you become aware in other ways of the "real" requirements of the class? Have you changed your mind about the grade you think you might get?

2. *What kinds of patterns emerge from notes on what you do in class?* Do you do the same thing in every class, or does your activity vary? Have you consciously changed what you do in class? If so, why?

3. *Has the work returned to you so far (homework, tests, quizzes, papers, etc.) confirmed or revised what you thought it would take to do well in the course?* What have you learned about the teacher's expectations and preferences?

4. *How does the work you do outside class figure in?* Could you skip class and still do well? Do you do all the work or only certain assignments? Do you have a system for deciding what to do and not do? If so, how did you develop it? Do you meet with or talk to the teacher, the teaching assistant, or other students about the class?

5. *What patterns emerge from your observations of other students?*

6. *What are the main differences and similarities in the courses you have observed?* What is their significance?

Writing the Report

For this project, use a version of the standard format for reports.

- **Introduction.** Explain what you are investigating and the purpose of your research. Identify the class you observed, its enrollment, usual attendance, course requirements, and any other pertinent information. It can help readers to summarize this information in a diagram that accompanies your Introduction. (See Table 3.1. on p. 190)

- **Method.** Explain how you gathered data.

- ■ **Observations.** Summarize key points from your field log to establish patterns and to characterize your participation in the course. (See the sample Observations.)
- ■ **Conclusions.** Derive inferences and generalizations from your observations. (See sample Conclusions.)

OBSERVATIONS AND CONCLUSIONS FROM "CROSS-CURRICULAR UNDERLIFE: A COLLABORATIVE REPORT ON WAYS WITH ACADEMIC WORDS"

■■■— *Worth Anderson, Cynthia Best, Alycia Black, John Hurst, Brandt Miller, and Susan Miller*

> The following Observations and Conclusions come from a longer article written by a group of undergraduates at the University of Utah in an independent study course under the direction of Susan Miller, a faculty member in English and a prominent writing theorist. Following an introductory section, the article consists of observations and conclusions written by the various members of the research group.

SAMPLE OBSERVATIONS

Art History

1 On the first day of class, the professor urged us all to drop, said she was willing to dispense drop cards to everyone, launched into a lecture that filled the time, handed out a syllabus, and reminded us that it was not too late to drop. I promptly named her "Madame Battleaxe."

It got worse. She was the embodiment of objectivist theories: "There are these facts. They constitute Truth. I will speak. You will listen. You will emerge with Truth." She spoke quickly, had some funky uses for the word "sensuous." I take notes very poorly, so I just sat and listened. A friend who sat beside me and played stenographer was frustrated by this, but for me I did better by just listening.

I realized that I was having trouble memorizing dates on pictures, so I went to see her. We got to talking about Charles V, and amazingly, I liked her. She reassured me about the test, and explained how highly she valued coherent writing, composed with an eye to history. I

decided that she considered herself a historian, so her audience values would be in that community.

After our meeting, I was far more tolerant of her in class. On the midterm and final I wrote much more than anyone else, and emerged both times with the top grade. Serving up what she wanted worked.

Sociology

5 The teacher basically taught lecture one day—film one day—lecture one day. . . . I believe that it's good to develop a routine, but not a rut! At first people groaned when they found out we were going to be watching another film. Once the students realized how the class would be taught, they began walking out during the films and lectures. One day I counted twenty-two people who walked out during a film. Later, the students developed a different routine. They would come to class and stay only if there was a film (so they could answer the test questions). But they would leave if the teacher was lecturing because they felt they could get more from reading the book.

TABLE 3.1 Descriptions of Courses Observed

Student	Course Title	Enrollment and % Usual Attendance	Course Requirements and Student Interpretations of them (MC=Multiple Choice)
Worth	Anthropology	90 (60%)	Pass 2 MC midterms; take notes, attend, study notes; 1-pg. extra credit paper.
	Common Medicines	150 (90%)	2 MC tests: drug names, uses; memorize, memorize; good notes are critical; final cramming will not do here.
	International Studies: Africa	55 (90%)	4 short ans. tests; 6-pg. paper. Study ugly stuff like population distribution.
	Art History	100 (95%)	Midterm and Final, both essay. Memorize names and dates; concepts not a problem.
Cynthia	Anthropology	76 (60%)	Read for weekly quizzes, watch films, pass MC midterm and final; 1-pg. book review for extra credit.
	Intellectual Trad. of the West (Medieval)	25 (90%)	Write 4 papers, essay midterm and final. Read, attend.
	Sociology	400 (50%)	3 MC tests. Read, take notes, watch films.
Alycia	Intellectual Trad. of the West (Medieval)	25 (80%)	1 paper; midterm, final with take-home essay. 150–200 pp./wk. reading.
	Critical Literature	22 (60–75%)	3 papers; response paragraphs; 15–60 min. reading/night to practice analyzing.
	Law	20 (95%)	10 1-page papers; research on topic about church and state.
John	Astronomy	105 (60%)	MC tests. Attend, read text, extra credit for 1000-word report.
	Psychology	155 (70–75%)	MC tests. Attend, read text, extra credit for being a subject in dept. experiments.
	Basic Acting II	9 (100%)	Perform 2 scenes, one monologue; attend 3 plays, review 2 of them.
Brandt	Calculus	35 (80%)	Problem sets. Take notes; geometrically interpret concepts; review and keep up.
	Chemistry	450 (70%)	Problems sets and MC test; read to get high grades on tests.
	History of Science	20 (97%)	Essay midterm and final; paper. Take notes and refer to them when reading; research final paper (use Wr. 210 skills); do well on final by catching up.

The teacher lectured from an outline of key words on the overhead projector. Several people commented that his lectures were hard to follow, but I thought they weren't too difficult because he followed the book. In fact, at times he read straight from it! The professor had the habit of leaning on the lectern while he lectured and placing his hand on his chin. (It almost covered his mouth!) One day I observed, "Five people walked out of the lecture early. I assume from the time that had elapsed that it was after they'd copied the outline. I noticed people who simply copied the outline of key words and then just sat there in a kind of stupor."

In such a large class I noticed diverse student behaviors. One day during the film, as I counted the twelve people who left early, the girl to my left did homework for another class, the guy in front of me ate yogurt, and the guy to my right organized his Franklin Day Planner. I rarely took notes on the films because they were irrelevant, but some people took notes anyway. One girl's notes consisted of "Boring—Big Time!"

Calculus

I would go early to hear students discuss assignments and compare solutions to take-home quizzes, but this seemed almost a formality rather than a concern over concepts. When the professor began to work rapidly on the board, the lead flew across my notebook. She may not be exceptionally exciting, but unless you pay attention, you get lost fast. There was only moderate interaction between students and instructor by way of questions. Amazingly few questions are raised about such complex material.

There were several overlapping communities of student interaction in this class. Although it was a small class, there were many students whose names I didn't know, and could barely recognize by sight. I think this was because math is an independent discipline. You only need to interact with a few students to find the right answer. I took notes the whole time. After class, I would talk to students who could explain concepts like double integration a little better than what I had understood.

10 Math is a very sequential subject. When I had had trouble understanding the last assignment, I knew it would only compound with a new one. Today's concepts would be based on what we learned yesterday, which was based on the day before. Students had a tough time when they hadn't been here. Dr. A. covers the new material by relating it to yesterday's material, which makes it easier. Dr. A. becomes a narrator for the strange mathematical figures that appear on the board.

When Dr. A. explained what kind of questions there would be on tests, she sometimes let us use a "cheat sheet," so we knew it would be hard. I would meet with other students to study.

SAMPLE CONCLUSIONS

A. In ITW, I learned both on my own and in class. I learned as I read the assignments alone, and then my knowledge was expanded when the professor expounded on the material. Sections of this course are taught by teachers from different disciplines, so students who take more than one part of the sequence learn about ideas and about professors' specific fields. This section was actually "taught." The history professor who taught it connected ideas to historical background. But in Sociology, I learned the most from the text. The instructor's lectures were helpful, but I gained very little from the films. Ironically though, I preferred the films to the lectures. As I wrote one day, "I enjoyed the film simply because I didn't have to listen to another lecture." Anthropology was not "taught." The professor simply spouted facts each day. In considering where the learning occurred here, I've decided I learned most from the text. The films were informative and very helpful, but they were never shown at the right times. I really struggled with the professor's lectures, yet I learned from my notes because that's the only place that certain material was given.

School is a contract between a student and a teacher. Each must share a mutual respect for the other for learning to occur. In my liberal education courses, the teachers were not as concerned about the classes as they should have been. I got the impression that these teachers were being punished. They were bored because the material was so fundamental to their disciplines. But to the students, the material is new. If the professor shows excitement and projects a positive attitude, students will tend to be more interested in learning. Large classes require more effort from both students and teachers.

B. Generally, the crucial part of learning in any classroom is digging up what the professor expects. I find that all classes require exceptional note-taking and analytical reading. Not all classes "require" attendance; in some I learn more from reading than from going to class. Poorly attended classes are those where the professor reads the text and gives no additional information. Well attended classes are taught by professors who enjoy the subject and make the students feel comfortable with it.

15   Although most of the students' learning must be done outside of class, an attitude toward learning is developed in the classroom. The professor's role is crucial because the students will be as active as the teacher is. Many of my peers say that the average student counts on having at least one "blow-off" class. If a teacher is strict, the students will make greater efforts and follow the teacher's guidelines. If a teacher is dull and doesn't include fun tidbits or allow us to express varying views, the students will find the material dull and difficult to study. But if the professor is excited, encourages us to voice different opinions, and interacts with us, the students will be excited about the subject and have an easier time.

MINING THE ARCHIVE

Textbooks from the Past

A Doll for Jane

"Hello, Father," said Dick.

"Jane will have a birthday soon.

Please get a new doll for Jane.

Get a baby doll that talks.

Please get a doll that talks."

15

Text and illustrations pp. 18–19 from *The New Fun with Dick and Jane* by William S. Gray, et al. Illustrated by Keith Ward and Eleanor Campbell. Scott Foresman, copyright 1956.

One way to get a sense of schooling in an earlier time is to take a look at that period's textbooks. Two of the most famous and popular series were designed to teach reading: *McGuffey's Eclectic Readers,* used by millions of American children during the nineteenth century, and the Dick and Jane primers, used from the 1930s to the 1960s. Each series offers a fascinating view of how elementary school students learned to read as well as the kinds of social values transmitted through the reading lessons. On the one hand, the McGuffey readers were anthologies of essays, poems, speeches, and stories filled with moral advice, patriotic ideas, and religious instruction. Heavily didactic in tone, the content of the readers was meant to be morally uplifting. The Dick and Jane readers, on the other hand, created a child's world of fun and surprise. Dick and Jane, along with their little sister, Sally, dog, Spot, and kitten, Puff, lived in an American dream of white-picket-fenced suburban homes, loving parents, laughter, and security. Most college and large public libraries will have copies of *McGuffey's Eclectic Reader* and some will have Dick and Jane readers as well. You can also find selections from the two textbook series in Elliot J. Gorn, ed., *The McGuffey Readers: Selections from the 1879 Edition* (Boston: Bedford, 1998), and Carol Kismaric and Marvin Heiferman, *Growing Up with Dick and Jane: Learning and Living the American Dream* (San Francisco: Collins Publishers, 1996). Researching these textbooks can lead to writing projects that focus on a range of topics. Below are a few examples; take these or design your own:

- Nineteenth-century reading instruction.
- The Protestant middle-class values of the McGuffey readers.
- Gender stereotypes in Dick and Jane.
- The postwar American dream in the Dick and Jane primers.

CHAPTER FOUR

Images

> In no other form of society in history has there been such a concentration of images, such a density of visual messages.
>
> —John Berger, *Ways of Seeing*

Photo courtesy of *Nation* magazine.

We are surrounded daily by the image. On billboards, in magazines, on television, in film and video, on our computer screens, and in nearly every public and private space, visual messages of all sorts compete for our attention. They carry information from corporate advertisers, nonprofit organizations, public and private institutions, friends and family, and they ask us to buy, to give, to believe, to subscribe, to respond, to understand, to act.

Visual communication has, of course, been an important part of communication practices for centuries. Throughout human history such images as paintings, drawings, designs, sketches, and icons did not merely decorate the insides of caves, temples, palaces, and the like but also chronicled family and community life; taught lessons in religion, culture, and politics; and even gave directions.

What is different in our experience with images today are the vast numbers and many kinds available and the ease with which they can be reproduced, imitated, parodied, reconstructed, and distributed. Also new is the aggressive nature of the image. Unless we purposefully isolate ourselves from the industrial world, it is difficult to avoid ads on street corners, buses, trains—nearly every public surface. Airlines now show a continuous loop of advertising even on some short flights, assuring themselves of a captive audience. Recently, the *New York Times* reported on a company that managed to create what the *Times* called "billboards that look back." These billboards are equipped "with tiny cameras that gather details about passers-by—their gender, approximate age and how long they looked at the billboard. These details are transmitted to a central database." From the scans, the billboard can change the message to suit the viewer. According to the report, the aim is "to tailor a digital display to the person standing in front of it—to show one advertisement to a middle-aged white woman, for example, and a different one to a teenage Asian boy." Such technology illustrates one perhaps inevitable outcome of an advertising industry in heavy competition for consumers' attention.

As you look at and consider the visual messages around you, remember that you don't have to be mindless consumers of visual culture. You are a producer as well, and you can make your own visual messages. One thing that bothers many people when they look at ads is the assuredness with which advertisers sell lifestyles and attempt to create new interests. Knowing that most people let ads go by without reading them closely, some activists write over ads to attract the public's attention to the alternative or oppositional readings possible in an ad campaign. You will find some of those rewrites in this chapter, in the feature "Visual Essay: Rewriting the Image," where you will have the opportunity to do some rewrites of your own. While many rewrites comment on advertising or art tastes, others simply take advantage of familiar images to make new statements. Take, for example, the cover on the January 3, 2005, issue of the *Nation* magazine (the opening image for this chapter). Cover designers took the extremely popular Depression-era Dorothea Lange photograph of Florence Thompson (see the Visual Guide, pp. 6–13), often called "Migrant Madonna," to comment on current economic conditions. They relied on their readers recognizing this as a reference to the Great Depression. They updated the clothing just slightly and added a Wal-Mart employee's badge to the outfit. In that way, the image alone signals the theme of the magazine's January 2005 issue. In that way, the image looks back to the past (the Great Depression) to link that past with current economic conditions.

This chapter raises a number of questions about images—how they work; whom they are addressing; what influence they do or do not have on the ways we imagine our world; even whether or not they tell the truth. Many of the visuals we cover here are taken from print ads and photography because most students and faculty have fairly easy access to still images, and still images can be studied carefully for long periods of time. However, the power of the visual to convey messages is not at all limited to advertising and photography. Television, film, music videos, YouTube, even the very layout of the page—all of these convey meaning and contribute to how a culture imagines itself. The fact that there has been a rapid rise in visual communication of all sorts signals, as well, an increased demand for all of us to become active readers and producers of visual text.

IN THE SHADOW OF THE IMAGE

— Stuart Ewen and Elizabeth Ewen

Stuart Ewen and Elizabeth Ewen have each written several books and articles on the history and meaning of popular culture. Cultural scholar Stuart Ewen's work includes *All Consuming Images: The Politics of Style in Contemporary Culture* and *Captains of Consciousness.* Historian Elizabeth Ewen's work includes *Immigrant Women in the Land of Dollars* (1985). *Channels of Desire* (1982), from which the following selection is taken, is their first full-length collaboration. The Ewens argue that much of what Americans understand about self-image is actually a reflection of mass-media images. As this essay illustrates, today's culture is one living "in the shadow of the image," whether the image is present in advertising, news reporting, or popular television and film. Everywhere people go, they see images created for mass consumption but aimed at individuals. Sometimes consciously but mostly not, people measure their looks, their moods, their success or lack of it against the appearances that surround them daily.

SUGGESTION FOR READING In preparation for class discussion, take a personal product inventory. What major brands do you notice in the clothes you wear, in the food you buy, or in hair products you use? What ads do you see during most days? Notice whether you and your friends talk about going, say, to lunch or going to McDonald's (or another chain restaurant brand). How much of your attachment to specific brands is conscious and how much seems to go without saying (shopping for an iPod, for example, instead of an MP3 player)? What are the predominant ad images in your personal product inventory? Bring your inventory to class for discussion.

1 Maria Aguilar was born twenty-seven years ago near Mayagüez, on the island of Puerto Rico. Her family had lived off the land for generations. Today she sits in a rattling IRT subway car, speeding through the iron-and-rock guts of Manhattan. She sits on the train, her ears dazed by the loud outcry of wheels against tracks. Surrounded by a galaxy of unknown fellow strangers, she looks up at a long strip of colorful signboards placed high above the bobbing heads of the others. All the posters call for her attention.

Looking down at her, a blond-haired lady cabdriver leans out of her driver's side window. Here is the famed philosopher of this strange urban world, and a woman she can talk to. The tough-wise eyes of the cabby combine with a youthful beauty, speaking to Maria Aguilar directly:

Estoy sentada 12 horas al dia.
Lo último que necesito son hemorroides.
(I sit for twelve hours a day. The last thing I
need are hemorrhoids.)

Under this candid testimonial lies a package of Preparation H ointment, and the promise *"Alivia dolores y picasonas. Y ayuda a reducir la hinchazón."* (Relieves pain and itching. And helps reduce swelling.) As her mind's eye takes it all in, the train sweeps into Maria's stop. She gets out; climbs the stairs to the street; walks to work where she will spend her day sitting on a stool in a small garment factory, sewing hems on pretty dresses.

Every day, while Benny Doyle drives his Mustang to work along State Road Number 20, he passes a giant billboard along the shoulder. The billboard is selling whisky and features a woman in a black velvet dress stretching across its brilliant canvas.

5 As Benny Doyle downshifts by, the lounging beauty looks out to him. Day after day he sees her here. The first time he wasn't sure, but now he's convinced that her eyes are following him.

The morning sun shines on the red-tan forehead of Bill O'Conner as he drinks espresso on his sun deck, alongside the ocean cliffs of La Jolla, California. Turning through the daily paper, he reads a story about Zimbabwe.

"Rhodesia," he thinks to himself.

The story argues that a large number of Africans in Zimbabwe are fearful about black majority rule, and are concerned over a white exodus. Two black hotel workers are quoted by the article. Bill puts this, as a fact, into his mind.

Later that day, over a business lunch, he repeats the story to five white business associates, sitting at the restaurant table. They share a superior laugh over the ineptitude of black African political rule. Three more tellings, children of the first, take place over the next four days. These are spoken by two of Bill O'Conner's luncheon companions; passed on to still others in the supposed voice of political wisdom.

10 Barbara and John Marsh get into their seven-year-old Dodge pickup and drive twenty-three miles to the nearest Sears in Cedar Rapids. After years of breakdowns and months of hesitation they've decided to buy a new washing machine. They come to Sears because it is there, and because they believe that their new Sears machine will be steady and reliable. The Marshes will pay for their purchase for the next year or so.

Barbara's great-grandfather, Elijah Simmons, had purchased a cream-separator from Sears, Roebuck in 1897 and he swore by it.

When the clock-radio sprang the morning affront upon him, Archie Bishop rolled resentfully out of his crumpled bed and trudged slowly to the john. A few moments later he was unconsciously squeezing toothpaste out of a mess of red and white Colgate packaging. A dozen scrubs of the mouth and he expectorated a white, minty glob into the basin.

Still groggy, he turned on the hot water, slapping occasional palmfuls onto his gray face.

A can of Noxzema shave cream sat on the edge of the sink, a film of crud and whiskers across its once neat label. Archie reached for the bomb and filled his left hand with a white creamy mound, then spread it over his beard. He shaved, then looked with resignation at the regular collection of cuts on his neck.

15 Stepping into a shower, he soaped up with a soap that promised to wake him up. Groggily, he then grabbed a bottle of Clairol Herbal Essence Shampoo. He turned the tablet-shaped bottle to its back label, carefully reading the "Directions."

"Wet hair."

He wet his hair.

"Lather."

He lathered.

20 "Rinse."

He rinsed.

"Repeat if necessary."

Not sure whether it was altogether necessary, he repeated the process according to directions.

Late in the evening, Maria Aguilar stepped back in the subway train, heading home to the Bronx after a long and tiring day. This time, a poster told her that "The Pain Stops Here!"

25 She barely noticed, but later she would swallow two New Extra Strength Bufferin tablets with a glass of water from a rusty tap.

Two cockroaches in cartoon form leer out onto the street from a wall advertisement. The man cockroach is drawn like a hipster, wearing shades and a cockroach zoot-suit. He strolls hand-in-hand with a lady cockroach, who is dressed like a floozy and blushing beet-red. Caught in the midst of their cockroach-rendezvous, they step sinfully into a Black Flag Roach Motel. Beneath them, in Spanish, the words:

> *Las Cucarachas entran . . . pero non pueden salir.*
> (In the English version: Cockroaches check in . . . but they don't check out.)

The roaches are trapped; sin is punished. Salvation is gauged by one's ability to live roach-free. The sinners of the earth shall be inundated by roaches. Moral tales and insects encourage passersby to rid their houses of sin. In their homes, sometimes, people wonder whether God has forsaken them.

Beverly Jackson sits at a metal and tan Formica table and looks through the *New York Post*. She is bombarded by a catalog of horror. Children are mutilated . . . subway riders attacked . . . . Fanatics are marauding and noble despots lie in bloody heaps. Occasionally someone steps off the crime-infested streets to claim a million dollars in lottery winnings.

Beverly Jackson's skin crawls; she feels a knot encircling her lungs. She is beset by immobility, hopelessness, depression.

30 Slowly she walks over to her sixth-floor window, gazing out into the sooty afternoon. From the empty street below, Beverly Jackson imagines a crowd yelling "Jump! . . . Jump!"

Between 1957 and 1966 Frank Miller saw a dozen John Wayne movies, countless other westerns and war dramas. In 1969 he led a charge up a hill without a name in Southeast Asia. No one followed; he took a bullet in the chest.

Today he sits in a chair and doesn't get up. He feels that images betrayed him, and now he camps out across from the White House while another movie star cuts benefits for veterans. In the morning newspaper he reads of a massive weapons buildup taking place.

Gina Concepcion now comes to school wearing the Jordache look. All this has been made possible by weeks and weeks of afterschool employment at a supermarket checkout counter.

Now, each morning, she tugs the decorative denim over her young legs, sucking in her lean belly to close the snaps.

These pants are expensive compared to the "no-name" brands, but they're worth it, she reasons. They fit better, and she fits better.

35 The theater marquee, stretching out over a crumbling, garbage-strewn sidewalk, announced "The Decline of Western Civilization." At the ticket window a smaller sign read "All seats $5.00."

It was ten in the morning and Joyce Hopkins stood before a mirror next to her bed. Her interview at General Public Utilities, Nuclear Division, was only four hours away and all she could think was "What to wear?"

A half hour later Joyce stood again before the mirror, wearing a slip and stockings. On the bed, next to her, lay a two-foot-high mountain of discarded options. Mocking the title of a recent bestseller, which she hadn't read, she said aloud to herself, "Dress for Success . . . What do they like?"

At one o'clock she walked out the door wearing a brownish tweed jacket; a cream-colored Qiana blouse, full-cut with a tied collar; a dark beige skirt, fairly straight and hemmed (by Maria Aguilar) two inches below the knee; shear fawn stockings, and simple but elegant reddish-brown pumps on her feet. Her hair was to the shoulder, her look tawny.

When she got the job she thanked her friend Millie, a middle manager, for the tip not to wear pants.

40 Joe Davis stood at the endless conveyor, placing caps on a round-the-clock parade of automobile radiators. His nose and eyes burned. His ears buzzed in the din. In a furtive moment he looked up and to the right. On the plant wall was a large yellow sign with THINK! printed on it in bold type. Joe turned back quickly to the radiator caps.

Fifty years earlier, in another factory, in another state, Joe's grandfather, Nat Davis, had looked up and seen another sign:

A Clean Machine Runs Better.
Your Body Is a Machine.
KEEP IT CLEAN.

Though he tried and tried, Joe Davis' grandfather was never able to get the dirt out from under his nails. Neither could his great-grandfather, who couldn't read.

In 1952 Mary Bird left her family in Charleston to earn money as a maid in a Philadelphia suburb. She earned thirty-five dollars a week, plus room and board, in a dingy retreat of a ranch-style tract house.

Twenty-eight years later she sits on a bus, heading toward her small room in North Philly. Across from her, on an advertising poster, a sumptuous meal is displayed. Golden fried chicken, green beans glistening with butter and flecked by pimento, and a fluffy cloud of rice fill the greater part of a calico-patterned dinner plate. Next to the plate sit a steaming boat of gravy, and an icy drink in an amber tumbler. The plate is on a quilted blue placemat, flanked by a thick linen napkin and colonial silverware.

45 As Mary Bird's hungers are aroused, the wording on the placard instructs her: "Come Home to Carolina."

Shopping List

paper towels
milk
eggs
rice crispies
chicken
snacks for kids (twinkies, chips, etc.)
potatoes
coke, ginger ale, plain soda
cheer
brillo
peanut butter
bread
ragu (2 jars)
spaghetti
saran wrap
salad
get cleaning, bank, must pay electric!!!

On his way to Nina's house, Sidney passed an ad for Smirnoff vodka. A sultry beauty with wet hair and beads of moisture on her smooth, tanned face looked out at him. "Try a Main Squeeze." For a teenage boy the invitation transcended the arena of drink; he felt a quick throb-pulse at the base of his belly and his step quickened.

In October of 1957, at the age of two and a half, Aaron Stone was watching television. Suddenly, from the black screen, there leaped a circus clown, selling children's vitamins, and yelling "Hi! boys and girls!" He ran, terrified, from the room, screaming.

For years after, Aaron watched television in perpetual fear that the vitamin clown would reappear. Slowly his family assured him that the television was just a mechanical box and couldn't really hurt him, that the vitamin clown was harmless.

Today, as an adult, Aaron Stone takes vitamins, is ambivalent about clowns, and watches television, although there are occasional moments of anxiety.

50 These are some of the facts of our lives; disparate moments, disconnected, dissociated. Meaningless moments. Random incidents. Memory traces. Each is an unplanned encounter, part of day-to-day existence. Viewed alone, each by itself, such spaces of our lives seem insignificant, trivial. They are the decisions and reveries of survival; the stuff of small talk; the chance preoccupations of our eyes and minds in a world of images—soon forgotten.

Viewed together, however, as an ensemble, an integrated panorama of social life, human activity, hope and despair, images and information, another tale unfolds from these vignettes. They reveal a pattern of life, the structures of perception.

As familiar moments in American life, all of these events bear the footprints of a history that weighs upon us, but is largely untold. We live and breathe an atmosphere where mass images are everywhere in evidence; mass produced, mass distributed. In the streets, in our homes, among a crowd, or alone, they speak to us, overwhelm our vision. Their presence, their messages are given; unavoidable. Though their history is still relatively short, their prehistory is, for the most part, forgotten, unimaginable.

The history that unites the seemingly random routines of daily life is one that embraces the rise of an industrial consumer society. It involves explosive interactions between modernity and old ways of life. It includes the proliferation, over days and decades, of a wide, repeatable vernacular of commercial images and ideas. This history spells new patterns of social, productive, and political life.

EXPLORATORY WRITING

Although the bulk of this selection consists of fictional vignettes—stories about people encountering advertising and how those repeated encounters affect their thinking, the Ewens shift to a direct argument near the end. They write, "The history that unites the seemingly random routines of daily life is one that embraces the rise of an industrial consumer society. It involves explosive interactions between modernity and old ways of life. It includes the proliferation, over days and decades, of a wide, repeatable vernacular of commercial images and ideas. This history spells new patterns of social, productive, and political life." To explore the larger implications of this statement for your work on advertising images, begin by writing an explanation of what you understand the authors to be arguing and how that argument plays out in your experience. What "explosive interactions between modernity and old ways of life" are set up by the heavy bombardment of advertising? What "new patterns of social, productive, and political life" are set up by this history? In order to do this, you'll need to reread several of the vignettes and make notes on what those vignettes seem to be getting at. Then reread the conclusion—especially the passage quoted here—and write in your own words what the Ewens are arguing. Quote passages or refer to specific vignettes to make sure your restatement of the argument matches what the Ewens are getting at in their piece.

TALKING ABOUT THE READING

Some ad images are so effective that they become almost an unconscious part of the culture. Take, for example, Apple's "Hi, I'm a Mac" image of the cool, laid back Justin Long as the look for Mac (and hipness) while the insecure, suit-wearing image of John Hodgman ("And I'm a PC") has become synonymous with older, stuffy, and rigid values that don't work well. That is how the "Jordache look" from the Ewens' Gina Concepcion vignette also works to help Gina "fit in" at school.

For a discussion of the role advertising images play in people's lives, join with a group of your classmates to create a list of products and product images that identify with a specific lifestyle, personality, or look. If you took a personal product inventory before class, use that inventory to help create your group lists. What are some of the looks you and your group would identify as popular from ads you see today?

WRITING ASSIGNMENTS

1. Write a series of vignettes about the daily encounters that you, your friends, and your family have with ad images. Pay attention to how the Ewens structure their piece. The

vignettes lead to a summary statement in which the authors briefly explain what such a sequence of encounters might mean. Include a statement that draws your reader away from the vignettes and sums up the stories with a commentary on your daily encounters with visual messages of all sorts.

2. If you have not taken a personal product inventory, begin this assignment by making a list of name-brand products in your closets, the foods you purchase, your personal hygiene products, your digital and electronic equipment, the car you drive, and the places you eat, for example. If you have already taken inventory, review your list and, if necessary, add to it. Choose 4–6 of these products for an essay in which you examine the images associated with them. What economic, age, gender, or regional appeals are apparent in the visuals? For example, do they portray a certain image of beauty, of patriotism, of youth, of economic success? How do the visuals convey those appeals?

3. For this assignment, choose a commonly used product like dog food or laundry detergent or flat-screen televisions, and analyze the visuals you find in ads for the product to determine its target market (the people the company is pitching its advertising to). Baby food ads, for example, are obviously pitched at parents in general, usually mothers. Some ads, however, are now pitched at stay-at-home fathers, first-time parents, or grandparents. Some products use different visuals to pitch to very different market sectors, depending on where the ad will appear. Ads for automobiles in family magazines might highlight safety features while the same car in *Road and Driver* would feature performance and the same in the *New Yorker* might feature luxury. Collect 5–7 ads from different sources for your analysis. Make sure you refer to specific features in the ads to support your concusion.

WHEN YOU MEET ESTELLA SMART, YOU BEEN MET!

■■—*Vertamae Smart-Grosvenor*

Vertamae Smart-Grosvenor describes herself as a "poet, culinary anthropologist and writer." She has written books and numerous essays, poems, and articles for national magazines and newspapers, including the *New York Times,* the *Washington Post, Redbook,* and *Ebony.* Her autobiographical cookbook *Vibration Cooking or the Travel Notes of a Geechee Girl* was first published in 1970 and reissued in 1986 and again in 1992. For several years, she was a commentator on NPR's *All Things Considered* and served as host of their documentary series *Horizons.* The following essay appeared in 1994 in the Deborah Willis collection *Picturing Us: African American Identity in Photography.*

SUGGESTION
FOR READING
Smart-Grosvenor's essay uses a photograph of her grandmother to prompt memories about the grandmother and about growing up. Most of the memories she has of those people and times are not in pictures, though she tells us she wishes she did have photographs of some of them. Before you read, think of a family story or a person in your past you wish you had a picture of.

1 If family stories were photographs, I'd need a small museum to house them, but a shoe box could hold all the photos I have of my family. Devastation by fire was a common occurrence in the wooden-frame houses where my family lived in rural South Carolina—besides which, photo opportunities were few and far between. Few photos survived.

Estella Smart.

Memories are our photos. The family history is told in stories; and I mean those Geechee people tell some stories!

I would do the hucklebuck in Macy's window for a photo of my great-grandfather Mott. They say he was a seven-feet-tall African man who could jump so high that his heels clicked three times before he came down. And they say his voice was so powerful that when he called "quitting time" you could hear him on plantations in the next county.

Not too long ago a bank was running TV spots called "First Americans." The idea was to talk about a person in your family who was or did something unusual and succeeded. I submitted Granddaddy Mott's name. He was a first American, and succeeded in spite of bitter southern oppression to live to be ninety-five years old.

5   I never heard from the bank. I'm convinced it's because I didn't have a photo.

On the other hand, I do have a picture of my grandmother, and it is one of my most treasured possessions.

Estella Smart was my grandmother on my father's side. I could say she was my paternal grandmother, but I like the way they say it back home.

For sure the picture was taken in Philadelphia where my grandmother, like many other southern blacks, migrated in the forties in search of a better life.

And I believe it was taken in the 1100 block of Girard Avenue. On visits to my grandmother I remember seeing a studio there, where on the weekend a steady stream of southern migrants came, eager to have the camera catch their likeness, to send home so everybody could see how well they were doing in the promised land.

10 Like most of the southern arrivals, my grandmother worked as a domestic when she first came to Philadelphia.

She hated it.

"I can't stand cleaning my own house, so you know I didn't want to clean nobody else's!"

So she worked as a domestic by day, and at night went to school to learn factory sewing, eventually getting the factory job she held until she retired in the sixties.

They say that children don't know that their lives or family circumstances are weird or different. To them that's what it is. I'm not sure that's always true. I knew straightaway my grandmother was different.

15 She just didn't or wouldn't do things the way everybody did, and it didn't seem to bother her. But it bothered almost everybody else. They had moved north to better themselves, and one of the first ways to do that was to get rid of those country ways, and Geechees were the *country-est* of all country people, the butt of numerous jokes. It was painful to be called "a bad-talking rice eater."

But Estella Smart wasn't about to get rid of nothing that was worth keeping. She continued to eat her rice every day, say "goober" for peanut, "kiver" for cover, "britches" for pants, and any other Geechee thing she wanted.

"They can ki-ki [a Gullah word meaning gossip] this and ki-ki that about me as much as they please, I'll talk about them on my knees," she said.

"Hit'a sin and a shame."

"Going to the market with a homemade basket, instead of shopping bag like everybody else, up here."

20 "Ain't hit the truth!"

"Did you see what she was wearing?"

"Lord knows hit's a shame."

"She make 'em!"

"Think she is something! She ain't no better than nobody else."

25 "There's was a way to act and that's all there is to it!"

It wasn't only the way she acted, it was her presence.

Langston Hughes must have had her in mind when he wrote, "There are people (you've probably noted it also) who have the unconscious faculty of making the world spin around themselves, throb and expand, contract and go dizzy."

But magic is threatening and, for many, a little Estella Smart went a long way. Those who knew her when would always allow with a certain edge in their voice, "She always been like that."

Estella, or Telly, as she was called, was the youngest of eight children born to Sam and Rina Myers, in the Atlantic coastal city of Port Royal, South Carolina. Her parents were former slaves. She used to tell me, "Many days us shed tears of sorrow" when we talked about slavery time.

30 According to family legend, young Telly was "oomanish"—meaning she was sassy.

She married twenty-four-year-old Cleveland Smart, a wheelwright, when she was fourteen. And as family legend has it, Mr. Smart had his hands full.

His independent and strong-willed bride didn't "act right." For one thing, she balked at working by the sun in the fields with her husband as most wives were expected to do, and did. Cleveland Smart went to see his father-in-law and asked him to do something with this peculiar-acting bride. But Sam Myers couldn't help him.

"Us never could do nuthin wid Telly, she just don't take no tea for the fever. Takes after her grandmama who she named for, and they couldn't do nuthin wid her either. Now if you don't want Telly bring her home. And anyhow we didn't name her to be no mule."

Cleveland Smart kept his bride and they had five children. Now according to some more legend, Estella birthed all five by herself without a midwife. I don't know if it's true, but if you ever met Estella Smart you would believe it could be true.

35   There is a lot of mystery surrounding Cleveland Smart's life. They say he was a big black man. "A saltwater African" who was adopted. By whom, and from whom? They say the Smarts lived in the swamp in a house surrounded by a moat and that they had a safe in the house. Why?

Still I would love to see a photograph of Cleveland Smart. Legend is he was a dreamer. . . . When Cleveland Smart dreamt something and told you this and that was going to happen, it did!

When my mother was "that way" he had a dream and told her she would have a girl and to name her Verta.

Well to make a very long story short, Mama did have a girl and a boy, so it looked like Cleveland Smart's dream didn't come true. But the baby boy died, and of course they named me Verta. Still I could never understand why they did, because Gullah people pronounce *v*'s like *w*'s and everybody called me "Werta."

I couldn't call Estella Smart "Grandmama," like I called my other grandmother. I was to call her "Mother Dear," which came out sounding like "Mudear." This was alright around other Geechees, but as I got older and integrated with blacks from other places, I was, as they say, "too shame to say it." But Estella Smart didn't have no shame around "siddy" blacks or white folks. She was confident and self-assured around everybody.

40   In 1970, when my first book came out, she came to the book party in New York. A slightly drunk and very condescending white man came up to her and said, "Haven't I met you before?"

"If you had met me you would have know it, cause when you meet Estella Smart, you've been met!"

I think that is the quality I admire most about my grandmother, her sense of self. Where did she get it? It certainly wasn't easy for an eccentric Geechee woman with a second-grade education. . . . I asked her about it, but she didn't think "sense of self" was something people could give you.

"Yes," I would say, "but it's not easy in these hard times." She would look at me with her eyes the color of iced tea and say, "If colored people didn't have hard times, they wouldn't have no times, so keep your eyes on the prize and git on up and keep yourself to yourself."

I also admire the way Estella Smart took on the challenge of living in Philadelphia, a woman apart from Carolina. She and the others who came to the city from the country were real urban pioneers.

45   I have no idea how old my grandmother was at the time the photograph was taken. She always said, "A woman who will tell her age will tell anything."

I didn't discover her age until she died in 1985, a week before her hundredth birthday.

Now that I know her age, I think of what it must have been to go from cooking in a fireplace to a gas stove, from kerosene lamps to electric lights, and from driving a horse and buggy to driving a car. Unbeknownst to the family, Estella Smart took driving lessons. I was in high school the day she asked us to come with her outside the house. We did and she stepped into the car and drove off.

Estella Smart was not an easy grandmother to have. She had little patience, and not the greatest sense of humor. Saturdays, when other children were going to the movies, I was at her house helping her clean and sew. I had to bring my own lunch because she didn't cook.

She never remembered birthdays and didn't give Christmas presents. But I was enchanted by her.

50   My favorite memories of Mudear are of the good times we had in Atlantic City.

She would take me to Atlantic City to "catch the sea breeze and bathe in the salt water, cause we come from saltwater people."

We didn't have money to rent a room, so we undressed on the beach.

Estella Smart looked normal until she peeled off her clothes down to the two-piece bathing suit made of cretonne-print upholstery fabric that she had made. Then she was a mermaid.

She would swim way out on her back. The lifeguards would blow their whistles. She kept on swimming.

55 The lifeguards would look scared, afraid they might have to swim out that far to get her. But they never did.

When they would blow the whistle, folks would crowd around as folks will and ask, "What happened?"

Once someone asked me, "Who is that woman out there?"

"That's no woman," I said, "That's Mudear riding the waves."

For a picture of that I would do the hucklebuck naked in Macy's window.

EXPLORATORY WRITING

Smart-Grosvenor's essay, though it seems to tell a straightforward story about her grandmother, is actually framed by much larger issues—class and racial difference in the context of family and personal history. Write a brief (1000–1200 word) discussion of what each part of the essay does to contribute to those larger issues. Look carefully at the specifics of this essay. What role does the photograph play in telling the story? Why write about lost photos and no photos? What does the story about great-grandfather Mott have to do with the rest of the essay? Why bring a reference to Langston Hughes into a description of her grandmother? What is Smart-Grosvenor saying when she writes (twice) that for a certain picture, "I would do the hucklebuck in Macy's window"? In your writing, refer to passages that move the story from a simple personal memory to a piece that speaks to a larger audience.

TALKING ABOUT THE READINGS

Photographs of family and friends constitute at least part of a personal history in pictures. When, for example, people put together wedding albums, vacation albums, or baby books, the photos are chosen to tell a story of the event or the people in the pictures. With a group of your classmates, share the details of a story, an event, or a person in your life you wish you had a picture of. In your group, discuss what makes some people or events in families special enough so that we want to look at them later in a photograph. What photographs do people generally want to keep? Why?

WRITING ASSIGNMENTS

1. As you discovered in your exploratory writing, this essay is about more than Vertamae Smart-Grosvenor's photo of her grandmother. It is also more than an essay about social history. At its center is the photograph of Estella Smart and an examination of what photos can reveal about people, especially the people in our lives. Choose a photograph from your family or from a time and place of your childhood. Write an essay that, like Smart-Grosvenor's, uses the photograph as a starting point for an examination of what was important about that person or place or time. Remember that the photo you choose is the centerpiece for your essay, so take time to write specifically about the details of that photo and what those details tell you about the person, place, or event you have chosen to write about.

2. Photo portraits are not important only in family histories. They are often used to identify certain qualities (both positive and negative) of famous personalities. Choose a photo portrait of a historical figure. You can choose any historical figure—Martin Luther King Jr., Hitler, Jacqueline Kennedy, Teddy Roosevelt, John Muir, for example—but the photo

should be one that you find particularly compelling or one that is especially good at revealing character. Examine the photo carefully. What does it seem to reveal about the person? Is there something trustworthy in the face? A sadness? Wisdom? A sense of humor? How do you know? Write an essay in which you read that portrait for what it seems to convey about the person.

3. Make a photo essay of your own family history and write an accompanying essay in which you explain what absolutely has to be included, what is left out, and what stories photos can tell about the people in our lives.

SUGGESTIONS FOR READING ADVERTISING

Much of this chapter asks you to read and write about ad images—where they occur, what they are selling, but especially how ad images speak to consumers. You can begin collecting ads now even before you have decided on a topic for writing. Thumb through popular and specialty magazines. Notice ads online. Take pictures, make sketches of, or write detailed descriptions of billboards, outdoor ad screens, and corporate murals. The more images you have to work with, the easier it will be to make choices when you decide on a focus.

Always remember to note carefully where you found the ad—the publication, date, and page number or the exact location of and date on which you saw an outdoor ad.

Once you do begin writing, start by asking fairly simple questions like those we have listed here. Depending on what you write, you aren't likely to use your responses to all of these questions, but you can use this list to record important information, generate ideas, and find your focus.

1. What is the product being sold, and what is that product used for?

2. What does the ad promise? What claim does the ad make about the product?

3. What visuals are used in the ad? Do they illustrate the product claim or promise, or do they associate the product with something else—for example, a lifestyle or a celebrity?

4. Who is the target audience? Who is likely to buy the product? Is age or gender an important issue for the ad or the product? Is cost an issue? How can you tell?

5. Where does the ad appear? If it is a magazine or newspaper ad, who reads that publication? If it is a billboard, where is it placed? Who is likely to be the target audience for that publication or location?

6. How are people depicted in the ad image? Do they conform to or break with stereotypes?

7. Can you identify the cultural significance of this product? Is it a product that has been around for several generations? Is it associated with a particular idea or ideal about American culture or family life? Is it new to the

market and suddenly popular with teens or young children? Does the ad refer to current events in the news or to popular films or media events?

8. Is this ad more text than image or more image than text? In other words, does the advertiser think the audience wants more information about the product, or is the audience one that will more likely be persuaded by the visual appeal of the ad? For example, ads in electronics equipment magazines give readers quite a bit of text—the details of the equipment—suggesting that advertisers assume the readers know something about the product and are looking for specific features. Ads for clothing, cosmetics, soap products, or cigarettes rarely provide much information beyond the product name, the product claim—"softer, younger-looking skin"—and the advertising image.

9. Does the ad look familiar to you? Does it remind you of other ads or other media? If it does, what is that association?

MAKING CONNECTIONS   Images of Gender

Media analyst Jean Kilbourne has written, "The aspect of advertising most in need of analysis and change is the portrayal of women," and certainly John Berger and Richard Leppert, whose writing appears in this section, would seem to agree with that. In the sequence of readings and assignments that follow, you will be asked to think and write about images that contribute to and help construct the ways we see each other. Such images are sometimes called "cultural constructions"—the ideas and ideals that become cultural norms through repetition, reproduction, and circulation. Advertising is, of course, one of the primary circulators of popular images that reinforce culturally constructed ideas and ideals. Advertisers don't come up with these ideals alone, however. Such constructions have been a part of the culture, in some cases, for many generations.

The readings here focus primarily on images of women and men, but you can use these readings as a way to consider other visual cultural constructions, such as images of age or race or wealth or ethnicity. You can also consider how images of gender have begun to change with changing times.

WAYS OF SEEING

— *John Berger*

John Berger is a British novelist, poet, and art critic. *Ways of Seeing,* from which the following selection has been taken, first appeared as a British Broadcasting Company television series of the same name in the early 1970s. The book based on that series appeared in 1972 and has since been recognized as an important statement about the cultural foundations of all visual representation, especially high-art representations. Instead of holding high art apart from the popular, Berger argues that it should be understood as an expression of cultural values—"ways of seeing" or of understanding the world around us. In the selection that follows, Berger argues that the images we see of women today—images that appear in contemporary ads, especially—have their origins in the tradition of the nude in European art.

SUGGESTION FOR READING Begin a collection of images of women in advertising. You can collect ads online and in popular magazines. You might also consider television ads for your collection. If you have time, extend your collection to include images of women in art. You can find reproductions of famous artwork in any simple web search. Berger mentions several artists, including Titian, Ingres, Rembrandt, and Manet. Search using those artists' names and others working in the same tradition, or do an image search by topic: female nude in European art history, for example. Bring a selection of the images you have collected to class for discussion. Remember to document where you found the ad—the magazine title, date, and page number; the website URL and date; or, the location of and date when you saw outdoor ads, for example.

1   According to usage and conventions which are at last being questioned but have by no means been overcome, the social presence of a woman is different in kind from that of a man. A man's presence is dependent upon the promise of power which he embodies. If the promise is large and credible his presence is striking. If it is small or incredible, he is found to have little presence. The promised power may be moral, physical, temperamental, economic, social, sexual—but its object is always exterior to the man. A man's presence suggests what he is capable of doing to you or for you. His presence may be fabricated, in the sense that he pretends to be capable of what he is not. But the pretence is always towards a power which he exercises on others.

By contrast, a woman's presence expresses her own attitude to herself, and defines what can and cannot be done to her. Her presence is manifest in her gestures, voice, opinions, expressions, clothes, chosen surroundings, taste—indeed there is nothing she can do which does not contribute to her presence. Presence for a woman is so intrinsic to her person that men tend to think of it as an almost physical emanation, a kind of heat or smell or aura.

To be born a woman has been to be born, within an allotted and confined space, into the keeping of men. The social presence of women has developed as a result of their ingenuity in living under such tutelage within such a limited space. But this has been at the cost of a woman's self being split into two. A woman must continually watch herself. She is almost continually accompanied by her own image of herself. Whilst she is walking across a room or whilst she is weeping at the death of her father, she can scarcely avoid envisaging herself walking or weeping. From earliest childhood she has been taught and persuaded to survey herself continually.

And so she comes to consider the *surveyor* and the *surveyed* within her as the two constituent yet always distinct elements of her identity as a woman.

5   She has to survey everything she is and everything she does because how she appears to others, and ultimately how she appears to men, is of crucial importance for what is normally thought of as the success of her life. Her own sense of being in herself is supplanted by a sense of being appreciated as herself by another.

Men survey women before treating them. Consequently how a woman appears to a man can determine how she will be treated. To acquire some control over this process, women must contain it and interiorize it. That part of a woman's self which is the surveyor treats the part which is the surveyed so as to demonstrate to others how her whole self would like to be treated. And this exemplary treatment of herself by herself constitutes her presence. Every woman's presence regulates what is and is not "permissible" within her presence. Every one of her actions—whatever its direct purpose or motivation—is also read as an indication of how she would like to be treated. If a woman throws a glass on the floor, this is an example of how she treats her own emotion of anger and so of how she would wish it to be treated by others. If a man does the same, his action is only read as an expression of his anger. If a woman makes a good joke this is an example of how she treats the joker in herself and accordingly of how she as a joker-woman would like to be treated by others. Only a man can make a good joke for its own sake.

One might simplify this by saying: *men act* and *women appear*. Men look at women. Women watch themselves being looked at. This determines not only most relations between men and women but also the relation of women to themselves. The surveyor of woman in herself is male: the surveyed female. Thus she turns herself into an object—and most particularly an object of vision: a sight.

In one category of European oil painting women were the principal, ever-recurring subject. That category is the nude. In the nudes of European painting we can discover some of the criteria and conventions by which women have been seen and judged as sights.

The first nudes in the tradition depicted Adam and Eve. It is worth referring to the story as told in Genesis:

And when the woman saw that the tree was good for food, and that it was a delight to the eyes, and that the tree was to be desired to make one wise, she took of the fruit thereof and did eat; and she gave also unto her husband with her, and he did eat.

And the eyes of them both were opened, and they knew that they were naked; and they sewed fig-leaves together and made themselves aprons. . . . And the Lord God called unto the man and said unto him, "Where are thou?" And he said, "I heard thy voice in the garden, and I was afraid, because I was naked; and I hid myself. . . .

Unto the woman God said, "I will greatly multiply thy sorrow and thy conception; in sorrow thou shalt bring forth children; and thy desire shall be to thy husband and he shall rule over thee".

10   What is striking about this story? They became aware of being naked because, as a result of eating the apple, each saw the other differently. Nakedness was created in the mind of the beholder.

The second striking fact is that the woman is blamed and is punished by being made subservient to the man. In relation to the woman, the man becomes the agent of God.

In the medieval tradition the story was often illustrated, scene following scene, as in a strip cartoon.

During the Renaissance the narrative sequence disappeared, and the single moment depicted became the moment of shame. The couple wear fig-leaves or make a modest gesture with their hands. But now their shame is not so much in relation to one another as to the spectator.

Later the shame becomes a kind of display.

15   When the tradition of painting became more secular, other themes also offered the opportunity of painting nudes. But in them all there remains the implication that the subject (a woman) is aware of being seen by a spectator.

She is not naked as she is.

She is naked as the spectator sees her.

Often—as with the favourite subject of Susannah and the Elders—this is the actual theme of the picture. We join the Elders to spy on Susannah taking her bath. She looks back at us looking at her.

Susannah and the Elders by Tintoretto

Susannah and the Elders by Tintoretto 1518–1594

Nell Gwynne by Lely 1618–1680

In another version of the subject by Tintoretto, Susannah is looking at herself in a mirror. Thus she joins the spectators of herself.

20   The mirror was often used as a symbol of the vanity of woman. The moralizing, however, was mostly hypocritical.

You painted a naked woman because you enjoyed looking at her, you put a mirror in her hand and you called the painting *Vanity*, thus morally condemning the woman whose nakedness you had depicted for your own pleasure.

The real function of the mirror was otherwise. It was to make the woman connive in treating herself as, first and foremost, a sight.

The Judgement of Paris was another theme with the same Inwritten idea of a man or men looking at naked women.

But a further element is now added. The element of judgement. Paris awards the apple to the woman he finds most beautiful. Thus Beauty becomes competitive. (Today The Judgement of Paris has become the Beauty Contest.) Those who are not judged beautiful are *not beautiful*. Those who are, are given the prize.

25   The prize is to be owned by a judge—that is to say to be available for him. Charles the Second commissioned a secret painting from Lely. It is a highly typical image of the tradition. Nominally it might be a Venus and Cupid. In fact it is a portrait of one of the King's mistresses, Nell Gwynne. It shows her passively looking at the spectator staring at her naked.

This nakedness is not, however, an expression of her own feelings; it is a sign of her submission to the owner's feelings or demands. (The owner of both woman and painting.) The painting, when the King showed it to others, demonstrated this submission and his guests envied him.

It is worth noticing that in other non-European traditions—in Indian art, Persian art, African art, Pre-Columbian art—nakedness is never supine in this way. And if, in these traditions, the theme of a work is sexual attraction, it is likely to show active sexual love as between two people, the woman as active as the man, the actions of each absorbing the other.

We can now begin to see the difference between nakedness and nudity in the European tradition. In his book on The Nude Kenneth Clark maintains that to be naked is simply to be without clothes, whereas the nude is a form of art. According to him, a nude is not the starting point of a painting, but a way of seeing which the painting achieves. To some degree, this is true—although the way of seeing "a nude" is not necessarily confined to art: there are also nude photographs, nude poses, nude gestures. What is true is that the nude is always conventionalized—and the authority for its conventions derives from a certain tradition of art.

What do these conventions mean? What does a nude signify? It is not sufficient to answer these questions merely in terms of the art-form, for it is quite clear that the nude also relates to lived sexuality.

30   To be naked is to be oneself.

To be nude is to be seen naked by others and yet not recognized for oneself. A naked body has to be seen as an object in order to become a nude. (The sight of it as an object stimulates the use of it as an object.) Nakedness reveals itself. Nudity is placed on display.

To be naked is to be without disguise.

To be on display is to have the surface of one's own skin, the hairs of one's own body, turned into a disguise which, in that situation, can never be discarded. The nude is condemned to never being naked. Nudity is a form of dress.

In the average European oil painting of the nude the principal protagonist is never painted. He is the spectator in front of the picture and he is presumed to be a man. Everything is addressed to him. Everything must appear to be the result of his being there. It is for him that the figures have assumed their nudity. But he, by definition, is a stranger—with his clothes still on.

35   Consider the Allegory of Time and Love by Bronzino.

The complicated symbolism which lies behind this painting need not concern us now because it does not affect its sexual appeal—at the first degree. Before it is anything else, this is a painting of sexual provocation.

The painting was sent as a present from the Grand Duke of Florence to the King of France. The boy kneeling on the cushion and kissing the woman is Cupid. She is Venus. But the way her body is arranged, has nothing to do with their kissing. Her body is arranged in the way it is, to display it to the man looking at the picture. This picture is made to appeal to *his* sexuality. It has nothing to do with her sexuality. (Here and in the European tradition generally, the convention of not painting the hair on a woman's body helps towards the same end. Hair is associated with sexual power, with passion. The woman's sexual passion needs to be minimized so that the spectator may feel that he has the monopoly of such passion.) Women are there to feed an appetite, not to have any of their own.

Compare the expressions of these two women:

La Grande Odalisque by Ingres 1780–1867

Venus, Cupid, Time, and Love by Bronzino 1503–1572

one the model for a famous painting by Ingres and the other a model for a photograph in a girlie magazine.

Is not the expression remarkably similar in each case? It is the expression of a woman responding with calculated charm to the man whom she imagines looking at her—although she doesn't know him. She is offering up her femininity as the surveyed.

40 It is true that sometimes a painting includes a male lover.

Bacchus. Ceres and Cupid by Von Aachen 1552–1615

But the woman's attention is very rarely directed towards him. Often she looks away from him or she looks out of the picture towards the one who considers himself her true lover—the spectator-owner.

There was a special category of private pornographic paintings (especially in the eighteenth century) in which couples making love make an appearance. But even in front of these it is clear that the spectator-owner will in fantasy oust the other man, or else identify with him. By contrast the image of the couple in non-European traditions provokes the notion of many couples making love. "We all have a thousand hands, a thousand feet and will never go alone."

Almost all post-Renaissance European sexual imagery is frontal—either literally or metaphorically—because the sexual protagonist is the spectator-owner looking at it.

The absurdity of this make flattery reached its peak in the public academic art of the nineteenth century.

Les Oreades by Bouguereau 1825–1905

45 Men of state, of business, discussed under paintings like this. When one of them felt he had been outwitted, he looked up for consolation. What he saw reminded him that he was a man.

There are a few exceptional nudes in the European tradition of oil painting to which very little of what has been said above applies. Indeed they are no longer nudes—they break the norms of the art-form; they are paintings of loved women, more or less naked. Among the hundreds of thousands of nudes which make up the tradition there are perhaps a hundred of these exceptions. In each case the painter's personal vision of the particular women he is painting is so strong that it makes no allowance for the spectator. The painter's vision binds the woman to him so that they become as inseparable as couples in stone. The spectator can witness their relationship—but he can do no more: he is forced to recognize himself as the outsider he is. He cannot deceive himself into believing that she is naked for him. He cannot turn her into a nude The way the painter has painted her includes her will and her intentions in the very structure of the image, in the very expression of her body and her face.

Danäe by Rembrandt 1606–1669

The typical and the exceptional in the tradition can be defined by the simple naked/nude antinomy, but the problem of painting nakedness is not as simple as it might at first appear.

What is the sexual function of nakedness in reality? Clothes encumber contact and movement. But it would seem that nakedness has a positive visual value in its own right: we want to *see* the other naked: the other delivers to us the sight of themselves and we seize upon it—sometimes quite regardless of whether it is for the first time or the hundredth. What does this sight of the other mean to us, how does it, at that instant of total disclosure, affect our desire?

Their nakedness acts as a confirmation and provokes a very strong sense of relief. She is a woman like any other: or he is a man like any other: we are overwhelmed by the marvellous simplicity of the familiar sexual mechanism.

We did not, of course, consciously expect this to be otherwise: unconscious homosexual desires (or unconscious heterosexual desires if the couple concerned are homosexual) may have led each to half expect something different. But the "relief" can be explained without recourse to the unconscious.

We did not expect them to be otherwise, but the urgency and complexity of our feelings bred a sense of uniqueness which the sight of the other, as she is or as he is, now dispels. They are more like the rest of their sex than they are different. In this revelation lies the warm and friendly—as opposed to cold and impersonal—anonymity of nakedness.

One could express this differently: at the moment of nakedness first perceived, an element of banality enters: an element that exists only because we need it.

Up to that instant the other was more or less mysterious. Etiquettes of modesty are not merely puritan or sentimental: it is reasonable to recognize a loss of mystery. And the explanation of this loss of mystery may be largely visual. The focus of perception shifts from eyes, mouth, shoulders, hands—all of which are capable of such subtleties of expression that the personality expressed by them is manifold—it shifts from these to the sexual parts, whose formation suggests an utterly compelling but single process. The other is reduced or elevated—whichever you prefer—to their primary sexual category: male or female. Our relief is the relief of finding an unquestionable reality to whose direct demands our earlier highly complex awareness must now yield.

We need the banality which we find in the first instant of disclosure because it grounds us in reality. But it does more than that. This reality, by promising the familiar, proverbial mechanism of sex, offers, at the same time, the possibility of the shared subjectivity of sex.

The loss of mystery occurs simultaneously with the offering of the means for creating a shared mystery. The sequence is: subjective—objective—subjective to the power of two.

We can now understand the difficulty of creating a static image of sexual nakedness. In lived sexual experience nakedness is a process rather than a state. If one moment of that process is isolated, its image will seem banal and its banality, instead of serving as a bridge between two intense imaginative states, will be chilling. This is one reason why expressive photographs of the naked are even rarer than paintings. The easy solution for the photographer is to turn the figure into a nude which, by generalizing both sight and viewer and making sexuality unspecific, turns desire into fantasy.

Let us examine an exceptional painted image of nakedness. It is a painting by Rubens of his young second wife whom he married when he himself was relatively old.

Helene Fourment in a Fur Coat by Rubens 1577–1640

We see her in the act of turning, her fur about to slip off her shoulders. Clearly she will not remain as she is for more than a second. In a superficial

sense her image is as instantaneous as a photograph's. But, in a more profound sense, the painting "contains" time and its experience. It is easy to imagine that a moment ago before she pulled the fur round her shoulders, she was entirely naked. The consecutive stages up to and away from the moment of total disclosure have been transcended. She can belong to any or all of them simultaneously.

Her body confronts us, not as an immediate sight, but as experience—the painter's experience. Why? There are superficial anecdotal reasons: her dishevelled hair, the expression of her eyes directed towards him, the tenderness with which the exaggerated susceptibility of her skin has been painted. But the profound reason is a formal one. Her appearance has been literally re-cast by the painter's subjectivity. Beneath the fur that she holds across herself, the upper part of her body and her legs can never meet. There is a displacement sideways of about nine inches: her thighs, in order to join on to her hips, are at least nine inches too far to the left.

60   Rubens probably did not plan this: the spectator may not consciously notice it. In itself it is unimportant. What matters is what it permits. It permits the body to become impossibly dynamic. Its coherence is no longer within itself but within the experience of the painter. More precisely, it permits the upper and lower halves of the body to rotate separately, and in opposite directions, round the sexual centre which is hidden: the torso turning to the right, the legs to the left. At the same time this hidden sexual centre is connected by means of the dark fur coat to all the surrounding darkness in the picture, so that she is turning both around and within the dark which has been made a metaphor for her sex.

Apart from the necessity of transcending the single instant and of admitting subjectivity, there is, as we have seen, one further element which is essential for any great sexual image of the naked. This is the element of banality which must be undisguised but not chilling. It is this which distinguishes between voyeur and lover. Here such banality is to be found in Rubens's compulsive painting of the fat softness of Hélène Fourment's flesh which continually breaks every ideal convention of form and (to him) continually offers the promise of her extraordinary particularity.

The nude in European oil painting is usually presented as an admirable expression of the European humanist spirit. This spirit was inseparable from individualism. And without the development of a highly conscious individualism the exceptions to the tradition (extremely personal images of the naked), would never have been painted. Yet the tradition contained a contradiction which it could not itself resolve. A few individual artists intuitively recognized this and resolved the contradiction in their own terms, but their solutions could never enter the tradition's *cultural* terms.

The contradiction can be stated simply. On the one hand the individualism of the artist, the thinker, the patron, the owner: on the other hand, the person who is the object of their activities—the woman—treated as a thing or an abstraction.

Dürer believed that the ideal nude ought to be constructed by taking the face of one body, the breasts of another, the legs of a third, the shoulders of a fourth, the hands of a fifth—and so on.

65   The result would glorify Man. But the exercise presumed a remarkable indifference to who any one person really was.

In the art-form of the European nude the painters and spectator-owners were usually men and the persons treated as objects, usually women. This unequal relationship is so deeply embedded in our culture that it still structures the consciousness of many women. They do to themselves what men do to them. They survey, like men, their own femininity.

In modern art the category of the nude has become less important. Artists themselves began to question it. In this, as in many other respects, Manet represented a turning point. If one compares his Olympia with Titian's original, one sees a woman, cast in the traditional role, beginning to question that role, somewhat defiantly.

The Venus of Urbino by Titian C 1487–1576

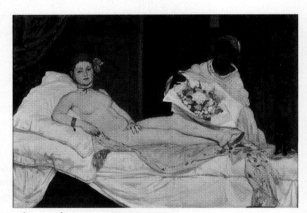

Olympia by Manet 1832–1883

The ideal was broken. But there was little to replace it except the "realism" of the prostitute—who became the quintessential woman of early avant-garde twentieth-century painting. (Toulouse-Lautrec, Picasso, Rouault, German Expressionism, etc.) In academic painting the tradition continued.

Today the attitudes and values which informed that tradition are expressed through other more widely diffused media—advertising, journalism, television.

70   But the essential way of seeing women, the essential use to which their images are put, has not changed. Women are depicted in a quite different way from men—not because the feminine is different from the masculine—but because the

"ideal" spectator is always assumed to be male and the image of the woman is designed to flatter him. If you have any doubt that this is so, make the following experiment. Choose from this book an image of a traditional nude. Transform the woman into a man. Either in your mind's eye or by drawing on the reproduction. Then notice the violence which that transformation does. Not to the image, but to the assumptions of a likely viewer.

EXPLORATORY WRITING

One of Berger's primary arguments in this reading is that "the social presence of a woman is different in kind from that of a man" and that difference is especially apparent in the images of women typical in the history of European painting. Write an explanation of how Berger makes his argument. What, for example, is his distinction between *naked* and *nude* and why does that distinction matter for his argument? What, given the evidence he provides, does he mean when he writes "Men act. Women appear"? How does he use images to support his argument? Be sure to explain, as well, the point he is making with his discussion of "exceptional nudes in the European tradition of oil painting." Throughout your explanation, be sure to point to specific passages or places in the selection that support your explanation.

TALKING ABOUT THE READING

With a group of your classmates, share 5–7 examples of the of ads and art images you have begun to collect. In what ways do your examples reinforce the argument Berger makes about representations of women in art and in contemporary culture as a whole? In what ways would you say the images you found contradict or depart from those arguments? How? In what circumstances?

WRITING ASSIGNMENT

Choose a product that typically uses the kinds of images of women Berger describes here. Write an argument for changing the way women are depicted in this product's ad campaign. In your argument, pitch an idea for a new ad campaign that breaks with the stereotype but that is just as appealing as the current advertising that relies on stereotyped portrayals of women and girls. Present your ad campaign idea to the class using mock ads to illustrate your new image for this product.

THE FEMALE NUDE: SURFACES OF DESIRE

— *Richard Leppert*

Richard Leppert is Morse Alumni Distinguished Teaching Professor in the Department of Cultural Studies and Comparative Literature at the University of Minnesota. He is the author of a number of books on art, music, and culture, including *The Sight of Sound: Music, Representation, and the History of the Body* (1993), *Art and the Committed Eye: The Cultural Functions of Imagery* (1996) from which this excerpt is taken, and *The Nude: The Cultural Rhetoric of the Body in the Art of Western Modernity* (2007).

SUGGESTION FOR READING This passage from *Art and the Committed Eye* serves as a response to John Berger's argument in *Ways of Seeing*. In preparation for reading, review the Berger selection. Then, as you read Leppert, mark places in the text where he addresses Berger's position directly.

1   In painting, nude or naked: What to call it? What are the stakes of the difference? A generation ago Sir Kenneth Clark, in his monumental study of nudity and nakedness in art, established the principles defining a difference. Nakedness, he said, describes a state of being without clothes; nudity, by contrast, is a category of artistic representation. The former, he argues, "implies some sort of embarrassment" most people feel from being deprived of clothes, but the latter "carries, in educated usage, no uncomfortable overtone. The vague image it projects into the mind is not of a huddled and defenseless body, but of a balanced, prosperous, and confident body: the body re-formed." Nudity for Clark operates as a manifestation of aesthetics, as representation and at a remove from mundane reality. The claim to aesthetics provides Clark with the source of his book's subtitle: "A Study in Ideal Form." Clark developed his project along formalist lines, investigating the representation of the naked human body in art as a type of painted or sculpted composition—which to be sure it is—governed by the regularities and symmetries of geometry.

Within the confines of a broadly defined Western tradition, Clark universalized the body as an unproblematic entity, divorced from history other than the history of art and art-making. In particular, he ignored any specific investigation of the function of the nude (the "why" question) or of the act of spectatorship (the "who's looking" question). As a result, his book (immensely insightful regarding formalist art history) oddly separates the nude from discourses about power and, a little ironically, from the politics of gender difference. Further, it identifies but quickly backs away from eroticism's role as a driving force to portray the nude in art from time immemorial. "It is necessary to labor the obvious," Clark says, "and say that no nude, however abstract, should fail to arouse in the spectator some vestige of erotic feeling, even though it be only the faintest shadow—and if it does not do so, it is bad art and false morals." The pleasure of looking at beautiful naked bodies in art, for Clark, is principally contemplative, not physical, a view predicated upon preserving "in educated usage" a sharp division between mind and body.

The first substantial, if brief, critique of Clark's book was mounted by the art critic John Berger in 1972. He argues that the nude in art responds to, and in turn reinforces, the principal power differential that partly defines the social and cultural functions of gender hierarchy. He reasons that man's "presence" in the world articulates a "power which he exercises on others," whereas a woman's presence articulates "what can and cannot be done to her" (while effectively critiquing Clark, Berger perpetuated a male discourse concerning women's supposed lack of agency). As far as art is concerned, he relates gender difference to the separate acts of looking and of being looked at: A man's look is directed outward toward others, a woman's inward toward herself. One surveys and surveils; the other is surveyed and surveils herself. Berger sums up:

Men act and *women appear.* Men look at women. Women watch themselves being looked at. This determines not only most relations between men and women but also the relation of women to themselves. The surveyor of woman in herself is male: the surveyed female. Thus she turns herself into an object—and most particularly an object of vision: a sight.

5   Berger argues that the painted nude is, essentially, the painted nude female. Historically, however, this is the case only since the nineteenth century, before which there is a reasonably close balance between the sexes in representations of the nude. Berger further notes that the female's nakedness is not expressive of her own feelings but is a sign of "her submission to the [art] owner's feelings or demands." To be naked, Berger suggests, is to "be oneself"; but to be nude is to be seen by others "and yet not recognized for oneself. . . . Naked-ness reveals itself. Nudity is placed on display." Finally, Berger reiterates the character of power difference by

noting that female nudity in art conventionally, though by no means always, includes men who are clothed or no men at all, leaving but one man implicit, the spectator-owner of the image who stands, clothed, outside the frame. In sum, whereas Clark defines the nude in terms of beauty, Berger defines it in terms of politics.

Berger's thesis about the painted nude and spectatorship has its counterpart in film studies, in a famous essay by Laura Mulvey, written in 1973 (a year after *Ways of Seeing* appeared) and published in 1975. Employing the term scopophilia (pleasure in looking), she suggested that the conditions of watching movies, together with the narrative conventions of film, promote "the illusion of voyeuristic separation." Viewing a movie manifests itself as a private act in a darkened theater (looking in on a private world, like a Peeping Tom), with attention focused on the human form itself, upon which the spectator may project his own desires. The pleasure, and the anxiety, of film, she argues, derives from the gap that separates image from self-image, a divide that can be bridged at least temporarily by fantasy. (This is the same gap exploited by advertising.) The woman in film (her body and the character it reveals) receives Mulvey's principal attention, and her understanding of the woman's visual function is summarized by the following: "Traditionally, the woman displayed has functioned on two levels: as erotic object for the characters within the screen story, and as erotic object for the spectator within the auditorium, with a shifting tension between the looks on either side of the screen."

For Mulvey and Berger, and implicitly for Clark, woman *is* image, and man is the bearer of the *look* on that image. The former is passive, hence it lacks agency; the other is active hence it possesses agency.

WHO'S GOT THE LOOK?

Is it sufficient to suggest, like Berger, that there exist only a relative few "exceptional" female nudes painted by male artists that fall outside the parameters thus far described? What happens when women themselves look at painted female nudes—or when women artists paint male (or female) nudes? Can women in effect "look back"? The terms of debate have largely been defined by the academic discipline of art history, which for most of its existence has been practiced almost entirely by men who rarely saw a need to raise issues of the sort articulated by Berger, who is a critic, not an academic, or Mulvey, who is an academic, but not an art historian.

The seemingly obvious connection of the art nude to sociocultural questions about sexual difference was made an issue only with the advent of feminist art history in the early 1970s. The issue surfaced much as the result of the increased presence of women in the discipline who, through their own experience as women in the society at large and through experiences within the academy—historically not a site of empathy toward women—began to constitute a new discourse. Some of the most interesting new work of this sort has addressed the contradictions inherent in the male gaze.

10   Marcia Pointon, for example, alludes to the deep-seated anxiety embedded in the male look concerning female sexuality, calling upon an Freudian psychoanalytic account of the male fear of castration, first experienced in child-hood, generated by the appearance of physiological sexual difference—the female's "lack" of a penis. In other words, her account of the male gaze tacitly acknowledges not only strength but weakness. A difficulty with this formulation, however, is the degree to which it preserves the phallus as the locus of imagining the visible, or as Luce Irigaray puts it, "The male sex becomes *the* sex because it is very visible, the erection is spectacular" in a culture that privileges sight over other senses— though as I will suggest in the next chapter, the male phallus *in art* borders culturally on being unrepresentable.

Nonetheless, Pointon demonstrates through her own practice as an art historian—a professional "looker" at art—that she can "see through" the visual technologies that operate to objectify women, thereby helping to undercut or overcome the effect. Her own gaze possesses the power to name patriarchy and to demonstrate how its rhetoric operates in representation. This still acknowledges that the female nude is a category of painting mostly by and for men, of which "woman as spectator is offered the dubious satisfaction of identification with the heterosexual masculine gaze, voyeuristic, penetrating and powerful . . . negating women's own experience and identity."

Pointon's most important insight is to regard the female nude as a form of rhetoric in which the subject is not fully contained or controlled either by the (male) artist, or the "author," or by the (male) spectator, or the "reader." In essence, the female nude *exceeds* her characterization by men, and this excess is not simply the result of external analysis by feminist spectators but in fact is inherent in the object itself. Put perhaps too simply, the female nude, even (perhaps especially) in its most objectified and objectionable form—usually what we call pornographic—constitutes an acknowledgment by men of the ability of women to satisfy a desire that men cannot satisfy themselves. Moreover, the female nude represents an *imaginary* female body to which the male spectator has access only psychically, not physically. In representation, she remains explicitly out of reach, except in fantasy. In other words, the desire to look, and to "possess" by looking, in the end only demonstrates that looking is *not* the same as "having." Assuming for a moment that all representations of female nudes are sexist (a blatant falsehood), we would still be required to specify that men's domination of women develops simultaneously from both strength *and* weakness. The *need* to dominate is the surest socio-cultural indicator of the latter—and is no comfort to those being dominated, to be sure, but neither is it to those exercising that form of coercive power.

The desire of men to look at women, *and vice versa,* whether clothed or naked, is after all deeply informed by sexual necessity, an activity fully sanctioned by society when involving lovers. Herein, of course, lies the problem: There is no single road map for looking at the body of another. The look may define desires driven by love or hate, desires mutual and reciprocal or selfish and self-serving. Accordingly, the rhetoric of a given image is defined by more than itself, by more than what it is made to *look like*. It is driven by the function to which it is put. In the generation of my youth, boys' experiences with *National Geographic,* for example, were probably not always in line with the "official" discourses surrounding that magazine's exploration of the world and its myriad cultures. Yet however we account for the sexual desire produced by a woman's pictured body, whatever intentions her body may be designated to serve, the very act of picturing her, and not something else, marks the power her body possesses over her male counterpart, as Pointon has shown. What this adds up to, in the end, is that the female nude occupies a space that is inevitably open to contestation, hence that space is profoundly ambiguous. And for all the insightful talk about the male and his controlling gaze, whereby women are objectified, I would argue that the female nude also defines fundamental limits to the agency of the gaze and its ability to objectify. The dominating power of the male gaze rests on the same fragile foundation as male identity itself, and although this can neither explain away the actual psychical and physical battering many women experience at the hands of men, it can perhaps provide a less essentialist account of the complexities surrounding the problem. The trouble with much current theorization about the male gaze is that it is itself essentialist, a vast simplification alike of both female *and male* identity and subjectivity, as I hope to show.

EXPLORATORY WRITING

Richard Leppert reviews what he calls Berger's "thesis about the painted nude and spectator-ship." Beyond the single statement "Men act. Women appear," what is Berger's "thesis"? Write a brief summary of Leppert's response to that argument. Be sure to point to specific passages where Leppert engages Berger's thesis.

TALKING ABOUT THE READING

Leppert opens his discussion with this remark: "In painting, nude or naked: What to call it? What are the stakes of the difference?" With a group of your classmates, sort out what, according to Leppert's discussion, are the stakes of the difference? What is at stake in Leppert's treatment of Berger's thesis?

WRITING ASSIGNMENT

Near the end of this selection, Leppert writes, "There is no single road map for looking at the body of another. The look may define desires driven by love or hate, desires mutual and recip-rocal or selfish and self-serving. Accordingly, the rhetoric of a given image is defined by more than itself, by more than what it is made to look like. It is driven by the function to which it is put." Locate three different images of women or men for an essay in which you argue how the image might be seen depending on where it appears and what function it is meant to have. Is it an advertisement in a high-class fashion magazine? An illustration in a medical book? A painting in an art museum? You can use the images reprinted in "Reading the Gaze" or choose images you have located on your own for this essay. Your aim in what you write is to explore Leppert's contention that the way one looks at any given image of the naked form has more to do with the rhetorical function of the image than the image itself. To illustrate your point, you might try placing one of your images in different contexts and explaining how a specta-tor might respond to it given the context.

VISUAL ESSAY   Reading the Gaze: Gender Roles in Advertising

Much discussion over the years has drawn the public's attention to the image of women in advertising, and yet men have also been objectified in popular advertis-ing. This Visual Essay illustrates how advertisers use what is called *the gaze* to estab-lish a relationship between the reader and the person represented in the image. Though theorists first began talking about the gaze in reference to images of women, even a quick survey of today's ads will turn up images that subject men as well as women to the gaze. The ads reprinted here offer an illustration of how sophisticated advertisers can be as they both reinforce and challenge gender stereotypes.

As you examine images of men and women in advertising, notice that the way you as a viewer are being asked to relate to the person in the picture is often signaled by whether the person in the image is looking at or away from the camera (or you, as the imaginary viewer).

When the person in the image looks at you directly and at close range, a different relationship is set up than when the person is depicted looking down, away from, or beyond your gaze. Some images show the model only from behind, as if an imaginary viewer is looking at the model but the model is unaware of that intrusion (as in a lingerie or cologne ad). In that case, the viewer holds power over the model. It's almost as if the viewer is watching from a hidden place. These are the kinds of concerns raised, in particular, by Berger's discussion of the male gaze and the position of the female nude.

In *Reading Images: The Grammar of Visual Design* (1996), Gunther Kress and Theo van Leeuwen describe the position of the subject in an image as portraying either an *offer* or a *demand*. They explain the difference between the two in this way:

> When represented participants look at the viewer, vectors, formed by participants' eyelines, connect the participants with the viewer. Contact is established, even if it is only on an imaginary level. . . . [This representation] creates a visual form of direct address. It acknowledges the viewers explicitly, addressing them with a visual "you." . . . It is for this reason we have called this kind of image a "demand": the participant's gaze (and the gesture, if present) demands something from the viewer, demands that the viewer enter into some kind of imaginary relation with him or her. Exactly what kind of relation is then signified by other means, for instance by the facial expression of the represented participants. They may smile, in which case the viewer is asked to enter into a relation of social affinity with them; they may stare at the viewer with cold disdain, in which case the viewer is asked to relate to them, perhaps, as an inferior relates to a superior; they may seductively pout at the viewer, in which case the viewer is asked to desire them. The same applies to gestures. A hand can point at the viewer, in a visual "Hey, you there, I mean you," or invite the viewer to come closer, or hold the viewer at bay with a defensive gesture as if to say: stay away from me. In each case the image wants something from the viewers— wants them to do something (come closer, stay at a distance) or to form a pseudo-social bond of a particular kind with the represented participant. . . .
>
> Other pictures address us indirectly. Here the viewer is not object but subject of the look, and the represented participant is the object of the viewer's dispassionate scrutiny. No contact is made. The viewer's role is that of the invisible onlooker . . . we have called this kind of image an "offer"—it "offers" the represented participants to the viewer as items of information, objects of contemplation, impersonally, as though they were specimens in a display case. (122–124)

As you examine the collection of images reproduced here, keep in mind how the man or woman in each image looks at or away from you the viewer. (To learn more about vectors, review "Visual Culture: Picturing Schooldays" in Chapter 3.)

EXPLORATORY WRITING

Write a summary of this visual essay that explains what, taken together, the images reprinted on pp. 222–223 seem to argue. As you write, pay careful attention to each of the ads, noting especially the manner in which each model is posed looking at or away from the viewer. Which models seem to be individuals? Which seem to be types? What kind of relationship, as Kress and van Leeuwen describe it or as Leppert and Berger discuss it, is each image setting up with the viewer? How does the notion of "offer" or "demand," as Kress and van Leeuwen explain it, complicate both Berger's and Leppert's discussion of spectatorship?

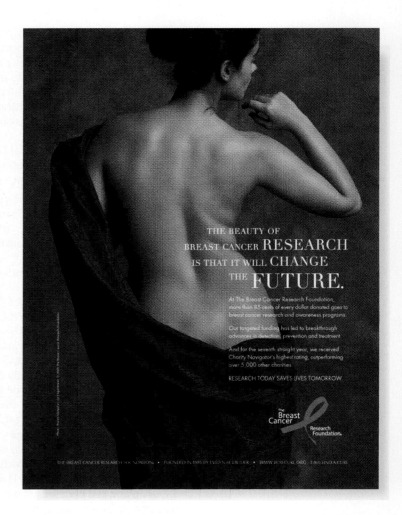

Breast cancer research ad in *Vogue,* June 2008.

Billboard ad for the Calvin Klein fragrance Obsession.

David and Victoria Beckham appear in the Intimately Beckham perfume ad.

From the "Got Milk" ad campaign.

TALKING ABOUT THE READING

Berger writes that, when men do appear with women, the woman is still offered for the viewer's pleasure. Look at the ads here that include both men and women. To what extent do they conform to that observation? How does the gaze work in ads like these? How might the gaze change if the viewer is a woman rather than a man? How does it change if, as Berger suggests, you change one of the female models in any of these ad images into a male model?

WRITING ASSIGNMENT

This Visual Essay is focused on stereotypes of gender in advertising and how those stereotypes are signaled by the way the model relates to (looks at or away from) the viewer. In general, the concept of the gaze asks readers to pay attention to how the subject of an image is treated—whether that subject seems to be an individual or just a body. Write an essay in which you imagine the look on the models reversed. That is, what would change if the woman posing in the breast cancer research ad were looking at the camera? What if the woman changed places with the man in the Armani ad?

WRITING SEQUENCE

1. Reread the exploratory writing you did in response to the Berger and Leppert pieces and the Visual Essay. (If you did not do the exploratory writing, write for 10 minutes on each,

noting down the arguments made in each of the readings.) Reread Berger and Leppert and the introduction to the Visual Essay, paying particular attention to what arguments or concerns each of the three have in common, how they comment on each other, or what they add to your understanding of the issue of visual representations of gender in art and advertising. When you have completed your rereading, write a new exploratory piece in which you bring the concerns of these three selections together. Where it is helpful, draw on the exploratory writing you have done for these readings. In your writing, be sure to point to specific passages from Berger and Leppert and to specific details from the ad images reprinted in the Visual Essay. Explain how each adds to or complicates arguments made in the others.

2. In a 2–3 page essay, explain how Berger's "thesis about the female nude and spectatorship" is addressed in Leppert's response as well as in the introduction to the Visual Essay. Notice that Leppert does not simply hold Berger up as a contrast to his own argument. What views do they have in common? What divides them? In your essay, choose a painting or other visual from Berger's text to illustrate how the two differ in their discussions. Your exploratory writing can help you with this essay, so review that writing and use anything from it that touches on the issue of spectatorship that Leppert takes up in his discussion.

3. As a culminating assignment, take the arguments surrounding the nature of the female nude and spectatorship and apply that discussion to images of the male nude. For this paper, you should show that you understand the argument Berger makes, Leppert's response to that argument, and the way the gaze functions as Kress and van Leeuwen explain it. Draw on any of the writing you have done leading up to and within this sequence when you need to.

   Leppert challenges his readers to go beyond what he calls the 19th century notion that, as Berger says of the female nude, "Men act. Women appear." He argues that "there is no single road map for looking at the body of another." Berger, on the other hand, would remind us that there are certain patterns or "ways of seeing" that are prevalent in any culture. From his point of view, the way we "see" a female nude is the product of a long cultural tradition of depicting women in a particular way. Kress and van Leeuwen would add that that way of seeing also contributes to the role of spectatorship.

   How might that discussion of the female nude help us read images of the male body or of men in general? That is the question you will address in this assignment.

   Begin by collecting images of men. These images should have appeared in the past 6–12 months in popular sources. Print advertisements, male fashion magazine spreads, sports magazine ads or photo shoots, for example, are all rich sources for this kind of study. After you have completed this step, collect several images of the male form from art history.

   Once you have a collection of 15–20 images to work with, present your own argument for how men today—especially the male body today—is depicted in popular culture. Does Berger's thesis still hold true, or has that pattern begun to change or shift? How might Richard Leppert write about current depictions of men, especially the male form? Are there precedents in art history for how the male nude continues to be depicted?

   Your paper should be longer than the writing leading up to this, and by the time you turn it in, it should also be finished (drafted, revised, and edited). Be sure, as well, to include visuals to help make your argument. These should be carefully reproduced, include a caption, and be cited, so keep careful records of where the image appeared and, where appropriate, who made the image. For example, if you are taking some examples from art history (Michaelangelo's David, for example), you will need to cite the artist, the medium, the title, the date it was made, and where it is currently housed in your works cited. Ads do not normally indicate who made them, but you should cite where they appeared—magazine title, date, page number, etc.

Public health campaigns take several forms, with messages that appear everywhere, from billboards and subway posters to newspaper and magazine ads to public service announcements on radio and television. Like advertising, public health messages are intended to persuade readers, viewers, and listeners to do something. In the case of public health publicity, however, the pitch is not to buy a product but to live a healthy lifestyle—to eat a balanced diet, stop smoking, drink in moderation, avoid drugs, exercise regularly, use a condom, immunize your kids, or have annual checkups.

Like advertising, public health publicity uses images that readers and viewers will recognize immediately to get its message across. The Candie's Foundation ad below, for example, uses a male model who looks like he could just as easily be in a fashion advertisement. This message ran in the magazine *Elle Girl,* the teen version of the upscale fashion magazine *Elle,* and obviously assumes that young people want to be sexy. It's an ad that argues for teen abstinence rather than safe sex while it draws from all of the codes of sultriness and sexuality these readers would be familiar with from ads in the same magazine.

As is true in all advertising, agencies designing public health messages face decisions about how to sell the message: should the publicity emphasize the negative consequences of unhealthy behavior or the positive benefits of a healthy lifestyle?

Some of the most interesting cases of how public health messages use images can be found in publicity concerning sexually transmitted diseases (STDs). This Visual Essay includes three examples: The two posters "Worst of the Three" and "She May Look Clean" were directed at men in the military during World War II. The third example, "Roses Have Thorns", is the cover of a pamphlet for teens on STDs.

IT DOESN'T MEAN YOU HAVE TO HAVE SEX ALMOST ONE MILLION TEENAGE GIRLS WILL BECOME PREGNANT THIS YEAR

be SEXY

the candie's foundation

SUGGESTION FOR READING

Before you read, look around your campus—in the dorms, the commons, the health service, any place where you are likely to find STD health messages—and bring examples of those (or take notes and bring descriptions of them) to class for discussion.

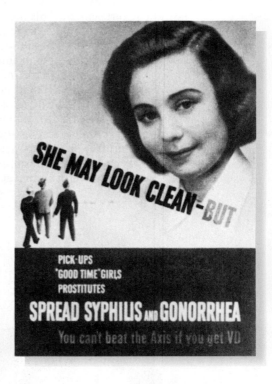

EXPLORATORY WRITING

The first two posters were part of a World War II campaign to stem the spread of syphilis and gonorrhea—the most widespread STDs, or venereal diseases (VDs)—among allied forces. Write a brief analysis of how these posters portray women. Notice that, in the first, a female death figure representing VD is accompanied by Hitler of Nazi Germany and Hirohito of Japan. What assumptions do these posters seem to make about the role of women in spreading STDs? What assumptions do they seem to make about male sexual behavior?

TALKING ABOUT THE READING

Share the public health messages you collected with a group of your classmates. How would you describe them? Do they conform to or break with the images of men and women and sexuality that you see in the Visual Essay? To what extent are some older attitudes preserved in newer messages? To what extent do newer messages break with those older themes and warnings? How effective are these newer messages?

WRITING ASSIGNMENTS

1. Examine the public health images reprinted here. Each is designed to appeal to a specific audience at a specific time. Choose one of these images for an analysis of how the ad targets that audience and what images, ideals, or ideas the ad takes advantage of from popular culture to create that message.

2. Work with two other classmates. Assemble several public health messages on STDs. (Your campus health center is a good resource, but also notice messages posted around campus or in other public places.) Analyze the kinds of images that appear in the public health publicity. Do the examples use familiar images? If so, are they used in expected or unexpected ways? Do the images seem to transmit messages about negative consequences or positive benefits (or some combination of the two)? How effective do you think the publicity is, given its intended audience? Prepare a written report that explains your findings.

3. Design your own public health publicity. Choose any health topic you find interesting and important (e.g., smoking, drugs, diet, exercise, STDs, alcohol). Decide on your intended audience—college students, teenagers, pregnant women, new mothers, or some other group. Fashion your message so that it speaks to the particular audience you have in mind. Choose carefully the image or images that can best convey your message. Be sure to review the suggestions for creating print ads reprinted here from Adbusters.org.

SUGGESTIONS FOR CREATING PRINT ADS

The following suggestions are adapted from the Web site Adbusters.org.

1. Decide on your communication objective. The communications objective is the essence of your message. If you want to tell people not to eat rutabagas because it's cruel, then that's your communications objective. A word of caution: though perhaps the most important of your 8 steps, this is also the one that beginners tend most to neglect. A precise and well-defined objective is crucial to a good ad. If your objective isn't right on, then everything that follows will be off as well.

2. **Decide on your target audience.** Who is your message intended for? If you're speaking to kids, then your language and arguments will have to be understandable to kids. On the other hand, if you're speaking to high-income earners (for example, if you're writing an ad to dissuade people from wearing fur coats), then your language will have to be more sophisticated. So define who your target audience is, because that will decide how your message is conveyed.

3. **Decide on your format.** Is it going to be a poster, a half-page magazine ad, or a tiny box in the corner of a newspaper? Make this decision based on the target audience you're trying to reach and the amount of money you can afford to spend. If you're talking to kids, a poster in one high school will not only cost less, it will actually reach more of your target audience than a full-page ad in the biggest paper in town. When it comes to deciding on the size of your ad, the larger it is, the more expensive it will be to produce and run. Don't let that discourage you. You can do a lot with a small ad so long as it's strong, clear, and properly targeted.

4. **Develop your concept.** The concept is the underlying creative idea that drives your message. Even in a big ad campaign, the concept will typically remain the same from one ad to another, and from one medium to another. Only the execution of that concept will change. So by developing a concept that is effective and powerful, you open the door to a number of very compelling ads. So take your time developing a concept that's strong.

Typically, an ad is made up of a photograph or a drawing (the "visual"), a headline, and writing (the "copy"). Whether you think of your visual or your headline first makes little difference. However, here are a few guidelines worth following.

5. **The visual.** Though you don't absolutely require a visual, it will help draw attention to your ad. Research indicates that 70 percent of people will only look at the visual in an ad, whereas only 30 percent will read the headline. So if you use a visual, then you're already talking to twice as many people as you otherwise might. Another suggestion is to use photographs instead of illustrations whenever possible. People tend to relate to realistic photographs more easily than unrealistic ones. But whether you choose a photograph or an illustration, the most important criterion is that the image be the most interesting one possible and at least half your ad whenever possible.

6. **The headline.** The most important thing to remember here is that your headline must be short, snappy, and must touch the people that read it. Your headline must affect readers emotionally, either by making them laugh, making them angry, making them curious, or making them think. If you can't think of a headline that does one of these four things, then keep thinking. Here's a little tip that might help: try to find an insight or inner truth to the message that you're trying to convey, something that readers will easily relate to and be touched by. It might be tempting to write a headline like: "Stop Exploiting These Migrant Workers." However, with a little thought, a more underlying truth might be revealed—that migrant workers are as human as we are, and that our actions do hurt them. From that inner truth, you might arrive at the headline: "Do unto others as you would have them do unto you." The headline doesn't have to be biblical, though that in itself will add meaning and power for many people. Finally, whenever possible, avoid a headline longer than fifteen words. People just don't read as much as they used to.

7. **The copy.** Here's where you make the case. If you have compelling arguments, make them. If you have persuasive facts, state them. But don't overwhelm with information. Two strong arguments will make more of an impression than a dozen weaker ones. Finally, be clear, be precise, and be honest. Any hint of deception will instantly detract from your entire message. Position your copy beneath the headline, laid out in two blocks two or three inches in length. Only about 5 percent of people will read your copy, whereas 30 percent will read your headline. By positioning your copy near your heading, you create a visual continuity which will draw more people to the information you want to convey. Use a serif typeface for your copy whenever possible. Those little lines and swiggles on the letters make the reading easier and more pleasing to the eye.

- **Subheads.** If you have lots of copy, break it up with interesting subheads. This will make your ad more inviting, more organized, and easier to read.

- **The signature.** This is where the name of the organization belongs, along with the address and phone number. If you don't have an organization, then think of a name that will help reinforce the message you're trying to convey. Perhaps "Citizens for Fairness to Migrant Workers" would work. Your organization doesn't have to be incorporated or registered for it to be real.

8. **Some mistakes to avoid.** The single most common mistake is visual clutter. Less is always better than more. So if you're not certain whether

something is worth including, leave it out. If your ad is chaotic, people will simply turn the page, and your message will never be read. The second most common mistake is to have an ad that's unclear or not easily understood. Haven't you ever looked at an ad and wondered what it was for? The best way to safeguard against this is to do some rough sketches of your visual with the headline and show it around. If people aren't clear about your message, it's probably because your message is unclear. And however tempting, don't argue with them or assume that they're wrong and that your ad is fine. You'll be in for an unpleasant surprise. Proofread your ad, then give it to others to proofread, then proofread it yet again. Typographical errors diminish your credibility and have an uncanny habit of creeping into ads when you least expect it.

PHOTOGRAPHIC ICONS: FACT, FICTION, OR METAPHOR?

— *Philip Gefter*

Philip Gefter is a senior picture editor at the *New York Times,* where he has served as the culture picture editor and the page-one picture editor. His writing on such major figures in photography as Robert Capa, John Szarkowski, and Robert Frank has appeared in a number of newspapers, journals, and magazines, including *Aperture,* where the article reprinted here originally appeared (winter 2006). In it, Gefter explores the place of photography in shaping public memory.

SUGGESTION FOR READING Gefter's article is about photos that have become iconic in history. Before you read, look up the meaning of *iconic* and write a brief reflection on how a photograph of any sort might take on an iconic status.

1 Truth-telling is the promise of a photograph—as if fact itself resides in the optical precision with which the medium reflects our native perception. A photograph comes as close as we get to witnessing an authentic moment with our own eyes while not actually being there. Think of all the famous pictures that serve as both documentation and verification of historic events: Mathew Brady's photographs of the Civil War; Lewis Hine's chronicle of industrial growth in America; the birth of the Civil Rights movement documented in a picture of Rosa Parks on a segregated city bus in Montgomery, Alabama. Aren't they proof of the facts in real time, moments in history brought to the present?

Of course, just because a photograph reflects the world with perceptual accuracy doesn't mean it is proof of what spontaneously transpired. A photographic image might look like actual reality, but gradations of truth are measured in the circumstances that led up to the moment the picture was taken.

The viewer's expectation about a picture's veracity is largely determined by the context in which the image appears. A picture published in

For more information or to order the book please visit www.aperture.org. Aperture is a not-for-profit public foundation dedicated to promoting photography as a unique form of artistic expression.

a newspaper is believed to be fact; an advertising image is understood to be fiction. If a newspaper image turns out to have been set up, then questions are raised about trust and authenticity. Still, somewhere between fact and fiction—or perhaps hovering slightly above either one—is the province of metaphor, where the truth is approximated in renderings of a more poetic or symbolic nature.

The impulse to define, perfect, or heighten reality is manifest in a roster of iconic photographs that have come to reside in the world as "truth." While Mathew Brady is known for his Civil War pictures, he rarely set foot on a battlefield. He couldn't bear the sight of dead bodies. In fact, most pictures of the battlefield attributed to Brady's studio were taken by his employees Alexander Gardner and Timothy O'Sullivan—both of whom were known to have moved bodies around for the purposes of composition and posterity.

5   In *Home of a Rebel Sharpshooter, Gettysburg* (1863), a picture by Gardner, the body of a dead soldier lies in perfect repose. His head is tilted in the direction of the camera, his hand on his belly, his rifle propped up vertically against the rocks. There would be no question that this is a scene the photographer happened upon, if it weren't for another picture by Gardner of the same soldier, this time his face turned away from the camera and his rifle lying on the ground.

In the Library of Congress catalog, the photograph *Dead Soldiers at Antietam* (1862) is listed twice, under the names of both Brady and Gardner. In the image, approximately two dozen dead soldiers lie in a very neat row across the field. Could they possibly have fallen in such tidy succession? Knowing what we do about Gardner's picture of the rebel soldier, the possibility lingers that he moved some of these bodies to create a better composition. Or it could be that other soldiers had lined the bodies up before digging a mass grave for burial. But whatever the circumstances that led to this picture, it is verifiable that the battle of Antietam took place on this field. We

Mathew Brady/Alexander Gardner, *Bodies of Confederate Dead Gathered for Burial*, Battle of Antietam, September 1862.

know that numbers of soldiers were killed. Evidence of the battle remains—the soldiers that died on that date, the battlefield on which they fought, the clothes they wore, and so on. Just how much of the subject matter does the photographer have to change before fact becomes fiction, or a photograph becomes metaphor?

"Mathew Brady used art to forge a relationship between photography and history, but when the memory of Brady the artist vanished, we came to accept his images as fact," Mary Panzer wrote in her 1997 book *Mathew Brady and the Image of History.* "Acknowledged or not, Brady's careful manipulation of his subjects continues to influence our perception, and still shapes the way in which we see his era, and the story of the nation."

Lewis Hine's 1920 photograph of a powerhouse mechanic symbolizes the work ethic that built America. The simplicity of the photograph long ago turned it into a powerful icon, all the more poignant because of its "authenticity." But in fact, Hine—who was interested in the human labor aspect of an increasingly mechanized world, and once claimed that "there is an urgent need for intelligent interpretation of the world's workers"—posed this man in order to make the portrait. Does that information make the picture any less valid?

We see in the first shot that the worker's zipper is down. Isn't it a sad fact that the flaws in daily life should prevent reality from being the best version of how things really are? In our attempt to perfect reality, we aim for higher standards. A man with his zipper down is undignified, and so the

— Variant of Lewis Hine's photograph of a powerhouse mechanic.

—Hine's iconic powerhouse mechanic working on a steam pump, 1920.

famous icon, posed as he is, presents an idealized version of the American worker—dignity customized, but forever intact. Still, the mechanic did work in that powerhouse and his gesture is true enough to his labor. The reality of what the image depicts is indisputable, and whether Hine maintained a fidelity to what transpired in real time may or may not be relevant to its symbolic import.

10   *Le Baiser de l'Hôtel de Ville* (Kiss at the Hôtel de Ville, 1950) by Robert Doisneau, despite its overexposure on posters and postcards, has long served as an example of how photography can capture the spontaneity of life. What a breezy testament to the pleasure of romance! How lovely the couple is, how elegant their gesture and their clothing, how delightful this perspective from a café in Paris! It makes you believe in romantic love: you want to be there, as if you, too, would surely witness love blossoming all around you— or even find it yourself—while sitting at a café in the City of Light.

But despite the story this picture seems to tell—one of a photographer who just happened to look up from his Pernod as the enchanted lovers walked by—there was no serendipity whatsoever in the moment. Doisneau had seen the man and woman days earlier, near the school at which they were studying acting. He was on assignment for *Life* magazine, for a story on romance in Paris, and hired the couple as models for the shot. This information was not brought to light until the early 1990s, when lawsuits demanding compensation were filed by several people who claimed to be the models in the famous picture. Does the lack of authenticity diminish the photograph? It did for me, turning its promise of romance into a beautifully crafted lie.

Ruth Orkin was in Florence, Italy, in the early 1950s when she met Jinx Allen, whom she asked to be the subject of a picture Orkin wanted to submit to the *Herald Tribune. American Girl in Italy* was conceived inadvertently when Orkin

— Ruth Orkin, *American Girl in Italy,* 1951.

noticed the Italian men on their Vespas ogling Ms. Allen as she walked down the street. Orkin asked her to walk down the street again, to be sure she had the shot. Does a second take alter the reality of the phenomenon? How do you parse the difference between Doisneau's staged picture and Orkin's re-creation?

Iwo Jima, Old Glory Goes Up on Mt. Suribachi was taken in 1945 by Joe Rosenthal, an Associated Press photographer. As documentation of a World War II victory, the picture immediately assumed symbolic significance—indeed, it won Rosenthal a Pulitzer Prize, and is one of the most enduring images of the twentieth century. For some time, it was considered a posed picture, but this was due to a misunderstanding. The famous image was the first of three pictures Rosenthal took of the flag being raised. For the last shot, he asked the soldiers to pose in front of the raised flag, thinking that the newspapers back home would expect a picture in which the soldiers' faces were visible. Later, asked if his picture of Iwo Jima was posed, he said yes—referring in his mind to that third frame, not the one that had been published. Still, that the moment captured in the well-known picture occurred just as we see it today surely confirms the truth-telling capability of photography.

The birth of the Civil Rights movement is often dated back to a moment in 1955 when Rosa Parks, a black woman, refused to give up her seat on a crowded city bus to a white man in

Rosa Parks sits in the front of a bus in Montgomery, Alabama. Parks was arrested on December 1, 1955 for refusing to give up her seat in the front of a bus in Montgomery. The man sitting behind Parks is Nicholas C. Chriss, a reporter for United Press International out of Atlanta.

Montgomery, Alabama. (While she was not the first black bus rider to refuse to give up her seat, her case became the one on which the legal challenge was based.) Many people assume that the famous picture of Parks sitting on a city bus is an actual record of that historic moment. But the picture was taken on December 21, 1956, a year after she refused to give up her seat, and a month after the U.S. Supreme Court ruled Montgomery's segregated bus system illegal. Before she died, Parks told Douglas Brinkley, her biographer, that she posed for the picture. A reporter and two photographers from *Look* magazine had seated her on the bus in front of a white man. Similar photo opportunities were arranged on the same day for other members of the Civil Rights community, including Martin Luther King. Here is a staged document that has become a historic reference point, and a revealing parable about the relationship of history to myth.

15   As a witness to events, the photojournalist sets out to chronicle what happens in the world as it actually occurs. A cardinal rule of the profession is that the presence of the camera must not alter the situation being photographed. Four years ago, Edward Keating, among the best staff photographers at the *New York Times,* was fired because of questions raised about one picture he took that ended up in the newspaper. This correction was published in the *Times* five days later:

> A picture in the early editions on September 20, 2002, showed a 6-year-old boy aiming a toy pistol alongside a sign reading "Arabian Foods" outside a store in Lackawanna, N.Y., near Buffalo. The store was near the scene of two arrests in a raid described by the authorities as a pre-emptive strike against a cell of Al Qaeda, and the picture appeared with an article recounting the life stories of the detainees. The picture was not relevant to the article and should not have appeared.

The correction went on to say that photographers on the scene from other news organizations had reported that Keating asked the young boy to aim the toy pistol. Upon further inquiry and a full inspection of the images from the entire photo assignment, the "editors concluded, and Mr. Keating acknowledged, that the boy's gesture had not been spontaneous." Altering the reality of the situation is a violation of journalistic policy, and it turned Keating's image from fact to illustration—a potent editorial statement about the Arabic community at a highly sensitive moment.

Paradoxically, looking through the photography archives of the *New York Times,* one is struck by the numbers of prints in which one or more people have been airbrushed out of the picture. The technique has been used at times to highlight an individual relevant to a particular news story, or simply to sharpen a line for better reproduction on newsprint. Other pictures have red-pencil crop marks, with which the art director or picture editor isolated only that part of the image relevant to the news story. To be fair, these changes were made not for the sake of censorship, but rather as part of an editing process simply to filter out unwanted information—perhaps no more egregious than cutting down a subject's spoken quotation to its salient points.

In 1839, the invention of photography provided a revolutionary method of replicating reality in accurate visual terms. What a great tool for artists and painters to construct images with greater perceptual facility. The history of art is a continuum of constructed images that depict *reality* as it was truly, or else as it was imagined in ideal terms. Photography did not change that continuum; it only made the difference between perception and reality more difficult to determine.

EXPLORATORY WRITING

Gefter writes, "Truth-telling is the promise of a photograph—as if fact itself resides in the optical precision with which the medium reflects our native perception." What follows from this is Gefter's discussion of what truths the camera can and cannot tell. Write a summary of how Gefter works with that opening statement as he moves through iconic photographs as fact, fiction, or metaphor. What examples does he use, and what do those examples illustrate? Is there no truth possible in a photograph?

TALKING ABOUT THE READING

Gefter offers several examples of photos that have become historical and cultural icons but which have been posed or altered to some extent. Among those are the Lewis Hine factory photo, the Matthew Brady Civil War photo, the news photo of Rosa Parks, the Robert Doisneau photo of lovers in Paris, and the Ruth Orkin photo of an American woman in Italy. With a group of your classmates, choose one of those photos for a discussion of iconic photography as fact, fiction, or metaphor.

WRITING ASSIGNMENTS

1. Gefter argues that "the promise of the photograph" is truth-telling. If you have done the exploratory writing that follows this reading, draw on it to complete this new exploratory writing. In it explain what Gefter is saying about the possibilities of photographing truth or evidence. Evidence of what? What history can a photo like those reprinted in this article uncover? What can a photo never reveal?

2. Gefter concludes his article with the statement that, "The history of art is a continuum of constructed images that depict reality as it was truly, or else as it was imagined in ideal terms. Photography did not change that continuum; it only made the difference between perception and reality more difficult to determine." On first reading, that statement might seem to contradict everything we know about photography, especially when a photograph is used in a news story or as evidence at a trial or as a record of family or public events. Write a fuller explanation of how, given the examples Gefter offers, photography can make reality not less difficult to see but rather more difficult. Use any of the photographs from this essay to illustrate your explanation.

3. Gefter makes the point that where a photograph appears and what use is made of the photograph makes all the difference in how much "truth" the photo carries. Write an essay in which you test out Gefter's argument by changing the way an iconic photograph is presented. Choose either a photo from Gefter's essay or another that you have access to and place it in more than one context. Place it in an advertisement for a product, in a news story, as an illustration in a novel, on a political poster, etc. Where you place it or how you change it is up to you. You might colorize a black and white photo or use a photo manipulation program to add something into the photo or remove something from it. When you have finished write an analysis of how the image changes with each change you make. Are there certain contexts or changes that give this photo higher truth value? Refer back to Gefter's discussion of the truth-value of photography for your discussion.

VISUAL ESSAY   Rewriting the Image

Advertising doesn't just create "images," it constructs differences between men and women, which operate under the assumption that they reflect a universal timeless truth. And so it is never merely a case of a good image versus a bad image. Looking itself has to be rewritten. . . .

It is time for some interventions in the belly of the beast.

There are many methods for upsetting the echelons of imagery. There is no one perfect way to intervene, not when the gospel of perfection is the very text being tampered with. From critiques to billboard activism, the creation of alternative imagery to boycotts and protests, strategic intervention is needed on all fronts. Humor and the unexpected are always good tools for deconstructing the codes the advertising world operates under.—Katherine Dodds, writing in Adbusters Magazine

Writing over, remaking, or talking back to an image is a tactic that has been around for a long time. Look, for example, at Marcel Duchamp's remake of Leonardo's *Mona Lisa*. The Da Vinci portrait had been held up for so long as a masterpiece of Renaissance art that Duchamp, trying to change the way people see the classics, did the unthinkable: he painted a mustache on the *Mona Lisa* (well, actually, on a reproduction of the *Mona Lisa*). It was, it could be argued, one of the most effective acts of graffiti ever created. It shocked many in the art world and those who considered the masterpieces sacred, and it made the public laugh. At the same time, it also made a statement about how art had to change, new voices had to be heard, and new images had to be accepted.

In the same way, the Canadian-based organization Adbusters advocates rewriting ads that represent unhealthy products, products that promote stereotypes, and products that exploit workers. In the article from which Katherine Dodds's statement is taken, she writes of the importance of this act of taking control of advertising images, many of which you have read and written about in this chapter.

Sometimes, though, a rewrite isn't meant to change attitudes or attack stereotypes at all. Sometimes a rewrite is simply necessary, in a world so thick with images, if anyone is ever to say something new, or to revise the ways people see each other, or even to laugh at themselves. Rewriting the image can be activism, as Dodds suggests, but it can also be a way of understanding how images function so that people aren't simply consumers but are also producers of the image.

Of course, if people are going to complain about what's produced out there, then the best way to change it is to change it.

SUGGESTION FOR READING

Because parody depends on knowledge of the original to make its point, the message that results from the parody or rewriting threatens to change one's response to the original. Duchamp, for example, certainly wanted to change the way viewers saw the *Mona Lisa*. As you look at the images here, write some notes on how the rewrite makes you rethink the original image.

Girl with the Pearl Earring, Johannes Vermeer.

L.H.O.O.Q. by Marcel Duchamp, 1930. © 2005 Artists Rights Society (ARS), New York/ADAGP, Paris/Succession.

Girl with the Pearl Nose Ring, Garrett LaCivita.

The Grand Odalisque, by Jean Auguste Dominique Ingres, 1814.

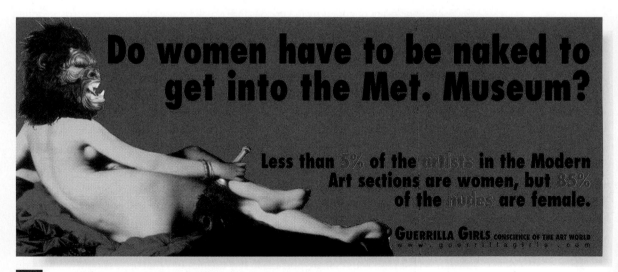

Guerrilla Girls' poster displayed on New York City buses.

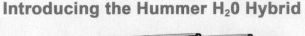

Introducing the Hummer H₂0 Hybrid

Now greener means BIGGER! Using advanced hybrid technology and a smaller 12 litre engine, the H20 gets up to double* the fuel economy of our standard H2 SUV. Ease your conscience today. You deserve it. Shop on-line at www.GreenBling.com

* The Hummer Hybrid is EPA rated at 2 mpg highway. 0 mpg city

 Hummer ad.

TALKING ABOUT THE READING

1. With a group of classmates, exchange the notes you made on how the rewrites of Da Vinci's *Mona Lisa* and Ingres's *Odalisque* change the way you read the original. With your group, make a list of popular paintings, advertisements, or photographs that could be "rewritten." How would a rewrite change those images? What images would your group consider "out of bounds" for parody or satire of this sort? Why?

2. Some people are offended by the images that are the result of writing over classic paintings. Others find the rewrites funny or powerful statements about the originals. What is your response to the Guerrilla Girls' rewrite of Ingres's *Odalisque*? How would you account for your response?

3. With a group of your classmates, choose a popular image to rewrite or parody. Present your rewrite to the class, and explain what your group wanted to accomplish with the image that you created.

WRITING ASSIGNMENTS

1. Choose an advertisement or series of ads that illustrates Dodds's statement that advertising "constructs differences between men and women, which operate under the assumption that they reflect a universal timeless truth." Write a brief explanation of what Dodds means, then use your ad or ads to explain how, as Dodds suggests, "Looking itself has to be rewritten." To do that, write over the ads, creating a parody, or explain what a reader needs to understand to look at these images differently.

2. When you rewrite an advertisement, your purpose usually is to bring to the surface the oppositional readings that are possible in any ad image. What oppositional readings do you find in the Hummer spoof ad reproduced here? How does the ad take on a new

meaning? Find an ad image that you would like to rewrite, and redo the image in a way that clearly draws on the original yet brings to the surface a new and oppositional reading of the original.

3. Choose any kind of image—on a T-shirt, poster, cereal box, magazine cover, commercial, famous painting, cover from a textbook or novel. Rewrite the image so that you bring an alternate reading of that image to the surface or so that you create an entirely new meaning. One T-shirt rewrite that has become a popular tourist souvenir, for example, is the shirt that reads, "My parents went to Paris and all I got was this lousy T-shirt." It's a rewrite because it acknowledges the habit of buying souvenir T-shirts as gifts to placate family and friends left at home. As well, Duchamp's rewrite of *Mona Lisa* only makes its point if you think *Mona Lisa* is a great work of art that shouldn't be changed. First-year Virginia Tech student Garrett LaCivita saw some of the same possibilities for visual rewrite in the very popular Jan Vermeer painting *The Girl with the Pearl Earring.* To bring the painting up-to-date, she rewrote it for her generation. Thus, *The Girl with the Pearl Earring* became *The Girl with the Pearl Nose Ring.* Notice that her rewrite both acknowledges the original and makes a statement of her own—changing the delicate elegance of the pearl to the edgy style of the nose ring and changing the muted style of dress to the hoodie of the streets. Still, in both her title and her composition, the rewrite makes a very specific reference to the original.

To make your own rewrite, you will have to understand the original message, so pay attention to that as you use the original to create your own image. The image you choose and the meaning you make with that image depend on your interests and on the interests of your intended audience. For whom are you making this image? Classmates? Parents? A particular teacher? An identifiable consumer group? You decide and then rewrite the image to speak to that group.In order for any visual parody or rewrite to be at all successful, it has to be a rewrite of an image your audience will immediately recognize. Your message also has to be clear. Keep that in mind as you design your rewrite.

FILM CLIP   Camera Work: Screening the Gaze

In the selection from *Art and the Committed Eye* in this chapter, Richard Leppert writes that the power of the gaze is not just an issue in art and advertising but also in other visual forms, significantly in film. In a number of films—especially horror or suspense films—we see the action from the point of view of the villain, the voyeur, or the lead character. When the camera positions itself so that the viewer seems to be looking through the eyes of one of the characters, that person becomes the subject of "the gaze." Think, for example, of Alfred Hitchcock's *Psycho* (1960) as Norman Bates peers through a peephole in the wall to watch his victim. When he presses his eye to the wall, the camera suddenly takes his point of view so that the viewer is now seeing what Bates sees. The same is true with a number of horror films like *Halloween, Friday the 13th,* and others that allow the viewer to look through the eyes of one of the characters—essentially taking the visual position of that character. The classic example of this kind of camera work is Alfred Hitchcock's *Rear Window* (1954), in which Jimmie Stewart's character, bored from being confined in a wheelchair while his broken leg mends, passes the time watching his neighbors, sometimes using a pair of binoculars or even a high-power camera lens. *Rear Window* was certainly the inspiration of the 2007 teen horror film *Disturbia*. In both, the camera work allows viewers to see through the protagonist's eyes, often playing the role of voyeur. In both of these films, the protagonist's girlfriend accuses him of voyeurism—of playing the Peeping Tom.

SUGGESTED ASSIGNMENT

For this paper, choose a film that uses the camera technique described above—often called "optical point of view" or "point of view shot," which allows the viewer to look through the eyes of a character in the film. Richard Leppert writes that, for critics Berger and Clark, "woman *is* image, and man is the bearer of the *look* on that image. The former is passive, hence it lacks agency; the other is active, hence it possesses agency." In other words, the character doing the looking always has power over the character being looked at unawares. Of course, what Leppert calls "the look" is much more complex, especially in film, than simply a shot of someone looking at or away from the camera. In film, we read the look in conjunction with what we know of the characters, the plot, the action, and even the film genre—horror film or romantic comedy, for example.

In your essay, choose a sequence of scenes or an extended scene that uses optical point of view as a visual technique, and examine how that point of view sets up certain power relations in the context of this film. What is the situation? Who is doing the looking? Who is being observed? What is the effect of seeing other characters through the eyes of a single character?

Some possible choices:

Secret Window	Halloween
Peeping Tom	Dark Passage
The Eyes of Laura Mars	Lady in the Lake
Dressed to Kill	Nightmare on Elm Street
Disturbia	Friday the 13th

CAMERA WORK AND EDITING: SOME USEFUL TERMS

Camera angle—the angle of view in relation to the subject being filmed. The perspective of the viewer shifts depending on whether the camera shoots at a low angle, a high angle, or level with the subject.

Camera distance—the apparent distance of the camera from the frame. In an extreme long shot, the person in the frame is just visible; a long shot brings the person in closer view but the background still predominates the frame. In a medium long shot, the figure is framed from about knees up and there is less background visible in the frame; a medium shot frames the body from about waist up; a medium close-up is from about chest up. A close-up shot is primarily the head or face filling the frame; an extreme close-up moves in on a small part of the body—the eye or mouth, for example.

Editing—the process of joining a series of shots to make scenes and then of moving from shot to shot or scene to scene.

Establishing shot—usually a long shot at the beginning of a film that establishes context for upcoming scenes.

Fade—the gradual disappearance or appearance of one image. To fade out, the image ends in black screen. To fade in, an image appears gradually onscreen.

Framing—the space of the film image; what the viewer sees through the camera's frame.

Montage—transitional sequences of a quick series of shots, often to suggest the passage of time or to establish a particular theme.

Off-screen space—the space not visible but assumed outside the frame.

Scene—a unit of film composed of a number of shots, usually a completed episode in the storyline.

Shot/reverse shot—often used during dialogue when the camera shoots one actor then shoots the second actor in the opposite space speaking or looking back in the direction of the first shot.

Shot—an unedited strip of film from the time the camera starts until it stops.

Two-shot—a medium shot that features two actors in the same frame.

FIELDWORK   Taking Inventory

We began this chapter by asserting that visual messages surround us and are so ubiquitous that we barely notice how many we read in our daily routine. Several of the authors in this chapter have said much the same. In our assignment suggestions, we have asked you to look for and keep track of the visuals you see during your normal daily routine. As you might already have realized, that is a big job, because the visual messages that surround us have increased significantly over the years and because most of us are so used to those signs, we take them for granted.

Fieldwork is meant to be more thorough and careful in detailing what is actually out there than a personal journal might be. For this project, you should join with a work group of three or four of your classmates. Your aim will be to get as accurate a count as you can of the number and types of visuals that are typically available in a particular place—in your classroom building, in designated areas of the campus, or in the local town or city where you are doing your work, for example. In other words, you are testing the premise of this chapter by doing fieldwork of your own.

When you have completed your count, write up your report, including schematic diagrams of the area each group member examined and where visuals occurred in those areas. You might also want to indicate on your diagram where the highest concentration of visuals occurred. Present your report to the class.

To be as representative as possible, each member of your group should choose a different part of the building, campus, town, or other location you have chosen for this project.

The space should be strictly limited. For example, if you were to focus on downtown, one member of your group should examine one block of the main street; another can work with a side street; a third might look at a local shopping spot. If you were to focus on your campus, ask different members of the group to focus on different buildings or different, clearly defined areas. Elect one person in the group to coordinate assignments, keep the project focused, and check the group's work for consistency.

1. Begin by surveying the area and noting down every visual message that you see—posters, icons for restrooms or to give directions, television monitors, artwork, etc.

2. Count the number of visual messages in your assigned area.

3. Identify the different media used to make or project the visual messages in the area. (Media refers to the technology used to create the message—television, digital display, neon, print, painting, etc.)

For your report:

1. Describe the area your group studied, making sure to indicate how you divided that area among group members. You should also indicate when you visited your site and how long your count took.

2. Provide the total number of visuals in the site as well as the different types or media, the places that held the highest concentration of visuals, and the places with the lowest concentration.

3. Explain, if you can, why different areas have more or fewer visuals.

4. When you present your findings to the class, provide examples of the different types of visuals (you can take digital photos or provide sketches) and project them so the entire class can see your samples.

For more information on writing up a report, see "Classroom Observation" in Chapter 3.

MINING THE ARCHIVE   Advertising Through the Ages

VIGILANCE IS THE PRICE OF BEAUTY

"Mum" is the word!

The Alluring Charm of a Dainty Woman

"Mum" prevents all body odors

Locate old copies of any popular magazine. *Good Housekeeping,* for example, began publication in January 1900, so it represents a full century of magazine design. You'll see a dramatic change, especially in advertising design, over these years.

Once you have found several ads ranging from the early, middle, and late twentieth century and now the twenty-first century, write a report on your findings. Compare the ad copy (written text) of older ads with current advertising. How do the claims of older ads compare with claims in today's advertisements for the same products? What role do pictorial elements play in those older ads? How would you describe the change in design over the years?

This kind of report is easier to write if you choose one type of product for a focus—for example, cosmetics, bath soaps, laundry detergent, cigarettes.

If you don't have access to a good library, you can find a stockpile of ads from newspapers and magazines between 1911 and 1955 at Duke University's Ad*Access Project. This project is housed in the Rare Book, Manuscript, and Special Collections room at the Duke University Library and can be accessed on the Internet at **http://scriptorium.lib.duke.edu/adaccess.** The site also includes useful information about copyright and fair use policies for using images for your class projects.

Style

Courtesy of Nirvana L.L.C.

In societies dominated by modern conditions of production, life is presented as an immense accumulation of spectacles. Everything that was directly lived has receded into a representation.

—Guy Debord

Americans live in a style-conscious culture, and even elementary school children know the difference between Nikes and cheaper imitations. By the time they enter junior high school, most American adolescents are already highly skilled at distinguishing between brand names. They know the difference, say, between the Gap and Wal-Mart, between a Ford Taurus and a BMW, not to mention between Nike, Vans, and Doc Marten as far as footwear goes. They have learned that brand differences *make a difference*.

Style matters. It matters what kind of music you listen to, how you wear your hair, whether you're tattooed or pierced, and what kind of food you eat. Mundane personal belongings—everyday-use objects, from staplers to toothbrushes to laptop computers—matter too. All of these things matter because the styles we follow and products we use send messages about who we are. They're part of the identity kits we put together to make up a self.

In many ways, this concern for brand names, personal styles, and the appearance of objects seems shallow and trivial. But style identifies. Whether consciously or unconsciously, we make judgments about people based on their appearance and style. By growing up in American culture, we acquire a sense of the style that goes with different walks of life—how, say, a high school teacher, a business executive, or a truck driver ought to look.

Style communicates messages about economic and social class, subcultures, and lifestyles because we share with others cultural codes that define what's normal and expected. For example, we expect wealthy professionals in metropolitan areas to be museum members, go to the opera, and enjoy gourmet food and fine wine. On the other hand, we are likely to expect that working-class men in the Midwest drink beer, listen to classic rock or country-western music, and support their local pro football team. This doesn't mean that everyone in a particular social group conforms to these cultural codes. What it does indicate, however, is that style carries cultural meanings that go beyond individual likes and dislikes.

If the styles we adopt seem to be freely taken personal choices, they are contained nonetheless in a larger system of cultural codes that organize the way we think about identity, social status, prestige, good (and bad) taste, tradition, and innovation. Fashion designers, graphic designers, and product designers understand this connection between style and identity. As they design corporate logos and brand trademarks, jeans and athletic shoes, computers and cars, their job is to match styles to people's identities and, at the same time, create styles that offer people new identities.

In this chapter, you will be asked to look at rebel designers, such as the punks of the 1970s and 1980s who created a new style and cultural identity, and professional designers whose work floods the contemporary marketplace. The idea of the chapter is to consider everyone a designer who puts together a style and identity.

STYLE IN REVOLT: REVOLTING STYLE

— *Dick Hebdige*

Dick Hebdige is a lecturer in communication at Goldsmith College, University of London. The following selection comes from *Subculture: The Meaning of Style* (1979), in which he examines the political and cultural importance of postwar British youth cultures, including the punk movement. In this excerpt, Hebdige looks at how the punks used style as a tool of disruption and revolt. This selection is also an introduction to the Visual Essay that follows, "Graphic Design in Rock Culture."

SUGGESTION FOR READING As you read, notice the range of evidence Hebdige brings forward to characterize the style of punk culture. Underline as many different examples of punk style as you can find. Notice how the final paragraph on graphic design and typography serves as an introduction to the graphic style of the rock posters and T-shirts in the Visual Essay.

Nothing was holy to us. Our movement was neither mystical, communistic nor anarchistic. All of these movements had some sort of programme, but ours was completely nihilistic. We spat on everything, including ourselves. Our symbol was nothingness, a vacuum, a void.

—*George Grosz on Dada*

We're so pretty, oh so pretty . . . vac-unt.

—*The Sex Pistols*

1 Although it was often directly offensive (T-shirts covered in swear words) and threatening (terrorist/guerilla outfits) punk style was defined principally through the violence of its cut ups. Like Duchamp's ready mades—manufactured objects which qualified as art because he chose to call them such, the most unremarkable and inappropriate items—a pin, a plastic clothes peg, a television component, a razor blade, a tampon—could be brought within the province of punk (un)fashion. Anything within or without reason could be turned into part of what Vivien Westwood called "confrontation dressing" so long as the rupture between "natural" and constructed context was clearly visible (i.e., the rule would seem to be: if the cap doesn't fit, wear it).

Objects borrowed from the most sordid of contexts found a place in the punks' ensembles: lavatory chains were draped in graceful arcs across chests encased in plastic bin-liners. Safety pins were taken out of their domestic "utility" context and worn as gruesome ornaments through the cheek, ear or lip. "Cheap" trashy fabrics (PVC, plastic, lurex, etc.) in vulgar designs (e.g., mock leopard skin) and "nasty" colours, long discarded by the quality end of the fashion industry as obsolete kitsch, were salvaged by the punks and turned into garments (fly boy drainpipes, "common" mini-skirts) which offered self-conscious commentaries on the notions of modernity and taste. Conventional ideas of prettiness were jettisoned along with the traditional feminine lore of cosmetics. Contrary to the advice of every woman's magazine, make-up for both boys and girls was worn to be seen. Faces became abstract

portraits: sharply observed and meticulously executed studies in alienation. Hair was obviously dyed (hay yellow, jet black, or bright orange with tufts of green or bleached in question marks), and T-shirts and trousers told the story of their own construction with multiple zips and outside seams clearly displayed. Similarly, fragments of school uniform (white brinylon shirts, school ties) were symbolically defiled (the shirts covered in graffiti, or fake blood; the ties left undone) and juxtaposed against leather drains or shocking pink mohair tops. The perverse and the abnormal were valued intrinsically. In particular, the illicit iconography of sexual fetishism was used to predictable effect. Rapist masks and rubber wear, leather bodices and fishnet stockings, implausibly pointed stiletto heeled shoes, the whole paraphernalia of bondage—the belts, straps and chains—were exhumed from the boudoir, closet and the pornographic film and placed on the street where they retained their forbidden connotations. Some young punks even donned the dirty raincoat—that most prosaic symbol of sexual "kinkiness"—and hence expressed their deviance in suitably proletarian terms.

Of course, punk did more than upset the wardrobe. It undermined every relevant discourse. Thus dancing, usually an involving and expressive medium in British rock and mainstream pop cultures, was turned into a dumb-show of blank robotics. Punk dances bore absolutely no relation to the desultory frugs and clinches which Geoff Mungham describes as intrinsic to the respectable working-class ritual of Saturday night at the Top Rank or Mecca.[1] Indeed, overt displays of heterosexual interest were generally regarded with contempt and suspicion (who let the BOF/wimp[2] in?) and conventional courtship patterns found no place on the floor in dances like the pogo, the pose and the robot. Though the pose did allow for a minimum sociability (i.e., it could involve two people) the "couple" were generally of the same sex and physical contact was ruled out of court as the relationship depicted in the dance was a "professional" one. One participant would strike a suitable cliché fashion pose while the other would fall into a classic "Bailey" crouch to snap an imaginary picture. The pogo forebade even this much interaction, though admittedly there was always a good deal of masculine jostling in front of the stage. In fact the pogo was a caricature—a reductio ad absurdum of all the solo dance styles associated with rock music. It resembled the "anti dancing" of the "Leapniks" which Melly describes in connection with the trad boom (Melly, 1972). The same abbreviated gestures—leaping into the air, hands clenched to the sides, to head an imaginary ball—were repeated without variation in time to the strict mechanical rhythms of the music. In contrast to the hippies' languid, free-form dancing, and the "idiot dancing" of the heavy metal rockers, the pogo made improvisation redundant: the only variations were imposed by changes in the tempo of the music—fast numbers being "interpreted" with manic abandon in the form of frantic on-the-spots, while the slower ones were pogoed with a detachment bordering on the catatonic.

The robot, a refinement witnessed only at the most exclusive punk gatherings, was both more "expressive" and less "spontaneous" within the very narrow range such terms acquired in punk usage. It consisted of barely perceptible twitches of the head and hands or more extravagant lurches (Frankenstein's first steps?) which were abruptly halted at random points. The resulting pose was held for several moments, even minutes, and the whole sequence was as suddenly, as unaccountably, resumed and re-enacted. Some zealous punks carried things one step further and choreographed whole evenings, turning themselves for a matter of hours, like Gilbert and George,[3] into automata, living sculptures.

5   The music was similarly distinguished from mainstream rock and pop. It was uniformly basic and direct in its appeal, whether through intention or lack of expertise. If the latter, then the punks certainly made a virtue of necessity

("We want to be amateurs"—Johnny Rotten). Typically, a barrage of guitars with the volume and treble turned to maximum accompanied by the occasional saxophone would pursue relentless (un)melodic lines against a turbulent background of cacophonous drumming and screamed vocals. Johnny Rotten succinctly defined punk's position on harmonics: "We're into chaos not music."

The names of the groups (the Unwanted, the Rejects, the Sex Pistols, the Clash, the Worst, etc.) and the titles of the songs: "Belsen was a Gas," "If You Don't Want to Fuck Me, Fuck Off," "I Wanna Be Sick on You," reflected the tendency towards willful desecration and the voluntary assumption of outcast status which characterized the whole punk movement. Such tactics were, to adapt Levi-Strauss's famous phrase, "things to whiten mother's hair with." In the early days at least, these "garage bands" could dispense with musical pretensions and substitute, in the traditional romantic terminology, "passion" for "technique," the language of the common man for the arcane posturings of the existing élite, the now familiar armoury of frontal attacks for the bourgeois notion of entertainment or the classical concept of "high art."

It was in the performance arena that punk groups posed the clearest threat to law and order. Certainly, they succeeded in subverting the conventions of concert and nightclub entertainment. Most significantly, they attempted both physically and in terms of lyrics and lifestyle to move closer to their audiences. This in itself is by no means unique: the boundary between artist and audience has often stood as a metaphor in revolutionary aesthetics (Brecht, the surrealists, Dada, Marcuse, etc.) for that larger and more intransigent barrier which separates art and the dream from reality and life under capitalism.[4] The stages of those venues secure enough to host "new wave" acts were regularly invaded by hordes of punks, and if the management refused to tolerate such blatant disregard for ballroom etiquette, then the groups and their followers could be drawn closer together in a communion of spittle and mutual abuse. At the Rainbow Theatre in May 1977 as the Clash played "White Riot," chairs were ripped out and thrown at the stage. Meanwhile, every performance, however apocalyptic, offered palpable evidence that things could change, indeed were changing: that performance itself was a possibility no authentic punk should discount. Examples abounded in the music press of "ordinary fans" (Siouxsie of Siouxsie and the Banshees, Sid Vicious of the Sex Pistols, Mark P of Sniffin Glue, Jordan of the Ants) who had made the symbolic crossing from the dance floor to the stage. Even the humbler positions in the rock hierarchy could provide an attractive alternative to the drudgery of manual labour, office work or a youth on the dole. The Finchley Boys, for instance, were reputedly taken off the football terraces by the Stranglers and employed as roadies.

If these "success stories" were, as we have seen, subject to a certain amount of "skewed" interpretation in the press, then there were innovations in other areas which made opposition to dominant definitions possible. Most notably, there was an attempt, the first by a predominantly working-class youth culture, to provide an alternative critical space within the subculture itself to counteract the hostile or at least ideologically inflected coverage which punk was receiving in the media. The existence of an alternative punk press demonstrated that it was not only clothes or music that could be immediately and cheaply produced from the limited resources at hand. The fanzines (*Sniffin Glue, Ripped and Torn,* etc.) were journals edited by an individual or a group, consisting of reviews, editorials and interviews with prominent punks, produced on a small scale as cheaply as possible, stapled together and distributed through a small number of sympathetic retail outlets.

The language in which the various manifestoes were framed was determinedly "working class" (i.e., it was liberally peppered with swear words) and typing errors and grammatical mistakes, misspellings and jumbled pagination were left uncorrected in the final proof. Those corrections and crossings out that were made before publication were left to be deciphered by the reader. The overwhelming impression was one of urgency and immediacy, of a paper produced in indecent haste, of memos from the front line.

10   This inevitably made for a strident buttonholing type of prose which, like the music it described, was difficult to "take in" in any quantity. Occasionally a written, more abstract item—what Harvey Garfinkel (the American ethnomethodologist) might call an "aid to sluggish imaginations"—might creep in. For instance, *Sniffin Glue,* the first fanzine and the one which achieved the highest circulation, contained perhaps the single most inspired item of propaganda produced by the subculture—the definitive statement of punk's do-it-yourself philosophy—a diagram showing three finger positions on the neck of a guitar over the caption: "Here's one chord, here's two more, now form your own band."

Even the graphics and typography used on record covers and fanzines were homologous with punk's subterranean and anarchic style. The two typographic models were graffiti which was translated into a flowing "spray can" script, and the ransom note in which individual letters cut up from a variety of sources (newspapers, etc.) in different type faces were pasted together to form an anonymous message. The Sex Pistols' "God Save the Queen" sleeve (later turned into T-shirts, posters, etc.) for instance incorporated both styles: the roughly assembled legend was pasted across the Queen's eyes and mouth which were further disfigured by those black bars used in pulp detective magazines to conceal identity (i.e., they connote crime or scandal). Finally, the process of ironic self abasement which characterized the subculture was extended to the name "punk" itself which, with its derisory connotations of "mean and petty villainy," "rotten," "worthless," etc. was generally preferred by hardcore members of the subculture to the more neutral "new wave."[5]

NOTES

1. In his P.O. account of the Saturday night dance in an industrial town, Mungham (1976) shows how the constricted quality of working-class life is carried over into the ballroom in the form of courtship rituals, masculine paranoia and an atmosphere of sullenly repressed sexuality. He paints a gloomy picture of joy-less evenings spent in the desperate pursuit of "booze and birds" (or "blokes and a romantic bus-ride home") in a controlled setting where "spontaneity is regarded by managers and their staff—principally the bouncers—as the potential hand-maiden of rebellion".

2. BOF = Boring Old Fart. Wimp = "wet."

3. Gilbert and George mounted their first exhibition in 1970 when, clad in identical conservative suits, with metallized hands and faces, a glove, a stick and a tape recorder, they won critical acclaim by performing a series of carefully controlled and endlessly repeated movements on a dais while miming to Flanagan and Allen's "Underneath the Arches." Other pieces with titles like "Lost Day" and "Normal Boredom" have since been performed at a variety of major art galleries throughout the world.

4. Of course, rock music had always threatened to dissolve these categories, and rock performances were popularly associated with all forms of riot and disorder—from the slashing of cinema seats by teddy boys through Beatlemania to the hippy happenings and festivals where freedom was expressed less aggressively in nudity, drug taking and general "spontaneity." However, punk represented a new departure.

5. The word "punk," like the black American "funk" and "superbad" would seem to form part of that "special language of fantasy and alienation" which Charles Winick describes (1959), "in which values are reversed and in which 'terrible' is a description of excellence." See also Wolfe (1969) where he describes the "cruising" scene in Los Angeles in the mid-60s—a subculture of custom-built cars, sweatshirts and "high-piled, perfect coiffure" where "rank" was a term of approval: Rank! Rank is just the natural outgrowth of Rotten . . . Roth and Schorsch grew up in the Rotten Era of Los Angeles teenagers. The idea was to have a completely rotten attitude towards the adult world, meaning, in the long run, the whole established status structure, the whole system of people organizing their lives around a job, fitting into the social structure embracing the whole community. The idea in Rotten was to drop out of conventional status competition into the smaller netherworld of Rotten Teenagers and start one's own league.

WORKS CITED

Melly, G. (1972), *Revolt into Style*, Penguin.

Mungham, G. (1976), "Youth in Pursuit of Itself," in G. Mungham and G. Pearson (eds.), *Working Class Youth Culture*, Routledge and Kegan Paul.

Winick, C. (1959), "The Uses of Drugs by Jazz Musicians," *Social Problems*, vol. 7, no. 3, Winter.

Wolfe, T. (1969), *The Pump House Gang*, Bantam.

VISUAL ESSAY   Graphic Design in Rock Culture

This Visual Essay gathers artifacts from rock culture—two posters, an AC/DC T-shirt, a Sex Pistol album cover, and the Nirvana decal at the beginning of the chapter. We have tried to choose examples of distinctive styles, including the psychedelic '60s, punk, heavy metal, grunge, and rave. As Dick Hebdige notes, rock culture does not consist of just the music but, as is the case with punk, can spawn an entire style that includes clothes, hairstyles, slang, fanzines, and visual design.

SUGGESTION FOR READING As you look through the various visual artifacts, consider the defining graphic style of each example. What does the graphic style seem to express about a particular style or movement in rock culture? What visual elements does it use?

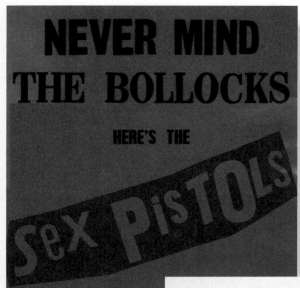

Design: Michael Szabo; Art Direction: DB + Scotto.

EXPLORATORY WRITING

Hebdige's work is primarily about British punks in the late 1970s, though punk style still has an influence on fashion, music, and graphics. If Hebdige were writing a book on American and/or British youth subcultures in the 2000s that are in revolt against the dominant culture, what groups and styles might he focus on (or would he find any at all)? What is the nature of the revolt? How is it expressed stylistically?

TALKING ABOUT THE READING

Make a list of all the examples of punk style you underlined in Hebdige's essay. Work with others in class to construct a table that starts with general categories (clothes, music, dancing, etc.) and then fill in the first column with examples from the punk movement. Add further columns on youth styles and subcultures since the punks. Name the subcultural style and give examples.

	PUNK	ALTERNATIVE	HIP HOP
Important bands/performers			
Dancing			
Hair			
Clothes			

WRITING ASSIGNMENTS

1. Use the table you constructed to identify an example of subcultural or group style that interests you. Pick a particular example—clothes, music, dancing, graphics, or something else—to serve as the topic of an essay. In the essay, explain who the group or subculture is and then show how the example you've chosen illustrates some central meaning about the group's style.

2. As Hebdige explains, punks used common objects and forms of dress in ways that departed from their originally intended uses to create new meanings. This kind of cultural recycling, however, is by no means limited to the punks. Others have recycled old styles to produce retro looks that are often both ironic and nostalgic. Write an essay about a group or style that recycles fashions and objects. Explain how the recycling creates new meanings for older styles.

3. It is possible to present here only a few examples of "Graphic Design in Rock Culture." To add to the Visual Essay, bring your own examples of posters, fanzines, T-shirts, and album covers to class. Be prepared to explain what your examples signify about a particular style in rock culture. Consider the visual elements—the style of font, the layout, images, and whether any aspects of the design are borrowed and recycled. Use Hebdige's analysis of punk graphics and typography as a model to analyze the graphic design of a visual artifact from rock culture. Use any of the examples in the Visual Essay or others you've brought to class or found on your own.

MAKING CONNECTIONS   Theme Parties

People like to dress in costumes—to go trick or treating on Halloween and to go to costume parties. There are interesting questions to ask about why we like to put on costumes and masks and to change our identities, if only briefly. What makes costumes so appealing? How do costumes take us out of our ordinary, day-to-day lives and transform us into other kinds of beings? What is the social function of parties that gather together people wearing costumes? These questions are the backdrop for a certain kind of party where individuals dress up according to themes—*Star Trek* parties (where people dress up as their favorite character), punk parties (where people spike their hair and put on spiked belts and ripped pants), and 1950s martini parties (where everyone puts on the fashions of the time and listens to Frank Sinatra).

Such theme parties are, for the most part, simply good fun—and have become a part of college students' repertoire of popular entertainment. The two following readings, however, focus on theme parties that are more problematical—and that raise further questions about why people put on costumes. As you will see, the first reading focuses on the controversy that arose when Prince Harry wore a Nazi costume to a " colonial or native" party in England. The second reading is a commentary on theme parties in the U.S.—in this case the "ghetto parties" staged by high school and college students.

THE VERY NASTY PARTY

■■■— *Mark Lawson*

Mark Lawson is a columnist for the *Guardian* (U.K.) and the author of the novels *Enough Is Enough or the Emergency Government* (2003) and *Going Out Live* (2002). What appears here is an excerpt from "The Very Nasty Party," the title of one of his pieces in the *Guardian* in 2005.

**SUGGESTION
FOR READING**   In many ways, the title of Mark Lawson's item in the *Guardian* tells the story: it was a "very nasty party." As you read, notice what exactly makes the "colonial or native" party "nasty" in Lawson's view. Consider the photograph taken on a cell phone by someone at the party. What visual clues does it offer to help answer the question about the party's "nastiness"?

1 It may be some consolation to the Prince of Wales that it could have been worse. The owner of Maud's Cotswold Costumes told the Sun that Prince Harry looked at SS costumes but "to be honest they all come in small sizes and there was no way any of them would have fitted him." So the Prince's father can be grateful that he inherited his mother's height because the third in line to the throne was forced to settle for a lower Nazi rank.

— Britain's Prince Harry in Nazi uniform.

Various defenders of the swastika prince have suggested that he has suffered enough criticism, and, while I think he deserves at least a few more days of burning ears, there's another aspect of the matter to be considered.

Every so often, something happens—an investigative documentary, a social worker's report into the murder of a child—that lifts up the British carpet to show the stamped-down filth. This is such a moment. While Harry's costume was shocking, it seems equally astonishing that, in 2005, there is a section of society in which it is not considered odd for a teenager to throw a

party with the theme of "colonial or native" and at which, according to some reports, young male guests blacked up their faces. The implication of much coverage is that Harry misjudged the party mood, but perhaps he merely took the nasty theme to its logical conclusion.

Equally perplexing is the revelation of the range available at Maud's Cotswold Costumes. Given that the Nazi kit was presumably not stocked just in case a prince of the realm wished to perpetrate a monstrous moral gaffe, the question arises of just who would hire it in normal circumstances. This calculation is made more complicated by the owner's quoted claim that the SS outfits "all come in small sizes."

5 Unless school theatre clubs or amateur dramatics groups for people of restricted growth are constantly putting on productions of Colditz throughout Gloucestershire, then it must be assumed that fancy-dress parties at which people wear Nazi uniforms are common in middle England, and that the chaps favouring this rig tend to be quite little. (This would be historically consistent, as few of the leading figures in the actual Nazi party were at risk of banging their heads on the ceiling.)

There has been some attempt by friends of Harry and the monarchy to mount what might be called the Mel Brooks defence. This line suggests that some confusion over matters of taste is understandable when one of the West End's hottest tickets is a musical in which the swastika is camply treated as a kind of drag. As the only reviewer in Britain who disliked The Producers (worried by the spectacle of an audience whooping at dancers in Nazi insignia), I have some sympathy with this view, but the musical's fans argue that Brooks is inoculated against the possibility of offence by being Jewish. Unless something lies in the royal bloodline beyond even the most lurid internet rumours, Prince Harry can hardly claim this exculpation.

But, if Harry Windsor has made a large miscalculation, Tony Blair may also have made a significant slip on this issue. The need to give the head of state's grandson a dressing down for dressing up was a tricky moment for the prime minister. Throughout his eight years in office, almost all his public pronouncements on prominent Britons have demanded praise of the recently dead. Even when he had cause to attack (Brown, Cook, Mandelson, etc), he has generally resisted for tactical reasons.

So he had no easy template to follow when calculating the government's response to Prince Harry's Germanic pantomime. Unable to say "he is the people's Nazi" or "this is no time for sound-bites, but I see the badge of history on his shoulder," Blair seems to have panicked and sent Lord Falconer on to Question Time to put foam on the fire: youthful enthusiasm, all woken up with regrets in our time and so on.

This was a continuation of Blair's longtime policy of supporting the monarchy wherever possible in order to give signals of moderation to middle England and the tabloids. But, on this occasion, the populist approach may well have been to box Harry's ears. The sight of the most famous British 20-year-old outside the Premiership wearing a Nazi armband was surely—please, hopefully—shocking to most people.

10   In calling for a fuller apology, Michael Howard may for once have outwitted Blair in a publicity game—although, as the most prominent Jewish politician in recent British history, he may also have cause for deep worry about the social subculture inadvertently revealed by the row. For, at the risk of political stereotype, do you think it likely that the kind of people whose kids have "colonial or native" parties fitted out by shops that stock SS costumes tend to be Labour or Liberal Democrat voters?

EXPLORATORY WRITING

Mark Lawson finds it "astonishing that, in 2005, there is a section of society in which it is not considered odd for a teenager to throw a party with the theme of 'colonial or native.' " But he doesn't really offer much analysis of the theme's meaning and significance, aside from saying that he thinks it is "shocking" to "most people." Use the photograph from the party to begin an analysis of what it means to dress up in blackface, Ku Klux Klan robes, and a Nazi uniform. What does the style of the party signify?

TALKING ABOUT THE READING

Bring to class a list of the costumes you have worn to parties at various points in the past. Work in a group with three or four other students. Compare the lists, noting where they overlap and diverge. Identify categories to label types of parties. Pick one type of party to analyze. Consider the occasion of the party. Why did it happen (e.g., Halloween, birthday, or other occasion)? What kinds of costumes did people wear? In what sense did wearing the costume amount to a change of identity, if only briefly? What fantasies were involved?

WRITING ASSIGNMENT

Consider Mark Lawson's report that Maud's Costume Company apparently had a number of Nazi costumes to rent. Why would anyone want to dress up in a Nazi costume? Write an essay that explains the significance of dressing up in Nazi gear. What is the allure of Nazi symbols? In what sense can this party be seen, in Dick Hebdige's words, as an example of "revolting style"? Who is revolting against whom and in what terms?

MISTAKEN IDENTITY: THE PERILS OF THEME PARTIES

— Shana Pearlman

Shana Pearlman was an undergraduate major in English and modern studies when "Mistaken Identities: The Perils of Theme Parties" was published in the *Declaration,* a student weekly tabloid of opinion at the University of Virginia in 1999. As you will see, she addresses the question of "ghetto parties" on college campuses, where students dress up as "pimps" and "hos."

SUGGESTION FOR READING As you read, consider why Shana Pearlman has responded to "ghetto parties" with a "mixture of horror and incredulity." Notice how she cites Eric Lott's analysis of the dependence of "cultural definitions of whiteness" on "cultural definitions of blackness."

1 Ah, the Greek system at the University. It's controversial and oft-debated from the outside looking in, but inside it is a pretty sweet deal. Life in the fraternities and sororities is as easy and simple as Chef Boyardee ravioli, as carefree as Leave It to Beaver, as comfortable as American Eagle pajamas. What these students really need, however, is a good party from time to time; as social organizations, the parties are what define fraternities and sororities. The form those parties take (the formal, semi-formal, and themed mixer) define them as well. What these parties provide is a chance to step outside normal, everyday life for an evening; how they provide that opportunity can sometimes take strange and disturbing twists and turns.

The web magazine Salon (www.salon-magazine.com) recently ran an article about a controversial party that took place among the Greek community at Dartmouth College. Last year something called a "ghetto party" was sponsored by several fraternities and sororities there, sending the participants "scurrying for Afro wigs, toy handguns, and crimping irons." When word of this party leaked to the larger community it caused quite a stink. There was an almost daily flurry of protests, demonstrations, and letters to the editor, according to the student newspaper The Dartmouth. African-American and Asian-American applicants to the Ivy League school dropped by 75 percent and 25 percent respectively; op-ed columnists hastened to blame the decrease on a hostile racial environment exemplified by events like the ghetto party.

I read about these happenings with a mixture of growing horror and incredulity. I was once in a sorority myself (before it was recolonized because its sisters weren't WASPy enough—but that's another story) and remembered that we too sponsored a "ghetto party." When we asked our social chair how one dressed for such a party, she blithely replied, "Oh, you know, track bottoms, sports bras, bandannas, a bottle of Colt 45 in your hand—pretty much like your average crack ho." During my "research" for this piece I happened across the Sigma Sigma Sigma web page and discovered in their pictures section a cheery little photograph entitled "Straight Out of Compton." Compton, for those of you who may not know, is a lower-class African-American neighborhood in Los Angeles, made famous by gangsta rap. In the picture are five white girls and one Asian girl at some sort of restaurant or bar, all wearing matching track bottoms, bandannas and sports bras and revealing a bit of tummy for an appreciative male who appears in the picture. It seems "ghetto parties" are a somewhat ordinary occurrence in the Greek system. Do they make only me grimace? Why isn't everyone else's stomach turning?

I realize that at this university the Greek and non-Greek communities are relatively separated and that neither really cares to know what goes on in the other. But just as fraternities and sororities care how they appear in print (and no doubt one or two will write to opine, "But other organizations have offensive parties too!"), we should all think about the way we choose to portray others. It's very easy to pick out an image or two to represent a culture for the purposes of dress-up, but what does that do to true members of a culture? What does it do to the people who appropriate that culture? What is the cultural significance if upper-middle-class white girls dress up as though they were "from the ghetto?"

5   The rules for a ghetto party for women mean that you are to dress as though you were a "crack ho," as though you came from Compton. But Compton is not just a symbol you find in gangsta rap, it's a real neighborhood where people live. What does it mean to equate "Compton," the neighborhood, with "crack ho," the image familiar from countless music videos? Does it imply that all working-class African-American women who live in Compton are "hos"? And since a woman from Compton can so easily be reduced to a costume and a drink, does that imply that ALL working-class African-American women can so easily be reduced? And if we follow that argument, we all know what that makes the male audience for which the women are dressing up. What does it mean when nice white boys take on the role of pimp? Considering the way the fraternities broker the Greek social scheme, and sororities live or die on being able to attract enough fraternities to have a full mixer schedule, it doesn't seem too far off the mark.

Whether or not the Greek system ought to be faulted for its lack of ethnic diversity isn't clear. What is clear is that it is largely white. Professor Eric Lott of the English Department has made a case for cultural definitions of whiteness being dependent on cultural definitions of blackness. White needs black as something against which it is identified. Lott uses examples such as minstrel shows and Al Jolson to demonstrate how this has happened throughout American history; the white aping of black culture sets whiteness apart while conversely demonstrating a curious dependence upon and solidarity with it. The trouble is that in practical terms, minstrel shows were racist and employed negative racial stereotypes for entertainment. The same politics are at work in ghetto parties. White girls and boys dress up according to popular African-American images to underscore their whiteness, yet they are racist and misogynist. Representations of African Americans in popular culture are few and far between—the ones that prevail are often those that are the most suspect. Yet in order to use blackness to define whiteness, those are the images that have to be used.

This article won't stop ghetto parties, nor will it cause protests on the Lawn to occur. What I hope it will do is bring about awareness of how we represent other people. This kind of exchange shouldn't be simply behind closed doors; it's important to understand the appeal behind being a ho or a pimp. In other words, we had better know what we mean when we say we're "Straight Out of Compton" via the manicured lawns and freshly scrubbed Jeeps of sweet suburbia.

EXPLORATORY WRITING

"Ghetto parties" have become commonplace events for high school and college students. (You can find photos from "ghetto parties" by doing a Google search.) What is Shana Pearlman's evaluation of this cultural phenomenon? Consider her discussion of the relationship between "whiteness" and "blackness" in American culture as the "politics at work in ghetto parties."

TALKING ABOUT THE READING

Pearlman links ghetto parties to a longer history of blackface and minstrel shows where whites ape black culture. Explore what Pearlman sees as the problem of "how we represent other people." What is the "appeal behind being a pimp or a ho" that Pearlman notes in the final paragraph? What other examples of whites imitating black culture can you think of? What is the appeal in these instances? How do these examples play out the relationship between whiteness and blackness in the United States?

WRITING ASSIGNMENT

Use Pearlman's analysis of whiteness and blackness in American culture to examine an instance of "the white aping of black culture." In your analysis, consider the complex dynamic Pearlman describes whereby "the white aping of black culture sets whiteness apart while conversely demonstrating a curious dependence upon and solidarity with" black culture. How does this dynamic play out in the example you're analyzing?

WRITING SEQUENCE

1. Both Lawson and Pearlman raise questions, implicitly or explicitly, about the appeal of theme parties and dressing up in "colonial or native" and "ghetto" styles. Begin with the exploratory (or any other) writing you've done so far to write a comparison of the two parties reported in the readings. (If you haven't done any exploratory writing, write for 10 minutes using the suggestion for exploratory writing that goes with each reading.) In an open-ended exploratory piece of writing, consider the appeal of the parties. What do they have in common? How do they differ? What identities and fantasies did the parties make available?

2. Use Shana Pearlman's analysis of whiteness and blackness to write a 2-page essay that examines the racial meanings of "colonial or native" parties. Note that the party took place in 2005, over fifty years after national liberation movements in India and Africa gained independence, ending the British empire, which had once conquered a sizable portion of the world. To work with Pearlman's terms, you'll need to move cultural definitions of whiteness and blackness from the American to a British context. (See the paired readings by Jamaica Kincaid, "Columbus in Chains," and George Orwell, "Shooting an Elephant," pp. 519–530, for a sense of the relations between "colonials" and "natives" in the British empire.)

3. Write a longer finished essay (drafted, revised, and edited) that analyzes a theme party you attended or know or read about. You can pick either of the parties in the readings or another one of your choice. Your task in the broadest sense is to explain the cultural significance of the party. The underlying dynamic of the party may have to do with whiteness and blackness, as in the case of ghetto parties, or with political power and domination, as in the colonial or native party. It may be a matter of masculinity and femininity or class character (as when the French queen Marie Antoinette and her court dressed up as peasants) or a subculture, such as *Star Trek* fans, that gives the party its particular identity. In any case, to determine the cultural significance of the party, you will need to explain the identities and fantasies played out at the party and in the costumes people wore.

WOMEN AND THE RISE OF RAUNCH CULTURE

—Ariel Levy

Ariel Levy is a journalist whose work has appeared in the *New York Times, Washington Post, Vogue,* and *Slate.* Her book *Female Chauvinist Pigs: Women and the Rise of Raunch Culture* (2005), from which this excerpt is taken, explores what Levy sees as a post-feminist cultural turn that resurrects stereotypes of female sexuality in style and sensibility.

SUGGESTION FOR READING In this excerpt, Levy wants to establish the new reality of "raunch culture." As you read, notice how she does this by presenting examples and anecdotes to show how "the culture shifted so drastically in such a short period of time."

1 I first noticed it several years ago. I would turn on the television and find strippers in pasties explaining how best to lap dance a man to orgasm. I would flip the channel and see babes in tight, tiny uniforms bouncing up and down on trampolines. Britney Spears was becoming increasingly popular and increasingly unclothed, and her undulating body ultimately became so familiar to me I felt like we used to go out.

Charlie's Angels, the film remake of the quintessential jiggle show, opened at number one in 2000 and made $125 million in theaters nationally, reinvigorating the interest of men and women alike in leggy crime fighting. Its stars, who kept talking about "strong women" and "empowerment," were dressed in alternating soft-porn styles—as massage parlor geishas, dominatrixes, yodeling Heidis in alpine bustiers. (The summer sequel in 2003—in which the Angels' perilous mission required them to perform stripteases—pulled in another $100 million domestically.) In my own industry, magazines, a porny new genre called the Lad Mag, which included titles like *Maxim, FHM,* and *Stuff,* was hitting the stands and becoming a huge success by delivering what *Playboy* had only occasionally managed to capture: greased celebrities in little scraps of fabric humping the floor.

This didn't end when I switched off the radio or the television or closed the magazines. I'd walk down the street and see teens and young women—and the occasional wild fifty-year-old—wearing jeans cut so low they exposed what came to be known as butt cleavage paired with miniature tops that showed off breast implants and pierced navels alike. Sometimes, in case the overall message of the outfit was too subtle, the shirts would be emblazoned with the Playboy bunny or say PORN STAR across the chest.

Some odd things were happening in my social life, too. People I knew (female people) liked going to strip clubs (female strippers). It was sexy and fun, they explained; it was liberating and rebellious. My best friend from college, who used to go to Take Back the Night marches on campus, had become captivated by porn stars. She would point them out to me in music videos and watch their (topless) interviews on *Howard Stern.* As for me, I wasn't going to strip clubs or buying *Hustler* T-shirts, but I was starting to show signs of impact all the same. It had only been a few years since I'd graduated from Wesleyan University, a place where you could pretty much get expelled for saying "girl" instead of "woman," but somewhere along the line I'd started saying "chick." And, like most chicks I knew, I'd taken to wearing thongs.

5 What was going on? My mother, a shiatsu masseuse who attended weekly women's consciousness-raising groups for twenty-four years, didn't own makeup. My father, whom she met as a student radical at the University of Wisconsin, Madison, in the sixties was a consultant for Planned Parenthood, NARAL, and NOW. Only thirty years (my lifetime) ago, our mothers were "burning their bras" and picketing Playboy, and suddenly we were getting implants and

wearing the bunny logo as supposed symbols of our liberation. How had the culture shifted so drastically in such a short period of time?

What was almost more surprising than the change itself were the responses I got when I started interviewing the men and—often—women who edit magazines like *Maxim* and make programs like *The Man Show* and *Girls Gone Wild*. This new raunch culture didn't mark the death of feminism, they told me; it was evidence that the feminist project had already been achieved. We'd *earned* the right to look at *Playboy;* we were *empowered* enough to get Brazilian bikini waxes. Women had come so far, I learned, we no longer needed to worry about objectification or misogyny. Instead, it was time for us to join the frat party of pop culture, where men had been enjoying themselves all along. If Male Chauvinist Pigs were men who regarded women as pieces of meat, we would outdo them and be Female Chauvinist Pigs: women who make sex objects of other women and of ourselves.

When I asked female viewers and readers what they got out of raunch culture, I heard similar things about empowering miniskirts and feminist strippers, and so on, but I also heard something else. They wanted to be "one of the guys"; they hoped to be experienced "like a man." Going to strip clubs or talking about porn stars was a way of showing themselves and the men around them that they weren't "prissy little women" or "girly-girls." Besides, they told me, it was all in fun, all tongue-in-cheek, and for me to regard this bacchanal as problematic would be old-school and uncool.

I tried to get with the program, but I could never make the argument add up in my head.

How is resurrecting every stereotype of female sexuality that feminism endeavored to banish *good* for women? Why is laboring to look like Pamela Anderson empowering? And how is imitating a stripper or a porn star—a woman whose *job* is to imitate arousal in the first place—going to render us sexually liberated?

Despite the rising power of Evangelical Christianity and the political right in the United States, this trend has only grown more extreme and more pervasive in the years that have passed since I first became aware of it. A tawdry, tarty, cartoonlike version of female sexuality has become so ubiquitous, it no longer seems particular. What we once regarded as a *kind* of sexual expression we now view *as* sexuality. As former adult film star Traci Lords put it to a reporter a few days before her memoir hit the bestseller list in 2003, "When I was in porn, it was like a back-alley thing. Now it's everywhere." Spectacles of naked ladies have moved from seedy side streets to center stage, where everyone—men and women—can watch them in broad daylight. *Playboy* and its ilk are being "embraced by young women in a curious way in a postfeminist world," to borrow the words of Hugh Hefner.

10   But just because we are post doesn't automatically mean we are feminists. There is a widespread assumption that simply because my generation of women has the good fortune to live in a world touched by the feminist movement, that means everything we do is magically imbued with its agenda. It doesn't work that way. "Raunchy" and "liberated" are not synonyms. It is worth asking ourselves if this bawdy world of boobs and gams we have resurrected reflects how far we've come, or how far we have left to go.

EXPLORATORY WRITING

At the heart of this selection is a debate between Ariel Levy and the women (and men) she interviewed who see sexually explicit styles and behaviors as "empowering" to women. Before you develop your own position, suspend judgment for a moment in order to describe the terms of the debate and the claims and evidence on both sides. As you write, consider the assumptions that have led people to take the positions they do and how those underlying beliefs divide them.

TALKING ABOUT THE READING

According to Levy, "raunchy" and "liberated" are not equivalent terms. But how are we to distinguish between them? Is it possible, as some of Levy's informants claim, to use stereotypes in dress, pornography, striptease, and so on in a self-conscious, tongue-in-cheek way that is liberating? Or are these forms of cultural expression by definition oppressive and degrading? If so, then how can female sexuality be expressed in positive and empowering ways? These are difficult questions to answer in the abstract. You need material to work with. To this end, bring to class a list of three examples and, if possible, the item itself (e.g., an image, a television show, a film, a product, an advertisement, clothing). One example should have what you consider a truly liberating image or message for women. The second should be unequivocally raunchy. And the third should have some ambiguity, where you find it difficult to determine whether the example is liberating or raunchy. Work in a group with three or four other students. Use your examples to see if you can reach a consensus about where the line is between raunchy and liberated. To what extent is this complicated by the ambiguous examples?

WRITING ASSIGNMENTS

1. Pick one of the examples Levy gives of raunch culture or choose one that's not mentioned. Write a double-column essay. On one side, explain what's wrong with the example in terms of the way it represents women and sexuality. On the other side, explain what's liberating or empowering about it for women.

2. Pick an example from class discussion that is ambiguous in terms of being raunchy or liberating. Write an essay that explains what makes it difficult to place the example in one category or the other.

3. Levy describes a cultural shift but, in this excerpt, does not explain what caused it. Assume that Levy is correct about the shift. Write an essay that offers some tentative reasons for the shift. Being tentative here allows you to try to out ideas and to evaluate what they explain and what they leave out.

MAKING CONNECTIONS   Geek Culture

While there are ongoing debates about exactly what the term "geek" means (and whether it is interchangeable with the term "nerd"), there is little question that geek and nerd culture has made its presence felt in contemporary culture. For many years in the United States, "geek" referred to a carnival performer who bit the head off a live chicken, and the term has kept the connotations of weirdness and freakishness. More recently, the term has been transferred to a subcultural style associated with an obsessive interest in high-tech computers and video games, science fiction (especially *Star Trek* and cyber-punk novels such as William Gibson's *The Neuromancer*), Dungeons and Dragons, and the Harry Potter series. A cultural stereotype of the geek has emerged, as may be seen in the journalist Julie Smith's definition of a geek which appeared in *New Orleans Beat:* "a bright young man turned inward, poorly socialized, who felt so little kinship with his own planet that he routinely traveled to the ones invented by his favorite authors, who thought of that secret, dreamy place his computer took him to as cyberspace—somewhere exciting, a place more real than his own life, a land he could conquer, not a drab teenager's room in his parents' house."

But more recently, geeks and nerds have been given a heightened place in the world—in, say, *Revenge of the Nerds,* TV shows like *Beauty and the Geek,* the success of Bill Gates and the Microsoft empire, and the rise of geek chic in fashion (with the mandatory plastic pocket protector) and geek rock bands (including "nerdcore" and "geeksta rap"). We have assembled a sequence of readings for you to explore the various meanings assigned to the terms geek and nerd and to the emergence of geek culture as a recognizable trend in American culture.

THE ALPHA GEEKS

— David Brooks

David Brooks is a columnist at the *New York Times* and the author of *Bobos in Paradise: The Upper Class and How They Got There* (2001) and *On Paradise Drive* (2005). He comments frequently in his columns on cultural style and social class in the United States. This reading is typical of his broad range of cultural references and his interest in characterizing new cultural trends from a sophisticated conservative perspective. "The Alpha Geeks" appeared in the *New York Times* on May 23, 2008.

SUGGESTION FOR READING   Notice that David Brooks is using the theme of status reversal to organize his piece. As you read, keep the final line—"the geek shall inherit the earth"—in mind, to consider how Brooks brings his readers to this conclusion.

1   In 1950, Dr. Seuss published a book called "If I Ran the Zoo." It contained the sentence: "I'll sail to Ka-Troo, and bring back an IT-KUTCH, a PREEP, and a PROO, a NERKLE, a NERD, and a SEERSUCKER, too!" According to the psychologist David Anderegg, that's believed to be the first printed use of the word "nerd" in modern English.

The next year, *Newsweek* noticed that nerd was being used in Detroit as a substitute for "square." But, as Anderegg writes in his book *Nerds,* the term didn't really blossom onto mass consciousness until The Fonz used it in "Happy Days" in the mid- to late-1970s. And thus began what you might call the ascent of nerdism in modern America.

At first, a nerd was a geek with better grades. The word described a high-school or college outcast who was persecuted by the jocks, preps, frat boys and sorority sisters. Nerds had their own heroes (Stan Lee of comic book fame), their own vocations (Dungeons & Dragons), their own religion (supplied by George Lucas and *Star Wars*) and their own skill sets (tech support). But even

as *Revenge of the Nerds* was gracing the nation's movie screens, a different version of nerd-dom was percolating through popular culture. Elvis Costello and The Talking Heads's David Byrne popularized a cool geek style that's led to Moby, Weezer, Vampire Weekend and even self-styled "nerdcore" rock and geeksta rappers.

The future historians of the nerd ascendancy will likely note that the great empowerment phase began in the 1980s with the rise of Microsoft and the digital economy. Nerds began making large amounts of money and acquired economic credibility, the seedbed of social prestige. The information revolution produced a parade of highly confident nerd moguls—Bill Gates and Paul Allen, Larry Page and Sergey Brin and so on.

5   Among adults, the words "geek" and "nerd" exchanged status positions. A nerd was still socially tainted, but geekdom acquired its own cool counterculture. A geek possessed a certain passion for specialized knowledge, but also a high degree of cultural awareness and poise that a nerd lacked.

Geeks not only rebelled against jocks, but they distinguished themselves from alienated and self-pitying outsiders who wept with recognition when they read *Catcher in the Rye*. If Holden Caulfield was the sensitive loner from the age of nerd oppression, then Harry Potter was the magical leader in the age of geek empowerment.

But the biggest change was not Silicon Valley itself. Rather, the new technology created a range of mental playgrounds where the new geeks could display their cultural capital. The jock can shine on the football field, but the geeks can display their supple sensibilities and well-modulated emotions on their Facebook pages, blogs, text messages and Twitter feeds. Now there are armies of designers, researchers, media mavens and other cultural producers with a talent for whimsical self-mockery, arcane social references and late-night analysis.

They can visit eclectic sites like Kottke.org and Cool Hunting, experiment with fonts, admire Stewart Brand and Lawrence Lessig and join social-networking communities with ironical names. They've created a new definition of what it means to be cool, a definition that leaves out the talents of the jocks, the M.B.A. types and the less educated. In *The Laws of Cool,* Alan Liu writes: "Cool is a feeling for information." When someone has that dexterity, you know it.

Tina Fey, who once was on the cover of *Geek Monthly* magazine, has emerged as a sym-bol of the geek who grows into a swan. There is now a cool geek fashion style, which can be found on shopping sites all over the Web (think Japanese sneakers and text-laden T-shirts). Schwinn now makes a retro-looking Sid/Nancy bicycle, which is sweet and clunky even though it has a faux-angry name. There are now millions of educated-class types guided by geek manners and status rules.

The news that being a geek is cool has apparently not permeated either junior high schools or the Republican Party. George Bush plays an interesting role in the tale of nerd ascent. With his professed disdain for intellectual things, he's energized and alienated the entire geek cohort, and with it most college-educated Americans under 30. Newly militant, geeks are more coherent and active than they might otherwise be.

Barack Obama has become the Prince Caspian of the iPhone hordes. They honor him with videos and posters that combine aesthetic mastery with unabashed hero-worship. People in the 1950s used to earnestly debate the role of the intellectual in modern politics. But the Lionel Trilling authority-figure has been displaced by the mass class of blog-writing culture producers.

So, in a relatively short period of time, the social structure has flipped. For as it is written, the last shall be first and the geek shall inherit the earth.

EXPLORATORY WRITING

David Brooks draws on a biblical reference in his last line when he says, "For as it is written, the last shall be first and the geek shall inherit the earth." How does he get to this conclusion? Consider the evidence he presents and how it fits into a narrative pattern of reversal, where the "social structure has flipped."

TALKING ABOUT THE READING

Brooks says that geeks have "created a new definition of what it means to be cool." Look back through Brooks's column to identify examples of geek cool. What are the criteria of selection Brooks uses? Can you add further examples to this list? Considering these various examples, what makes geek culture cool? How is geek coolness different from or similar to what cool means in other contexts, for other subcultures?

WRITING ASSIGNMENT

Write an essay that explains the heightened visibility of geeks in American culture. Consider what Brooks's explanation of geek ascendancy emphasizes. What, if anything, would you add or modify? Use the essay to engage Brooks and to locate your sense of geek culture in relation to his.

WHO'S A NERD, ANYWAY?

— Benjamin Nugent

Benjamin Nugent is the author of *American Nerd: The Story of My People* (2008). He played in the indie rock band the Cloud Room, was a reporter for *Time* magazine, and published *Elliott Smith and the Big Nothing* (2004), a biography of the late musician. This essay appeared in the *New York Times Magazine* on July 29, 2007.

SUGGESTION FOR READING In this essay, Nugent walks his readers through linguist Mary Bucholtz's research on the idea of nerdiness and her conclusion that it represents a form of "hyperwhiteness." As you read, notice how Nugent presents Bucholtz's view of nerdiness "first and foremost as a way of using language."

1 What is a nerd? Mary Bucholtz, a linguist at the University of California, Santa Barbara, has been working on the question for the last 12 years. She has gone to high schools and colleges, mainly in California, and asked students from different crowds to think about the idea of nerdiness and who among their peers should be considered a nerd; students have also "reported" themselves. Nerdiness, she has concluded, is largely a matter of racially tinged behavior. People who are considered nerds tend to act in ways that are, as she puts it, "hyperwhite."

While the word "nerd" has been used since the 1950s, its origin remains elusive. Nerds, however, are easy to find everywhere. Being a nerd has become a widely accepted and even proud identity, and nerds have carved out a comfortable niche in popular culture; "nerdcore" rappers, who wear pocket protectors and write paeans to computer routing devices, are in vogue, and TV networks continue to run shows with titles like *Beauty and the Geek*. As a linguist, Bucholtz understands nerdiness first and foremost as a way of using language. In a 2001 paper, "The Whiteness of Nerds: Superstandard English and Racial Markedness," and other works, including a book in progress, Bucholtz notes that the "hegemonic" "cool white" kids use a limited amount of African-American vernacular English; they may say "blood" in lieu of "friend," or drop the "g" in "playing." But the nerds she has interviewed, mostly white kids, punctiliously adhere to Standard English. They often favor Greco-Latinate words over Germanic ones ("it's my observation" instead of "I think"), a preference that lends an air of scientific detachment. They're aware they speak distinctively, and they use language as a badge of membership in their cliques. One nerd girl Bucholtz observed performed a typically nerdy feat when asked to discuss "blood" as a slang term; she replied: "B-L-O-O-D. The word is blood," evoking the format of a spelling bee. She went on, "That's the stuff which is inside of your veins," humorously using a literal definition. Nerds are not simply victims of the prevailing social codes about what's appropriate and what's cool; they actively shape their own identities and put those codes in question.

Though Bucholtz uses the term "hyperwhite" to describe nerd language in particular, she claims that the "symbolic resources of an extreme whiteness" can be used elsewhere. After all, "trends in music, dance, fashion, sports and language in a variety of youth subcultures are often traceable to an African-American source," but "unlike the styles of cool European American students, in nerdiness, African-American culture and language [do] not play even a covert role." Certainly, "hyperwhite" seems a good word for the sartorial choices of paradigmatic nerds. While a stereotypical black youth, from the zoot-suit era through the bling years, wears flashy clothes, chosen for their aesthetic value, nerdy clothing is purely practical: pocket protectors, belt sheaths for gadgets, short shorts for excessive heat, etc. Indeed, "hyperwhite" works as a description for nearly everything we intuitively associate with nerds, which is why Hollywood has long traded in jokes that try to capitalize on the emotional dissonance of nerds acting black (Eugene Levy saying, "You got me straight trippin', boo") and black people being nerds (the characters Urkel and Carlton in the sitcoms *Family Matters* and *The Fresh Prince of Bel-Air*).

By cultivating an identity perceived as white to the point of excess, nerds deny themselves the aura of normality that is usually one of the perks of being white. Bucholtz sees something to admire here. In declining to appropriate African-American youth culture, thereby "refusing to exercise the racial privilege upon which white youth cultures are founded," she writes, nerds may even be viewed as "traitors to whiteness." You might say they know that a culture based on theft is a culture not worth having. On the other hand, the code of conspicuous intellectualism in the nerd cliques Bucholtz observed may shut out "black students who chose not to openly display their abilities." This is especially disturbing at a time when African-American students can be stigmatized by other African-American students if they're too obviously diligent about school. Even more problematic, "Nerds' dismissal of black cultural practices often led them to discount the possibility of friendship with black students," even if the nerds were involved in political activities like protesting against the dismantling of affirmative action in California schools. If nerdiness, as Bucholtz suggests, can be a rebellion against the cool white kids and their use of black culture, it's a rebellion with a limited membership.

EXPLORATORY WRITING

Benjamin Nugent's essay amounts in many respects to a summary of Mary Bucholtz's 2001 paper "The Whiteness of Nerds: Superstandard English and Racial Markedness." To do this, Nugent has had to be selective in presenting the research and its findings. Write a summary of Nugent's summary, reducing it to one or two paragraphs that capture the main points.

TALKING ABOUT THE READING

Work in a group with three or four other students. Take turns reading aloud the summaries you have written. To what extent are they similar? How do they differ? Don't assume one is better than another or argue about accuracy. Instead, try to identify the principles of selection each person used. Discuss how others' summaries change or add to your understanding of Nugent's essay.

WRITING ASSIGNMENT

The article that Benjamin Nugent draws on for his essay, Mary Bucholtz's "The Whiteness of Nerds: Superstandard English and Racial Markedness," appeared in the *Journal of Linguistic Anthropology* 11, no. 1 (2001): 84–100. You can find a copy through your library's online journal service or at Bucholtz's Web site at the University of California, Santa Barbara, www.linguistics.ucsb.edu/faculty/bucholtz/articles/MB_JLA2001.pdf. Read her article. Be patient in your reading. Remember she is writing for an audience of specialists, so there may be terms and concepts that are unfamiliar to you. Write an essay that explains how Nugent worked with Bucholtz's article to make her findings and conclusions accessible to an audience of nonspecialists. Notice what he selects and what he leaves out—and the possible reasons he does so. Consider Nugent's style as an act of translation, to bring a specialized article to the attention of general readers. How does he work with Buchholtz's language—the discourse and vocabulary of an academic field—to write a popular essay?

GEEK LOVE

— *Adam Rogers*

> Adam Rogers is a senior editor at *Wired* magazine. "Geek Love" appeared in the *New York Times* on March 9, 2008, shortly after Gary Gygax, the co-creator of Dungeon and Dragons, died. Rogers uses this occasion to honor Gygax and to assess the influence of role-playing games on geek culture. Unlike the pieces by Brooks and Nugent, this one is written from the perspective of a self-identified geek.

SUGGESTION FOR READING As you read, notice how Rogers is making the case that we now live in a world Gary Gygax helped to create. Pay attention to the evidence and examples he presents to support this claim.

1 Gary Gygax died last week and the universe did not collapse. This surprises me a little bit, because he built it.

I'm not talking about the cosmological, Big Bang part. Everyone who reads blogs knows that a flying spaghetti monster made all that. But Mr. Gygax co-created the game Dungeons & Dragons, and on that foundation of role-playing and polyhedral dice he constructed the social and intellectual structure of our world.

Dungeons & Dragons was a brilliant pastiche, mashing together tabletop war games, the Conan-the-Barbarian tales of Robert E. Howard and a magic trick from the fantasy writer Jack Vance with a dash of Bulfinch's mythology, a bit of the Bible and a heaping helping of J. R. R. Tolkien.

Mr. Gygax's genius was to give players a way to inhabit the characters inside their games, rather than to merely command faceless hordes, as you did in, say, the board game Risk. Roll the dice and you generated a character who was quantified by personal attributes like strength or intelligence.

5 You also got to pick your moral alignment, like whether you were "lawful good" or "chaotic evil." And you could buy swords and fight dragons. It was cool.

Yes, I played a little. In junior high and even later. Lawful good paladin. Had a flaming sword. It did not make me popular with the ladies, or indeed with anyone. Neither did my affinity for geometry, nor my ability to recite all of *Star Wars* from memory.

Yet on the strength of those skills and others like them, I now find myself on top of the world. Not wealthy or in charge or even particularly popular, but in instead of out. The stuff I know, the geeky stuff, is the stuff you and everyone else has to know now, too.

We live in Gary Gygax's world. The most popular books on earth are fantasy novels about wizards and magic swords. The most popular movies are about characters from superhero comic books. The most popular TV shows look like elaborate role-playing games: intricate, hidden-clue-laden science fiction stories connected to impossibly mathematical games that live both online and in the real world. And you, the viewer, can play only if you've sufficiently mastered your home-entertainment command center so that it can download a snippet of audio to your iPhone, process it backward with beluga whale harmonic sequences and then podcast the results to the members of your Yahoo group.

Even in the heyday of Dungeons & Dragons, when his company was selling millions of copies and parents feared that the game was somehow related to Satan worship, Mr. Gygax's creation seemed like a niche product. Kids played it in basements instead of socializing. (To be fair, you needed at least three people to play—two adventurers and one Dungeon Master to guide the game—so Dungeons & Dragons was social. Demented and sad, but social.) Nevertheless, the game taught the right lessons to the right people.

10   Geeks like algorithms. We like sets of rules that guide future behavior. But people, normal people, consistently act outside rule sets. People are messy and unpredictable, until you have something like the Dungeons & Dragons character sheet. Once you've broken down the elements of an invented personality into numbers generated from dice, paper and pencil, you can do the same for your real self.

For us, the character sheet and the rules for adventuring in an imaginary world became a manual for how people are put together. Life could be lived as a kind of vast, always-on role-playing campaign.

Don't give me that look. I know I'm not a paladin, and I know I don't live in the Matrix. But the realization that everyone else was engaged in role-playing all the time gave my universe rules and order.

We geeks might not be able to intuit the subtext of a facial expression or a casual phrase, but give us a behavioral algorithm and human interactions become a data stream. We can process what's going on in the heads of the people around us. Through careful observation of body language and awkward silences, we can even learn to detect when we are bringing the party down with our analysis of how loop quantum gravity helps explain the time travel in that new *Terminator* TV show. I mean, so I hear.

Mr. Gygax's game allowed geeks to venture out of our dungeons, blinking against the light, just in time to create the present age of electronic miracles.

15   Dungeons & Dragons begat one of the first computer games, a swords-and-sorcery dungeon crawl called Adventure. In the late 1970s, the two games provided the narrative framework for the first fantasy-based computer worlds played by multiple, remotely connected users. They were called multi-user dungeons back then, and they were mostly the province of students at the Massachusetts Institute of Technology. But they required the same careful construction of virtual identities that Mr. Gygax had introduced to gaming.

Today millions of people are slaves to Gary Gygax. They play EverQuest and World of Warcraft, and someone must still be hanging out in Second Life. (That "massively multiplayer" computer traffic, by the way, also helped drive the development of the sort of huge server clouds that power Google.)

But that's just gaming culture, more pervasive than it was in 1974 when Dungeons & Dragons was created and certainly more profitable—today it's estimated to be a $40 billion-a-year business—but still a little bit nerdy. Delete the dragon-slaying, though, and you're left with something much more mainstream: Facebook, a vast, interconnected universe populated by avatars.

Facebook and other social networks ask people to create a character—one based on the user, sure, but still a distinct entity. Your character then builds relationships by connecting to other characters. Like Dungeons & Dragons, this is not a competitive game. There's no way to win. You just play.

This diverse evolution from Mr. Gygax's 1970s dungeon goes much further. Every Gmail login, every instant-messaging screen name, every public photo collection on Flickr, every blog-commenting alias is a newly manifested identity, a character playing the real world.

20   We don't have to say goodbye to Gary Gygax, the architect of the now. Every time I

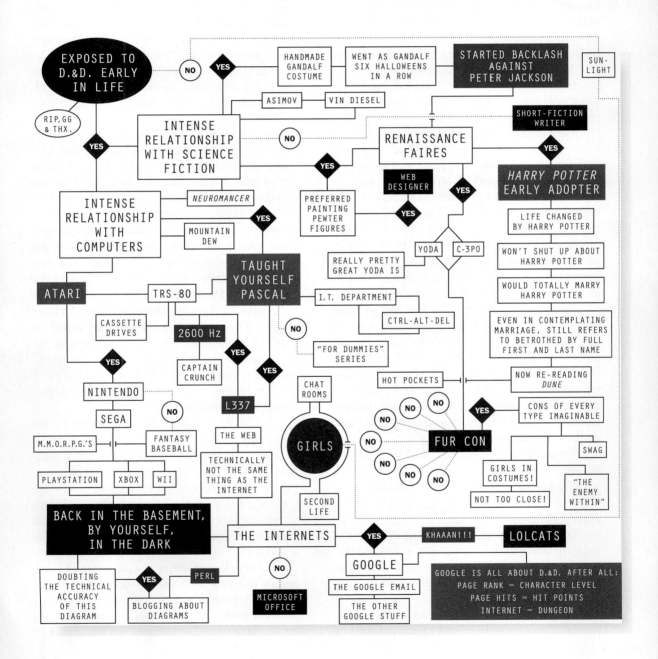

make a tactical move (like when I suggest to my wife this summer that we should see *Iron Man* instead of *The Dark Knight*), I'm counting my experience points, hoping I have enough dexterity and rolling the dice. And every time, Mr. Gygax is there—quasi-mystical, glowing in blue and bearing a simple game that was an elegant weapon from a more civilized age.

That was a reference to *Star Wars*. Cool, right?

EXPLORATORY WRITING

Embedded in Adam Rogers' article is a discussion of who geeks are and what they value. How does Rogers define geeks? How does his definition differ from those in the pieces by Brooks and Nugent?

TALKING ABOUT THE READING

Consider the diagram that accompanies Rogers's article. Reading it from top left to bottom right, explain the paths it lays out and the story it tells. How do all the possible routes contribute to the meaning of the diagram? Note, for example, where the path goes if you answer "no" to "exposed to D.&D. early in life." What representation of geek culture emerges from the diagram?

WRITING ASSIGNMENT

Rogers traces an evolution from Dungeons and Dragons to multiplayer computer games and video games to Facebook and blogs. What is the underlying thread in this evolution? Can you think of further examples of this evolution to support Rogers's claim "We live in Gary Gygax's world"? What about counter examples? Do they refute the claim or complicate it? Write an essay that evaluates Rogers's claim, whether you support it or find it needs modification.

WRITING SEQUENCE

1. Both Brooks and Rogers present a geek ascendancy. (Rogers says, "I now find myself on top of the world.") Reread each of the essays. Write 2–3 pages of exploratory writing that compares how each explains the triumph of geek culture. Notice where their reasons differ and overlap. What underlying assumptions are they making in their claims about geek culture? To what extent do they justify these assumptions, or do they imagine readers will take them for granted?

2. Nugent is the only one of the three writers who mentions race and how geek culture is linked to cultural definitions of whiteness and blackness. Reread Nugent's essay and any writing you have done on it so far. Write a 2-page essay that explains what Nugent adds to the discussion of geek culture found in the pieces by Brooks and Rogers.

3. Write your own analysis of geek culture. This culminating assignment is a longer finished essay (drafted, revised, and edited). Draw on the representations of geek culture in Brooks, Nugent, and Rogers to establish the context of issues for your perspective on geek culture. Your task here is to locate your thinking in relation to that of Brooks, Nugent, and Rogers as a way of identifying the central focus of your essay—the particular problem or question about geek culture that your writing engages.

THE AURA

— *Rob Walker*

Rob Walker writes a weekly feature about product design, "Consumed," for the *New York Times Sunday Magazine*. "The Aura" is an excerpt from a longer article on the iPod, "The Guts of the New Machine," that appeared in the *New York Times Sunday Magazine* in 2003, when it was clear that the iPod was an overwhelming commercial success and had become an icon of product design.

SUGGESTION FOR READING   Rob Walker uses two key words in this excerpt, "icon" and "aura." Before you begin reading, look up the words in a dictionary. As you read, notice how Walker uses the two terms to invest the iPod with nearly magical qualities.

1   If you want to understand why a product has become an icon, you of course want to talk to the people who dreamed it up and made it. And you want to talk to the design experts and the technology pros and the professors and the gurus. But what you really want to do is talk to Andrew Andrew. Andrew Andrew is a "highly diversified company" made of two personable young men, each named Andrew. They dress identically and seem to agree on everything; they say, among other things, that they have traveled from the future "to set things on the right course for tomorrow." They require interviewers to sign a form agreeing not to reveal any differences between Andrew and Andrew, because to do so might undermine the Andrew Andrew brand— and since this request is more interesting than whatever those differences might be, interviewers sign it.

Among other things, they do some fashion design and they are DJ's who "spin" on iPods, setting up participatory events called iParties. Thus they've probably seen more people interact with the player than anyone who doesn't work for Apple. More important, they put an incredible amount of thought into what they buy, and why: in a world where, for better or worse, aesthetics is a business, they are not just consumers but consumption artists. So Andrew remembers exactly where he was when he first encountered the iPod: 14th Street near Ninth Avenue in New York City. He was with Andrew, of course. A friend showed it to them. Andrew held the device in his hand. The main control on the iPod is a scroll wheel: you spin it with your thumb to navigate the long list of songs (or artists or genres), touch a button to pick a track and use the wheel again to adjust the volume. The other Andrew also tried it out. "When you do the volume for the first time, that's the key moment," says Andrew. "We knew: we had to have one." (Well, two.)

Before you even get to the surface of the iPod, you encounter what could be called its aura. The commercial version of an aura is a brand, and while Apple may be a niche player in the computer market, the fanatical brand loyalty of its customers is legendary. A journalist, Leander Kahney, has even written a book about it, "The Cult of Mac," to be published in the spring. As he points out, that base has supported the company with a faith in its will to innovate— even during stretches when it hasn't. Apple is also a giant in the world of industrial design. The candy-colored look of the iMac has been so widely copied that it's now a visual cliché.

But the iPod is making an even bigger impression. Bruce Claxton, who is the current president of the Industrial Designers Society of America and a senior designer at Motorola, calls the device emblematic of a shift toward products that are "an antidote to the hyper lifestyle," which might be symbolized by hand-held devices that bristle with buttons and controls that seem to promise a million functions if you only had time to figure them all out. "People are seeking out products that are not just simple to use but a joy to use." Moby, the recording artist, has been a high-profile iPod booster since the product's debut. "The kind of insidious revolutionary quality of the iPod," he says, "is that it's so elegant and logical, it becomes part of your life so quickly that you can't remember what it was like beforehand."

5   Tuesday nights, Andrew Andrew's iParty happens at a club called APT on the spooky, far western end of 13th Street. They show up at about 10 in matching sweat jackets and sneakers, matching eyeglasses, matching haircuts. They connect their matching iPods to a modest Gemini mixer that they've fitted with a white front panel to make it look more iPodish. The iPods sit on either side of the mixer, on their backs, so they look like tiny turntables. Andrew Andrew change into matching lab coats and ties. They hand out long song lists to patrons, who take a number and, when called, are invited up to program a seven-minute set. At around midnight, the actor Elijah Wood (Frodo) has turned up and is permitted to plug his own iPod into Andrew Andrew's system. His set includes a Squarepusher song.

Between songs at APT, each Andrew analyzed the iPod. In talking about how hard it was, at first, to believe that so much music could be stuffed into such a tiny object, they came back to the scroll wheel as the key to the product's initial seductiveness. "It really bridged the gap." Andrew observed, "between fantasy and reality."

The idea of innovation, particularly technological innovation, has a kind of aura around it, too. Imagine the lone genius, sheltered from the storm of short-term commercial demands in a research lab somewhere, whose tinkering produces a sudden and momentous breakthrough. Or maybe we think innovation begins with an epiphany, a sudden vision of the future. Either way, we think of that one thing, the lightning bolt that jolted all the other pieces into place. The Walkman came about because a Sony executive wanted a high-quality but small stereo tape player to listen to on long flights. A small recorder was modified, with the recording pieces removed and stereo circuitry added. That was February 1979, and within six months the product was on the market.

The iPod's history is comparatively free of lightning-bolt moments. Apple was not ahead of the curve in recognizing the power of music in digital form. It was practically the last computer maker to equip its machines with CD burners. It trailed others in creating jukebox software for storing and organizing music collections on computers. And various portable digital music players were already on the market before the iPod was even an idea. Back when Napster was inspiring a million self-styled visionaries to predict the end of music as we know it, Apple was focused on the relationship between computers and video. The company had, back in the 1990's, invented a technology called FireWire, which is basically a tool for moving data between digital devices—in large quantities, very quickly. Apple licensed this technology to various Japanese consumer electronics companies (which used it in digital camcorders and players) and eventually started adding FireWire ports to iMacs and creating video editing software. This led to programs called iMovie, then iPhoto and then a conceptual view of the home computer as a "digital hub" that would complement a range of devices. Finally, in January 2001, iTunes was added to the mix.

And although the next step sounds prosaic—we make software that lets you organize the music on your computer, so maybe we should make one of those things that lets you take it with you—it was also something new. There were companies that made jukebox software, and companies that made portable players, but nobody made both. What this meant is not that the iPod could do more, but that it would do less. This is what led to what Jonathan Ive, Apple's vice president of industrial design, calls the iPod's "overt simplicity." And this, perversely, is the most exciting thing about it.

EXPLORATORY WRITING

Rob Walker opens with the question of understanding why a product such as the iPod has become an icon. What does he mean by "icon"? What other products might be considered icons? How does the design of the product contribute to its iconic status?

TALKING ABOUT THE READING

Bring to class a product that you think is iconic. Work in a group of three or four. Your task here is to use Walker's key words "icon" and "aura" to explain the appeal of the products. Consider that both words have religious or spiritual connotations. Icons, for example, refer to small paintings of sacred figures in many religious traditions. (See the reading "Photographic Icons: Fact, Fiction, or Metaphor?" pp. 230–237, on the nature of iconicity.) An aura is the otherworldly glow that surrounds people and objects toward which we have a sense of awe and reverence. For Walter Benjamin, aura means the originality and authenticity of an artwork before the era of mechanical (and now digital) reproduction, before endless copies of the work could be made and circulated, when the only way to see a work of art was to encounter it in person. Aura, for Benjamin, is the sense of singularity and irreplaceability viewers experienced when encountering a work of art. The question for you is how are the immaterial qualities invoked by the terms "icon" and "aura" transferred to material objects in product design and use?

WRITING ASSIGNMENTS

1. To explain the appeal of the iPod, Walker quotes Moby's remarks that the "insidious revolutionary quality of the iPod is that . . . it becomes a part of your life so quickly that you can't remember what it was like beforehand." Write an essay on a product that insinuated itself into your life or people's lives in this manner. Take into account what it was like before the product and after. Explain the reasons for the shift.

2. A number of critical observers have argued that the iPod is a retreat from sociability and shared experience, a retreat from or defense against the world and interactions with other people. Write an essay that addresses this analysis of the iPod. To what extent do the critics have a reasonable point? How do you think Walker would respond to their argument?

3. Write an essay on a product that has, in one way or another, become an icon. What is the aura that surrounds the product, the sense of reverence and awe that consumers feel toward it. Consider what the iconic status of the product reveals about contemporary American culture and the lifestyles of the people who use the product.

VISUAL ESSAY   Reading Labels, Selling Water

The next time a client questions the value of brand positioning and clever packaging, instead of backpedaling, I'm going to take him straight to the bottled water aisle of my grocery store. Amongst the shelves of Evian, Voss, Aquapod, Aquafina, Dasani, SmartWater, Propel and the dozens of other bottled water brands, I'm going to ask him to compare the price of the most expensive brand, at $5.99, to tap water that's essentially free from any faucet.

—Maureen Hall, Advertising Age Online Posting, September 24, 2007

According to a 2008 report from the Beverage Marketing Corporation, the market for bottled water in the United States grew from just over $6 million a year in 2000 to well over $12 million in 2008. By any standard, that is a fast-growing and profitable industry, especially for a product that is distinguishable almost solely by its package design. Take, for example, the water brand Bling H2O. Bottled in Dandridge, Tennessee, Bling H2O sells for as much as $40–$60 a bottle and has become a favorite among the Hollywood elite. It comes in a frosted, corked bottle with the brand name spelled out with Swarovski crystal. One *Washington Post* reporter calls this "the push to turn water into the new wine" ("What's Colorless and Tasteless and Smells Like . . . Money?" June 30, 2008).

There are other, even more expensive bottled waters, but the water most of us are likely to pick up in our local grocery or deli, though much less pricey, must still distinguish itself from other brands by its label and package design alone. Why choose a $2 bottle when the generic brand sells for less than a dollar? Why choose bottled water at all when much of it is simple tap water, something we can, as Maureen Hill points out, get for free in our kitchens or at any public drinking fountain?

Labels and package design are meant to persuade consumers to buy, and with a product like water, the appeal is often prestige or the promise of pure, refreshing water from underground springs in places like Maine or northern Wisconsin—places associated with clean air and healthy lifestyles.

SUGGESTION FOR READING Notice that our readings of these labels first take into account the message that the label sends. We then consider the market that message addresses. Think about how the design of the labels sets up a relationship between message and reader.

The "ethos" design sells to a consumer's conscience. The cause is described on the back in tiny, hard-to-read white text, so it has to be the text on the front— "Helping children get clean water"—that sells a vague social agenda. The bottle itself is clear, tall, and uncluttered. The simple text uses Helvetica for the brand name, to make it clear and clean. The social message is in a handwriting font, to make it personal and direct. Text takes up only about a third of the front of the bottle. The rest of this package is clear water and clean lines. You can see through it; the product's ethos, its character, is meant to be up front and uncomplicated.

Target Market: Environmentally conscious, upper-middle-class adults with spending money, probably in the twenty-something and thirty-something range.

The Pellegrino label says Old World. If you go into the bottled water aisle, this one will be on a top shelf with the imported waters. The green glass bottle (not plastic) marks it as the sort of product you would find in good restaurants. The label—blue background with a red star at the center—has the appearance of a customs stamp or an official document of some sort. The town of San Pellegrino Terme and the founding date of the company—1899—are featured on a smaller stamp near the top of the bottle.

Target Market: Upscale people who have or hope to soon have money and see themselves as having cosmopolitan tastes.

When the shape of the bottle and the label of a store brand echo Dasani or Aquafina, the design is selling a low-cost alternative to those. There is nothing fancy here, just "Water" as the label says, but the design also makes a direct reference to popular brand names as if to say, "Our water is just as good as theirs, only cheaper." There is no attempt to name a specific source for the water or to claim anything except that it has been purified.

Target Market: The cost-conscious consumer who drinks bottled water but doesn't want to and perhaps can't afford to spend $2 or more for a brand name.

EXPLORATORY WRITING

Look carefully at the bottled waters featured in this Visual Essay and reread the analysis of each. In a brief writing, identify which visual features of the design seem to be important in the analysis. What is the connection between the design and the target market? Why would particular designs appeal to particular segments of the bottled water market?

TALKING ABOUT THE VISUAL ESSAY

Work in a group with three or four other students and pick a product you are familiar with that has competing brands. Bring at least four examples of the product to class to make a presentation. Follow the example of the bottled water, and explain the message on the label and the target market implied by the design.

WRITING ASSIGNMENTS

1. Using this Visual Essay as a guide, write your own essay on the visual design of bottled water. Make explicit how the advertising pitch connects to the targeted audience. Pick 2–3 bottled water designs, and explain how the visual design is related to a particular aspect of the market targeted by each.

2. Following the example we have presented here, compose your own visual essay on the designs of 3–5 similar products. Make sure you identify both the message conveyed by the design and the targeted audience.

3. Design a label for a product. Accompany your design with a written explanation or an oral presentation (depending on what your teacher asks for) of the message on the label and the market you have targeted. Think in terms of how to distinguish what is basically the same product from other products of the same type.

FILM CLIP

Makeup and Costumes: Monsters and the Middle Ages

The style of a film depends in part on makeup artists and costume designers who work closely with directors and actors to give a movie its particular look. The work of makeup artists ranges from highlighting the natural features of a film star to changing altogether actors' appearances to fit the characters they portray. In the black and white era of filmmaking, movies favored stars such as Katharine Hepburn and Lauren Bacall whose angular faces and prominent cheekbones caught the light and cast lovely shadows. With the advent of color, the emphasis shifted to the glowing complexion of Marilyn Monroe, Grace Kelly, and Kim Novak. The job of the makeup artist, in either case, was to prepare these stars to face the camera by accentuating the telling features. At the same time, makeup artists have also created totally new faces for actors, making them seem older or younger and, in the case of horror films, turning normal people into vampires, werewolves, mummies, or other monsters.

One way to think about the work of makeup artists is to look at how they have created film monsters. To do this, you might trace the various film versions of Dracula, Frankenstein, or the Phantom of the Opera. In turn, you could compare these classic film monsters to more recent figures such as Freddy Krueger of a *Nightmare on Elm Street* or Jason of the *Friday the 13th* series.

Costuming plays a key role in enabling movie-goers to visualize the identities of actors and the historical period a film recreates. In some cases, such as the *Godfather* trilogy, *Malcolm X, Titanic,* or *Gangs of New York,* costume design creates a sense of authenticity about the time in which the film is set. In other cases, costuming seems to be a comment on an actor's character, such as the disheveled look of Jeff Bridges in a bathrobe in *The Big Lebowski* or the cool style of George Clooney and the rest of the cast in the *Ocean's* series.

From such extravaganzas as *Gone With the Wind* in 1939 to *Vanity Fair* in 2004 and more recent films, Hollywood has produced many costume dramas. One of the historical periods Hollywood keeps coming back to is the Middle Ages—the era of knights, chivalry, and romance. To think about the work of costume designers, you could examine a number of films that portray the Middle Ages, such as *Knights of the Round Table* (1953), *El Cid* (1961), *Lion in Winter* (1968), *Monty Python and the Holy Grail* (1975), *Excalibur* (1981), *The Return of Martin Guerre* (1984), *Braveheart* (1995), and *King Arthur* (2004).

MINING THE ARCHIVE   Race and Branding

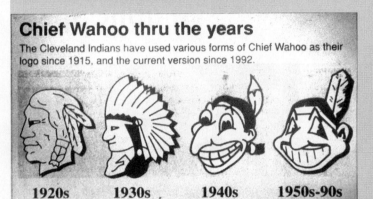

Chief Wahoo thru the years

The Cleveland Indians have used various forms of Chief Wahoo as their logo since 1915, and the current version since 1992.

1920s   1930s   1940s   1950s-90s

The history of branding by companies and sports teams in the United States is deeply implicated in the racial politics of the nation. Companies have for years used images of African Americans such as Aunt Jemima and Uncle Ben as familiar and reassuring symbols of product quality, and critics have argued that these representations perpetuate racial stereotypes of blacks as cooks and servants to whites. A similar issue has arisen about Native American nicknames and logos used for professional baseball and football teams such as the Cleveland Indians, the Atlanta Braves, the Washington Redskins, and the Kansas City Chiefs. Do these images invoke a powerful identity for their teams as warriors, or do they contribute to the myth of Native Americans as a savage, vanishing race? In recent years, several high schools and colleges have changed their nicknames and logos.

There are several archival sources you can consult to examine this issue. To find out more about the representation of African Americans in branding, check out *Aunt Jemima, Uncle Ben, and Rastus: Blacks in Advertising, Yesterday, Today, and Tomorrow* by Marilyn Kern-Foxworth; on Aunt Jemima, see *Slave in a Box* by M. M. Manring. Also visit the Uncle Ben Web site, www.unclebens.com, to see Ben in his office as company chairman. It is possible that your own college or high school or one nearby has a Native American nickname and logo. If that is the case, research the original decision to name the school teams and any stylistic changes that occur over time, as you can see here in the evolution of the Cleveland Indians' "mascot," Chief Wahoo.

CHAPTER
SIX

Public Space

Photo courtesy SPARC. www.sparcmurals.org.

La Familia, detail from *Chicano Time Trip* by East Los Streetscapers (Wayne Alaniz Healy and David Rivas Botello), 1977. 18′ × 26′ panel (total mural is 18′ × 90′). Lincoln Heights, East Los Angeles. City Wide Mural Project.

In wildness, is the preservation of the world.

—Henry David Thoreau

When you go up to the city, you better have some cash, 'cause the people in the city don't mess around with trash.

—Traditional blues lyric

One way of examining how a culture lives and what it values is to look at its public spaces—its streets, parks, sports arenas, shopping malls, museums—all those places where people gather to do business and play and loiter. For many people, public space means open land, wilderness holdings, national parks, and other areas held by the government in the public trust. For others, public space is the space on city streets—the parks, the town halls, the courthouses. It matters little if your background is rural or urban or suburban. If you have visited historical monuments, spent any time in a major city, attended a ball game, watched a parade, shopped in a mall, eaten in a fast food restaurant, or simply attended a church bazaar or school dance, you already know a good deal about how public space is organized in contemporary America, and you probably make more judgments about public spaces than you think.

To say a space is public is to suggest it belongs to everyone—a space for a community, not simply for private use. Yet more and more spaces that at first seem to be open to the public aren't at all public in the strictest sense. Malls, for example, are often credited with becoming the new "town square," but a town square is a space where people in the community have certain rights, such as the right to free speech. Malls are private property. You cannot distribute campaign literature or any other kinds of materials without the permission of mall owners, and many of those owners are very careful about letting anyone into their space who might threaten business as usual by diverting the public's attention from the stores to political or social issues. So even though a mall might invite a Senior Mall Walker's Club to come and exercise before stores open for business, that is not the same as walking out your door and taking your morning jog through the neighborhood. The mall owners can rescind the invitation at any time and bar from the property anyone they feel interferes with business. Even public streets are not so free to the public as one might imagine. In the 1990s, demonstrators at both Republican and Democratic national conventions found themselves segregated into small groups, many quite far from the convention site, as city officials attempted to control the unexpected.

What's more, the tension between public use of public space and private land ownership is a serious one, especially when it comes to wilderness land holdings. In the West, cattle ranchers fight attempts to limit their access to or increase usage fees on grazing land within national parks. The debate over whether to open the Black Hills to more gold mining is an ongoing one. The national parks system has even begun to privatize many of its services. It is a conflict not easily resolved: Americans want public spaces but value private use.

Much of what you write depends on what you have already experienced and what you already think about the topic. Take time, then, to mine your memory about public spaces. What spaces would you expect to be "public"? What space is definitely private? Who should make decisions about how public space is designed and what it is used for? What spaces do you wish would never change? Why? These are the kinds of questions you can begin to consider as you explore the subject of public space.

THE CENTER OF THE UNIVERSE

▬— *Tina McElroy Ansa*

Tina McElroy Ansa is a journalist, novelist, and teacher who grew up in middle Georgia in the 1950s hearing, she says, her grandfather's stories on the porch of her family home and strangers' stories downtown in her father's juke joint. Her first novel, *Baby of the Family* (2002), was listed by the state of Georgia as one of the twenty-five books every Georgian should read. Her articles and op-ed pieces have appeared in a number of newspapers and magazines across the country, including the *Los Angeles Times*, the *Atlanta Constitution*, *Ms. Magazine*, and *Essence*. "The Center of the Universe" (2003) is about Ansa's memories of growing up in Macon, Georgia. In it she raises the question of place and belonging—especially for African Americans growing up in the South.

SUGGESTION FOR READING Before you read, write a brief description of what you would call small-town America in the 1950s. Think about where you get the impression of what that place should look like, what the people are like, and whether or not you believe this place really ever existed.

1   On the way home from school one day when I was seven or eight years old—a black child growing up in Macon, Georgia, in the 1950s—my father, Walter McElroy, took me to a huge fountain in a city park. At the edge of the fountain, he pointed to the water and said very seriously, "That is the exact center of Georgia."

It was a momentous revelation for me. Since that instant, I have always thought of myself being at the center of my universe, enveloped in the world around me. From that day, I have imagined myself standing at that fountain surrounded by my African American community of Pleasant Hill, in my hometown of Macon, in middle Georgia, with the muddy Ocmulgee River running nearby, with the entire state of Georgia around me, then all of the southeastern section of the continental United States, then the country, the Western Hemisphere, then the world.

The image has always made me feel safe. Sheltered by my surroundings, enveloped in the arms of "family" of one kind or another, mostly southern family. That is how I see myself, a southerner.

For some folks, my discussing my southernness makes them downright uncomfortable. I mean really, the very idea, a black person, an African American over the age of thirty-five, going on and on about the South and her place in it as if she weren't aware of the region, its past, and all it stands for.

5   Doesn't she know history? she seems to think. And she's a writer, too. It's almost embarrassing.

As if a black person does not belong in the South, to the South. In a couple of decades of moving up and down the United States' eastern seaboard, I found there was no place else I *did belong*.

Of course I know the region's history, I want to tell folks looking askance at me. I know it because I am a part of the history. My parents were part of that history. And their parents were part of it.

My father's people came from Wrightsville, in the south-central part of the state. They were farming people, like most black people at the turn of the twentieth century. At that time, black folks owned nearly twenty million acres of farmland in the United States. When my father's father, Frank, left the farm nearly one hundred years ago for the city of Macon and work on the M-D-S—the Macon-Dublin-Savannah train line, which connected those three Georgia cities— his brother Isadore (whom we called "Uncle Sunshine") and his family remained there on the farm. As a child, when my parents, two older brothers and two older sisters, and I piled into our green woodie station wagon and left the "city" for a few days in summer to visit the "country," it was to Uncle Sunshine's farm we went.

My mother's people—the Lees—were also from middle Georgia. But they were "city people," they were not farmers. They were school-teachers and tradespeople and semiprofessionals. Everyone in town knew my great-grandfather as "Pat, the barber." All I have to do now is say that name to make my mother smile with nostalgia and begin telling me stories surrounding the antique red leather barbershop chair that sat on my great-aunt's back porch for decades. Patrick Lee's maiden daughter, Elizabeth, not only took over her father's barbershop when he died in the 1930s. She also taught folks in middle Georgia from the cradle to the grave. During the day, she led her own private kindergarten class. During the evenings, she taught illiterate adults to read. "All I want to do is learn to read the Bible," they would tell her. She always chuckled: "Lord, some of the most difficult words and concepts in the world are in the Bible."

10   In childhood, I always thought of her as just a stern religious old maid who didn't even drink Coca-Colas or take aspirin because they were "dope" or let you sleep in any bed in her house past sunup lest you get "the big head." I thank the Holy Spirit that she and I both lived long enough for me to see her for the extraordinary African American woman that she was. She was one of the reasons my mother loved reading and passed that love on to her children.

Today, every word I write, I write on a computer atop the old pedal-motored Singer sewing machine console that once sat in Auntie's bedroom.

It is no wonder that in my childhood family house—a big old brick two-story house with an attic and basement—there were books everywhere: in the bedrooms, the bathroom, the living room, and the kitchen. When I was a child, the joke in our family was to shove a copy of the tiny Macon telephone book under the door of the bathroom when someone hollered out for some new reading material. Whenever that happened to me, I happily sat there with my legs dangling off the toilet and amused myself by reading that phone book, looking up my friends' numbers and addresses, coming upon interesting names, making up stories about the people and streets I encountered there.

When I was growing up, I thought the entire world was made up of stories. My mother gossiping on the phone was to my ear my mother weaving stories. The tales of love and woe that I overheard from the customers at my father's juke joints and liquor store down on Broadway and Mulberry Street, as I sat at the end of the bar in my Catholic school uniform doing my homework, were to me stories. My grandfather Walter McElroy's ghost stories of cats wearing diamond rings sticking their hands into blazing campfires. My Baptist great-auntie Elizabeth Lee relating how she always wanted to go to the Holy Land but had no intention of crossing any water to get there. My mother telling me over and over as she whipped up batter for one of her light-as-air, sweet-as-mother's-love desserts how she made her first cake when she was only seven.

I draw sustenance from these stories, in the same way I draw nourishment from knowing that my father's people farmed land right up the road in Wrightsville, Georgia. In my southern mind, I can see Uncle Sunshine drawing his bony mule under the hot shade of a tall Georgia pine and wiping his brow when I gaze at the pine trees around my house. I never cross a railroad track without recalling my grandfather's years with the M-D-S line and the first time my father put me on the famed "Nancy Hanks" train for a trip to Savannah by myself. After my father handed me over to the care of the train's porters, they asked, pointing to my father's retreating back, "Who was that boy?" I replied indignantly, "That's no boy! That's my daddy!" The black men looked at each other and just beamed. Then proceeded to getting me cold Coca-Colas and sneaking me sandwiches from the whites-only dining car. For the rest of the four-hour trip, they treated me like a princess, heaping on me the loving attention usually thought of as the preserve of little white girls traveling on the southern train system. In fact, they treated me better. They treated me like family.

15 Family. As a writer, a novelist, it is all that I write about. My first novel, *Baby of the Family*, is not just about my retaining that special place of the last born in my household. It is also about the ties, the connections, the stories, the food, the rituals, the seasons, the minutiae that go into forming the family unit.

Like all of us, I carry my childhood with me.

No matter where I go or in what time zone I find myself, at eleven o'clock Eastern Standard Time Sunday mornings, I think of St. Peter Claver Church sitting at the top of Pleasant Hill and the sacrament of the Eucharist being celebrated there. Sunday morning mass in my childhood parish is still the quintessential Sunday morning to me. Just as that fountain in the middle of Tatnall Square Park is the primary bellwether for my place in the universe.

When I write, I still envision myself standing at that fountain surrounded by my family, my community, my hometown, my state, my country, and the world.

From time to time, my mother will wistfully remind some old friend of hers who asks about me, "Tina doesn't live in Macon anymore."

20 My Mama is right. I *don't* live in Macon anymore.

Macon lives in me.

EXPLORATORY WRITING

At the beginning of her essay, Ansa poses a question for her readers: why would an African American love the South? After all, the history of that region should make it very difficult for any African American to want to claim it as home. Write an account of how Ansa responds to that question.

TALKING ABOUT THE READING

With a group of your classmates, share the piece you wrote before you read this essay. What does each person in your group identify as the idealized place called "small-town America"? What are the characteristics of that place? How do the descriptions differ? What do they have in common? To what extent do individuals' experiences growing up today and in different places influence their impressions of small-town America as it has been idealized?

WRITING ASSIGNMENTS

1. Write your own account of how you do or do not carry the place or places where you grew up with you. What role do those early places in your life play in the way you think people should live or what you think towns or cities should look like? What role do the popular media play in the way most of us envision a good place (and its opposite) for living or raising children?

2. "Family," writes Ansa. "As a writer, a novelist, it is all that I write about." This essay is certainly a story about family, but it is also about place. What role does place play in the childhood that Ansa says she carries with her?

3. Most readers would say that Ansa's description of small-town Georgia in the 1950s is an idealized one. Write an essay in which you examine this essay as an extension of the media or idealized image of U.S. small towns in the 1950s. What makes Ansa's description seem idealized? What about it strikes you as real? In your essay, refer to specific films or televisions programs that portray that 1950s small-town America.

CARING FOR THE WOODS

—Barry Lopez

Award-winning author Barry Lopez is a widely recognized and well respected nature writer. Among his many awards in both fiction and nonfiction, he is the recipient of a National Book Award, a Pushcart Prize, and a Guggenheim Fellowship. Lopez is perhaps best known for such nonfiction works as *Arctic Dreams: Imagination and Desire in the Northern Landscape* (1986), *Of Wolves and Men* (1978), and *Crossing Open Ground* (1989). He has contributed to a number of magazines and newspapers, including *Harper's* where he served as a contributing editor, the *New York Times, Paris Review, Orion,* and *Audubon Magazine,* where the essay reprinted here originally appeared in 1995.

SUGGESTION FOR READING Lopez traces both his family history and a brief cultural history of the area in his essay about the importance of caring for the woods. As you read, keep track of those two histories and pay attention to how they figure into Lopez's views on land development and the preservation of wild places. You can do this either by underlining and making annotations in the margins or by keeping notes.

1 My family has been in the Americas for almost five centuries. Marín López, a shipwright on my father's side, was in the Caribbean with Cortés in 1511. My mother's English and German ancestors began farming on the Pennsylvania side of the Delaware River valley in the 1650s. A scion of that group later moved to Virginia (where the Holston River still bears the family name); his progeny moved into the Carolinas and eastern Alabama, where my mother was born on a plantation in 1914. One relative in that clan moved on to New Mexico at the close of the 19th century and then dropped from sight. He is recalled as a man obsessed with killing Indians.

My father's family, originally tobacco farmers in Cuba, eventually came to St. Louis and New York as tobacco merchants, though they maintained close ties with Asturias, their homeland in northern Spain. Neither the Romans nor the Moors, my father is still proud to say, ever conquered Asturias. He traces his lineage there back to Rodrigo Díaz de Vivar—El Cid. In her last years my mother followed her own path back as far, to a baron of Somerset who ratified the Magna Carta at Runnymede.

All these centuries later, the wandering, the buying up, the clearing, the planting, and the harvesting of land in my single branch of the family has come down to a parcel in Oregon: 35 acres of mixed old-growth forest, rising quickly into the foothills of the Cascade Mountains from the north bank of the McKenzie River. These woods harbor Roosevelt elk and mountain lion, suites of riparian and mixed-forest birds, and an assortment of insects, wildflowers, and mushrooms that trails off into a thousand species.

I understand the desire to own the land, the dream of material wealth that brought each of my lines of descent to the Americas. I respect the determination, the tenacity, and the uses to which the land-profit was put—formal education, for example. But I've come to believe, at the age of 49, that sacrificing the biological integrity of land to abet human progress is a practice my generation must end. If we do not, I believe the Americas will finally wash into the sea like Haiti, leaving behind a social nightmare.

5 My wife, Sandra, and I have lived on the right bank of the river for 24 years. We want to keep this single wooded slope of land in the West undeveloped and uncut. We want to pass it on like a well-read book, not the leavings of someone's meal.

The enormous trees and the river, because of their scale, dominate what we see here, but the interstices of this landscape are jammed with life: hummingbirds, spiders, butterflies, cutthroat trout, wild ginger, skinks, the cascading blossoms of wild rhododendron. In the 1940s some of the larger trees—Douglas fir, western hemlock, and western red cedar, four to six feet in diameter—were selectively logged. The selective logging and a fire that burned a long stretch of the north bank of the McKenzie in 1855 created a forest with a few tall, rotting stumps; dense patches of younger Douglas fir; and several dozen massive, isolated, towering trees, 300 to 400 years old, all standing among many fewer Pacific yew, chinquapin, bigleaf maple, red alder, Pacific dogwood, California hazel, and the odd Pacific madrone.

In 1989 a neighbor who owned this slope put 32 acres of it up for sale. Timber companies that intended to clear-cut the property were the most active bidders, and Sandra and I were forced to match money and wits with them. But in 1990 we were able to add these acres to three we'd bought in 1976. We then completed a legal arrangement to prevent the land from being either logged or developed after we passed away. Good intention toward an individual stretch of land has now become well-meaning of another kind in my family.

We did not set out to preserve these woods. From the start we felt it a privilege, also a kind of wonder, to live here. Twenty-inch spring chinook spawn on a redd in front of the house in September every year. Wild bleeding heart, yellow violets, white flowers such as trillium and wood sorrel, and the red flowers of coralroot are brilliant in the deep, green woods in April and May. I find bear scat, beaver-clipped willows, and black-tailed deer prints regularly on my walks. On the same night we've listened to northern spotted owls, western screech owls, and northern saw-whet owls call. Spotted skunks and a short-tail weasel have tried to take up residence in the house. On summer nights, when we leave the windows open, bats fly through.

From a certain perspective, this wooded hill with its unnamed creek and marvelous creatures—I nearly stepped on a rubber boa one morning on the way to the toolshed—is still relatively unmanipulated; but I try not to let myself be fooled by the thought. The number of songbirds returning each spring I would guess to be half what it was a decade ago. The number of chinook on the redd, though it fluctuates, has also fallen off in recent years. And I've taken hundreds of dead animals off the road along the river—raccoon, brush rabbit, even Steller's jay and mink. People new to the area are apt to log the few Douglas firs left on their property, to roll out fresh lawns and plant ornamental trees in their place. Their house cats leave shrews, white-footed mice, and young birds strewn in the woods like so much litter.

10   Driftnets that snag salmon in the far-off Pacific, industrial logging in Central America that eliminates migratory-bird habitat, speeding trucks and automobiles, attractive prices for timber— all of it directly affects these acres. There is no way to fence it out.

The historical detail that might make vivid what, precisely, occurred in the McKenzie River valley after its location in 1812 by Donald MacKenzie—a trapper and kinsman of the Canadian explorer Alexander MacKenzie—is hard to come by, but the story is similar to those told of a hundred other valleys in the West. Beaver trappers were the first whites to sleep in these woods. (Molala and Kalapuya Indians, from the east and west side of the Cascades respectively, apparently camped along the McKenzie in summer, when salmon were running and openings in the heavily forested mountains were crowded with ripening blue and red huckleberries, soft thimbleberries, strawberries, orange salmonberries, blue and red elderberries, and trailing blackberries.) When the free trappers and the company trappers were gone, gold and silver miners filtered in. Toward the end of the 19th century some homestead settlement followed small-scale logging operations along the river, though steep mountains and dense forests made farming and grazing in the area impractical. Clear-cutting in modern times, with its complicated attendant problems—siltation smothering salmon redds, "predator control" programs directed against black bears—has turned the road between our house and Eugene, 40 miles downriver, into as butchered a landscape as any I know in the Cascades.

In the 1980s, when the price of Douglas fir reached $300 for 1,000 board feet, some small-property owners succumbed—two or three trees might bring them $2,500. The resulting harvest has grown to look like mange on the hills. Hand in hand with that has come real estate promotion, the hundreds of FOR SALE signs along the road a sort of Muzak.

I am not a cynical man, but watching the quick spread of suburban logging and seeing the same house put up for sale every few years—with a little more landscaping, a higher fence, and another $30,000 to $40,000 added to the price—pushes me closer to it than anything else I know. A long-term commitment to the place, knowledge of its biological limits, or concern for the valley's fate—these do not appear to be a part of the transactions. The hacking away at natural growth, the incessant prettifying with rosebushes and trimmed hedges, and the imposition of incongruous antebellum architecture look like a scatter of bad marriages—reigning husbands with presentable wives.

If I had answers to these problems, or if I felt exempt in this mess, I would be angry about it more often than I am. As it is, Sandra and I pace ourselves. We work on initiatives to control real estate development and rein in logging along the river. We provide a place for the release of rehabilitated raptors, including spotted owls. We work amicably with the state highway department and the Bonneville Power Administration (BPA), which maintain corridors across the land we occupy. We have had to threaten a lawsuit to curb the recklessness of the highway department with chainsaws and heavy equipment, and we have had to insist through an attorney that the BPA not capriciously fall "danger trees" along its power-line right-of-way.

15   But these agencies, whose land-management philosophies differ so strikingly from our own, have slowly accommodated us. Instead of flooding the roadside with herbicides and flailing at it with oversize brush cutters, the highway department now permits us (and others along the river) to trim back by hand what brush actually threatens motor traffic. And the regional director of the BPA wrote into a recent contract that I could accompany his fallers, to be certain no felled tree was sent crashing needlessly into other trees.

Sandra and I ourselves, of course, have not left the place untouched. In January 1991 two windstorms felled about 30 trees. We logged them out with horses and put the money toward the land payment. I have felled standing dead trees that threatened the house. We compost our kitchen waste, laundry lint, and woodstove ashes in the woods. We've planted gardens and built outbuildings. But it is our habit to disturb these acres very little and to look after them in a way only humans can: by discouraging or preventing the destruction other humans bring. I've asked my neighbors to stop dumping refuse on our place. (They had done it for years because it was only "the woods," a sort of warehouse for timber, deer, and fish, and a dumping ground for whatever one wanted to abandon—cars, bedsprings, fuel drums, mall packaging.) I've asked another neighbor's children not to shoot at birds or chop down trees. I've asked unwitting fishermen not to walk through the salmon redd. And, reluctantly, I've gated and posted the land to keep out wanton hunters and people in four-wheel-drives looking for something to break down or climb over.

We know we cannot fence off the endangered chinook redd without attracting curious passersby. Neither I nor anyone can outlaw the product advertising (or foolish popular history) that contributes to images of men taming a violent West. Neither I nor anyone, I fear, can soon change human sentiment to put lands that are unharvested, unhunted, unroaded, or untenanted on the same footing with lands that are domesticated or industrialized. So the birds and animals, the fish and spiders, the wild orchids and other flowers will not have these shields.

Piece by piece, however, as a citizen and as a writer, I want to contest the obsessions that I believe imperil American landscapes—the view that they are principally sources of material wealth or scenic backdrops for a more important human drama. I want to consider the anomalies that lie at the heart of our incessant desire to do good. And I want to see how to sidestep despair, by placing my faith in something larger than my own ideas.

Sandra and I know we do not own these 35 acres. The Oregon ash trees by the river, in whose limbs I have seen flocks of 100 Audubon's warblers, belong also to the families in Guatemala in whose forests these birds winter. The bereavement I feel at the diminishment of life around me is also a bereavement felt by men and women and children I don't know, living in cities I've never visited. And the exhilaration I experience seeing fresh cougar tracks in mud by a creek is an emotion known to any person in love who hears the one-who-is-loved speak.

20   There is more mystery to be contemplated, there are more lessons to be absorbed, on these 35 acres than all the people in my lineage going back to Runnymede and medieval Asturias could manage, should the study be pursued another 1,000 years. My generation's task, I believe, is to change the direction of Western civilization in order to make such a regard practicable.

When I rise in the morning I often walk down to the riverbank. If it's summer I'm likely to see mergansers, tree swallows, and osprey. I see first light brightly reflected on alder twigs stripped by beaver. I feel the night movement of cool air downriver and see deer-head orchid and blue gilia blooming in the dark-green salal and horsetail rushes.

I am acutely aware, winter or summer, that these waters have come from farther east in the mountains, that in a few days they will cross the bar at the mouth of the Columbia and become part of the Pacific. The ancient history alone of this river, this animate and elusive business of rain and snow and gravity, gives me hope.

Walking back to the house in this serene frame of mind, I know that to love life, to swear an allegiance to what is alive, is the essence of what I am after. I'm moved to forgive whoever does not find in these acres what I do. I glance into the moving picket of trees and shadow, alert for what I've never noticed before, in a woods I'm trying to take care of—as in its very complicated way it is taking care of me.

EXPLORATORY WRITING

Using the notes or annotations you made as you read the essay, write a brief summary of Lopez's argument and how he uses family history and cultural history to make that argument. How do those histories inform his decision to preserve as much of the woods as he can? Where does he position himself in these histories?

TALKING ABOUT THE READING

With a group of your classmates, make a chart in which you identify the stakeholders (both past and present) in Lopez's argument about how the woods should be used or taken care of. Under each person or group, list what is actually at stake in how the woods are used. Lopez and his wife, for example, could be called stakeholders. The trappers and different Indian tribes could be on your chart. Present your chart to the class for a discussion of what is actually at stake in the ways we use our forests or undeveloped natural spaces.

WRITING ASSIGNMENTS

1. Lopez reaches back in time in his writing to set up a context for how these woods came to be threatened. He writes about the role of explorers and trappers and developers in the ways nature is endangered today. He also occasionally identifies his own role in the development of natural spaces. Write an essay in which you examine how Lopez establishes his authority. How would you describe his character—his ethos? How does he represent others and their motives or desires? Point to specific passages in the essay where Lopez positions himself on this issue. You might find it helpful before you begin this essay to look back at the Exploratory Writing in which you identified how Lopez represents himself within the larger history of this place.

2. Some readers might object to Lopez's position on preservation and land development because, they would argue, he is being selfish. He wants places to be left alone because that is how he lives best; that is what he prefers. Moreover, Lopez can afford to buy up tracts of land and leave it undeveloped while others cannot. Write an essay in which you examine to what extent Lopez leaves himself open to those charges. Given what he writes here, how would he respond to those charges?

3. Write an essay about a place you know well that you have seen change over the years. In your essay, describe the place as you remember it before the change and what it is today. How has the change affected the people and the areas around this place? Who are the stakeholders in this development?

SHOPPING FOR PLEASURE: MALLS, POWER, AND RESISTANCE

— *John Fiske*

John Fiske is a professor of communication at the University of Wisconsin, Madison. He is among the many scholars today who make use of the artifacts of daily life to interpret modern culture. For Fiske, as well as others engaging in cultural studies, the analysis of popular culture can help reveal how a society produces meaning from its social experience. The following selection, taken from *Reading the Popular* and written in 1989, demonstrates how phenomena we take for granted in our everyday lives, such as shopping malls, are a part of that cultural production of meaning.

SUGGESTION FOR READING   Notice as you read that Fiske makes reference to other studies from which he has drawn ideas, interpretations, and information. He uses those references to give scholarly weight to his argument and to acknowledge his use of others' work in building his own interpretation. If you are not familiar with the names (he usually uses last names only), don't let that stop your reading. The context in which the name is used can usually give you enough information to allow you to continue. As you read, underline passages in which Fiske distinguishes his own view from that of other scholars.

1   Shopping malls are cathedrals of consumption—a glib phrase that I regret the instant it slides off my pen. The metaphor of consumerism as a religion, in which commodities become the icons of worship and the rituals of exchanging money for goods become a secular equivalent of holy communion, is simply too glib to be helpful, and too attractive to those whose intentions, whether they be moral or political, are to expose the evils and limitations of bourgeois materialism. And

yet the metaphor is both attractive and common precisely because it does convey and construct a knowledge of consumerism; it does point to one set of "truths," however carefully selected a set.

Truths compete in a political arena, and the truths that the consumerism-as-contemporary-religion strives to suppress are those that deny the difference between the tenor and vehicle of the metaphor. Metaphor always works within that tense area within which the forces of similarity and difference collide, and aligns itself with those of similarity. Metaphor constructs similarity out of difference, and when a metaphor becomes a cliché, as the shopping mall-cathedral one has, then a resisting reading must align itself with the differences rather than the similarities, for clichés become clichés only because of their centrality to common sense: the cliché helps to construct the commonality of common sense.

So, the differences: the religious congregation is powerless, led like sheep through the rituals and meanings, forced to "buy" the truth on offer, all the truth, not selective bits of it. Where the interests of the Authority on High differ from those of the Congregation down Low, the congregation has no power to negotiate, to discriminate: all accommodations are made by the powerless, subjugated to the great truth. In the U.S. marketplace, 90 percent of new products fail to find sufficient buyers to survive (Schudson 1984), despite advertising, promotions, and all the persuasive techniques of the priests of consumption. In Australia, Sinclair (1987) puts the new product failure rate at 80 percent—such statistics are obviously best-guesstimates: what matters is that the failure rate is high. The power of consumer discrimination evidenced here has no equivalent in the congregation: no religion could tolerate a rejection rate of 80 or 90 percent of what it has to offer.

Religion may act as a helpful metaphor when our aim is to investigate the power of consumerism; when, however, our focus shifts to the power of the consumer, it is counterproductive. . . . Shopping is the crisis of consumerism: it is where the art and tricks of the weak can inflict most damage on, and exert most power over, the strategic interests of the powerful. The shopping mall that is seen as the terrain of guerrilla warfare looks quite different from the one constructed by the metaphor of religion.

Pressdee (1986), in his study of unemployed youth in the South Australian town of Elizabeth, paints a clear picture of both sides in this war. The ideological practices that serve the interests of the powerful are exposed in his analysis of the local mall's promotional slogan, which appears in the form of a free ticket: "Your ticket to a better shopping world: ADMITS EVERYONE." He comments:

> The words "your" and "everyone" are working to socially level out class distinction and, in doing so, overlook the city's two working class groups, those who have work and those who do not. The word "admits" with a connotation of having to have or be someone to gain admittance is cancelled out by the word "everyone"—there are no conditions of admittance; everyone is equal and can come in.

This pseudoticket to consumerism denies the basic function of a ticket—to discriminate between those who possess one and those who do not—in a precise moment of the ideological work of bourgeois capitalism with its denial of class difference, and therefore of the inevitability of class struggle. The equality of "everyone" is, of course, an equality attainable only by those with purchasing power: those without are defined out of existence, as working-class interests (derived from class *difference*) are defined out of existence by bourgeois ideology. "The ticket to a better shopping world does not say 'Admits everyone with at least some money to spend' . . . ; money and the problems associated with getting it conveniently disappear in the official discourse" (Pressdee 1986: 10–11).

Pressdee then uses a variation of the religious metaphor to sum up the "official" messages of the mall:

> The images presented in the personal invitation to all in Elizabeth is then that of the cargo cult. Before us a lightshaft beams down from space,

which contains the signs of the "future"; "Target", "Venture"—gifts wrapped; a table set for two. But beamed down from space they may as well be, because . . . this imagery can be viewed as reinforcing denial of the production process— goods are merely beamed to earth. The politics of their production and consumption disappear.

Yet his study showed that 80 percent of unemployed young people visited the mall at least once a week, and nearly 100 percent of young unemployed women were regular visitors. He comments on these uninvited guests:

> For young people, especially the unemployed, there has been a congregating within these cathedrals of capitalism, where desires are created and fulfilled and the production of commodities, the very activity that they are barred from, is itself celebrated on the altar of consumerism. Young people, cut off from normal consumer power, are invading the space of those with consumer power. (p. 13)

Pressdee's shift from the religious metaphor to one of warfare signals his shift of focus from the powerful to the disempowered.

10   Thursday nights, which in Australia are the only ones on which stores stay open late, have become the high points of shopping, when the malls are at their most crowded and the cash registers ring up their profits most busily, and it is on Thursday nights that the youth "invasion" of consumer territory is most aggressive. Pressdee (1986) describes this invasion vividly:

> Thursday nights vibrate with youth, eager to show themselves:—it belongs to them, they have possessed it. This cultural response is neither spectacular nor based upon consumerism itself. Nor does it revolve around artifacts or dress, but rather around the possession of space, or to be more precise the possession of consumer space where their very presence challenges, offends and resists.
>
> Hundreds of young people pour into the centre every Thursday night, with three or four hundred being present at any one time. They parade for several hours, not buying, but presenting, visually, all the contradictions of

employment and unemployment, taking up their natural public space that brings both life and yet confronts the market place. Security men patrol all night aided by several police patrols, hip guns visible and radios in use, bringing a new understanding to law and order.

> Groups of young people are continually evicted from this opulent and warm environment, fights appear, drugs seem plentiful, alcohol is brought in, in various guises and packages. The police close in on a group of young women, their drink is tested. Satisfied that it is only coca-cola they are moved on and out. Not wanted. Shopkeepers and shoppers complain. The security guards become agitated and begin to question all those seen drinking out of cans or bottles who are under 20, in the belief that they must contain alcohol. They appear frightened, totally outnumbered by young people as they continue their job in keeping the tills ringing and the passage to the altar both free and safe. (p. 14)

Pressdee coins the term "proletarian shopping" (p. 16) to describe this window shopping with no intention to buy. The youths consumed images and space instead of commodities, a kind of sensuous consumption that did not create profits. The positive pleasure of parading up and down, of offending "real" consumers and the agents of law and order, of asserting their difference within, and different use of, the cathedral of consumerism became an oppositional cultural practice.

The youths were "tricksters" in de Certeau's terms—they pleasurably exploited their knowledge of the official "rules of the game" in order to identify where these rules could be mocked, inverted, and thus used to free those they were designed to discipline. De Certeau (1984) points to the central importance of the "trickster" and the "guileful ruse" throughout peasant and folk cultures. Tricks and ruses are the art of the weak that enables them to exploit their understanding of the rules of the system, and to turn it to their advantage. They are a refusal to be subjugated:

> The actual order of things is precisely what "popular" tactics turn to their own ends, without

any illusion that it will change any time soon. Though elsewhere it is exploited by a dominant power . . . here order is tricked by an art. (de Certeau 1984: 26)

This trickery is evidence of "an ethics of tenacity (countless ways of refusing to accord the established order the status of a law, a meaning or a fatality)" (p. 26).

Shopping malls are open invitations to trickery and tenacity. The youths who turn them into their meeting places, or who trick the security guards by putting alcohol into some, but only some, soda cans, are not actually behaving any differently from lunch hour window shoppers who browse through the stores, trying on goods, consuming and playing with images, with no intention to buy. In extreme weather people exploit the controlled climate of the malls for their own pleasure—mothers take children to play in their air-conditioned comfort in hot summers, and in winter older people use their concourses for daily walks. Indeed, some malls now have notices welcoming "mall walkers," and a few have even provided exercise areas set up

with equipment and instructions so that the walkers can exercise more than their legs.

15   Of course, the mall owners are not entirely disinterested or altruistic here—they hope that some of the "tricky" users of the mall will become real economic consumers, but they have no control over who will, how many will, how often, or how profitably. One boutique owner told me that she estimated that 1 in 30 browsers actually bought something. Shopping malls are where the strategy of the powerful is most vulnerable to the tactical raids of the weak.

REFERENCES

De Certeau, M. (1984). *The Practice of Everyday Life*. Berkeley: University of California Press.

Pressdee, M. (1986). "Agony or Ecstasy: Broken Transitions and the New Social State of Working-Class Youth in Australia." Occasional Papers, S. Australian Centre for Youth Studies, S.A. College of A.E., Magill, S. Australia.

Schudson, M. (1984). *Advertising: The Uneasy Persuasion*. New York: Basic Books.

Sinclair, J. (1987). *Images Incorporated: Advertising as Industry and Ideology*. London: Croom Helm.

EXPLORATORY WRITING

Write a 1–2 page summary of Fiske's argument. In your summary, take into account the cathedral metaphor Fiske raises as one way of talking about mall culture as well as his challenge of that metaphor. Note how Fiske moves from his discussion of metaphor to his argument about malls as spaces of resistance, especially but not solely for young people.

TALKING ABOUT THE READING

Share your summary with a group of your classmates. As you read others' summaries, take note of ideas or details they picked up that you did not. Once you have finished your discussion, come to a consensus on what your group would identify as Fiske's most important assertions in his argument. In your group's experience with malls, where would you say his argument might break down? How, for example, does your group respond to his assertion that "Shopping malls are where the strategy of the powerful is most vulnerable to the tactical raids of the weak"?

WRITING ASSIGNMENTS

1. In 2006, the following BBC news item appeared in papers across the United Kingdom:

   Mozart's music is being brought to a new wave of listeners in the 250th anniversary year of his birth, but it is not intended to be inspirational.

Luton Borough Council plans to play classical music in the town centre to discourage teenagers from gathering around shops and becoming a nuisance. Research shows young people can be deterred by classical music. They tend to move away from music they do not like and it is alleged Mozart is particularly effective.

The borough council is also using equipment designed to drive away mosquitoes to discourage the youths from gathering.

The mosquito units are small sound generators that give out a high frequency sound which, it is claimed, only young people under the age of 25 can hear, because of the density of their inner ear bones.

Classical music will be played outside the shops at Sundon Park parade, while mosquito units will be on trial at Wigmore Lane and St Dominic's Square, both areas experiencing problems with anti-social behaviour.

Since that report, more businesses in the UK, Australia, and some in the United States have experimented with classical music and (increasingly) mosquito units to drive young people away from shops when they are not buying anything but, instead, just hanging out or "loitering." In the United States, this device is distributed through a Web site called *KidsBeGone.com*, which advertises itself as the "exclusive North American importer for the Mosquito Kid Deterrent Device" and promises business owners that this device, aimed at teenagers, is "the most effective tool in our fight against anti social behavior."

Write an essay in which you examine the underlying assumptions about young people in public places that the use of such a device indicates. Why target people under 25, especially teens? Why not drive senior mall walkers out with loud hip-hop music or a sound device aimed at elderly eardrums? In your essay, consider your group's discussion of Fiske's claim that "Shopping malls are where the strategy of the powerful is most vulnerable to the tactical raids of the weak." How might this move to chase young people off be one way of acknowledging that vulnerability?

2. Fiske's analysis of mall culture turns our attention away from the store owners and mall managers who make the rules and hope to profit from their investments to an analysis of how people actually use the mall. He writes, "Shopping malls are open invitations to trickery and tenacity. The youths who turn them into their meeting places, or who trick the security guards by putting alcohol into some, but only some, soda cans, are not actually behaving any differently from lunch hour shoppers who browse through the stores, trying on goods, consuming and playing with images, with no intention to buy."

Choose a public space other than a mall that people use for their own purposes rather than or in addition to the purpose for which it was designed, and write an essay that explains what it is about the place that lends itself to "trickery and tenacity," as Fiske says malls do. For this essay, rely on your own recollection of and experience with the place for your analysis. Remember to bring in events you have witnessed or things you and your friends or family have done in that place. You can also draw on Fiske's analysis of the way the public uses mall space to help you explain the way the public uses the place you have chosen. You might be able to draw on your written summaries and class discussions to help you begin your own analysis of public spaces as sites of resistance.

3. With at least two of your classmates, visit a local mall. Spend time watching who is there, who is buying, who is hanging out, eating lunch, mall walking, or window shopping. To get the best sense of mall use, your group will need to visit the mall at different times of the day and week, so you might want to begin your work by dividing up tasks and observation times. As well, make a list of the kinds of activities you are looking for. Gather any information about this mall that seems useful for your project. For example, someone in

your group might visit the mall office and ask for a copy of mall rules. (These are often posted in the mall area itself but sometimes not.)

With your group, write a report on how visitors to the mall use the space and what restrictions are placed on mall visitors. Refer to Fiske's argument in your report. To what extent would you say the mall you observed conforms to his analysis? In your report, be sure to say how much time you spent in the space, what days you went there, what different groups of people you saw (teens, mothers with small children, seniors, business people, etc.), and any other information relevant to your findings. Report your findings to the class. Be sure to indicate to what extent your observations correspond to Fiske's.

FORTRESS LOS ANGELES: THE MILITARIZATION OF URBAN SPACE

—Mike Davis

> Mike Davis, a professor of history at the University of California, Irvine, is the author of a number of books and articles that examine the politics of public space. His book *City of Quartz: Excavating the Future of Los Angeles* (1990), from which this selection was taken, is a study of how urban space in Los Angeles has been configured to echo local and racial politics.

SUGGESTION FOR READING Davis opens this selection with the following statement: "In Los Angeles—once a paradise of free beaches, luxurious parks, and 'cruising strips'—genuinely democratic space is virtually extinct." As you read, underline and annotate those passages where Davis explains specifically what he means by that.

1 In Los Angeles—once a paradise of free beaches, luxurious parks, and "cruising strips"—genuinely democratic space is virtually extinct. The pleasure domes of the elite Westside rely upon the social imprisonment of a third-world service proletariat in increasingly repressive ghettos and barrios. In a city of several million aspiring immigrants (where Spanish-surname children are now almost two-thirds of the school-age population), public amenities are shrinking radically, libraries and playgrounds are closing, parks are falling derelict, and streets are growing ever more desolate and dangerous.

Here, as in other American cities, municipal policy has taken its lead from the security offensive and the middle-class demand for increased spatial and social insulation. Taxes previously targeted for traditional public spaces and recreational facilities have been redirected to support corporate redevelopment projects. A pliant city government—in the case of Los Angeles, one ironically professing to represent a liberal biracial coalition—has collaborated in privatizing public space and subsidizing new exclusive enclaves (benignly called "urban villages"). The celebratory language used to describe contemporary Los Angeles—"urban renaissance," "city of the future," and so on—is only a triumphal gloss laid over the brutalization of its inner-city neighborhoods and the stark divisions of class and race represented in its built environment. Urban form obediently follows repressive function. Los Angeles, as always in the vanguard, offers an especially disturbing guide to the emerging liaisons between urban architecture and the police state.

FORBIDDEN CITY

Los Angeles's first spatial militarist was the legendary General Harrison Gray Otis, proprietor of the *Times* and implacable foe of organized labor. In the 1890s, after locking out his union printers and announcing a crusade for "industrial freedom," Otis retreated into a new *Times* building designed as a fortress with grim turrets and battlements crowned by a bellicose bronze eagle. To emphasize his truculence, he later had a small, functional cannon installed on the hood of his Packard touring car. Not surprisingly, this display of aggression produced a response in kind. On October 1, 1910, the heavily fortified *Times* headquarters—the command-post of the open shop on the West Coast—was destroyed in a catastrophic explosion, blamed on union saboteurs.

Eighty years later, the martial spirit of General Otis pervades the design of Los Angeles's new Downtown, whose skyscrapers march from Bunker Hill down the Figueroa corridor. Two billion dollars of public tax subsidies have enticed big banks and corporate headquarters back to a central city they almost abandoned in the 1960s. Into a waiting grid, cleared of tenement housing by the city's powerful and largely unaccountable redevelopment agency, local developers and offshore investors (increasingly Japanese) have planted a series of block-square complexes: Crocker Center, the Bonaventure Hotel and Shopping Mall, the World Trade Center, California Plaza, Arco Center, and so on. With an increasingly dense and self-contained circulation system linking these superblocks, the new financial district is best conceived as a single, self-referential hyperstructure, a Miesian skyscape of fantastic proportions.

5   Like similar megalomaniacal complexes tethered to fragmented and desolate downtowns—such as the Renaissance Center in Detroit and the Peachtree and Omni centers in Atlanta—Bunker Hill and the Figueroa corridor have provoked a storm of objections to their abuse of scale and composition, their denigration of street life, and their confiscation of the vital energy of the center, now sequestered within their subterranean concourses or privatized plazas. Sam Hall Kaplan, the former design critic of the *Times,* has vociferously denounced the antistreet bias of redevelopment; in his view, the superimposition of "hermetically sealed fortresses" and random "pieces of suburbia" onto Downtown has "killed the street" and "dammed the rivers of life."

Yet Kaplan's vigorous defense of pedestrian democracy remains grounded in liberal complaints about "bland design" and "elitist planning practices." Like most architectural critics, he rails against the oversights of urban design without conceding a dimension of foresight, and even of deliberate repressive intent. For when Downtown's new "Gold Coast" is seen in relation to other social landscapes in the central city, the "fortress effect" emerges, not as an inadvertent failure of design, but as an explicit—and, in its own terms, successful—socio-spatial strategy.

The goals of this strategy may be summarized as a double repression: to obliterate all connection with Downtown's past and to prevent any dynamic association with the non-Anglo urbanism of its future. Los Angeles is unusual among major urban centers in having preserved, however negligently, most of its Beaux Arts commercial core. Yet the city chose to transplant—at immense public cost—the entire corporate and financial district from around Broadway and Spring Street to Bunker Hill, a half-dozen blocks further west.

Photographs of the old Downtown in its 1940s prime show crowds of Anglo, black, and Mexican shoppers of all ages and classes. The contemporary Downtown "renaissance" renders such heterogeneity virtually impossible. It is intended not just to "kill the street" as Kaplan feared, but to "kill the crowd," to eliminate that democratic mixture that Olmsted believed was America's antidote to European class polarization. The new Downtown is designed to ensure a seamless continuum of middle-class work, consumption, and recreation, insulated from the city's "unsavory" streets. Ramparts and battlements, reflective glass and elevated pedways, are tropes in an architectural language warning off the underclass Other. Although architectural critics are usually blind to this militarized syntax, urban pariah groups—whether young black men, poor Latino immigrants, or elderly homeless white females—read the signs immediately.

MEAN STREETS

This strategic armoring of the city against the poor is especially obvious at street level. In his famous study of the "social life of small urban spaces," William Whyte points out that the quality of any urban environment can be measured, first of all, by whether there are convenient, comfortable places for pedestrians to sit. This maxim has been warmly taken to heart by designers of the high corporate precincts of Bunker Hill and its adjacent "urban villages." As part of the city's policy of subsidizing the white-collar residential colonization of Downtown, tens of millions of dollars of tax revenue have been invested in the creation of attractive, "soft" environments in favored areas. Planners envision a succession of opulent piazzas, fountains, public art, exotic shrubbery, and comfortable street furniture along a ten-block pedestrian corridor from Bunker Hill to South Park. Brochures sell Downtown's "livability" with idyllic representations of office workers and affluent tourists sipping cappuccino and listening to free jazz concerts in the terraced gardens of California Plaza and Grand Hope Park.

10 In stark contrast, a few blocks away, the city is engaged in a relentless struggle to make the streets as unlivable as possible for the homeless and the poor. The persistence of thousands of street people on the fringes of Bunker Hill and the Civic Center tarnishes the image of designer living Downtown and betrays the laboriously constructed illusion of an urban "renaissance." City Hall has retaliated with its own version of low-intensity warfare.

Although city leaders periodically propose schemes for removing indigents *en masse*—deporting them to a poor farm on the edge of the desert, confining them in camps in the mountains,

or interning them on derelict ferries in the harbor—such "final solutions" have been blocked by council members' fears of the displacement of the homeless into their districts. Instead the city, self-consciously adopting the idiom of cold war, has promoted the "containment" (the official term) of the homeless in Skid Row, along Fifth Street, systematically transforming the neighborhood into an outdoor poorhouse. But this containment strategy breeds its own vicious cycle of contradiction. By condensing the mass of the desperate and helpless together in such a small space, and denying adequate housing, official policy has transformed Skid Row into probably the most dangerous ten square blocks in the world. Every night on Skid Row is Friday the 13th, and, unsurprisingly, many of the homeless seek to escape the area during the night at all costs, searching safer niches in other parts of Downtown. The city in turn tightens the noose with increased police harassment and ingenious design deterrents.

One of the simplest but most mean-spirited of these deterrents is the Rapid Transit District's new barrel-shaped bus bench, which offers a minimal surface for uncomfortable sitting while making sleeping impossible. Such "bumproof" benches are being widely introduced on the periphery of Skid Row. Another invention is the aggressive deployment of outdoor sprinklers. Several years ago the city opened a Skid Row Park; to ensure that the park could not be used for overnight camping, overhead sprinklers were programmed to drench unsuspecting sleepers at random times during the night. The system was immediately copied by local merchants to drive the homeless away from (public) storefront sidewalks. Meanwhile Downtown restaurants and markets have built baroque enclosures to protect their refuse from the homeless. Although no one in Los Angeles has yet proposed adding cyanide to the garbage, as was suggested in Phoenix a few years back, one popular seafood restaurant has spent $12,000 to build the ultimate bag-lady-proof trash cage: three-quarter-inch steel rod with alloy locks and vicious out-turned spikes to safe-guard moldering fishheads and stale french fries.

Public toilets, however, have become the real frontline of the city's war on the homeless. Los Angeles, as a matter of deliberate policy, has fewer public lavatories than any other major North American city. On the advice of the Los Angeles police, who now sit on the "design board" of at least one major Downtown project, the redevelopment agency bulldozed the few remaining public toilets on Skid Row. Agency planners then considered whether to include a "free-standing public toilet" in their design for the upscale South Park residential development; agency chairman Jim Wood later admitted that the decision not to build the toilet was a "policy decision and not a design decision." The agency preferred the alternative of "quasi-public rest-rooms"—toilets in restaurants, art galleries, and office buildings—which can be made available selectively to tourists and white-collar workers while being denied to vagrants and other unsuit-ables. The same logic has inspired the city's trans-portation planners to exclude toilets from their designs for Los Angeles's new subway system.

Bereft of toilets, the Downtown badlands east of Hill Street also lack outside water sources for drinking or washing. A common and troubling sight these days is the homeless men—many of them young refugees from El Salvador—washing, swimming, even drinking from the sewer effluent that flows down the concrete channel of the Los Angeles River on the eastern edge of Downtown. The city's public health department has made no effort to post warning signs in Spanish or to mobi-lize alternative clean-water sources.

15   In those areas where Downtown profession-als must cross paths with the homeless or the working poor—such as the zone of gentrification along Broadway just south of the Civic Center—extraordinary precautions have been taken to ensure the physical separation of the different classes. The redevelopment agency, for example, again brought in the police to help design "twenty-four-hour, state-of-the-art security" for the two new parking structures that serve the *Los Angeles Times* headquarters and the Ronald Reagan State Office Building. In contrast to the mean streets outside, both parking structures incorporate beautifully landscaped microparks, and one even boasts a food court, picnic area, and historical exhibit. Both structures are intended to function as "confidence-building" circulation systems that allow white-collar work-ers to walk from car to office, or from car to bou-tique, with minimum exposure to the public street. The Broadway-Spring Center, in particu-lar, which links the two local hubs of gentrifica-tion (the Reagan Building and the proposed Grand Central Square) has been warmly praised by architectural critics for adding greenery and art to parking. It also adds a considerable dose of menace—armed guards, locked gates, and ubiquitous security cameras—to scare away the homeless and the poor.

The cold war on the streets of Downtown is ever escalating. The police, lobbied by Downtown merchants and developers, have broken up every attempt by the homeless and their allies to create safe havens or self-governed encampments. "Justiceville," founded by homeless activist Ted Hayes, was roughly dispersed; when its inhabi-tants attempted to find refuge at Venice Beach, they were arrested at the behest of the local coun-cil member (a renowned environmentalist) and sent back to Skid Row. The city's own brief exper-iment with legalized camping—a grudging response to a series of deaths from exposure dur-ing the cold winter of 1987—was abruptly termi-nated after only four months to make way for the construction of a transit maintenance yard. Current policy seems to involve perverse play upon the famous irony about the equal rights of the rich and poor to sleep in the rough. As the for-mer head of the city planning commission explained, in the City of the Angels it is not against the law to sleep on the street per se—"only to erect any sort of protective shelter." To enforce this proscription against "cardboard condos," the police periodically sweep the

Nickel, tearing down shelters, confiscating possessions, and arresting resisters. Such cynical repression has turned the majority of the homeless
into urban bedouins. They are visible all over
Downtown, pushing their few pathetic possessions in stolen shopping carts, always fugitive,
always in motion, pressed between the official
policy of containment and the inhumanity of
Downtown streets.

SEQUESTERING THE POOR

An insidious spatial logic also regulates the lives
of Los Angeles's working poor. Just across the
moat of the Harbor Freeway, west of Bunker Hill,
lies the MacArthur Park district—once upon a
time the city's wealthiest neighborhood.
Although frequently characterized as a no-
man's-land awaiting resurrection by developers,
the district is, in fact, home to the largest Central
American community in the United States. In the
congested streets bordering the park, a hundred
thousand Salvadorans and Guatemalans, including a large community of Mayan-speakers, crowd
into tenements and boarding houses barely adequate for a fourth as many people. Every morning at 6 A.M. this Latino Bantustan dispatches
armies of sewing *operadoras,* dishwashers, and
janitors to turn the wheels of the Downtown
economy. But because MacArthur Park is
midway between Downtown and the famous
Miracle Mile, it too will soon fall to redevelopment's bulldozers.

Hungry to exploit the lower land prices in
the district, a powerful coterie of developers, represented by a famous ex-councilman and the former president of the planning commission, has
won official approval for their vision of "Central
City West": literally, a second Downtown com-
prising 25 million square feet of new office and
retail space. Although local politicians have
insisted upon a significant quota of low-income
replacement housing, such a palliative will
hardly compensate for the large-scale population
displacement sure to follow the construction of
the new skyscrapers and yuppified "urban vil-

lages." In the meantime, Korean capital, seeking
lebensraum for Los Angeles's burgeoning
Koreatown, is also pushing into the MacArthur
Park area, uprooting tenements to construct
heavily fortified condominiums and office complexes. Other Asian and European speculators
are counting on the new Metrorail station, across
from the park, to become a magnet for new
investment in the district.

The recent intrusion of so many powerful
interests into the area has put increasing pressure upon the police to "take back the streets"
from what is usually represented as an occupying army of drug-dealers, illegal immigrants, and
homicidal homeboys. Thus in the summer of
1990 the LAPD announced a massive operation
to "retake crime-plagued MacArthur Park" and
surrounding neighborhoods "street by street,
alley by alley." While the area is undoubtedly a
major drug market, principally for drive-in Anglo
commuters, the police have focused not only on
addict-dealers and gang members, but also on
the industrious sidewalk vendors who have
made the circumference of the park an exuber-
ant swap meet. Thus Mayan women selling such
local staples as tropical fruit, baby clothes, and
roach spray have been rounded up in the same
sweeps as alleged "narcoterrorists." (Similar
dragnets in other Southern California communities have focused on Latino day-laborers congre-
gated at street-corner "slave markets.")

By criminalizing every attempt by the
poor—whether the Skid Row homeless or
MacArthur Park venders—to the public space for
survival purposes, law-enforcement agencies
have abolished the last informal safety-net separating misery from catastrophe. (Few third-world
cities are so pitiless). At the same time, the police,
encouraged by local businessmen and property
owners, are taking the first, tentative steps toward
criminalizing entire inner-city communities. The
"war" on drugs and gangs again has been the
pretext for the LAPD's novel, and disturbing,
experiments with community blockades. A large
section of the Pico-Union neighborhood, just

south of MacArthur Park, has been quarantined since the summer of 1989; "Narcotics Enforcement Area" barriers restrict entry to residents" on legitimate business only." Inspired by the positive response of older residents and local politicians, the police have subsequently franchised "Operation Cul-de-Sac" to other low-income Latino and black neighborhoods.

Thus in November 1989 (as the Berlin Wall was being demolished), the Devonshire Division of the LAPD closed off a "drug-ridden" twelve-block section of the northern San Fernando Valley. To control circulation within this largely Latino neighborhood, the police convinced apartment owners to finance the construction of a permanent guard station. Twenty miles to the south, a square mile of the mixed black and Latino Central-Avalon community has also been converted into Narcotic Enforcement turf with concrete roadblocks. Given the popularity of these quarantines—save amongst the ghetto youth against whom they are directed—it is possible that a majority of the inner city may

eventually be partitioned into police-regulated "no-go" areas.

The official rhetoric of the contemporary war against the urban underclasses resounds with comparisons to the War in Vietnam a generation ago. The LAPD's community blockades evoke the infamous policy of quarantining suspect populations in "strategic hamlets." But an even more ominous emulation is the reconstruction of Los Angeles's public housing projects as "defensible spaces." Deep in the Mekong Delta of the Watts-Willowbrook ghetto, for example, the Imperial Courts Housing Project has been fortified with chain-link fencing, restricted entry signs, obligatory identity passes—and a substation of the LAPD. Visitors are stopped and frisked, the police routinely order residents back into their apartments at night, and domestic life is subjected to constant police scrutiny. For public-housing tenants and inhabitants of narcotic-enforcement zones, the loss of freedom is the price of "security."

EXPLORATORY WRITING

Write a brief explanation of what Davis means by "genuinely democratic space." In preparation for this writing, review the underlinings and annotations you made as you read.

TALKING ABOUT THE READING

Davis writes, "The American city is being systematically turned inward. The 'public' spaces for the new megastructures and supermalls have supplanted traditional streets and disciplined their spontaneity." This statement represents a judgment about what American cities once were as well as an opinion about what they should be. With a group of your classmates, examine that judgment. How well does it correspond to your own notion of what American cities should be like. Do events like the September 11, 2001, attack on New York's World Trade Towers change your expectations for freedom and spontaneity in public spaces? How?

WRITING ASSIGNMENTS

1. Review your annotations and your exploratory writing in preparation for writing a summary of Davis's argument. What are his primary reasons for arguing that "The pleasure domes of elite Westside rely upon the social imprisonment of a third-world service proletariat in increasingly repressive ghettos and barrios"?

2. One of the issues current in urban planning is how to deal with the growing number of homeless men and women on the streets. Many city planners believe that any space that

has a lot of visible homeless people is going to keep others away. Create a "mental" map of your home town, your campus, or any place you have lived long enough to know well. Start with a real map of the place and identify four kinds of areas: (1) Areas where you will not go; (2) Areas you consider "ethnic"; (3) Areas of conflict; (4) Areas you consider "normal." Rewrite that original map so that your new map clearly identifies those four places.

After you have completed your map, write a key for it that explains what identifies each of these areas as safe or unsafe, comfortable or uncomfortable, foreign or familiar. Then write an introduction to your map in which you reflect on why certain places make you uncomfortable while others do not. What assumptions do you carry with you about place or the people you encounter that inform your way of thinking about these spaces? Consider, in your reflection, how the people in spaces that make you uncomfortable might feel in spaces that you feel are friendly and comfortable.

3. Davis levels strong charges against city planners, corporate interests, the city council, and other official agencies that have anything to do with how Los Angeles is divided, how public services are distributed and maintained, and where "urban renewal" programs will be sited. His analysis is based partially but not solely on his familiarity with the city he writes about. He also has spent time finding out the history of Los Angeles's urban developments, where funding is directed, what areas of the city are in most serious disrepair, and what the ethnic and racial demographics are in each section of the city.

You might not be able to do all of that, but you can map out the areas you think ought to be of most concern in the place where you grew up or the place with which you are most familiar. Choose a place (small town, city, subdivision, etc.) you know well or want to know well. Sketch a map of that place and explain what you consider the most important issues to emerge from examining how the place is planned and where most funding or development seems to be directed. Is there a "genuinely democratic space" available in this place? Does one section of the place seem to be segregated economically or racially from other sections? If you created a mental map for the previous writing assignment, draw on what you discovered about place from creating that map to help you make your decisions about what it takes to create a place where people from different walks of life and backgrounds might all feel safe. Write a report of what you found in your investigations. Present your report to the class.

SIGNS FROM THE HEART: CALIFORNIA CHICANO MURALS

■■—*Eva Sperling Cockcroft and Holly Barnet-Sánchez*

In his full-length work on Chicano culture in Los Angeles (*Anything but Mexican: Chicanos in Contemporary Los Angeles*), Rodolfo Acuña writes that "no space in East Lost Angeles is left unused or unmarked." For Acuña, Chicano or Latino culture has claimed, if not always the physical space, at least interpretive space—signs and images that mark a place as belonging to a certain group or person. Interpretive space is claimed in East Los Angeles primarily through the Los Angeles mural movement, which was begun in the 1960s, carried on today under the direction of the Social and Public Arts Resource Center (SPARC), and headed by artist and activist Judy Baca. In the following selection, artists Eva Cockcroft and Holly

Barnet-Sánchez write of the origins of the mural movement in Los Angeles. Their essay appeared in 1993 in the book *Signs from the Heart: California Chicano Murals.*

SUGGESTION FOR READING   Throughout this selection, Cockcroft and Barnet-Sánchez remind their readers that, though mural painting might have been considered high art in earlier periods when it was funded by church or state, by the time the Chicano mural movement had come to California, these highly realistic, working-class, public wall paintings were no longer valued by the art world. Instead, the mural movement became a part of the *barrioscape*—a sign of Chicano culture and a statement about Chicano politics. As you read, note how Cockcroft and Barnet-Sánchez explain the fall of murals from high to low in the art world. After you have completed your reading, write an informal response in which you speculate on why artists or art collectors care whether or not such public art is considered "high culture." Note down, as well, how you would differentiate "art" from "wall paintings"?

1   A truly "public" art provides society with the symbolic representation of collective beliefs as well as a continuing re-affirmation of the collective sense of self. Paintings on walls, or "murals" as they are commonly called, are perhaps the quintessential public art in this regard. Since before the cave paintings at Altamira some 15,000 years before Christ, wall paintings have served as a way of communicating collective visions within a community of people. During the Renaissance in Italy, considered by many to be the golden age of Western Art, murals were regarded as the highest form in the hierarchy of painting. They served to illustrate the religious lessons of the church and to embody the new Humanism of the period through artistic innovations like perspective and naturalistic anatomy.

After the Mexican Revolution of 1910–1917, murals again served as the artistic vehicle for educating a largely illiterate populace about the ideals of the new society and the virtues and evils of the past. As part of a re-evaluation of their cultural identity by Mexican-Americans during the Chicano movement for civil rights and social justice that began in the mid-1960s, murals again provided an important organizing tool and a means for the reclamation of their specific cultural heritage.

The desire by people for beauty and meaning in their lives is fundamental to their identity as human beings. Some form of art, therefore, has existed in every society throughout history. Before the development of a significant private picture market in Seventeenth Century Holland, most art was public, commissioned by royalty, clergy, or powerful citizens for the greater glory of their country, church, or city and placed in public spaces. However, after the Industrial Revolution and the development of modern capitalism with its stress on financial rather than social values, the art world system as we know it today with galleries, critics, and museums gradually developed. More and more, art became a luxury object to be enjoyed and traded like any other commodity. The break-up of the stable structures of feudal society and the fluidity and dynamism of post-Industrial society was reflected symbolically in art by the disruption of naturalistic space and the experimentation characteristic of Modernism.

Modernism has been a mixed blessing for art and artists. Along with a new freedom for innovation and the opportunity to express an individual vision that resulted from the loss of direct control by patrons of artistic production, artists experienced a sense of alienation from the materialistic values of capitalism, loss of a feeling of clearly defined social utility, and the freedom to starve. This unstable class situation and perception of isolation from society was expressed in the attitude of the bohemian *avant garde* artist who scorns both the crass commercialism of the bourgeoisie and the unsophisticated tastes of the working class, creating work exclusively for the appreciation of a new aristocracy of taste. Especially in the United States of the 1960s, for most people art had become an irrelevant and mysterious thing enjoyed only by a small educated elite.

5   When muralism emerged again as an important art movement in Mexico during the 1920s, the murals served as a way of creating a new national consciousness—a role quite similar to that of the religious murals of the Renaissance although directed toward a different form of social cohesion. Unlike the murals of the Italian Renaissance which expressed the commonly held beliefs of both rulers and masses, the Mexican murals portrayed the ideology of a worker, peasant, and middle class revolution against the former ruling class: capitalists, clergy, and foreign interests. Since that time in the eyes of many, contemporary muralism has been identified with poor people, revolution, and communism. This association has been a major factor in changing muralism's rank within the hierarchy of the "fine arts" from the highest to the lowest. Once the favored art of popes and potentates, murals, especially Mexican-style narrative murals, now considered a "poor people's art," have fallen to a level of only marginal acceptance within the art world.

The three great Mexican artists whose names have become almost synonymous with that mural renaissance, Diego Rivera, Jose Clemente Orozco, and David Alfaro Siqueiros, were all influenced by stylistic currents in European modernism—Cubism, Expressionism, and Futurism—but they used these stylistic innovations to create a new socially motivated realism. Rather than continuing to use the naturalistic pictorial space of Renaissance murals, the Mexicans explored new forms of composition. Rivera used a collage-like discontinuous space which juxtaposed elements of different sizes; Orozco employed non-naturalistic brushwork, distorted forms, and exaggerated light and dark, while Siqueiros added expressive uses of perspective with extreme foreshortening that made forms burst right out of the wall. The stylistic innovations of the Mexicans have provided the basis for a modern mural language

and most contemporary muralism is based to some extent or another on the Mexican model. The Mexican precedent has been especially important in the United States for the social realist muralists of the Works Progress Administration (WPA) and Treasury Section programs of the New Deal period and the contemporary mural movement that began in the late 1960s.

More than 2500 murals were painted with government sponsorship during the New Deal period in the United States. By the beginning of World War II however, support for social realist painting, and muralism in general, had ended. During the Cold War period that followed, realistic painting became identified with totalitarian systems like that of the Soviet Union, while abstraction, especially New York–style Abstract Expressionism, was seen as symbolizing individual freedom in *avant garde* art circles. By the early 1960s, only the various kinds of abstract art from the geometric to the bio-morphic were even considered to really be art. Endorsed by critics and the New York museums, abstraction was promulgated abroad as the International Style and considered to be "universal"—in much the same way as straight-nosed, straight-haired blondes were considered to be the "universal" ideal of beauty. Those who differed or complained were dismissed as ignorant, uncultured, or anti-American.

The concept of a "universal" ideal of beauty was closely related to the "melting pot" theory, then taught in schools, which held that all the different immigrants, races and national groups which composed the population of the United States could be assimilated into a single homogeneous "American." This theory ignored the existence of separate cultural enclaves within the United States as well as blatant discrimination and racism. It also ignored the complex dialectic between isolation and assimilation and the problem of identity for people like the Mexican-Americans of California who were neither wholly "American" nor "Mexican" but a new, unique, and constantly changing composite variously called "American of Mexican descent," "Mexican-American," Latino or Hispanic. In the 1960s the term "Chicano" with its populist origins was adopted by socially conscious youth as a form of positive self-identification for Mexican-Americans. Its use became a form of political statement in and of itself.[1]

The dialectic between assimilation and separatism can be seen in the history of Los Angeles, for example, first founded in 1781 as a part of New Spain. In spite of constant pressure for assimilation including job discrimination and compulsory use of English in the schools, the Mexican-American population was able to maintain a culture sufficiently distinct so that, as historian Juan Gómez-Quiñones has frequently argued, a city within a city can be defined. This separate culture continues to exist as a distinct entity within the dominant culture, even though it is now approximately 150 years since Los Angeles was acquired by the United States. This situation, by itself, tends to discredit the melting pot concept.

10   The Civil Rights Movement, known among Mexican-Americans as the Chicano Movement or *el movimiento,* fought against the idea of a "universal" culture, a single ideal of beauty and order. It re-examined the common assumption that European or Western ideas represented the pinnacle of "civilization," while everything else, from the thought of Confucius to Peruvian portrait vases, was second-rate, too exotic, or "primitive." The emphasis placed by Civil Rights leaders on self-definition and cultural pride sparked a revision of standard histories to include the previously unrecognized accomplishments of women and minorities as well as a re-examination of the standard school curriculum. Along with the demonstrations, strikes, and marches of the political movement came an explosion of cultural expression.

As was the case after the Mexican Revolution, the Civil Rights Movement inspired a revival of muralism. However, this new mural movement differed in many important ways from the Mexican one. It was not sponsored by a successful revolutionary government, but came out of the struggle by the people themselves against the *status quo.* Instead of well-funded projects in government buildings, these new murals were located in the *barrios* and ghettos of the inner cities, where oppressed people lived. They served as an inspiration for struggle, a way of reclaiming a cultural heritage, or even as a means of developing self-pride. Perhaps most significantly, these murals were not the expression of an individual vision. Artists encouraged local residents to join them in discussing the content, and often, in doing the actual painting. For the first time, techniques were developed that would allow non-artists working with a professional to design and paint their own murals. This element of community participation, the placement of murals on exterior walls in the community itself, and the philosophy of community input, that is, the right of a community to decide on what kind of art it wants, characterized the new muralism.

Nowhere did the community-based mural movement take firmer root than in the Chicano communities of California. With the Mexican mural tradition as part of their heritage, murals were a particularly congenial form for Chicano artists to express the collective vision of their community. The mild climate and low, stuccoed buildings provided favorable physical conditions, and, within a few years, California had more murals than any other region of the country. As home to the largest concentration of Mexicans and people of Mexican ancestry anywhere outside of Mexico City, Los Angeles became the site of the largest concentration of Chicano murals in the United States. Estimates range from one thousand to fifteen hundred separate works painted between 1969 and the present. The Social and Public Art Resource Center's "California Chicano Mural Archive" compiled in 1984 documents close to 1000 mural projects throughout the state in slide form.

Because Chicano artists were consciously searching to identify the images that represented their shared experience they were continually led back to the *barrio*. It became the site for "finding" the symbols, forms, colors, and narratives that would assist them in the redefinition of their communities. Not interested in perpetuating the Hollywood notion that art was primarily an avenue of escape from reality, Chicano artists sought to use their art to create a dialogue of demystification through which the Chicano community could evolve toward cultural liberation. To this end, murals and posters became an ubiquitous element of the *barrioscape*. According to Ybarra-Frausto, they publicly represented the reclamation of individual Chicano minds and hearts through the acknowledgement and celebration of their community's identity through the creation of an art of resistance.

Prior to the Chicano movement, U.S. Mexicans were defined externally through a series of derogatory stereotypes with total assimilation as the only way to break out of the situation of social marginalization. Art that integrated elements of U.S. Mexican or *barrio* culture was also denigrated as "folk" art and not considered seriously. The explosion of Chicano culture and murals as a result of the political movement, provided new recognition and value for Chicano art which weakened the old barriers. According to Sánchez-Tranquilino, this experience allowed artists to figuratively break through the wall that confined artists either to the *barrio* or to unqualified assimilation. It gave them the confidence to explore new artistic forms and a new relationship to the dominant society.

NOTE

1. Throughout this book several terms are used to identify Americans of Mexican descent: "Mexican-Americans," "U.S. Mexicans," and "Chicanos." Each carries specific meanings and they are not used interchangeably. "Mexican-American" is primarily a post World War II development in regular use until the politicization of *el movimiento*, the Chicano civil rights movement of the 1960s and 1970s. Its use acknowledges with pride the Mexican heritage which was hidden by an earlier, less appropriate term, "Spanish-American." However, its hyphenated construction implies a level of equality in status between the Mexican and the American which in actuality belies the unequal treatment of Americans of Mexican descent within United States society.

U.S. Mexican is a term developed by essayist Marcos Sánchez-Tranquilino to replace the term Mexican-American with one that represents both more generally and clearly all Mexicans within the United States whether their families were here prior to annexation in 1848, have been here for generations, or for only two days. In other words, it represents all Mexicans living within U.S. borders regardless of residence or citizenship status.

The most basic definition of the term Chicano was made by journalist Ruben Salazar in 1970: "A Chicano is a Mexican-American who does not have an Anglo image of himself." It is a term of self-definition that denotes politicization.

EXPLORATORY WRITING

This selection consists of portions of an introduction to a collection of essays about California Chicano murals. The authors set the mural movement in the larger context of public art throughout history as a way of explaining what murals have meant in the past and what they have come to mean today. After you read this selection, write a detailed outline that traces the rise and fall of murals from high art to popular expression as described by Cockcroft and Barnet-Sánchez.

TALKING ABOUT THE READING

The introduction to this selection notes that Chicano murals have claimed an "interpretive space" in Los Angeles. As Cockcroft and Barnet-Sánchez write, these murals "publicly represented the reclamation of individual Chicano minds and hearts through the acknowledgment and celebration of their community's identity through the creation of an art of resistance." With a group of your classmates, discuss why it might be important for a group such as the one described in this selection to claim a space through art or signs or language or music (i.e., interpretive space). In what ways do other groups or people that you know claim interpretive space?

WRITING ASSIGNMENTS

1. Write an essay in which you discuss how a knowledge of the mural movement, as it is outlined in the selection above, either changes or reinforces the impression that you have of Los Angeles from television and film portrayals of that place.

2. Write an essay that examines why it might be important for marginalized groups to claim interpretive space through images or signs as in the mural movement. Do you know of any strategies similar to the mural movement that other groups use to claim interpretive space? Draw on your reading on Los Angeles and the mural movement to help you with this writing. You might also draw on experiences in your own town, city, or school to help you explain why those who feel like outsiders need to claim interpretive space with images or signs.

3. Cockcroft and Barnet-Sánchez write, "Prior to the Chicano movement, U.S. Mexicans were defined externally through a series of derogatory stereotypes." Watch a film that includes or deals with Latinos in the United States (e.g., *Selena, Mi Familia, The Bronze Screen,* or *A Walk in the Clouds*) and write an essay in which you address that comment. In what ways do the characters and their situations break with the familiar stereotypes? In what ways are those stereotypes perpetuated? Before you begin your essay (and even before you begin watching one of these films), make a list of familiar stereotypes. If you are unsure of the common Latino stereotypes, ask classmates, friends, and family to help you.

VISUAL ESSAY   Claiming Interpretive Space

In her *New Yorker* profile of Banksy (published May 14, 2007), writer Laura Collins describes the artist in this way:

> The British graffiti artist Banksy likes pizza, though his preference in toppings cannot be definitively ascertained. He has a gold tooth. He has a silver tooth. He has a silver earring. He's an anarchist environmentalist who travels by chauffeured S.U.V. He was born in 1978, or 1974, in Bristol, England—no, Yate. The son of a butcher and a housewife, or a delivery driver and a hospital worker, he's fat, he's skinny, he's an introverted workhorse, he's a breeze-shooting exhibitionist given to drinking pint after pint of stout. For a while now, Banksy has lived in London: if not in Shoreditch, then in Hoxton.

The Wikipedia entry on Banksy calls him a "pseudo-anonymous English graffiti artist." Even his own Web site (Banksy.co.uk) offers little more than samples of the artist's work and a manifesto detailing the origins of his radicalism. That, of course, is the way Banksy prefers things. Very little is known for certain about the graffiti artist who works at night to create detailed, radical statements about power and conflict—local and international.

In Banksy's introduction to *Wall and Piece,* a 2005 collection of his work, the artist challenges critics who would put graffiti in the category of vandalism rather than art. For Banksy, graffiti is not only art but the most democratic of art forms. He writes, "Graffiti is not the lowest form of art. Despite having to creep about at night and lie to your mum, it's actually the most honest artform available. There is no elitism or hype, it exhibits on some of the best walls a town has to offer, and nobody is put off by the price of admission." Banksy often uses his work to comment on that high-art/low-art divide so common in some critics' circles. In one piece, for example, Banksy depicts a city worker sandblasting cave-paintings—perhaps the earliest form of "graffiti." In another, he portrays a museum guard keeping an eye on graffiti—in this case, a painting of an art frame surrounding the scrawled words, "Smash the System."

Graffiti artists worldwide have long had to dodge police in order to make their art on public walls. For Banksy, the people's right to claim public walls as open space for free expression is inherent in a free society.

For that reason, Banksy uses his art to make bold—sometimes outrageous—statements on local politics, social conditions, and even on other art forms. One piece shows aid workers being held back while news reporters and documentary photographers take pictures of a small child, bleeding and standing among the rubble of what used to be a home. In one of his most famous acts of guerilla street art, Banksy managed to sneak up to the West Bank wall and paint what appeared to be a hole in the wall looking onto a calm and luxurious beach scene. In England, Banksy's graffiti art typically comments on police harassment, closed circuit surveillance cameras, and living conditions. Using detailed stencils prepared in advance, Banksy can work quickly to create remarkably detailed murals and signs.

Ironically, his art has become so popular and well-respected by many in the contemporary art world that local museums and village councils have acted to preserve and protect it. In several of these attempts, however, the council paints over what it considers the offensive part of the image, leaving behind a well-crafted painting with the satire blunted or eliminated entirely.

SUGGESTION FOR READING You can find image files for Banksy's art throughout the Internet and especially at Banksy's official website www.banksy.co.uk. Take some time to look over that site. Read Banksy's manifesto. As you look at the images reprinted here, consider what you see in relationship to Banksy's assertion that public walls are public spaces for all of us to use as places for free speech and free expression and especially as places to stand in opposition to the world of commerce.

EXPLORATORY WRITING

In his introduction to *Wall and Piece,* Banksy argues for the rights of (and even the necessity for) street artists to begin "speaking up." In a brief writing, simply describe what you see in the images reprinted here and suggest your own reading for what is going on in each and why the authorities might be so quick to want to remove them from public walls.

TALKING ABOUT THE VISUAL ESSAY

Share your exploratory writing with 2 or 3 of your classmates. How do your readings of these images differ? What does each reading add to the others?

WRITING ASSIGNMENTS

1. In his introduction to *Wall and Piece,* Banksy writes that "graffiti is only dangerous in the mind of three types of people: politicians, advertising executives, and graffiti writers." Write an essay in which you explain how that is the case. What, in the reprints of his work here, might seem dangerous to any of those?

2. In their discussion of the Chicano Mural Movement, Cockcroft and Barnet-Sánchez are careful to make a distinction between mural art and the mural movement and graffiti. The first they consider real "art." The second (graffiti) they would not classify as art at all. Write an essay in which you compare the aims of the mural movement as Cockcroft and Barnet-Sánchez explain it to the aims of graffiti as Banksy understands it. How are the two different? Where might they share common ground?

3. Banksy's work is clearly that of a social critic, someone who is consciously making visual statements about politics and social concerns. Look around the city or town where you live. Where is there graffiti? In what ways is it a protest? Is all graffiti protest of some sort?

What would Banksy say to that question? At the heart of this topic is the question "Who has the right to determine what is placed on public walls?" Write a review of the graffiti in your city or town that addresses these issues. How does it compare (not in skill but in purpose) to Banksy's work?

MAKING CONNECTIONS
Public Roadsides, Private Grief:
Roadside Memorials and Public Policy

Most of us have seen them along the highways and along back roads as we drive across the country: roadside crosses, wreathes, and other memorials marking the sites of fatal accidents. Every now and then, the roadside memorial features a grouping of crosses, each with the name of a victim, certainly a site where several people died. Most people don't stop to read these handmade memorials. They have become a part of the landscape in this country, where thousands of drivers and passengers are killed on highways every year. It might seem odd, then, that what is essentially a private expression of grief could be at the heart of a controversy. After all, what does it matter if someone wants to erect a memorial to a lost loved one?

The problem is that roadside memorials are placed on what is essentially public land—the state and local road system—and that alone puts them at the center of a dispute over what rights any of us have to place signs of any sort on public roads and highways and whether religious icons can be placed freely on public roads (most memorials are small wooden crosses, though some are elaborate shrines and some are large, sturdy structures).

These memorials are also at the center of cultural tradition for many people, especially those in the southwest regions of the country. Writer Rudolfo Anaya explains the origins of roadside memorials, called *descansos* in the Southwest:

> The first descansos were resting places where those who carried the coffin from the church to the camposanto paused to rest. In the old villages of New Mexico, high in the Sangre de Cristo Mountains or along the river valleys, the coffin was shouldered by four or six men.
>
> Led by the priest or preacher and followed by mourning women dressed in black, the procession made its way from the church to the cemetery. The rough hewn pine of the coffin cut into the shoulders of the men. If the camposanto was far from the church, the men grew tired and they paused to rest, lowering the coffin and placing it on the ground. The place where they rested was the descanso.
>
> The priest prayed; the wailing of the women filled the air; there was time to contemplate death. Perhaps someone would break a sprig of juniper and bury it in the ground to mark the spot, or place wild flowers in the ground. Perhaps someone would take two small branches of piñon and tie them together with a leather thong, then plant the cross in the ground.

Rested, the men would shoulder the coffin again, lift the heavy load, and the procession would continue. With time, the descansos from the church to the cemetery would become resting spots. . . .

Time touches everything with change. The old descanso became the new as the age of the automobile came to the provinces of New Mexico. How slow and soft and deeper seemed the time of our grandfathers. Horses or mules drew the wagons. "Voy a preparar el carro de vestia," my grandfather would say. I remember the sound of his words, the ceremony of his harnessing the horses.

Yes, there have always been accidents, a wagon would turn over, a man would die. But the journeys of our grandfathers were slow, there was time to contemplate the relationship of life and death. Now time moves fast, cars and trucks race like demons on the highways, there is little time to contemplate. Death comes quickly, and often it comes to our young. Time has transformed the way we die, but time cannot transform the shadow of death.

I remember very well the impact of the car on the people of the llano and the villages of my river valley. I remember because I had a glimpse of the old way, the way of my grandfather, and as a child I saw the entry of the automobile.

One word describes the change for me: violence. The cuentos of the people became filled with tales of car wrecks, someone burned by gasoline while cleaning a carburetor, someone crippled for life in an accident. The crosses along the country roads increased. Violent death had come with the new age. Yes, there was utility, the ease of transportation, but at a price. Pause and look at the cross on the side of the road, dear traveler, and remember the price we pay.

From "Introduction/Dios da y Dios quita," in *Descansos: An Interrupted Journey*, by Rudolfo Anaya, Juan Estevan Arellano, and Denise Chavez (1995).

As you read the following two articles on the debate over roadside memorials, keep in mind the complexity of this issue, one that touches private pain, public land rights, cultural traditions, separation of church and state, and even free speech issues.

ROADSIDE CROSSES: CENTURIES-OLD TRADITION CAN STIR CONTROVERSY

▬— L. Anne Newell

Anne Newell is a staff reporter for the *Arizona Daily Star*. The following story was printed in the *Star* on Tuesday, September 3, 2002.

SUGGESTION FOR READING Before you read, look up the Department of Transportation regulations for your state on roadside memorials or crosses.

1 It used to be that Michael Sanchez didn't think a lot about the eight white crosses standing near his family's house.

They'd been there since his family moved to the neighborhood in 1998, like silent soldiers, a lingering memory of a car collision that killed eight people, five of them children.

Then Sanchez's father died in February in a car accident at Interstate 10 and Palo Verde Road. The family put a cross there.

"I think they're really important," Sanchez, 18, says now. "It's a memorial for people to know what happened."

5   Roadways across the country are dotted with crosses and other markers. It's at least a centuries-old tradition, a Tucson folklorist said— a way for the living to remember those they have lost and a religious ceremony for some, to mark the holy spot where a soul has left a body.

But they're not without controversy. One such memorial is the focus of a court battle in Colorado. And officials across the country are finding different ways to handle the markers.

Tucson folklorist Jim Griffith said the memorials began in Arizona in the Catholic community for people who died without having the chance to be absolved of sin.

They lined trails in their early days, and passers-by would stop, light a candle or say a prayer, Griffith said.

In 1783, the bishop of Sonora asked Spanish military authorities to forbid the practice because it discouraged other settlers, Griffith said. It was forbidden, he said, but it didn't stop.

10   The state Highway Patrol used white crosses in the 1940s and 1950s to mark the places motorists died, Griffith said. It has stopped the practice, but the markers continue to be placed by others.

"There still are people who take these as an indication they should say a prayer for the repose of the people who died there," he said.

In New Mexico, where people have made grave markers out of flowers, pumpkins, tin cans and other materials since Spanish rule, memorials are protected as "traditional cultural properties" through the Historic Preservation Division.

Last year, roadside memorials, also known as descansos (resting places), crucitas and memorias, were banned as traffic hazards in North Carolina.

California memorials are "discreetly removed" as road hazards, except when a victim was killed by a drunken driver who is convicted. Then, the state will erect a sign for $1,000.

15   In Florida, the state will put up a nondenominational marker for free, upon request.

In West Virginia, memorials are protected by a 2000 statute and can remain indefinitely if registered with the state.

And in Idaho last year, legislators replaced a program under which gold stars were placed at accident sites with a policy allowing roadside memorials.

Arizona traffic officials say they don't mind the memorials—if they aren't permanent and don't cause traffic hazards or impede road maintenance.

"There's really not a law or a written policy," said Walt Gray, a state Transportation Department spokesman. "Our general policy is we leave them there."

20   Crews will even move a memorial rather than remove it.

"We recognize that it's something important to the families for their closure," Gray said.

Michael Graham, spokesman for the city's Transportation Department, and Carol Anton, in community relations in the county Transportation Department, said their agencies' stances are similar. They just ask people to be cautious in erecting the signs.

"This is a very sensitive issue," Graham said. "People are mourning, and they need an opportunity to mourn."

That opportunity has led to a court battle in Colorado.

25   Brian Rector, 18, died in March 1998 when his Ford Escort was hit by a semi.

After the cremation and funeral, a family friend took some 2-by-4s and paint and fashioned a 3-foot-tall white cross, inscribing it "Son, Brother, Friend."

Relatives added flowers and small angel figurines.

"Because we don't have a cemetery plot to go to," Rector's mother, Deena Breeden, said, "we definitely want to keep up the memorial forever."

A driver who often passed Rector's memorial and others disagreed—and took action one night in April 2000.

30   A state trooper saw Rodney Lyle Scott's truck on the side of the road with its hazard lights on. A collection of flowers and wooden crosses was in the bed.

Scott told the trooper he was "cleaning up the interstate." Thinking Scott had permission, the trooper let him go.

Soon, the Breedens and other families noticed their memorials missing and complained. They found a sympathetic ear at the office of Adams County District Attorney Robert Grant.

Scott, identified through his license number taken by the trooper, was charged with "desecration of a venerated object" and faced the possibility of six months in jail and a $750 fine.

"I had gone through a lot of personal turmoil myself," Scott said. "I didn't appreciate somebody else throwing their hurt and sorrow out for the public view, as if it was more important than someone else's."

35   Denver attorney Bob Tiernan, a member of the Madison, Wis.-based Freedom From Religion Foundation, offered to represent Scott for free.

The memorials "are using public property to endorse religion," Tiernan said. "It's a violation of the U.S. Constitution, as far as I'm concerned, and it's a serious distraction."

In April 2001, Tiernan won acquittal for Scott when a judge ruled the Rector memorial was "discarded refuse" and "unlawful advertising" under the law, not a venerated object.

The district attorney appealed and said he'll take the case to the state Supreme Court.

The memorials, he said, "are to venerate the life and passing of the person involved in the fatal accident, and at the same time serve the public purpose in getting people to slow down."

40   The Breedens were allowed to put a memorial back up—its cross removed, they said, to keep from offending anyone—without receiving a citation.

Michael Oscar Sanchez was 43 when he was thrown from his truck in February as it rolled across I-10 near Palo Verde.

He'd been eastbound on I-10 when he veered off the road, scraping along a guardrail for nearly 100 feet. He overcorrected, driving across the eastbound lanes and into the median, where his truck rolled and he was thrown outside. The vehicle flipped once and came to rest in the westbound lanes.

A white cross memorializes the spot now, marked with his name, birth date and death date.

"I think they should leave it there," Sanchez's son said as he stood outside his family's home, about 50 feet from the large collection of crosses at West Corona and South San Fernando roads.

45   Other memorials dot the streets in this South Side neighborhood. They mark the roads on the Tohono O'odham Reservation. And, increasingly, they're appearing all around Tucson, in various forms.

The one near the Sanchez house marks where Carlos Manuel Peralta ran a stop sign going about 65 mph in 1997, plowing into a minivan and killing eight members of two families. Peralta was sentenced to more than 200 years in prison.

It was one of the worst car crashes in Tucson's history. Neighbors have maintained the memorial since, and the victims' relatives still visit it. Stuffed animals, dried and silk flowers, and a rock border mark the spot, which Sanchez says he thinks of differently now.

But the Pima Community College freshman—who's studying administrative justice—doesn't think every state should be as lenient as Arizona.

He suggests standards for states where the memorials are being challenged.

50   "I think it should be a state-by-state decision," he said. "If it distracts someone, I don't think it should be there."

Joe Villa Jr., who raced out of his home to help the victims of the 1997 crash and whose family keeps watch over the memorial with other neighbors, said it's important to the neighborhood and the relatives of the victims.

"I think it shows a lot of people what can happen when you drink and do drugs and don't pay attention to the road signs," he said. "It's important for the family, too. They can leave a remembrance. They bring flowers or something. The spirits went to God in this spot."

EXPLORATORY WRITING

Although this might seem a straightforward news report on roadside memorials and state law, it actually touches on personal pain and the right to use publicly owned space to memorialize a loved one. Write an exploratory piece in which you detail the arguments each stakeholder makes in this controversy. Don't try to resolve those arguments. At this point, you simply want to sort them out.

TALKING ABOUT THE READING

Rudolfo Anaya makes it clear that, though these memorials are Catholic in origin, they also are a part of the culture of Mexicans and Indians who have lived in the Southwest for many generations. With a group of your classmates, discuss to what extent, then, the memorials (and the disputes surrounding them) should be thought of in terms of separation of church and state? Is this a religious issue? Why? Why not?

WRITING ASSIGNMENT

Write an essay in which you consider the many functions these memorials perform. Are they warnings to drivers? Religious proselytizing? Family memorials? Why, in addition to the difficulty many people have dealing with the sudden death of a loved one, would anyone want to display grief in this way? Look back at what the families Newell interviewed said to her. Use those statements to help you detail what function these memorials perform.

MEMORIALS CAUSE CONTROVERSY

██—*Jeff Burlew*

Jeff Burlew is a staff writer for the *Tallahassee Democrat*. This story appeared in that paper in November 2003. In it, Burlew reports on one memorial cross that sparked new regulations on all roadside markers in Florida.

SUGGESTION FOR READING As you read, underline and annotate the arguments each side uses in the controversy over roadside memorials.

1 After James H. "Jim" Ward Jr. was killed in a crash at Gum and Aenon Church roads, his family placed an 8-foot wooden cross near the scene to remember him.

Ward, 45, died March 18, 2002, when a Leon County school bus ran a stop sign in foggy weather and crashed into his pickup truck. Family members put up the custom-made cross in July 2002.

But about a year after the cross went up, the county's public works department took it down and placed it in storage because of complaints from a nearby business owner.

And last month, county commissioners unanimously approved a new memorial-marker policy that bans homemade crosses from county roadways. Under the policy, the county will erect round memorial markers at a family's request that say "Drive Safely" and list the crash victim's name.

5 Ward's widow, Lynn Ward of Greensboro, is upset by the removal of the cross and the new policy on roadside memorials. She said she got permission from the county and others before putting up the cross.

"I feel this is very unfair because our cross was up before this new policy came into effect," she wrote in a letter to the Democrat. "Does this mean others will have to fear that their cross will be taken down too. After all, what is it hurting to put up a cross in memory of someone you loved and lost."

Jeanie Lewis, owner of Jeanie's Beauty Salon, said she didn't object when the Ward family called and asked to put up a cross in front of her business. She and her husband, Larry, were among the first on the scene the morning of the crash.

But Lewis said the cross was too big and blocked her own business sign. She complained to the county and asked Commissioner Jane Sauls, who represents her district, for help.

"It was a beautiful cross, but it just needed to be somewhere else," Lewis said. "I've been here for 27 years. Why should I be blocked?"

10 County officials said they tried to be sensitive to the Ward family in handling the cross issue. And they said the policy was needed because homemade memorials can interfere with maintenance of the right of way and even pose dangers for motorists and mourners. They based their policy and the markers themselves on the Florida Department of Transportation's policy and signs.

"We want a way to honor those people that have lost their lives and do it in a way that doesn't obstruct signs or even your vision on the right of way," Sauls said. "We really looked at it as a positive thing."

The markers are 15 inches in diameter and stand about 31/2 feet high. None has gone up yet because no one has asked for one, according to Dale Walker, the county's road superintendent.

The signs cost the county about $100 to make and install but are offered to the public for free.

The policy states that all homemade memorials along county-maintained roads will be removed immediately, although both state and county officials said road crews don't aggressively look for them.

Family members or friends with family permission can ask the county to put up the new markers, which the county will maintain for a year. They must reapply after a year to keep them up.

15 This isn't the first time government policies over memorial markers have led to controversy. In 1997, the state decided against moving forward with a policy that would have replaced homemade memorials along state-maintained roads with white crosses, which also symbolize safety.

After atheist and Jewish groups complained about the crosses, the state came up with the round "Drive Safely" signs. Since then, more than 1,800 memorial signs have gone up across the state, according to DOT spokesman Dick Kane.

"I think it's been very successful for the families out there who want to memorialize their loved ones," Kane said, adding that the memorials also remind motorists to use caution behind the wheel.

But Ward and others said the county and state memorial signs are impersonal. The families of two boys killed in a 1988 crash on U.S. Highway 27 put up crosses on private property to remember them. Marsha Long, whose son, Stevie, died in the crash, said the round signs don't convey the same message as crosses.

"What is a little round circle sticking in the ground?" she asked. "It means nothing. If you see a cross, you know something happened."

20 Some, however, are happy to see roadside crosses go. Dan DeWiest contacted the Democrat recently to complain about two crosses placed off Apalachee Parkway near an entrance to Wal-Mart.

"While I believe in the freedom of religious expression," he wrote in an e-mail, "I don't think that [it] is fair to promote one religion over any other religion on public property."

Ward, however, still is hoping the county will let her put up the cross. Her attorney, J. C. O'Steen, said the family would rather not take legal action but hasn't ruled it out. Ward wrote that crosses should be allowed if they make grieving families feel better.

"Everyone should realize that it's not always someone else facing a tragedy," she wrote. "Sometimes, it's you."

EXPLORATORY WRITING

Write a summary of the issues at the center of this dispute over roadside memorials.

TALKING ABOUT THE READING

Burlew uses people's stories and reactions to set up the controversy raging over a specific memorial as well as spontaneous memorials in general. With a group of your classmates, discuss how those stories help Burlew cover the larger controversy. How does Burlew's choice of what to quote from his interviews contribute to how he characterizes this controversy? Could he tell this story as well without the individual stories and interviews?

WRITING ASSIGNMENT

With camera or sketchbook in hand, take a drive along your own local highways and take pictures of, sketch, or write a description of the roadside memorials you see. Which ones might be seen as a driving hazard? Do any of these memorials tell the story of what happened in that place? Are any maintained regularly? If you hadn't been looking for them, would you have noticed most of them? After you have finished your survey, report your findings to the class.

WRITING SEQUENCE

1. Reread each selection to refresh your memory on the nature of this controversy. If you did exploratory writing, review that before you begin this assignment. For this paper, write a longer exploratory essay in which you explain the complexities of this controversy as you understand them from your reading here. Don't settle for a "who is right" argument, and don't try to settle the dispute. Instead, explain the dimensions of this debate. Explain what Newell, Burlew, and Anaya (quoted in the introduction to this sequence) each contribute to an understanding of the dimensions of this debate.

2. For this essay, begin by reviewing the exploratory writing you just completed in which you set forth the issues and its many dimensions. Now go back to the news reports and reread several of the interviews that make up the bulk of each report. Write a 2–3 page essay in which you explain the role of these private and very painful stories in the way this controversy has been reported. To what extent do they clarify the controversy? To what extent do they muddy the issue?

3. If you followed our suggestion for reading before when you began this sequence, you have already looked up your state's Department of Transportation regulations on roadside memorials or crosses. If you did not, then begin this paper with a search of the state's DOT Web site. Most states post their regulations there. You can also contact the DOT in your state if you can't locate the regulations online. For this culminating assignment, write a longer essay (drafted, revised, and edited) in which you make an argument for how a state

should address this issue. In your discussion, explain the many public and private dimensions of this controversy and the difficulty any legislative body must have when making decisions on roadside memorials. Consider both the stories of people who erect the memorials and those who are offended by them. Make sure you take into account current state regulations and consider traditions or native practices if they apply in your state.

VISUAL CULTURE   The Troubled Landscape

Most of us have taken pictures of the places where we grew up or visited on vacation. The fact that Ansel Adams's landscape photographs of the West continue to be extremely popular—as calendar art, in museum retrospectives, as posters, and more—is a tribute to the beauty of those photographs and, perhaps, to the hopefulness of Adams's audience. Americans like to think of the land as something beautiful and free. Landscape photography, hearkening back to the great landscape paintings that came before it, has traditionally captured that sort of beauty. It very typically pictures an uninhabited land, one unmarred by human presence, unchanged by time. The very nature of landscape art, then, is to picture the ideal.

That convention of picturing the ideal has led more recent landscape photographers like Robert Adams and Richard Misrach to recreate this genre in an attempt to capture both beauty and the ravages of industrialization. Landscape in the context of growing industry, environmental health hazards, and the loss of the land as free and open space shares the haunting beauty of traditional landscapes at the same time that it reveals the reality of living with waste.

With the following essay by Jason Berry and the Richard Misrach photos that accompany it, we invite you to reconsider your notion of what landscape photography can be, especially in a land troubled by chemical spills, air and water pollution, and urban sprawl.

CANCER ALLEY: THE POISONING OF THE AMERICAN SOUTH

— Jason Berry—with photographs by Richard Misrach

Jason Berry is a freelance investigative reporter based in New Orleans. Richard Misrach has photographed the American desert for much of his career. His beautiful, startling photographs of such images as nuclear waste in a strikingly beautiful landscape can be both powerful and frightening. Like photographer Robert Adams before him, Misrach rarely photographs an untouched landscape. The photographs here appeared in *Aperture* (Winter 2001) along with Berry's essay "Cancer Alley."

SUGGESTION FOR READING In the library, look up the issue of the magazine *Aperture* (Winter 2001) where this essay and photographs originally appeared. Spend some time looking at all of the Misrach photographs that accompany the article. Berry also mentions Misrach's Desert Cantos photographs and the photographs of Clarence Laughlin. Look at those in the library or online so that you have a good notion of what Berry is talking about when he writes about Misrach's work.

1   "Baton Rouge was clothed in flowers, like a bride—no, much more so; like a greenhouse. For we were in the absolute South now," wrote Mark Twain of the vistas from a riverboat in his 1883 classic *Life on the Mississippi*. "From Baton Rouge to New Orleans," he continued, "the great sugar-plantations border both sides of the river all the way, and stretch their league-wide levels back to the dim forest of bearded cypress in the rear. The broad river lying between the two rows becomes a sort of spacious street."

Twain caught the ninety-mile river corridor between the old Capitol and New Orleans at a poignant moment. Plantations still harvested profits in cotton and sugarcane; the black field workers, no longer slaves, were sharecroppers or virtual serfs. The river flowed through a land riddled with injustice. Yet there was beauty in the waterway and surrounding landscape, and beauty—although burdened with an unsavory history—in those old houses of "the absolute South," with their porticoes and pillared balconies.

By the 1940s, when Clarence John Laughlin trained his lens upon the area, some of the mansions had been torn down and others lay in ruins. The wrecked buildings riveted his eye as much as the several dozen that were still preserved (then starting to shift from farming to tourist sites, which most remain today). A haunting sense of loss suffuses the black-and-white surrealism in Laughlin's remarkable book *Ghosts Along the Mississippi*.

Between the time of Twain's reportage and Laughlin's elegiac photographs from the mid-twentieth century, oil and petrochemical producers bought up vast pieces of land along the river and began grafting an industrial economy over the old agricultural estates. The refineries and plants—like the derricks that dot the Cajun prairie and the oil-production platforms in Louisiana coastal waters off the Gulf of Mexico—boosted the economies of communities once mired in poverty. The downside has been a political mentality blind to the ravages of pollution.

ORIGINS OF CANCER ALLEY

5   Standard Oil opened a refinery in 1909 on the fringes of Baton Rouge. In 1929 Governor Huey P. Long erected the new Capitol, a thirty-four-story Art Deco tower near the Standard plant. Today that political temple stands out in high relief from the expanded grid of pumping stacks and smoke clouds where Exxon (Standard's successor) functions like a city-within-the-city. The Capitol and the massive oil complex issuing pungent clouds have melded into an awesome symbol of Louisiana politics: pollution as the price of power.

Providence Plantation, which dated to the 1720s, was in the river town of Des Allemands, and on its grounds was a massive tree known as the Locke Breaux Live Oak, which was 36 feet around and 101 feet high, with a limb span of 172 feet. That majestic tree, estimated to be over three hundred years old, died from exposure to pollution in 1968: the new owner of its site, Hooker Chemical, had it cut up and removed.

The human toll has been even more harsh.

By the 1980s, according to the Louisiana Office of Conservation, thousands of oil-waste pits, many leaching toxic chemicals, were scattered across Louisiana; hundreds of them were seeping into areas of the fertile rice belt in Cajun country. As awareness spread about groundwater contamination and diseases in communities along the river's industrial corridor, activists began calling the area "Cancer Alley."

Although Louisiana ranks in the top 10 percent of states in terms of its cancer mortality rate, petrochemical interests dismiss the term "Cancer Alley" as factually unsupported, a provocation. Black irony coats their charge.

10   The Louisiana Chemical Association provided base funding for the state Tumor Registry, which assembles the data on cancers. The registry is undertaken by a division of the Louisiana State University Medical Center, which is a beneficiary of donations from polluting industries. Louisiana's Tumor Registry, unlike those in most other states, offers no reliable data on incidences of childhood cancer, or incidences by parish (county), or incidences on a yearly basis. It reports trends only in larger geographic groupings; as a result, disease clusters cannot be pinpointed. Rare forms of cancer can't be tracked geographically. Much information gathered by physicians who treat cancer patients is anecdotal.

And that, in the opinion of Dr. Patricia Williams, is just the way business and petrochemical lobbyists want it. "Without reliable data, no one can link disease patterns to pollution," says Williams, who is herself a professor at the LSU Medical School, and is at the forefront of attempts to change the system.

"We're being denied the raw data and it's unconscionable," says Williams. "Embryonic tumors are not being reported as they are diagnosed. Raw data, by parish, would allow prevention programs. If you see a particular trend of brain cancers, you could begin to sort out what's going on. . . . The same [holds true] with cancer clusters."

Despite the state's history of being at or near the top of statistical lists in categories of toxic emissions, plaintiff attorneys have a great deal of trouble getting medical data to prove the impact of pollution in a given community.

Like Clarence John Laughlin before him, Richard Misrach captures the tones of a culture in spiritual twilight—clinging to a past beauty in the old mansions and icons of Catholicism—now facing a darkness brought about by big oil. Misrach's use of color sets him apart from Laughlin stylistically, as does his striking sense of juxtapositions: the petrochemical specters shadowing fields, ponds, buildings, cemeteries, and basketball courts. Misrach's commitment to discovering the ravaged landscape, while conceptually similar to Laughlin's, is rooted in the land itself. His long-term exploration of the American West and its defilement, the epic "Desert Cantos," are relentlessly straightforward. The "Bravo 20" series of the late 1980s—photographs of Nevada's disturbingly stunning bombing ranges—allow the terrain to create its own dark metaphors. Misrach's work reveals the primary emblems and moods of these frightening landscapes; the Louisiana images are thus as mysterious as they are horrific.

CITIZENS TAKE A STAND

15   Clarence Laughlin was a romantic who saw industry in symbolic terms—machine against man. In 1980, he took a firm stand at a news conference in New Orleans, lashing out against a plan to put the world's largest toxic-waste incinerator next to the historic Houmas House plantation, in Ascension Parish, midway along the river corridor south of Baton Rouge. A California-based company called Industrial Tank (I.T.) had begun with a $350,000 grant from the state government in Baton Rouge for a site feasibility study. I.T. recommended the construction of a massive disposal complex on a piece of land that was a proven flood plain, below sea level, in an already congested industrial road fronting the Mississippi River. In a move that reeked of corrupt politics, state officials then awarded I.T. the necessary permits to build the complex—whose feasibility I.T. had just been paid to assess. (In fact, the company had put money down on the land before it even got the permits.)

Reports soon surfaced that I.T. had pollution problems at its California sites, and was utterly inexperienced in managing a project of the scope envisioned in Louisiana. A citizens' group filed suit against I.T. and the state. In 1984, the state Supreme Court threw out the permits, killing the project. By then, activists were challenging industry over other conflicts.

DYNAMICS OF CHANGE

Amos Favorite, a seventy-eight-year-old black man, is now retired after many years in the union at Ormet Aluminum. Favorite grew up speaking the Creole French patois in the town of Vacherie, where Fats Domino was born. He remembers when ponds were blue. As a teenager he moved to nearby Geismar, where he has lived ever since.

"This was a good place to live at one time," says Favorite. "All the meat was wild game. I was raised on rabbits, squirrels, and deer." He hated work in the fields, however, and when he came home from infantry in World War II, Favorite bought a dozen acres of Geismar plantation, which was being sold off at thirty-five dollars an acre. The town is named for the family that owned the estate. Favorite's nine children grew up on his acreage; one of his sons was building a handsome two story house next door to Amos Favorite's this past August.

One of his daughters, artist Malika Favorite, was the first black child to desegregate the local white school. Because of that, two KKK members tried to dynamite the family home. Before they could set the charge, Amos Favorite took his shotgun and started blasting. "I gave 'em the red ass, yes I did," he laughs. "They went runnin' to the sheriff, but that sheriff didn't do nothin' to me."

20   That was in 1968. A few years later, Favorite began to realize that people were getting sick from wells that drew water from the local aquifer, and he started speaking out against Ascension Parish's sacred cow: industry. BASF, the largest chemical company in the world, and Vulcan, which produces perchloroethylene (the chemical that goes into dry cleaning fluid) have plants in the area.

(Untitled), Norco, Louisiana, 1998 from "Cancer Alley" © Richard Misrach.

Playground and Shell refinery.

Holy Rosary Cemetery and Union Carbide complex.

Holy Rosary Cemetery and Union Carbide Complex, Taft, Louisiana, 1998 from "Cancer Alley" © Richard Misarach.

Despite opposition from management at thirteen major plants in Geismar, including BASF and Vulcan, Favorite won support from union members in those industries for his attempt to establish a public water system and separate district for Geismar. Favorite found a valuable ally in Willie Fontenot, the environmental investigator in the state attorney general's office. Fontenot has made a career of helping communities organize and gather research against polluters and unresponsive state agencies.

"The local government in Ascension had failed to provide adequate water," says Fontenot. "Amos Favorite and the Labor Neighbor project [a cross section of activists from various walks of life] broke the impasse and got the Baton Rouge water company to extend piping and set up a distribution system in Ascension to supplant the old private wells. . . . It was a pretty big victory for a ragtag citizens' group."

The most recent "ragtag" victory came in the town of Convent, where a company called Shintech wanted to build a huge chemical plant in an area of low-income black residents. Tulane University's Environmental Law Clinic helped the citizens challenge the state's operating permits, citing new EPA standards to guard against environmental racism. Shintech pulled out, and found another site, rather than risk being the first major test case of EPA's guidelines. The law clinic took a pounding from Governor Mike Foster and the State Supreme Court, which issued a ruling that severely restricts law students from working with community groups on environmental cases.

The people who live and work in this region of the Mississippi take a long view of their struggle. "The pendulum is going to swing," says Dr. Williams, who lives in LaPlace, twenty miles upriver from New Orleans. "Pollution is such a problem that people are becoming aware of cancers in their friends. They're becoming suspicious. Ten or fifteen years from now, what has happened to big tobacco companies is going to happen to industries that are polluting here." A surge of civil-damage suits against industry is inevitable, she predicts, "because there has been such a concerted effort to conceal what's happened."

TALKING ABOUT THE READING

With a group of your classmates, look carefully at Misrach's photos of "Cancer Alley" and then offer a reading of them as, in Berry's words, "geography, autobiography, and metaphor." One way to examine photos like the ones Misrach takes is to look for what they are saying about the place they depict. In photos detailing pollution or the consequences of heavy industry, there is the implication that the scene should (or did) appear different before the impact of industrial waste. In other words, we have the sense that either something is missing or that something is very out of line—like the photo of Holy Rosary cemetery with Union Carbide as a backdrop. Look carefully at this photo. How do you read it? What is Misrach trying to convey with the subject he has chosen and the way in which he framed the photo? What stands out? What contrasts or contradictions do you notice? What is the metaphor—the meaning outside the photo?

WRITING FROM THE READING

Berry writes, "Misrach's work reveals the primary emblems and moods of these frightening landscapes; the Louisiana images are thus as mysterious as they are horrific." Most of Misrach's photos are also quite beautiful. Write an essay in which you explain what Misrach achieves in finding beauty in this pollution. Is there a way in which the beautiful can undercut the history of abuse that Berry writes of?

SUGGESTED ASSIGNMENT

Photographer Robert Adams once wrote that we rely on landscape photography "to make intelligible to us what we already know." Make your own photographic record of a specific landscape as it has been affected by industry or development. Once you have completed your project, write a reflection in which you examine your photographs in terms of the truths they tell about the landscape and the way it is changing. In your reflection, consider what the photographs reveal that "we already know" but that is often hidden in calendar or postcard landscape photography.

FILM CLIP   Analyzing Set Design: Cities in Decay

For many filmmakers, set design plays as important a role in conveying the meaning, tone, and symbolic action of a film as does the story, acting, and camera work. Whether you are looking at the classic haunted castle and dark corridors of a horror film or the too-clean attempt at realism in small-town dramas, set design is one key to understanding what the filmmaker is getting at.

The dystopia film genre provides especially rich opportunities for analyzing set design. Contrary to a utopian vision that presents an impossibly ideal world, the dystopian world often seems impossibly broken. It is an image of a future world gone mad. From Fritz Lang's 1927 classic *Metropolis* to Ridley Scott's 1982 *Blade Runner* to Frank Miller's 2005 film adaptation of his graphic novel *Sin City,* the dystopic world is often an urban setting that has much in common with the city as we know it, though just a bit off. *The Eternal Sunshine of the Spotless Mind,* for example, looks more like our world than the Los Angeles of *Blade Runner,* and yet both are dystopias. On the other hand, the setting of *The Truman Show* seems to be a perfect little town until Truman discovers that he is not living in that world at all.

Choose one of the films listed here or another in the dystopia genre. Watch the film, paying particular attention to the film's set design. You can use the following questions to help you focus your analysis:

- Where is the film set?
- How would you describe the world in which the film takes place?
- To what extent is the set realistic? To what extent is it imaginary?
- What does the dystopic setting of this film say about the world we are currently living in?
- How does the setting contribute to the overall theme or storyline of the film?
- What features of the film's future world are recognizable to you so that that could be in any city or town today? What effect does that familiarity have for you as an audience to either accept or reject the world of the film?

Film Suggestions

Blade Runner	*Demolition Man*
Metropolis	*The Terminator*
Eternal Sunshine of the Spotless Mind	*Hellboy*
Sin City	*V for Vendetta*
Brazil	*I am Legend*

FIELDWORK   Observing the Uses of Public Space

In 1980, William Whyte published findings from nearly a decade of fieldwork in the streets of New York City which sought to reveal what Whyte called "the behavior of ordinary people on city streets." To do that, Whyte, as the director of the New York Street Life Project, set up teams of observers, used time-lapse photography to monitor activity in the streets, and mapped the spaces to see if the design of the space might influence how people use that space.

One of Whyte's most basic, though important discoveries in this study had to do with why people gather in some places and not in others. After observing people in several plazas similar in most respects except in the number of people who tended to hang around each space, Whyte's team came to this conclusion: *People tend to sit most where there are places to sit.*

> This may not strike you as an intellectual bombshell, and, now that I look back on our study, I wonder why it was not more apparent to us from the beginning. Sitting space, to be sure, is only one of the many variables, and, without a control situation as a measure, one cannot be sure of cause and effect. But sitting space is most certainly prerequisite. The most attractive fountains, the most striking designs, cannot induce people to come and sit if there is no place to sit.

> —From *The Social Life of Small Urban Spaces*

Whyte discovered that it didn't matter much whether there were actual chairs and benches. It just mattered if there were places to sit—even low walls with room to sit were enough to encourage people to hang around.

THE PROJECT

The purpose of your fieldwork project is to find a space where people hang out—a campus common area, for example, or a public park—and study how people use the space and what in the space actually invites people to sit and stay.

With a group of your classmates, make at least three visits—at different times of the day—to see how well the space is suited for gathering. Who hangs out there? How do they spend their time? Where do they sit? How long do they stay? When you have completed your project, present your observations to the class, making sure you focus on your conclusions about why this space is a popular one for gathering or just hanging out. Detail the features your group observed that make the space inviting and easy to rest or spend time in.

Mapping the Space

When you begin your observation, sketch a map of the space. Note the layout of the place. How large is the space? What kind of furniture, if any, is available for sitting? How is the furniture arranged? Can it be moved? How do people enter the space? Make any important notes about the way the space is arranged on this map. If there is no furniture, where do people sit? How comfortable is the space for gathering or finding privacy? If you reproduce your map on a transparency or put it in a program that will project images, you can use your sketch as a visual when you present your findings to the class.

Watching People

Begin by keeping as accurate a count of people as you can. Don't try to get too much information or guess at too much. Note how long people stay and where they sit. Your aim here is to get as accurate a picture as possible of how many people use the space, how easy it is for them to sit, where they sit, and for how long. Make sure you include the details of these observations in your report.

For more information on writing a report from fieldwork observations, review instructions on writing a report in the fieldwork assignment in Chapter 3 (p. 187).

MINING THE ARCHIVE   Take a Walking Tour

We normally think of an archive as a collection of papers or documents. Yet a city, town, or national park area can also function as a kind of archive—a place where you will find sites of historic, political, or cultural importance.

Certainly one of the best ways to learn about a public space and its archival potential is to take a walking tour. Cities, towns, local and national parks, botanical gardens, museums, campuses, cemeteries, and historical buildings across this country have walking tours designed to show visitors the history of the place; the best places to shop; popular restaurants; homes of poets, artists, and politicians; little-known places of historic interest; and more. These tours usually include a step-by-step guide to the places on the tour, an easy-to-follow map, and a thumbnail description of the importance of each stop.

Begin this project by locating several sample walking tours. Most travel guides in local bookstores and public libraries will include walking tours. For example, Frommer's guide to San Francisco includes a walking tour of Chinatown. *The Eyewitness Travel Guide to New York* includes walking tours of Greenwich Village, Lower Manhattan, and the Upper East Side. There are even alternative walking tours such as Bruce Kayton's *Radical Walking Tours of New York City,* whose maps include the homes of leftists, anarchists, and radicals who are often left out of the commercial guides or locally produced maps designed for most tourists.

Bring the walking tours you have located to class for a general discussion of what walking tours include, what they leave out, and how they identify public space.

A good walking tour should have the following:

- A focus or theme.
- A clear map.
- A brief description of each stop on the tour.
- Information about how to get there, how long the tour will take, and what difficulties a walker might encounter.

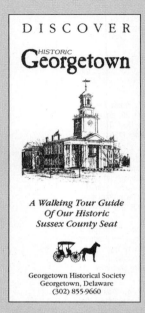

D I S C O V E R

HISTORIC
Georgetown

*A Walking Tour Guide
Of Our Historic
Sussex County Seat*

Georgetown Historical Society
Georgetown, Delaware
(302) 855-9660

Displayed here are portions of a walking tour of historic Georgetown, Delaware. Study the map and entries we have selected from the guide's description of each stop. When you have a good sense of what a walking tour entails, make a walking tour of a place you know well. Be sure to draw a clear map and time the walk. Give your tour a theme or focus. Your tour can focus on people, places, events, whatever ties the place together as a historical resource. You can even create an underground tour—of campus dorms or the library or the place where you grew up—that, like Bruce Kayton's *Radical Walking Tours of New York City*, highlights the people, places, and events in the history of that city not considered mainstream or not usually shown to visitors.

Georgetown was established in 1791 by an act of the Delaware General Assembly removing the Sussex County Seat of government from Lewes on the coast to a more central location. The site of the Town was purchased on May 9, 1791, and surveyed into 60 x 120 foot lots, which were sold to defray the cost of the land purchase.

The Town was eventually laid out in a circle one half mile in all directions from The Circle and it was governed directly by the legislature until the mid-1800s. The circular boundary was broken in 1986.

Although relatively young for many communities in Sussex County, Georgetown has some of the finest homes and unique architectural styles in Delaware.

Enjoy your tour through our historic County Seat.

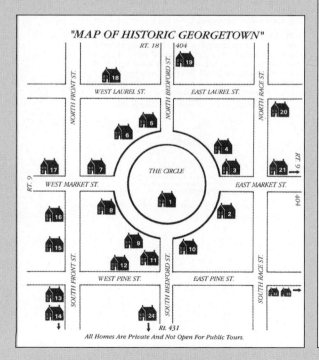

"MAP OF HISTORIC GEORGETOWN"

All Homes Are Private And Not Open For Public Tours.

1. **The Circle.** Or Public Square designed by Commissioner Rhoads Shankland following the purchase of 76 acres for the new Sussex County seat on May 9, 1791. Legend has it that a slave girl named Liz was responsible for plowing the center of the Town Square and planting the trees there. The Circle is on the National Register of Historic Places.

2. **New Sussex County Courthouse.** *1 The Circle.* Designed by renowned architect William Strickland, the structured was built between 1837-1839 on the same location as the Old Courthouse. The portico and cupola were added in 1914.

3. **Town Hall.** *39 The Circle.* Formerly the site of a Tavern built in 1820 and called the "Rising Sun," the brick structure was built in 1921 for the Delaware Trust Company. The building was donated to the Town in 1965 by Wilmington Trust Company.

4. **Old Fire Hall.** *37 The Circle.* The first fire apparatus was purchased in 1831 and the Georgetown Fire Company was organized in 1903. The company moved to the old firehall building on The Circle in 1930 and to their new building on South Bedford Street in 1966.

5. **The Mansion House.** *28 The Circle.* The Greek Revival style of the front section of the structure dates to 1830-1866. The older back portion is believed to have been constructed in 1799. The home was once owned by Charles Sudler Richards, who served as Delaware Secretary of State and Chief Justice of the State Supreme Court.

6. **The Paynter House.** *26 The Circle.* Constructed in the early 1800s, the house was occupied by the Paynter Family, which owned Clayfield Farm for a time. The Paynter Family included physicians, a bank president, and a Delaware Supreme Court Justice.

7. Dr. Joseph B. Waples House. *4 West Market Street.* Constructed in the 1800s, the house was home to the Town's dedicated physician. His office was next to his home adjacent to Sussex County Family Court.

8. The Brick Hotel. *18 The Circle.* The inn was constructed in 1836 and served as the Sussex County Courthouse during construction of the new Courthouse.

9. Old Farmers Bank. *13 The Circle.* Farmer's Bank was chartered in 1807 and a fine brick structure built in 1852. The present Georgian-style structure was constructed in 1971. Farmers Bank was sold in 1981. Mellon Bank acquired the bank in 1983.

10. Old Georgetown Post Office. *2 The Circle.* After 33 separate postmasters and post offices scattered throughout the Town, the cornerstone of the old post office was laid on June 4, 1932 and cost $63,452. The structure was acquired in 1994 by the Sussex County Council as meeting chambers and councilmanic offices.

11. Old Sussex County Courthouse. *10 South Bedford Street.* Constructed in 1791-1792 to meet the exact dimensions of the former County Courthouse in Lewes and moved from its original Circle location in 1837 to make way for the present courthouse. The structure was restored in 1976 and is the oldest wooden Courthouse still in use by the court system (on occasion). The building is open for public tours on the first Wednesday of each month and by appointment. For tour information call 855-9660.

12. New Century Club Building. *10 West Pine Street.* Constructed in 1926, the building now houses the Georgetown Library.

13. The Sorden-Rollins House. *103 West Pine Street.* The Greek Revival style structure was constructed between 1791-1801.

14. Clayfield Farm. *228 South Front Street.* The home was built in 1841 by the son of U.S. Senator William Wells and once owned by Judge James M. Tunnell, Jr., a Delaware Supreme Court Justice.

15. The Benton Harris House. *14 South Front Street.* The front section of the house was constructed in 1795 by Georgetown's first storekeeper. When he became postmaster in 1799, the home became the post office as was the custom at the time.

16. Dr. Stephen Green House. *8 South Front Street.* The oldest section of the house dates to before 1810 and in about 1868 had a three-bay section added. Dr. Green was a physician and served as Justice of the Peace in 1836 and 1851.

17. The Judges. *104 West Market Street.* Built in 1809 by Judge Peter Robinson, the Early-Georgian structure has served as the home of several judges, State Supreme Court Justices and two Delaware Secretary's of State.

18. The Peter S. Faucett House. *11 West Laurel Street.* An excellent example of joining two separate 3-bay houses, the oldest section was believed to have been constructed about 1830.

19. The Alfred Robinson House. *112 North Bedford Street.* Constructed on The Circle before 1800, this grand residence was moved to its present location in 1857. The giant Magnolia tree is said to have been a gift of a sea captain in the late 1850s.

20. Wesley United Methodist Church. *10 North Race Street.* It is said that Francis Asbury preached in what would become the Town as early as 1779, although no edifice was constructed until 1802 on West Pine Street near the Church cemetery. Two church buildings later, the present sanctuary was constructed in 1896. The parsonage was added in 1907.

21. Masonic Lodge. *151 East Market Street.* Constructed in 1843, the Masonic Hall was called the Georgetown Academy and was built with funds raised through a lottery approved by the Legislature for construction of the school on the first floor. The Academy closed in 1885 and the portico was added in 1920.

22. St. Paul's Episcopal Church. *122 East Pine Street.* Organized in 1794, a wood frame structure was built in 1804. The brick structure was constructed in 1844. A fire in 1987 destroyed the parish house in the rear. It was rebuilt in 1990.

23. The Old Academy. *104 East Pine Street.* Private school instruction began in Georgetown in 1812 and its first building was constructed in 1836, it was so named to distinguish it from the Masonic Hall, called the New Academy. Near St. Paul's Church, Georgetown School was constructed in 1885.

24. Nutter D. Marvel Museum. *508 South Bedford Street.* A collection of unique structures displaying memorabilia and photographs of old Georgetown and Sussex County and several historic horse drawn carriages assembled by Mr. Marvel and donated to the Town of Georgetown after his death in 1988. The Museum is operated by the Georgetown Historical Society. For tour information call 855-9660.

Cover art courtesy of local artist Ellen H. Rice.

SUSSEX COUNTY
CONVENTION & TOURISM COMMISSION

Funding for this project was provided in part by the Association of Sussex County Chambers of Commerce and Convention and Visitors Bureau, Inc.

Storytelling

Tomine/The New Yorker, © Conde Nast Publications.

PRICE $4.50   **THE**   FEB. 25, 2008

NEW YORKER

Experience which is passed on from mouth to
mouth is the source from which all storytellers
have drawn. And among those who have
written down the tales, it is the great ones
whose written version differs least from the
speech of the many nameless storytellers.

—Walter Benjamin, *The Storyteller*

"Why to think of it, we're in the same tale still!
It's going on. Don't the great tales never end?"
"No, they never end as tales," said Frodo. "But
the people in them come, and go when their
part's ended. Our part will end later—or
sooner."

—J. R. R. Tolkein, *The Two Towers*

S torytelling is a persistent form of popular entertainment, whether people tell
ghost stories around a campfire or watch the electronic glow of a television set.
Every culture has its own storytelling tradition of myths, legends, epics, fables,
animal stories, fairy tales, and romances. Listeners take delight in the mythic powers
of their heroes, laugh at the comic predicaments clowns and tricksters get themselves

into, and feel awe—and sometimes terror—when they hear stories of unseen worlds and the supernatural. In every storytelling tradition, there is a repertoire of stock characters and plots that listeners recognize immediately—and know how to respond to through laughter, tears, excitement, fear, and grief.

But the fact that people everywhere, in all known cultures, tell stories only raises a series of questions we will ask you to explore in this chapter. We will be asking you to recall stories from the past and present to think about the functions storytelling performs, the occasions on which stories are told, and the people who tell stories. The reading and writing assignments in this chapter will ask you to look at some of the stories circulating today.

One of the key functions of storytelling, aside from entertaining listeners, is a pedagogical one. Stories teach. As one of the oldest forms of human communication, stories are important ways young people learn about the world and what their culture values. In early societies, stories were passed along orally from generation to generation. The elders were responsible for initiating young people into the lore of the tribe or culture. In many respects, the same is true today in the mass-media world of contemporary America. To be an adult and a full member of society means knowing the stories a particular culture tells about the world and about itself.

What's more, the kinds of stories people tell teach them as much about who they want to be and how they want to live as about who they are now. The stories uncover fears and desires. They comfort and disturb. Even the fantasy worlds storytellers create look amazingly like the real world they live in—only much better—with heroes who know what to do and villains so evil it's impossible not to know they are the bad guys. Storytelling is, then, as much about understanding and reordering the world as it is about entertaining.

People love to tell and listen to stories about politicians, celebrities, and professional athletes—who is dating whom, who is getting divorced, who is checking into a drug or alcohol abuse clinic, who is under investigation for what. These kinds of stories—personal anecdotes, gossip, bits and pieces of the evening news—may seem so trivial that they don't really merit the title of storytelling. But although telling and listening to these stories may appear to be no more than a way to pass the time with family, neighbors, coworkers, and friends, in fact this type of storytelling performs a useful social function within local communities. As people tell and listen to stories, perhaps without fully recognizing it, they are working out their own attitudes and evaluations of a wide range of social realities, from relations between the sexes to politics.

If you have seen such popular television and film genres as family sitcoms, hospital dramas, soap operas, action adventure stories, science fiction, mysteries, westerns, and slasher flicks, you already know about many of the conventions of storytelling. In each, the cast of characters is a familiar one: interracial cop teams, superheroes, cyberpunks, urban vigilantes, gangsters, android terminators, martial arts masters, hard-boiled private eyes, cowboys, swinging singles, career women, men behaving badly, dumb parents, and precocious kids. These popular figures inhabit fictional worlds—the western frontier, the criminal underworld, interstellar space, the mean streets of the city, the middle-class homes of the suburbs—where they are working out the aspirations and anxieties of average people while dealing with whichever conflict threatens to overturn their/our world.

RED SKY IN THE MORNING

—*Patricia Hampl*

Patricia Hampl is Regents' Professor at the University of Minnesota, where she teaches creative writing. She is a poet and memoirist, a writer who tells stories of her own life. She teaches in Minneapolis and lives in St. Paul, where she has spent most of her life. In 1990, she was awarded a prestigious MacArthur Fellowship in part for her first book-length memoir *A Romantic Education* (1981). "Red Sky in the Morning" appeared in *I Could Tell You Stories* (1999), Hampl's collection of essays devoted to memoir.

SUGGESTION FOR READING Although many people associate storytelling with fiction, most of us have also experienced the long tradition of storytelling that is characteristic of family or town stories, stories that recall local or family history and the people that made up that history. In her brief essay on memoir, Hampl raises the question of what kinds of incidents, people, or memories make it into the family stories we tell. Before you read, think about a story you remember an adult in your life telling—one you would be willing to share with others. Write about why that story stays with you. Is the story about family? About the person who told it? About how people treat one another? Why do you think it is worth remembering or not?

1 Years ago, in another life, I woke to look out the smeared window of a Greyhound bus I had been riding all night, and in the still-dark morning of a small Missouri river town where the driver had made a scheduled stop at a grimy diner, I saw below me a stout middle-aged woman in a flowered housedress turn and kiss full on the mouth a godlike young man with golden curls. But I've got that wrong: *he* was kissing *her*. Passionately, without regard for the world and its incomprehension. He had abandoned himself to his love, and she, stolid, matronly, received this adoration with simple grandeur, like a socialist-realist statue of a woman taking up sheaves of wheat.

Their ages dictated that he must be her son, but I had just come out of the cramped, ruinous half sleep of a night on a Greyhound and I was clairvoyant: This was that thing called love. The morning light cracked blood red along the river.

Of course, when she lumbered onto the bus a moment later, lurching forward with her two bulging bags, she chose the empty aisle seat next to me as her own. She pitched one bag onto the overhead rack, and then heaved herself into the seat as if she were used to hoisting sacks of pota-

toes onto the flatbed of a pickup. She held the other bag on her lap, and leaned toward the window. The beautiful boy was blowing kisses. He couldn't see where she was in the dark interior, so he blew kisses up and down the side of the bus, gazing ardently at the blank windows. "Pardon me," the woman said without looking at me, and leaned over, bag and all, to rap the glass. Her beautiful boy ran back to our window and kissed and kissed, and finally hugged himself, shutting his eyes in an ecstatic pantomime of love-sweet-love. She smiled and waved back.

Then the bus was moving. She slumped back in her seat, and I turned to her. I suppose I looked transfixed. As our eyes met she said, "Everybody thinks he's my son. But he's not. He's my husband." She let that sink in. She was a farm woman with hands that could have been a man's; I was a university student, hair down to my waist. It was long ago, as I said, in another life. It was even another life for the country. The Vietnam War was the time we were living through, and I was traveling, as I did every three weeks, to visit my boyfriend who was in a federal prison. "Draft dodger," my brother said.

"Draft resister," I piously retorted. I had never been kissed the way this woman had been kissed. I was living in a tattered corner of a romantic idyll, the one where the hero is willing to suffer for his beliefs. I was the girlfriend. I lived on pride, not love.

5 My neighbor patted her short cap of hair, and settled in for the long haul as we pulled onto the highway along the river, heading south. "We been married five years and we're happy," she said with a penetrating satisfaction, the satisfaction that passeth understanding. "Oh," she let out a profound sigh as if she mined her truths from the bountiful, bulky earth, "Oh, I could tell you stories." She put her arms snugly around her bag, gazed off for a moment, apparently made pensive by her remark. Then she closed her eyes and fell asleep.

I looked out the window smudged by my nose which had been pressed against it at the bus stop to see the face of true love reveal itself. Beyond the bus the sky, instead of becoming paler with the dawn, drew itself out of a black line along the Mississippi into an alarming red flare. It was very beautiful. The old caution—*Red sky in the morning, sailor take warning*—darted through my mind and fell away. Remember this, I remember telling myself, hang on to this. I could feel it all skittering away, whatever conjunction of beauty and improbability I had stumbled upon.

It is hard to describe the indelible bittersweetness of that moment. Which is why, no doubt, it had to be remembered. The very word—*Remember!*—spiraled up like a snake out of a basket, a magic catch in its sound, the doubling of the m—*re memmemem*—setting up a low murmur full of inchoate associations as if a loved voice were speaking into my ear alone, occultly.

Whether it was the unguarded face of love, or the red gash down the middle of the warring country I was traveling through, or this exhausted farm woman's promise of untold tales that bewitched me, I couldn't say. Over it all rose and remains only the injunction to remember. This, the most impossible command we lay upon ourselves, claimed me and then perversely disappeared, trailing an illusive silken tissue of meaning, without giving a story, refusing to leave me in peace.

Because everyone "has" a memoir, we all have a stake in how such stories are told. For we do not, after all, simply *have* experience; we are entrusted with it. We must do something—make something—with it. A story, we sense, is the only possible habitation for the burden of our witnessing.

10 The tantalizing formula of my companion on the Greyhound—*oh, I could tell you stories*—is the memoirist's opening line, but it has none of the delicious promise of the storyteller's "Once upon a time . . . " In fact, it is a perverse statement. The woman on the bus told me nothing— she fell asleep and escaped to her dreams. For the little sentence inaugurates nothing, and leads nowhere after its *dot dot dot* of expectation. Whatever experience lies tangled within its seductive promise remains forever balled up in the woolly impossibility of telling the-truth-the-whole-truth of a life, any life.

Memoirists, unlike fiction writers, do not really want to "tell a story." They want to tell it *all*—the all of personal experience, of consciousness itself. That includes a story, but also the whole expanding universe of sensation and thought that flows beyond the confines of narrative and proves every life to be not only an isolated story line but a bit of the cosmos, spinning and streaming into the great, ungraspable pattern of existence. Memoirists wish to tell their mind, not their story.

The wistfulness implicit in that conditional verb—*I could tell*—conveys an urge more primitive than a storyteller's search for an audience. It betrays not a loneliness for someone who will listen but a hopelessness about language itself and a sad recognition of its limitations. How much reality can subject-verb-object bear on the frail shoulders of the sentence? The sigh within the statement is more like this: I could tell you stories—if only stories could tell what I have in me to tell.

For this reason, autobiographical writing is bedeviled. It is caught in a self which must become a world—and not, please, a narcissistic world. The memoir, once considered a marginal literary form, has emerged in the past decade as the signature genre of the age. "The triumph of memoir is now established fact," James Atlas trumpeted in a cover story on "The Age of the Literary Memoir" in the *New York Times Magazine.* "Fiction," he claimed, "isn't delivering the news. Memoir is."

With its "triumph," the memoir has, of course, not denied the truth and necessity of fiction. In fact, it leans heavily on novelistic assumptions. But the contemporary memoir has reaf-firmed the primacy of the first person voice in American imaginative writing established by Whitman's "Song of Myself." Maybe a reader's love of memoir is less an intrusive lust for confession than a hankering for the intimacy of this first-person voice, the deeply satisfying sense of being spoken to privately. More than a story, we want a voice speaking softly, urgently, in our ear. Which is to say, to our heart. That voice carries its implacable command, the ancient murmur that called out to me in the middle of the country in the middle of a war—remember, remember (*I dare you, I tempt you*).

15 Looking out the Greyhound window that red morning all those years ago, I saw the improbable face of love. But even more puzzling was the cryptic remark of the beloved as she sat next to me. I think of her more often than makes sense. Though he was the beauty, she is the one who comes back. How faint his golden curls have become (he also had a smile, crooked and charming, but I can only remember the idea of it—the image is gone). It is she, stout and unbeautiful, wearing her flowery cotton housedress with a zipper down the middle, who has taken up residence with her canny eye and her acceptance of adoration. To be loved like that, loved improbably: of course, she had stories to tell. She took it for granted in some unapologetic way, like being born to wealth. Take the money and run.

But that moment before she fell asleep, when she looked pensive, the red morning rising over the Mississippi, was a wistful moment. *I could tell you stories*—but she could not. What she had to tell was too big, too much, too *something*, for her to place in the small shrine that a story is.

When we met—if what happened between us was a meeting—I felt nothing had ever happened to me and nothing ever would. I didn't understand that riding this filthy Greyhound down the middle of bloodied America in the middle of a mutinous war was itself a story and that something *was* happening to me. I thought if something was happening to anybody around me it was happening to people like my boyfriend: They were the heroes, according to the lights that shined for me then. I was just riding shotgun in my own life. I could not have imagined containing, as the farm woman slumped next to me did, the sheer narrative bulk to say, "I could tell you stories," and then drifting off with the secret heaviness of experience into the silence where stories live their real lives, crumbling into the loss we call remembrance.

The boastful little declaration, pathetically conditional (not "I'll tell you a story" but "I could") wavered wistfully for an instant between us. The stranger's remark, launched in the dark of the Greyhound, floated across the human landscape like the lingering tone of a struck bell from a village church, and joined all the silence that ever was, as I turned my face to the window where the world was rushing by along the slow river.

EXPLORATORY WRITING

In the middle of this essay, Hampl writes, "Because everyone 'has' a memoir, we all have a stake in how such stories are told. For we do not, after all, simply *have* experience; we are entrusted with it. We must do something—make something—with it. A story, we sense, is the only possible habitation for the burden of our witnessing." Write an explanation of that statement. How does it serve as a summary for what Hampl is saying about memoir and storytelling?

TALKING ABOUT THE READING

With a group of your classmates, retell the parts of Hampl's story that you remember best. Why did they stick out for you? Compare what you remember to what others remember. How does each group member's memory of the story differ? How does Hampl characterize herself in this story? What details from the story serve to build that characterization for you?

WRITING ASSIGNMENTS

1. On one level, "Red Sky in the Morning" is a simple memory piece—memoir. In it, the author recounts a chance meeting with a woman whose words—"*I could tell you stories*"—haunt her. On a more important level, this essay (and the story within it) is about storytelling. Write an essay in which you explain the nature of storytelling as Hampl's story reveals it. Why, for example, does she remember the woman better than anything else? What is it that she did not understand then (as she tells us near the end of the essay) that she now understands better—about herself, about storytelling, about expectations? You might want to use the woman's words—"*I could tell you stories*"—as a focus for your essay.

2. Within the story of the woman and her husband is the story of Hampl, her boyfriend, and the temper of the times—a country in the middle of an unpopular war. Write an essay in which you explain the importance of that background for the story. Besides being the reason for Hampl's bus trip, what other purpose does that background serve? Keep in mind the several places in the essay where Hampl explains what a memoirist does. For example, "Memoirists wish to tell their mind, not their story." Use that and other statements like it to help frame your essay.

3. Write your own story from the story you wrote before you read Hampl's essay. Keep in mind Hampl's notion that stories are things we are entrusted with. To make them useful for others, we must shape them. Tell your story so that it is meaningful for others outside your circle of family and friends. Remember that your story should "tell your mind," not your story.

MAKING CONNECTIONS   Urban Legends

One of the most persistent kinds of storytelling is what has come to be called the urban legend, a story that is widely circulated as true but actually is fictional. Many of these urban legends are the stuff of camp stories—tales meant to scare listeners. Some are warnings, often to those traveling alone at night or trusting the wrong person. The key feature of an urban legend is its persistence. "The Killer in the Backseat," for example, is a story that has been told for decades but is always told as though it happened recently, nearby, and to a person known through a friend or reported in a local news story. Many urban legends have gone digital, circulating in e-mail chain letters or on Web sites like YouTube.com. These myths have become so common that the Web site snopes.com has dedicated itself to verifying or debunking stories that circulate in this way.

In the readings that follow, folklorist Jan Brunvand and sociologist Patricia Turner each write of urban legends and the roles they play in shaping cultural myths or revealing cultural fears. As you read, begin a list of the urban legends you have heard or seen circulated in email or in internet chatrooms.

"THE HOOK" AND OTHER TEENAGE HORRORS
— *Jan Harold Brunvand*

Jan Harold Brunvand is a folklorist and professor emeritus of English at the University of Utah. "'The Hook' and Other Teenage Horrors" is a chapter from Brunvand's book *The Vanishing Hitchhiker: American Urban Legends and Their Meaning* (1981). In *The Vanishing Hitchhiker* and its two sequels, *The Choking Doberman* (1986) and *The Mexican Pet* (1988), Brunvand has gathered examples of contemporary storytelling—strange, scary, funny, macabre, and embarrassing tales storytellers relate as true accounts of real-life experience. Brunvand calls these stories "urban legends" because they are, by and large, set in contemporary America and, like all legends, are alleged to be about real people and real events. These legends, often about someone that the narrator knows or the "friend of a friend," are passed on by word of mouth, forming an oral tradition in the midst of America's mass-media culture. As Brunvand says, urban legends "survive by being as lively and 'factual' as the television evening news, and, like the daily newscasts, they tend to concern deaths, injuries, kidnappings, tragedies, and scandals." Stories such as "The Hook" are told and are believed—or at least are believable—as "human interest" stories that capture some of the fears and anxieties of contemporary America.

SUGGESTION FOR READING As a folklorist, Brunvand is interested in interpreting urban legends as well as in gathering them. As you read through "'The Hook' and Other Teenage Horrors," underline and annotate the passages where Brunvand offers his own interpretations or those of other folklore scholars.

GROWING UP SCARED

1 People of all ages love a good scare. Early childlore is full of semiserious spooky stories and ghastly threats, while the more sophisticated black humor of Little Willies, Bloody Marys, Dead Babies, and other cycles of sick jokes enters a bit later. Among the favorite readings at school are Edgar Allan Poe's blood-soaked tales, and favorite stories at summer camp tell of maniacal ax-murderers and deformed giants lurking in the dark forest to ambush unwary Scouts.

Halloween spook houses and Hollywood horror films cater to the same wish to push the level of tolerable fright as far as possible.

The ingredients of horror fiction change little through time, but the style of such stories does develop, even in oral tradition. In their early teens young Americans apparently reject the overdramatic and unbelievable juvenile "scaries" and adopt a new lore of more plausible tales with realistic settings. That is, they begin to enjoy urban legends, especially those dealing with "folks" like themselves—dating couples, students, and baby-sitters—who are subjected to grueling ordeals and horrible threats.

One consistent theme in these teenage horrors is that as the adolescent moves out from home into the larger world, the world's dangers may close in on him or her. Therefore, although the immediate purpose of many of these legends is to produce a good scare, they also serve to deliver a warning: Watch out! This could happen to you! Furthermore, the horror tales often contain thinly disguised sexual themes which are, perhaps, implicit in the nature of such plot situations as parking in a lovers' lane or baby-sitting (playing house) in a strange home. These sexual elements furnish both a measure of further entertainment and definite cautionary notices about the world's actual dangers. Thus, from the teenagers' own major fears, concerns, and experiences, spring their favorite "true" oral stories.

The chief current example of this genre of urban legend—one that is even older, more popular, and more widespread than "The Boyfriend's Death"—is the one usually called "The Hook."

"THE HOOK"

5 On Tuesday, November 8, 1960, the day when Americans went to the polls to elect John F. Kennedy as their thirty-fifth president, thousands of people must have read the following letter from a teenager in the popular newspaper column written by Abigail Van Buren:

Dear Abby: If you are interested in teenagers, you will print this story. I don't know whether it's true or not, but it doesn't matter because it served its purpose for me:

A fellow and his date pulled into their favorite "lovers' lane" to listen to the radio and do a little necking. The music was interrupted by an announcer who said there was an escaped convict in the area who had served time for rape and robbery. He was described as having a hook instead of a right hand. The couple became frightened and drove away. When the boy took his girl home, he went around to open the car door

for her. Then he saw—a hook on the door handle! I don't think I will ever park to make out as long as I live. I hope this does the same for other kids.

Jeanette

This juicy story seems to have emerged in the late 1950s, sharing some common themes with "The Death Car" and "The Vanishing Hitchhiker" and then . . . influencing "The Boyfriend's Death" as that legend developed in the early 1960s. The story of "The Hook" (or "The Hookman") really needed no national press report to give it life or credibility, because the teenage oral-tradition underground had done the job well enough long before the election day of 1960. Teenagers all over the country knew about "The Hook" by 1959, and like other modern legends the basic plot was elaborated with details and became highly localized.

One of my own students, originally from Kansas, provided this specific account of where the event supposedly occurred:

Outside of "Mac" [McPherson, Kansas], about seven miles out towards Lindsborg, north on old highway 81 is an old road called "Hookman's Road." It's a curved road, a traditional parking spot for the kids. When I was growing up it [the legend] was popular, and that was back in the '60's, and it was old then.

Another student told a version of the story that she had heard from her baby-sitter in Albuquerque in 1960:

over the radio came an announcement that a crazed killer with a hook in place of a hand had escaped from the local insane asylum. The girl got scared and begged the boy to take her home. He got mad and stepped on the gas and roared off. When they got to her house, he got out and went around to the other side of the car to let her out. There on the door handle was a bloody hook.

But these two students were told, after arriving in Salt Lake City, that it had actually occurred *here* in Memory Grove, a well-wooded city park. "Oh, no," a local student in the class insisted. "This couple was parked outside of Salt Lake City *in a mountain canyon* one night, and . . . "

It turned out that virtually every student in the class knew the story as adapted in some way to their hometowns.

10   Other folklorists have reported collecting "The Hook" in Maryland, Wisconsin, Indiana, Illinois, Kansas, Texas, Arkansas, Oregon, and Canada. Some of the informants' comments echo Dear Abby's correspondent in testifying to the story's effect (to discourage parking) even when its truth was suspect. The student said, "I believe that it *could* happen, and this makes it seem real," or "I don't really [believe it], but it's pretty scary; I sort of hope it didn't happen."

Part of the great appeal of "The Hook"—one of the most popular adolescent scare stories—must lie in the tidiness of the plot. Everything fits. On the other hand, the lack of loose ends would seem to be excellent testimony to the story's near impossibility. After all, what are the odds that a convicted criminal or crazed maniac would be fitted with a hook for a missing hand, that this same threatening figure would show up precisely when a radio warning had been broadcast of his escape, and that the couple would drive away rapidly just at the instant the hookman put his hook through the door handle? Besides, why wouldn't he try to open the door with his good hand, and how is it that the boy—furious at the interruption of their lovemaking—is still willing to go around politely to open the girl's door when they get home? Too much, too much—but it makes a great story.

In an adolescent novel titled *Dinky Hocker Shoots Smack!*, M. E. Kerr captured the way teenagers often react to such legends—with cool acceptance that it might have happened, and that's good enough:

> She told Tucker this long story about a one-armed man who was hanging around a lovers' lane in Prospect Park [Brooklyn]. There were rumors that he tried to get in the cars and carry off the girls. He banged on the windshields with his hooked wooden arm and frothed at the mouth. He only said two words: *bloody murder*; and his voice was high and hoarse.

> Dinky claimed this girl who went to St. Marie's was up in Prospect Park one night with a boyfriend. The girl and her boyfriend began discussing the one-armed man while they were parked. They both got frightened and decided to leave. The boy dropped the girl off at her house, and drove home. When he got out of his car, he found this hook attached to his door handle.

> Dinky said, "They must have driven off just as he was about to open the door."

> "I thought you weren't interested in the bizarre, anymore," Tucker said.

> "It's a true story."

> "It's still bizarre."

A key detail lacking in the *Dinky Hocker* version, however, is the boyfriend's frustrated anger resulting in their leaving the scene in a great hurry. Almost invariably the boy guns the motor and roars away: " . . . so he revs up the car and he goes torquing out of there." Or, "The boy floored the gas pedal and zoomed away," or "Her boyfriend was annoyed and the car screeched off. . . ." While this behavior is essential to explain the sudden sharp force that tears loose the maniac's hook, it is also a reminder of the original sexual purpose of the parking, at least on the boy's part. While Linda Dégh saw "the natural dread of the handicapped," and "the boy's disappointment and suddenly recognized fear as an adequate explanation for the jump start of the car," folklorist Alan Dundes disagreed, mainly because of the curtailed sex quest in the plot.

Dundes, taking a Freudian line, interpreted the hook itself as a phallic symbol which penetrates the girl's door handle (or bumps seductively against her window) but which is torn off (symbolic of castration) when the car starts abruptly. Girls who tell the story, Dundes suggests, "are not afraid of what a man lacks, but of what he has"; a date who is "all hands" may really want to "get his hooks into her." Only the girl's winding up the window or insisting upon going home at once saves her, and the date has to "pull out fast" before he begins to act like a sex maniac himself. The radio—turned on originally for soft, romantic background music—introduces instead "the consciencelike voice from society," a warning that the girl heeds and the boy usually scorns. Dundes concluded that this popular legend "reflects a very real dating practice, one which produces anxiety . . . particularly for girls."

"THE KILLER IN THE BACKSEAT"

A similar urban legend also involves cars and an unseen potential assailant; this time a man threatens a woman who is driving alone at night. The following version of "The Killer in the Backseat" was contributed in 1967 by a University of Utah student who had heard other versions set in Denver and Aurora, Colorado:

A woman living in the city [i.e., Salt Lake City] was visiting some friends in Ogden. When she got into her car in front of this friend's house, she noticed that a car started up right behind her car. It was about 2:00 in the morning, and there weren't any other cars on the road. After she had driven to the highway, she began to think that this car was following her. Some of the time he would drive up real close to her car, but he wouldn't ever pass. She was really scared to death and kept speeding to try to get away from him.

When she got to Salt Lake, she started running stop lights to get away from him, but he would run right through them too. So when she got to her driveway she pulled in really fast, and this guy pulled in right behind her. She just laid on the horn, and her husband came running out. Just then, the guy jumped out of the car, and her husband ran over and said, "What the hell's goin' on here?" So he grabbed the guy, and his wife said, "This man's followed me all the way from Ogden." The man said, "I followed your wife because I was going to work, and as I got into my car, I noticed when I turned my lights on, a man's head bob down in her back seat." So the husband went over to her backseat, opened the door, and pulled this guy from out of the backseat.

15   This legend first appeared in print in 1968 in another version, also—coincidentally—set in

Ogden, Utah, but collected at Indiana University, Bloomington. (This shows how the presence of folklorists in a locality will influence the apparent distribution patterns of folk material.) Twenty further texts have surfaced at Indiana University with, as usual, plenty of variations and localizations. In many instances the pursuing driver keeps flashing his headlights between the high and low beam in order to restrain the assailant who is popping up and threatening to attack the driver. Sometimes the pursuer is a burly truck driver or other tough-looking character, and in several of the stories the supposed would-be attacker (the pursuing rescuer) is specifically said to be a black man. (Both motifs clearly show white middle class fears of minorities or of groups believed to be socially inferior.)

In a more imaginative set of these legends the person who spots the dangerous man in back is a gas station attendant who pretends that a ten dollar bill offered by the woman driver in payment for gas is counterfeit. With this ruse he gets her safely away from her car before calling the police. In another version of the story, a passing motorist sharply warns the woman driver to roll up her window and follow him, driving in exactly the same manner he does. She obeys, speeding and weaving along the highway, until a suspected assailant—usually carrying an ax—is thrown from his perch on the roof of her car.

"THE BABY-SITTER AND THE MAN UPSTAIRS"

Just as a lone woman may unwittingly be endangered by a hidden man while she is driving at night, a younger one may face the same hazard in a strange home. The horror legend of "The Baby-sitter and the Man Upstairs," similar in structure to "The Killer in the Backseat," is possibly a later variation of the same story relocated to fit teenagers' other direct experiences. This standard version is from a fourteen-year-old Canadian boy (1973):

There was this baby-sitter that was in Montreal baby-sitting for three children in a big house.

She was watching TV when suddenly the phone rang. The children were all in bed. She picked up the phone and heard this guy on the other end laughing hysterically. She asked him what it was that he wanted, but he wouldn't answer and then hung up. She worried about it for a while, but then thought nothing more of it and went back to watching the movie.

Everything was fine until about fifteen minutes later when the phone rang again. She picked it up and heard the same voice laughing hysterically at her, and then hung up. At this point she became really worried and phoned the operator to tell her what had been happening. The operator told her to calm down and that if he called again to try and keep him on the line as long as possible and she would try to trace the call.

Again about fifteen minutes later the guy called back and laughed hysterically at her. She asked him why he was doing this, but he just kept laughing at her. He hung up and about five seconds later the operator called. She told the girl to get out of the house at once because the person who was calling was calling from the upstairs extension. She slammed down the phone and just as she was turning to leave she saw the man coming down the stairs laughing hysterically with a bloody butcher knife in his hand and meaning to kill her. She ran out onto the street but he didn't follow. She called the police and they came and caught the man, and discovered that he had murdered all the children.

The storyteller added that he had heard the story from a friend whose brother's girlfriend was the baby-sitter involved.

By now it should come as no surprise to learn that the same story had been collected two years earlier (1971) some 1500 miles southwest of Montreal, in Austin, Texas, and also in Bloomington, Indiana, in 1973 in a college dormitory. These three published versions are only samples from the wide distribution of the story in folk tradition. Their similarities and differences provide another classic case of folklore's variation within traditional boundaries. In all

three legend texts the hour is late and the baby-sitter is watching television. Two of the callers make threatening statements, while one merely laughs. In all versions the man calls three times at regular intervals before the girl calls the operator, then once more afterwards. In both American texts the operator herself calls the police, and in the Indiana story she commands "Get out of the house immediately; don't go upstairs; don't do anything; just leave the house. When you get out there, there will be policemen outside and they'll take care of it." (One is reminded of the rescuers' orders not to look back at the car in "The Boyfriend's Death.") The Texas telephone operator in common with the Canadian one gives the situation away by adding, "The phone call traces to the upstairs." The murder of the child or children (one, two, or three of them—no pattern) is specified in the American versions: in Texas they are "chopped into little bitty pieces"; in Indiana, "torn to bits." All of the storytellers played up the spookiness of the situation—details that would be familiar to anyone who has ever baby-sat—a strange house, a television show, an unexpected phone call, frightening sounds or threats, the abrupt orders from the operator, and finally the shocking realization at the end that (as in "The Killer in the Backseat") the caller had been there in the house (or behind her) all the time. The technical problems of calling another telephone from an extension of the same number, or the actual procedures of call-tracing, do not seem to worry the storytellers.

20   Folklorist Sue Samuelson, who examined hundreds of unpublished "Man Upstairs" stories filed in American folklore archives, concluded that the telephone is the most important and emotionally-loaded item in the plot: the assailant is harassing his victim through the device that is her own favorite means of communication. Baby-sitting, Samuelson points out, is an important socializing experience for young women, allowing them to practice their future roles, imposed on them in a male-dominated society,

as homemakers and mothers. Significantly, the threatening male figure is upstairs—on top of and in control of the girl—as men have traditionally been in the sexual relationship. In killing the children who were in her care, the man brings on the most catastrophic failure any mother can suffer. Another contributing factor in the story is that the baby-sitter herself is too intent on watching television to realize that the children are being murdered upstairs. Thus, the tale is not just another scary story, but conveys a stern admonition to young women to adhere to society's traditional values.

Occasionally these firmly believed horror legends are transformed from ghastly mysteries to almost comical adventures. The following Arizona version of "The Baby-sitter and the Man Upstairs," collected in 1976, is a good example:

It was August 8, 1969. She was going to baby-sit at the Smiths who had two children, ages five and seven. She had just put the children to bed and went back to the living room to watch TV.

The phone began to ring; she went to answer it; the man on the other end said, "I'm upstairs with the children; you'd better come up."

She hung the phone up immediately, scared to death. She decided that it must be a prank phone call; again she went to watch TV. The phone rang again; she went to answer it, this time more scared than last.

The man said, "I'm upstairs with the children," and described them in detail. So she hung up the phone, not knowing what to do. Should I call the police? Instead she decided, "I'll call the operator. They can trace these phone calls." She called the operator, and the operator said that she would try and do what she could. Approximately ten minutes later the phone rang again; this time she was shaking.

She answered the phone and the man again said, "I'm upstairs with the children; you'd better come quick!" She tried to stay on the phone as long as she could so that the operator could trace the call; this time the man hung up.

She called back, and the operator said, "Run out of the house; the man is on the extension."

She didn't quite know what to do; should she go and get the children? "No," she said, "he's up there; if I go and get the children, I'll be killed too!!" She ran next door to the neighbor's house and called the police. The sirens came—there must have been at least ten police cars. They went inside the house, ran upstairs, and found not a man, but a seven-year-old child who was sitting next to the phone with a tape recorder. Later they found that a boy down the street had told this young boy to do this next time he had a baby-sitter. You see the boy didn't like his parents going out, and he didn't like having baby-sitters. So he felt this was the only way he could get rid of them. The boys [sic] don't have baby-sitters anymore; now they go to the nursery school.

"THE ROOMMATE'S DEATH"

Another especially popular example of the American adolescent shocker story is the widely known legend of "The Roommate's Death." It shares several themes with other urban legends. As in "The Killer in the Backseat" and "The Baby-sitter and the Man Upstairs," it is usually a lone woman in the story who is threatened—or thinks she is—by a strange man. As in "The Hook" and "The Boyfriend's Death," the assailant is often said to be an escaped criminal or a maniac. Finally, as in the latter legend, the actual commission of the crime is never described; only the resulting mutilated corpse is. The scratching sounds outside the girl's place of refuge are an additional element of suspense. Here is a version told by a University of Kansas student in 1965 set in Corbin Hall, a freshman women's dormitory there:

These two girls in Corbin had stayed late over Christmas vacation. One of them had to wait for a later train, and the other wanted to go to a fraternity party given that night of vacation. The dorm assistant was in her room—sacked out. They waited and waited for the intercom, and then they heard this knocking and knocking outside in front of the dorm. So the girl thought it was her date and she went down. But she didn't come back and she didn't come back. So real late that night this other girl heard a scratching and gasping down the hall. She couldn't lock the door, so she locked herself in the closet. In the morning she let herself out and her roommate had had her throat cut, and if the other girl had opened the door earlier, she [the dead roommate] would have been saved.

At all the campuses where the story is told the reasons for the girls' remaining alone in the dorm vary, but they are always realistic and plausible. The girls' homes may be too far away for them to visit during vacation, such as in Hawaii or a foreign country. In some cases they wanted to avoid a campus meeting or other obligation. What separates the two roommates may be either that one goes out for food, or to answer the door, or to use the rest room. The girl who is left behind may hear the scratching noise either at her room door or at the closet door, if she hides there. Sometimes her hair turns white or gray overnight from the shock of the experience (an old folk motif). The implication in the story is that some maniac is after her (as is suspected about the pursuer in "The Killer in the Backseat"); but the truth is that her own roommate needs help, and she might have supplied it had she only acted more decisively when the noises were first heard. Usually some special emphasis is put on the victim's fingernails, scratched to bloody stumps by her desperate efforts to signal for help.

A story told by a California teenager, remembered from about 1964, seems to combine motifs of "The Baby-sitter and the Man Upstairs" with "The Roommate's Death." The text is unusually detailed with names and the circumstances of the crime:

Linda accepted a baby-sitting job for a wealthy family who lived in a two-story home up in the hills for whom she had never baby-sat for before. Linda was rather hesitant as the house was rather isolated and so she asked a girlfriend, Sharon, to go along with her, promising Sharon half of the baby-sitting fee she would earn. Sharon accepted Linda's offer and the two girls went up to the big two-storey house.

The night was an especially dark and windy one and rain was threatening. All went well for the girls as they read stories aloud to the three little boys they were sitting for and they had no problem putting the boys to bed in the upstairs part of the house. When this was done, the girls settled down to watching television.

It was not long before the telephone rang. Linda answered the telephone, only to hear the heavy breathing of the caller on the other end. She attempted to elicit a response from the caller but he merely hung up. Thinking little of it and not wanting to panic Sharon, Linda went back to watching her television program, remarking that the caller had dialed a wrong number. Upon receiving the second call at which time the caller first engaged in a bit of heavy breathing and then instructed them to check on the children, the two girls became frightened and decided to call the operator for assistance. The operator instructed the girls to keep the caller on the line as long as possible should he call again so that she might be able to trace the call. The operator would check back with them.

The two girls then decided between themselves that one should stay downstairs to answer the phone. It was Sharon who volunteered to go upstairs. Shortly, the telephone rang again and Linda did as the operator had instructed her. Within a few minutes, the operator called back telling Linda to leave the house immediately with her friend because she had traced the calls to the upstairs phone.

Linda immediately hung up the telephone and proceeded to run to the stairway to call Sharon. She then heard a thumping sound coming from the stairway and when she approached the stairs she saw her friend dragging herself down the stairs by her chin, all of her limbs severed from her body. The three boys also lay dead upstairs in their beds.

25   Once again, the Indiana University Folklore Archive has provided the best published report on variants of "The Roommate's Death," Linda Dégh's summary of thirty-one texts and several

subtypes and related plots collected since 1961. The most significant feature, according to her report, is the frequent appearance of a male rescuer at the end of the story. In one version, for example, two girls are left behind alone in the dorm by their roommate when she goes downstairs for food; they hear noises, and so stay in their room all night without opening the door. Finally the mailman comes around the next morning, and they call him from the window:

> The mailman came in the front door and went up the stairs, and told the girls to stay in their room, that everything was all right but that they were to stay in their rooms [sic]. But the girls didn't listen to him cause he had said it was all right, so they came out into the hall. When they opened the door, they saw the girlfriend on the floor with a hatchet in her head.

In other Indiana texts the helpful male is a handyman, a milkman, or the brother of one of the roommates.

According to folklorist Beverly Crane, the male-female characters are only one pair of a series of significant opposites, which also includes home and away, intellectual versus emotional behavior, life and death, and several others. A male is needed to resolve the female's uncertainty—motivated by her emotional fear—about how to act in a new situation. Another male has mutilated and killed her roommate with a blow to her head, "the one part of the body with which women are not supposed to compete." The girls, Crane suggested, are doubly out of place in the beginning, having left the haven of home to engage in intellectual pursuits, and having remained alone in the campus dormitory instead of rejoining the family on a holiday. Ironically, the injured girl must use her fingernails, intended to be long, lovely, feminine adornments,

in order to scratch for help. But because her roommate fails to investigate the sound, the victim dies, her once pretty nails now bloody stumps. Crane concluded this ingenious interpretation with these generalizations:

> The points of value implicit in this narrative are then twofold. If women wish to depend on traditional attitudes and responses they had best stay in a place where these attitudes and responses are best able to protect them. If, however, women do choose to venture into the realm of equality with men, they must become less dependent, more self-sufficient, more confident in their own abilities, and, above all, more willing to assume responsibility for themselves and others.

One might not expect to find women's liberation messages embedded in the spooky stories told by teenagers, but Beverly Crane's case is plausible and well argued. Furthermore, it is not at all unusual to find up-to-date social commentary in other modern folklore—witness the many religious and sexual jokes and legends circulated by people who would not openly criticize a church or the traditional social mores. Folklore does not just purvey the old codes of morality and behavior; it can also absorb newer ideas. What needs to be done to analyze this is to collect what Alan Dundes calls "oral-literary criticism," the informants' own comments about their lore. How clearly would the girls who tell these stories perceive—or even accept—the messages extrapolated by scholars? And a related question: Have any stories with clear liberationist themes replaced older ones cautioning young women to stay home, be good, and—next best—be careful, and call a man if they need help?

EXPLORATORY WRITING

Look back at the underlinings and annotations you made as you read. Use those to help you compose a summary statement on Brunvand's interpretations of urban legends. What, according to Brunvand, are urban legends really about?

TALKING ABOUT THE READING

Work together with classmates to create your own collection of urban legends. Which of the stories that Brunvand tells have you heard before? Where, when, and from whom did you hear a particular story? When you heard them, how were the details adapted to local conditions? What stories would you add to the list that Brunvand does not tell here? What fears, concerns, or experiences do those stories seem to reflect?

WRITING ASSIGNMENT

Reread "'The Hook' and Other Teenage Horrors," and notice how Brunvand interprets each of the urban legends he writes about. Pick one of the interpretations that you find particularly interesting or striking. Write an essay in which you summarize the interpretation and explain why it seems adequate or inadequate. What alternative interpretations might be offered?

I HEARD IT THROUGH THE GRAPEVINE

— *Patricia A. Turner*

Patricia A. Turner is vice provost of undergraduate studies and professor of folklore in the Department of African American and African Studies at the University of California, Davis. Her work includes the book-length study *Ceramic Uncles and Celluloid Mammies: Black Images and Their Influence on Culture* (1994), *Whispers on the Color Line: Rumor and Race in America* (2001) with Gary Alan Fine, and *I Heard It Through the Grapevine: Rumor in African-American Culture* (1993), from which the following selection has been excerpted. Turner's work takes its start from Brunvand's claim in his introduction to *The Vanishing Hitchhiker* that urban legends are "an integral part of white Anglo-American culture." Turner traces African American contemporary legends and rumors to the earliest slave ships and argues that the stories emerging from that experience, and from periods of racial discord since, function as a tool of resistance for the African Americans who tell them.

SUGGESTION FOR READING Like Brunvand, Turner recounts rumors and contemporary legends that are horrifying and unlikely but somehow believable. Where Brunvand would emphasize how urban legends are used to keep sexually active teens aware of potential dangers surrounding their activities, Turner argues that African American rumors are linked to racial strife and arise from actual horrors that African Americans have faced since the beginnings of the slave trade. As you did when you read Brunvand, mark specific passages in Turner's essay where she offers interpretations of these legends. Make note of how her interpretation identifies these stories as specific to African American lives.

1 I was teaching Introduction to Black Literature at the University of Massachusetts at Boston in February 1986. Like most folklorists, I rely on folk material for examples in even my nonfolklore courses. After telling the students about the popular contemporary legend known as the Kentucky Fried Rat, Wayne, an intelligent young African-American, raised his hand to say, "Oh well, I guess that's like what they say about eating at Church's Chicken—you know the Klan owns it and they do something to the chicken so that when black men eat there they become sterile. Except that I guess it isn't really like the one about the Kentucky Fried Rat because it is true about Church's. I know because a friend of mine saw the story on '60 Minutes.'" Several other

black students nodded in silent agreement; the white students looked at them in rapt disbelief, while the remaining black students seemed to be making a mental note not to eat at Church's. After class I sprinted to my office and began calling folklore colleagues. No professional folklorists (all white) had heard any version of the Church's text, but throughout the remainder of the day I was able to collect several variations from black students and black members of the university staff.

Several months later, as I was finishing an article on the Church's cycle, I found myself discussing it with another class. An African-American student raised her hand and said, "Well, if you don't believe that one, you probably don't believe that the FBI was responsible for the deaths of all those children in Atlanta. I heard that they were taking the bodies to the Centers for Disease Control in Atlanta to perform interferon experiments on them." As I began research on *that* story, also unknown to my white colleagues, I confirmed my earlier suspicions that these contemporary texts were not mere ephemera lacking in historical antecedents. Indeed, a provocative corpus of related material can be traced back to the early sixteenth century, when white Europeans began to have regular contact with sub-Saharan Africa. I realized that this discourse was sufficiently rich to explore in book-length form.

A white colleague familiar with my work on the Church's and Atlanta Child Killer stories then pointed out that the increasingly common claim that the AIDS virus was the product of an anti-black conspiracy fit the pattern of my research. And in early 1989 I was querying a black studies class about the Church's item when one student raised her hand and said, "I don't know about the Klan owning Church's, but I do know that they are supposed to own Troop clothing." Other African-American students expressed agreement, while white students sat perplexed by this unfamiliar news. With this text the students had a real advantage over me because I had never even heard of the popular line of clothing apparently marketed quite aggressively to young black consumers.

I was convinced that these items fit into the category dubbed by folklorists as "urban" or "contemporary legend." Interestingly enough, Jan Harold Brunvand, a prolific writer on urban legend, referred to such stories as "an integral part of *white* [emphasis added] Anglo-American culture and are told and believed by some of the most sophisticated 'folk' of modern society—young people, urbanites, and the well-educated." The fact that no in-depth investigation of the texts that circulate among African-Americans has been conducted is not surprising. Most folklorists are white, and they have not discovered the black urban legend tradition.

5   The following is a representative sampling of rumors known to many African-Americans from all over the United States during this era:

Text #1: Church's [fast food chicken franchise] is owned by the Ku Klux Klan [KKK], and they put something in it to make black men sterile.

Text #2: I remember hearing that the killings [of twenty-eight African-Americans] in Atlanta were related to genocide of the black race. The FBI [Federal Bureau of Investigation] was responsible and using the bodies for interferon research.

Text #3: I have heard that U.S. scientists created AIDS in a laboratory (possibly as a weapon to use against enemy in the event of war), and they needed to test the virus, so they go to Africa, as they [Africans] are expendable, introduce the disease, and then are unable to control its spread to Europeans and Americans.

Text #4: Troop [a popular brand of athletic wear] is owned by the Ku Klux Klan. They are using the money they make from the products to finance the lawsuit that they lost to the black woman whose son was killed by the Klan.

Text #5: Reebok is made in South Africa. All of the money they make off of those shoes goes to support whites in South Africa.

Text #6: The production and mass distribution of drugs is an attempt by the white man to keep blacks who are striving to better themselves from making it in the world. So many blacks take drugs in order to find release and escape from the problems they face in life. By taking drugs, blacks are killing themselves, and by selling them they are bringing about the imminent destruction of their race. Overall, the white man has conspired to wipe out the black population by using them [blacks] to destroy themselves.

Text #7: Tropical Fantasy [a fruit-flavored soft drink] is made by the KKK. There is a special ingredient in it that makes black men sterile.

CONTAMINATION

Let us now look at texts in which the conspiracy in question is intended specifically to contaminate blacks in a physical way, either directly or indirectly. The majority of people who spoke with me about the Church's rumor, for example, allege much more than a simple KKK plot to capitalize monetarily on a product preferred by African-Americans. The first informant who shared the item told me, "They're doing something to the chicken so that when black men eat it, they become sterile," and this comment accusing the KKK of imposing a sinister form of ethnic birth control pervades my fieldwork. The same motif dominates the Tropical Fantasy cycle. Many informants who claim that the FBI was responsible for the Atlanta child murders elaborate by reporting that the bodies were taken to the Centers for Disease Control in Atlanta for biological experiments. A college-aged African-American female said, "I remember hearing that the killings in Atlanta were related to the genocide of the black race. The FBI was responsible and using the bodies for interferon during research." (Interferon is an antiviral glycoprotein produced by human cells exposed to a virus; according to certain research reports of the late 1970s and early 1980s, the scientific community

was well on its way to testing it so that it could be marketed as a genuine "miracle drug.")

In some folk items, contamination is a much more prominent motif than conspiracy. Growing public awareness of the threat implicit in the acquired immune deficiency syndrome (AIDS) epidemic caused various contemporary legends to arise connecting this fatal, sexually transmitted disease with an ethnically based contamination plot. Some informants, for instance, claimed that AIDS was developed from experiments having to do with disease, chemical, or germ warfare. These experiments were supposedly conducted in Haiti or West Africa, populations that the experimenters (usually identified as some group affiliated with "the government") perceived to be expendable. As one informant reported, "The United States government was developing germ warfare when it got out of control. AIDS was the project, and they tried it out in Africa first to see if it would work. It did." Others claim even more heinous motives, saying that the disease was developed for the express purpose of limiting the growth of third world populations. A New England–born thirty-nine-year-old African-American female offered this succinct version: "AIDS originated in Africa by the [U.S.] government in that it was a conspiracy to kill off a lot of black people."

DANGEROUS CHICKEN

Approximately half of my informants claimed that the Klan's goal in its ownership of Church's was to put something (spices, drugs) into the chicken (either into the batter or flour coating, or, by injections, directly into the chicken) that would cause sterility in black male eaters. Similar aims and tactics were true of the Tropical Fantasy conspiracy. This motif contains the specificity and narrative closure that folklorists often find in contemporary legend texts. However, the other texts I collected lacked any such closure. Most informants used the present tense and described the contamination as an ongoing, relatively unfocused conspiracy. Typical of the comments I collected was, "I heard that the Klan owns Church's chicken and has been lacing the batter with a spermicide." Several people suggested that the KKK's goal was to "make blacks infertile." Thus both men and women have something to fear. One black female informant claimed that eating the chicken "makes something go wrong with pregnant black women so that their children come out retarded."

Typically, food contamination rumors and contemporary legends are associated either with instances of accidental, incidental contamination (the Kentucky Fried Rat, the mouse in the Coke bottle) or with premeditated food substitution, ostensibly for the purpose of increasing the company's profit ("wormburgers," the use of dog food on fast food pizzas). In the latter case, the company is not trying to hurt its customers, but rather to decrease costs through the use of socially distasteful but essentially safe ingredients. In the Church's rumor, by contrast, greed is not stated as a strong motive for the Klan. Although a few informants contributed versions that lacked any contamination motif, maintaining merely that the KKK owned the company, not a single informant speculated on how much money the Klan could make by selling fast food fried chicken to African-Americans. The white supremacist organization's goal, simply put, was to implement domestic genocide.

10   To those outside the rumor's public, the mechanism of contamination makes the accusation seem highly implausible. I encountered very few white informants who were familiar with the rumor. Upon hearing a summary, most responded by asking, "How is this mysterious substance supposed to distinguish between white male eaters and black male eaters?" When this question is posed to blacks, a common explanation is that most Church's franchises are located in black neighborhoods. Similarly, those who believe the Tropical Fantasy rumors note that the beverage is sold in inner-city ma-and-pa grocery stores, not at downtown soda counters. Hence, the KKK runs very little risk of sterilizing white male consumers. Other informants suggest that a substance has

been discovered that impedes the production of sperm in black males but is harmless when consumed by whites.

When the Church's rumor surfaced in San Diego in 1984, Congressman Jim Bates arranged to have the Food and Drug Administration test the chicken using gas chromatography and mass spectrometry. After finding no evidence of foreign materials, an assistant of Bates together with two West Coast Church's officials held a press conference to share their findings with the public. Tropical Fantasy was tested in 1991. A female informant told me that the Klan had probably "fixed things up with the FDA" so that the test on Church's would come out negative. Although I performed no scientific investigation of the chicken myself, I queried University of Massachusetts biologists and chemists about the possibility of such tampering. They maintained that there is no known tasteless, odorless substance that could be disguised in the chicken that would result in sterilization with no discernible side effects. I asked a black male student who overheard one of these conversations if he still believed the rumor. He said he did not. I asked him if he would patronize the nearby Church's. He said he would not.

To better understand the appeal of the contamination motif in the Church's and Tropical Fantasy rumors, it is useful to look at a very similar rumor. In speculating on just how the alleged sterilization agent in the chicken could function, none of my informants made any specific reference to the "ethnic weapon." This is the label that the U.S. intelligence community applied to rumors alleging that government scientists had developed a substance that could kill blacks but leave whites unharmed. These rumors, which appeared in leftist publications in the mid-1980s, caused great concern for the United States Information Agency (USIA). However, officials charged with exploring the reports drew no connections between them and other items of folk belief concerning people of color; rather, they claimed that the Soviet Union had designed and disseminated the rumors. In a publication familiarizing members of Congress with the scope of communist propaganda activity, the agency introduced the segment on the ethnic weapon thus:

> Since at least 1980, the Soviet press has been circulating claims that the United States is conducting research on or has developed a so-called "ethnic weapon," which would kill only non-whites. The Soviet media typically also charges that the South Africans—or less frequently the Israelis—are supposedly collaborating with the United States in this research. The Soviet goal in this campaign seems clear: to make it appear as if the United States and its alleged collaborators are pursuing racist, genocidal policies.
>
> The Soviet charge is absurd on the face of it. Even if the U.S. government wanted to produce such a weapon, it would make no sense to do so, given the multi-ethnic composition of the American population and the armed forces. The only plausible group that would want to produce such a weapon would be unregenerate white supremacists—a portrait of the U.S. government that Soviet disinformation specialists apparently want their audiences to believe.

These comments are followed by various statements by scientific authorities explaining why such a substance could not be developed, as well as forty-five references in left-wing and communist publications to the U.S. government's role in the development of such a weapon.

Because none of my over two hundred Church's and Tropical Fantasy informants mentioned the "ethnic weapon" by name, I can only conclude that this rumor was not embraced by the African-American population. Whether communist-inspired journalists actually planted the rumor or simply reported one that was gaining popularity is less relevant, in my view, than the fact that the item did not capture the African-American imagination. Why did a rumor alleging the KKK's malevolent involvement in a fast food company find more acceptance than one claiming the government was manufacturing a weapon for racial genocide?

15   In the various left-wing print references cited in the USIA pamphlet, the so-called ethnic weapon is either a perfected substance or one still under development. Except in one item linking it to the AIDS virus, there are no hints that the weapon has been deployed. Nor are there any real indications of how, when, or why it would be used. The threat is in its mere existence—in the possibility that the U.S. government might want to have such a weapon, in the fact that it could not be used in a clandestine manner, and in the fact that the potential victims have no control over its implementation. In the Church's and Tropical Fantasy texts, by contrast, a form of random deployment is at work. Any African-American who chances to eat at Church's or sip a Tropical Fantasy soft drink is a potential victim. Yet in these cases, people can avoid victimization by refusing to purchase the product. The Church's and Tropical Fantasy rumors, in short, give people some control over their fate, whereas the ethnic weapon texts do not.

The other primary difference between the Church's rumor—as well as the other contamination rumors—and the ethnic weapon item resides in the mode of contamination. With the ethnic weapon, there is no clue as to how the victims will be infected with the deadly substance or what modus operandi will govern the weapon's use. In the other items, however, the contamination is more specifically rendered: poisoned food or soft drinks, postmortem intrusions, and sexual intercourse are concrete threats. In short, rumors that contain specific physical consequences are more likely to seize the interest of a public than ambiguous, unspecific ones.

With motifs pinpointing a particular company, a known antiblack conspiratorial group, a familiar prepared food, and a detrimental outcome, the Church's rumor contains all of the nuances the ethnic weapon rumor lacks. Because a person can do something about the threat contained in the Church's item simply by not patronizing the restaurant, it is ultimately a much less ominous rumor. No informants who professed belief in the Church's story believed themselves to have been sterilized permanently because they consumed the chicken before they heard the item. No one said anything like, "It's too late for me now." Instead they merely observed, "So I haven't eaten any since."

Like other folk groups, African-Americans assign food and its preparation symbolic importance; food choice is part of the ordering process by which humans endow the environment with meaning and feeling. At first glance, a fast food chain that provides decent, familiar foods at a friendly price is offering a fair service and product. But by removing the preparation of an ethnic food from the home kitchens most strongly identified with it, the Church's corporation unwittingly intruded on sacred territory.

Ethnic foods, as a rule, are prepared and consumed by the very people who have created the dishes or by descendants who have had the recipes handed down to them. On special occasions or in special settings, these foods are shared with outsiders eager to participate in "equal opportunity eating." Church's created a new, public context for the sharing of what had thus far been considered communal foods—and foods, moreover, that carried with them strong symbolic associations. Nor are these associations necessarily positive. American popular culture has long perpetuated a stereotype in which blacks are portrayed as inordinately fond of foods that can be eaten without utensils, such as fried chicken and watermelon. Given this background, it is not surprising that blacks wish to approach these foods, particularly when offered outside the home, cautiously. The anthropologist Mary Douglas has pointed out that people with a minority status in their society are often suspicious of cooked foods as well as protective of the body's orifices: "If we treat ritual protection of bodily orifices as a symbol of social preoccupations about exits and entrances," she writes, "the purity of cooked food becomes important. I suggest that food is not likely to be polluting at all unless the external boundaries of the social system are under pressure."

20   The popularity of the Church's rumor indicates that the black community perceives itself as vulnerable to the hostile desires of the majority population, which, it seems, will stop at nothing to inhibit the growth of the minority population—including the use of polluted food to weaken individual sexual capacity. In this case, indeed, the threat to fertility comes from a source that employs the name of the very religious structure presumed by the black community to offer the most safety: the church.

The key to understanding the item's popularity, however, resides in the power it bestowed upon its public to seize control over a perceived threat to all African-American people. In the spring of 1990, an African-American female Californian discussed it as if it were ancient history. She recalled first hearing it "a long time ago," and concluded her commentary by stating, with obvious satisfaction, "A lot of these Church's have closed up now." Like many other informants who used similar closing motifs, she believed that a battle had been "won."

EXPLORATORY WRITING

After you have read this selection, go back through your underlinings and annotations to use in an exploratory writing in which you summarize her interpretations of the legends she relates.

TALKING ABOUT THE READING

With a group of your classmates, compare the exploratory writings you each wrote in response to this selection. As a group, discuss how the rumors Turner recounts compare with the urban legends Brunvand collects. In what ways are they similar? How do they differ?

WRITING ASSIGNMENT

In her introduction to *I Heard It Through the Grapevine*, Turner argues that African American contemporary legends and rumors go beyond teenage scare stories to function as "tools of resistance" in the African American community. Once a conspiracy story is circulated widely, the conspiracy can no longer be carried out because too many people know about it. Write an essay in which you examine how stories of contamination or KKK conspiracy might function as tools of resistance. In your discussion, consider how the power shifts to the teller of the story as it is circulated through a community.

WRITING SEQUENCE

1. Go back over the underlinings, notes, and exploratory writings you did as you read the pieces by Brunvand and Turner. For this assignment, create a chart or table in which you list Brunvand's urban legends on one side and Turner's on the other. Once you have them listed, write a summary statement in which you comment on the similarities and differences in the two sets of legends. Be as specific as you can. Who are the people affected in each set of stories? Who are the perpetrators? What, if anything, is the overarching theme of each set of legends?

2. Turner makes it clear that African American rumors, like all urban legends, begin with a seed of truth. In Brunvand's stories, you can see how adult worries over teenage sexuality, for example, can feed into the perpetuation of stories such as "The Hook" or all of those baby-sitter stories. Turner's stories, however, connect with fears of genocide and racism. Use your chart and summary statement to write an essay in which you compare the stories Brunvand tells with the stories Turner tells. Is one story more believable than another? More serious? More likely to be taken as fact by only some groups and not others? Why? What makes a rumor or legend believable to some and not to others?

3. As Jan Harold Brunvand writes, "People of all ages love a good scare." Write a culminating essay that explains why people enjoy being scared by ghost stories, horror films, thrillers, and urban legends. Draw on both Brunvand's and Turner's explanations of urban legends to develop your discussion. In it, you might compare the horror story with another kind of storytelling, such as fairy tales or adventure stories. Or begin with the kinds of stories that scare you but that you read or watch anyway. What is it that draws you to them? What kinds of stories did you and your friends tell to scare each other as you were growing up? Considering how they interpret urban legends, how would you say Turner and Brunvand might interpret the appeal of stories that frighten us? This should be a 4–6 page finished essay (drafted, revised, and edited). Any references to the readings or any other sources should be carefully cited.

WHY HEATHER CAN WRITE: MEDIA LITERACY AND THE HARRY POTTER WARS

—*Henry Jenkins*

Henry Jenkins is the DeFlorz Professor of Humanities and director of the Comparative Media Studies Program at MIT. His work in media studies has appeared in a number of books, newspaper and scholarly articles, and online sources, including his official Web log *Confessions of an Aca-Fan* (an academic who is also a fan) at http://www.henryjenkins.org. His most recent books include *From Barbie to Mortal Kombat: Gender and Computer Games* with Justine Cassell (2000), *The Wow Climax: Tracing the Emotional Impact of Popular Culture* (2006), *Fans, Bloggers, and Gamers: Media Consumers in a Digital Age* (2006), and *Convergence Culture: Where Old and New Media Collide* (2006), from which the following selection has been excerpted.

SUGGESTION FOR READING   Before you read, take time to write a brief summary of what you know or have heard about "the Potter Wars"—either the fight by some groups to keep the *Harry Potter* series out of libraries and schools or the debate over fans' rights to use the characters or settings in fan fiction and books about the series. If you have never heard about these battles, do a quick library or online search on the disagreements over the *Harry Potter* series to familiarize yourself with some of the controversies surrounding the books.

HOGWARTS AND ALL

1   When she was thirteen, Heather Lawver read a book that she says changed her life: *Harry Potter and the Sorcerer's Stone.*[1] Inspired by reports that J. K. Rowling's novel was getting kids to read, she wanted to do her part to promote literacy. Less than a year later, she launched *The Daily Prophet* (http://www.dprophet.com), a Web-based "school newspaper" for the fictional Hogwarts. Today, the publication has a staff of 102 children from all over the world.

Lawver, still in her teens, is its managing editor. She hires columnists who cover their own "beats" on a weekly basis—everything from the latest quidditch matches to muggle cuisine. Heather personally edits each story, getting it ready for publication. She encourages her staff to closely compare their original submissions with the edited versions and consults with them on issues of style and grammar as needed. Heather initially paid for the site through her allowances until someone suggested opening a post office box where participants could send their contributions; she still runs it on a small budget, but at least she can draw on the allowances of her friends and contributors to keep it afloat during hard times.

Lawver, by the way, is home schooled and hasn't set foot in a classroom since first grade. Her family had been horrified by what they saw as racism and anti-intellectualism, which they encountered when she entered first grade in a rural Mississippi school district. She explained,

"It was hard to combat prejudices when you are facing it every day. They just pulled me and one of my brothers out of school. And we never wanted to go back."

A girl who hadn't been in school since first grade was leading a worldwide staff of student writers with no adult supervision to publish a school newspaper for a school that existed only in their imaginations.

5   From the start, Lawver framed her project with explicit pedagogical goals that she used to help parents understand their children's participation. In an open letter to parents of her contributors, Lawver describes the site's goals:

> *The Daily Prophet* is an organization dedicated to bringing the world of literature to life. . . . By creating an online "newspaper" with articles that lead the readers to believe this fanciful world of *Harry Potter* to be real, this opens the mind to exploring books, diving into the characters, and analyzing great literature. By developing the mental ability to analyze the written word at a young age, children will find a love for reading unlike any other. By creating this faux world we are learning, creating, and enjoying ourselves in a friendly utopian society.[2]

Lawver is so good at mimicking teacherly language that one forgets that she has not yet reached adulthood. For example, she provides reassurances that the site will protect children's actual identities and that she will screen posts to ensure that none contain content inappropriate for younger participants.[3] Lawver was anxious to see her work recognized by teachers, librarians, and her fellow home schoolers. She developed detailed plans for how teachers can use her template to create localized version of a Hogwarts school newspaper as class projects. A number of teachers have taken up her offer.

Whether encountered inside or outside formal education, Lawver's project enabled kids to immerse themselves into the imaginary world of Hogwarts and to feel a very real sense of connection to an actual community of children around the world who were working together to produce *The Daily Prophet*. The school they were inventing together (building on the foundations of J. K. Rowling's novel) could not have been more different from the one she had escaped in Mississippi. Here, people of many different ethnic, racial, and national backgrounds (some real, some imagined) formed a community where individual differences were accepted and where learning was celebrated.

The point of entry into this imaginary school was the construction of a fictional identity, and subsequently these personas get woven into a series of "news stories" reporting on events at Hogwarts. For many kids, the profile is all they would write—having a self within the fiction was enough to satisfy the needs that brought them to the site. For others, it was the first step toward constructing a more elaborate fantasy about their life at Hogwarts. In their profiles, kids often combined mundane details of their everyday experiences with fantastical stories about their place within J. K. Rowling's world:

I recently transferred from Madame McKay's Academy of Magic in America to come to Hogwarts. Lived in southern California for most of my life, and my mother never told my father that she was a witch until my fifth birthday (he left shortly afterwards).

Orphaned when at 5 when her parents died of cancer, this pure blood witch was sent to live with a family of wizards associated with the Ministry of Magic.

The image of the special child being raised in a mundane (in this case, muggle) family and discovering their identities as they enter school age is a classic theme of fantasy novels and fairy tales, yet here there are often references to divorce or cancer, real-world difficulties so many kids face. From the profiles themselves, we can't be sure whether these are problems they have confronted personally or if they are anxious possibilities they are exploring through their fantasies. Heather has suggested that many kids come to *The Daily Prophet* because their schools and families have failed them in some way; they use the new school community to work through their feelings about some traumatic event or to compensate for their estrangement from kids in their neighborhoods. Some children are drawn toward some of the fantasy races—elves, goblins, giants, and the like—while other kids have trouble imagining themselves to be anything other than muggle-born, even in their fantasy play. Children use stories to escape from or reaffirm aspects of their real lives.[4]

Rowling's richly detailed world allows many points of entry. Some kids imagine themselves as related to the characters, the primary ones like Harry Potter or Snape, of course, but also minor background figures—the inventors of the quidditch brooms, the authors of the textbooks, the heads of referenced agencies, classmates of Harry's mother and father, any affiliation that allows them to claim a special place for themselves in the story. In her book, *Writing Superheroes* (1997), Anne Haas Dyson uses the metaphor of a "ticket to play" to describe how the roles provided by children's media properties get deployed by children in a classroom space to police who is allowed to participate and what roles they can assume.[5] Some children fit comfortably within the available roles; others feel excluded and have to work harder to insert themselves into the fantasy. Dyson's focus has to do with divisions of gender and race, primarily, but given the global nature of *The Daily Prophet* community, nationality also was potentially at stake. Rowling's acknowledgment in subsequent books that Hogwarts interacted with schools around the world gave students from many countries a "ticket" into the fantasy: "Sirius was born in India to Ariel and Derek Koshen. Derek was working as a Ministry of Magic ambassador to the Indian Ministry. Sirius was raised in Bombay, and speaks Hindi fluently. While he was in Bombay he saved a stranded Hippogriff from becoming a jacket, cementing his long-lasting love of magical creatures. He attended Gahdal School of Witchcraft and Wizardry in Thailand." Here, it helps that the community is working hard to be inclusive and accepts fantasies that may not comfortably match the world described within the novels.

One striking consequence of the value placed on education in the *Harry Potter* books is that almost all of the participants at *The Daily Prophet* imagine themselves to be gifted students. Kids who read recreationally are still a subset of the total school population, so it is very likely that many of these kids are teacher's pets in real life. Hermione represented a particularly potent role model for the studiously minded young girls who were key contributors to *The Daily Prophet*. Some feminist critics argue that she falls into traditional feminine stereotypes of dependency and nurturance.[6] This may be true, but this character provides some point of identification for female readers within a book otherwise so focused on young boys. Here's how one young writer framed her relationship to the character:

My name is Mandi Granger. I am 12 yrs old. I am also muggle born. Yes, I am related to Hermione Granger. I am Hermione's cousin. I am attending Hogwarts School for Witchcraft and Wizardry. This is my third year at Hogwarts. I am doing this article between all my studies. I guess I pick up my study habits from my cousin. I am in the Gryffindor house just like my just like my cousin. I do know Harry Potter personally by my cousin. My cousin took him to my house before I went to Hogwarts. We mostly talk about Hogwarts and the Weasley's children.

10 Through children's fantasy play, Hermione takes on a much more active and central role than Rowling provided her. As Ellen Seiter notes in regard to girl-targeted series such as *Strawberry Shortcake* (1981), feminist parents sometimes sell their daughters short by underestimating their ability to extend beyond what is represented on the screen and by stigmatizing the already limited range of media content available to them.[7] Female readers are certainly free to identify across gender with a range of other characters— and one can see the claims of special family ties as one way of marking those identifications. Yet, at an age when gender roles are reinforced on all sides, transgressing gender roles through the fantasy may be harder than reconstructing the characters as vehicles for your own empowerment fantasies.

In some cases, the back stories for these characters are quite elaborate with detailed accounts of their wands, the animal familiars, their magical abilities, their favorite classes, their future plans, and the like. These fictional personas can contain the seeds of larger narratives, suggesting how the construction of an identity may fuel subsequent fan fiction:

I'm the only sister of Harry Potter, and I am going to play for the Gryffindor quidditch team this year as a chaser. My best friend is Cho Chang, and I am dating Draco Malfoy (although Harry's not happy about that). One of my other good friends is Riley Ravenclaw, a co-writer. I have a few pets, a winged Thestral named Bostrio, a unicorn foal named Golden, and a snowy owl (like Hedwig) named Cassiddia. I was able to escape the Lord Voldemort attack on my family for the reason that I was holidaying with my Aunt Zeldy in Ireland at the time, though I mourn the loss of my mum and dad. I was mad about the awful things Ms. Skeeter wrote about my little brother, and I have sent her her own little package of undiluted bubotuber pus. HA!

As *The Daily Prophet* reporters develop their reports about life at Hogwarts, they draw each other's personas into their stories, trying to preserve what each child sees as its special place within this world. The result is a jointly produced fantasy—somewhere between a role-playing game and fan fiction. The intertwining of fantasies becomes a key element of bonding for these kids, who come to care about one another through interacting with these fictional personas.

What skills do children need to become full participants in convergence culture? Across this book, we have identified a number—the ability to pool knowledge with others in a collaborative enterprise (as in *Survivor* spoiling), the ability to share and compare value systems by evaluating ethical dramas (as occurs in the gossip surrounding reality television), the ability to make connections across scattered pieces of information (as occurs when we consume *The Matrix*, 1999, or *Pokémon*, 1998), the ability to express your interpretations and feelings toward popular fictions through your own folk culture (as occurs in *Star Wars* fan cinema), and the ability to circulate what you create via the Internet so that it can be shared with others (again as in fan cinema). The example of *The Daily Prophet* suggests yet another important cultural competency: role-playing both as a means of exploring a fictional realm and as a means of developing a richer understanding of yourself and the culture around you. These kids came to understand *Harry Potter* by occupying a space within Hogwarts; occupying such a space helped them to map more fully the rules of this fictional world and the roles that various characters played within it. Much as an actor builds up a character by combining things discovered through research with things learned through personal introspection, these kids were drawing on their own experiences to flesh out various aspects of Rowling's fiction. This is a kind of intellectual mastery that comes only through active participation. At the same time, role-playing was providing an inspiration for them to expand other kinds of literacy skills—those already valued within traditional education.

What's striking about this process, though, is that it takes place outside the classroom and beyond any direct adult control. Kids are teaching kids what they need to become full participants in convergence culture. More and more, educators are coming to value the learning that occurs in these informal and recreational spaces, especially as they confront the constraints imposed on learning via educational policies that seemingly value only what can be counted on a standardized test. If children are going to acquire the skills needed to be full participants in their culture, they may well learn these skills through involvement in activities such as editing the newspaper of an imaginary school or teaching one another skills needed to do well in massively multiplayer games or any number of others things that teachers and parents currently regard as trivial pursuits.

. . .

DEFENSE AGAINST THE DARK ARTS

15   J. K. Rowling and Scholastic, her publisher, had initially signaled their support for fan writers, stressing that storytelling encouraged kids to expand their imaginations and empowered them to find their voices as writers. Through her London-based agent, the Christopher Little Literary Agency, Rowling had issued a statement in 2003 describing the author's long-standing policy of welcoming "the huge interest that her fans have in the series and the fact that it has led them to try their hand at writing."[8] When Warner Bros. bought the film rights in 2001, however, the stories entered a second and not so complimentary intellectual property regime.[9] The studio had a long-standing practice of seeking out Web sites whose domain names used copyrighted or trademarked phrases. Trademark law was set up to avoid "potential confusions" about who produces particular goods or content; Warner felt it had a legal obligation to police sites that emerged around their properties. The studio characterized this as a "sorting out" process in which each site was suspended until

the studio could assess what the site was doing with the *Harry Potter* franchise. Diane Nelsen, senior vice president of Warner Bros. Family Entertainment, explained:

> When we dug down under some of these domain names, we could see clearly who was creating a screen behind which they were exploiting our property illegally. With fans you did not have to go far to see that they were just fans and they were expressing something vital about their relationship to this property. . . . You hate to penalize an authentic fan for the actions of an inauthentic fan, but we had enough instances of people who really were exploiting kids in the name of *Harry Potter*.

In many cases, the original site owner would be issued permission to continue to use the site under the original name, but Warner Bros. retained the right to shut it down if they found "inappropriate or offensive content."

The fans felt slapped in the face by what they saw as the studio's efforts to take control over their sites. Many of those caught up in these struggles were children and teens, who had been among the most active organizers of the *Harry Potter* fandom. Heather Lawver, the young editor of *The Daily Prophet,* formed the American-based organization, Defense Against the Dark Arts, when she learned that some fan friends had been threatened with legal action: "Warner was very clever about who they attacked. . . . They attacked a whole bunch of kids in Poland. How much of a risk is that? They went after the 12 and 15 year olds with the rinky-dink sites. They underestimated how interconnected our fandom was. They underestimated the fact that we knew those kids in Poland and we knew the rinky dink sites and we cared about them." Heather herself never received a cease-and-desist letter, but she made it her cause to defend friends who were under legal threats. In the United Kingdom, fifteen-year-old Claire Field emerged as the poster girl in the fans' struggle against Warner Bros. She and her parents had hired a solicitor after she received a cease-and-desist letter for her site,

www.harrypotterguide.co.uk, and in the process, took the struggle to the British media. Her story was reported worldwide, and in each location other teen Webmasters who had been shut down by Warner's legal representatives also came public.[10] Lawver joined forces with Field's British supporters, helping to coordinate media outreach and activism against the studio.

Defense Against the Dark Arts argued that fans had helped to turn a little known children's book into an international best-seller and that the rights holders owed them some latitude to do their work. The petition ends with a "call to arms" against studios that fail to appreciate their supporters: "There are dark forces afoot, darker even than He-Who-Must-Not-Be-Named, because these dark forces are daring to take away something so basic, so human, that it's close to murder. They are taking away our freedom of speech, our freedom to express our thoughts, feelings, and ideas, and they are taking away the fun of a magical book."[11] Lawver, the passionate and articulate teen, debated a Warner Bros. spokesman on MSNBC's *Hardball with Chris Matthews* (1997). As Lawver explained, "We weren't disorganized little kids anymore. We had a public following and we had a petition with 1500 signatures in a matter of two weeks. They [Warner Bros.] finally had to negotiate with us."

As the controversy intensified, Diane Nelson, senior vice president of Warner Bros. Family Entertainment, publicly acknowledged that the studio's legal response had been "naïve" and "an act of miscommunication."[12] Nelson, now executive vice president for Global Brand Management, told me, "We didn't know what we had on our hands early on in dealing with *Harry Potter*. We did what we would normally do in the protection of our intellectual property. As soon as we realized we were causing consternation to children or their parents, we stopped it." Out of the conflict, the studio developed a more collaborative policy for engaging with *Harry Potter* fans, one similar to the ways that Lucas was seeking to collaborate with *Star Wars* fan filmmakers:

Heather is obviously a very smart young woman and did an effective job drawing attention to the issue. . . . She brought to our attention fans who she felt had been victims of these letters. We called them. In one instance, there was a young man she was holding up as a poster child for what we were doing wrong. He was a young man out of London. He and two of his friends from school had started a Triwizard Tournament on the internet. They were having contests through their sites. . . . Ultimately, what we did with them was the basis of what we did with subsequent fans. We deputized them. We ended up sponsoring their tournament and paying for their P.O. box for off line entries to this contest. . . . We were not at all opposed to his site or what he was doing on it or how he was expressing himself as a fan. In fact, we believed from day one that those sites were critical to the success of what we were doing and the more of them the better. We ended up giving him official sanction and access to materials to include on the site so that we could keep him within the family and still protect *Harry Potter* materials appropriately.

Many *Potter* fans praised Warner for admitting its mistakes and fixing the problems in their relations with fans. Lawver remains unconvinced, seeing the outcome more as an attempt to score a public relations victory than any shift in their thinking. She has recently added a section to *The Daily Prophet* designed to provide resources for other fan communities that wish to defend themselves against studio restrictions on their expression and participation.[13]

Heather Lawver and her allies had launched their children's campaign against Warner Bros. under the assumption that such fan activism had a long history. She explained: "I figured with the history that *Star Wars* and *Star Trek* fan writers had, people would have done this before. I didn't think much of it. I thought we had precedence but apparently not." Other groups had tried, but not with nearly the same degree of success. After several decades of aggressive studio attention, there is literally no case law concerning fan fiction. The broad claims sometimes asserted by the studios have never been subjected to legal contestation. Studios threaten, fans back down, and none of the groups that would normally step forward to defend free expression rights consider it part of their agenda to defend amateur creators. Free-speech organizations, including the American Civil Liberties Union and the Electronic Frontier Foundation, joined Muggles for Harry Potter, a group created to support teachers who wanted to keep the *Harry Potter* books in the classroom, but failed to defend the fan fiction writers who asserted their rights to build their fantasies around Rowling's novel. The Stanford Center for Internet and Society posted a statement—explicitly supportive, implicitly condescending—about fan fiction on its Chilling Effects Web site (http://www.chillingeffects.org/fanfic). The statement in effect concedes most of the claims made by the studio attorneys.[14] Adopting a similar position, Electronic Frontier Foundation chairman of the board Brad Templeton writes, "Almost all 'fan fiction' is arguably a copyright violation. If you want to write a story about Jim Kirk and Mr. Spock, you need Paramount's permission, pure and simple."[15] Note how Templeton moves from legal hedge words like "arguably" in the first sentence to the moral certainty of "plain and simple" by the second. With friends like these, who needs enemies?

20   The fan community includes plenty of lawyers, some informed, some otherwise, who have been willing to step up where the public interest groups have failed, and to offer legal advice to fans about how to contest efforts to shut down their Web sites.[16] Fan activists, for example, support Writers University, a Web site that, among other services, provides periodic updates on how a range of different media franchises and individual authors have responded to fan fiction, identifying those who welcome and those who prohibit participation.[17] The site's goal

is to allow fans to make an informed choice about the risks they face in pursuing their hobbies and interests. Legal scholars Rosemary J. Coombe and Andrew Herman note that fans have found posting their cease-and-desist letters on the Web to be an effective tactic, one that forces media companies to publicly confront the consequences of their actions, and one that helps fans see the patterns of legal action that might otherwise be felt only by those Webmistresses directly involved.[18]

Nobody is sure whether fan fiction falls under current fair-use protections. Current copyright law simply doesn't have a category for dealing with amateur creative expression. Where there has been a "public interest" factored into the legal definition of fair use—such as the desire to protect the rights of libraries to circulate books or journalists to quote or academics to cite other researchers—it has been advanced in terms of legitimated classes of users and not a generalized public right to cultural participation. Our current notion of fair use is an artifact of an era when few people had access to the marketplace of ideas, and those who did fell into certain professional classes. It surely demands close reconsideration as we develop technologies that broaden who may produce and circulate cultural materials. Judges know what to do with people who have professional interests in the production and distribution of culture; they don't know what to do with amateurs, or people they deem to be amateurs.

Industry groups have tended to address copyright issues primarily through a piracy model, focusing on the threat of file sharing, rather than dealing with the complexities of fan fiction. Their official educational materials have been criticized for focusing on copyright protections to the exclusion of any reference to fair use. By implication, fans are seen simply as "pirates" who steal from the studios and give nothing in return. Studios often defend their actions against fans on the grounds that if they do not actively enforce their copyrights they will be vulnerable to commercial competitors encroaching on their content.

The best legal solution to this quagmire may be to rewrite fair-use protections to legitimate grassroots, not-for-profit circulation of critical essays, and stories that comment on the content of mass media. Companies certainly are entitled to protect their rights against encroachment from commercial competitors, yet under the current system, because other companies know how far they can push and are reluctant to sue each other, they often have greater latitude to appropriate and transform media content than amateurs, who do not know their rights and have little legal means to defend them even if they did. One paradoxical result is that works that are hostile to the original creators and thus can be read more explicitly as making critiques of the source material may have greater freedom from copyright enforcement than works that embrace the ideas behind the original work and simply seek to extend them in new directions. A story where Harry and the other students rose up to overthrow Dumbledore because of his paternalistic policies is apt to be recognized by a judge as political speech and parody, whereas a work that imagines Ron and Hermione going on a date may be so close to the original that its status as criticism is less clear and is apt to be read as infringement.

In the short run, change is more likely to occur by shifting the way studios think about fan communities than reshaping the law, and that's why the collaborative approaches we've seen across the past two chapters seem like important steps in redefining the space of amateur participation. Nelson said that the *Harry Potter* controversy was instrumental in starting conversations within the studio between business, public relations, creative, and legal department staffers, about what principles should govern their relations with their fans and supporters: "We are trying to balance the needs of other creative stakeholders, as well as the fans, as well as our own legal obligations, all within an arena which is new and changing and there are not clear precedents about how things should be interpreted or how they would be acted upon if they ever reached the courts."

25   In the course of the interview, she described fans as "core shareholders" in a particular property and the "life blood" of the franchise. The studio needed to find ways to respect the "creativity and energy" these fans brought behind a franchise, even as they needed to protect the franchise from encroachment from groups who wanted to profit for their efforts, to respond quickly to misinformation, or, in the case of material aimed at the youth market, to protect children from access to mature content. As far as fan fiction goes,

We recognize that it is the highest compliment in terms of the fans inserting themselves into the property and wanting to express their love for it. We are very respectful of what that means. There is a degree to which fan fiction is acceptable to authors and there is a degree to which it moves into a place where it does not feel appropriate, respectful, or within the rights of fans. A lot has to do with how a fan wants to publish and whether they want to benefit commercially off of that fan fiction. If it is purely just an expression for others to read and experience and appreciate, I think that is generally pretty tolerable by a studio rights holder and a creator. The more broadly the fan wants to see that fan fiction disseminated or trade upon it for revenue, promotion, or publicity, the less tolerant the studio or creator might be.

But, as Nelson acknowledged, the fan's "sense of ownership over a particular property" posed challenges for the studio:

When we stray from the source material or what fans perceive as the true roots of a property, we are under their scrutiny. They can become either advocates for what we are doing or strong dissenters. They can shift the tide of how a property is introduced into the market place depending on whether they perceive us as having presented it carefully, respectfully, and accurately. . . . Fans may be trying to promote the property on the internet in their terms but they can sometimes compromise our responsibility to protect that intellectual property so as to keep it pure and to keep our legal rights in tact.

There is still—and perhaps may always be—a huge gap between the studio's assumptions about what constitutes appropriate fan participation and the fans' own sense of moral "ownership" over the property. The studios are now, for the most part, treating cult properties as "love marks" and fans as "inspirational consumers" whose efforts help generate broader interests in their properties. Establishing the fans' loyalty often means lessening traditional controls that companies might exert over their intellectual properties and thus opening up a broader space for grassroots creative expression.

NOTES

1. Unless otherwise noted, all quotes from Heather Lawver taken from interview with author, August 2003.

2. Heather Lawver, "To the Adults," http://www.dprophet.com/hq/openletter.html.

3. Lawver, "To the Adults."

4. For more on the ways younger children use stories to work through reallife concerns, see Henry Jenkins, "Going Bonkers! Children, Play, and Pee-Wee," in Constance Penley and Sharon Willis (eds.), *Male Trouble* (Minneapolis: University of Minnesota Press, 1993).

5. Anne Haas Dyson, *Writing Superheroes: Contemporary Childhood, Popular Culture, and Classroom Literacy* (New York: Teacher's College Press, 1997).

6. See, for example, Christine Schoefer, "Harry Potter's Girl Trouble," *Salon,* January 13, 2000, http://dir.salon.com/books/feature/2000/01/13/potter/index.html?sid = 566202. For a rebuttal, see Chris Gregory, "Hands Off Harry Potter! Have Critics of J. K. Rowling's Books Even Read Them?" *Salon,* March 1, 2000, http://www.salon.com/books/feature/2000/03/01/harrypotter.

7. Ellen Seiter, *Sold Separately: Children and Parents in Consumer Culture* (New Brunswick, N.J.: Rutgers University Press, 1993).

8. Tracy Mayor, "Taking Liberties with Harry Potter," *Boston Globe Magazine,* June 29, 2003.

9. Stephanie Grunier and John Lippman, "Warner Bros. Claim Harry Potter Sites," *Wall Street Journal Online,* December 20, 2000, http://zdnet.com.com/2102-11_ 2-503255.html; "Kids 1—Warner Bros. 0: When the Big Studio Set Its Hounds on Some *Harry Potter* Fan Web Sites, It Didn't Bargain on the Potterhead Rebellion," *Vancouver Sun,* November 17, 2001.

10. Claire Field, interview with author, August 2003.

11. "Defense Against the Dark Arts," http://www.dprophet.com/dada/.

12. Ryan Buell, "Fans Call for War; Warner Bros. Claim Misunderstanding!" http://www.entertainment-rewired.com/fan_appology.htm.

13. See http://www.dprophet.com/dada/.

14. "Fan Fiction, Chilling Effects," http://www.chilling effects.org/fanfic.

15. Brad Templeton, "10 Big Myths about Copyright Explained," http://www.templetons.com/brad/copymyths.html.

16. See, for example, Rebecca Tushnet, "Legal Fictions: Copyright, Fan Fiction, and a New Common Law," *Loyola of Los Angeles Entertainment Law Journal,* 1977, accessed online at http://www.tushnet.com/law/fanficarticle.html; A. T. Lee, "Copyright 101: A Brief Introduction to Copyright for Fan Fiction Authors," *Whoosh!,* October 1998, http://www.whoosh.org/issue25/leee1.html.

17. Katie Dean, "Copyright Crusaders Hit Schools," *Wired,* August 13, 2004, http://www.wired.com/news/digiwood/0,1412,64543,00.html.

18. Rosemary Coombe and Andrew Herman, "Defending Toy Dolls and Maneuvering Toy Soldiers: Trademarks, Consumer Politics and Corporate Accountability on the World Wide Web," presented at MIT Communication Forum, April 12, 2001, accessed at http://web.mit.edu/m-i-t/forums/trademark/index_ paper.html.

EXPLORATORY WRITING

As Jenkins explains in a portion of his essay that was not included here, the J. K. Rowling series created conflicts after the first book was published, and even more so after Warner Bros. purchased the film rights to the series: "On the one hand, there was the struggle of teachers, librarians, book publishers, and civil liberty groups to stand up against efforts by the religious right to have the *Harry Potter* books removed from school libraries and banned from local bookstores. On the other, there were the efforts of Warner Bros. to rein in fan appropriations of the *Harry Potter* books on the grounds that they infringed on the studio's intellectual property." Jenkins argues that both of these efforts threatened children's rights to participate in the imaginative world of Harry Potter. Write an essay in which you explain how Jenkins uses Heather's story to make that argument. What does he believe Heather and her online community achieve with *The Daily Prophet*?

TALKING ABOUT THE READING

Although it might at first seem odd for a teenager to create an entire online community in which participants become a part of a fictional world, it is actually quite common and has been for many years. Children play at Superman or Spider Man or Star Wars. Teens and adults write fanzines and create online fan communities based on soap operas, television shows, and favorite celebrities. Members of the Society for Creative Anachronism attempt to recreate pre-seventeenth-century Europe in games, costumes, and participatory stories. With a group of your classmates, make a list of stories or characters that so influenced you and your friends, you imagined yourselves in those worlds through games or fan fiction or costuming. What makes those stories and characters particularly rich for fan participation?

WRITING ASSIGNMENTS

1. Henry Jenkins sees Heather's *Daily Prophet* site as an example of what he calls "convergence culture," that place where old and new media come together to make something altogether different. In the case of *The Daily Prophet,* the *Harry Potter* series of books is the old media and the ability to create online fan communities is the new. Jenkins suggests that sites like this one are creating a generation of writers. Write an essay in which you examine Jenkins's claims for this convergence culture as it emerges in online fan fiction. What, for example, would Jenkins say that Heather's site and sites like hers do that reading groups or writing groups or school cannot do?

2. At the end of this excerpt, Jenkins writes, "There is still—and perhaps may always be—a huge gap between the studio's assumptions about what constitutes appropriate fan participation and the fans' own sense of moral 'ownership' over the property." Some companies attempt to control fan ownership by creating corporate-sponsored fan sites. The American Girls Co., for example, began building this kind of corporate-based fan "ownership" of its characters very early by selling dolls with stories and then girls' clothing that matched the dolls' clothing. The company has a Web site where fans can participate, occasionally even creating stories for the American Girls dolls. Visit this or other corporate-sponsored fan sites. Write an analysis of the site in which you examine the amount of control the corporation has over the product and the control allowed to fans. In what ways are sites like these both like and different from the kind of site for fan fiction that Jenkins describes?

3. Visit *The Daily Prophet* site (http://www.dprophet.com) as well as another fan fiction site. You can find thousands of them at http://www.fanfiction.net, which has shown over 360,000 hits for *Harry Potter* and 260 hits for *Robin Hood*. Write a review of *The Daily Prophet* in which you compare it to other fan sites. Be sure to use Jenkins's discussion of the promise of interactive fan fiction and new technology in your review.

THE SHOOTOUT OVER HIDDEN MEANINGS IN VIDEO GAMES

—David Itzkoff

David Itzkoff has worked as an editor at *Maxim* and *Spin*. He is the author of the book *Lads: A Memoir of Manhood* (2004), both the story of his beginnings as an editor and also a searing look at *Maxim* and the world of men's magazines. He is a frequent contributor to the *New York Times,* writing for the *Times* book blog *Paper Cuts* and as an occasional popular culture reviewer. His review of the video game *Metal Gear Solid 4: Guns of the Patriot* first appeared as an "Ideas and Trends" column in the *Times* on June 22, 2008.

SUGGESTION FOR READING Before you read, write a brief account of your own experience with video games and their storytelling possibilities. If you don't play video games or aren't familiar with many games, write about your current knowledge of or attitude toward video games.

1 If there's a subject that's as contentious as war itself, it might be a video game about war.

It's been just over a week since the release of Metal Gear Solid 4: Guns of the Patriots, the latest chapter in the popular video game series about a covert military agent named Solid Snake. And already, fans are exchanging rhetorical fusillades on the Internet, teasing out what the underlying political and philosophical messages of Metal Gear Solid 4 might be.

Encrypted within this discussion is a more sophisticated argument about the nascent medium of video games. Can it tell a story as satisfyingly as a work of cinema or literature?

Is the Sisyphean mission of Solid Snake—to rid the world of a robotic nuclear tank called Metal Gear—a parable about the futility of war or about its necessity? A critique of America's domination of the global stage? A metaphor for the struggle between determinism and free will? If the creator of the Metal Gear Solid series, Hideo Kojima, has answers to these questions, he isn't telling.

5   "He doesn't interview very much," said Leigh Alexander, an associate editor at Kotaku.com, a video game blog. "Sometimes he will speak about it, and other times it's left to the critical peanut gallery to disassemble what his intentions might have been."

Devoted players have no shortage of opinions about what Mr. Kojima's games are saying. The original Metal Gear Solid, released in 1998 for Sony's PlayStation console, combined stealth combat with cinematic intermission scenes, full of dialogue and imagery that directly invoked the bombing of Hiroshima and the birth of atomic weapons. The game called attention to the scourge of nuclear proliferation, and forced players to consider the morality of their own lethal actions.

These messages were complicated by a pair of sequels: Metal Gear Solid 2: Sons of Liberty, released in late 2001, introduced a shadowy supernational group called the Patriots, so powerful that even the president of the United States answers to it. (A commentary on the disputed 2000 election? The cabal theories of post-9/11 politics?) And Metal Gear Solid 3: Snake Eater, released in 2004, explored the cold war origins of its characters, whose personal stories are intertwined with the rise of the military-industrial complex.

"This is a just-off-center world that gamers can almost believe in," said Rob Smith, the editor in chief of PlayStation: The Official Magazine. "All the important world history of the 20th century matches up in ways that say, 'If we'd gone down this path then, this is what we'd now be facing.'"

Metal Gear Solid 4, released for the PlayStation 3 console, further upends traditional notions of heroism and villainy: in this game Solid Snake (think James Bond meets Rambo) has aged considerably, as have several of his archenemies; the forces he battles are not the soldiers of identifiable nations but the mercenaries on the payroll of private military companies. "The issue of good guys and bad guys doesn't exist anymore," Mr. Smith said. "It's just: here's the guys."

10   Even as gamers ponder what this symbolism means (an allegory of war in the era of Blackwater Worldwide and stateless enemy combatants?), they are also debating whether the story of Metal Gear Solid 4 is a satisfying one, and if its storytelling techniques are used effectively.

"You get so caught up in just figuring out, Does this story need to be here?" said Stephen Totilo, an MTV News reporter who covers video games. "That's not a question you wind up asking yourself when you're reading a novel. Of course the story needs to be there! Otherwise you don't have a novel."

Players like Shawn Elliott, the senior executive editor of the gaming Web site 1up.com, have criticized the game for its preachiness, and for its reliance on lengthy cinematic interludes that can run 30 minutes or longer.

"It can basically become a movie for long stretches," Mr. Elliott said. "It's not necessarily a game catching up with movies, but a game kind of cheating and using a language that isn't native to its own medium."

Others object to the sheer density of the story, spanning seven games released over 20 real-world years, that players are asked to master. "Let's just say it's not something any of us gamers are nearly as used to doing when we're playing a game as when we're reading a novel," Mr. Totilo said.

15   Players can skip over the storytelling elements in Metal Gear Solid and still play the game.

But unrepentant fans like Ms. Alexander of Kotaku.com argue that, coherent or not, the narrative of Metal Gear Solid 4 is an inseparable part of the "package experience" that makes it an evolutionary step beyond fare like Halo 3, a first-person shooting game designed to soothe itchy trigger fingers.

Metal Gear Solid, Ms. Alexander said, "has the characters and the narrative, the symbolism and the metaphors, and all of the lore that ties it together," whereas Halo is popular "not because of any of its peripheral elements or anything else about it, other than that you shoot people."

EXPLORATORY WRITING

David Itzkoff opens his review by saying, "If there's a subject that's as contentious as war itself, it might be a video game about war." In a short paper, show how Itzkoff develops that claim. What features of the game *Metal Gear Solid 4: Guns of the Patriot* are, according to this review, especially contentious in terms of its politics or storyline?

TALKING ABOUT THE READING

Although the earliest video games remained frozen for years in the world of *Pac Man* and other computer dexterity games, they were always at least loosely tied to the world of story-telling. After all, if you have to rescue the victim, shoot the enemy, or find your way into the castle, you are a part of a story. With role-playing games and games like the *Sims,* which ask players to create the entire world of the game, storytelling becomes an even more vital component. In his review, Itzkoff writes that one underlying question about games like this one is, "Can it tell a story as satisfyingly as a work of cinema or literature?"

With a group of your classmates, make a list of video games that you know. Which games definitely have a storyline? Which have a definite political message or underlying meaning? How active are players in creating that storyline? How important are the politics of the game in your desire to play or continue playing the game? Can this game "tell a story as satisfyingly as cinema or literature?" How? Or why not?

WRITING ASSIGNMENTS

1. With a group of two or three classmates, review a video game in terms of its appeal as a storytelling game and as a game that evokes or avoids discussion about underlying meaning. In your review, make sure you compare the game to others created around the same time and aimed at some of the same audience. What makes the game popular (or not)? What makes it innovative (or not)? What makes players want to argue about the meanings in its storyline (or not)? Present your review, with sample clips from the game, to the class.

2. Many popular films and television programs have generated video games. *Matrix, Lord of the Rings, Star Wars, CSI, Lost,* even *American Idol* all have generated companion video games. Choose one of these and familiarize yourself with both the original and the video game. Write an essay on the game in which you examine it in terms of its ability to tell a complex story, one in which underlying meanings or messages are debated by users. In other words, how much of the game picks up not just the action but the complexity of the original story?

3. Sometimes films are created from video games. *Lara Croft: Tomb Raider* is one of the first video games to become a movie, but there are others. Choose a film that originated as a video game. Watch the film and familiarize yourself with the game (both forms are available at film rental firms). Write an essay in which you examine what the film story-line and characters retain from the original game. What changes? What can you identify in the game that seems to lend itself easily to popular film? Itzkoff, at one point, quotes MTV reporter Stephen Totilo as saying, "You get so caught up in just figuring out, Does this story need to be here? That's not a question you wind up asking yourself when you're reading a novel. Of course the story needs to be there! Otherwise you don't have a novel." As you consider the video game-turned-film, think about that statement. Did the story have to be in the original? It obviously cannot be left out of the film, but what does it contribute to the game?

A few games that became films are:

Lara Croft: Tomb Raider	*In the Name of the King: A Dungeon Siege Tale*
Mortal Kombat	*Far Cry*
Resident Evil	*Street Fighter: The Legend of Chun Li*
Doom	

THE GANGSTER AS TRAGIC HERO

—Robert Warshow

Robert Warshow was a film critic and one of the first American intellectuals to write seriously about popular culture. The following essay, "The Gangster as Tragic Hero," is taken from his book *The Immediate Experience*, published posthumously in 1962. (Warshow died in 1955.) The essay, though brief, is considered by many to be a classic example of film criticism and cultural analysis. Since the 1950s, when Warshow was writing, any number of gangster films have appeared: *Bonnie and Clyde,* the famous *Godfather* trilogy, *Goodfellas,* a remake of *Scarface* (starring Al Pacino this time), a film version of the TV show *The Untouchables,* black gangster films such as *New Jack City* and *American Gangster.* On television, HBO's series *The Sopranos, The Wire,* and *Deadwood* have drawn large and loyal audiences.

SUGGESTION FOR READING As you read, keep the title of the essay—"The Gangster as Tragic Hero"—in mind. Underline/highlight and annotate passages in the essay where Warshow explains what makes gangsters tragic figures.

1 America, as a social and political organization, is committed to a cheerful view of life. It could not be otherwise. The sense of tragedy is a luxury of aristocratic societies, where the fate of the individual is not conceived of as having a direct and legitimate political importance, being determined by a fixed and supra-political—that is, non-controversial—moral order or fate. Modern equalitarian societies, however, whether democratic or authoritarian in their political forms, always base themselves on the claim that they are making life happier; the avowed function of the modern state, at least in its ultimate terms, is not only to regulate social relations, but also to determine the quality and the possibilities of human life in general. Happiness thus becomes the chief political issue—in a sense, the only political issue—and for that reason it can never be treated as an issue at all. If an American or a Russian is unhappy, it implies a certain reprobation of his society, and

therefore, by a logic of which we can all recognize the necessity, it becomes an obligation of citizenship to be cheerful; if the authorities find it necessary, the citizen may even be compelled to make a public display of his cheerfulness on important occasions, just as he may be conscripted into the army in time of war.

Naturally, this civic responsibility rests more strongly upon the organs of mass culture. The individual citizen may still be permitted his private unhappiness so long as it does not take on political significance, the extent of this tolerance being determined by how large an area of private life the society can accommodate. But every production of mass culture is a public act and must conform with accepted notions of the public good. Nobody seriously questions the principle that it is the function of mass culture to maintain public morale, and certainly nobody in the mass audience objects to having his morale maintained. At a time when the normal condition of the citizen is a state of anxiety, euphoria spreads over our culture like the broad smile of an idiot. In terms of attitudes towards life, there is very little difference between a "happy" movie like *Good News,* which ignores death and suffering, and a "sad" movie like *A Tree Grows in Brooklyn,* which uses death and suffering as incidents in the service of a higher optimism.

But, whatever its effectiveness as a source of consolation and a means of pressure for maintaining "positive" social attitudes, this optimism is fundamentally satisfying to no one, not even to those who would be most disoriented without its support. Even within the area of mass culture, there always exists a current of opposition, seeking to express by whatever means are available to it that sense of desperation and inevitable failure which optimism itself helps to create. Most often, this opposition is confined to rudimentary or semiliterate forms: in mob politics and journalism, for example, or in certain kinds of religious enthusiasm. When it does enter the field of art, it is likely to be disguised or attenuated: in an unspecific form of expression like jazz, in the basically harmless nihilism of the Marx Brothers, in the continually reasserted strain of hopelessness that often seems to be the real meaning of the soap opera. The gangster film is remarkable in that it fills the need for disguise (though not sufficiently to avoid arousing uneasiness) without requiring any serious distortion. From its beginnings, it has been a consistent and astonishingly complete presentation of the modern sense of tragedy.

In its initial character, the gangster film is simply one example of the movies' constant tendency to create fixed dramatic patterns that can be repeated indefinitely with a reasonable expectation of profit. One gangster film follows another as one musical or one Western follows another. But this rigidity is not necessarily opposed to the requirements of art. There have been very successful types of art in the past which developed such specific and detailed conventions as almost to make individual examples of the type interchangeable. This is true, for example, of Elizabethan revenge tragedy and Restoration comedy.

5   For such a type to be successful means that its conventions have imposed themselves upon the general consciousness and become the accepted vehicles of a particular set of attitudes and a particular aesthetic effect. One goes to any individual example of the type with very definite expectations, and originality is to be welcomed only in the degree that it intensifies the expected experience without fundamentally altering it. Moreover, the relationship between the conventions which go to make up such a type and the real experience of its audience or the real facts of whatever situation it pretends to describe is of only secondary importance and does not determine its aesthetic force. It is only in an ultimate sense that the type appeals to its audience's experience of reality; much more immediately, it appeals to previous experience of the type itself: it creates its own field of reference.

Thus the importance of the gangster film, and the nature and intensity of its emotional and aesthetic impact, cannot be measured in terms of the place of the gangster himself or the importance of the problem of crime in American life. Those European movie-goers who think there is a gangster on every corner in New York are certainly deceived, but defenders of the "positive" side of American culture are equally deceived if they think it relevant to point out that most Americans have never seen a gangster. What matters is that the experience of the gangster *as an experience of art* is universal to Americans. There is almost nothing we understand better or react to more readily or with quicker intelligence. The Western film, though it seems never to diminish in popularity, is for most of us no more than the folklore of the past, familiar and understandable only because it has been repeated so often. The gangster film comes much closer. In ways that we do not easily or willingly define, the gangster speaks for us, expressing that part of the American psyche which rejects the qualities and the demands of modern life, which rejects "Americanism" itself.

The gangster is the man of the city, with the city's language and knowledge, with its queer and dishonest skills and its terrible daring, carrying his life in his hands like a placard, like a club. For everyone else, there is at least the theoretical possibility of another world—in that happier American culture which the gangster denies, the city does not really exist; it is only a more crowded and more brightly lit country—but for the gangster there is only the city; he must inhabit it in order to personify it: not the real city, but that dangerous and sad city of the imagination which is so much more important, which is the modern world. And the gangster—though there are real gangsters—is also, and primarily, a creature of the imagination. The real city, one might say, produces only criminals; the imaginary city produces the gangster: he is what we want to be and what we are afraid we may become.

Thrown into the crowd without background or advantages, with only those ambiguous skills which the rest of us—the real people of the real city—can only pretend to have, the gangster is required to make his way, to make his life and impose it on others. Usually, when we come upon him, he has already made his choice or the choice has already been made for him, it doesn't matter which: we are not permitted to ask whether at some point he could have chosen to be something else than what he is.

The gangster's activity is actually a form of rational enterprise, involving fairly definite goals and various techniques for achieving them. But this rationality is usually no more than a vague background; we know, perhaps, that the gangster sells liquor or that he operates a numbers racket; often we are not given even that much information. So his activity becomes a kind of pure criminality: he hurts people. Certainly our response to the gangster film is most consistently and most universally a response to sadism; we gain the double satisfaction of participating vicariously in the gangster's sadism and then seeing it turned against the gangster himself.

10   But on another level the quality of irrational brutality and the quality of rational enterprise become one. Since we do not see the rational and routine aspects of the gangster's behavior, the practice of brutality—the quality of unmixed criminality—becomes the totality of his career. At the same time, we are always conscious that the whole meaning of this career is a drive for success: the typical gangster film presents a steady upward progress followed by a very precipitate fall. Thus brutality itself becomes at once the means to success and the content of success—a success that is defined in its most general terms, not as accomplishment or specific gain, but simply as the unlimited possibility of aggression. (In the same way, film presentations of businessmen tend to make it appear that they achieve their success by talking on the telephone and holding conferences and that success *is* talking on the telephone and holding conferences.)

From this point of view, the initial contact between the film and its audience is an agreed conception of human life: that man is a being with the possibilities of success or failure. This principal, too, belongs to the city; one must emerge from the crowd or else one is nothing.

On that basis, the necessity of the action is established, and it progresses by inalterable paths to the point where the gangster lies dead and the principal has been modified: there is really only one possibility—failure. The final meaning of the city is anonymity and death.

In the opening scene of *Scarface*, we are shown a successful man; we know he is successful because he has just given a party of opulent proportions and because he is called Big Louie. Through some monstrous lack of caution, he permits himself to be alone for a few moments. We understand from this immediately that he is about to be killed. No convention of the gangster film is more strongly established than this: it is dangerous to be alone. And yet the very conditions of success make it impossible not to be alone, for success is always the establishment of an *individual* preeminence that must be imposed on others, in whom it automatically arouses hatred; the successful man is an outlaw. The gangster's whole life is an effort to assert himself as an individual, to draw himself out of the crowd, and he always dies *because* he is an individual; the final bullet thrusts him back, makes him, after all, a failure. "Mother of God," says the dying Little Caesar, "Is this the end of Rico?"—speaking of himself thus in the third person because what has been brought low is not the undifferentiated *man*, but the individual with a name, the gangster, the success; even to himself he is a creature of the imagination. (T. S. Eliot has pointed out that a number of Shakespeare's tragic heroes have this trick of looking at themselves dramatically; their true identify, the thing that is destroyed when they die, is something outside themselves—not a man, but a style of life, a kind of meaning.)

At bottom, the gangster is doomed because he is under the obligation to succeed, not because the means he employs are unlawful. In the deeper layers of the modern consciousness, *all* means are unlawful, every attempt to succeed is an act of aggression, leaving one alone and guilty and defenseless among enemies: one is *punished* for success. This is our intolerable dilemma: that failure is a kind of death and success is evil and dangerous, is—ultimately—impossible. The effect of the gangster film is to embody this dilemma in the person of the gangster and resolve it by his death. The dilemma is resolved because it is *his* death, not ours. We are safe; for the moment, we can acquiesce in our failure, we can choose to fail.

EXPLORATORY WRITING

Warshow writes that for the gangster, "the whole meaning of [his] career is a drive for success." Write an explanation of what he means by that statement. What, in particular, does "success" mean in this context? How does he develop that claim?

TALKING ABOUT THE READING

According to Warshow, the gangster film is "a consistent and astonishingly complete presentation of the modern sense of tragedy." With a group of your classmates, discuss what Warshow means by tragedy in this context? In what sense are gangster films tragic? With your group, choose a gangster film you are familiar with (*Road to Perdition*, for example). Does it fit Warshow's definition of tragedy? How might his definition be updated for films today?

WRITING ASSIGNMENTS

1. According to Warshow, gangsters are more attractive figures than the "good guys." Why is this so? Write an essay that explains why the gangster—or any other hero who lives outside the law—is such a popular figure in the American imagination.

2. Use Warshow's definition of tragedy to analyze a film or TV show featuring the gangster as a tragic hero. Films that feature gangster-hero types range from the campy *Kill Bill* (volumes I and II) to more traditional stories like the 1970s bio-pic *Bonnie and Clyde*. Does the film or television character actually meet the criteria Warshow sets up? How does seeing the gangster as a tragic hero influence the way viewers respond to the story?

3. Think of other films besides gangster movies that have a tragic ending for the main character or characters (such as *Titanic, American Beauty, Vanilla Sky, American History X, Road to Perdition, There Will Be Blood,* or *No Country for Old Men*). Pick one in which the tragic end represents something interesting and important about the limits of American culture. Write an essay that explains the tragedy in the film. What was the main character or characters striving to do? Why was the tragic end inevitable? What does this tragic end tell about American culture?

MAKING CONNECTIONS   Film Reviews: The Case of *Hancock*

One of the most frequently read genres of writing today is the film review. Movie-goers consult reviews online, in magazines, on television, and in regular film review columns in national and local newspapers. In the first decade of the twenty-first century, superhero films drew movie-goers to the theaters. *Superman* returned, *Spider Man* remained popular for at least three film runs, *Iron Man, The Dark Knight, Hellboy II,* and others became blockbusters and super-blockbusters. In 2008, perhaps the strangest superhero of all emerged in *Hancock,* where Will Smith portrayed a drunken bum of a hero suffering from image problems and a bad attitude. As the reviews here illustrate, responses to the film and the character were mixed. Was this a superhero for our times or a very bad mistake for the filmmakers? Where does a superhero like Hancock belong in the mythology of superheroes?

ABLE TO LEAP TALL BUILDINGS, EVEN IF HUNGOVER

— *Manohla Dargis*

Manohla Dargis writes film reviews for the *New York Times,* where this review appeared on July 2, 2008. She has also written for the *Village Voice,* served as film critic for the *Los Angeles Times,* and was editor of the film section at *LA Weekly.*

SUGGESTION FOR READING Before you read, take time to write down your assumptions about superheroes. You might think here of the heroes you grew up watching or reading about, what they stood for and how they acted or were supposed to act. Or, you might simply write about what you expect out of a film that features a superhero.

1   Soon into the superhero spectacular *Hancock,* before the machinery has fully kicked in, and the story is still wreathed in blissful ambiguity, you see the star Will Smith sprawled on a Los Angeles bench. Dirty, disheveled, in full distressed costume and character, and within easy sloshing reach of a bottle, he looks lost and alone, much like all the human detritus that washes up in every city and remains mostly unnoticed. But there's no ignoring Hancock, who has amazing powers. He can fly, for starters, and soon enough he's blasting straight into the heavens, the first homeless superhero in movies—Superbum!

Alas (bummer), though he can look the part, Hancock isn't literally homeless, just rootless, troubled and bedeviled. He drinks hard, swears at children (who curse him in turn), rarely shaves, never smiles. Worse, he has lousy superhero style, with sneakers and shorts (no cape), a grubby watch cap pulled over his forehead and buggy sunglasses that hide his (X-ray?) eyes. His takeoffs and landings are a mess: sloppy and violent, they invariably leave a heap of trouble and general rubble in his wake. He's Pothole Man, Train Wreck Man, but mainly he's Seriously Ticked Off Man, which, given that he's also a black man in Los Angeles, suggests that this superhero story comes with some bite, even a few nibbling sharp teeth.

Although whatever teeth it had have mostly been pulled, *Hancock* makes for one unexpectedly satisfying and kinky addition to Hollywood's superhero chronicles. Touching and odd, laden with genuine twists and grounded by three appealing lead performances, it was ably directed by Peter Berg and written by Vy Vincent Ngo and Vince Gilligan. It's a curious movie for the week of July 4, when the air is traditionally filled with the rockets' red glare and muscular box office heroics. There's a real jolt in the choking, splenetic exhaust of a disgruntled blockbuster anti-hero, especially one played by the affable Mr. Smith, who 12 years ago this very week helped save the world in *Independence Day,* a movie that made blowing up the White House into a joke.

That was then, this is now, and while it would be a stretch to say that this summertime amusement has much on its mind, it does have a little something percolating between its big bangs and gaudy effects. Most of that something isn't overtly political, despite the setup (Super Angry Black Man), a few winking asides and Mr. Berg's downbeat tendencies. Mr. Smith may be playing a provocative role in a city famous for its troubled race relations, but he's also a megastar and largely shielded from everyday stings, which, as it happens, is also true of his character. Hancock kicks back in a couple of derelict trailers (the Shack of Solitude) instead of a mansion, but his pain is existential, not material. He suffers at his leisure.

5   Engineered for broad, knowing laughs, with lots of kablooey, *Hancock* is principally a comedy and for a while plays out that way, notably when Mr. Smith is interacting with Jason Bateman. Their characters meet cute when Hancock saves Ray (Mr. Bateman) from being flattened by a freight train. In typical fashion, Hancock botches the save. He plucks Ray from death, but in the process derails the train and, also true to bad form, receives an invective-laced earful from the gathering mob. Struck by the crowd's hostility, Ray, a public relations guy with a do-gooder streak and a knockout wife, Mary (Charlize Theron), decides to rescue Hancock in turn by giving him a superhero makeover, one that follows a course blazed by many a fallen star (contrition, redemption, fabulousness).

Mr. Berg, who explored heroism of a different stripe in his poignant high school football movie, *Friday Night Lights,* and showed off terrific action chops in the underrated flick *The Kingdom,* is not a comedy natural. He squeezes laughs out of *Hancock*—Mr. Bateman needs no goosing—though some of its biggest yuks are fairly yucky, like a cringing bit involving a bizarre variant on prison rape. (That's entertainment?) For the most part, what Mr. Berg does is bring gravity to *Hancock,* a heaviness that can feel lugubrious even in midair though it often seems just right for a lonely, walking-if-usually-flying, seemingly self-loathing question mark. Mr. Berg takes the character's complications to heart, and Mr. Smith, his charm and smile dimmed, does the same.

The extent of that complexity doesn't emerge until the big reveal, which involves Ms. Theron's character and is so surprising that I heard several grown men loudly gasp. ("No way!") I was more struck by Ms. Theron, an actress who, I think, is capable of greater depth than most of her performances require, even those that try to rub the glamour off her. She helps Mr. Smith enrich the story's emotional texture, which is no small thing, since the movie itself starts to falter just when it begins to deepen. That's too bad because while *Hancock* is far from perfect—it feels overly rushed, particularly toward its chaotic end—it has a raggedness that speaks honestly to the fundamental human fragility that makes the greatest heroes super.

EXPLORATORY WRITING

Dargis does not come right out and say that *Hancock* is a good or a bad film. Write a summary of her review. What does she see in this film that makes it "one unexpectedly satisfying and kinky addition to Hollywood's superhero chronicles"?

TALKING ABOUT THE READING

With a group of your classmates, read each others' exploratory writings and then go back over Dargis's review. Discuss what Dargis identifies as the flaws or weaknesses of this film. What does she seem to expect from this kind of film?

WRITING ASSIGNMENT

Using the assumptions you wrote down before you read about superheroes and superhero films and your exploratory writing about Dargis's expectations for these films, write an essay in which you describe what a superhero movie would have to do to break with audience expectations.

DESPERATE MEN

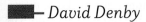— *David Denby*

David Denby is a regular film reviewer for the *New Yorker,* where the review reprinted here first appeared, in the July 7, 2008 issue. He is the author of a number of articles and books, including *Great Books: My Adventures with Homer, Rousseau, Woolf, and Other Indestructible Writers of the Western World* (1996), about the Great Books Curriculum at Columbia University, and *American Sucker* (2003), a book about investing during the dot-com boom and bust. His writing on film has also appeared in a wide variety of newspapers and magazines, including the *Atlantic Monthly, New York Review of Books,* and *New Republic.*

SUGGESTION FOR READING If you haven't done this yet, before you read Denby's review, watch *Hancock* and a second superhero movie like *The Dark Knight Returns* or *Iron Man.*

1 After *Speed Racer, Iron Man, Indiana Jones, The Incredible Hulk,* and *Get Smart* (which is so innocuous that you forget the jokes before you hit the street), it seemed clear that this year's big summer movies, however spectacular, had lost all interest in making even a minimal emotional connection to the moviegoer. But *Hancock,* starring Will Smith, is a surprisingly resonant spectacle that places three people with recognizable feelings in the middle of a wild fantasy. For one thing, *Hancock* has the grace to acknowledge the audience's increasing impatience with digital wonders. Hancock (Smith), a lonely superhero in Los Angeles, can't fly anywhere without making a mess. Carelessly, he punches holes in glass-tower office buildings, and, when he lands on the street in some pleasant suburban neighborhood, he tears up the pavement. The public hates him, and the Dickensian TV lawyer Nancy Grace, of the curling lip and ferocious eye, is on his case. Consider this: A fellow named Ray Embrey (Jason Bateman) is stuck in his car at a railway crossing, and Hancock saves him from an oncoming train by putting up his hands and bringing the locomotive to a jolting halt. The trouble is, the piled-up cars behind the locomotive jackknife and fall off the tracks. Hancock doesn't mean any harm, but he's out of it—a heedless, drunken-slob nihilist who just happens to have supernatural abilities. Unlike a comic-book hero, he has no "normal" placid self; he's always an airborne bum. The grateful Ray, however, has a scheme for saving him. A good-hearted P.R. man, he insists that Hancock "interface with the public." He persuades him to wear tight-fitting rubber suits, like a proper comic-book hero, and to make smiling appearances at West Hollywood clubs.

Hancock was written by Vy Vincent Ngo and Vince Gilligan, directed by Peter Berg (*The Kingdom*), and produced by such shrewd Hollywood talents as Michael Mann, Jonathan Mostow, and Akiva Goldsman (among others), and, like the people who made *You Don't Mess with the Zohan,* these filmmakers realize that it's time to transform digital into meta-digital. If everyone knows that digital has tossed realism overboard, then why not turn that knowingness into a joke? Hancock flips an obnoxious neighborhood kid into the sky and, looking up now and then, carries on a conversation with Ray, only to put out an arm and catch the howling towhead as he falls to earth. That's a pretty funny trick, and there are others just as good, but when Ray introduces Hancock to his wife, Mary (Charlize Theron), the movie, adding sexual tension and emotional power to its visual gags, reaches a new level. Theron looks at Smith with an uncanny mixture of alarm and attraction. What's going on with her? He may be a superhero, but he smells of booze. We're also puzzled by Berg's visual style, which, in these intimate scenes, depends on a handheld camera, restlessly moving yet pinned to the actors in super-tight closeups. It's as if he were making a Cassavetes psychodrama.

Suddenly, we realize why he stays so close. We are watching genuine actors at work, not well-paid hired hands filling up the space between agitated zeroes and ones. For the first time in his life, Will Smith doesn't flirt with the audience. He doesn't smile and tease and drawl; he stays in character as a self-hating lonely guy, and, in Berg's closeups, the planes of his face seem massive, almost sculpted. Charlize Theron undergoes her own kind of conversion. In such recent movies as *Monster, North Country,* and *In the Valley of Elah,* Theron has drawn on rage— perhaps the anger that a beautiful woman feels toward an industry that initially wanted to confine her to decorative roles. In *Monster,* she covered her face with prosthetics and tattoo ink, and in *Elah* and parts of *North Country* she was severe and drab. But Theron isn't running away from her good looks anymore. Wearing a simple sleeveless red shift, her blond hair hanging around her shoulders, she's a knockout in *Hancock,* and she gives the sexiest performance of her career. The currents flowing between her and Smith are reminiscent of the heat generated by Gable and Harlow, say, or Bogart and Bacall. It turns out that there's a bond between these two (which I won't reveal), and the rest of the movie, which includes some superb comic invention as well as scarily turbulent scenes, grows out of it.

Hancock suggests new visual directions and emotional tonalities for pop. It's by far the most enjoyable big movie of the summer.

EXPLORATORY WRITING

Denby offers high praise in his review of *Hancock,* calling it "the most enjoyable big movie of the summer." Write a brief summary of this review in which you identify specifically what Denby likes about this film.

TALKING ABOUT THE READING

Denby begins his review by comparing *Hancock* to a series of summer movies that came out in 2008—*The Incredible Hulk, Iron Man, Get Smart, Speed Racer,* and the latest film in the *Indiana Jones* series. He doesn't say much about them but implies a good deal in the way he writes about *Hancock.* With a group of your classmates, discuss what comparisons Denby is making with those films. Notice that he ends by calling this the most enjoyable "big movie of the summer." What is he telling his reader about his evaluation of the movie with the opening and closing comparisons?

WRITING ASSIGNMENT

Often the first—and sometimes the only—impression we have of films comes in the trailers or previews posted online and shown in theaters and during commercial breaks on television. Locate and watch trailers for *Hancock.* You can find them by making a simple online search, by going to the official film site, or by going to online reviews. (The *New York Times* review by Dargis, for example, also includes trailers and clips from the film if you go to the online version of the paper.) After you have watched trailers of *Hancock,* write your own impression of what this movie is like. In what ways do the trailers indicate (or not) any of the complexity these two reviewers found? How do the trailers construct an audience for the film? Who would you say the film is aimed at, given the trailers?

WRITING SEQUENCE

1. Often a review is written in response to assumptions the reviewer brings to a film even before seeing it. If you began this sequence by writing down your own assumptions about and expectations of superhero movies, then read over what you wrote. (If you didn't write those down, do that before you go on to the rest of this assignment. Also, if you haven't seen *Hancock* yet, be sure to do that before you write. It is widely available for rental.) After reading over your earlier writing and considering your own response to the film, write a new and longer exploratory piece in which you detail your expectations for superhero films and explain how those expectations influence the way you responded to *Hancock.* Did it meet those expectations? In what ways?

2. Notice that these two critics cover some of the same ground in their reviews. For example, they both measure *Hancock* against other superhero movies coming out at the same time. They both consider the lead acting performances, though Dargis focuses on Will Smith while Denby points out Charlize Theron's performance for special attention. They comment on the director's work both on this film and in previous work. They each mention character development and whether the film's writers achieved comedy or complexity. They also work within basic assumptions about what a superhero is and what a summer blockbuster is or ought to be. Review your exploratory writings and reread the

two reviews. Then write a 2–3 page essay that examines the criteria these two critics use for their reviews. In what ways are they similar? Where do they differ? When does personal preference or personal taste seem to come into play in their assessments?

3. For this culminating assignment, write your own review of a superhero movie. This review should be 3–4 pages in length and aimed at readers of your student newspaper. In preparation, review the essay you wrote in which you examined the two reviews printed here. Notice what they pay attention to in a review and cover some of that same ground in your own review. For example, pay attention to the story, the characters, and how convincing the acting and the action sequences are. How does the film conform (or not) to the superhero film genre as you understand it and as the two reviewers here indicate what constitutes that genre? Does the subject of the movie appeal to a specific audience or age group, or does it have a broader audience appeal, even for a superhero movie? Does the film draw on interests, concerns, fears, or desires that seem current to you? What is your recommendation to your readers? Should they see this movie or pass it up? Be sure your review is finished and has gone through drafting, revising, and editing before you turn it in for the final time. (For more information on writing film reviews, refer to the Film Clip feature in Chapter 3.)

VISUAL CULTURE   The Graphic Novel: Reader Participation

Although storytelling is usually considered an oral or written form, people have been telling stories with pictures—making visual narratives—since ancient times. Prehistoric cave paintings tell hunting stories or detail rituals. Medieval church murals and windows narrate the lives of saints. Even today, many modes of storytelling are visual ones. Obviously, television and film carry much of the story through pictures, but still pictures—cartoons, comic books, children's books, and much print advertisement—depend on visual sequencing and arrangement to move the narrative (the story) along. With very little dialogue, the reader must follow the logic of the panel sequence.

Graphic novels work because readers fill in the information that is not expressly drawn or written in the panels. For example, in the second panel of the story reprinted here, Marjane Satrapi tells us that she is in the picture, although we cannot see her because she has been cut off. We see only a bit of her veil. Satrapi is depending here on the reader's ability to put her into the picture, especially since she gives us a complete drawing of herself in the panel before. In this way, the reader relies on both the sequencing of the two panels (panel 1 with a complete drawing of Satrapi as a child, followed by panel 2 with Satrapi cut off but identified as being "in" the picture) and the reader's ability to imagine outside the panel to fill in the image. That is how *reader participation* works in comics and in graphic novels.

The following excerpts are from Marjane Satrapi's autobiographical graphic novel *Persepolis: The Story of a Childhood*. This graphic novel works very much like a visual memoir, drawing on the conventions of comics and visual narrative to tell a young girl's story of growing up in Iran during the Islamic revolution there. In what follows, we have reprinted Satrapi's introductory essay that sets the scene and historic context for this memoir and "The Veil," the opening chapter of *Persepolis*.

THE VEIL

—*Marjane Satrapi*

Marjane Satrapi was born in 1969 in Rasht, Iran. She grew up in Tehran, where she studied at the Lycée Française before leaving for Vienna and going to Strasbourg to study illustration. She has written several children's books, and her illustrations appear in newspapers and magazines throughout the world, including the *New Yorker* and the *New York Times. Persepolis,* a memoir of growing up in Iran during the Islamic revolution, was first published in 2000. Satrapi has called it an autobiographical novel in graphic novel form. This excerpt, "The Veil," is the opening chapter in *Persepolis.*

SUGGESTION FOR READING Before you begin reading, write what you already know about or think about Iran, the Islamic revolution there, and the Islamic practice of requiring women to wear the veil.

1 In the second millennium B.C., while the Elam nation was developing a civilization alongside Babylon, Indo-European invaders gave their name to the immense Iranian plateau where they settled. The word "Iran" was derived from "Ayryana Vaejo," which means "the origin of the Aryans." These people were semi-nomads whose descendants were the Medes and the Persians. The Medes founded the first Iranian nation in the seventh century B.C.; it was later destroyed by Cyrus the Great. He established what became one of the largest empires of the ancient world, the Persian Empire, in the sixth century B.C. Iran was referred to as Persia—its Greek name—until 1935 when Reza Shah, the father of the last Shah of Iran, asked everyone to call the country Iran.

Iran was rich. Because of its wealth and its geographic location, it invited attacks: from Alexander the Great, from its Arab neighbors to the west, from Turkish and Mongolian conquerors, Iran was often subject to foreign domination. Yet the Persian language and culture withstood these invasions. The invaders assimilated into this strong culture, and in some ways they became Iranians themselves.

In the twentieth century, Iran entered a new phase. Reza Shah decided to modernize and westernize the country, but meanwhile a fresh source of wealth was discovered: oil. And with the oil came another invasion. The West, particularly Great Britain, wielded a strong influence on the Iranian economy. During the Second World War, the British, Soviets, and Americans asked Reza Shah to ally himself with them against Germany. But Reza Shah, who sympathized with the Germans, declared Iran a neutral zone. So the Allies invaded and occupied Iran. Reza Shah was sent into exile and was succeeded by his son, Mohammad Reza Pahlavi, who was known simply as the Shah.

In 1951, Mohammed Mossadeq, then prime minister of Iran, nationalized the oil industry. In retaliation, Great Britain organized an embargo on all exports of oil from Iran. In 1953, the CIA, with the help of British intelligence, organised a coup against him. Mossadeq was overthrown and the Shah, who had earlier escaped from the country, returned to power. The Shah stayed on the throne until 1979, when he fled Iran to escape the Islamic revolution.

5 Since then, this old and great civilization has been discussed mostly in connection with fundamentalism, fanaticism, and terrorism. As an Iranian who has lived more than half of my life in Iran, I know that this image is far from the truth. This is why writing *Persepolis* was so important to me. I believe that an entire nation should not be judged by the wrongdoings of a few extremists. I also don't want those Iranians who lost their lives in prisons defending freedom, who died in the war against Iraq, who suffered under various repressive regimes, or who were forced to leave their families and flee their homeland to be forgotten.

One can forgive but one should never forget.

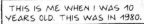

THIS IS ME WHEN I WAS 10 YEARS OLD. THIS WAS IN 1980.

AND THIS IS A CLASS PHOTO. I'M SITTING ON THE FAR LEFT SO YOU DON'T SEE ME. FROM LEFT TO RIGHT: GOLNAZ, MAHSHID, NARINE, MINNA.

IN 1979 A REVOLUTION TOOK PLACE. IT WAS LATER CALLED "THE ISLAMIC REVOLUTION".

THEN CAME 1980: THE YEAR IT BECAME OBLIGATORY TO WEAR THE VEIL AT SCHOOL.

WEAR THIS!

WE DIDN'T REALLY LIKE TO WEAR THE VEIL, ESPECIALLY SINCE WE DIDN'T UNDERSTAND WHY WE HAD TO.

IT'S TOO HOT OUT!

EXECUTION IN THE NAME OF FREEDOM.

OOH! I'M THE MONSTER OF DARKNESS.

GIVE ME MY VEIL BACK!

YOU'LL HAVE TO LICK MY FEET!

GIDDYAP!

EVERYWHERE IN THE STREETS THERE WERE DEMONSTRATIONS FOR AND AGAINST THE VEIL.

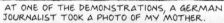

AT ONE OF THE DEMONSTRATIONS, A GERMAN JOURNALIST TOOK A PHOTO OF MY MOTHER.

I WAS REALLY PROUD OF HER. HER PHOTO WAS PUBLISHED IN ALL THE EUROPEAN NEWSPAPERS.

AND EVEN IN ONE MAGAZINE IN IRAN. MY MOTHER WAS REALLY SCARED.

HAVE YOU SEEN THIS?

DON'T WORRY, DARLING.

SHE DYED HER HAIR,

AND WORE DARK GLASSES FOR A LONG TIME.

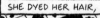

LIKE ALL MY PREDECESSORS I HAD MY HOLY BOOK.

THE FIRST THREE RULES CAME FROM ZARATHUSTRA. HE WAS THE FIRST PROPHET IN MY COUNTRY BEFORE THE ARAB INVASION.

YOU MUST BASE EVERYTHING ON THESE THREE RULES: BEHAVE WELL, SPEAK WELL, ACT WELL.

I ALSO WANTED US TO CELEBRATE THE TRADITIONAL ZARATHUSTRIAN HOLIDAYS. LIKE THE FIRE CEREMONY,

BEFORE THE PERSIAN NEW YEAR, NOROUZ, ON MARCH 21ST, THE FIRST DAY OF SPRING.

ONLY MY GRANDMOTHER KNEW ABOUT MY BOOK.

RULE NUMBER SIX: EVERYBODY SHOULD HAVE A CAR.

RULE NUMBER SEVEN: ALL MAIDS SHOULD EAT AT THE TABLE WITH THE OTHERS.

RULE NUMBER EIGHT: NO OLD PERSON SHOULD HAVE TO SUFFER.

IN THAT CASE, I'LL BE YOUR FIRST DISCIPLE.

REALLY?

BUT TELL ME HOW YOU'LL ARRANGE FOR OLD PEOPLE NOT TO SUFFER?

IT WILL SIMPLY BE FORBIDDEN.

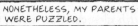

TALKING ABOUT THE READING

With a group of your classmates share what you each already know about the Islamic revolution in Iran. How does that previous knowledge help you read this visual narrative? How does Satrapi make her story clear even to readers who know little or nothing about that history?

WRITING FROM THE READING

In her introduction to *Persepolis*, Marjane Satrapi writes that the old and great civilization that was Iran is, from the outside, seen "mostly in connection with fundamentalism, fanaticism, and terrorism. As an Iranian who has lived more than half of my life in Iran, I know that this image is far from the truth. This is why writing *Persepolis* was so important to me."

Write an essay in which you examine your own preconceptions Iran and the Middle East in general. How does this graphic memoir figure into the way you think of Iran? In your piece, consider how telling this story as a graphic novel from the point of view of a small child might influence the way readers respond to this history. What is gained in the decision to tell the story visually? What is lost?

SUGGESTED ASSIGNMENT

Drawing from a well-known short story, play, short novel, or film, create your own graphic novel. Or make your own graphic memoir by telling a story in your life using the techniques of a graphic novel. You do not have to be an artist to make a visual narrative. You could use computer programs such as PowerPoint to arrange clip art. Or use photographs arranged in a sequence, or use images cut from magazines. Or make your own drawings or paintings that you arrange in a sequence to tell a story.

Tips on composing your graphic narrative:

1. Choose a story that you have read and liked and that seems to lend itself well to being told in pictures. If you are writing your own original story or memoir rather than adapting a story you already know, reread Patricia Hampl's essay on memoir reprinted earlier in this chapter. A memoir must be about something more than just the story. It should, as Hampl suggests, tell your mind, not just the story. Satrapi, for example, is telling a story about a people. Her part in the story is interesting and sometimes funny and sometimes sad, but it is not a story about her. It is a story about everything around her.

2. Write down the basics of the story. Make sure you write out the parts of the story that you believe are crucial to telling this story well. If you are working with a novel, you very likely can work only with one chapter rather than the entire novel. Decide which chapter is key for understanding the story.

3. Make a list of the key scenes in your story. Your visual narrative cannot convey every detail in the story, so you have to decide which parts of the story make for good visual narration. What can you show? Decide on the number of scenes. Choose scenes that are crucial for telling the story and that have good potential for visual impact.

4. Arrange your scenes. On paper, or in a computer program with storyboard capabilities, make a storyboard. Fill in your storyboard with general sketches or notes on what scenes must go in each space. Sequencing is important in the way you tell your story, so pay attention to the order of your scenes.

5. Present the completed story to your classmates. Be sure that you can project the story in a computer program or on transparencies so that the entire class can see clearly. In your presentation, talk about what choices you had to make to turn a written story into a graphic novel. Use the following questions to guide your preparations for the presentation:

   ■ What does the story gain when you change it from the written version to the visual?

   ■ What does it lose?

   ■ What in the original story seemed to lend itself to being told as a graphic novel?

   ■ What roles do color, line, and sequence play in telling the story?

   ■ When did you have to use dialogue, caption, and sounds?

   ■ When could you rely on image and sequence alone to tell the story?

FILM CLIP   The Art of Adaptation

One of the comments most of us have heard about film adaptations of books is: "The movie is never as good as the book." What that statement usually means is that the reader misses both the experience of reading the book and the events (and sometimes whole plotlines and characters) as they are portrayed in the book.

A good film adaptation, however, is not a faithful rendering of the pages of a novel, short story, or play. Storytelling in film is different because the medium is different. For one thing, film depends on the visual to make many of the connections that are spelled out in a book. Popular film also has difficulty if a story contains too many plotlines that threaten to distract or confuse viewers. When the very popular *Lord of the Rings* trilogy was adapted into three films by Peter Jackson, Fran Walsh, and Phillipa Boyens, each film was about three hours long, and their extended DVD editions run over four hours. But these films do not come close to reproducing everything in the three novels. Most movies are limited to just about two hours, so time constraints will affect the way a book is adapted into film. Moreover, production companies want to make movies that appeal to the widest audiences possible, so popular films often maintain a faster pace than many novels.

If you think of film adaptations of books as interpretations of those stories rather than faithful renderings of what is on the page, then you have a notion of what it means to translate a story from a book onto screen. The filmmaker and scriptwriters are forced to make choices about what they can leave in and what must go. Jackson, for example, has talked of his interpretation of *The Lord of the Rings* as being "Frodo-centric," meaning that the scriptwriting team cut from the storyline anything that did not directly relate to Frodo and his mission. Other filmmakers do much the same. They make a decision about how to interpret events of a novel, play, or short story, and that interpretation shapes the way the film is written, acted, shot, and edited.

Watch a film adaptation of a novel, short story, play, or comic book or graphic novel, and write an essay in which you examine the way the film interprets the original. You can write this sort of essay doing one of the following:

- Choose a story that has been filmed more than once (*Pride and Prejudice, David Copperfield, Sense and Sensibility, The Importance of Being Earnest, Hamlet, Jane Eyre, Wuthering Heights, Frankenstein,* or *Dracula,* for example) and compare two film interpretations of the work. What does each emphasize? What does each cut? Is anything added? What is the purpose of the cut or the addition?

- Choose a novel, short story, play, comic book, or graphic novel that you know well and like. Watch a film adaptation of that piece of literature. How does the filmmaker interpret characters, important events, setting, and central themes or conflicts? Write an essay in which you examine the film interpretation of the written work. *Lord of the Rings, Harry Potter, The Hitchhiker's Guide to the Galaxy, Do Androids Dream of Electric Sheep?* (filmed as *Blade Runner*), *Sin City,* and *The Road to Perdition* are all popular stories that have been interpreted through film.

- Choose a film version of a novel, short story, play, comic book, or graphic novel that has been remade so that it is changed for very new audiences. For example, *Clueless* is a reworking of the novel and film versions of Jane Austen's *Emma. Bridget Jones' Diary* and the Bollywood film *Bride and Prejudice* are both rewritings of Austen's *Pride and Prejudice. Apocalypse Now* is a rewriting of Joseph Conrad's *Heart of Darkness. Forbidden Planet* and *Prospero's Books* are reworkings of Shakespeare's *The Tempest.* Write an essay in which you examine the update as an interpretation of the original. What does it emphasize? What does it change? What does the story gain in the update? What do you think is lost?

FIELDWORK	**Writing a Questionnaire**

We all have strong preferences when it comes to what we like to read, what we hate, what we think is too sappy or gory or outright boring. And since each of us knows what we like and why, it's often difficult to imagine other people's preferences. Who reads those romance novels? What is the audience for cyberfiction? Does anybody, outside of English teachers, still read *Silas Marner* for pleasure?

One way to find out what people like to read is, quite simply, to ask them. For this assignment, you will be doing just that by designing and distributing a questionnaire that asks people what they read for pleasure and how their reading tastes have changed over the years.

Design this questionnaire either on your own, with a small group of classmates, or as an entire class. If you do it on your own, try to get 15–25 responses. If you work with a small group, each person should get 10 responses to compile a fairly large sampling. If the entire class uses the same questionnaire, each person can get 10 responses and the class will have a substantial amount of information to sort through. Even if you have only 25 responses to your questionnaire, you will have more than your own and your classmates' impressions from which to draw. That kind of information can help you broaden your own response and begin to account for the differences as well as the similarities that you see around you.

DESIGNING A QUESTIONNAIRE

1. *Make it brief and readable.* It is best to limit your questionnaire to one page. The simpler it seems to your audience members, the more likely they will be to fill it out. Make it readable. Don't try to crowd too many questions on the page or make instructions complicated. There should be plenty of white space, and the language should be simple and direct.

2. *Write different kinds of questions to get different kinds of answers.* The kind of questions you ask will determine the kind of information you receive. If you ask questions that can be answered with a yes or a no, then you will likely get more responses but less specific information. If you ask people to write quite a bit, you may not get as many participants and you might have trouble summarizing your findings.

3. *Decide who will answer your questionnaire.* If you want to know what a certain age group is reading—middle school or high school or college age students, for example—target that audience. You might, however, want to know what older adults are reading and how their reading interests have changed over the years. Or you might want to know what women read or what men read.

You could also ask about a certain kind of reading. Stephen King says that people love a good scare, but not everyone does, just as not everyone is fond of romance novels or stories about superheroes or fantasy and science fiction. You can create one kind of questionnaire to focus on a particular kind of story—such as science fiction—and try to get at what it is in those stories that appeals to the audience.

It's probably best that you decide as a class or as a group what information you hope to get from your questionnaire. The sample questionnaire below is adapted from Janice Radway's *Reading the Romance*, a study of women whose favorite reading for pleasure is the romance novel.

Sample Questionnaire

1. At what age did you begin reading for pleasure?
   a. _____ 5–10
   b. _____ 11–20
   c. _____ 21–30
   d. _____ 31 or above

2. Age today:
   a. _____ 18–21
   b. _____ 22–30
   c. _____ 31–45
   d. _____ 46–55
   e. _____ over 55

3. What kinds of books did you read for pleasure when you were a teenager?
   a. _____ biography
   b. _____ historical fiction
   c. _____ romances
   d. _____ westerns
   e. _____ mysteries
   f. _____ comic books
   g. _____ sports stories
   h. _____ other (specify)

4. What kind of book do you read for pleasure now?
   a. _____ biography
   b. _____ historical fiction
   c. _____ romances
   d. _____ westerns
   e. _____ mysteries
   f. _____ comic books
   g. _____ sports stories
   h. _____ other (specify)

5. What kinds of books do you never read for pleasure?
   a. _____ biography
   b. _____ historical fiction
   c. _____ romances
   d. _____ westerns

e. _____ mysteries
f. _____ comic books
g. _____ sports stories
h. _____ other (specify)

6. What book or story have you read most recently for pleasure?

Remember that your questionnaire should be designed to answer the questions you and your classmates have about reading for pleasure. Some or all of these questions might be useful, but be sure to target your audience, decide on what you want to know, and ask questions that can get at that information.

Report on Your Findings

Once you have completed your questionnaire, report your findings to the rest of the class. Write a report, give a presentation, or design a chart or graph that visually illustrates your findings.

MINING THE ARCHIVE   Comic Strips and Comic Books

Comic strips started to appear in daily newspapers and the Sunday papers in the late 1890s and early 1900s, establishing a new medium of storytelling that brings together three key ingredients: a narrative sequence of pictures, speech balloons, and a regular cast of characters. The Yellow Kid (1895)—a bald, gap-toothed street urchin dressed in a yellow nightshirt—became the first comic-strip celebrity, followed by the Katzenjammer Kids (1897), Happy Hooligan (1900), Mutt and Jeff (1907), and Krazy Kat (1910).

Examples of these early joke-a-day gag strips that anticipate Pogo (1949), Peanuts (1950), Doonesbury (1970), Cathy (1976), and Dilbert (1989) are in Robert C. Harvey's books *The Art of the Funnies: An Aesthetic History* (1994) and *Children of the Yellow Kid: The Evolution of the American Comic Strip* (1998). The Web site Krazy Kat Daily Strips at rrnet.com/-nakamura/soba/kat/day/ contains thirty enlargements of Krazy Kat strips. As you look at old comic strips, consider how the narrative sequencing from panel to panel sets up the humor and how cartooning styles give the characters their particular identities.

You can also find examples in Harvey's two books of detective and adventure themes in comic strips such as Dick Tracy (1931), Terry and the Pirates (1934), Prince Valiant (1937), and Steve Canyon (1947), as well as domestic sitcoms such as Bringing Up Father (1913), Gasoline Alley (1918), Little Orphan Annie (1924), and Blondie (1930).

In the 1930s, the narrative techniques of the comic strip found a new outlet in comic books. In 1938, Superman—the first of the great comic-book heroes—made his appearance, followed quickly by Batman, Green Lantern, Wonder Woman, Captain America, and Plastic Man. You can find examples of these superheroes in Jules Feiffer's *The Great Comic Book Heroes* (1965) and Robert C. Harvey's *The Art of the Comic Book: An Aesthetic History* (1996). Comic books offer opportunities to think about how the integration of the visual and the verbal has created new narrative possibilities in graphic storytelling.

Work

Wear comfortable clothes and properly fitted shoes while working around the house.

Don't be shy about pulling something you like out of the trash.

—from Northwest Airline's tip sheet *101 Ways to Save Money,* distributed to employees in August 2006 after they had been warned to prepare for major lay-offs

I'm goin' . . . where they hung the jerk who invented work on the Big Rock Candy Mountain.

—Harry McClintock

Historically, Americans have had a love/hate relationship with their jobs. That may be due partially to something called the "Protestant work ethic," a philosophy of living that has formed a part of this nation's character from the first European settlements. According to this ethic, "Idle hands are the devil's tool." The contrast between fruitful labor and wasteful leisure is one the Puritans brought with them as they traveled to the New World to explore and to settle in this country. Its message is a simple (and simplistic) one: success is the reward for diligence; failure is the consequence of idleness.

Of course, success and failure are never so easily explained away, but a cultural myth—even one as readily dispelled as this one—is difficult to ignore. For many American workers, getting a good job and keeping it is a measure of success. Losing a job, for whatever reason, means failure. Workers who lose their jobs might well have been fired or laid off through no fault of their own, but the suspicion often remains that those let go may somehow have deserved it.

Many people feel that their identities are linked to the jobs they hold or want to hold. After all, from the time children start school, parents and teachers ask them what they want to be when they grow up. By adulthood, they are expected to have a "career"—a job that will support a family, provide opportunities for professional advancement, buy leisure time, perhaps contribute to community well-being, signal status, and be fulfilling, all at once.

Despite the popularity of television shows set in the workplace—*The Office*; *CSI*; *Gray's Anatomy*—the real history of labor has been a story of struggle between management and workers over issues most of us now take for granted. A forty-hour week, the minimum wage, child labor regulations, health and safety issues, and the rights of workers to organize were all established only after hard-fought labor wars in the nineteenth and early twentieth centuries. Disputes that may have seemed settled for American workers in the first half of the twentieth century have now reemerged as global struggles, with companies outsourcing (or "off-shoring") their labor to countries where sweatshop conditions and lower wages are commonplace. Moreover, the move into a global marketplace has had a direct effect on labor/management relations, on attitudes toward immigrant labor, and on the continuing battle over what constitutes a living wage.

Work, as you will see, is rarely just as simple as a place to go to earn a paycheck. Workers' identities are often tied to the work they do or the work they would like to do. We may have moved beyond the simple logic of the Protestant work ethic, but this is a culture concerned at some level with the dignity of work. That concern for dignity and fair play comes into nearly every discussion about work.

THE FIRST JOB

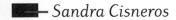— *Sandra Cisneros*

Sandra Cisneros was born in Chicago, the daughter of a Mexican father and a Mexican American mother. She has been a poet in the schools, a teacher for high school dropouts, and an arts administrator. Cisneros is the author of *My Wicked Ways* (1987), a volume of poetry; two collections of short stories—*The House on Mango Street* (1985), from which the following selection has been excerpted, and *Woman Hollering Creek* (1991)—and the novel *Caramelo* (2002).

SUGGESTION FOR READING   Write a brief description of a time when you found yourself in a situation that was uncomfortable—a place where you did not know what to expect. After you have read Cisneros's story, use your own memory piece to help you focus on what the event that she writes of means to you.

1 It wasn't as if I didn't want to work. I did. I had even gone to the social security office the month before to get my social security number. I needed money. The Catholic high school cost a lot, and Papa said nobody went to public school unless you wanted to turn out bad. I thought I'd find an easy job, the kind other kids had, working in the dime store or maybe a hotdog stand. And though I hadn't started looking yet, I thought I might the week after next. But when I came home that afternoon, all wet because Tito had pushed me into the open water hydrant—only I had sort of let him—Mama called me in the kitchen before I could even go and change, and Aunt Lala was sitting there drinking her coffee with a spoon. Aunt Lala said she had found a job for me at the Peter Pan Photo Finishers on North Broadway where she worked and how old was I and to show up tomorrow saying I was one year older and that was that.

So the next morning I put on the navy blue dress that made me look older and borrowed money for lunch and bus fare because Aunt Lala said I wouldn't get paid 'til the next Friday and I went in and saw the boss of the Peter Pan Photo Finishers on North Broadway where Aunt Lala worked and lied about my age like she told me to and sure enough I started that same day.

In my job I had to wear white gloves. I was supposed to match negatives with their prints, just look at the picture and look for the same one on the negative strip, put it in the envelope, and do the next one. That's all. I didn't know where these envelopes were coming from or where they were going. I just did what I was told.

It was real easy and I guess I wouldn't have minded it except that you got tired after a while and I didn't know if I could sit down or not, and then I started sitting down only when the two ladies next to me did. After a while they started to laugh and came up to me and said I could sit when I wanted to and I said I knew.

5 When lunch time came I was scared to eat alone in the company lunchroom with all those men and ladies looking, so I ate real fast standing in one of the washroom stalls and had lots of time left over so I went back to work early. But then break time came and not knowing where else to go I went into the coatroom because there was a bench there.

I guess it was time for the night shift or middle shift to arrive because a few people came in and punched the time clock and an older Oriental man said hello and we talked for a while about my just starting and he said we could be friends and next time to go in the lunchroom and sit with him and I felt better. He had nice eyes and I didn't feel so nervous anymore. Then he asked if I knew what day it was and when I said I didn't he said it was his birthday and would I please give him a birthday kiss. I thought I would because he was so old and just as I was about to put my lips on his cheek, he grabs my face with both hands and kisses me hard on the mouth and doesn't let go.

EXPLORATORY WRITING

Reread Cisneros's piece and notice how abruptly her story ends, and especially how the attitude of the narrator shifts suddenly in that last paragraph. Write an explanation of how that sudden shift changes the story. How does that ending affect the way that you understand what this story is about?

TALKING ABOUT THE READING

In many ways, this story is about situation, nagging responsibilities, and naiveté. With a group of your classmates, discuss the narrator's motivation for getting a job, why she says, "It wasn't as if I didn't want to work," and how she got herself into the situation that ends the story. In what ways is this story about workplace conditions? In what ways might it be about women and young girls in the workplace?

WRITING ASSIGNMENTS

1. As a reader, you may understand or relate to stories because they touch on something that you already have experienced or an emotion that you have felt. Cisneros's story about a young woman's first day on a new job describes a brief and confusing encounter with an adult world of which she had no prior knowledge. In an exploratory piece of writing, examine the narrator's response to this world of work and human inter-action using your own experiences in the working world or in situations that seemed out of your control. Even if you have experienced nothing like this, you probably have a reaction to or an understanding of how the young woman in this story felt. If it seems useful, draw on the writing you did in preparation for reading this story to complete this assignment.

2. Write a brief character analysis of the narrator. Who is she? What are her motiva-tions? What are her errors? How do you know? In your analysis, take into account both what she says about herself and her family situation and the events that unfold in the story.

3. Tell a story about one of the first jobs you ever held (whether it was a paying job or some new responsibility you were asked to take on in your family or community, your peer group, an organization, or for school or church). Try to convey what the job meant to you and how you did or didn't fit into this new world. Choose a moment that sticks with you because it seemed to represent your entire experience with the world of work or the world of adults. In preparation for this writing, spend some time listing jobs you did and jotting memories of people, places, and events connected to those jobs. Notice how Cisneros manages to tell a great deal about why she began working, about the work-place, and about the event that concludes this story in a short piece of writing. Before you begin composing your story, reread Cisneros to see how the form of her narrative might help you to plan your own.

I STAND HERE IRONING

— *Tillie Olson*

Tillie Olsen was born in 1912, began writing in the 1930s, and is considered a major voice for women in twentieth-century American literature. Olsen stopped writing for twenty years to raise four children and to work at a series of low-paying jobs to help support the family. She didn't return to writing as a profession until she was in her mid-forties and her last child had started school. The title story in the collection *Tell Me a Riddle* (1961), from which the follow-ing selection has been taken, won an O'Henry Prize for short fiction. "I Stand Here Ironing" has become a classic statement of the tensions women face between motherhood and the need to make a living outside the home.

SUGGESTION This story has little or no real "action." The woman telling it remains at the ironing board
FOR READING throughout as she recalls the story of her daughter's life. Keep track of that story as you read.

1   I stand here ironing, and what you asked me moves tormented back and forth with the iron.

"I wish you would manage the time to come and talk with me about your daughter. I'm sure you can help me understand her. She's a youngster who needs help and whom I'm deeply interested in helping."

"Who needs help." . . . Even if I came, what good would it do? You think because I am her mother I have a key, or that in some way you could use me as a key? She has lived for nineteen years. There is all that life that has happened outside of me, beyond me.

And when is there time to remember, to sift, to weigh, to estimate, to total? I will start and there will be an interruption and I will have to gather it all together again. Or I will become engulfed with all I did or did not do, with what should have been and what cannot be helped.

5   She was a beautiful baby. The first and only one of our five that was beautiful at birth. You do not guess how new and uneasy her tenancy in her now-loveliness. You did not know her all those years she was thought homely, or see her poring over her baby pictures, making me tell her over and over how beautiful she had been—and would be, I would tell her—and was now, to the seeing eye. But the seeing eyes were few or nonexistent. Including mine.

I nursed her. They feel that's important nowadays. I nursed all the children, but with her, with all the fierce rigidity of first motherhood, I did like the books then said. Though her cries battered me to trembling and my breasts ached with swollenness, I waited till the clock decreed.

Why do I put that first? I do not even know if it matters, or if it explains anything.

She was a beautiful baby. She blew shining bubbles of sound. She loved motion, loved light, loved color and music and textures. She would lie on the floor in her blue overalls patting the surface so hard in ecstasy her hands and feet would blur. She was a miracle to me, but when she was eight months old I had to leave her daytimes with the woman downstairs to whom she was no miracle at all, for I worked or looked for work and for Emily's father, who "could no longer endure" (he wrote in his good-bye note) "sharing want with us."

I was nineteen. It was the pre-relief, pre-WPA world of the depression. I would start running as soon as I got off the streetcar, running up the stairs, the place smelling sour, and awake or asleep to startle awake, when she saw me she would break into a clogged weeping that could not be comforted, a weeping I can hear yet.

10   After a while I found a job hashing at night so I could be with her days, and it was better. But it came to where I had to bring her to his family and leave her.

It took a long time to raise the money for her fare back. Then she got chicken pox and I had to wait longer. When she finally came, I hardly knew her, walking quick and nervous like her father, looking like her father, thin, and dressed in a shoddy red that yellowed her skin and glared at the pockmarks. All the baby loveliness gone.

She was two. Old enough for nursery school they said, and I did not know then what I know now—the fatigue of the long day, and the lacerations of group life in the kinds of nurseries that are only parking places for children.

Except that it would have made no difference if I had known. It was the only place there was. It was the only way we could be together, the only way I could hold a job.

And even without knowing, I knew. I knew the teacher that was evil because all these years it has curdled into my memory, the little boy hunched in the corner, her rasp, "why aren't you outside, because Alvin hits you? that's no reason, go out, scaredy." I knew Emily hated it even if she did not clutch and implore "don't go Mommy" like the other children, mornings.

15   She always had a reason why we should stay home. Momma, you look sick. Momma, I feel sick. Momma, the teachers aren't there today, they're sick. Momma, we can't go, there was a fire there last night. Momma, it's a holiday today, no school, they told me.

But never a direct protest, never rebellion. I think of our others in their three-, four-year-oldness—the explosions, the tempers, the denunciations, the demands—and I feel suddenly ill. I put the iron down. What in me demanded that goodness in her? And what was the cost, the cost to her of such goodness?

The old man living in the back once said in his gentle way: "You should smile at Emily more when you look at her." What *was* in my face when I looked at her? I loved her. There were all the acts of love.

It was only with the others I remembered what he said, and it was the face of joy, and not of care or tightness or worry I turned to them—too late for Emily. She does not smile easily, let alone almost always as her brothers and sisters do. Her face is closed and sombre, but when she wants, how fluid. You must have seen it in her pantomimes, you spoke of her rare gift for comedy on the stage that rouses laughter out of the audience so dear they applaud and applaud and do not want to let her go.

Where does it come from, that comedy? There was none of it in her when she came back to me that second time, after I had had to send her away again. She had a new daddy now to learn to love, and I think perhaps it was a better time.

20 Except when we left her alone nights, telling ourselves she was old enough.

"Can't you go some other time, Mommy, like tomorrow?" she would ask. "Will it be just a little while you'll be gone? Do you promise?"

The time we came back, the front door open, the clock on the floor in the hall. She rigid awake. "It wasn't just a little while. I didn't cry. Three times I called you, just three times, and then I ran downstairs to open the door so you could come faster. The clock talked loud. I threw it away, it scared me what it talked."

She said the clock talked loud again that night I went to the hospital to have Susan. She was delirious with the fever that comes before red measles, but she was fully conscious all the week I was gone and the week after we were home when she could not come near the new baby or me.

She did not get well. She stayed skeleton thin, not wanting to eat, and night after night she had nightmares. She would call for me, and I would rouse from exhaustion to sleepily call back: "You're all right, darling, go to sleep, it's just a dream," and if she still called, in a sterner voice, "now go to sleep, Emily, there's nothing to hurt you." Twice, only twice, when I had to get up for Susan anyhow, I went in to sit with her.

25 Now when it is too late (as if she would let me hold and comfort her like I do the others) I get up and go to her at once at her moan or restless stirring. "Are you awake, Emily? Can I get you something?" And the answer is always the same: "No, I'm all right, go back to sleep, Mother."

They persuaded me at the clinic to send her away to a convalescent home in the country where "she can have the kind of food and care you can't manage for her, and you'll be free to concentrate on the new baby." They still send children to that place. I see pictures on the society page of sleek young women planning affairs to raise money for it, or dancing at the affairs, or decorating Easter eggs or filling Christmas stockings for the children.

They never have a picture of the children so I do not know if the girls still wear those gigantic red bows and the ravaged looks on the every other Sunday when parents can come to visit "unless otherwise notified"—as we were notified the first six weeks.

Oh it is a handsome place, green lawns and tall trees and fluted flower beds. High up on the balconies of each cottage the children stand, the girls in their red bows and white dresses, the boys in white suits and giant red ties. The parents stand below shrieking up to be heard and the children shriek down to be heard, and between them the invisible wall: "Not to Be Contaminated by Parental Germs or Physical Affection."

There was a tiny girl who always stood hand in hand with Emily. Her parents never came. One visit she was gone. "They moved her to Rose Cottage," Emily shouted in explanation. "They don't like you to love anybody here."

30   She wrote once a week, the labored writing of a seven-year-old. "I am fine. How is the baby. If I write my leter nicly I will have a star. Love." There never was a star. We wrote every other day, letters she could never hold or keep but only hear read—once. "We simply do not have room for children to keep any personal possessions," they patiently explained when we pieced one Sunday's shrieking together to plead how much it would mean to Emily, who loved so to keep things, to be allowed to keep her letters and cards.

Each visit she looked frailer. "She isn't eating," they told us.

(They had runny eggs for breakfast or mush with lumps, Emily said later, I'd hold it in my mouth and not swallow. Nothing ever tasted good, just when they had chicken.)

It took us eight months to get her released home, and only the fact that she gained back so little of her seven lost pounds convinced the social worker.

I used to try to hold and love her after she came back, but her body would stay stiff, and after a while she'd push away. She ate little. Food sickened her, and I think much of life too. Oh she had physical lightness and brightness, twinkling by on skates, bouncing like a ball up and down up and down over the jump rope, skimming over the hill; but these were momentary.

35   She fretted about her appearance, thin and dark and foreign-looking at a time when every little girl was supposed to look or thought she should look a chubby blonde replica of Shirley Temple. The doorbell sometimes rang for her, but no one seemed to come and play in the house or be a best friend. Maybe because we moved so much.

There was a boy she loved painfully through two school semesters. Months later she told me how she had taken pennies from my purse to buy him candy. "Licorice was his favorite and I brought him some every day, but he still liked Jennifer better'n me. Why, Mommy?" The kind of question for which there is no answer.

School was a worry to her. She was not glib or quick in a world where glibness and quickness were easily confused with ability to learn. To her overworked and exasperated teachers she was an overconscientious "slow learner" who kept trying to catch up and was absent entirely too often.

I let her be absent, though sometimes the illness was imaginary. How different from my now-strictness about attendance with the others. I wasn't working. We had a new baby, I was home anyhow. Sometimes, after Susan grew old enough, I would keep her home from school, too, to have them all together.

Mostly Emily had asthma, and her breathing, harsh and labored, would fill the house with a curiously tranquil sound. I would bring the two old dresser mirrors and her boxes of collections to her bed. She would select beads and single earrings, bottle tops and shells, dried flowers and pebbles, old postcards and scraps, all sorts of oddments; then she and Susan would play Kingdom, setting up landscapes and furniture, peopling them with action.

40   Those were the only times of peaceful companionship between her and Susan. I have edged away from it, that poisonous feeling between them, that terrible balancing of hurts and needs I had to do between the two, and did so badly, those earlier years.

Oh there are conflicts between the others too, each one human, needing, demanding, hurting, taking—but only between Emily and Susan, no, Emily toward Susan that corroding resentment. It seems so obvious on the surface, yet it is not obvious. Susan, the second child, Susan, golden- and curly-haired and chubby, quick and articulate and assured, everything in appearance and manner Emily was not; Susan, not able to resist Emily's precious things, losing or sometimes clumsily breaking them; Susan telling jokes and riddles to company for applause while Emily sat silent (to say to me later: that was *my* riddle, Mother, I told it to Susan); Susan, who for all the five years' difference in age was just a year behind Emily in developing physically.

I am glad for that slow physical development that widened the difference between her and her contemporaries, though she suffered over it. She was too vulnerable for that terrible world of youthful competition, of preening and parading, of constant measuring of yourself against every other, of envy, "If I had that copper hair," "If I had that skin . . . " She tormented herself enough about not looking like the others, there was enough of the unsureness, the having to be conscious of words before you speak, the constant caring—what are they thinking of me? without having it all magnified by the merciless physical drives.

Ronnie is calling. He is wet and I change him. It is rare there is such a cry now. That time of motherhood is almost behind me when the ear is not one's own but must always be racked and listening for the child cry, the child call. We sit for a while and I hold him, looking out over the city spread in charcoal with its soft aisles of light. "*Shoogily,*" he breathes and curls closer. I carry him back to bed, asleep. *Shoogily*. A funny word, a family word, inherited from Emily, invented by her to say: *comfort.*

In this and other ways she leaves her seal, I say aloud. And startle at my saying it. What do I mean? What did I start to gather together, to try and make coherent? I was at the terrible, growing years. War years. I do not remember them well. I was working, there were four smaller ones now, there was not time for her. She had to help be a mother, and housekeeper, and shopper. She had to set her seal. Mornings of crisis and near hysteria trying to get lunches packed, hair combed, coats and shoes found, everyone to school or Child Care on time, the baby ready for transportation. And always the paper scribbled on by a smaller one, the book looked at by Susan

then mislaid, the homework not done. Running out to that huge school where she was one, she was lost, she was a drop; suffering over the unpreparedness, stammering and unsure in her classes.

45   There was so little time left at night after the kids were bedded down. She would struggle over books, always eating (it was in those years she developed her enormous appetite that is legendary in our family) and I would be ironing, or preparing food for the next day, or writing V-mail to Bill, or tending the baby. Sometimes, to make me laugh, or out of her despair, she would imitate happenings or types at school.

I think I said once: "Why don't you do something like this in the school amateur show?" One morning she phoned me at work, hardly understandable through the weeping: "Mother, I did it. I won, I won; they gave me first prize; they clapped and clapped and wouldn't let me go."

Now suddenly she was Somebody, and as imprisoned in her difference as she had been in anonymity.

She began to be asked to perform at other high schools, even in colleges, then at city and statewide affairs. The first one we went to, I only recognized her that first moment when thin, shy, she almost drowned herself into the curtains. Then: Was this Emily? The control, the command, the convulsing and deadly clowning, the spell, then the roaring, stamping audience, unwilling to let this rare and precious laughter out of their lives.

Afterwards: You ought to do something about her with a gift like that—but without money or knowing how, what does one do? We have left it all to her, and the gift has as often eddied inside, clogged and clotted, as been used and growing.

50   She is coming. She runs up the stairs two at a time with her light graceful step, and I know she is happy tonight. Whatever it was that occasioned your call did not happen today.

"Aren't you ever going to finish the ironing, Mother? Whistler painted his mother in a rocker.

I'd have to paint mine standing over an ironing board." This is one of her communicative nights and she tells me everything and nothing as she fixes herself a plate of food out of the icebox.

She is so lovely. Why did you want me to come in at all? Why were you concerned? She will find her way.

She starts up the stairs to bed. "Don't get me up with the rest in the morning." "But I thought you were having midterms." "Oh, those," she comes back in, kisses me, and says quite lightly, "in a couple of years when we'll all be atom-dead they won't matter a bit."

She has said it before. She *believes* it. But because I have been dredging the past, and all that compounds a human being is so heavy and meaningful in me, I cannot endure it tonight.

55   I will never total it all. I will never come in to say: She was a child seldom smiled at. Her father left me before she was a year old. I had to work her first six years when there was work, or I sent her home and to his relatives. There were

years she had care she hated. She was dark and thin and foreign-looking in a world where the prestige went to blondeness and curly hair and dimples, she was slow where glibness was prized. She was a child of anxious, not proud, love. We were poor and could not afford for her the soil of easy growth. I was a young mother, I was a distracted mother. There were other children pushing up, demanding. Her younger sister seemed all that she was not. There were years she did not want me to touch her. She kept too much in herself, her life was such she had to keep too much in herself. My wisdom came too late. She has much to her and probably little will come of it. She is a child of her age, of depression, of war, of fear.

Let her be. So all that is in her will not bloom—but in how many does it? There is still enough left to live by. Only help her to know—help make it so there is cause for her to know—that she is more than this dress on the ironing board, helpless before the iron.

EXPLORATORY WRITING

Write a brief summary in which you sort out the details of Olson's story. What is the setting? Who is the narrator and who is she talking to? What is the situation? What does the narrator mean when she says, "Even if I came, what good would it do? You think because I am her mother I have a key . . . ? There is all that life that has happened outside of me, beyond me."

TALKING ABOUT THE READING

At the end of the story, Emily says, "Whistler painted his mother in a rocker. I'd have to paint mine standing over an ironing board." What does Emily mean by that? Is she joking? Is she criticizing? In terms of how you imagine she spent most of her time, choose a woman in your life and explain how you would "paint" her. What characterizes the way she spends her days?

WRITING ASSIGNMENTS

1. Write Emily's side of this story. What would she have noticed in her mother's life? What might she have missed? How would she describe her relationship with her mother?

2. This story ends with a plea: "Only help her to know—help make it so there is cause for her to know—that she is more than this dress on the ironing board, helpless before the iron." Write an explanation for that final comment. How does it summarize the dilemma this narrator finds herself in? How might it represent the conflict many mothers have felt over the years as they worked to raise a family and to support that family?

3. Write an analysis of the role that work plays in the narrator's life. How does she use work to explain her daughter? To what extent does she describe herself through work? How does her work or her need to work determine the kind of mother she can be to Emily?

OUR LITTLE WOMEN PROBLEM

— *Stacy Schiff*

Stacy Schiff is an award-winning biographer whose work includes *The Great Improvisation: Franklin, France, and the Birth of America* (2005); *Vera (Mrs. Vladimir Nabokov),* which won the Pulitzer Prize for biography (2000); and *Saint-Exupéry: A Biography,* a 1995 Pulitzer Prize nominee. She has been a frequent guest columnist for the *New York Times,* where the following column appeared on June 18, 2005. In it, Schiff wonders whether women looking for strong role models in the work world have misread a classic girls' role model—Jo March, from *Little Women.*

SUGGESTION FOR READING Schiff uses Jo March from Louisa May Alcott's *Little Women* as a role model that, she suggests, may have misled generations of young women who believed that because Jo was strong and independent, they could be, too. To prepare you for this reading, write down briefly what you know about *Little Women* and the character of Jo March. To what extent would you consider her a role model for working mothers?

If you do not know the character, find out what you can about her. You can do this with a simple Internet search or by using a source like the *Larousse Dictionary of Literary Characters* or the *Chambers Dictionary of Literary Characters* available in most college and university libraries. Bring your writing to class with you for discussion.

1 As it seems to be the way things are done around here, I asked my spouse's opinion. Could this working mother thing ever be mastered? "On two conditions," he said, but the rest of the sentence was drowned out by a wail from the other room, where the youngest had raced out of bed so fast that she had collided with her door.

She was also in the mood for poached eggs, which—my husband helpfully pointed out—Robert Novak was presumably not making this morning. If he was, I wonder if he too was under strict instructions to keep the yolks runny, and to position the eggs in the precise center of each slice of toast. The 5-year-old is a gourmand and a tyrant, equally exacting in her menus as she is stern in her conviction that mothers do not go to their offices on weekends.

This is especially galling as the little tyrant is named for a feminist icon, in a novel I clearly should have read more closely. Jo March represented many of our first encounters with a capable, independent-minded heroine. She stands alone in a field crowded with submissive women.

She isn't sitting around with dwarfs or sweeping floors. She is waiting neither for a fairy godmother nor a handsome prince. She makes choices—and seemingly perverse ones, too. Perhaps most significantly, she is the first girl in literature with a room of her own.

5 Or so I remember it.

Writing in the May 16 [2005] *New Republic,* Deborah Friedell offers a startling revelation. I have misread *Little Women.* It is true that Jo is spunky, thirsty for adventure and grappling with her "disappointment in not being a boy." It's also true that—15 years later—she has entirely reconciled herself to her disappointment. Having relinquished her dreams, she looks from stout husband to unruly children and pronounces herself happier than she has ever been.

She is philosophical about her early ambition: "the life I wanted then seems selfish, lonely and cold to me now." One day she may well write a good book—as indeed she will, in a sequel—but she has no qualms. Nor does she care that she has kissed the tenure track goodbye.

How could I have got this so entirely wrong? It's like holding up Emma Bovary as an emblem of marital bliss. In part I have conflated the Jo of *Little Women* with the Jo of the sequels. And in part I've had help from Hollywood, which has filmed *Little Women* three times, and three times blessed Jo with both career and children.

Friedell feels that Alcott was not so much swayed by market pressures as she was eager to spare Jo her own fate. She lent her heroine the domestic bliss she would have preferred. (She also allows Jo the luxury of not working, something she could never afford.) So it was that from the proto-feminist, the single woman who put in 14-hour days at her desk, supported her extended family, and died of overwork, we got Rapunzel redux.

10   Two volumes later Jo indeed finds work she loves, and success, and money to spare. But the realization of her "wildest and most cherished dream" comes at a price. It is exhausting, and a strain on the domestic front. The feather duster brings more satisfaction than the fan mail. Alcott's message is loud and clear. Evidently it does not in fact require testosterone to deliver an opinion.

It helps, though. "First of all," resumed my husband, swabbing the counter, "two parents have to know how to make breakfast." Yes, and 75 percent of male executives have non-working wives. Seventy-four percent of female executives have working husbands. Guess who's making breakfast? "And," he continued, "the women who manage well will be the ones whose fathers listened to them."

I suspect he's reading this stuff while I'm wielding the feather duster. But the research bears him out. Mr. Alcott was a case in point. John Munder Ross, clinical professor of medical psychology at Columbia College of Physicians and Surgeons, is among those who have argued that for the Jos in this world to manage work and love, they need fathers who teach them to think—and to think that they deserve to marry their equals. Those men are as crucial to a girl's development, Ross holds, as the frantic mother who brings in a paycheck.

It could well be the route to the Hollywood version of *Little Women*. Happy Father's Day.

EXPLORATORY WRITING

Schiff sets her commentary on working mothers in her own kitchen, with her husband and children in the background. Write a summary of her argument. In your piece, note how Schiff uses her husband in this column. What role does he play in her discussion of the promise and possibilities for women who are trying to succeed in a professional career while also raising and caring for a family? What does he mean, for example, when he points out to her that Robert Novak is probably not cooking eggs in the morning?

TALKING ABOUT THE READING

With a group of your classmates, share what you each wrote about *Little Women* and Jo March before you read Schiff's column. How do your impressions of this novel and character differ? To what extent are they the same? How much of a role model for professional women is Jo March, given what you and your classmates have remembered or found out about the character?

WRITING ASSIGNMENTS

1. Reread your exploratory writing in which you examined how Schiff structures her commentary and how she sets the scene for her reader. In a follow-up writing drawing (when it is useful) on your exploratory writing, explain what Schiff means by her title, "Our Little Women Problem"? Whose problem? Problem with what?

2. Write an essay in which you examine where your own role models have come from. Do you see or admire those same characteristics in fictional characters? Politicians? Sports stars? Parents? Grandparents? How have those role models affected your decisions in school or in choosing a career goal or shaping values you consider important for your life?

3. During the 2008 primary election season, Hillary Clinton often spoke of the presidency as this country's "highest glass ceiling." According to a report in the *Christian Science Monitor* (June 6, 2008), "over 88 percent of voters agreed with the statement, 'I am glad to see a woman as a serious contender for president.' " That is up from a 1984 poll after Geraldine Ferraro's run for vice president, when only 62 percent of those polled by CBS said they were glad to see a woman candidate for high office. Even so, the same report mentions a moment during the campaign in New Hampshire when a young man from the audience called out to Clinton, "Iron my shirt!"

   With a group of three of your classmates, conduct your own, limited poll of attitudes among local college-age students toward the possibility of electing a woman for president. Each member of the group should poll at least 10 individuals in the 18–26 age range. Create a question that allows for a quick answer that is easy for your group to tabulate— for example, "I believe a woman could be elected U.S. President today." Tabulate your results, and report them to your classmates. In your report, speculate (as the *Christian Science Monitor* report does) on what you believe your results might suggest about local attitudes among your peers toward women running for high office.

ALABANZA: IN PRAISE OF LOCAL 100

— *Martín Espada*

Martín Espada is a poet, essayist, and translator. His collection *Alabanza: New and Selected Poems (1982–2002),* from which we have taken the title poem, appeared in 2003. It was awarded the Paterson Award for Sustained Literary Achievement and was named an American Library Association Notable Book. An earlier collection of Espada's work, *Imagine the Angels of Bread* (1996), won an American Book Award. *Rebellion Is the Circle of a Lover's Hands* (1990) received the Paterson Poetry Prize and a PEN/Revson Fellowship. Other awards include the Robert Creeley Award and two NEA Fellowships. His poems have appeared in the *New York Times Book Review, Harper's,* the *Nation,* and *The Best American Poetry.* Much of his writing arises from his Puerto Rican heritage and his work experiences, ranging from bouncer to tenant lawyer. He is also the editor of *Poetry Like Bread: Poets of the Political Imagination* from Curbstone Press. Espada is a professor of English at the University of Massachusetts, Amherst, where he teaches creative writing, Latino poetry, and the work of Pablo Neruda. Espada is also a lawyer who has acted as an advocate for the Latino community and for immigrants.

The word *alabanza* is Spanish for "praise" and comes from the Latin *alabar,* meaning "to celebrate with words." This poem is dedicated to the forty-three members of Local 100 of the Hotel Employees and Restaurant Employees union who were working in the Windows on the World restaurant at the top of the World Trade Center and were killed when that building was attacked on September 11, 2001.

SUGGESTION FOR READING   This poem functions, in part, as a eulogy to the restaurant workers who died in the World Trade Center. Before you read, look up the features common to a *eulogy*. Write a brief description of what expectations you bring with you when you listen to or deliver a eulogy.

For the 43 members of Hotel Employees and Restaurant Employees Local 100, working at the Windows on the World restaurant, who lost their lives in the attack on the World Trade Center

1 *Alabanza.* Praise the cook with a shaven head
and a tattoo on his shoulder thatsaid Oye,
a blue-eyed Puerto Rican with people from Fajardo,
the harbor of pirates centuries ago.
5 Praise the lighthouse in Fajardo, candle
glimmering white to worship the dark saint of the sea.
Alabanza. Praise the cook's yellow Pirates cap
worn in the name of Roberto Clemente, his plane
that flamed into the ocean loaded with cans for Nicaragua,
10 for all the mouths chewing the ash of earth-quakes
Alabanza. Praise the kitchen radio, dial clicked
even before the dial on the oven, so that music and Spanish
rose before bread. Praise the bread. *Alabanza.*

Praise Manhattan from a hundred and seven flights up,
15 like Atlantis glimpsed through the windows of an ancient aquarium.
Praise the great windows where immigrants from the kitchen
could squint and almost see their world, hear the chant of nations:
Ecuador, México, Republica Dominicana,
Haiti, Yemen, Ghana, Bangladesh.
20 *Alabanza.* Praise the kitchen in the morning,

where the gas burned blue on every stove
and exhaust fans fired their diminutive propellers,
hands cracked eggs with quick thumbs
or sliced open cartons to build an altar of cans.
25 *Alabanza.* Praise the busboy's music, the chime-chime
of his dishes and silverware in the tub.
Alabanza. Praise the dish-dog, the dishwasher
who worked that morning because another dishwasher
could not stop coughing, or because he needed overtime
30 to pile the sacks of rice and beans for a family
floating away on some Caribbean island plagued by frogs.
Alabanza. Praise the waitress who heard the radio in the kitchen
and sang to herself about a man gone. *Alabanza.*

After the thunder wilder than thunder,
35 after the shudder deep in the glass of the great windows,
after the radio stopped singing like a tree full of terrified frogs,
after night burst the dam of day and flooded the kitchen,
for a time the stoves glowed in darkness like the lighthouse in Fajardo,
like a cook's soul. Soul I say, even if the dead cannot tell us
40 about the bristles of God's beard because God has no face,
soul I say, to name the smoke-beings flung in constellations

across the night sky of this city and cities to
come.
Alabanza I say, even if God has no face.

Alabanza. When the war began, from Manhattan
and Kabul
45 two constellations of smoke rose and drifted to
each other,

mingling in icy air, and one said with an Afghan
tongue:
Teach me to dance. We have no music here.
And the other said with a Spanish tongue:
I will teach you. Music is all we have.

EXPLORATORY WRITING

Paraphrase this poem so that someone who doesn't read much poetry would be able to understand what it is saying. A paraphrase is a rewriting of the original in your own words.

TALKING ABOUT THE READING

Reread the final stanza of this poem. It might be clear that, in Kabul where war continues,
workers would feel that there is no music—nothing beautiful. With a group of your classmates, discuss why immigrant workers in the United States might feel that the only thing they
have is music.

WRITING ASSIGNMENTS

1. Drawing on the paraphrase you wrote in your exploratory writing, write an essay in
   which you explain in what ways this poem functions as a eulogy and in what ways it functions as a political statement about what kinds of work are valued in America and what
   kinds tend to be invisible.

2. In an interview with PBS, Espada spoke of one reason to call attention to the restaurant
   workers of Local 100: "when we think of these buildings, the WTC, these were, after
   all, office buildings in Manhattan. And a shadow army passes through every office
   building in Manhattan, making those buildings run and providing what we need. What
   could be more basic than food, than feeding us? That is what those food service workers were doing that very morning." For one day, keep a record of the hidden tasks,
   and the people who do them, that make your day what it is. Your list might include food
   service workers, computer systems administrators, janitors and housekeepers, power
   plant workers, and more. You won't be able to list them all, but do your best. Then write
   an essay in which you explain how much of your daily life depends on a "hidden army"
   of workers.

3. This poem is about individuals who lost their lives in a terrible tragedy, but it is also about
   low-wage jobs that go primarily to immigrants in this country, many of whom speak little or no English and have connections to other countries and other cultures. Write an
   essay in which you examine how these workers are depicted in the poem. Who are they?
   What do they care about? What connects them to each other and to the world as a
   whole? How does the last stanza of the poem characterize them and their living and working situations?

Working-Class Heroes

THE REAL STORY OF THE SUPERHEROES

— *Dulce Pinzón*

Dulce Pinzón was born in Mexico City in 1974. She studied mass media communications at the Universidad de Las Americas in Puebla, Mexico, and photography at Indiana University in Pennsylvania. In 1995, she moved to New York, where she studied at the International Center of Photography. Her work has been published and exhibited in Mexico, the United States, Australia, Argentina, and Europe. In 2002, she won the prestigious Jovenes Creadores grant for her work. She won an honorific mention in the Santa Fe project competition in 2006 with "The Real Story of the Superheroes" series, from which the photographs here were taken.

SUGGESTION FOR READING   Before you read Pinzón's statement about the exhibit (taken from her Web site), spend time looking carefully at each of these photographs. What do you notice about each? Write a brief reaction to the photos.

1 After September 11, the notion of the "hero" began to rear its head in the public consciousness more and more frequently. The notion served a necessity in a time of national and global crisis to acknowledge those who showed extraordinary courage or determination in the face of danger, sometimes even sacrificing their lives in an attempt to save others. However, in the whirlwind of journalism surrounding these deservedly front-page disasters and emergencies, it is easy to take for granted the heroes who sacrifice immeasurable life and labor in their day to day lives for the good of others, but do so in a somewhat less spectacular setting.

The Mexican immigrant worker in New York is a perfect example of the hero who has gone unnoticed. It is common for a Mexican worker in New York to work extraordinary hours in extreme conditions for very low wages which are saved at great cost and sacrifice and sent to families and communities in Mexico who rely on them to survive.

The Mexican economy has quietly become dependent on the money sent from workers in the US. Conversely, the US economy has quietly become dependent on the labor of Mexican immigrants. Along with the depth of their sacrifice, it is the quietness of this dependence which makes Mexican immigrant workers a subject of interest.

The principal objective of this series is to pay homage to these brave and determined men and women that somehow manage, without the help of any supernatural power, to withstand extreme conditions of labor in order to help their families and communities survive and prosper.

5 This project consists of 20 color photographs of Mexican immigrants dressed in the costumes of popular American and Mexican superheroes. Each photo pictures the worker/superhero in their work environment, and is accompanied by a short text including the worker's name, their hometown in Mexico, the number of years they have been working in New York, and the amount of money they send to Mexico each week.

Photo courtesy Dulce Pinzón, www.dulcepinzon.com.

Maria Luisa Romero from the State of Puebla works in a laundromat in Brooklyn, New York. She sends 150 dollars a week.

Photo courtesy Dulce Pinzón, www.dulcepinzon.com.

Bernabe Mendez from the State of Guerrero works as a professional window cleaner in New York. He sends 500 dollars a month.

Photo courtesy Dulce Pinzón, www.dulcepinzon.com.

Noe Reyes from the State of Puebla works as a delivery boy in Brooklyn, New York. He sends 500 dollars a week.

EXPLORATORY WRITING

Each of these photographs represents a worker as a superhero: Superman, Spider Man, and Wonder Woman. Drawing on the reaction piece you wrote before reading Pinzón's statement, write your own account of the people she has chosen to photograph and the way she has chosen to represent them—the costumes she asks them to wear and the situations and settings for each. What statement is she making that is individual for each?

TALKING ABOUT THE VISUAL ESSAY

Divide the class into groups, each group working with a different photograph from this series. In your group, begin by assembling what you all know about Wonder Woman, Superman, or Spider Man, depending on which photo your group is responsible for. With your group, discuss how Pinzón works both with and against the image of the superhero to create her own superhero in the photograph. Present your discussion to the class. Listen to the other group reports, and then, as a class, discuss what a knowledge of the superhero character adds to your reading of these photos as a collection.

WRITING ASSIGNMENTS

1. In her description of the series, Pinzón writes, "The principal objective of this series is to pay homage to these brave and determined men and women that somehow manage, without the help of any supernatural power, to withstand extreme conditions of labor in order to help their families and communities survive and prosper." Write an

essay in which you examine these photographs in light of that comment. How does the series pay homage to these workers? What comment does it make on heroes and super-heroes in general?

2. Like Martín Espada in "Alabanza," Dulce Pinzón asks her audience to pay attention to the people we normally take for granted in our everyday lives—the people who are often unacknowledged when great tragedy strikes or ignored when we are looking for role models. Write an essay in which you examine how the poem "Alabanza" and the Superhero photographs work together as a statement about immigrant labor, service workers, and the kinds of work this culture seems to value. How does Pinzón's work shed light on Espada's and Espada's heighten the effect of Pinzón's?

3. Create your own folio of working-class heroes. Who are the people, what are the kinds of work you value that you think others do not notice? Take a series of photographs and intro-duce them with a brief commentary indicating what you hope your audience sees in them.

MAKING CONNECTIONS   Off-Shoring the Great American Dream

According to a Reuters report, December 2004 marked the first time in thirty years that the median salary for an electrical engineer in the United States dropped. That report cited the practice of "offshoring" high-skill technology jobs to take advantage of the lower wages in overseas markets. In the articles that follow, Thomas L. Friedman and David Moberg explore the implications of offshoring made possible by advances in high-speed digital technology.

THE GREAT INDIAN DREAM

— Thomas L. Friedman

Thomas L. Friedman, a columnist for the *New York Times,* has won three Pulitzer Prizes for commentary. He is the author of *From Beirut to Jerusalem* (1989), which won the National Book Award for nonfiction, and *The Lexus and the Olive Tree* (2000), which won an Overseas Press Club award. His book *The World Is Flat: A Brief History of the Twenty-first Century* (2005) argues that globalization and the digital revolution have leveled the playing field so that devel-oping nations now can compete successfully in the global market and even change the bal-ance of economic power. "The Great Indian Dream" first appeared in Friedman's *New York Times* column on March 11, 2004. In it, Friedman credits the free market, globalization, and the digital revolution for changing the economic outlook of places like Bangalore, India.

SUGGESTION FOR READING In this column, Friedman argues that Bangalore's recent success in the marketplace can be traced to good timing, hard work, talent, and luck. Highlight/underline and annotate those places in the column where he explains that argument.

1 Nine years ago, as Japan was beating America's brains out in the auto industry, I wrote a column about playing a computer geography game with my daughter, then 9 years old. I was trying to help her with a clue that clearly pointed to Detroit, so I asked her, "Where are cars made?" And she answered, "Japan." Ouch.

Well, I was reminded of that story while visiting an Indian software design firm in Bangalore, Global Edge. The company's marketing manager, Rajesh Rao, told me he had just made a cold call to the vice president for engineering of a U.S. company, trying to drum up business. As soon as Mr. Rao introduced himself as calling from an Indian software firm, the U.S. executive said to him, "Namaste"—a common Hindi greeting. Said Mr. Rao: "A few years ago nobody in America wanted to talk to us. Now they are eager." And a few even know how to say hi in proper Hindu fashion. So now I wonder: if I have a granddaughter one day; and I tell her I'm going to India, will she say, "Grandpa, is that where software comes from?"

Driving around Bangalore you might think so. The Pizza Hut billboard shows a steaming pizza under the headline "Gigabites of Taste!" Some traffic signs are sponsored by Texas Instruments. And when you tee off on the first hole at Bangalore's KGA golf course, your playing partner points at two new glass-and-steel buildings in the distance and says: "Aim at either Microsoft or I.B.M."

How did India, in 15 years, go from being a synonym for massive poverty to the brainy country that is going to take all our best jobs? Answer: good timing, hard work, talent and luck.

5 The good timing starts with India's decision in 1991 to shuck off decades of socialism and move toward a free-market economy with a focus on foreign trade. This made it possible for Indians who wanted to succeed at innovation to stay at home, not go to the West. This, in turn, enabled India to harvest a lot of its natural assets for the age of globalization.

One such asset was Indian culture's strong emphasis on education and the widely held belief here that the greatest thing any son or daughter could do was to become a doctor or an engineer, which created a huge pool of potential software technicians. Second, by accident of history and the British occupation of India, most of those engineers were educated in English and could easily communicate with Silicon Valley. India was also neatly on the other side of the world from America, so U.S. designers could work during the day and e-mail their output to their Indian subcontractors in the evening. The Indians would then work on it for all of their day and e-mail it back. Presto: the 24-hour workday.

Also, this was the age of globalization, and the countries that succeed best at globalization are those that are best at "glocalization"—taking the best global innovations, styles and practices and melding them with their own culture, so they don't feel overwhelmed. India has been naturally glocalizing for thousands of years.

Then add some luck. The dot-com bubble led to a huge overinvestment in undersea fiber-optic cables, which made it dirt-cheap to transfer data, projects or phone calls to far-flung places like India, where Indian techies could work on them for much lower wages than U.S. workers. Finally, there was Y2K. So many companies feared that their computers would melt down because of the Year 2000 glitch they needed software programmers to go through and recode them. Who had large numbers of programmers to do that cheaply? India. That was how a lot of Indian software firms got their first outsourced jobs.

So if you are worried about outsourcing, I've got good news and bad news. The good news is that a unique techno-cultural-economic perfect storm came together in the early 1990's to make India a formidable competitor and partner for certain U.S. jobs—and there are not a lot of other Indias out there. The bad news, from a competition point of view, is that there are 555 million Indians under the age of 25, and a lot of them want a piece of "The Great Indian Dream," which is a lot like the American version.

10   As one Indian exec put it to me: The Americans' self-image that this tech thing was their private preserve is over. This is a wake-up call for U.S. workers to redouble their efforts at education and research. If they do that, he said, it will spur "a whole new cycle of innovation, and we'll both win. If we each pull down our shutters, we will both lose."

EXPLORATORY WRITING

Friedman argues that part of India's success is due to "glocalization." From what you have read here, write a brief explanation of the term *glocalization* as Friedman explains it.

TALKING ABOUT THE READING

Friedman opens with an anecdote about his daughter, who had identified Japan rather than Detroit as the place where cars are made. He ends by asking if his granddaughter will one day identify India as "where software comes from." With a group of your classmates, identify what Friedman's attitude is toward this shift in economic power and identification. What in the article indicates that attitude?

WRITING ASSIGNMENT

Friedman claims that India has been "naturally glocalizing for years." Write an essay in which you examine that claim as a challenge to U.S. economic policy.

HIGH-TECH HIJACK

— David Moberg

David Moberg is a senior editor for *In These Times,* where he has been on staff since 1976, covering the labor movement. In 2003, Moberg received the Max Steinbock Award from the International Labor Communications Association and, in 1993, a Project Censored Award for his coverage of labor issues. His writing has also appeared in the *Nation, New York Times, Chicago Tribune, Boston Globe,* and many other national publications. "High-tech Hijack" appeared in the January 2005 issue of *In These Times.*

SUGGESTION FOR READING As you read, keep in mind how Friedman interprets the phenomenon of offshoring in the previous reading. Note in the margins where Friedman and Moberg share similar concerns on this issue. Where do they depart?

1 Stephen Gentry had worked as a programmer for Boeing for 15 years before he was laid off in July 2003. His last project was training his replacements, software engineers from India. They were working in Seattle on temporary visas before returning home to do Gentry's job at Infosys, one of India's leading subcontractors of information technology (IT) services.

Eighteen months later, Gentry, 52, who earned a computer sciences degree while working as a construction worker, still hasn't found a job. "American corporations," he says, "are so greedy and cutthroat-oriented they don't care about me, you or anybody else except their bottom line."

Gentry is not alone. The offshoring of work once done by Americans is growing rapidly. Over the past few years, corporations have shifted roughly a half million business service and IT jobs, many highly skilled, to developing countries. This has kept high-tech unemployment up, driven down wages, sparked widespread job anxieties, depressed support for free trade and generated a political backlash.

Elite apologists for globalization had long assured workers that they had a secure future with a college degree and a service job, especially anything computer-related. Now fewer Americans share the blind faith that the market will supply new and better jobs, as corporations cut costs by sending work—ranging from customer services to reading X-rays—to countries like India, where wages are often one-tenth the level in the United States.

5   Nobody knows precisely how many high-tech service jobs have been moved offshore. The number is still much less than the number of manufacturing jobs moved overseas, but future prospects are grim. Multinational companies are speeding up plans either to outsource more jobs to overseas contractors—including both U.S. multinationals and fast-growing foreign firms like Infosys—or to set up their own offshore service operations. IDC, a private IT research firm, predicts that IT offshoring will increase by more than 500 percent by 2007, and, according to the company's senior vice president for research, Frank Gens, China—now moving into services—"represents a wild card that could well accelerate the U.S. offshoring trend." Forrester Research predicts 3.3 million service jobs—a third of them in the highest-paying fifth of the job market—will go overseas by 2015. And a University of California Berkeley study estimates that that 14 million service jobs are vulnerable.

"If you work behind a computer screen, your job is up for grabs," says Sanjay Kumar, former CEO of Computer Associates, a leading management software company.

END OF THE LINE

Offshoring service work is the latest chapter in the history of capitalist reorganization of work. Early capitalists subdivided and routinized tasks so they could be performed by less-skilled—and lower-paid—workers. With digitization of information and standardization of software, the strategies behind dividing the manufacture of widgets can be applied to bytes of information relating to insurance claims, financial accounting, tax preparation, and hundreds of other tasks.

This new division of work meshes with two other growing trends: first, outsourcing, or subcontracting, of tasks to other companies, including even core tasks like manufacturing and design of products and, second, the shift of production overseas. Manufacturing was the first to go global, but with the expansion of high-speed Internet links and plummeting international telecommunication costs, the stage was set for offshoring services.

Multinational service corporations had long expected to globalize, mainly by setting up foreign branches to provide services. A few, like General Electric and American Express, began using technical and service workers in low-wage countries to cut costs for their own global operations or, later, to provide services for other companies. Now a wide range of multinationals can digitally fragment their work, outsourcing to many different worldwide suppliers in a search for the lowest cost. Consultants—many with a financial stake in outsourcing services—promoted offshoring as the wave of the future.

10   Over the past decade, companies in developing countries have become major offshoring players as well. Indian software companies in particular expanded by taking advantage of tens of thousands of English-speaking Indian engineers, who had worked in the United States on temporary visas, to develop a skilled workforce and knowledge of American business. Their reputation for good, cheap work was boosted by the surge of contracts to fix Y2K software problems. Meanwhile, Indian universities have been churning out thousands of graduates, and the government relaxed controls on foreign businesses and service exporters.

WINNERS AND LOSERS

Offshoring services hasn't always been as smooth or as cheap as promised, but companies have prospered. An Institute for Policy Studies/United for a Fair Economy study found that executive pay for the 50 largest outsourcers of service jobs increased dramatically in 2003 to 28 percent above the average for large-company CEOs.

But will offshoring be good for everyone else? Here's the pro-offshoring argument: Businesses that offshore jobs will save money, cut prices, expand sales, make more profit and then reinvest in new, high value-added, high-skilled jobs—if only redundant workers will just retrain themselves. But that scenario has its skeptics. Marcus Courtney, president of WashTech, an IT local of the Communications Workers, asks, "Everybody assumes they'll reinvest here, but why wouldn't they reinvest where it's cheaper?" Indeed, Philip Mattera of the Corporate Research Project reports that venture capitalists now ask IT start-up companies to present their offshoring strategy.

High-level American IT jobs are still growing. However, overall IT employment declined in recent years even after corporate IT spending rebounded. The threat of offshoring has also depressed IT wages, and college IT enrollment is dropping. Meanwhile, offshore firms are moving higher up the services skill ladder.

SILICON CEILING

Most new U.S. jobs, according to the Economic Policy Institute (EPI), are not steps up: they pay 21 percent less on average than job-losing industries. Six of the 10 occupations that the Bureau of Labor Statistics forecasts will provide the largest number of new jobs through 2012 require no college education and typically pay low wages. Foreign investment—contrary to hype about "insourcing" of jobs to the United States—is no solution. Foreign investors have mainly acquired existing U.S. companies, according to EPI, resulting in a net loss of jobs and a rising trade deficit, while generating a measly 25,000 jobs a year from new enterprises. And stirring up a hornet's nest among economists, Nobel Prize winner Paul Samuelson last summer pointed out that the U.S. economy could end up losing, not winning, from

expanded free trade if low-wage foreign competitors drive down the price of products where the United States theoretically has a comparative advantage. That seems increasingly possible.

WHAT'S THE SOLUTION?

15 In the short run, legislation has been introduced at the state and federal level to restrict outsourcing of public jobs, tighten tech visa controls, increase disclosure of offshoring, ensure privacy of information and otherwise regulate offshoring of services. But such legislation, while useful, would have limited effect. Meanwhile, two Indian union leaders recently toured the United States, advocating transnational labor action to raise labor standards in India—call centers can be oppressive operations—and slow offshoring. But tech and business service workers are largely unorganized in both countries.

The U.S. government could spur new job creation by increasing scientific research funding (which Bush is cutting) and linking corporate use of federal research to investment in the United States. It could also expand trade adjustment to cover now-excluded service workers and provide all displaced workers more comprehensive education (which Bush opposes).

In the long run, however, workers and communities must win a greater voice in corporate strategic decisions through federal reform of corporate governance, shifting of more of the financial burden from displaced workers and their communities to corporations, collective bargaining and putting pressure on pension funds. Pension funds and corporate reformers should also try to reduce Wall Street's focus on short-run profits. And any national economic benefits from globalization must be shared with everyone—such as through universal health care, improved pensions and higher service sector wages—not hoarded by a tiny elite.

The crisis looming from the massive offshoring of the service industry may make these currently utopian notions politically feasible—and a matter of practical national survival.

EXPLORATORY WRITING

Notice that while Friedman tells this story from the point of view of Bangalore's gain, Moberg tells it from the point of view of American workers. In a brief writing, explain how this shift in perspective changes the way a reader might respond to globalization in the digital revolution.

TALKING ABOUT THE READING

Low-tech jobs have been outsourced for many years now. With a group of your classmates, discuss how high-tech, high-skill job outsourcing (offshoring) is or is not more serious. Where possible, draw on both Friedman and Moberg in your discussion.

WRITING ASSIGNMENT

Write an essay in which you make a clear distinction between Moberg's and Friedman's concerns about offshoring.

WRITING SEQUENCE

1. For this longer exploratory writing, begin by rereading the articles by Friedman and Moberg and review any notes, underlinings, or earlier writings you did in response to your first reading. In this exploratory piece, detail the basic arguments each makes, noting particularly where the two seem to meet on common ground as well as where their positions depart. What is the issue at stake in this discussion?

2. Friedman writes from the point of view of a rising Bangalore market. Moberg comes at this issue from the point of view of American workers. Using your longer exploratory writing as a base from which to begin, write a 2–3 page analysis of the two articles in which you examine how the discussion changes depending on whose point of view the story of offshoring is written from. Pay attention in your analysis to how point of view determines what each writer will focus on as a central issue, concern, or advantage of the move toward offshoring, how it shapes the way the argument is made.

3. For this culminating assignment, use your previous writing and discussions to write an essay in which you use Moberg to speak back to Friedman or Friedman to speak back to Moberg. In other words, use the arguments one makes (drawing directly from passages in that writer's article) to address specific concerns the other raises. Make sure you quote directly from each and cite your source when you do. In preparation for this essay, review both your longer exploratory writing in which you set out the issues as each writer represents them and your analysis in which you examine how the argument changes depending on whose point of view you take. This essay, then, draws on those two pieces to put these two writers in a conversation. What, for example, would Moberg say about Friedman's discussion of what he calls "glocalization"? What would Friedman say to Moberg in response to Moberg's charge that U.S. jobs have been "hijacked"? This should be a 3–5 page finished essay (drafted, revised, and edited).

WORKED AND OVERWORKED

— *Steven Greenhouse*

Steven Greenhouse serves as the labor and workplace reporter for the *New York Times*. His writing on labor issues has appeared widely in a number of newspapers and online sites, including Slate magazine and Talking Points Café (talkingpointsmemo.com). *The Big Squeeze: Tough Times for the American Worker* (2008) is Greenhouse's first book-length investigation of current workplace conditions.

SUGGESTION FOR READING The selection reprinted here is from the first chapter of *The Big Squeeze*. Greenhouse opens with a series of workplace scenarios, telling stories of workers who have personally felt the squeeze of current economic conditions. Notice, as you read, where Greenhouse shifts from anecdotal evidence to research on the status of workers today. Highlight or annotate those places where Greenhouse uses that research to comment on individual stories.

1   In his job at a Wal-Mart in Texas, Mike Michell was responsible for catching shoplifters, and he was good at it, too, catching 180 in one two-year period. But one afternoon things went wildly awry when he chased a thief—a woman using stolen checks—into the parking lot. She jumped into her car, and her accomplice gunned the accelerator, slamming the car into Michell and sending him to the hospital with a broken kneecap, a badly torn shoulder, and two herniated disks. Michell was so devoted to Wal-Mart that he somehow returned to work the next day, but a few weeks later he told his boss that he needed surgery on his knee. He was fired soon afterward, apparently as part of a strategy to dismiss workers whose injuries run up Wal-Mart's workers' comp bills.[1]

Immediately after serving in the army, Dawn Eubanks took a seven-dollar-an-hour job at a call center in Florida. Some days she was told to clock in just two or three hours, and some days she was not allowed to clock in during her whole eight-hour shift. The call center's managers warned the workers that if they went home, even though they weren't allowed to clock in, they would be viewed as having quit.

Twenty-eight-year-old John Arnold works in the same Caterpillar factory in Illinois as his father, but under the plant's two-tier contract, the maximum he can ever earn is $14.90 an hour, far less than the $25 earned by his father. Caterpillar, long a symbol of America's industrial might, insists that it needs a lower wage tier to remain competitive. "A few people I work with are living at home with their parents," Arnold said. "Some are even on food stamps."

At a Koch Foods poultry plant in Tennessee, the managers were so intent on keeping the line running all out that Antonia Lopez Paz and the other workers who carved off chicken tenders were ordered not to go to the bathroom except during their lunch and coffee breaks. When one desperate woman asked permission to go, her supervisor took off his hard hat and said, "You can go to the bathroom in this." Some women ended up soiling themselves.

5   Don Jensen anticipated a relaxing life of golf after retiring from his human resources post with Lucent Technologies in New Jersey, where he was in charge of recruiting graduates from Stanford, Cornell, MIT, and other top universities. But when Lucent increased its retirees' health insurance premiums to $8,280 a year, up from $180, Jensen was forced to abandon his retirement. He took a job as a ten-dollar-an-hour bank teller.

As part of her software company's last-lap sprint to get new products out the door, Myra Bronstein sometimes had to work twenty-four hours straight testing for bugs. She felt great loyalty to the Seattle-area company because its executives had repeatedly promised, "As long as we're in business, you have a job." But one Friday morning the company suddenly fired Bronstein and seventeen other quality assurance engineers. The engineers were told that if they wanted to receive severance pay, they had to agree to spend the next month training the workers from India who would be replacing them.

One of the least examined but most important trends taking place in the United States today is the broad decline in the status and treatment of American workers—white-collar and blue-collar workers, middle-class and low-end workers—that began nearly three decades ago, gradually gathered momentum, and hit with full force soon after the turn of this century. A profound shift has left a broad swath of the American workforce on a lower plane than in decades past, with health coverage, pension benefits, job security, workloads, stress levels, and often wages growing worse for millions of workers.

That the American worker faces this squeeze in the early years of this century is particularly troubling because the squeeze has occurred while the economy, corporate profits, and worker productivity have all been growing robustly. In recent years, a disconcerting disconnect has emerged, with corporate profits soaring while workers' wages stagnated.

The statistical evidence for this squeeze is as compelling as it is disturbing. In 2005, median income for nonelderly households failed to increase for the fifth year in a row, after factoring in inflation. That is unprecedented in a time of economic growth.[2] In 2006, median income for those households did finally rise, but it still remained lower—$2,375 lower—than six years earlier.[3] That, too, is unprecedented. Even though corporate profits have doubled since recession gave way to economic expansion in November 2001, and even though employee productivity has risen more than 15 percent since then, the average wage for the typical American worker has inched up just 1 percent (after inflation). With the subprime mortgage crisis threatening to pull the economy into recession, some economists say this may be the first time in American history that the typical working household goes through an economic expansion without any increase in income whatsoever.

10   This, unfortunately, is the continuation of a long-term squeeze. Since 1979, hourly earnings for 80 percent of American workers (those in private-sector, nonsupervisory jobs) have risen by just 1 percent, after inflation.[4] The average hourly wage was $17.71 at the end of 2007. For male workers, the average wage has actually slid by 5 percent since 1979. Worker productivity, meanwhile, has climbed 60 percent.[5] If wages had kept pace with productivity, the average full-time worker would be earning $58,000 a year; $36,000 was the average in 2007.[6] The nation's economic pie is growing, but corporations by and large have not given their workers a bigger piece.[7]

The squeeze on the American worker has meant more poverty, more income inequality, more family tensions, more hours at work, more time away from the kids, more families without health insurance, more retirees with inadequate pensions, and more demands on government and taxpayers to provide housing assistance and health coverage. Twenty percent of families with children under six live below the poverty line, and 22 million full-time workers do not have health insurance.[8] Largely as a result of the squeeze, the number of housing foreclosures and personal bankruptcies more than tripled in the quarter century after 1979.[9] Economic studies show that income inequality in the United States is so great that it more closely resembles the inequality of a third world country than that of an advanced industrial nation.[10]

Many families *are* enjoying higher incomes, enabling them to buy a plasma-screen TV or take a vacation in Orlando, but this is frequently because fathers have taken on second jobs or more overtime hours or because mothers, even with toddlers, have opted for full-time paid employment. Millions of households have not slipped further behind only because Americans are working far harder than before. A husband and wife in the average middle-class household are, taken together, working 540 hours or three months more per year than such couples would have a quarter century ago, mainly because married women are working considerably longer hours than before.[11]

Viewed another way, the American worker's financial squeeze has translated into a time squeeze. In a survey by the Families and Work Institute, two-thirds of employed parents responded that they didn't have enough time with their kids, and just under two-thirds said they didn't have enough time with their spouses.[12] The typical American worker toils 1,804 hours a year, 135 hours more per year than the typical British worker, 240 hours more than the average French worker, and 370 hours (or nine full-time weeks) more than the average German worker.[13] No one in the world's advanced economies works more. Aggravating the time squeeze is a phenomenon known as job creep in which our jobs have spilled increasingly into our leisure time. Americans are finishing work memos on their home computers at eleven p.m., they are reading office e-mails on Saturdays and Sundays, and they are using their cell phones and BlackBerries to answer their bosses' queries while on vacation. The Conference Board, the business research group, found that Americans are less satisfied with their jobs—just 47 percent are satisfied—than at any time since it started tracking the numbers two decades ago. "The breadth of dissatisfaction is unsettling," the Conference Board wrote, its director of research adding, "The demands in the workplace have increased tremendously."[14]

Americans are going deeper into debt than ever before. Millions of households have supersized their credit card balances, and many have taken cash out of their homes by obtaining second mortgages, arguably unhealthy ways to try to maintain a comfortable lifestyle on a less-than-comfortable income.[15] In 2005, for the first time since the Great Depression, the nation's personal savings rate sank below zero, meaning that Americans were actually spending more than they were earning.[16] As a result, among the bottom two-fifths of households, nearly one in four spends at least 40 percent of its monthly income paying down its debts.[17] And foreclosure filings, spurred by the sub-prime mortgage crisis, are expected to soar to as many as two million by the end of 2008. Two million would represent one in sixty-two households.[18]

Even as wages stagnated in recent years, many government officials triumphantly boasted that consumer spending had continued to rise. But this increase was largely due to soaring incomes at the top. From 1979 to 2005, a period when national output more than doubled, after-tax income inched up just 6 percent for the bottom fifth of American households after accounting for inflation, while it rose 21 percent for the middle fifth. For the top fifth, income jumped 80 percent and for the top 1 percent it more than tripled, soaring by 228 percent.[19] A 2007 report by the Congressional Budget Office found that the top 1 percent of households had pre-tax income in 2005 that was more than two-fifths larger than that of the bottom 40 percent. (After taxes, the top 1 percent's income in 2005 was still nearly 10 percent greater than the bottom 40 percent's.)[20] As Paul Krugman wrote, "It's a great economy if you're a high-level corporate executive or someone who owns a lot of stock. For most other Americans, economic growth is a spectator sport."[21]

The nation appears to be on the threshold of recession, and as a result, America's workers are likely to be squeezed not just by stagnant wages but also by rising unemployment. One of the most worrisome—and puzzling—aspects of the economic expansion that began in November 2001 is that wages have remained stubbornly flat, after factoring in inflation, even though the jobless rate has been low by historical standards. That wages have gone nowhere in a tight labor market underlines the American worker's declining ability to command higher wages, and now with unemployment increasing, workers' leverage to push for higher wages is bound to grow even weaker.

The squeeze is of course worst for those on the lowest rungs, including millions of workers who are part of our everyday lives: fast food workers, cashiers, child care workers, hotel maids, and nurse's aides. Nearly 33 million workers—almost one-fourth of the American workforce—earn less than ten dollars an hour, meaning their wages come to less than the poverty line for a family of four ($20,614 in 2006).[22] Despite strong economic growth, the number of Americans living in poverty jumped by 15 percent from 2000 to 2006—an increase of 5.4 million to 36.5 million.[23] For millions of low-income workers, the promise of America has been broken: the promise that if you work hard, you will be rewarded with a decent living, the promise that if you do an honest day's work, you will earn enough to feed, clothe, and shelter your family.

Not only do workers on the bottom rungs lack money, but they often lack basic benefits. Three out of four low-wage workers in the private sector do not have employer-provided health insurance, while eight out of nine do not participate in a pension plan.[24] Three-fourths of low-wage workers do not receive paid sick days, so if they need to miss two days' work because they are sick or their child is sick, they receive no pay for those days—and often risk getting fired.[25]

A study sponsored by the Ford, Rockefeller, and Annie E. Casey foundations, "Working Hard, Falling Short," concluded, "More than one out of four American working families now earn wages so low"—defined as income of less than twice the poverty line for a family of four ($41,200 in 2006)—"that they have difficulty surviving financially." The study continued, "While our economy relies on the service jobs these low-paid workers fill . . . our society has not taken adequate steps to ensure that these workers can make ends meet and build a future for their families, no matter how determined they are to be self-sufficient."[26] In her book *Nickel and Dimed*, Barbara Ehrenreich described these workers as "the major philanthropists of our society." Ehrenreich wrote, "They neglect their own children so the children of others will be cared for; they live in substandard housing so that other homes will be shiny and perfect."[27] Across America more than 50 million people live in near poor households, those with incomes between $20,000 and $40,000 a year. Katherine Newman, a Princeton sociologist, has described this large but often overlooked group as "the missing class." The mass of workers who are barely getting by is likely to grow only larger, because the Bureau of Labor Statistics forecasts that low-wage jobs will account for six of the top ten categories in overall job growth between now and 2014: janitors, nursing home aides, waiters, home-health aides, retail sales workers including cashiers, and food-prep and fast food workers.[28]

20   America's ailing health care system is a big part of the worsening squeeze. From 2000 to 2006, the number of Americans without health insurance climbed by 8.6 million, to 47 million.[29] One study found that more than two-fifths of moderate-income, working-age Americans went without health insurance for at least part of 2005.[30] Not only that, for employees who want coverage, companies are requiring them to pay more for it, and as a result, the cost of family coverage has soared 83 percent in just six years.[31] As health costs consume more and more of the nation's economic output—they account for 16 percent of gross domestic product, or GDP, up from 5 percent in 1960—that necessarily leaves less money for wage increases.

Pensions, the other pillar of employee benefits, are under assault as never before. In May 2005, a bankruptcy judge allowed United Airlines to default on its pension plans and dump them on the federal agency that protects retirement benefits. Because that agency guarantees pensions only up to a certain amount, many United pilots will receive only half what they expected when they retire. United's move was the biggest pension default in American history, releasing it from paying $3.2 billion in obligations over the following five years. One of United's lawyers predicted that more and more companies would use this "strategic tool" to increase their competitiveness.[32] Since then, US Airways and Delta have followed suit. When Delphi, the auto parts giant, filed for bankruptcy in October 2005, its chief executive, Robert S. Miller, threatened to slash the company's pensions unless the workers agreed to massive wage concessions.

As part of this assault on pensions, Hewlett-Packard, IBM, Verizon, Sears, Motorola, and many other companies have embraced a riskier, far less generous type of retirement plan, 401(k)s, while turning away from the traditional plans that promised workers a specific monthly benefit for life after they retired.[33] When Hewlett-Packard took that step, a company spokesman said, "Pension plans are kind of a thing of the past."[34]

With pensions growing ever scarcer, more and more workers are convinced that they won't have enough money to retire. Ominously, some economists have begun to warn that millions of Americans might have to continue working into their seventies.

Even though this is an era of increased economic volatility, the federal government has decided to let Americans fend increasingly for themselves. Just one-third of laid-off workers receive unemployment benefits, down from 50 percent a generation ago. And even though workers' skills are becoming obsolete faster than ever because of new technologies and globalization, funding for the main federal program for retraining has been reduced by more than $10 billion in the last quarter century.[35] "Americans increasingly find themselves on an economic tightrope, without an adequate safety net if—as is ever more likely—they lose their footing," wrote Jacob S. Hacker, author of *The Great Risk Shift*.[36]

25 Business executives say they have been forced to tighten their belts on wages and every-

thing else because they face ever-fiercer competition. That is true, but corporate profits have nonetheless soared, climbing 13 percent a year in the six years after the 2001 recession ended, while wages have remained flat. (Employee productivity has also far outpaced wages, rising 15 percent from 2001 through 2007.) Corporate profits have climbed to their highest share of national income in sixty-four years, while the share going to wages has sunk to its lowest level since 1929.[37]

"This is the most pronounced several years of labor's share declining," said Lawrence Katz, an economics professor at Harvard. "For as long as we've had a modern economy, this is the worst we've seen it."[38]

Very simply, corporations, along with their CEOs, are seizing a bigger piece of the nation's economic pie for themselves, leaving the nation's workers and their families diminished.

Many Americans are feeling the squeeze as part of a growing wave of worker exploitation. Faster line speeds at the nation's meat and poultry plants are causing workers' bodies to break down and leading to more amputations. Workers have died at construction sites when scaffolding or trenches collapsed because supervisors ignored the most elementary precautions.[39] Inside some of the nation's best-known retail stores, immigrant janitors have been forced to work 365 days a year.

Exploitation is of course nothing new, as Upton Sinclair's writings, Lewis Hines's photographs, and the Triangle Shirtwaist fire all made clear. In the decades after the Great Depression, exploitation declined as the United States created the world's most prosperous middle class and as business, labor, and government often worked hand in hand to improve workplace conditions. In recent years, however, worker mistreatment has been on the rise, spurred by a stepped-up corporate focus on minimizing costs and by an influx of easy-to-exploit immigrants. Corporate executives, intent on maximizing profits, often assign rock-bottom labor budgets to the managers who run their stores and restaurants, and those managers in turn often squeeze their workers relentlessly.

30   A steady decline in workplace regulation has opened the door to greater exploitation. Even though the workforce has grown from 90 million to 145 million over the past three decades, the number of federal wage and hour investigators has fallen. Seven hundred eighty-eight federal wage and hour inspectors are responsible for ensuring compliance at the nation's 8.4 million business establishments.[40] George W. Bush's labor secretary, Elaine Chao, signaled her ambivalent views about enforcement when she said, "Sometimes it's not what you do, but what you refrain from doing that is important."[41] The infamous Sago Mine in West Virginia had been cited 273 times for safety violations in the two years before an explosion there killed twelve miners in 2006. But none of those fines exceeded $460, and many were just $60—a minuscule amount considering that the company that owned Sago had $110 million in annual profits. In the five years before, the Mine Safety and Health Administration, then run by former industry executives appointed by President Bush, failed to collect fines in almost half the cases in which it had levied them.[42]

The rising tide of exploitation has taken countless forms. Target, Safeway, Albertsons, and Wal-Mart have all hired cleaning contractors who required janitors to work the midnight shift thirty days a month. These contractors systematically broke the law by virtually never paying Social Security or unemployment insurance taxes, and they almost never paid janitors time and a half for overtime even though the janitors often worked fifty-five hours or more each week.[43] These contractors sometimes dumped badly injured workers in front of a hospital or at a bus station with a ticket back to Mexico.

At Taco Bell, Wal-Mart, and Family Dollar, many employees complained that managers forced them to work five or more unpaid hours off the clock each week. The workers who were cheated often earned just $12,000 to $18,000 a year. At an A&P in Westchester County, New York, Wilfredo Brewster, a customer service manager, said he worked from six a.m. to six p.m. Monday through Friday, sixty hours, but was paid for only forty. Managers pressured him to donate his Saturdays to the store as well, telling him it would help him earn a promotion. Under federal and state law, he, as an hourly employee, was supposed to be paid overtime for those Saturdays.

Stylists at SmartStyle, the nation's largest hair salon company, said that pressure to minimize payroll costs was so intense that on days when there were few customers, managers often ordered stylists to clock out, then clean up the salon. Several hairdressers said they were occasionally paid for only half the hours they worked, their earnings sometimes slipping to $2.50 an hour, less than half the $5.15 federal minimum wage at the time.[44]

According to many workers and supervisors at Pep Boys, Toys "R" Us, Family Dollar, Wal-Mart, and other companies, some managers illegally tampered with time clock records to erase hours that employees had worked.[45] Dorothy English, a payroll assistant at a Wal-Mart in Louisiana, said that if an employee had clocked forty-three hours in a week, her boss often ordered her to delete three hours from the worker's time records to avoid paying time and a half. "I told them this wasn't right," she said. "But they said, 'This is how we keep people to forty hours.'"[46]

35   At dozens of upscale supermarkets in Manhattan, including Food Emporium and Gristede's, deliverymen often worked seventy-five hours a week but were paid just two hundred dollars, or less than three dollars an hour. They were told they were independent contractors, a group that is not covered by minimum wage and overtime laws.[47]

Some call centers deduct pay for every minute a worker spends in the bathroom. Workers at Wal-Mart and the Cheesecake Factory complained that managers often refused to give them the lunch breaks and fifteen-minute rest breaks that state law required.[48] Bella Blaubergs, a diabetic who worked at a Wal-Mart in Washington State, said she nearly fainted several times from low blood sugar because managers often would not let her take breaks.[49] At numerous Abercrombie & Fitch stores, African American, Asian, and Hispanic workers complained that they were relegated to back-of-the-store jobs, doing stockroom work and inventory, while white employees were given jobs up front—all to promote Abercrombie's preppy, fraternity, all-American look.[50]

Some cleaning workers at several of the hottest software companies in Silicon Valley earn so little that they live in rented garages in someone else's home. Rosalba Ceballos, a divorced immigrant from Mexico, was one of them; she lived with her three daughters—ages one, three, and seven—in an absurdly cluttered, windowless garage just outside Palo Alto.

Middle-class workers have not been immune. On a day in 2003 that Circuit City workers remember as "Bloody Wednesday," the retailer fired 3,900 senior commissioned salespeople—some earned $50,000 a year—having concluded that their commissions and wages were too high. Circuit City simultaneously hired 2,100 replacement salespeople who were to receive lower wages and far lower commissions.[51] Then in 2007, Circuit City laid off another 3,400 employees because they, in the company's words, earned "well above the market-based salary range for their role." Many of those laid off were earning around $29,000 a year. Circuit City announced that these workers could reapply for their jobs ten weeks later, but if rehired, they would come back at the lower "market rate."

In her ten years at the Circuit City in Hoover, Alabama, Julie Godette was considered a model employee, assigned to train new hires and receiving repeated raises that brought her up to $16.40 an hour. She, too, was suddenly laid off. "To work that long for a company and to be let go because you did a good job really hurts," Godette said.[52]

40   At JP Morgan Chase, Barbara Parkinson, a customer service representative in the global investment services department in New York City, said managers had repeatedly complained when workers submitted time sheets listing several hours' overtime. To avoid management's continued wrath, she and other workers decided to forgo the overtime pay due them.[53]

At RadioShack's headquarters in Fort Worth, four hundred workers were fired by e-mail. "The workforce reduction notification is currently in progress," the e-mail dryly informed recipients. "Unfortunately your position is one that has been eliminated."[54]

Northwest Airlines gave laid-off workers a booklet entitled "101 Ways to Save Money." But the booklet added insult to financial injury. "Borrow a dress for a big night out" and "Shop at auctions or pawn shops for jewelry" were among the tips it offered. And then it suggested, "Don't be shy about pulling something you like out of the trash."[55]

Rarely have so many economic and social forces been arrayed against the American worker. Downsizing, rightsizing, and reengineering have increasingly made job security an obsolete notion. Many workers fear pink slips so much that they are frightened to ask for raises or protest oppressive workloads. Globalization, including the recent rush to offshore hundreds of thousands of white-collar jobs, has increased such fears. Layoffs have become a fact of life. Nowadays, on nearly a daily basis, some company announces that it is laying off several thousand employees, and except for the workers and their families, virtually everyone who hears about it ignores it.

America has lost one-fifth of its factory jobs since 2000, jobs that have long been a stepping-stone to the middle class. There has been a concomitant decline in the labor movement to its lowest point in decades, undermining the one force that, for all its faults, created some semblance of balance between workers and management during the second half of the twentieth century. The massive influx of immigrants has created a huge pool of easy-to-bully workers that has given managers greater leverage—most visibly in construction and meatpacking—to squeeze wages and worsen conditions for *all* workers. Many companies have embraced the just-in-time workforce—a mass of temps, freelancers, and on-call occasionals whose lower pay and unstable status often undercut the wages, benefits, and job security of the traditional year-round workforce.

45   The position of the American worker has been further undermined by the economy's evolution from industrial capitalism to financial capitalism. Industrialists were once firmly in control, intent on maximizing production and market share, but now investment bankers, mutual fund managers, hedge fund managers, and, increasingly, managers of private-equity funds wield great power and are forever pressuring the companies that they've invested in to maximize profits and take whatever steps are necessary to keep stock prices at their highest. Companies, in response, often skimp on wages, lay off workers, and close operations.

Wal-Mart, founded in a small Arkansas town in 1962, has spearheaded the rise of a less caring, less generous, and often less law-abiding management style. Wal-Mart employs nearly 1.4 million workers in the United States, far more than any other company. With its phenomenal growth, it has become the world's largest retailer, and its low wages and benefits—it provides health insurance to just half of its workers—have created a downward pull on the way that many companies treat their workers. (For that reason, we will examine Wal-Mart in great detail.) The Wal-Mart effect could be seen most starkly when the three largest supermarket chains in California—Safeway, Albertsons, and Ralphs—grew alarmed about Wal-Mart's plans to open dozens of supercenters in California that would sell groceries

in addition to general merchandise. The supermarket chains demanded lower wages and far less generous health benefits for all future hires, and after a bitter four-and-a-half-month strike and lockout in 2003–4, the chains got their way. The California supermarkets said they couldn't compete when their cashiers earned $17.90 an hour on average and Wal-Mart's earned $8.50 an hour.

The squeeze on the American worker has been further exacerbated by corporate America's growing sway over politics and policy, making it harder for beleaguered workers to turn to government for help. When investigators unearthed serious child labor violations at a dozen Wal-Marts, officials in the Bush Labor Department signed a highly unusual secret agreement promising to give Wal-Mart fifteen days' advance notice whenever inspectors planned to visit a Wal-Mart store to look for more such violations. Wal-Mart officials had been major donors to the Republican Party.

As a result of business's strong influence over President George W. Bush and Republicans in Congress, the federal minimum wage remained stuck at $5.15 for nearly a decade. A full-time worker who earns $5.15 an hour grosses $10,712 a year, far below the $16,079 poverty line for a family of three. In 2007, the $5.15 minimum wage, after adjusting for inflation, was 33 percent below its 1979 level.[56] In 2007, the Democratic Congress raised the minimum wage to $7.25 an hour over two years.

Nor have the tax policies emanating from Washington been very friendly to workers. President Bush and Republicans in Congress pushed vigorously to minimize taxes on investors, that is, taxes on dividends and capital gains, while urging elimination of the estate tax. Bush's tax cuts saved the average middle-class taxpayer $744 a year, while saving $44,212 a year for the top 1 percent of taxpayers and $230,136 for the top one-tenth of 1 percent of households.[57]

NOTES

1. Michell and more than a dozen other Wal-Mart workers said in interviews that they were terminated or pushed out after being injured on the job. Wal-Mart denies having a policy to eliminate injured workers.

2. U.S. Bureau of the Census, *Income, Poverty, and Health Insurance Coverage in the United States 2006* (Washington, D.C.: GPO, 2007), p. 6. Median household income for nonelderly households slid to $54,001 in 2005, down $3,100 or 5.4 percent from five years earlier, after accounting for inflation (in 2006 dollars). For all households, including elderly households, median income rose by 1.1 percent in 2005, after having slid the previous five years. The figure for all households, including elderly households, was down 2.7 percent from 2000.

3. U.S. Bureau of the Census, *Income, Poverty, and Health Insurance 2006*, p. 5. In 2006, median income for nonelderly households was $54,726, up $725 or 1.3 percent from the previous year. For all households, median income was $48,201, up $360 or .7 percent.

   The economist Stephen Rose argues that median household income has been held down by numerous factors, including more single-parent households, more elderly widows, and more young adults living on their own. Stephen Rose, "Does Productivity Growth Still Benefit Working Americans?: Unraveling the Income Growth Mystery to Determine How Much Median Incomes Trail Productivity Growth," Washington, D.C., Information Technology and Innovation Foundation, June 2007.

4. Lawrence Mishel, Jared Bernstein, and Sylvia Allegretto, *The State of Working America 2006/2007* (Ithaca: Cornell University Press, 2007), p. 119.

5. Mishel, Bernstein, and Allegretto, *State of Working America 2006/2007*, p. 115.

6. Within the economics profession there is a debate over just how much wages have stagnated, with some economists arguing that the consumer price index overstates inflation and that as a result wages have risen somewhat faster than official Bureau of Labor Statistics (BLS) figures indicate.

7. Perhaps the most compelling statistic showing the economy's increased tilt against workers is the decline in the share of national income going to wages and salaries. The wage share fell to its lowest level on record in 2006, with data going back to 1929, while the share going to overall employee compensation, including health and pension benefits, slid to its lowest point in four decades, except for 1997. But the share of national income going to corporate profits has climbed to its highest level since 1942. Steven Greenhouse and David Leonhardt, "Real Wages Fail to Match a Rise in Productivity," *New York Times,* Aug. 28, 2006, p. A1; Aviva Aron-Dine and Isaac Shapiro, "Share of National Income Going to Wages and Salaries at Record Low in 2006," Center on Budget and Policy Priorities, Washington, D.C., March 29, 2007.

8. U.S. Bureau of the Census, *Income, Poverty, and Health Insurance 2006*, pp. 12, 21.

9. Elizabeth Warren and Amelia W. Tyagi, *The Two-Income Trap* (New York: Perseus Books, 2003), p. 20. Warren and Tyagi show that foreclosures were increasing even before the subprime mortgage crisis. Many bankers asserted that one reason for the increase in bankruptcies was that many Americans were taking advantage of lenient provisions in the bankruptcy laws.

10. Richard B. Freeman, *America Works: The Exceptional U.S. Labor Market* (New York: Russell Sage Foundation, 2007), pp. 41–45.

11. Mishel, Bernstein, and Allegretto, *State of Working America 2006/2007*, p. 91.

12. Ellen Galinsky, James T. Bond, and E. Jeffrey Hill, "When Work Works," New York, Families and Work Institute, April 2004, p. 1.

13. *OECD Employment Outlook 2007* (Paris: Organization for Economic Co-operation and Development, 2007), table F, p. 263.

14. Michael Mandel, "Which Way to the Future?" *BusinessWeek,* Aug. 20, 2007, p. 45, quoting Lynn Franco, director of consumer research for the Conference Board; "In Pursuit of Satisfaction: U.S. Job Satisfaction Declines," News Release, Conference Board, Feb. 23, 2007.

15. Bob Davis, "Extra Credit: Lagging Behind the Wealthy, Many Use Debt to Catch Up," *Wall Street Journal,* May 17, 2005, p. A1.

16. At the same time, household debt soared to a record 132 percent of disposable income, an all-time record, up from 74 percent a quarter century earlier. Mishel, Bernstein, and Allegretto, *State of Working America,* p. 271.

17. Brian K. Bucks, Arthur B. Kennickell, and Kevin B. Moore, "Recent Changes in U.S. Family Finances:

Evidence from the 2001 and 2004 Survey of Consumer Finances," *Federal Reserve Bulletin,* 2006, p. A35.

18. Vikas Bajaj and Edmund L. Andrews, "Broader Losses from Mortgages," *New York Times,* Oct. 25, 2007, p. A1. The Joint Economic Committee of Congress estimated up to two million foreclosures. The Bush administration predicted up to 500,000, which, in itself, would be a tidal wave compared with recent years.

19. Congressional Budget Office, *Historical Effective Federal Tax Rates* (Washington, D.C.: GPO, 2007), table 1C. As a result of such trends, the share of the nation's overall income going to the top 1 percent of earners has leaped from 9 percent in 1980 to 22 percent in 2005, reaching heights not seen since the Roaring Twenties. Thomas Piketty and Emmanuel Saez, "Income Inequality in the United States: 1913–1998," *Quarterly Journal of Economics* 68, no. 1 (Feb. 2003): 1–39 (elsa.berkeley.edu/ ~ saez/pikettyqje.pdf). An updated series can be found at elsa.berkeley.edu/ ~ saez/TabFig2005prel.xls. Also see David Cay Johnston, "Income Gap Is Widening, Data Shows," *New York Times,* March 29, 2007, p. C1.

20. Congressional Budget Office, *Tax Rates,* table 1C. President Bush has been able to boast that average income is up—the upper crust's income boom has pulled up everyone else's mean income. But there's a catch: *median* income, with half of Americans above and half below, has remained depressingly flat. According to a 2007 study based on IRS data, income for the bottom 90 percent of Americans fell in 2005, before government payments are included, while income for the top 1 percent—they average $1.1 million a year—climbed by $139,000 on average. Piketty and Saez, "Income Inequality."

21. Paul Krugman, "Left Behind Economics," *New York Times,* July 14, 2006, p. 19.

22. Mishel, Bernstein, and Allegretto, *State of Working America 2006/2007,* p. 121.

23. U.S. Bureau of the Census, *Income, Poverty, and Health Insurance 2006,* p. 12. The earned income tax credit has certainly been a salve to many low-income families, giving them a few thousand extra dollars, but even with this boost, far too many Americans—12.3 percent—remain in poverty.

There is considerable debate about how to define the poverty threshold. Based on recommendations of the National Academy of Sciences, the Census Bureau calculated that the poverty rate in 2003 would have been 16 percent if one added housing subsidies, food stamps, subsidized school lunches, and the income tax credit to family income and then subtracted federal and state taxes, child care, and commuting costs. Another Census Bureau calculation would figure in the imputed return of home equity for homeowners, and that would have reduced the 2003 rate to 9 percent. See David Wessel, "Counting the Poor: Methods and Controversy," *Wall Street Journal,* June 15, 2006, p. A10.

24. Mishel, Bernstein, and Allegretto, *State of Working America 2006/2007,* pp. 135, 138; Alicia H. Munnell and Pamela Perun, "An Update on Private Pensions," Center for Retirement Research at Boston College, Aug. 2006, p. 2.

25. Beth Shulman, *The Betrayal of Work* (New York: New Press, 2005), p. 31.

26. Tom Waldron, Brandon Roberts, and Andrew Reamer, "Working Hard, Falling Short: America's Working Families and the Pursuit of Economic Security," Working Poor Families Project, Oct. 2004, p. 3.

27. Barbara Ehrenreich, *Nickel and Dimed* (New York: Henry Holt, 2001), p. 221.

28. U.S. Bureau of Labor Statistics, "2004–14 Employment Projections," USDL News Release 05-2276, Dec. 7, 2005 (www.bls.gov/news.release/ecopro.nro.htm).

29. U.S. Bureau of the Census, *Income, Poverty, and Health Insurance 2006,* p 21.

30. Sara R. Collins, Karen Davis, Michelle M. Doty, Jennifer L. Kriss, and Alyssa L. Holmgren, "Gaps in Health Insurance: An All-American Problem," Commonwealth Fund, April 2006, p. vii. The study defined moderate-income as having household income of $20,000 to $40,000 a year.

31. Kaiser Family Foundation and Health Research and Educational Trust, "Survey of Employer Health Benefits 2007," Sept. 11, 2007, charts 4 and 5.

32. "Can You Afford to Retire?" *Frontline,* Public Broadcasting System, May 16, 2006. In an interview with correspondent Hedrick Smith, the lawyer for United Airlines was James H. M. Sprayregen, who said, "Chapter Eleven has become somewhat of a more accepted strategic tool than just companies filing who are about to go out of business, or something like that."

33. Donald L. Bartlett and James B. Steele, "The Broken Promise: It Was Part of the American Dream," *Time,* Oct. 31, 2005, p. 32.

34. Brian Bergstein, "HP Struggling with Pension Costs," Associated Press, July 19, 2005.

35. Peter G. Gosselin, "If America Is Richer, Why Are Its Families So Much Less Secure?" *Los Angeles Times,* Oct. 10, 2004, p. A1. Gosselin has done extraordinary work on the growing risks that American workers face.

36. Jacob S. Hacker, "The Privatization of Risk and the Growing Economic Insecurity of Americans," Social Science Research Council, posted Feb. 14, 2006. (privatizationofrisk.ssrc.org/Hacker/). See also Jacob S. Hacker, *The Great Risk Shift: The Assault on American Jobs, Families, Health Care and Retirement—and How You Can Fight Back* (New York: Oxford University Press, 2006).

37. At the same time, the share of national income going to employee compensation overall—wages and benefits taken together—has, except for 1997, sunk to its lowest level since 1968. The wage share fell to 51.6 percent of national income in 2006, from 55 percent in 2001, while the share of employee compensation fell to 64 percent, from 66.2 percent in 2001. Aron-Dine and Shapiro, "Share of National Income Going to Wages and Salaries at Record Low in 2006."

38. Telephone interview with Lawrence Katz, April 6, 2005.

39. For a haunting account of this problem, see David Barstow, "A Trench Caves In; a Young Worker Is Dead. Is It a Crime?" *New York Times,* Dec. 21, 2003, p. 1.

40. This means that if each investigator visited one establishment per workday, it would take forty-two years to inspect every single one. Annette Bernhardt and Siobhan McGrath, "Trends in Wage and Hour Enforcement by the U.S. Department of Labor, 1975–2004," Brennan Center for Justice, Sept. 3, 2005 (www.brennancenter.org/programs/downloads/trendswageshours.pdf). Although many critics say the Labor Department's wage and hour division should be far more aggressive, it did collect a record $221 million in back wages in fiscal 2007, including $181 million for minimum wage and overtime violations.

41. "Remarks by Labor Secretary Elaine Chao on the National Day of Prayer," Federal News Service, May 4, 2006.

42. Ian Urbina and Andrew W. Lehren, "U.S. Is Reducing Safety Penalties for Mine Flaws," *New York Times,* March 2, 2006, p. A1.

43. Steven Greenhouse, "Among Janitors, Violations Go with the Job," *New York Times,* July 13, 2005, p. A1.

44. Steven Greenhouse, "Forced to Work off the Clock, Some Fight Back," *New York Times,* Nov. 19, 2004, p. A1.

45. Steven Greenhouse, "Altering of Worker Time Cards Spurs Growing Number of Suits," *New York Times,* April 4, 2004, p. A1.

46. Steven Greenhouse, "Suits Say Wal-Mart Forces Workers to Toil off the Clock," *New York Times,* June 25, 2002, p. A1.

47. Steven Greenhouse, "Neighbors Take Up Cause of Higher Pay at Some Stores," *New York Times,* Oct. 18, 2004, p. B1.

48. Steven Greenhouse, "In-House Audit Says Wal-Mart Violated Labor Laws," *New York Times,* Jan. 13, 2004, p. A16; Rachel Osterman, "Lunch and the Law; Workers Split on Timing of Breaks," *Sacramento Bee,* Dec. 29, 2004, p. D1.

49. Greenhouse, "In-House Audit."

50. Steven Greenhouse, "Abercrombie & Fitch Bias Case Is Settled," *New York Times,* Nov. 17, 2004, p. A16; Steven Greenhouse, "Clothing Chain Accused of Discrimination," *New York Times,* June 17, 2003, p. A21.

51. Carlos Tejada and Gary McWilliams, "New Recipe for Cost Savings: Replace Expensive Workers—In a Tight Market, Employers Are Finding Job Seekers Willing to Accept Less," *Wall Street Journal,* June 11, 2003, p. A1.

52. Sherri C. Goodman, "Fired Worker Feels Betrayed by Circuit City; 17 Employees in Area Laid Off," *Birmingham News,* April 12, 2007, p. 1D.

53. Greenhouse, "Forced to Work off the Clock."

54. Rachel Williams, "400 Workers 'Eliminated' by Email," Press Association, Aug. 31, 2006.

55. Joel J. Smith, "NWA Layoff Tips Offend Workers," *Detroit News,* Aug. 17, 2006, p. 1C.

56. Jared Bernstein and Isaac Shapiro, "Buying Power of Minimum Wage at 51-Year Low," Washington, D.C., Economic Policy Institute and Center on Budget and Policy Priorities, June 20, 2006 (www.epinet.org/issuebriefs/224/ib224/pdf#search = %22economic%20policy%20institute%20minimum%20wage%20cbpp%22).

57. Tax Policy Center "Combined Effect of the 2001–2006 Tax Cuts." Washington. D.C., table T06-0279, Nov. 13, 2006.

EXPLORATORY WRITING

This opening chapter from Greenhouse's book *The Big Squeeze* sets forth a series of concerns about today's labor market. In a 3-page paper, identify what those concerns are. Are they directed solely at manual-labor jobs? At outsourcing? At factory conditions? What does Greenhouse identify as "the big squeeze" on American labor today?

TALKING ABOUT THE READING

With a group of 3–4 of your classmates, share the exploratory writing you each did in response to Greenhouse's piece. Then make a group outline of the issues Greenhouse sets out as crucial to understanding what he has called the "big squeeze." When you have completed your outline, go back and review some of the anecdotal evidence Greenhouse offers (the stories of men and women in the workplace). As a group, discuss how that anecdotal evidence works to set up Greenhouse's argument that "one of the least examined but most important trends taking place in the United States today is the broad decline in the status and treatment of American workers."

WRITING ASSIGNMENTS

1. Drawing on your exploratory writing and your group outline, write a summary of Greenhouse's article, taking care to pinpoint the specific issues he presents as contributing to the "broad decline in the status and treatment of American workers" today. In your summary, explain how Greenhouse actually makes his argument. How does he use anecdotal evidence? What claims require him to use research? How does he balance anecdotal evidence with his research?

2. One underlying assumption in Greenhouse's discussion is that of worker expectations. The events Greenhouse relates here would not seem surprising or of much concern if Americans didn't have certain expectations about how workers should be treated in both manual labor and professional positions. Write an essay in which you examine your own expectations for future work or professional life. What, in terms of workplace conditions and treatment of workers, do you assume you ought to be able to count on as a worker— white collar or blue collar—in this country? In many ways, this is an essay written in response to Greenhouse, but it is not an argument with his research. You should refer back to some of the charges he makes about workplace conditions, but don't get distracted by trying to prove him right or wrong. Instead, examine your own expectations. How do your expectations match or depart from those Greenhouse suggests are being undermined in the big squeeze?

3. In the final chapter of *The Big Squeeze,* Greenhouse offers some possible responses to the problems he details throughout his study. He writes that American workers need to be part of the public conversation about wages, workplace conditions, health care, retirement, and more. Part of that conversation should be about raising the minimum wage: "There are two schools of thought regarding the minimum wage. One argues that only the market should set wages and that whatever a worker's wages are, no matter how low, is fair because that's where the market set them. The other school of thought holds that every full-time worker should earn enough to assure a life of dignity."

    For this assignment, join with 2–3 of your classmates to research both the current state of the minimum wage and estimates of what would amount to a "living wage" and a "poverty wage" for the area where you are now living or a place where you would like to live. To do that, you will need to find out what the minimum wage is, what exceptions there are for who must be paid a minimum wage, and what local estimates are for making a living wage. There are a number of resources both online and in your library where you can find that information. The Web site Poverty in America: The Living Wage Calculator (http://www.livingwage.geog.psu.edu/) will make those calculations for you once you enter place information, but there are other sources for this same information if you do a simple search for "Standard of Living" or "Cost of Living."

When you have completed your research, write a report in which you identify what the cost of living is for the place you have researched, what constitutes a living wage, a poverty wage, and what the average wage is for that place. What would the minimum wage have to be in order for a worker to support a family of four working one full-time job? How much of a discrepancy exists between the cost of living in the place you researched and the minimum wage? Present your report to the class.

VISUAL CULTURE   Reading Documentary Photography

Documentary photography has been at the center of social and political change since the late nineteenth century when reporter Jacob Riis photographed living conditions in the New York City tenement district. His photos of dangerous and horrifying living conditions have long been credited with spurring housing reform at the time. Since then, photographers like Lewis Hine whose photographs documented child labor conditions, Walker Evans who photographed tenant farmers during and after the Great Depression, and Danny Lyon whose photos recorded some of the worst abuses of the civil rights movement have all been credited with opening the public's eyes to events and conditions not readily available in the mainstream press.

Documentary photography is meant to actually document—to record—events as the photographer sees them. To do that, documentary photography offers visual evidence of how people are living or that an event occurred in a particular way. The documentarist is a historian, a reporter, and sometimes an artist.

Social historian James Curtis lists the following questions as key to reading documentary photography:

- Who took the photograph? (What do you know about the photographer?)
- Why and for whom was it taken?
- What message is being sent in the photograph?
- How was the photograph taken? (Was it posed? Did the subjects know they were being photographed?)
- What do companion images tell us about the message of the photograph?
- How was the photograph presented? (Is it in a pamphlet advocating change, for example? Is there a caption? How do viewers know what the photograph is about?)

CAMERA OF DIRT

— *Charles Bowden*

Charles Bowden is a contributing editor for *Esquire* and *Harper's* magazines and the author of more than a dozen books, including *Juárez: The Laboratory of Our Future* (1998). He is the recipient of the Lannan Literary Award for Nonfiction and the Sidney Hillman Award. "Camera of Dirt" first appeared in the photography magazine *Aperture* (Spring 2000).

SUGGESTION FOR READING *Maquiladoras*—the subject of these photos—are foreign-owned and largely untaxed assembly plants located in Mexico along the border between Mexico and the United States. They are not subject to duties or tariffs or to the same labor or environmental regulations that apply in the United States, though most of these plants are U.S. owned. Families might live in cardboard shacks. Young children are allowed to work in these factories. They are typically closed to all outside press.

1   He rises, his lean body unfolds from the chair in the hubbub of the market, and he moves with feline grace, camera in hand. The table hosts short, dark teenagers from Oaxaca, country people who have come up more than a thousand miles to the border because they have heard rumors of work. The boys wear watches, the girls new clothes. He leans into them, his voice soft, face smiling. They have been here six months, they have a shack they share, they have jobs, and today they have Sunday off and can eat in the public market and enjoy the throb of the city. The camera comes up, he slowly bends toward the targets, the film whirls and Julián Cardona feeds. He has been at this for almost twenty years. No one asked him to do this work. That does not matter; he is about his business and his business is this border city of bruises, death, dirt, and love.

Talking about dirt, dust in the air chewing the city, dirt choking the lungs on a windy day, streets of dirt, yards of dirt, a city of dirt and mud and dust, talking about Juárez, two million people huddling in shacks on the flanks of the dunes to the south and west, talking about dirt and dust and mud and Juárez, the city Julián Cardona loves.

"This street," he says, "this street is where I walked with my girl."

The *calle* is dust, rock, and ruts. Here, he wants it known, here when he was a boy, a teenager, he walked with his girl, down this dirt street, and see?—she lived over there, and down there and up the hill, that's where he lived, back then, when he was young and in love in the city of dirt. Smoke from cooking fires floods the air, night is falling, the wind blows, he is in love, he is back there, walking with his girl. The turf is K-13, the most vicious of the hundreds of gangs in the city of dirt. No matter. Love. Here, then, and now.

5   El Paso lights up in the dusk, not even a mile away. He hates it there, it is too cold, he explains. With a ninth-grade education, he managed to learn English. "Do you know this essay," he asks, "by Gore Vidal?" The dust coats the tongue, the smoke sweetens the air, a stench comes off the privies.

He was two, he thinks, when he declared his life for beauty. Ten when he gave up on eternity. About twenty when he was working in a factory here and he stumbled into photography, bought magazines, got a camera, taught himself everything. After that came a time working for blood-and-guts working-class tabloids, finally the move up to the daily paper, and now, at thirty-nine, the life of beauty. Beauty is everywhere, even in a pebble he spied at age two. Eternity is incomprehensible, there is only now. The photograph, the thing curators call *the image,* is now, this moment of beauty that exists for a second. Until devoured by the camera and made into comprehensible eternity. That's it, it is that simple.

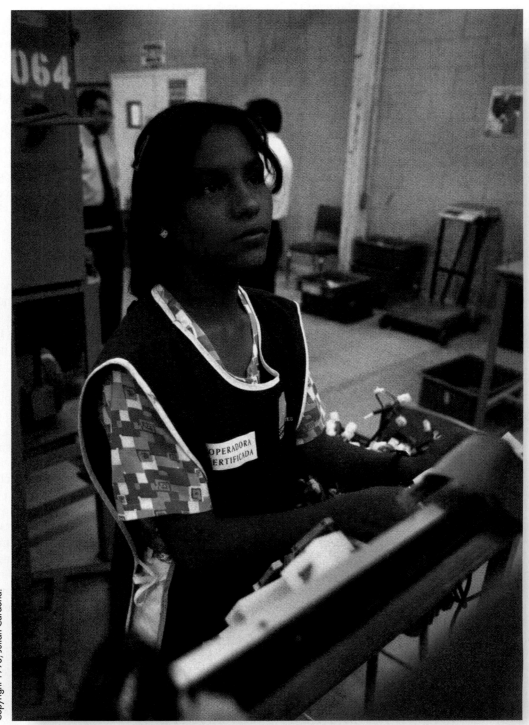

A young girl at work. Electrical Wire (ECM plant).

◼◼◼— A canal of agues negras (contaminated water) separates one of the ca. 352 maquiladoras in Cd. Juárez from the new home of seven-year-old Guadalupe Valenzuela Rosales, who lives with her parents, two sisters, and brother in a caraboard-and-wood house.

◼◼◼— Hosiery discarded by El Paso shopkeepers is bought, mended, dyed, and dried in the sun by a Cd. Juárez woman living in Colonia Puerlo de Anapra, who then resells the stockings for the equivalent of about $1.

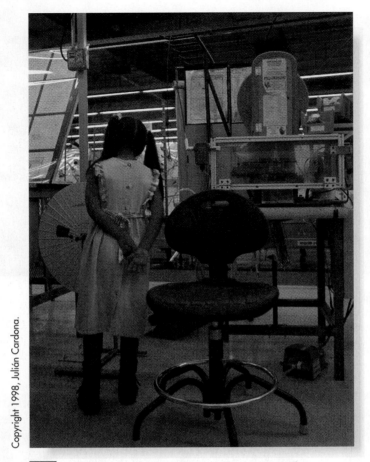

— UTA#158 (one of the former Essex plants in Juárez.)
United Technologies Automotive, UTC.

The girl he used to walk with, she married someone else. Julián Cardona lives alone and says with a laugh that the camera is his wife. And the beauty is here, in this sprawling slum of a city packed with workers in cardboard shacks, racked by drug killings, ruled by endless corruption, ignored by the rest of the planet. Beauty is here in the city of dirt and dust and mud and love and Julián Cardona is here to prove it and taste it and capture it and admire it and love it in turn.

Talking about dirt.

He is a brown man in a brown city. Juárez lacks water and is first and last dust. Grass, trees, flowers, they are for somewhere else. The city is a holding pen for cheap labor sucked north from the hopeless interior of Mexico. Hundreds of factories, mainly owned by Americans, assemble goods for the U.S. market safe within the tariff wall of NAFTA. The wages are 25 to 50 bucks a week. No one can live on them. No one. Turnover runs from 11 percent to 25 percent a week in the plants. And they are plants—General Motors alone has thirty in Juárez. Cheap labor, impossible living conditions, the bottomless U.S. market, violence, and dirt. There is nothing more to say about it, except to tell lies.

10   "I have witnessed a lot of deaths," he offers, "and when you are a photographer you have a

chance to die so many times. You see a kid of eleven playing an accordion in the street—what will he become? What if he is you? The woman is dying. What if she is your sister? Photography is a mirror of yourself."

Julián lives in a cement building of two rooms he threw together himself. The patio, a cement slab waiting for some next phase with no due date, looks down on the other little houses and shacks huddling on the bare hillside. Julián Cardona opens a bottle of red wine from Zacatecas. He is a quiet man, a pair of eyes that takes things in and feels no need to speak of what he sees. In his monk's room are a few books of photography with plates he studies, and a simple cot. The other room is a kitchen.

Out here are red wine, night, and talk.

He offers, "I think a photograph uncovers what is hidden and then what is hidden comes before the public eye. You must confront yourself in this mirror of reality. And the photo must seek beauty in even the worst things, it must capture the primitive things that move a human being—loneliness, hope and love. Dreams."

In the *mercado publico,* he eats *menudo* amid the din of Sunday shoppers. A band of old men plays country songs. His eye drifts, the girl two tables away has fine cheekbones and the face of a child. He moves, talks, sits with her. The camera comes up and feeds. She is a teenager working in an American factory and her face shines with experiments in cosmetics. He never stops. Her name, phone number. He will visit and take yet more images. The photo will nail her in his vision of eternity.

15   He never knew his father, and his mother left Julián to the care of her parents. His grandfather was a farmer who formed an *ejido,* a collective, after the revolution. He tried to teach Julián the earth and its animals. When Julián was in his early twenties, he faltered after working for five years in a *maquiladora* (one eye is permanently damaged from those years of leaning over a lathe), and with two friends he decided to go back to the *ejido* his grandfather had founded. The peasants

agreed to let him join and have ground out of respect for his grandfather. It all came to nothing. His friends fell away from the scheme, Julián fell in love with a beautiful and rich woman. So it ends this way: he gives his patch of ground to another peasant and asks that, if possible, someday the *ejido* build a library or clinic and name it after his grandfather because, he says, "He was like millions of farmers and animals. No one will ever know they existed and who they were."

The beautiful rich woman marries someone else. Julián lives on the streets of Juárez for months. He does not explain this period except to make the point that he had it easy since he had money for food. Then he returns to the camera, the beauty. He takes that first shot; two men dressed as clowns standing one atop the other's shoulders in traffic and begging for change. The man on top juggles. The camera clicks. It is twilight, forever.

He spends day after day haunting the central city, the market, the whores, the cathedral, the plaza. He is the thin, silent man, the one almost unnoticed. See him, right over there, in those shadows, that man holding a camera. These spells come and go but now he is in the midst of one. He will capture that eternity, that beauty amid the stench and dust and dirt and broken glass and painted lips on the young girls soliciting in the doorways. And finally, as always, he is broken, worn out, and so he does what he must do. Sometimes he goes to his aunt's house and leaves his camera with her. The house is teeming with cousins and their wives and their children. Everyone sleeps in shifts, everyone works in the *maquiladoras.* This is the safe house for Julián. So he leaves the camera for two weeks.

Then he can rest for a while.

But he can't keep his eyes closed. He retrieves his camera, and creeps into the *maquiladoras,* a zone of work barred to the press except for company-controlled publicity shots. Julián has learned to shoot secretly in low light and so a flow of photographs begins, men and women looking blankly at the camera with eyes chastened by a five-and-a-half-day week. They are a nation of

Mexicans from the interior suddenly meeting the culture of the machine and being broken to the habits of presses, drills, and assembly lines. Julián at night leans over the tiny light table in his room and stares at the slides of the place he escaped, the dull grind he fled for the *ejido,* and then the streets and finally the marriage to his camera. No one wants these images. The press of Juárez is in thrall to the economic might of the *maquiladoras.* The press of the United States is oblivious to the carnage just below the surface of the pat phrase "Free Trade." No matter. Julián is on his mission, and he takes his wife, the camera, with him into the mills. And finds the beauty in dead-end lives.

20 For Julián Cardona the entire city of Juárez is the *maquiladora,* a giant factory breathing to the rhythm of the machines. He is the lover of this factory called a city. Forget everything else. Forget the theory, the art of the print, the function of the curator, the various zones. Talking dirt now. Two million people with low wages and constant songs. Young girls everywhere fresh as flowers and growing out of the din. There will be no folio. There will be no cantos. There will be no show. There will be no audience. The work is instantaneous, a bullet passing through the market and ripping faces off the people. A shot fired in the sterlie void of the factories where brown people meet the machine and wear smocks and sport blank eyes. He is there, everywhere, working with the light or the absence of light.

The photo essay is dead. The video camera is the tool of light now. Julián keeps shooting. He says his camera is his wife. Talking dirt now.

The question is not why he keeps shooting. The question is why not? Like all good questions, it is not asked. Or answered. There is this street where he once walked with his girl. There is this street where he looked down at age two and saw a pebble and it was beautiful. The clock ticks. Do not listen to it. Now, this second, savor eternity, lick it with your tongue.

You gotta wonder. Not why he takes pictures. But why everyone does not walk around with a camera.

Drinking late at night, more of the red wine from Zacatecas, the smoke of the cook-fires drifting up to his tiny house hanging on the dirt of the hillside. He tries to explain why he will not go north, through that nearby fence, into the land of the U.S. and of money. "Mexico is a loose way of living," he says, "a bohemian way of life. We enjoy love. We look at a woman and we say, '*Te adoro,*' I adore you. My pictures are slices of Mexican beauty, but these slices of beauty ask questions. It is a question of love, a love of your country and your people, and by those acts, a love of myself. I know just a little bit of Mexico but it is like knowing just a little bit of a woman you love, still you love her for that little bit. But at the same time, I hate Mexico because I want to change it. But this is impossible because as a lover you must take your love as it is."

TALKING ABOUT THE READING

With two or three of your classmates discuss what you learn about the photographer from Bowden's description. How does knowing that Cordona had to sneak into factories to take the pictures change how you might read them? How does the fact that he lived most of his life in Juárez influence the way you read his photos?

WRITING ABOUT THE READING

In a brief essay, compare Julián Cordona's photograph of a young girl at work with Lewis Hine's photograph of a young girl working in a textile mill that appears in Mining the Archive at the end of this chapter. In your essay, consider how the two are alike. How do they differ?

In what way might Cordona's decision to shoot these photos in color change how readers respond to these pictures as documentary? How would Cordona's photographs read differently if it were in black and white?

SUGGESTED ASSIGNMENT

Make your own photo documentary of work. You can photograph school work, the workers on campus, a local business, any kind of work that interests you and about which you have something important to say. The kind of work matters much less than what you have to say about it. What is your message? Is it about working conditions? About who does the work? About a lost skill? About uncovering work that must go on daily but that most people don't notice? Present your documentary to the class with a brief explanation of what you were trying to convey with your photo documentary. (In the case of an assignment like this, it is best to get people's permission before you photograph them.)

FILM CLIP · Documentary Film and the Narrator

Like documentary photography, documentary film has been one of the most popular ways to convey labor issues to a large, popular audience. The documentary is meant to tell a factual story about the subject of the film. To do that, a filmmaker might follow a story as it happens, in the same way a reporter would for a film news report. The footage would then be edited to tell the story of the event or situation—a strike, or changed working conditions, for example—in the time allotted for the film. Or the filmmaker might take archival footage and work the history of the issue into the actual events to flesh out the story, shape the way the audience understands the story, and give the film historical relevance.

The way the story is narrated, however, might be the element that most influences the way an audience reads a film documentary. Documentary film often uses what is called the *voice-over narrator*—someone who does not appear onscreen but who tells the audience what is happening. A key question for examining the narrator in a documentary, then, is to ask what the narrator's relationship is to the events portrayed in the film.

For this assignment, choose one of the films below. Watch it and then write an essay in which you examine the film's point of view as it is signaled by the narrator. As you watch the film, pay attention to the following questions concerning the narrator:

■ Is the narrator a character in the documentary and thus a part of the story?

■ Is the narrator what is called a *noncharacter,* a voice that has sometimes been called "the voice of God" in film circles?

■ How does the narrator shape the way you receive the events in the film?

■ What position does the narrator take in relation to the events of the film?

The following documentaries all cover labor issues and are widely available for rental:

Roger and Me

Harlan County, USA

American Dream

Wal-Mart: The High Cost of Low Price

FIELDWORK — Reconstructing the Network of a Workplace

In any job you hold, negotiating the workplace involves more than performing the work you were hired to do. You need to understand your coworkers and how they do their jobs, how they relate to each other and to you, how they have established unspoken rules for daily routines and interactions, and where you fit into all of that. As the narrator in Sandra Cisneros's story "The First Job" discovered, the people who have worked at a place for some time seem to know almost automatically how to act, when to speak, when to sit, and when to make sure they are working diligently.

This is what's known as the "social network" established in any job that involves more than two people. Most of these unspoken rules are unique to each workplace and are unknown to those on the outside. If, for example, you entered an office, stood in front of what you thought was the receptionist's desk, and felt frustrated or confused when the person behind the desk pointedly ignored you until you discovered that the receptionist was at the next desk, you probably stumbled onto one of the unspoken rules that has evolved from the social network in that office. Customers often are confused by such networks and, for example, might call the waitress assigned to another area to their table in a restaurant or ask the stocker rather than a sales clerk at a discount store to help them purchase an item. New workers must learn to negotiate these social networks quickly or they are likely to make mistakes in front of the supervisor that veterans in that workplace would never make.

One way that anthropologists have studied the culture of the workplace is to try to understand the social networks established on the job. To do so, they have relied on interviews and on participant-observation studies, such as the one described in the selection by James Spradley and Brenda Mann.

THE COCKTAIL WAITRESS

— *James P. Spradley and Brenda J. Mann*

James Spradley, a professor of anthropology at MacAlaster College in St. Paul, Minnesota, and Brenda Mann, who has worked as a senior product analyst at Dialog Information Services, spent a year studying the culture of the workplace from the point of view of "cocktail waitresses," as waitresses in bars were still called in 1975 when this study was completed. The selection

reprinted below, from *The Cocktail Waitress,* illustrates how workers almost automatically interpret their own workplace so they know whom to go to for information, whom to avoid, or what
tasks will hang them up.

SUGGESTION Spradley and Mann make a clear distinction between the "social structure" that has been
FOR READING established in Brady's bar and the "social network." Underline/highlight and annotate those
places in the selection where Spradley and Mann provide examples or explanations for each.
After you complete your reading, review your annotations and use them to write a short explanation of the difference between the two.

1 Denise moves efficiently through her section, stopping at a few of her tables. "Another round here?" she asks at the first table. They nod their assent and she moves on. "Would you like to order now?" "Two more of the usual here?" She takes orders from four of the tables and heads back to the bar to give them to the bartender. The work is not difficult for her now, but when she first started at Brady's, every night on the job was confusing, frustrating, embarrassing, and exhausting. Now it is just exhausting.

Her first night was chaos. When introduced to the bartender, Mark Brady, he responded with: "Haven't I seen you somewhere before?" Flustered, she shook her head. "He's not going to be one of those kind, is he?" she thought. Then later, following previous instruction, she asked two obviously underaged girls for identi-fication, which they didn't have. As she was ask-ing them to leave Mark called Denise over and told her not to card those two particular girls. Embarrassed, Denise returned to their table, explained they could stay, and took their order. A customer at the bar kept grabbing her every time she came to her station, and tried to engage her in conversation. Not knowing what to do, she just smiled and tried to look busy. She asked one customer what he wanted to drink and he said, "the usual" and she had to ask him what that was. An older man seated at the bar smiled and said, "Hello, Denise," as he put a dollar bill on her tray. Again, she didn't know what to say or do so she just smiled and walked away, won-dering what she had done or was supposed to do to make her worth the dollar. Another customer at a table grabbed her by the waist each time she

walked past his table and persistently questioned her: "Are you new here?" "What nights do you work?" "What are you doing after work?" And so went the rest of the evening. It wasn't until sev-eral nights later and following similar encounters that she began to sort out and make sense of all this. She began to learn who these people were, what special identities they had in the bar cul-ture, and where each one was located in the social structure of Brady's Bar.

The bartender's initial question, albeit a rather standard come-on, had been a sincere and friendly inquiry. The two girls she carded were *friends of the Brady family* and often drank there despite their young age. The grabby and talka-tive customer at the bar was Jerry, a *regular cus-tomer* and harmless drinker. The dollar tip came from *Mr. Brady,* the patriarch of the business. The man with the hands and persistent ques-tions was a *regular* from the University who had a reputation with the other waitresses as a *hustler* to be avoided. These people were more than just customers, as Denise had initially cat-egorized them. Nor could she personalize them and treat each one as a unique individual. They were different *kinds* of people who came into Brady's, and all required different kinds of serv-ices and responses from her.

SOCIAL STRUCTURE

Social structure is a universal feature of culture. It consists of an organized set of social identities and the expected behavior associated with them. Given the infinite possibilities for organizing people, anthropologists have found it crucial to discover the particular social structure in each society they study. It is often necessary to begin by asking informants for the social identity of specific individuals. "He is a *big man*." "That's my *mother*." "She is my *co-wife*." "He is my *uncle*." "She is my *sister*." Then one can go on to examine these categories being used to classify people. A fundamental feature of every social structure is a set of such categories, usually named, for dividing up the social world. In the area of kinship, for example, some societies utilize nearly 100 categories, organizing them in systematic ways for social interaction.

5   When we began our research at Brady's Bar, the various categories of the social structure were not easy to discern. Of course the different activities of waitresses, bartenders, and customers suggested these three groupings, but finer distinctions were often impossible to make without the assistance of informants. At first we thought it would be possible to arrange all the terms for different kinds of people into a single folk taxonomy, much like an anthropologist might do for a set of kinship terms. With this in mind, we began listening, for example, to the way informants talked about customers and asked them specifically, "What are all the different kinds of customers?" This procedure led to a long list of terms, including the following:

girl	regular	cougar
jock	real regular	sweetie
animal	person off street	waitress
bartender	policeman	loner
greaser	party	female
businessman	zoo	drunk
redneck	bore	Johnny
bitch	pig	hands
creep	slob	couple
bastard	hustler	king and his
obnoxo	Annie	court

This list was even more confusing as we checked out the various terms. For example, we asked, "Would a waitress say that a bartender is a kind of customer?" Much to our surprise, the answer was affirmative. Then we discovered that a *regular* could be an *obnoxo* or a *bore*, a *party* could be a *zoo*, a *cougar* was always a *jock*, but a *jock* could also be a *regular* or *person off the street*. Even though it seemed confusing, we knew it was important to the waitresses to make such fine distinctions among types of customers and that they organized all these categories in some way. As our research progressed it became clear that waitresses operated with several different sets of categories. One appeared to be the basis for the formal social structure of the bar, the others could only be understood in terms of the specific social networks of the waitresses. Let us examine each briefly.

The formal social structure included three major categories of people *customers, employees,* and *managers*. When someone first enters the bar and the waitresses look to see who it is, they quickly identify an individual in terms of one or another category in this formal social structure. The terms used form a folk taxonomy shown in Figure 1. Waitresses use these categories to identify who people are, anticipate their behavior, and plan strategies for performing their role.

Although waitresses often learn names and individual identities, it is not necessary. What every girl must know is the category to which people belong. It is essential, for example, to distinguish between a real regular and a person off the street. Both are customers, but both do not receive identical service from her. For example, a waitress should not have to ask a real regular what he's drinking, she should expect some friendly bantering as she waits on him, and she won't be offended if he puts his arm around her waist. A person off the street, however, receives only minimal attention from the waitress. Denise will have to inquire what he or she wants to drink, she won't be interested in spending her time talking with him, and she will be offended if he makes physical advances. It is important that Denise recognize these differences and not confuse the two kinds of customers. Being a good waitress means she can make such

Kinds of people at Brady's Bar	Managers			
	Employees	Bartenders		Night bartenders
				Day bartenders
		Bouncers		
		Waitresses		Day waitresses
				Night waitresses
	Customers	Regulars		Real regulars
				Regulars
		People off the street		Loners
				Couples
				Businessmen
				People off the street
				Drunks
		Female customers		

FIGURE 1

important distinctions. Although a knowledge of this formal social structure is essential to waitresses, it is not sufficient for the complexities of social interaction in Brady's Bar. In order to understand the other categories for identifying people and also to see how waitresses use the social structure, we need to examine the nature of *social networks.*

SOCIAL NETWORK

Social network analysis shifts our attention from the social structure as a formal system to the way it is seen through the eyes of individual members, in this case, the cocktail waitresses. Each waitress is at the center of several social networks. [See Figure 2] Some link her to specific individuals in the bar; other networks have strands that run outside the bar to college professors, roommates, friends, and parents. In addition to the formal social structure, we discovered at least three different sets of identities that make up distinct social networks. Only through an awareness of these networks is it possible to understand the way waitresses view their social world.

10   The first is a social network determined by the behavioral attributes of people. As the girls make their way between the bar and tables each night, identities such as *customer, waitress,* and *bartender* become less significant than ones like *bitch* and *obnoxo* based on specific actions of individuals. Sue returns to a table of four men as she balances a tray of drinks. No sooner has she started placing them on the table than she feels a hand on her leg. In the semidarkness no one knows of this encounter but the customer and the waitress. Should she ignore it or call attention to this violation of her personal space? She quietly steps back and the hand disappears, yet every time she serves the table this regular makes a similar advance. By the middle of the evening Sue is saying repeatedly, "Watch the hands." When Sandy takes over for her break, Sue will point out *hands,* a man who has taken on a special social identity in the waitresses' network. The real regular, businessman, loner, person off the street, or almost any kind of male customer can fall into the same network category if his behavior warrants it. A customer who peels paper off the beer

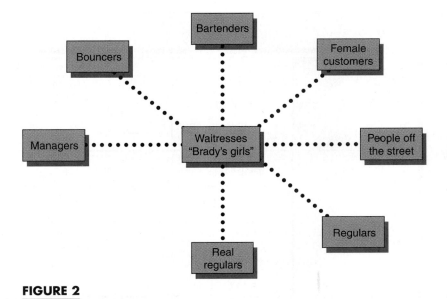

FIGURE 2

bottles and spills wax from the candle becomes a *pig*. The person who slows down the waitress by always engaging her in conversation, perhaps insisting that she sit at his table and talk, becomes a *bore*. As drinking continues during an evening, the behavior of some individuals moves so far outside the bounds of propriety that they become *obnoxos*. *Hustlers* gain their reputation by seeking to engage the waitress in some after-work rendezvous. The bartender who is impatient or rude becomes someone for the waitress to avoid, a real *bastard*. Even another waitress can be a *bitch* by her lack of consideration for the other girls. When a new waitress begins work, she doesn't know what kind of actions to expect nor how to evaluate them. Part of her socialization involves learning the categories and rules for operating within this network.

A second social network is based on social identities from outside the bar itself. Holly's roommate from college often visits the bar and one or another waitress serves her. Although she is a *customer*, they treat her as one of the other girl's *roommates* who has a special place in this social network. Each waitress will reciprocate when the close friends of other waitresses come

to the bar, offering special attention to these customers. The colleges attended by customers and employees provide another basis for identifying people. "That's a table of Annie's," Joyce will say about the girls from St. Anne's College. *Cougars* are customers who also play on the university football team. Even *bartenders* and *waitresses* can be terms for kinds of customers when they have these identities from other bars where they work.

Finally, there is a special network of insiders that crosscuts the formal social structure. This is *the Brady family,* made up of managers, employees, and customers—especially real regulars. The new waitress does not know about this select group of people when she first starts work. Sooner or later she will end up hanging around after work to have a drink on the house and talk. In this inner circle she will no longer think of the others as waitresses, bartenders, or customers, but now they are part of the Brady family. This network overarches all the specific categories of people in a dualistic kind of organization, a system not uncommon in non-Western societies. For example, a Nuer tribesman in Africa organizes people primarily on the basis of kinship. He has dozens of kinship terms to sort people into various identities and to anticipate their behavior. But every fellow tribesman, in a general sense, is either *both* or *mar*, distinctions that are important for social interaction. For the waitress, everyone in the bar is either in the Brady family or outside of it.

The social life of Brady's Bar derives its substance and form from the formal social structure as well as the various networks that waitresses and others activate for special purposes. Each waitress finds herself linked in some way to others in the bar with varying degrees of involvement.

TALKING ABOUT THE READING

1. Although this selection opens with a scene of a particular waitress working Brady's Bar, Spradley and Mann are not writing a story of the bar or a description of the shift of one waitress. Why provide this opening scene? How does it help readers to understand the information and analysis provided in the rest of the selection?

2. Recall a place where you have worked or think about the place where you currently work. What are some of the types of people who make up that workplace? Make a "single folk taxonomy" list, the way Spradley and Mann do for Brady's Bar. In what way might your list be divided into a more formal social structure, as the researchers divided their list of types at Brady's?

3. From what you have read here, explain how the social network at Brady's functions to help waitresses do their job and, at the same time, creates what Spradley and Mann call the "social life" of the bar.

FIELDWORK PROJECT

For this assignment, reconstruct the social network in a workplace, much like Spradley and Mann did. Do this assignment whether or not you are currently holding a job. If you currently hold a job (even if it is volunteer work, campus work, or work for an organization that is paid or unpaid), spend some time taking field notes (see "Participant Observation Fieldwork" in Chapter 3) and keep the questions below in mind. If you currently do not hold a job, write about one you have done before and use the questions below to help you recall details of that workplace. Divide your report into three sections: Background, Analysis, and Conclusion.

Background

Begin your report by giving your audience a general background summary of the workplace. The questions below can help you prepare that summary:

1. What is the nature of this business or organization?

2. When did you begin working there? What was/is your job? What difficulties did you encounter during the initial stages of the job?

3. Who are the people in this workplace, and how many employees typically are on the job at one time?

4. Who supervises the workplace? Is that person always present or only occasionally present?

5. What is the pay, if it is a paying position; if it is not, how many volunteer hours are expected of those who work there?

6. What do people expect from employees in this workplace? (For example, do customers expect to be waited on or are they left to themselves to browse?)

7. What is the workspace like? Describe it. How large is it? Is there enough room here for workers to do a job comfortably? Is there anything in particular that is important to mention about the space? (For example, is it exceptionally dark or open or crowded?)

Analysis: Reconstructing the Social Network of the Workplace

Your aim in this central section of your report is to reconstruct the social network of the workplace. Spradley and Mann use visual diagrams and descriptive analysis to explain how workers and customers interact in the bar to form the social network at Brady's. You can do the same. Begin by visually mapping out relationships and follow that diagram with a description of the social network you have reconstructed. The following questions can help you with your analysis:

1. Who is in charge (either by actually having a position above others or by virtue of less formal or unstated determinations)? Is the boss or supervisor always in control, or do subordinates have their own ways of doing what they want?

2. How do workers spend their time while on the job?

3. How do workers know what to do and when to do it?

4. What kinds of things happen that help or impede the work done in this place? Are there certain people you would identify as interfering with work and others you would say facilitate the work being done?

5. What seems to be the attitude of those working as they are doing their job?

6. How do workers interact with each other? Do they interact with customers or outside people coming into the workspace? For example, what are the typical informal as well as formal interactions among employees, employees and customers, staff and supervisors, and so on?

7. Is there a person (supervisor or not) who must be pleased or not crossed? How do workers know that?

8. What are some things that go on in the job that you only learned on your own after working there for a time?

9. What are the unspoken rules of this workplace, and how does the social network that has evolved there seem to convey and sustain those rules?

Conclusion

The concluding paragraph of the Spradley and Mann selection offers a quick summary of their descriptive analysis: "The social life of Brady's Bar derives its form from the formal social structure as well as the various networks that waitresses and others activate for special purposes. Each waitress finds herself linked in some way to others in the bar with varying degrees of involvement." Your conclusion ought to do the same. Summarize your analysis quickly in this concluding portion of the report.

MINING THE ARCHIVE

Lewis Hine and the Social Uses of Photography

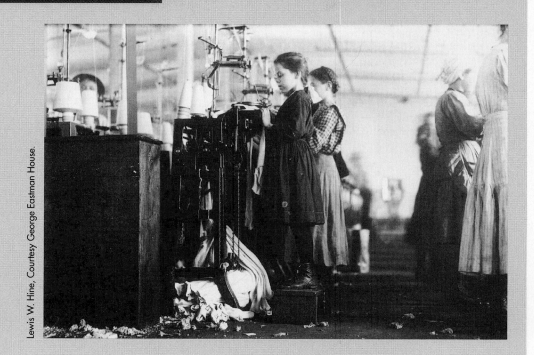

Lewis W. Hine, Courtesy George Eastman House.

American photographer Lewis Hine believed that photography had an educational and social role to play, and he used his photographs to educate Americans about the conditions of working life in the United States in the first part of the twentieth century. For many years, Hine did work for the National Child Labor Committee. Historian Alan Trachtenberg has written that, for Hine, "social photography means that the photography itself performed a social act, made a particular communication." Hine believed that pictures could make a difference in the way people thought about issues, such as those surrounding child labor laws. He saw photography as a means of interpreting and revealing the world of work to the public at large.

In 1907, Hine was invited to participate in what came to be called "The Pittsburgh Survey," an investigation of labor conditions in Pittsburgh at the time. Hine's photos from that project were used in six volumes of the *Survey* magazine, a new publication that had originally been called *Charities and the Commons.* Hine's work was also a familiar feature of the *Survey Graphic,* a monthly magazine begun in 1921. Both of these publications are still available in many local and college libraries. Check your library for these publications, and locate Hine's photographs in the early volumes. If the magazines are not available, enter "Lewis Hine" into the image search engine on your computer and find examples of his work at Web sites for the George Eastman House, Library of Congress, New York Public Library, University of Georgia Libraries, and Chicago Historical Society, among others.

Once you have located photographs by Lewis Hine and information on him and his work, use that material to report on the world of child labor as Hine interpreted it in his photos. In your report, discuss what is distinctive about Lewis Hine's vision of child labor in America and speculate about why his photographs remain in the public eye today, even showing up occasionally in labor publicity.

History

One of the marks of a good professional historian is the consistency with which he reminds his readers of the purely provisional nature of his characterization of events, agents, and agencies found in the always incomplete historical record.

—Hayden White, *Tropics of Discourse*

H istory is the collective memory of a culture which seeks to come to terms with its past, to represent where it stands in the present, and to imagine its future possibilities and directions. By linking past, present, and future together, history offers what Raymond Williams calls a "selective tradition." In the United States, we encounter the American past through a selective historical tradition that appears in many places and forms: in school textbooks; in statues, monuments, and murals; in scholarly work by professional historians; in TV docudramas and Hollywood films; in museum exhibits and lectures at local libraries; and in festivals, historical pageants, and reenactments. In this chapter, you will be asked to begin with the idea that history is not just an academic subject; it is constantly performed live, televised, and remembered in public places. History surrounds us and shapes the way we understand what it means to live in the United States.

Until fairly recently, the selective tradition of American history told a tale of national destiny—of how hard-working Americans developed a democratic society in the New World and how America prospered and grew bigger and stronger to become an industrial and geopolitical superpower in the twentieth century. According to this story, the expansion of America's borders and productivity was simply the natural growth of the nation, the inevitable unfolding of the country's role in history. This sense of destiny was linked closely to Americans' image of themselves and their mission as a people, shaping the collective memory by telling of the founding events, heroic acts, and tragic sacrifices that made this country a powerful nation.

Over the past quarter-century, this version of American history, which had prevailed in schools and textbooks since the nineteenth century, has been called into question. Historians started to reread the historical record from the bottom up, to represent voices that were silenced and social, cultural, and political movements that were ignored in the story of America's national development. The presence of Native Americans, African Americans, Latinos, Asian Americans, women, gays and lesbians, working people of all sorts, rural and urban, adds forms of consciousness to America's collective memory, ways of seeing and experiencing the past that were simply not available in prior accounts.

For example, once you take the presence of Native Americans into account, the westward expansion looks less like the progressive development of the land and its agricultural and mineral resources and more like a history of massacres, military conquest, the occupation of tribal land, relocation, the reservation system, and urban poverty. To make the multitudes of people who had been ignored in the selective tradition visible in American history complicates the way we see the past and understand its aftermath in the class relations and racial, ethnic, and sexual hierarchies that form American culture.

The purpose of this chapter is to investigate how representations of history, in writing and other media, shape our memories of the past and our sense of the present. You will be asked to read, think, and write about how we remember the past and how historians work to fashion a past that, in Alan Trachtenberg's words, is "intelligible and usable."

MORE THAN JUST A SHRINE: PAYING HOMAGE TO THE GHOSTS OF ELLIS ISLAND

■■—*Mary Gordon*

Mary Gordon is an acclaimed novelist and short-story writer who teaches at Barnard College. Her novels *Final Payments, The Company of Women,* and *The Other Side* explore the history and culture of Irish Catholics in America. In the following selection, an essay originally published in the *New York Times* (1987), Gordon offers her personal reflections on the history of immigration that brought her ancestors—Irish, Italian, and Lithuanian Jews—to the United States by way of Ellis Island, the point of entry in New York Harbor for more than 16 million immigrants between 1892 and 1924. In her essay, Gordon suggests that history is a living relationship to the past, in this case to the "ghosts of Ellis Island" that she wants to honor.

SUGGESTION FOR READING   As you read, notice that Mary Gordon provides a good deal of historical information about Ellis Island, and yet her main point is to establish her own personal connection to this American landmark. Mark passages where Gordon locates herself in relation to what took place in the past.

1   I once sat in a hotel in Bloomsbury trying to have breakfast alone. A Russian with a habit of compulsively licking his lips asked if he could join me. I was afraid to say no; I thought it might be bad for détente. He explained to me that he was a linguist and that he always liked to talk to Americans to see if he could make any connection between their speech and their ethnic background. When I told him about my mixed ancestry—my mother is Irish and Italian, my father was a Lithuanian Jew—he began jumping up and down in his seat, rubbing his hands together and licking his lips even more frantically.

"Ah," he said, "so you are really somebody who comes from what is called the boiling pot of America." Yes, I told him; yes, I was; but I quickly rose to leave. I thought it would be too hard to explain to him the relation of the boiling potters to the main course, and I wanted to get to the British Museum. I told him that the only thing I could think of that united people whose backgrounds, histories, and points of view were utterly diverse was that their people had landed at a place called Ellis Island.

I didn't tell him that Ellis Island was the only American landmark I'd ever visited. How could I describe to him the estrangement I'd always felt from the kind of traveler who visits shrines to America's past greatness, those rebuilt forts with muskets behind glass and sabers mounted on the walls and gift shops selling maple sugar candy in the shape of Indian headdresses, those reconstructed villages with tables set for fifty and the Paul Revere silver gleaming? All that Americana—Plymouth Rock, Gettysburg, Mount Vernon, Valley Forge—it all inhabits for me a zone of blurred abstraction with far less hold on my imagination than the Bastille or Hampton Court. I suppose I've always known that my uninterest in it contains a large component of the willed: I am American, and those places purport to be my history. But they are not mine.

Ellis Island is, though; it's the one place I can be sure my people are connected to. And so I made a journey there to find my history, like any Rotarian traveling in his Winnebago to Antietam to find his. I had become part of that humbling democracy of people looking in some site for a past that has grown unreal. The monument I traveled to was not, however, a tribute to some old glory. The minute I set foot upon the island I could feel all that it stood for: insecurity, obedience, anxiety, dehumanization, the terrified and careful deference of the displaced. I hadn't traveled to the Battery and boarded a ferry across from the Statue of Liberty to raise flags or breathe a richer, more triumphant air. I wanted to do homage to the ghosts.

5   I felt them everywhere, from the moment I disembarked and saw the building with its high-minded brick, its hopeful little lawn, its ornamental cornices. The place was derelict when I arrived; it had not functioned for more than thirty years—almost as long as the time it had operated at full capacity as a major immigration center. I was surprised to learn what a small part of history Ellis Island had occupied. The main building was constructed in 1892, then rebuilt between 1898 and 1900 after a fire. Most of the immigrants who arrived during the latter half of the nineteenth century, mainly northern and western Europeans, landed not at Ellis Island but on the western tip of the Battery, at Castle Garden, which had opened as a receiving center for immigrants in 1855.

By the 1880s, the facilities at Castle Garden had grown scandalously inadequate. Officials looked for an island on which to build a new immigration center, because they thought that on an island immigrants could be more easily protected from swindlers and quickly transported to railroad terminals in New Jersey. Bedloe's Island was considered, but New Yorkers were aghast at the idea of a "Babel" ruining their beautiful new treasure, "Liberty Enlightening the World." The statue's sculptor, Frédéric-Auguste Bartholdi, reacted to the prospect of immigrants landing near his masterpiece in horror; he called it a "monstrous plan." So much for Emma Lazarus.

Ellis Island was finally chosen because the citizens of New Jersey petitioned the federal government to remove from the island an old naval powder magazine that they thought dangerously close to the Jersey shore. The explosives were removed; no one wanted the island for anything. It was the perfect place to build an immigration center.

I thought about the island's history as I walked into the building and made my way to the room that was the center in my imagination of the Ellis Island experience: the Great Hall. It had been made real for me in the stark, accusing photographs of Louis Hine and others, who took those pictures to make a point. It was in the Great Hall that everyone had waited—waiting, always, the great vocation of the dispossessed. The room was empty, except for me and a handful of other visitors and the park ranger who showed us around. I felt myself grow insignificant in that room, with its huge semicircular windows, its air, even in dereliction, of solid and official probity.

I walked in the deathlike expansiveness of the room's disuse and tried to think of what it might have been like, filled and swarming. More than sixteen million immigrants came through that room; approximately 250,000 were rejected. Not really a large proportion, but the implications for the rejected were dreadful. For some, there was nothing to go back to, or there was

certain death; for others, who left as adventurers, to return would be to adopt in local memory the fool's role, and the failure's. No wonder that the island's history includes reports of three thousand suicides.

10   Sometimes immigrants could pass through Ellis Island in mere hours, though for some the process took days. The particulars of the experience in the Great Hall were often influenced by the political events and attitudes on the mainland. In the 1890s and the first years of the new century, when cheap labor was needed, the newly built receiving center took in its immigrants with comparatively little question. But as the century progressed, the economy worsened, eugenics became both scientifically respectable and popular, and World War I made American xenophobia seem rooted in fact.

Immigration acts were passed; newcomers had to prove, besides moral correctness and financial solvency, their ability to read. Quota laws came into effect, limiting the number of immigrants from southern and eastern Europe to less than 14 percent of the total quota. Intelligence tests were biased against all non-English-speaking persons, and medical examinations became increasingly strict, until the machinery of immigration nearly collapsed under its own weight. The Second Quota Law of 1924 provided that all immigrants be inspected and issued visas at American consular offices in Europe, rendering the center almost obsolete.

On the day of my visit, my mind fastened upon the medical inspections, which had always seemed to me most emblematic of the ignominy and terror the immigrants ensured. The medical inspectors, sometimes dressed in uniforms like soldiers, were particularly obsessed with a disease of the eyes called trachoma, which they checked for by flipping back the immigrants' top eyelids with a hook used for buttoning gloves—a method that sometimes resulted in the transmission of the disease to healthy people. Mothers feared that if their children cried too much, their red eyes would be mistaken for a symptom of the disease and the whole family would be sent home. Those immigrants suspected of some physical disability had initials chalked on their coats. I remembered the photographs I'd seen of people standing, dumbstruck and innocent as cattle, with their manifest numbers hung around their necks and initials marked in chalk upon their coats: "E" for eye trouble, "K" for hernia, "L" for lameness, "X" for mental defects, "H" for heart disease.

I thought of my grandparents as I stood in the room: my seventeen-year-old grandmother, coming alone from Ireland in 1896, vouched for by a stranger who had found her a place as a domestic servant to some Irish who had done well. I tried to imagine the assault it all must have been for her; I've been to her hometown, a collection of farms with a main street—smaller than the athletic field of my local public school. She must have watched the New York skyline as the first- and second-class passengers were whisked off the gangplank with the most cursory of inspections while she was made to board a ferry to the new immigration center.

What could she have made of it—this buff-painted wooden structure with its towers and its blue slate roof, a place *Harper's Weekly* described as "a latter-day watering place hotel"? It would have been the first time she had heard people speaking something other than English. She would have mingled with people carrying baskets on their heads and eating foods unlike any she had ever seen—dark-eyed people, like the Sicilian she would marry ten years later, who came over with his family at thirteen, the man of the family, responsible even then for his mother and sister. I don't know what they thought, my grandparents, for they were not expansive people, nor romantic; they didn't like to think of what they called "the hard times," and their trip across the ocean was the single adventurous act of lives devoted after landing to security, respectability, and fitting in.

15   What is the potency of Ellis Island for someone like me—an American, obviously, but one who has always felt that the country really belonged to the early settlers, that, as J. F. Powers wrote in *Morte D'Urban,* it had been "handed down to them by the Pilgrims, George Washington and others, and that they were taking a risk in letting you live in it." I have never been the victim of overt discrimination; nothing I have wanted has been denied me because of the accidents of blood. But I suppose it is part of being an American to be engaged in a somewhat tiresome but always self-absorbing process of national definition. And in this process, I have found in traveling to Ellis Island an important piece of evidence that could remind me I was right to feel my differentness. Something had happened to my people on that island, a result of the eternal wrongheadedness of American protectionism and the predictabilities of simple greed. I came to the island, too, so I could tell the ghosts that I was one of them, and that I honored them—their stoicism, and their innocence, the fear that turned them inward, and their pride. I wanted to tell them that I liked them better than I did the Americans who made them pass through the Great Hall and stole their names and chalked their weaknesses in public on their clothing. And to tell the ghosts what I have always thought: that American history was a very classy party that was not much fun until they arrived, brought the good food, turned up the music, and taught everyone to dance.

EXPLORATORY WRITING

Mary Gordon describes the "estrangement I'd always felt from the kind of traveler who visits shrines to America's past greatness" and goes on to say that "those places purport to be my history. But they are not mine." Why does Gordon feel this way? What is she suggesting about the way that people experience the history of America? What historical landmarks have you visited with your family or on class trips in elementary or high school? What were your feelings about those trips? Compare your experience with Gordon's. Did you experience these historical sites as part of your history?

TALKING ABOUT THE READING

Gordon says that Ellis Island is "the one place I can be sure my people are connected to." Name a place to which your people are connected, where you could, as Gordon puts it, "do homage to the ghosts." Work with three or four other students. Compare the place to those your classmates have named. To what extent are these places alike or different? How would you explain the significance of these similarities and differences?

WRITING ASSIGNMENTS

1. Mary Gordon says the one thing that unifies her ancestors—Irish, Italian, and Lithuanian Jews "whose backgrounds, histories, and points of view were utterly diverse"—is that they all landed at Ellis Island. Write an essay that explores the diversity among your ancestors and considers whether there is something—a place such as Ellis Island or a historical event such as immigration—that unites them.

2. Use Gordon's account of her visit to Ellis Island as a model to write an essay that explains your response to visiting a historical site. Explain the historical importance of the place you visited, but also follow Gordon's example to explain your own relation to that history. Did you experience the place as part of a history to which you felt connected, or did you, for some reason, feel estranged?

3. Gordon's essay suggests that history is as much a matter of paying "homage to the ghosts" as it is learning a chronology of events. Pick a historical figure, place, or event in American history with which you feel a strong personal identification. Describe it and then explain the reasons for your identification. Use the essay as an occasion to pay homage—to explain your personal allegiances and why the person, place, or event seems important to you.

MAKING A MEMORY OF WAR: BUILDING THE VIETNAM VETERANS MEMORIAL

—Kristen Ann Hass

Kristen Ann Hass teaches in the American Culture Program at the University of Michigan, Ann Arbor. The selection "Making a Memory of War: Building the Vietnam Veterans Memorial" is taken from her book *Carried to the Wall: American Memory and the Vietnam Veterans Memorial* (1998). Hass is interested in how the American public has grappled with the problem of memorializing the 58,000 soldiers killed in a long and unpopular war, and how unresolved feelings about the Vietnam War played a powerful role in debates about the architect Maya Lin's design of the Vietnam Veterans Memorial in Washington, D.C.

SUGGESTION FOR READING   At the end of the first section, Hass asks why so many visitors to the Wall have left things. The purpose of her book *Carried to the Wall* is to provide analysis and interpretation to answer this question. As you read, notice how Hass's discussion of the memorial's design complicates her question and anticipates her answers.

American materialism is . . . the materialism of action and abstraction.

—*Gertrude Stein,* in Gertrude Stein's America

1   In 1971 angry Vietnam veterans gathered outside the White House gates and on the steps of Capitol Hill. Chanting and jeering, they hurled their Purple Hearts, their Bronze Stars, their awards of valor and bravery, over the White House fence and against the limestone Capitol. In a radical breach of military and social decorum, these highly decorated military men spit back their honors. They had been betrayed, lied to, and abandoned. They had had no chance to be Hollywood heroes; instead they had fought an ugly war, survived, and lost.

In 1982, in the calm of the Constitution Gardens, these medals started to appear at the base of the Vietnam Veterans Memorial. They were set carefully under a name (or a group of names of soldiers who lost their lives together) by the owners of the medals and the fathers of the dead. Chances are good that there was no chanting or jeering as the medals were laid down; the Wall is a startlingly quiet place. And although the medals and ribbons were sometimes accompanied by a photograph or a note hastily written on stationery from a local hotel, the awards were left at the Wall one at a time. At first, they were set down without publicity or organized purpose. Thousands of Americans had the same unanticipated response to the memorial. They came and left their precious things. Why?

Hurling your Purple Heart at the powers that be and setting it at the foot of a memorial to your dead friends are very different acts. The veterans' throwing of their medals is not difficult to interpret as the rejection of an honor, a disdainful public protest against betrayal. However defiant, these veterans were still acting within commonly understood social codes. The things they threw had clearly defined social meanings.

The things offered at the memorial were given new meaning in a much less clear social context. Mainstream funerary and memorial traditions in American culture do not involve the offering of things. Flowers and flags are for memorials. Medals of valor and old cowboy boots are for mantels and attics. This new response to a veterans memorial, then, raises some fascinating questions. Why did so many people have the same unconventional, unanticipated response to the memorial? Where did it come from? What meaning do these things have? Are these offerings left for the dead or the living? Is the medal left as a show of respect? Or of anger?

5   More than 20 million visitors, about one in ten Americans, have visited the Wall, and every day for fifteen years some of these visitors have left offerings. The flowers and flags have been accompanied by long letters to the dead, poems, teddy bears, wedding rings, human remains, photographs, ravaged military uniforms, high school yearbooks, fishing lures, cans of beer, collections of stories, Bibles, and bullets. In November of 1990, eight years after the dedication of the monument, nearly six hundred objects were left, including seventy military medals, one urn containing human ashes, and a large sliding glass door. Why?

THE MEMORIAL

Dear Smitty,

Perhaps, now I can bury you; at least in my soul. Perhaps now I won't again see you night after night when the war reappears and we are once more amidst the myriad hells that Vietnam engulfed us in. . . . I never cried. My chest becomes unbearably painful and my throat tightens so I can't even croak, but I haven't cried. I wanted to, just couldn't. I think I can today. Damm, I'm crying now. Bye Smitty. Get some rest.

Anonymous note left at the Wall

The average age of the soldiers killed in Vietnam was nineteen; most of those who died had been drafted. The Vietnam Veterans Memorial was born out of a clear vision of what was to be represented: the dead, the veterans, and the sense of community that had made the war palatable to some Americans between 1957 and 1975. The problem, however, of what the death, the veterans, and the lost community suggested together and how they might be represented was the subject of many public and private battles. The work of any memorial is to construct the meaning of an event from fragments of experience and memory. A memorial gives shape to and consolidates public memory; it makes history. As historian James Mayo argues, "how the past is commemorated through a country's war memorials mirrors what people want to remember, and lack of attention reflects what they wish to forget." The veterans fighting to shape the meaning of the Vietnam War found that their efforts to commemorate this country's longest war were met with all of the conflicting emotions and ideologies expressed about the war itself. There was no consensus about what the names represented, about what to remember or what to forget.

The deeply controversial nature of the war, its unpopularity, and the reality that it was lost created an enormous void of meaning that compounded the difficult work of memorializing. What it meant to die in this war was as unclear as what it meant to fight in it. Moreover, the duration of the war, the military's system of rotation, and the defeat precluded the ticker-tape parades young boys going to war might have anticipated. Veterans came home to changing ideas about patriotism and heroism; they returned

to a society riven by the civil rights movement, Watergate, and the assassinations of the men who had inspired many of them to fight. There was no clear ideology around which a community of grief could have formed. It was a muddled, lost war waiting to be forgotten even before it was over. People who lost their children, husbands, father, sisters, and their own hearts were without a public community for the expression of grief or rage or pride. This lack of community not only made them deeply crave a remembrance of the experience of Americans in Vietnam but also made the work of remembering especially difficult. Commemorating the war and the deaths required giving new shape to the broken meanings of the war. It required a reimagination of the nation.

In March of 1979 Jan Scruggs, a vet and the son of a rural milkman, went to see *The Deer Hunter*. He came home terrified and inspired. This Hollywood movie, about the horrors of the war, the impossibility of coming home, and the struggles of a small, working-class Pennsylvania community to come to terms with its losses, convinced Scruggs that it was time for the nation to publicly remember the war. In the movie a community shattered by the war regains its bearings in a tentative return to the patriotic ideals that had inspired its boys to fight. It is a troubling response, but it offered Scruggs some hope; the possibility of a community healing itself inspired in him the idea of building a memorial. So with a few of his veteran friends, Scruggs formed the Vietnam Veterans Memorial Fund (VVMF) in April of 1979.

10 The fund's first attempts to gain public support were not entirely successful. No more than a dozen reporters showed up for the first press conference, on May 28, 1979. Scruggs and his friends tried to launch a national fundraising campaign, but they received a handful of heartwrenching letters and worn dollar bills instead of the generous checks for which they had hoped. The veterans fighting for a memorial were angry and determined, but they were not

socially or politically powerful; and their cause was not easily or quickly embraced. They did, however, attract the attention of a few influential Vietnam veterans. Jack Wheeler, a Harvard- and Yale-educated West Pointer, joined the VVMF and began to draw in Vietnam veterans from high places throughout Washington. And although the founders of the VVMF had wanted to oppose the power structures whose work they were trying to memorialize, they learned that they could not raise public interest—let alone funds—without the aid of a few Washington power brokers. The fund's first major contributions came after a brunch for defense contractors organized by Senator John Warner.

The men and women who came to form the core of the VVMF were by no means politically or socially unified. Some had protested after serving in the war, and others continued to believe in the ideals of the conflict; nearly all, however, were white veterans who were keenly aware of their outcast social position as survivors of a deeply unpopular war. They wanted a national monument to help them reclaim a modicum of recognition and social standing.

As the money began to trickle in, the VVMF made several key decisions that determined a great deal about the character of the memorial and the kind of community that it rebuilt. The fund wanted a monument that listed all the names of those killed, missing in action, or still held as prisoners of war in Vietnam. Although the dead became the heart of the project because they were, in an important sense, all these veterans could agree upon, there was no easy agreement about how the memorial should remember the dead. The fund imagined a *veterans* memorial not a *war* memorial; the former would ensure a memory that emphasized the contributions of the soldiers rather than the federal government. The members of the fund did not ask for federal money because they did not want to be perceived as more Vietnam vets looking for a handout and because after Ronald Reagan cut $12 million from the Veterans Administrations

budget in 1980, the vets did not trust his administration to give them the kind of memorial they hoped for. Building it with private contributions would also prove that a larger American public wanted to remember, and they wanted the memorial built on the Mall in Washington, D.C., to assure the memory of the veterans a place of national prominence.

The VVMF found itself in a complicated political position. The fund expected strong opposition from the antiwar movement and from the Washington bureaucracy; so it had to negotiate a public memory without either celebrating or explicitly renouncing the war, which would have been politically disastrous for any administration. As a result, strange alliances were formed at every step of the memorializing process. In 1980 the VVMF raised money through letters from Bob Hope calling for a reward for sacrifices made. Gerald Ford, Rosalynn Carter, Nancy Reagan, James Webb, Admiral James Stockdale, General William Westmoreland, and George McGovern made unlikely companions on the fund's letterhead. Few of the alliances were easily made, and not all of them held.

Early on the average donation to the $10 million project was $17.93 and envelopes were sent in with $2 change. Eventually, however, the campaign worked, and the success clearly demonstrated to the VVMF organizers that there was a population that wanted to publicly remember this war. Building this community of supportees and contributors, tenuous though it may have been, was an essential first step in the work of making a public meaning of the war. To memorialize the war, to solidify its shape and meaning, the fund had to bring together diverse experiences and ideologies. The seeming impossibility of the project was not only in facing the "myriad hells that Vietnam engulfed" the country in but also in repairing the social and political understandings that the war had fractured. In the end, the design of the memorial was a response to the problem of making memory in the wake of the Vietnam War; this is the history they made.

THE DESIGN

I came down today to pay respects to the good
friends of mine. Go down to visit them
sometime. They are on panel 42E, lines 22 and
26. I think that you will like them.

Anonymous note left at the Wall

15   Most war memorials in America—statues,
schools, stadiums, bridges, parks—proudly salute
American triumph. How do you memorialize a
painfully mired, drawn-out defeat that called
into question the most fundamental tenets of
American patriotism?

The design of the Vietnam Memorial was
bound to be controversial. Its promoters understood that it would be impossible to find a representation of the war that could satisfy a deeply
polarized society. The leaders of the VVMF
decided to hold an open juried contest because
they knew that without the participation of some
recognized bearers of cultural capital they would
never get a design through Washington's notoriously difficult architectural gatekeepers—the
National Planning Commission. Choosing the
jury was difficult, though. Who should decide
how the war would be represented? There was
some noise made about including a Vietnam veteran, an African American, and a woman; but it
was feared that jurors might defer too much to
the opinions of a vet, and, oddly, they were
unable to locate a qualified woman or a qualified
African American. So the decision was turned
over to the most traditional bearers of culture:
early in 1981 a panel of distinguished architects,
landscape architects, sculptors, and critics
was organized by Washington architect Paul
Spreiregen. The unpaid veterans who had
worked long hours to bring the memorial to this
point were impressed by the prestige of the jury
but nervous about turning their project over to
men "the same age as the people who sent
[them] to 'Nam."

The jury and the contestants were given
only a few simple, if wildly ambitious, instructions: the design should "(1) be reflective and
contemplative in character; (2) harmonize with
its surroundings; (3) contain the names of those
who had died in the conflict or who were still
missing; and (4) make no political statement
about the war." The most important task of the
design, however, was the creation of a memorial
that would, as Scruggs wrote, "begin a healing
process, a reconciliation of the grievous divisions
wrought by the war." One of the great ironies of
these guidelines is that Vietnam's death toll of
fifty-eight thousand is, compared with that
of most other American wars, so low that all of
the names could actually be reproduced on one
memorial. (The effect is overwhelming, of
course, but possible only because so relatively
few Americans died.)

By April 26, 1981, more than fourteen hundred designs had been entered. On May 1, 1981,
the jurors, after remarkably little deliberation,
unanimously selected a simple black granite V,
set into a small hill in the Constitution Gardens,
carved with the name of every man and woman
who never came back from Vietnam. They were
impressed with the eloquence and the simplicity of the design. The jurors, one of whom
noted of the designer, "he knows what he's
doing, all right," were no doubt startled to discover that their winner was a remarkable
impossibility: a twenty-one-year-old art student
at Yale University—young, intellectual, female,
and Chinese American.

In imagining her design, Maya Ying Lin
made a clear decision not to study the history of
the war, or to enmesh herself in the controversies
surrounding it. Her design lists the names of the
men and women killed in Vietnam in the order
in which they were killed. The names are carved
into black granite panels that form a large V at a
125-degree angle and suggest the pages of an
open book. The first panel cuts only a few inches
into the gently sloping hillside, but each panel is
longer than the last and cuts more deeply into the
ground, so that you walk down-hill toward the
apex, at which point the black panels tower three
or four feet above your head. At the center you

are half buried in a mass of names; pulled toward the black granite, you see yourself and the open lawns of the mall behind you reflected in the memorial. The center of the monument is a strangely private, buffered public space. Literally six feet into the hillside you are confronted simultaneously with the names and with yourself. The black granite is so highly reflective that even at night visitors see their own faces as they look at the Wall. The Wall manages to capture the unlikely simultaneous experiences of reflection and burial. This brilliant element of the design asks for a personal, thoughtful response. As you exit, the panels diminish in size, releasing you back into the daylight. Lin's design did not initially include the word "Vietnam"; she gave form not to the event that caused the deaths but to the names of the dead, to the fact of the deaths.

20   The names are carved out of polished granite from Bangalore, India. The carving invites tangible interaction. Each name has a physical presence. It asks to be touched. Lin wanted visitors to be able to feel the names in many different ways, and she wanted people to be able to take something of the Wall away with them—a rubbing of a name.

The Wall tries to make a somehow individuated memory of a war. The events in Vietnam are remembered through the names of the dead: these men and women—many of whom, even those drafted against their will, might have imagined, at least in part, that their experience would be like that portrayed in the movie *How I Won the War with John Wayne*—are each remembered as tragically fallen individuals. The power of the design lies in the overwhelming presence of individual names, which represent complicated human lives cut short. This attention to individual lives lost would not, however, be as potent if it were separated from the black expanse of all of the names together, the effect of which is so overwhelming that it both foregrounds the individual names and hides them. Lin's organization of the names also contributes to this tension between particular names and the whole formed by the names together. The dead appear on the Wall not alphabetically but rather in the order in which they died in Vietnam. Soldiers who died together are listed together on the Wall, so that on every line on every panel stories of particular times and places are inscribed with the names. This placement of the names, however, makes finding an individual name in the list impossible without the aid of the phone book–like alphabetical indexes at the entrances to the memorial. Although the index provides information about every name—including hometown, birth date, and death date—it requires a certain amount of participation on the part of any visitor interested in a particular name.

Maya Lin's design earned her a B in her funerary architecture class at Yale, but that was the least of her troubles. She was thrown into a noisy "firestorm of the national heart." Her design was dubbed the "black gash of shame." Its shape was considered an affront to veteran and conservative manhood especially when compared to the shape of the neighboring Washington Monument: the V shape hinted at the peace sign, or a reference to the Vietcong; the black stone was more mournful than heroic. It seemed to many too clear an admission of defeat. The public outcry reflected outrage with Lin's design and with the principles that the VVMF required of all designs: the Wall was too abstract, too intellectual, too reflective. It was, in the minds of many, high art, the art of the class that lost the least in the war. It was not celebratory, heroic, or manly. James Webb, a member of the VVMF's National Sponsoring Committee, called it a "wailing Wall for future anti-draft and anti-nuclear demonstrators." Tom Carhart, a veteran who had been awarded a Purple Heart and had submitted a design of his own, coined a key phrase for those who hated the design when he wrote in a *New York Times* op-ed piece that it was "pointedly insulting to the sacrifices made for their country by all Vietnam veterans . . . by this we will be remembered: a black gash of shame and sorrow, hacked into the national visage that is the mall."

The popular press offered some support for the design, but the conservative press was enraged by it. In the *Moral Majority Weekly* Phyllis Schlafly called it a "tribute to Jane Fonda." *National Review* described it as an "Orwellian glob." In an open letter to President Reagan, Republican Representative Henry Hyde complained that it was "a political statement of shame and dishonor." And in September of 1981 an editorial in *National Review* demanded that Reagan intervene, arguing: "Okay, we lost the Vietnam war, okay the thing was mismanaged from start to finish. But American soldiers who died in Vietnam fought for their country and for the freedom of others, and they deserve better than the outrage that has been approved as their memorial . . . the Reagan administration should throw the switch on the project."

Its implicit admission that the war was disastrous, of course, is precisely what others loved about the design. A great many Vietnam veterans reacted with cautious approval. The VVMF and all leading veterans organizations, including the Veterans of Foreign Wars and the American Legion, officially approved of the design. The best evidence of the reaction of the larger community of veterans was their continued effort to support the monument despite the barrage of bitter publicity about the design. Veterans held garage sales, bingo games, and "pass the helmet" campaigns to raise funds for construction. At one of these events in Matoon, Illinois, a vet remarked to Scruggs that "everything Vietnam touches seems to go sour. . . . I may never have the money to get to D.C., but it would make me feel good to know that my buddies' names are up there."

25   Of course, since the official dedication of the Wall in 1982 volumes of praise have been written for the design and the reflection that it has inspired. The Wall's emphasis on the tragedy of each death has appealed to critics and supporters alike. Strong hopes that this monument will guard against future wars have been expressed: James Kilpatrick, a nationally syndicated colum-

nist, wrote, "this will be the most moving memorial even erected . . . each of us may remember what he wishes to remember—the cause, the heroism, the blunders, or the waste." One vet carried a sign at the memorial's opening that expressed a commonly held sentiment: "I am a Vietnam Veteran / I like the memorial / And if it makes it difficult to send people to battle again / I like it even more." A *New York Times* editorial reprinted in the Gold Star Mothers Association newsletter argued, "Nowadays, patriotism is a complicated matter. Ideas about heroism, or art, for that matter, are no longer what they were before Vietnam. . . . But perhaps the V-shaped, black granite lines merging gently with the sloping earth make the winning design seem a lasting and appropriate image of dignity and sadness."

Understanding the design as an attempt to represent a new, complicated patriotism may have appealed to many veterans and Gold Star Mothers, but to the newly elected leaders of the "Reagan revolution" it was an abomination. The design flew in the face of the recently revived strain of relentlessly nostalgic patriotism that had sent them to the capital. It is not surprising that in this political climate, the czars of American conservatism resented the abstraction and the ambiguity of the proposed war memorial, or that opposition to the design came from high places in Washington. James Watt, then secretary of the interior, was a key figure in the design controversy. It was Watt—with the support of irate VVMF contributor H. Ross Perot—who demanded that Lin's deign be supplemented, if not supplanted, by a more heroic, representational, figural memorial. Watt would not let the Wall be *the* Vietnam War memorial. Sculptor Frederick Hart made himself and his concrete bronze design, *The Three Fightingmen*, readily available to Watt, Perot, and the press. His intense lobbying efforts were well rewarded. Watt took to Hart's figures and threatened to hold up construction indefinitely unless the VVMF agreed to use the sculpture. With their backs against the wall, the VVMF decided that the memorial was worth the compromise.

Ultimately, this compromise reflects the impossibility of finding a single design that could represent the Vietnam War for all Americans. Hart's figural sculpture satisfied powerful voices that required concrete representation, but it did not solve the problem of representation presented by the war. His figures, a white man flanked by an African American man and a third man whose race is unclear, stand a hundred feet away facing the Wall, apparently transfixed by its power. They are strong, highly masculinized, and heroic. The white man holds his hands out slightly to his side as if to warn his companions, in a patrician gesture that mimics the imperial nature of the war, of some impending danger. Although frozen, they, like the human figures who walk the memorial's path, are drawn to the black granite that recedes into the earth and then delivers into the light. Hart had intended the figures to look warily into the distance for the ubiquitous, hidden Vietnamese enemy, but the negotiations involved in the addition of the sculpture turned their gaze on the Wall and opened up a broad range of interpretive possibilities. This ironic fate for Hart's symbolically stable, heroic figures is indicative of the difficulty he faced in trying to divert attention from Lin's design. The sculpture in the end dramatizes the difficulties of representation and the power of the names; the main attraction of the memorial continues to be the Wall.

Even after the addition of the figures in 1984, the official commemoration of the war was not yet finished. In 1993, nearly ten years later, another battle over the memory of the war took shape on the Mall. After years of struggling to raise money and interest, Vietnam veteran Diane Carlson Evans presided over the dedication of the Vietnam Women's Memorial. This memorial is the first national memorial to female veterans. Its four figures—a prone, blindfolded, injured male soldier, a white nurse who holds him in her arms, an African American woman comforting

the nurse and looking to the sky, and a third woman kneeling over medical equipment—stand about three hundred feet from the Wall, sheltered in a grove of tall trees. It is a very straightforward figural memorial. And while the sculptor, Glenna Goodacre, was swiftly written off by art critics for whom her pietà is uninspiring, the principal argument against a memorial to the women who served in Vietnam was that it would set a precedent for a whole slew of other "special interest memorials." This complaint, as hollow as it might seem in light of the utter lack of memorials to the sacrifices made by American women at war, held considerable sway with the Park Service and the Fine Arts Commission; it is a reminder of the strength of the ideal that one symbolic gesture should be able to make a memory of this twenty-year war.

Evans wanted a women's memorial because the Wall did not heal the particular, complicated alienation of women veterans she had experienced, and it did not make women visible at the memorial. But her efforts to make the work of women in this war an obvious part of its official memory became a struggle against the firmly held ideal of a singular public memory. This struggle was particularly frustrating because the monument already included two sculptures and because women's war work in the United States has been invisible for so long despite the central role of women in the forging of public memory. The Mount Vernon Ladies' Association of the Union, the Daughters of the Confederacy, the Gold Star Mothers Association, and other women's volunteer associations have been essential to the history of memorializing in America. They have worked to ensure that national memories have been preserved and respected, but their contributions to the history of commemoration have not been recorded. Their roles in the work of making memory have been carefully prescribed—they have nurtured the memories of war as mothers, daughters, wives, and sisters but have not been seen as participants worth remembering. Women were undoubtedly a part of the life of the Vietnam Veterans Memorial in its first ten years, but they were principally visible as grievers, not as veterans. Diane Evans wanted to rewrite the history with the figure of a nurse.

30   Maya Lin sagely observed about the first statue, "In a funny sense, the compromise brings the memorial closer to the truth. What is also memorialized is that people still cannot resolve the war, nor can they separate the issues, the politics from it." This is true about both of the added statues. Hart's sculpture memorializes a need to remember these veterans as manly and heroic; Goodacre's sculpture, eight years later, memorializes a victory for women veterans over the perceived threat to patriotism posed by the idea of making any memory of war that is not singular and masculine. Hart's and Goodacre's additions to the Wall commemorate the difficulty of making memory in the midst of shifting cultural values. It is, in part, this sense of the impossibility of representation that pulls personal, individual memorials from visitors to the Wall; with their things people are bringing the monument "closer to the truth."

In the statement she submitted with her design proposal, Maya Lin wrote, "it is up to each individual to resolve or to come to terms with this loss. For death is in the end a personal and private matter and the area containing this within the memorial is a quiet place, meant for personal reflection and private reckoning." Lin was entirely right. She probably could not have anticipated the extent to which visitors to this memorial would take on the responsibility for the memory of the war, but she did appreciate the constantly unfinished, contested nature of the memory of this war. She understood that memorializing the war necessarily meant undoing the traditional idea of patriotic nationalism in the shape of a singular, heroic memorial. The multiplication of memorials, names, and objects at the Wall has, indeed, replaced the possibility of a singular memory of the war; the single figure of the male citizen embodying the nation has been supplanted by three official memorials and a steady stream of combat boots, bicycle parts, and St. Christophers. People come to this memorial and they make their own memorials.

EXPLORATORY WRITING

In the final line of this selection, Hass says, "People come to this memorial and they make their own memorials." Consider this statement in light of the questions Hass begins with concerning why people leave things at the Wall. Trace her line of reasoning through the two sections "The Memorial" and "The Design." How does her discussion in these middle sections provide the groundwork for the answer she offers at the end? What evidence links her closing answer to her opening question?

TALKING ABOUT THE READING

Hass notes that in 1984, two years after the Wall was built, another memorial—Frederick Hart's *The Three Fightingmen*—was added. Then a third memorial was completed in 1993, Glenda Goodacre's *Vietnam Women's Memorial.* (You can find images of the three memorials by doing a search at Google Images.) Work together with three or four other students. Consider the designs of the three memorials. What does each seem to signify on its own? What do they signify when taken together? How do they differ in the way they ask us to remember the Vietnam War? What does Hass see as the significance of the addition of two memorials to the Wall? How do these memorials compare to earlier war memorials, such as the Marine Corps War Memorial, which is based on the iconic photo of the flag raising at Iwo Jima?

WRITING ASSIGNMENTS

1. Kristen Hass sees the addition of the two memorials—*The Three Fightingmen* and the Vietnam Women's Memorial—as a compromise that reflects "the impossibility of finding a single design that could represent the Vietnam War for all Americans." Write an essay that works with Hass's analysis of the three memorials and the lack of consensus they reveal in American memories of the Vietnam War. Consider what her perspective brings to light about the visual design of each memorial and what the visual designs signify when all three memorials are taken together.

2. Monuments and statues are not the only forms of cultural expression that reflect and shape how Americans remember the Vietnam War. Films are also important repositories of historical memory. Some of the best-known films about the Vietnam War are *Coming Home, The Deer Hunter, Platoon, Born on the Fourth of July, Full Metal Jacket,* and the *Rambo* series. Watch one or more of these films. Write an essay that explains the historical memory of the Vietnam War that the film offers viewers. Keep in mind the issue is not whether the film is historically accurate but the vision of the past it provides.

3. As a group project, locate memorials in the town or city where your college is. You are likely to find a number of war memorials, but don't limit yourself to commemorations of the military dead. Americans have also memorialized events such as the Great Famine, the Holocaust, and the AIDS epidemic, as well as abolitionists, Native American leaders, industrialists, civil rights and women's rights activists, trade unionists, philanthropists, writers, artists, judges, and politicians among others. Once you have surveyed the memorials, develop a proposal for a new memorial to commemorate someone or some event that has been left out of the selective tradition of historical memory created by existing memorials. To do this, you will need first to describe existing memorials and explain the vision of the past they embody. Then you will need to make a case for the person or event you want to see memorialized and what type of memorial would be fitting.

READING AMERICAN PHOTOGRAPHS

—Alan Trachtenberg

Alan Trachtenberg is a distinguished professor of English and American Studies at Yale and the author of many articles and books, including *The Incorporation of America: Culture and Society in the Gilded Age* (1982). The following selection is an excerpt from the preface to his book *Reading American Photographs: Images as History, Mathew Brady to Walker Evans* (1989). Trachtenberg holds that the historian and photographer share a similar task, namely "how to make the random, fragmentary, and accidental details of everyday existence meaningful without loss of the details themselves."

SUGGESTION FOR READING As you read, consider what Trachtenberg means when he says that "photographs are not simple depictions but constructions." When you are finished reading, summarize Trachtenberg's argument in 3–4 sentences.

1 My argument throughout is that American photographs are not simple depictions but constructions, that the history they show is inseparable from the history they enact: a history of photographers employing their medium to make sense of their society. It is also a history of photographers

seeking to define themselves, to create a role for photography as an American art. How might the camera be used for social commentary and cultural interpretation? Consisting of images rather than words, photography places its own constraints on interpretation, requiring that photographers invent new forms of presentation, of collaboration between image and text, between artist and audience.

For the reader of photographs there is always the danger of overreading, of too facile a conversion of images into words. Speaking of "the camera's affinity for the indeterminate," Kracauer remarks that, "however selective," photographs are still "bound to record nature in the raw. Like the natural objects themselves, they will therefore be surrounded by a fringe of indistinct multiple meanings." All photographs have the effect of making their subjects seem at least momentarily strange, capable of meaning several things at once, or nothing at all. Estrangement allows us to see the subject in new and unexpected ways. Photographs entice viewers by their silence, the mysterious beckoning of another world. It is as enigmas, opaque and inexplicable as the living world itself, that they most resemble the data upon which history is based. Just as the meaning of the past is the prerogative of the present to invent and choose, the meaning of an image does not come intact and whole. Indeed, what empowers an image to represent history is not just what it shows but the struggle for meaning we undergo before it, a struggle analogous to the historian's effort to shape an intelligible and usable past. Representing the past, photographs serve the present's need to understand itself and measure its future. Their history lies finally in the political visions they may help us realize.

VISUAL ESSAY American Photographs

As Alan Trachtenberg notes, photographs do not simply depict but rather construct events. Single photographic images have taken on the power to contain and represent whole historical events. This Visual Essay features some of these iconic images, and it also directs you to other famous historical photographs that appear later in this chapter and in other places in *Reading Culture*.

From T. H. O'Sullivan's photographs of the American Civil War (p. 502) to present-day photojournalism, photographs have created immediately recognizable images of complex historical forces that have been captured in the concrete details of a moment. For example, Alfred Stieglitz's "The Steerage" (1907), which appears at the opening of the chapter, seems to distill the waves of immigration from southern and eastern Europe from 1880 to 1920 in a single frame, the "huddled masses" who have left the old world and are about to disembark in the new.

By the same token, the Great Depression of the 1930s has come to be known and remembered through the photographs of the Farm Security Administration. Dorothea Lange's "Migrant Mother, Florence Thompson and Her Children" (p. 6) has become an enduring icon, a modern madonna figure who embodies the suffering and resilience of rural people displaced from their land and turned into migrants by the American Dustbowl. People think of photos from the Depression as a reliable source, a documentary account of the life experience of workers, sharecroppers, Dustbowl migrants, and the unemployed. These photos have taken on the authority to bring the past to life and to show how things really were.

Photographs offer viewers moments of identification as well as information. When people look at a photograph of the flag raising at Iwo Jima (p. 502), for example, they are likely to recall the story of World War II as one of national unity to fight the "good war." In a sense, the photo seeks to recruit viewers—to have them join the just cause and commemorate American victory. On the other hand, the photo from the Vietnam War—the image of Colonel Loan executing a Viet Cong suspect (p. 503)—prompted for many Americans at the time feelings of shock, outrage, and horror and a crisis of confidence in the government's war policies. To say that these two photos have become iconic is to see the power they have to sum up in a single image the entire history of a war and the way it united or divided the country.

The photographs that appear in the Visual Essay have been chosen because they pose, at different historical moments and in different ways, this question of identification and division and how photographs produce memories that align our allegiances to the past.

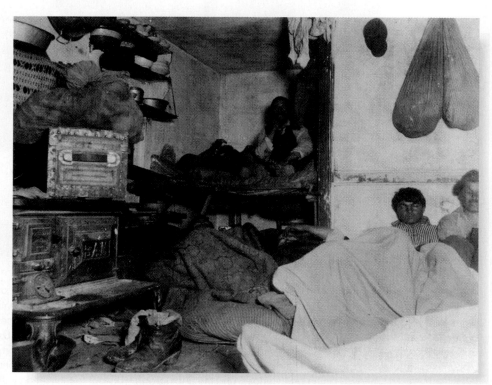

The issue of identification and division is evident in the title of Jacob Riis's investigation of the "lower depths" of New York City, *How the Other Half Lives,* from 1890. Riis is a pioneer of photojournalism; he was a police reporter in New York City whose crusading exposés of life in slum tenements prompted social reform. His often sensationalistic pictures of poverty, crime, and vice raise questions about Riis's relationship to his subjects and how he represents them. One of Riis's most famous pictures, "Five Cents a Spot," reveals the startled faces of lodgers crowded in a Bayard Street basement, as Riis—in what he called a "raiding party" of the photographers, public health inspectors, and occasionally policemen who accompanied him on his tours of the slums—burst in unannounced and unbidden to photograph the conditions of the poor.

In the picture of Tommy Smith and John Carlos raising their fists on the victory stand at the 1968 Olympics in Mexico City, the insurgent force of the photograph can precipitate a crisis of identification. Viewers at the time responded with celebration, fear, anxiety, outrage, pleasure, identification, or some combination of mixed feelings to this powerful image of black power and the freedom struggle of the 1960s. Part of the power of the image comes from the classic tableau of the Olympic victory stand and how it makes Smith and Carlos monumental figures, symbolizing the nobility of athletic excellence that goes back to the original Olympics in ancient Greece. The way Smith and Carlos—and the photograph—disrupt identification with such a classic image gives the picture its political impact, pushing the viewer to integrate their act of rebellion.

■—— This image of working-class militancy, from the Minneapolis general strike of 1934, provides another picture of the Great Depression, one that contains the iconic power to sum up in a single photograph the labor activism of the 1930s. City-wide general strikes in San Francisco, Toledo, and Minneapolis in 1934, the drive to organize new industry-wide unions by the Congress of Industrial Organization, the 1936–1937 autoworkers sit-down strike in Flint, mass labor meetings and street demonstrations—all reflected the growing sense among working people across the nation of the power of labor. And yet, photographs like this one, of workers in struggle, are less well known from the Depression than pictures of stoic individuals, dust storms, breadlines, and the unemployed, raising questions about the images that are available to remember the past, that distill a historical period into a single shot.

EXPLORATORY WRITING

Alan Trachtenberg says, "what empowers an image to represent history is not just what it shows but the struggle for meaning we undergo before it, a struggle analogous to the historian's effort to shape an intelligible and usable past." Use Trachtenberg's sense of the "struggle for meaning" to explain your reading of one of the photographs mentioned in the Visual Essay. How does the photograph call on you "to shape an intelligible and usable past"?

DESIGNING A VISUAL ESSAY

Work together in groups of four or five. Assemble a file of photographs about Hurricane Katrina and its aftermath in New Orleans. The more photos you can bring together, the better. Your task is to design a visual essay of four photos that provide a way of remembering the event. In your selection, look for iconic images that have the power to distill the meaning of the event in a single picture. Present your visual to the class, explaining how your selection makes Katrina an "intelligible" and "usable" moment in history. Compare your account with those from other groups. In what sense are the various visual essays a "struggle for meaning" about how we remember Hurricane Katrina?

WRITING ASSIGNMENTS

1. In his introduction to *How the Other Half Lives* (1996), David Levitan writes, "Riis's blend of sensationalism, melodrama, and realism . . . tends to confuse readers, forcing them to ask themselves, once again, if they are to pity the plight of the poor or fear their spread." Levitan notes, "In fact, Riis wanted his readers to do both." Write an essay that examines Levitan's claim that Riis's photos elicited mixed feelings from viewers. What is it about the nature of the photos that prompts both pity and fear? Consider how Riis uses a "blend of sensationalism, melodrama, and realism" in his photos. Do some research on Riis to develop your thinking about his relationship to his subjects and how he wanted to position his middle-class readers in relation to the poor of New York. You can find examples of Riis's photographs online.

2. Write an essay that compares two of the photographs mentioned in the Visual Essay (or find your own pair) in terms of what gives each its iconic character. Part of the task here is the selection of photos, to pair two that can provide interesting grounds for comparison and contrast. Given the examples in *Reading Culture,* you could look, for instance, at how Dorothea Lange's "Migrant Mother" and the photo of the Minneapolis General Strike of 1934 represent the Depression, or you could compare Jacob Riis's representations of the poor to Alfred Stieglitz's "The Steerage" or one of the photos by Lewis Hine. What photo would be good to pair with the black power salute by Tommy Smith and John Carlos at the 1968 Olympics?

3. Design a visual essay of 8–10 photos, combined with an introductory commentary, to characterize in word and image a particular year or decade in American history. You might, for example, do the year of your birth, to assemble images of the world you were born into, or a decade like the Roaring Twenties. This will take some research into the history of the year or decade and the photographs that were taken at the time. In your commentary, explain how the photos go together to form a memory of the year or decade. Say something about each of the photos' capacity to distill the meaning of a significant event in that year or decade.

"INDIANS": TEXTUALISM, MORALITY, AND THE PROBLEM OF HISTORY

—*Jane Tompkins*

Jane Tompkins is a professor of English and education at the University of Illinois, Chicago. She is well known for her literary criticism, including the two books *Sensational Designs: The Cultural Work of American Fiction, 1790–1860* (1985) and *West of Everything: The Inner Life of Westerns* (1992). The following essay was written for the journal of literary criticism *Critical Inquiry* and originally appeared in 1986. As you will see, the essay reports on how Tompkins dealt with the conflicting historical interpretations that she encountered in her research on the Puritans' relation with Native Americans.

SUGGESTION FOR READING   Notice that Tompkins's essay can be divided into three parts. The first raises the problem of conflicting interpretations. The second—the longest part of the essay—reports on her research and the differing assumptions, perspectives, and interpretations that she found. In the final part, Tompkins explains how she found a "way out" of the difficulties that these "irreconcilable points of view" posed for her. As you read, annotate the essay to help you keep track of what Tompkins is doing.

1   When I was growing up in New York City, my parents used to take me to an event in Inwood Park at which Indians—real American Indians dressed in feathers and blankets—could be seen and touched by children like me. This event was always a disappointment. It was more fun to imagine that you were an Indian in one of the caves in Inwood Park than to shake the hand of an old man in a headdress who was not overwhelmed at the opportunity of meeting you. After staring at the Indians for a while, we would take a walk in the woods where the caves were, and once I asked my mother if the remains of a fire I had seen in one of them might have been left by the original inhabitants. After that, wandering up some stone steps cut into the side of the hill, I imagined I was a princess in a rude castle. My Indians, like my princesses, were creatures totally of the imagination, and I did not care to have any real exemplars interfering with what I already knew.

I already knew about Indians from having read about them in school. Over and over we were told the story of how Peter Minuit had bought Manhattan Island from the Indians for twenty-four dollars' worth of glass beads. And it was a story we didn't mind hearing because it gave us the rare pleasure of having someone to feel superior to, since the poor Indians had not known (as we eight-year-olds did) how valuable a piece of property Manhattan Island would become. Generally, much was made of the Indian presence in Manhattan; a poem in one of our readers began: "Where we walk to school today / Indian children used to play," and we were encouraged to write poetry on this topic ourselves. So I had a fairly rich relationship with Indians before I ever met the unprepossessing people in Inwood Park. I felt that I had a lot in common with them. They, too, liked animals (they were often named after animals); they, too, made mistakes—they liked the brightly colored trinkets of little value that the white men were always offering them; they were handsome, war-like, and brave and had led an exciting, romantic life in the forest long ago, a life such as I dreamed of leading myself. I felt lucky to be living in one of the places where they had definitely been. Never mind where they were or what they were doing now.

My story stands for the relationship most non-Indians have to the people who first populated this continent, a relationship characterized by narcissistic fantasies of freedom and adventure, of a life lived closer to nature and to spirit than the life we lead now. As Vine Deloria Jr. has pointed out, the American Indian Movement in the early seventies couldn't get people to pay attention to what was happening to Indians who were alive in the present, so powerful was this country's infatuation with people who wore loincloths, lived in tepees, and roamed the plains and forests long ago.[1] The present essay, like these fantasies, doesn't have much to do with actual Indians, though its subject matter is the histories of European-Indian relations in seventeenth-century New England. In a sense, my encounter with Indians as an adult doing "research" replicates the childhood one, for while I started out to learn about Indians, I ended up preoccupied with a problem of my own.

This essay enacts a particular instance of the challenge poststructuralism poses to the study of history. In simpler language, it concerns the difference that point of view makes when people are giving accounts of events, whether at first or second hand. The problem is that if all accounts of events are determined through and through by the observer's frame of reference, then one will never know, in any given case, what really happened.

5   I encountered this problem in concrete terms while preparing to teach a course in colonial American literature. I'd set out to learn what I could about the Puritans' relations with American Indians. All I wanted was a general idea of what had happened between the English settlers and the natives in seventeenth-century New England; poststructuralism and its dilemmas were the furthest thing from my mind. I began, more or less automatically, with Perry Miller, who hardly mentions the Indians at all, then proceeded to the work of historians who had dealt exclusively with the European-Indian encounter. At first, it was a question of deciding which of these authors to believe, for it quickly became apparent that there was no unanimity on the subject. As I read on, however, I discovered that the problem was more complicated than deciding whose version of events was correct. Some of the conflicting accounts were not simply contradictory, they were completely incommensurable, in that their assumptions about what counted as a valid approach to the subject, and what the subject itself was, diverged in fundamental ways. Faced with an array of mutually irreconcilable points of view, points of view which determined what was being discussed as well as the terms of the discussion, I decided to turn to primary sources for clarification, only to discover that the primary sources reproduced the problem all over again. I found myself, in other words, in an epistemological quandary, not only unable to decide among conflicting versions of events but also unable to believe that any such decision could, in principle, be made. It was a moral quandary as well. Knowledge of what really happened when the Europeans and the Indians first met seemed particularly important, since the result of that encounter was virtual genocide. This was the kind of past "mistake" which, presumably, we studied history in order to avoid repeating. If studying history couldn't put us in touch with actual events and their causes, then what was to prevent such atrocities from happening again?

For a while, I remained at this impasse. But through analyzing the process by which I had reached it, I eventually arrived at an understanding which seemed to offer a way out. This essay records the concrete experience of meeting and solving the difficulty I have just described (as an abstract problem, I thought I had solved it long ago). My purpose is not to throw new light on antifoundationalist epistemology—the solution I reached is not a new one—but to dramatize and expose the troubles antifoundationalism gets you into when you meet it, so to speak, in the road.

My research began with Perry Miller. Early in the preface to *Errand into the Wilderness,* while explaining how he came to write his history of the New England mind, Miller writes a sentence that stopped me dead. He says that what fascinated him as a young man about his country's history was "the massive narrative of the movement of European culture into the vacant wilderness of America."[2] "Vacant?" Miller, writing in 1956, doesn't pause over the word "vacant," but to people who read his preface thirty years later, the word is shocking. In what circumstances could someone proposing to write a history of colonial New England not take account of the Indian presence there?

The rest of Miller's preface supplies an answer to this question, if one takes the trouble to piece together its details. Miller explains that as a young man, jealous of older compatriots who had had the luck to fight in World War I, he had gone to Africa in search of adventure. "The adventures that Africa afforded," he writes, "were tawdry enough, but it became the setting for a sudden epiphany" (p. vii). "It was given to me," he writes, "disconsolate on the edge of a jungle of central Africa, to have thrust upon me the mission of expounding what I took to be the innermost propulsion of the United States, while supervising, in that barbaric tropic, the unloading of drums of case oil flowing out of the inexhaustible wilderness of America" (p. viii). Miller's picture of himself on the banks of the Congo furnishes a key to the kind of history he will write and to his mental image of a vacant wilderness; it explains why it was just there, under precisely these conditions, that he should have had his epiphany.

The fuel drums stand, in Miller's mind, for the popular misconception of what this country is about. They are "tangible symbols of [America's] appalling power," a power that everyone but Miller takes for the ultimate reality (p. ix). To Miller, "the mind of man is the basic factor in human history," and he will plead, all unaccommodated as he is among the fuel drums, for the intellect—the intellect for which his fellow historians, with their chapters on "stoves or bathtubs, or tax laws," "the Wilmot Proviso" and "the chain store," "have so little respect" (p. viii, ix). His preface seethes with a hatred of the merely physical and mechanical, and this hatred, which is really a form of moral outrage, explains not only the contempt with which he mentions the stoves and bathtubs but also the nature of his experience in Africa and its relationship to the "massive narrative" he will write.

10   Miller's experiences in Africa are "tawdry," his tropic is barbaric because the jungle he stands on the edge of means nothing to him, no more, indeed something less, than the case oil. It is the nothingness of Africa that precipitates his vision. It is the barbarity of the "dark continent," the obvious (but superficial) parallelism between the jungle at Matadi and America's "vacant wilderness" that releases in Miller the desire to define and vindicate his country's cultural identity. To the young Miller, colonial Africa and colonial America are—but for the history he will bring to light—mirror images of one another. And what he fails to see in the one landscape is the same thing he overlooks in the other: the human beings who people it. As Miller stood with his back to the jungle, thinking about the role of mind in human history, his failure to see that the land into which European culture had moved was not vacant but already occupied by a varied and numerous population, is of a piece with his failure, in his portrait of himself at Matadi, to notice who was carrying the fuel drums he was supervising the unloading of.

The point is crucial because it suggests that what is invisible to the historian in his own historical moment remains invisible when he turns his gaze to the past. It isn't that Miller didn't "see" the black men, in a literal sense, any more than it's the case that when he looked back he didn't "see" the Indians, in the sense of not realizing they were there. Rather, it's that neither the Indians nor the blacks *counted* for him, in a fundamental way. The way in which Indians can be seen but not counted is illustrated by an entry in Governor John Winthrop's journal, three hundred years before, when he recorded that there had been a great storm with high winds "yet through God's great mercy it did no hurt, but only killed one Indian with the fall of a tree."[3] The juxtaposition suggests that Miller shared with Winthrop a certain colonial point of view, a point of view from which Indians, though present, do not finally matter.

A book entitled *New England Frontier: Puritans and Indians, 1620–1675,* written by Alden Vaughan and published in 1965, promised to rectify Miller's omission. In the outpouring of work on the European-Indian encounter that began in the early sixties, this book is the first major landmark, and to a neophyte it seems definitive. Vaughan acknowledges the absence of Indian sources and emphasizes his use of materials which catch the Puritans "off guard."[4] His announced conclusion that "the New England

Puritans followed a remarkably humane, considerate, and just policy in their dealings with the Indians" seems supported by the scope, documentation, and methodicalness of his project (NEF, p. vii). The author's fair-mindedness and equanimity seem everywhere apparent, so that when he asserts "the history of interracial relations from the arrival of the Pilgrims to the outbreak of King Philip's War is a credit to the integrity of both peoples," one is positively reassured (NEF, p. viii).

But these impressions do not survive an admission that comes late in the book, when, in the course of explaining why works like Helen Hunt Jackson's *Century of Dishonor* had spread misconceptions about Puritan treatment of the Indians, Vaughan finally lays his own cards on the table.

> The root of the misunderstanding [about Puritans and Indians] . . . lie[s] in a failure to recognize the nature of the two societies that met in seventeenth century New England. One was unified, visionary, disciplined, and dynamic. The other was divided, self-satisfied, undisciplined, and static. It would be unreasonable to expect that such societies could live side by side indefinitely with no penetration of the more fragmented and passive by the more consolidated and active. What resulted, then, was not—as many have held—a clash of dissimilar ways of life, but rather the expansion of one into the areas in which the other was lacking. (NEF, p. 323)

From our present vantage point, these remarks seem culturally biased to an incredible degree, not to mention inaccurate: was Puritan society unified? If so, how does one account for its internal dissensions and obsessive need to cast out deviants? Is "unity" necessarily a positive culture trait? From what standpoint can one say that American Indians were neither disciplined nor visionary, when both these characteristics loom so large in the ethnographies? Is it an accident that ways of describing cultural strength and weakness coincide with gender stereotypes—active/passive, and so on? Why is one

culture said to "penetrate" the other? Why is the "other" described in terms of "lack"?

15   Vaughan's fundamental categories of apprehension and judgment will not withstand even the most cursory inspection. For what looked like evenhandedness when he was writing *New England Frontier* does not look that way anymore. In his introduction to *New Directions in American Intellectual History,* John Higham writes that by the end of the sixties

> the entire conceptual foundation on which [this sort of work] rested [had] crumbled away. . . . Simultaneously, in sociology, anthropology, and history, two working assumptions . . . came under withering attack: first, the assumption that societies tend to be integrated, and second, that a shared culture maintains that integration. . . . By the late 1960s all claims issued in the name of an "American mind" . . . were subject to drastic skepticism.[5]

"Clearly," Higham continues, "the sociocultural upheaval of the sixties created the occasion" for this reaction.[6] Vaughan's book, it seemed, could only have been written before the events of the sixties had sensitized scholars to questions of race and ethnicity. It came as no surprise, therefore, that ten years later there appeared a study of European-Indian relations which reflected the new awareness of social issues the sixties had engendered. And it offered an entirely different picture of the European-Indian encounter.

Francis Jennings's *The Invasion of America* (1975) rips wide open the idea that the Puritans were humane and considerate in their dealings with the Indians. In Jennings's account, even more massively documented than Vaughan's, the early settlers lied to the Indians, stole from them, murdered them, scalped them, captured them, tortured them, raped them, sold them into slavery, confiscated their land, destroyed their crops, burned their homes, scattered their possessions, gave them alcohol, undermined their systems of belief, and infected them with diseases that wiped out ninety percent of their numbers within the first hundred years after contact.[7]

Jennings mounts an all-out attack on the essential decency of the Puritan leadership and their apologists in the twentieth century. The Pequot War, which previous historians had described as an attempt on the part of Massachusetts Bay to protect itself from the fiercest of the New England tribes, becomes, in Jennings's painstakingly researched account, a deliberate war of extermination, waged by whites against Indians. It starts with trumped-up charges, is carried on through a series of increasingly bloody reprisals, and ends in the massacre of scores of Indian men, women, and children, all so that Massachusetts Bay could gain political and economic control of the southern Connecticut Valley. When one reads this and then turns over the page and sees a reproduction of the Bay Colony seal, which depicts an Indian from whose mouth issue the words "Come over and help us," the effect is shattering.[8]

But even so powerful an argument as Jennings's did not remain unshaken by subsequent work. Reading on, I discovered that if the events of the sixties had revolutionized the study of European-Indian relations, the events of the seventies produced yet another transformation. The American Indian Movement, and in particular the founding of the Native American Rights Fund in 1971 to finance Indian litigation, and a court decision in 1975 which gave the tribes the right to seek redress for past injustices in federal court, created a climate within which historians began to focus on the Indians themselves. "Almost simultaneously," writes James Axtell, "frontier and colonial historians began to discover the necessity of considering the American natives as real determinants of history and the utility of ethnohistory as a way of ensuring parity of focus and impartiality of judgment."[9] In Miller, Indians had been simply beneath notice; in Vaughan, they belonged to an inferior culture; and in Jennings, they were the more or less innocent prey of power-hungry whites. But in the most original and provocative of the ethnohistories, Calvin Martin's *Keepers of the Game,*

Indians became complicated, purposeful human beings, whose lives were spiritually motivated to a high degree.[10] Their relationship to the animals they hunted, to the natural environment, and to the whites with whom they traded became intelligible within a system of beliefs that formed the basis for an entirely new perspective on the European-Indian encounter.

20   Within the broader question of why European contact had such a devastating effect on the Indians, Martin's specific aim is to determine why Indians participated in the fur trade which ultimately led them to the brink of annihilation. The standard answer to this question had always been that once the Indian was introduced to European guns, copper kettles, woolen blankets, and the like, he literally couldn't keep his hands off them. In order to acquire these coveted items, he decimated the animal populations on which his survival depended. In short, the Indian's motivation in participating in the fur trade was assumed to be the same as the white European's—a desire to accumulate material goods. In direct opposition to this thesis, Martin argues that the reason why Indians ruthlessly exploited their own resources had nothing to do with supply and demand, but stemmed rather from a breakdown of the cosmic worldview that tied them to the game they killed in a spiritual relationship of parity and mutual obligation.

The hunt, according to Martin, was conceived not primarily as a physical activity but as a spiritual quest, in which the spirit of the hunter must overmaster the spirit of the game animal before the kill can take place. The animal, in effect, *allows* itself to be found and killed, once the hunter has mastered its spirit. The hunter prepared himself through rituals of fasting, sweating, or dreaming which revealed the identity of his prey and where he can find it. The physical act of killing is the least important element in the process. Once the animal is killed, eaten, and its parts used for clothing or implements, its remains must be disposed of in ritually prescribed fashion, or the game boss, the "keeper" of that species, will not permit more animals to be killed. The relationship between Indians and animals, then, is contractual; each side must hold up its end of the bargain, or no further transactions can occur.

What happened, according to Martin, was that as a result of diseases introduced into the animal population by Europeans, the game suddenly disappeared, began to act in inexplicable ways, or sickened and died in plain view, and communicated their diseases to the Indians. The Indians, consequently, believed that their compact with the animals had been broken and that the keepers of the game, the tutelary spirits of each animal species whom they had been so careful to propitiate, had betrayed them. And when missionization, wars with the Europeans, and displacement from their tribal lands had further weakened Indian society and its belief structure, the Indians, no longer restrained by religious sanctions, in effect, turned on the animals in a holy war of revenge.

Whether or not Martin's specific claim about the "holy war" was correct, his analysis made it clear to me that, given the Indians' understanding of economic, religious, and physical processes, an Indian account of what transpired when the European settlers arrived here would look nothing like our own. Their (potential, unwritten) history of the conflict could bear only a marginal resemblance to Eurocentric views. I began to think that the key to understanding European-Indian relations was to see them as an encounter between wholly disparate cultures, and that therefore either defending or attacking the colonists was beside the point since, given the cultural disparity between the two groups, conflict was inevitable and in large part a product of mutual misunderstanding.

But three years after Martin's book appeared, Shepard Krech III edited a collection of seven essays called *Indians, Animals, and the Fur Trade*, attacking Martin's entire project. Here the authors argued that we don't need an ideological or religious explanation for the fur trade. As Charles Hudson writes,

The Southeastern Indians slaughtered deer (and were prompted to enslave and kill each other) because of their position on the outer fringes of an expanding modern world-system. . . . In the modern world-system there is a core region which establishes *economic* relations with its colonial periphery. . . . If the Indians could not produce commodities, they were on the road to cultural extinction. . . . To maximize his chances for survival, an eighteenth-century Southeastern Indian had to . . . live in the interior, out of range of European cattle, forestry, and agriculture. . . . He had to produce a commodity which was valuable enough to earn him some protection from English slavers.[11]

25   Though we are talking here about Southeastern Indians, rather than the subarctic and Northeastern tribes Martin studied, what really accounts for these divergent explanations of why Indians slaughtered the game are the assumptions that underlie them. Martin believes that the Indians acted on the basis of perceptions made available to them by their own cosmology; that is, he explains their behavior as the Indians themselves would have explained it (insofar as he can), using a logic and a set of values that are not Eurocentric but derived from within Amerindian culture. Hudson, on the other hand, insists that the Indians' own beliefs are irrelevant to an explanation of how they acted, which can only be understood, as far as he is concerned, in the terms of a Western materialist economic and political analysis. Martin and Hudson, in short, don't agree on what counts as an explanation, and this disagreement sheds light on the preceding accounts as well. From this standpoint, we can see that Vaughan, who thought that the Puritans were superior to the Indians, and Jennings, who thought the reverse, are both, like Hudson, using Eurocentric criteria of description and evaluation. While all three critics (Vaughan, Jennings, and Hudson) acknowledge that Indians and Europeans behave differently from one another, the behavior differs, as it were, within the order of the same: all three assume, though only Hudson makes the assumption explicit,

that an understanding of relations between the Europeans and the Indians must be elaborated in European terms. In Martin's analysis, however, what we have are not only two different sets of behavior but two incommensurable ways of describing and assigning meaning to events. This difference at the level of explanation calls into question the possibility of obtaining any theory-independent account of interaction between Indians and Europeans.

At this point, dismayed and confused by the wildly divergent views of colonial history the twentieth-century historians had provided, I decided to look at some primary materials. I thought, perhaps, if I looked at some firsthand accounts and at some scholars looking at those accounts, it would be possible to decide which experts were right and which were wrong by comparing their views with the evidence. Captivity narratives seemed a good place to begin, since it was logical to suppose that the records left by whites who had been captured by Indians would furnish the sort of firsthand information I wanted.

I began with two fascinating essays based on these materials written by the ethnohistorian James Axtell, "The White Indians of Colonial America" and "The Scholastic Philosophy of the Wilderness."[12] These essays suggest that it would have been a privilege to be captured by North American Indians and taken off to Canada to dwell in a wigwam for the rest of one's life. Axtell's reconstruction of the process by which Indians taught European captives to feel comfortable in the wilderness, first taking their shoes away and giving them moccasins, carrying the children on their backs, sharing the scanty food supply equally, ceremonially cleansing them of their old identities, giving them Indian clothes and jewelry, assiduously teaching them the Indian language, finally adopting them into their families, and even visiting them after many years if, as sometimes happened, they were restored to white society—all of this creates a compelling portrait of Indian culture and helps to explain the

extraordinary attraction that Indian culture apparently exercised over Europeans.

But, as I had by now come to expect, this beguiling portrait of the Indians' superior humanity is called into question by other writings on Indian captivity—for example, Norman Heard's *White into Red,* whose summation of the comparative treatment of captive children east and west of the Mississippi seems to contradict some of Axtell's conclusions:

> The treatment of captive children seems to have been similar in initial stages. . . . Most children were treated brutally at the time of capture. Babies and toddlers usually were killed immediately and other small children would be dispatched during the rapid retreat to the Indian villages if they cried, failed to keep the pace, or otherwise indicated a lack of fortitude needed to become a worthy member of the tribe. Upon reaching the village, the child might face such ordeals as running the gauntlet or dancing in the center of a throng of threatening Indians. The prisoner might be so seriously injured at this time that he would no longer be acceptable for adoption.[13]

One account which Heard reprints is particularly arresting. A young girl captured by the Comanches who had not been adopted into a family but used as a slave had been peculiarly mistreated. When they wanted to wake her up the family she belonged to would take a burning brand from the fire and touch it to her nose. When she was returned to her parents, the flesh of her nose was completely burned away, exposing the bone.[14]

30   Since the pictures drawn by Heard and Axtell were in certain respects irreconcilable, it made sense to turn to a firsthand account to see how the Indians treated their captives in a particular instance. Mary Rowlandson's "The Soveraignty and Goodness of God," published in Boston around 1680, suggested itself because it was so widely read and had set the pattern for later narratives. Rowlandson interprets her captivity as God's punishment on her for failing to

keep the Sabbath properly on several occasions. She sees everything that happens to her as a sign from God. When the Indians are kind to her, she attributes her good fortune to divine Providence; when they are cruel, she blames her captors. But beyond the question of how Rowlandson interprets events is the question of what she saw in the first place and what she considered worth reporting. The following passage, with its abrupt shifts of focus and peculiar emphases, makes it hard to see her testimony as evidence of anything other than the Puritan point of view:

> Then my heart began to fail: and I fell weeping, which was the first time to my remembrance, that I wept before them. Although I had met with so much Affliction, and my heart was many times ready to break, yet could I not shed one tear in their sight: but rather had been all this while in a maze, and like one astonished: but not I may say as, Psal. 137.1. *By the Rivers of Babylon, there we sate down; yea, we wept when we remembered Zion.* There one of them asked me, why I wept, I could hardly tell what to say: yet I answered, they would kill me: No, said he, none will hurt you. Then came one of them and gave me two spoon-fulls of Meal to comfort me, and another gave me half a pint of Pease; which was more worth than many Bushels at another time. Then I went to see King Philip, he bade me come in and sit down, and asked me whether I woold smoke it (a usual Complement nowadayes among Saints and Sinners) but this no way suited me. For though I had formerly used Tobacco, yet I had left it ever since I was first taken. It seems to be a Bait, the Devil layes to make men loose their precious time: I remember with shame, how formerly, when I had taken two or three pipes, I was presently ready for another, such a bewitching thing it is: But I thank God, he has now given me power over it; surely there are many who may be better imployed than to ly sucking a stinking Tobacco-pipe.[15]

Anyone who has ever tried to give up smoking has to sympathize with Rowlandson, but it is nonetheless remarkable, first, that a passage which begins with her weeping openly in front of her captors, and comparing herself to Israel in

Babylon, should end with her railing against the vice of tobacco; and, second, that it has not a word to say about King Philip, the leader of the Indians who captured her and mastermind of the campaign that devastated the white population of the English colonies. The fact that Rowlandson has just been introduced to the chief of chiefs makes hardly any impression on her at all. What excites her is a moral issue which was being hotly debated in the seventeenth century: to smoke or not to smoke (Puritans frowned on it, apparently, because it wasted time and presented a fire hazard). What seem to us the peculiar emphases in Rowlandson's relation are not the result of her having screened out evidence she couldn't handle, but of her way of constructing the world. She saw what her seventeenth-century English Separatist background made visible. It is when one realizes that the biases of twentieth-century historians like Vaughan or Axtell cannot be corrected for simply by consulting the primary materials, since the primary materials are constructed according to *their* authors' biases, that one begins to envy Miller his vision at Matadi. Not for what he didn't see—the Indian and the black—but for his epistemological confidence.

Since captivity narratives made a poor source of evidence for the nature of European-Indian relations in early New England because they were so relentlessly pietistic, my hope was that a better source of evidence might be writings designed simply to tell Englishmen what the American natives were like. These authors could be presumed to be less severely biased, since they hadn't seen their loved ones killed by Indians or been made to endure the hardships of captivity, and because they weren't writing propaganda calculated to prove that God had delivered his chosen people from the hands of Satan's emissaries.

The problem was that these texts were written with aims no less specific than those of the captivity narratives, though the aims were of a different sort. Here is a passage from William

Wood's *New England's Prospect,* published in London in 1634.

To enter into a serious discourse concerning the natural conditions of these Indians might procure admiration from the people of any civilized nations, in regard of their civility and good natures. . . . These Indians are of affable, courteous and well disposed natures, ready to communicate the best of their wealth to the mutual good of one another; . . . so . . . perspicuous is their love . . . that they are as willing to part with a mite in poverty as treasure in plenty. . . . If it were possible to recount the courtesies they have showed the English, since their first arrival in those parts, it would not only steady belief, that they are a loving people, but also win the love of those that never saw them, and wipe off that needless fear that is too deeply rooted in the conceits of many who think them envious and of such rancorous and inhumane dispositions, that they will one day make an end of their English inmates.[16]

However, in a pamphlet published twenty-one years earlier, Alexander Whitaker of Virginia has this to say of the natives:

These naked slaves . . . serve the divell for feare, after a most base manner, sacrificing sometimes (as I have heere heard) their own Children to him. . . . They live naked in bodie, as if their shame of their sinne deserved no covering: Their names are as naked as their bodie: They esteem it a virtue to lie, deceive and steale as their master the divell teacheth to them.[17]

35 According to Robert Berkhofer in *The White Man's Indian,* these divergent reports can be explained by looking at the authors' motives. A favorable report like Wood's, intended to encourage new emigrants to America, naturally represented Indians as loving and courteous, civilized and generous, in order to allay the fears of prospective colonists. Whitaker, on the other hand, a minister who wishes to convince his readers that the Indians are in need of conversion, paints them as benighted agents of the devil. Berkhofer's commentary constantly implies

that white men were to blame for having represented the Indians in the image of their own desires and needs.[18] But the evidence supplied by Rowlandson's narrative, and by the accounts left by early reporters such as Wood and Whitaker, suggests something rather different. Though it is probably true that in certain cases Europeans did consciously tamper with the evidence, in most cases there is no reason to suppose that they did not record faithfully what they saw. And what they saw was not an illusion, was not determined by selfish motives in any narrow sense, but was there by virtue of a way of seeing which they could no more consciously manipulate than they could choose not to have been born. At this point, it seemed to me, the ethnocentric bias of the firsthand observers invited an investigation of the cultural situation they spoke from. Karen Kupperman's *Settling with the Indians* (1980) supplied just such an analysis.

Kupperman argues that Englishmen inevitably looked at Indians in exactly the same way that they looked at other Englishmen. For instance, if they looked down on Indians and saw them as people to be exploited, it was not because of racial prejudice or antique notions about savagery, it was because they looked down on ordinary English men and women and saw them as subjects for exploitation as well.[19] According to Kupperman, what concerned these writers most when they described the Indians were the insignia of social class, of rank, and of prestige. Indian faces are virtually never described in the earliest accounts, but clothes and hairstyles, tattoos and jewelry, posture and skin color are. "Early modern Englishmen believed that people can create their own identity, and that therefore one communicates to the world through signals such as dress and other forms of decoration who one is, what group or category one belongs to."[20]

Kupperman's book marks a watershed in writings on European-Indian relations, for it reverses the strategy employed by Martin two years before. Whereas Martin had performed an ethnographic analysis of Indian cosmology in order to explain, from within, the Indians' motives for engaging in the fur trade, Kupperman performs an ethnographic study of seventeenth-century England in order to explain, from within, what motivated Englishmen's behavior. The sympathy and understanding that Martin, Axtell, and others extend to the Indians are extended in Kupperman's work to the English themselves. Rather than giving an account of "what happened" between Indians and Europeans, like Martin, she reconstructs the worldview that gave the experience of one group its content. With her study, scholarship on European-Indian relations comes full circle.

It may well seem to you at this point that, given the tremendous variation among the historical accounts, I had no choice but to end in relativism. If the experience of encountering conflicting versions of the "same" events suggests anything certain it is that the attitude a historian takes up in relation to a given event, the way in which he or she judges and even describes "it"— and the "it" has to go in quotation marks because depending on the perspective, that event either did or did not occur—this stance, these judgments and descriptions are a function of the historian's position in relation to the subject. Miller, standing on the banks of the Congo, couldn't see the black men he was supervising because of his background, his assumptions, values, experiences, goals. Jennings, intent on exposing the distortions introduced into the historical record by Vaughan and his predecessors stretching all the way back to Winthrop, couldn't see that Winthrop and his peers were not racists but only Englishmen who looked at other cultures in the way their own culture had taught them to see one another. The historian can never escape the limitations of his or her own position in history and so inevitably gives an account that is an extension of the circumstances from which it springs. But it seems to me that when one is confronted with this particular succession of stories, cultural and historical relativism is not a position that one can comfortably assume. The

phenomena to which these histories testify— conquest, massacre, and genocide, on the one hand; torture, slavery, and murder on the other— cry out for judgment. When faced with claims and counterclaims of this magnitude one feels obligated to reach an understanding of what actually did occur. The dilemma posed by the study of European-Indian relations in early America is that the highly charged nature of the materials demands a moral decisiveness which the succession of conflicting accounts effectively precludes. That is the dilemma I found myself in at the end of this course of reading, and which I eventually came to resolve as follows.

After a while it began to seem to me that there was something wrong with the way I had formulated the problem. The statement that the materials on European-Indian relations were so highly charged that they demanded moral judgment, but that the judgment couldn't be made because all possible descriptions of what happened were biased, seemed to contain an internal contradiction. The statement implied that in order to make a moral judgment about something, you have to know something else first— namely, the facts of the case you're being called upon to judge. My complaint was that their perspectival nature would disqualify any facts I might encounter and that therefore I couldn't judge. But to say as I did that the materials I had read were "highly charged" and therefore demanded judgment suggests both that I was reacting to something real—to some facts—*and* that I had judged them. Perhaps I wasn't so much in the lurch morally or epistemologically as I had thought. If you—or I—react with horror to the story of the girl captured and enslaved by Comanches who touched a firebrand to her nose every time they wanted to wake her up, it's because we read this as a story about cruelty and suffering, and not as a story about the conventions of prisoner exchange or the economics of Comanche life. The *seeing* of the story as a cause for alarm rather than as a droll anecdote or a piece of curious information is evidence of values we already hold, of judgments already made, of facts already perceived as facts.

40   My problem presupposed that I couldn't judge because I didn't know what the facts were. All I had, or could have, was a series of different perspectives, and so nothing that would count as an authoritative source on which moral judgments could be based. But, as I have just shown, I did judge, and that is because, as I now think, I did have some facts. I seemed to accept as facts that ninety percent of the native American population of New England died after the first hundred years of contact, that tribes in eastern Canada and the northeastern United States had a compact with the game they killed, that Comanches had subjected a captive girl to casual cruelty, that King Philip smoked a pipe, and so on. It was only where different versions of the same event came into conflict that I doubted the text was a record of something real. And even then, there was no question about certain major catastrophes. I believed that four hundred Pequots were killed near Saybrook, that Winthrop was the Governor of the Massachusetts Bay Colony when it happened, and so on. My sense that certain events, such as the Pequot War, did occur in no way reflected the indecisiveness that overtook me when I tried to choose among the various historical versions. In fact, the need I felt to make up my mind was impelled by the conviction that certain things *had* happened that shouldn't have happened. Hence it was never the case that "what happened" was completely unknowable or unavailable. It's rather that in the process of reading so many different approaches to the same phenomenon I became aware of the difference in the attitudes that informed these approaches. This awareness of the interests motivating each version cast suspicion over everything, in retrospect, and I ended by claiming that there was nothing I could know. This, I now see, was never really the case. But how did it happen?

Someone else, confronted with the same materials, could have decided that one of these historical accounts was correct. Still another person might have decided that more evidence was needed in order to decide among them. Why did I conclude that none of the accounts was accurate because they were all produced from some particular angle of vision? Presumably there was something in my background that enabled me to see the problem in this way. That something, very likely, was poststructuralist theory. I let my discovery that Vaughan was a product of the fifties, Jennings of the sixties, Rowlandson of a Puritan worldview, and so on lead me to the conclusion that all facts are theory dependent because that conclusion was already a thinkable one for me. My inability to come up with a true account was not the product of being situated nowhere; it was the product of certitude that existed *somewhere else*, namely, in contemporary literary theory. Hence, the level at which my indecision came into play was a function of particular beliefs I held. I was never in a position of epistemological indeterminacy, I was never *en abyme*. The idea that all accounts are perspectival seemed to me a superior standpoint from which to view all the versions of "what happened," and to regard with sympathetic condescension any person so old-fashioned and benighted as to believe that there really was some way of arriving at the truth. But this skeptical standpoint was just as firm as any other. The fact that it was also seriously disabling—it prevented me from coming to any conclusion about what I had read—did not render it any less definite.

At this point something is beginning to show itself that has up to now been hidden. The notion that all facts are only facts within a perspective has the effect of emptying statements of their content. Once I had Miller and Vaughan and Jennings, Martin and Hudson, Axtell and Heard, Rowlandson and Wood and Whitaker, and Kupperman; I had Europeans and Indians, ships and canoes, wigwams and log cabins, bows and arrows and muskets, wigs and tattoos, whiskey and corn, rivers and forts, treaties and battles, fire and blood—and then suddenly all I had was a metastatement about perspectives. The effect of bringing perspectivism to bear on history was to wipe out completely the subject matter of history. And it follows that bringing perspectivism to bear in this way on any subject matter would have a similar effect; everything is wiped out and you are left with nothing but a single idea—perspectivism itself.

But—and it is a crucial but—all this is true only if you believe that there is an alternative. As long as you think that there are or should be facts that exist outside of any perspective, then the notion that facts are perspectival will have this disappearing effect on whatever it touches. But if you are convinced that the alternative does not exist, that there really are no facts except as they are embedded in some particular way of seeing the world, then the argument that a set of facts derives from some particular worldview is no longer an argument against that set of facts. If all facts share this characteristic, to say that any one fact is perspectival doesn't change its factual nature in the slightest. It merely reiterates it.

This doesn't mean that you have to accept just anybody's facts. You can show that what someone else asserts to be a fact is false. But it does mean that you can't argue that someone else's facts are not facts *because they are only the product of a perspective,* since this will be true of the facts that you perceive as well. What this means then is that arguments about "what happened" have to proceed much as they did before poststructuralism broke in with all its talk about language-based reality and culturally produced knowledge. Reasons must be given, evidence adduced, authorities cited, analogies drawn. Being aware that all facts are motivated, believing that people are always operating inside some particular interpretive framework or other is a pertinent argument when what is under discussion is the way beliefs are grounded. But it doesn't give one any leverage on the facts of a particular case.[21]

45   What this means for the problem I've been addressing is that I must piece together the story of European-Indian relations as best I can, believing this version up to a point, that version not at all, another almost entirely, according to what seems reasonable and plausible, given everything else that I know. And this, as I've shown, is what I was already doing in the back of my mind without realizing it, because there was nothing else I *could* do. If the accounts don't fit together neatly, that is not a reason for rejecting them all in favor of a metadiscourse about epistemology; on the contrary, one encounters contradictory facts and divergent points of view in practically every phase of life, from deciding whom to marry to choosing the right brand of cat food, and one decides as best one can given the evidence available. It is only the nature of the academic situation which makes it appear that one can linger on the threshold of decision in the name of an epistemological principle. What has really happened in such a case is that the subject of debate has changed from the question of what happened in a particular instance to the question of how knowledge is arrived at. The absence of pressure to decide what happened creates the possibility for this change of venue.

The change of venue, however, is itself an action taken. In diverting attention from the original problem and placing it where Miller did, on "the mind of man," it once again ignores what happened and still is happening to American Indians. The moral problem that confronts me now is not that I can never have any facts to go on, but that the work I do is not directed toward solving the kinds of problems that studying the history of European-Indian relations has awakened me to.

NOTES

1. See Vine Deloria Jr., *God Is Red* (New York, 1973), pp. 39–56.

2. Perry Miller, *Errand into the Wilderness* (Cambridge, Mass., 1964), p. vii; all further references will be included in the text.

3. This passage from John Winthrop's *Journal* is excerpted by Perry Miller in his anthology *The American Puritans: Their Prose and Poetry* (Garden City, N.Y., 1956), p. 43.

In his headnote to the selections from the *Journal*, Miller speaks of Winthrop's "characteristic objectivity" (p. 37).

4. Alden T. Vaughan, *New England Frontier: Puritans and Indians, 1620–1675* (Boston, 1965), pp. vi–vii; all further references to this work, abbreviated NEF, will be included in the text.

5. John Higham, intro. to *New Directions in American Intellectual History,* ed. Higham and Paul K. Conkin (Baltimore, 1979), p. xii.

6. Higham, *New Directions in American Intellectual History*.

7. See Francis Jennings, *The Invasion of America: Indians, Colonialism, and the Cant of Conquest* (New York, 1975), pp. 3–31. Jennings writes: "The so-called settlement of America was a resettlement, reoccupation of a land made waste by the diseases and demoralization introduced by the newcomers. Although the source data pertaining to populations have never been compiled, one careful scholar, Henry F. Dobyns, has provided a relatively conservative and meticulously reasoned estimate conforming to the known effects of conquest catastrophe. Dobyns has calculated a total aboriginal population for the western hemisphere within the range of 90 to 112 million, of which 10 to 12 million lived north of the Rio Grande" (p. 30).

8. Jennings, fig. 7, p. 229; and see pp. 186–229.

9. James Axtell, *The European and the Indian: Essays in the Ethnohistory of Colonial North America* (Oxford, 1981), p. viii.

10. See Calvin Martin, *Keepers of the Game: Indian-Animal Relationships and the Fur Trade* (Berkeley and Los Angeles, 1978).

11. See the essay by Charles Hudson in *Indians, Animals, and the Fur Trade: A Critique of "Keepers of the Game,"* ed. Shepard Krech III (Athens, Ga., 1981), pp. 167–69.

12. See Axtell, "The White Indians of Colonial America" and "The Scholastic Philosophy of the Wilderness," *The European and the Indian*, pp. 168–206 and 131–67.

13. J. Norman Heard, *White into Red: A Study of the Assimilation of White Persons Captured by Indians* (Metuchen, N.J., 1973), p. 97.

14. See Heard, *White into Red*, p. 98.

15. Mary Rowlandson, "The Soveraignty and Goodness of God, Together with the Faithfulness of His Promises Displayed; Being a Narrative of the Captivity and Restauration of Mrs. Mary Rowlandson (1676)," in *Held Captive by Indians: Selected Narratives, 1642–1836,* ed. Richard VanDerBeets (Knoxville, Tenn., 1973), pp. 57–58.

16. William Wood, *New England's Prospect,* ed. Vaughan (Amherst, Mass., 1977), pp. 88–89.

17. Alexander Whitaker, *Goode Newes from Virginia* (1613), quoted in Robert F. Berkhofer Jr., *The White Man's Indian: Images of the American Indian from Columbus to the Present* (New York, 1978), p. 19.

18. See, for example, Berkhofer's discussion of the passages he quotes from Whitaker (*The White Man's Indian,* pp. 19, 20).

19. See Karen Ordahl Kupperman, *Settling with the Indians: The Meeting of English and Indian Cultures in America, 1580–1640* (Totowa, N.J., 1980), pp. 3, 4.

20. Kupperman, *Settling with the Indians,* p. 35.

21. The position I've been outlining is a version of neopragmatism. For an exposition, see *Against Theory: Literary Studies and the New Pragmatism,* ed. W. J. T. Mitchell (Chicago, 1985).

EXPLORATORY WRITING

Return to Tompkins's essay and notate each of the historians or first-person witnesses discussed in the long middle section. What interpretation of European–Indian relations in colonial New England does each offer? What differing assumptions does each make? It may help to create a chart that notes each historian or eyewitness and the interpretations and assumptions.

TALKING ABOUT THE READING

Think of an occasion or two when you encountered conflicting and irreconcilable interpretations of an event. The event could be one that you studied in a history class or one from personal experience. What differing perspectives and points of view produced the conflicting interpretations? How did you deal with these conflicting interpretations? Explain how Tompkins deals with conflicting interpretations in the final section of the essay. In what sense has she found the "way out" that she describes in the opening section? Compare her resolution of the issue with the way that you handled conflicting interpretations. What do you see as the main similarities and differences? How do you account for them?

WRITING ASSIGNMENTS

1. Write an essay that uses Jane Tompkins's account of her research as a model. Choose a research project that you did for a class in school—for example, a term paper, a report, or a history fair exhibit. Following Tompkins's style, explain the connections between the topic that you researched and your personal experience. Then take readers behind the scenes to explain how you did the research and how you dealt with any differing points of view or conflicting interpretations that you encountered. Use your account as a way to pose the problem of historical research and working with other people's accounts of the past.

2. Write a critical review of the historians' points of view and the interpretations that Tompkins presents in her essay. Provide an introduction that generally explains the problems and issues that the historians as a group are addressing. Assess the perspective that each historian brings to his or her research—what it helps you to see and what it obscures—and compare the strengths and weaknesses of the historians' various interpretations. As you review the historians' accounts, explain how you might piece them together and what view of Indian–settler relations in colonial New England ultimately emerges for you.

3. Consult American history textbooks that are used in high school and college and compare their treatment of European–Indian relations in seventeenth-century New England with the perspectives of the various historians in Tompkins's essay. (You can focus on just one textbook or extend your research to several texts.) What point of view and what assumptions seem to determine the treatment of Indians and Europeans in the textbook? How is this treatment similar to or different from the interpretations that you have read in Tompkins's essay? What perspectives seem to dominate? The textbook may well present this material as a factual account. If so, read between the lines to identify the perspective that the textbook author or authors bring to Indian–settler relations in colonial New England.

NECESSARY FICTIONS: WARREN NEIDICH'S EARLY AMERICAN COVER-UPS

▰▰—*Christopher Phillips*

Christopher Phillips is a photography critic who has published in *October, Art in America,* and elsewhere. "Necessary Fictions" introduces the Visual Essay that follows—Warren Neidich's "Contra Curtis: Early American Cover-Ups."

SUGGESTION FOR READING Edward Sheriff Curtis's images, as Christopher Phillips notes, are "elegiac" depictions of a "vanishing race" of American Indians, seemingly caught in a timeless, aboriginal past. As you read this selection and Neidich's photographic essay, keep in mind Phillips's comments on how images can enable people to forget as well as to remember.

STRATAGEMS FOR FORGETTING

1 "They from the beginning announced that they wanted to maintain their way of life. . . . And we set up these reservations so they could, and have a Bureau of Indian Affairs to help take care of them. . . . Maybe we made a mistake. Maybe we should not have humored them in wanting to stay in that kind of primitive lifestyle. Maybe we should have said, 'No, come join us.' . . . You'd be surprised. Some of them became very wealthy, because some of those reservations were overlaying great pools of oil. And so I don't know what their complaint might be." (Ronald Reagan, in response to a question at Moscow University about the condition of Native Americans, quoted in *Time,* June 13, 1988.)

A CHILDHOOD MEMORY

Only a few days after Reagan provided students in Moscow with this hallucinatory account of the winning of the West, an item in the *New York Times* (June 5, 1988) reported that the designer Oleg Cassini planned a vast "Navajo Nation" complex in Arizona to repackage for the tourist industry the history, art, and culture of that apparently willing tribe. This odd conjunction of events sent me back in thought to the several summers, long ago, when our family paid regular visits to the Appalachian resort town of Cherokee, North Carolina. We were usually accompanied by a friend of my parents . . . a woman whose interest in the trip sprang principally from the fact that one of her own friends, a New York dancer, migrated to Cherokee every summer to earn a few dollars performing in a popular "outdoor historical drama." Minus the feathers and war paint that went with his role as a leaping Cherokee warrior, Louis proved unremarkable, aside from a rasping Brooklyn accent and the purple sports car in which he raced around the mountain roads. I remember, though, being puzzled when I was taken backstage before one evening's performance, and discovered there an assortment of equally improbable characters donning their costumes and makeup.

Very interesting, I thought, but where were the real Indians?

The play itself proposed a relatively bland answer to that question. Situated in a past so hazy as to be utterly remote from the concerns of the present day, it unfolded in a series of melodramatic incidents the tale of the Cherokees' encounter with the homespun agents of Manifest Destiny, their expulsion from their mountain homeland, and their arduous trek to a new, ostensibly happier home on the plains of Oklahoma. Nevertheless another, more ominous possibility was planted in my already suspicious ten-year-old mind each time we passed a crowded burger drive-in situated in the heart of Cherokee. It announced its specialty in brazenly flashing red letters that I can still see: Squawburgers.

CONTRA CURTIS

It's from a similar unmarked crossroads of historical representation and popular memory that Warren Neidich's "Contra Curtis" photographs begin. Disinterred from the vast necropolis of American culture comprised of late-night TV's reruns of the pulp entertainment of earlier decades, Neidich's images are at once perfectly innocuous and painfully provoking. All-too-typical examples of the estimated 17,000 acts of mediated mayhem witnessed by all of us who have grown up in the television era, these achingly familiar specimens focus on moments of ritualized violence directed against "Indians." Of course we know that these aren't real Indians being burned, shot, knifed, or burst asunder, but actors, actresses, and stuntmen dressed up for the part. These figures serve as stand-ins or surrogates for a "historical actor" long pushed off the main stage of American life, but preserved in cultural memory in the long line of phantasmic Others against whom any violence is permitted.

5   It's the way that such phantasms weave in and out of our culture's interlocking networks of personal memory, popular memory, and archival memory that furnishes the real subject of much

of Neidich's work. But aside from this general predilection, "Contra Curtis" has a more specific target in mind. Neidich seems clearly to wish that these photographs be attached as permanently as a shadow to the famous body of work produced around the turn of the century by the celebrated photographer Edward Sheriff Curtis. Curtis's elegiac images of Native American tribes turned a benign paternal gaze upon the "picturesque" tribespeople whom he singled out, costumed, and directed for his camera. Printed (like Neidich's) on platinum paper, Curtis's photographs were circulated in lavish volumes and portfolios to such discerning patrons as J. P. Morgan and Teddy Roosevelt. Neidich, using images drawn from a later, less discreet cultural sector, suggests the bloody historical preliminaries that were genteelly elided in Curtis's nostalgic account of a "vanishing race." Indeed, like that flashing red sign in Cherokee, his images disclose, behind Curtis's veil of tasteful exoticism, an oblique vision of the return of the historically repressed.

COGITO INTERRUPTUS

Once the very embodiment of the qualities of objectivity, precision, and fidelity, the photographic image occupies an increasingly unstable place in the systems which today generate cultural memory. Certainly the photograph's partaking of the prestige of the indexical sign seemed until very recently to exempt it from the so-called referential illusion that had mired so many other sign-systems in the Slough of Undecidability. Only a decade ago reputable philosophers of history still argued that observing a Brady photograph of the Civil War was, for all practical purposes, equivalent to observing the historical scene itself.

But too often photographs convey a dangerously weak sense of the past . . . substituting a mute and fleeting commemoration for the more active, critical processes of remembering, interrogating, and understanding. Nearly three decades ago Alain Resnais in "Last Year at Marienbad" shared his suspicion that personal memory and photographic images might well lead in different, equally untrustworthy directions. By the 1980s, with the film "Blade Runner" (based on Philip K. Dick's novel) we find android "replicants" conspicuously outfitted with ersatz family snapshots, which provide them with pre-packaged "memories" of a human past that blocks their discovery of their real mechanical origin. This film's implicit allusion to the human condition . . . still camped in Plato's cave . . . is hardly inappropriate as we move into the age of the digitally edited, electronically generated photocomposite: an image indistinguishable from a "real" photograph, an image which renders superfluous the remaining distinctions between photographic fact and fiction.

THE PACIFICATION OF THE PAST

If the camera's images no longer compel unflinching conviction, they nonetheless retain their currency as the standard visual language of the spectacle. Where Warren Neidich's previous work evidenced a fascination with the possibility of fabricating ersatz historical photographs, "Contra Curtis" points not only to the structuring absences of the historical archive but to the historical residue that can be gleaned from spectacle itself. Taking a cue from Duchamp and Breton, these photographs could perhaps be considered "compensation documents," provisional stand-ins for images too often erased from the official picture of the American past.

In regard to the contending claims of the image and the historical sense, Guy Debord's recent "Commentaries on the Society of the Spectacle" affords considerable insight, if small consolation. Writing twenty years after he identified the "spectacle" as the succession of images that provides the contemporary world with its distorting mirror, Debord points out that during the past two decades the discrediting of the historical sense has been increasingly adopted as a tactic of power. He notes that such recently fashionable slogans as "the ruins of post-history" can only bring comfort to those who exercise power now, to all those who can avail themselves of the flagrant historical lie in assurance that no correction will be registered. The self-serving flight of fantasy cited at the head of this essay was dutifully reproduced in Time magazine, after all, without commentary or correction . . . sign of an extraordinary public prudence in regard to power, or confirmation of a jaded reluctance to bother to point to the chasm between fact and phantasmagoria.

CIRCUIT BREAKERS

10   To interrupt the precipitous succession of mutually canceling images that hurdle past us each day, to replace that rhythm, if only for a moment, with another . . . such is the recurrent dream of the art of the 1980s. If they were not disguised as art, Neidich's photographs might be described as attempts at visual sedition, or local campaigns of "critical disinformation." It remains to be determined, of course, whether they (or any other artwork today) can break out of that subcircuit of activity that Debord shrugs off as the "spectacular critique of the spectacle." For the moment, Neidich's photographs modestly propose that the recycled images of popular history available on every channel can be recycled yet again . . . this time to provide an ironic corrective to at least a few of the more transparent idiocies which today parade as public discourse.

VISUAL ESSAY   ## Contra Curtis: Early American Cover-Ups

— *Warren Neidich*

Warren Neidich is a photographer living in New York and Los Angeles; his photographs have been exhibited in and collected by museums in Europe and the United States. Neidich is known for his work on the media saturation surrounding the O. J. Simpson murder trial and on Calico, a restored silver mining town in Barstow, California. An ophthalmologist by training, Neidich is interested in cognitive science and sight. Presented here are selections from his photographic essay "Contra Curtis: Early American Cover-Ups" that appear in his book *American History Reinvented* (1989).

As the title "Contra Curtis" indicates, Neidich locates his work in relation to Edward Sheriff Curtis, the well-known photographer of American Indians in the early twentieth century. Neidich uses platinum prints, just as Curtis did, which give the images an antique glow that seems to assign them to a vanished past. At the same time, Neidich wants to make these images relevant to the present. You can find photographs from Curtis's twenty-volume *The North American Indian* at curtis.library.northwestern.edu.

Warren Neidich, "Contra Curtis: Early American Cover-Ups," Number 2

Warren Neidich, "Contra Curtis," Number 5

— Warren Neidich, "Contra Curtis," Number 9

— Warren Neidich, "Contra Curtis," Number 14

EXPLORATORY WRITING

Warren Neidich joins together two visual codes—the platinum prints Edward Sheriff Curtis used in his photographs and the conventions of the Hollywood western. How do these go together? What viewer responses do they provoke?

TALKING ABOUT THE VISUAL ESSAY

In a group with three or four other students, compare Neidich's photographs with those of Curtis. Do Curtis's photographs prompt historical amnesia, as Christopher Phillips suggests? In what sense are Neidich's photographs a critique of Curtis? What is Neidich asking the viewer to remember?

WRITING ASSIGNMENTS

1. Christopher Phillips says Neidich's photographs "might be described as an act of visual sedition." What does he mean? Write an essay that explains why and how Neidich's photographs are seditious.

2. Write your own introduction to Neidich's photographs. Explain his purposes and the means he has chosen to carry out these purposes.

3. Both Jane Tompkins and Warren Neidich are trying to develop new understandings of the "Indian" in American history. Write an essay that compares the strategies they use— Neidich's project to "reinvent" American history and Tompkins's efforts to come to terms with what eyewitnesses and historians have written. You want to explain what each is trying to do, but your essay should go beyond simply summarizing to consider the significance of the similarities and differences in their perspectives on American history. What do they bring to light about how we might understand the past?

MAKING CONNECTIONS

Two Speeches on Race and Racism in the United States

Issues of race and racism are deeply embedded in American history—in a legacy of slavery and Jim Crow, the massacre and relocation of Native Americans, the Mexican-American War of 1846, anti-Chinese legislation, and the internment of Japanese Americans during World War II. The fact that racism remains an unresolved question in American memories of the past may be seen in the two speeches we include here: Frederick Douglass's "What to the Slave Is the Fourth of July?" delivered in 1852, and Barack Obama's "A More Perfect Union," from the presidential primary campaign of 2008. Both speeches rely on a reading of American history to put the matter of race and racism in context, using the the past to shape a politics of the present.

RHETORICAL STANCE

In the following assignments, you will be asked to examine and compare the rhetorical stance of Douglass and Obama. Rhetorical stance means, in the most general sense, how a speaker or writer responds to a rhetorical situation, the sense of exigence or urgency he or she experiences. A speaker's or writer's rhetorical stance can be analyzed as the coordination of three distinct but overlapping appeals to their readers, drawing on terms from classical rhetoric:

■ **Ethos**. *Ethos* refers to the way a speaker or writer projects his or her character, to establish credibility, authority, good will, and so on. Ethos has to do with the presentation of self.

■ **Pathos**. *Pathos* refers to the emotions and responses a speech or piece of writing arouses. It offers a way to analyze what the speaker or writer anticipates as their audience's state of mind and what listeners or readers have invested in the topic at hand.

■ **Logos**. *Logos* refers to what is said or written, the speaker's or writer's message and the line of reasoning it follows.

WHAT TO THE SLAVE IS THE FOURTH OF JULY?

■■— *Frederick Douglass*

Frederick Douglass (1817–1895) was born a slave and, following his escape from bondage in 1838, became a prominent abolitionist, orator, writer, and newspaper publisher. At the time of his death, Douglass was considered the most important African American leader in the U.S. *The Narrative of the Life of Frederick Douglass* (the first of three autobiographies) appeared in 1845 and played an important role in publicizing the abolitionist crusade against slavery. In 1852, the Ladies Anti-Slavery Society in Rochester, New York asked Douglass to give a Fourth of July address. The Fugitive Slave Law that Douglass condemns in his oration had been passed two years earlier, denying the right of habeas corpus and trial by jury to those accused of being fugitive slaves, threatening the kidnapping of free blacks, and requiring the cooperation of state and local officials in the return of runaway slaves to their masters—all of which were highly unpopular in parts of the North, where they were seen as an unprincipled collaboration with the slaveholders brought about by the 1850 Missouri Compromise. Against this backdrop of rising sectional tensions, Douglass delivered what is widely considered one of the greatest speeches in American history.

SUGGESTION FOR READING Pay attention to how Douglass arranges the parts of his speech. We have marked the three main sections. Notice how Douglass treats the celebration of national independence in the opening section, then shifts from past to present to catalog the evils of slavery in the middle section, and finally returns to the Declaration of Independence in the closing section.

1 *[Section One: Douglass establishes the occasion of his speech, praises the Founding Fathers, and gives honor to the celebration of national independence.]*

Mr. President, Friends and Fellow Citizens: He who could address this audience without a quailing sensation, has stronger nerves than I have. I do not remember ever to have appeared as a speaker before any assembly more shrinkingly, nor with greater distrust of my ability, than I do this day. A feeling has crept over me, quite unfavorable to the exercise of my limited powers of speech. The task before me is one which requires much previous thought and study for its proper performance. I know that apologies of this sort are generally considered flat and unmeaning. I trust, however, that mine will not be so considered. Should I seem at ease, my appearance would much misrepresent me. The little experience I have had in addressing public meetings, in country schoolhouses, avails me nothing on the present occasion.

The papers and placards say, that I am to deliver a 4th [of] July oration. This certainly sounds large, and out of the common way, for it is true that I have often had the privilege to speak in this beautiful Hall, and to address many who now honor me with their presence. But neither their familiar faces, nor the perfect gage I think I have of Corinthian Hall, seems to free me from embarrassment.

The fact is, ladies and gentlemen, the distance between this platform and the slave plantation, from which I escaped, is considerable—and the difficulties to be overcome in getting from the latter to the former, are by no means slight. That I am here to-day is, to me, a matter of astonishment as well as of gratitude. You will not, therefore, be surprised, if in what I have to say. I evince no elaborate preparation, nor grace my speech with any high sounding exordium. With little experience and with less learning, I have been able to throw my thoughts hastily and imperfectly together; and trusting to your patient and generous indulgence, I will proceed to lay them before you.

5 This, for the purpose of this celebration, is the 4th of July. It is the birthday of your National Independence, and of your political freedom. This, to you, is what the Passover was to the emancipated people of God. It carries your minds back to the day, and to the act of your great deliverance; and to the signs, and to the wonders, associated with that act, and that day. This celebration also marks the beginning of another year of your national life; and reminds you that the Republic of America is now 76 years old. I am glad, fellow-citizens, that your nation is so young. Seventy-six years, though a good old age for a man, is but a mere speck in the life of a nation. Three score years and ten is the allotted time for individual men; but nations number their years by thousands. According to this fact, you are, even now, only in the beginning of your national career, still lingering in the period of childhood. I repeat, I am glad this is so. There is hope in the thought, and hope is much needed, under the dark clouds which lower above the horizon. The eye of the reformer is met with angry flashes, portending disastrous times; but his heart may well beat lighter at the thought that America is young, and that she is still in the impressible stage of her existence. May he not hope that high lessons of wisdom, of justice and of truth, will yet give direction to her destiny? Were the nation older, the patriot's heart might be sadder, and the reformer's brow heavier. Its future might be shrouded in gloom, and the hope of its prophets go out in sorrow. There is consolation in the thought that America is young. Great streams are not easily turned from channels, worn deep in the course of ages. They may sometimes rise in quiet and stately majesty, and inundate the land, refreshing and fertilizing the earth with their mysterious properties. They may also rise in wrath and fury, and bear away, on their angry waves, the accumulated wealth of years of toil and hardship. They, however, gradually flow back to the same old channel, and flow on as serenely as ever. But, while the river may not be turned aside, it may dry up, and

leave nothing behind but the withered branch, and the unsightly rock, to howl in the abyss-sweeping wind, the sad tale of departed glory. As with rivers so with nations.

Fellow-citizens, I shall not presume to dwell at length on the associations that cluster about this day. The simple story of it is that, 76 years ago, the people of this country were British subjects. The style and title of your "sovereign people" (in which you now glory) was not then born. You were under the British Crown. Your fathers esteemed the English Government as the home government; and England as the fatherland. This home government, you know, although a considerable distance from your home, did, in the exercise of its parental prerogatives, impose upon its colonial children, such restraints, burdens and limitations, as, in its mature judgment, it deemed wise, right and proper.

But, your fathers, who had not adopted the fashionable idea of this day, of the infallibility of government, and the absolute character of its acts, presumed to differ from the home government in respect to the wisdom and the justice of some of those burdens and restraints. They went so far in their excitement as to pronounce the measures of government unjust, unreasonable, and oppressive, and altogether such as ought not to be quietly submitted to. I scarcely need say, fellow-citizens, that my opinion of those measures fully accords with that of your fathers. Such a declaration of agreement on my part would not be worth much to anybody. It would, certainly, prove nothing, as to what part I might have taken, had I lived during the great controversy of 1776. To say now that America was right, and England wrong, is exceedingly easy. Everybody can say it; the dastard, not less than the noble brave, can flippantly discant on the tyranny of England towards the American Colonies. It is fashionable to do so; but there was a time when to pronounce against England, and in favor of the cause of the colonies, tried men's souls. They who did so were accounted in their day, plotters of mischief, agitators and rebels, dangerous men.

To side with the right, against the wrong, with the weak against the strong, and with the oppressed against the oppressor! here lies the merit, and the one which, of all others, seems unfashionable in our day. The cause of liberty may be stabbed by the men who glory in the deeds of your fathers. But, to proceed.

Feeling themselves harshly and unjustly treated by the home government, your fathers, like men of honesty, and men of spirit, earnestly sought redress. They petitioned and remonstrated; they did so in a decorous, respectful, and loyal manner. Their conduct was wholly unexceptionable. This, however, did not answer the purpose. They saw themselves treated with sovereign indifference, coldness and scorn. Yet they persevered. They were not the men to look back.

As the sheet anchor takes a firmer hold, when the ship is tossed by the storm, so did the cause of your fathers grow stronger, as it breasted the chilling blasts of kingly displeasure. The greatest and best of British statesmen admitted its justice, and the loftiest eloquence of the British Senate came to its support. But, with that blindness which seems to be the unvarying characteristic of tyrants, since Pharaoh and his hosts were drowned in the Red Sea, the British Government persisted in the exactions complained of.

10   The madness of this course, we believe, is admitted now, even by England; but we fear the lesson is wholly lost on our present ruler.

Oppression makes a wise man mad. Your fathers were wise men, and if they did not go mad, they became restive under this treatment. They felt themselves the victims of grievous wrongs, wholly incurable in their colonial capacity. With brave men there is always a remedy for oppression. Just here, the idea of a total separation of the colonies from the crown was born! It was a startling idea, much more so, than we, at this distance of time, regard it. The timid and the prudent (as has been intimated) of that day, were, of course, shocked and alarmed by it.

Such people lived then, had lived before, and will, probably, ever have a place on this planet; and their course, in respect to any great change, (no matter how great the good to be attained, or the wrong to be redressed by it), may be calculated with as much precision as can be the course of the stars. They hate all changes, but silver, gold and copper change! Of this sort of change they are always strongly in favor.

These people were called Tories in the days of your fathers; and the appellation, probably, conveyed the same idea that is meant by a more modern, though a somewhat less euphonious term, which we often find in our papers, applied to some of our old politicians.

Their opposition to the then dangerous thought was earnest and powerful; but, amid all their terror and affrighted vociferations against it, the alarming and revolutionary idea moved on, and the country with it.

15   On the 2d of July, 1776, the old Continental Congress, to the dismay of the lovers of ease, and the worshipers of property, clothed that dreadful idea with all the authority of national sanction. They did so in the form of a resolution; and as we seldom hit upon resolutions, drawn up in our day whose transparency is at all equal to this, it may refresh your minds and help my story if I read it. "Resolved, That these united colonies are, and of right, ought to be free and Independent States; that they are absolved from all allegiance to the British Crown; and that all political connection between them and the State of Great Britain is, and ought to be, dissolved."

Citizens, your fathers made good that resolution. They succeeded; and to-day you reap the fruits of their success. The freedom gained is yours; and you, therefore, may properly celebrate this anniversary. The 4th of July is the first great fact in your nation's history—the very ring-bolt in the chain of your yet undeveloped destiny.

Pride and patriotism, not less than gratitude, prompt you to celebrate and to hold it in perpetual remembrance. I have said that the Declaration of Independence is the ring-bolt to the chain of your nation's destiny; so, indeed, I regard it. The principles contained in that instrument are saving principles. Stand by those principles, be true to them on all occasions, in all places, against all foes, and at whatever cost.

From the round top of your ship of state, dark and threatening clouds may be seen. Heavy billows, like mountains in the distance, disclose to the leeward huge forms of flinty rocks! That bolt drawn, that chain broken, and all is lost. Cling to this day—cling to it, and to its principles, with the grasp of a storm-tossed mariner to a spar at midnight.

The coming into being of a nation, in any circumstances, is an interesting event. But, besides general considerations, there were peculiar circumstances which make the advent of this republic an event of special attractiveness.

20   The whole scene, as I look back to it, was simple, dignified and sublime.

The population of the country, at the time, stood at the insignificant number of three millions. The country was poor in the munitions of war. The population was weak and scattered, and the country a wilderness unsubdued. There were then no means of concert and combination, such as exist now. Neither steam nor lightning had then been reduced to order and discipline. From the Potomac to the Delaware was a journey of many days. Under these, and innumerable other disadvantages, your fathers declared for liberty and independence and triumphed.

Fellow Citizens, I am not wanting in respect for the fathers of this republic. The signers of the Declaration of Independence were brave men. They were great men too—great enough to give fame to a great age. It does not often happen to a nation to raise, at one time, such a number of truly great men. The point from which I am compelled to view them is not, certainly, the most favorable; and yet I cannot contemplate their great deeds with less than admiration. They were statesmen, patriots and heroes, and for the good they did, and the principles they contended for, I will unite with you to honor their memory.

They loved their country better than their own private interests; and, though this is not the highest form of human excellence, all will concede that it is a rare virtue, and that when it is exhibited, it ought to command respect. He who will, intelligently, lay down his life for his country, is a man whom it is not in human nature to despise. Your fathers staked their lives, their fortunes, and their sacred honor, on the cause of their country. In their admiration of liberty, they lost sight of all other interests.

They were peace men; but they preferred revolution to peaceful submission to bondage. They were quiet men; but they did not shrink from agitating against oppression. They showed forbearance; but that they knew its limits. They believed in order; but not in the order of tyranny. With them, nothing was "settled" that was not right. With them, justice, liberty and humanity were "final;" not slavery and oppression. You may well cherish the memory of such men. They were great in their day and generation. Their solid manhood stands out the more as we contrast it with these degenerate times.

25   How circumspect, exact and proportionate were all their movements! How unlike the politicians of an hour! Their statesmanship looked beyond the passing moment, and stretched away in strength into the distant future. They seized upon eternal principles, and set a glorious example in their defense. Mark them!

Fully appreciating the hardship to be encountered, firmly believing in the right of their cause, honorably inviting the scrutiny of an on-looking world, reverently appealing to heaven to attest their sincerity, soundly comprehending the solemn responsibility they were about to assume, wisely measuring the terrible odds against them, your fathers, the fathers of this republic, did, most deliberately, under the inspiration of a glorious patriotism, and with a sublime faith in the great principles of justice and freedom, lay deep the corner-stone of the national superstructure, which has risen and still rises in grandeur around you.

Of this fundamental work, this day is the anniversary. Our eyes are met with demonstra-

tions of joyous enthusiasm. Banners and pennants wave exultingly on the breeze. The din of business, too, is hushed. Even Mammon seems to have quitted his grasp on this day. The ear-piercing fife and the stirring drum unite their accents with the ascending peal of a thousand church bells. Prayers are made, hymns are sung, and sermons are preached in honor of this day; while the quick martial tramp of a great and multitudinous nation, echoed back by all the hills, valleys and mountains of a vast continent, bespeak the occasion one of thrilling and universal interests nation's jubilee.

Friends and citizens, I need not enter further into the causes which led to this anniversary. Many of you understand them better than I do. You could instruct me in regard to them. That is a branch of knowledge in which you feel, perhaps, a much deeper interest than your speaker. The causes which led to the separation of the colonies from the British crown have never lacked for a tongue. They have all been taught in your common schools, narrated at your firesides, unfolded from your pulpits, and thundered from your legislative halls, and are as familiar to you as household words. They form the staple of your national poetry and eloquence.

I remember, also, that, as a people, Americans are remarkably familiar with all facts which make in their own favor. This is esteemed by some as a national trait—perhaps a national weakness. It is a fact, that whatever makes for the wealth or for the reputation of Americans, and can be had cheap! will be found by Americans. I shall not be charged with slandering Americans, if I say I think the American side of any question may be safely left in American hands.

30   I leave, therefore, the great deeds of your fathers to other gentlemen whose claim to have been regularly descended will be less likely to be disputed than mine!

[Section Two: Douglass shifts to the present and, in a dramatic reversal, dissociates himself— and all African Americans—from the Fourth of July. Then he catalogs the evils of slavery and the

Fugitive Slave Law, and denounces the hypocrisy of churches in the United States and their failure to fight against slavery.]

My business, if I have any here to-day, is with the present. The accepted time with God and his cause is the ever-living now.

"Trust no future, however pleasant,
Let the dead past bury its dead;
Act, act in the living present,
Heart within, and God overhead."

We have to do with the past only as we can make it useful to the present and to the future. To all inspiring motives, to noble deeds which can be gained from the past, we are welcome. But now is the time, the important time. Your fathers have lived, died, and have done their work, and have done much of it well. You live and must die, and you must do your work. You have no right to enjoy a child's share in the labor of your fathers, unless your children are to be blest by your labors. You have no right to wear out and waste the hard-earned fame of your fathers to cover your indolence. Sydney Smith tells us that men seldom eulogize the wisdom and virtues of their fathers, but to excuse some folly or wickedness of their own. This truth is not a doubtful one. There are illustrations of it near and remote, ancient and modern. It was fashionable, hundreds of years ago, for the children of Jacob to boast, we have "Abraham to our father," when they had long lost Abraham's faith and spirit. That people contented themselves under the shadow of Abraham's great name, while they repudiated the deeds which made his name great. Need I remind you that a similar thing is being done all over this country to-day? Need I tell you that the Jews are not the only people who built the tombs of the prophets, and garnished the sepulchres of the righteous? Washington could not die till he had broken the chains of his slaves. Yet his monument is built up by the price of human blood, and the traders in the bodies and souls of men, shout—"We have Washington to our father." Alas! that it should be so; yet so it is.

"The evil that men do, lives after them,
The good is oft' interred with their bones."

Fellow-citizens, pardon me, allow me to ask, why am I called upon to speak here to-day? What have I, or those I represent, to do with your national independence? Are the great principles of political freedom and of natural justice, embodied in that Declaration of Independence, extended to us? and am I, therefore, called upon to bring our humble offering to the national altar, and to confess the benefits and express devout gratitude for the blessings resulting from your independence to us?

35 Would to God, both for your sakes and ours, that an affirmative answer could be truthfully returned to these questions! Then would my task be light, and my burden easy and delightful. For who is there so cold, that a nation's sympathy could not warm him? Who so obdurate and dead to the claims of gratitude, that would not thankfully acknowledge such priceless benefits? Who so stolid and selfish, that would not give his voice to swell the hallelujahs of a nation's jubilee, when the chains of servitude had been torn from his limbs? I am not that man. In a case like that, the dumb might eloquently speak, and the "lame man leap as an hart."

But, such is not the state of the case. I say it with a sad sense of the disparity between us. I am not included within the pale of this glorious anniversary! Your high independence only reveals the immeasurable distance between us. The blessings in which you, this day, rejoice, are not enjoyed in common. The rich inheritance of justice, liberty, prosperity and independence, bequeathed by your fathers, is shared by you, not by me. The sunlight that brought life and healing to you, has brought stripes and death to me. This Fourth [of] July is yours, not mine. You may rejoice, I must mourn. To drag a man in fetters into the grand illuminated temple of liberty, and call upon him to join you in joyous anthems, were inhuman mockery and sacrilegious irony. Do you mean, citizens, to mock me, by asking me to speak to-day? If so, there is a parallel to your conduct. And let me warn you that it is dangerous to copy the example of a nation whose crimes, lowering up to heaven, were thrown down by the breath of the Almighty, burying that nation in irrecoverable ruin! I can to-day take up the plaintive lament of a peeled and woe-smitten people!

"By the rivers of Babylon, there we sat down. Yea! we wept when we remembered Zion. We hanged our harps upon the willows in the midst thereof. For there, they that carried us away captive, required of us a song; and they who wasted us required of us mirth, saying, Sing us one of the songs of Zion. How can we sing the Lord's song in a strange land? If I forget thee, O Jerusalem, let my right hand forget her cunning. If I do not remember thee, let my tongue cleave to the roof of my mouth."

Fellow-citizens; above your national, tumultuous joy, I hear the mournful wail of millions! whose chains, heavy and grievous yesterday, are, to-day, rendered more intolerable by the jubilee shouts that reach them. If I do forget, if I do not faithfully remember those bleeding children of sorrow this day, "may my right hand forget her cunning, and may my tongue cleave to the roof of my mouth!" To forget them, to pass lightly over their wrongs, and to chime in with the popular theme, would be treason most scandalous and shocking, and would make me a reproach before God and the world. My subject, then fellow-citizens, is AMERICAN SLAVERY. I shall see, this day, and its popular characteristics, from the slave's point of view. Standing, there, identified with the American bondman, making his wrongs mine, I do not hesitate to declare, with all my soul, that the character and conduct of this nation never looked blacker to me than on this 4th of July! Whether we turn to the declarations of the past, or to the professions of the present, the conduct of the nation seems equally hideous and revolting. America is false to the past, false to the present, and solemnly binds herself to be false to the future. Standing with God and the

crushed and bleeding slave on this occasion, I will, in the name of humanity which is outraged, in the name of liberty which is fettered, in the name of the constitution and the Bible, which are disregarded and trampled upon, dare to call in question and to denounce, with all the emphasis I can command, everything that serves to perpetuate slavery—the great sin and shame of America! "I will not equivocate; I will not excuse;" I will use the severest language I can command; and yet not one word shall escape me that any man, whose judgment is not blinded by prejudice, or who is not at heart a slaveholder, shall not confess to be right and just.

But I fancy I hear some one of my audience say, it is just in this circumstance that you and your brother abolitionists fail to make a favorable impression on the public mind. Would you argue more, and denounce less, would you persuade more, and rebuke less, your cause would be much more likely to succeed. But, I submit, where all is plain there is nothing to be argued. What point in the anti-slavery creed would you have me argue? On what branch of the subject do the people of this country need light? Must I undertake to prove that the slave is a man? That point is conceded already. Nobody doubts it. The slaveholders themselves acknowledge it in the enactment of laws for their government. They acknowledge it when they punish disobedience on the part of the slave. There are seventy-two crimes in the State of Virginia, which, if committed by a black man, (no matter how ignorant he be), subject him to the punishment of death; while only two of the same crimes will subject a white man to the like punishment. What is this but the acknowledgement that the slave is a moral, intellectual and responsible being? The manhood of the slave is conceded. It is admitted in the fact that Southern statute books are covered with enactments forbidding, under severe fines and penalties, the teaching of the slave to read or to write. When you can point to any such laws, in reference to the beasts of the field, then I may consent to argue the manhood of the slave.

When the dogs in your streets, when the fowls of the air, when the cattle on your hills, when the fish of the sea, and the reptiles that crawl, shall be unable to distinguish the slave from a brute, their will I argue with you that the slave is a man!

40   For the present, it is enough to affirm the equal manhood of the Negro race. Is it not astonishing that, while we are ploughing, planting and reaping, using all kinds of mechanical tools, erecting houses, constructing bridges, building ships, working in metals of brass, iron, copper, silver and gold; that, while we are reading, writing and cyphering, acting as clerks, merchants and secretaries, having among us lawyers, doctors, ministers, poets, authors, editors, orators and teachers; that, while we are engaged in all manner of enterprises common to other men, digging gold in California, capturing the whale in the Pacific, feeding sheep and cattle on the hill-side, living, moving, acting, thinking, planning, living in families as husbands, wives and children, and, above all, confessing and worshipping the Christian's God, and looking hopefully for life and immortality beyond the grave, we are called upon to prove that we are men!

Would you have me argue that man is entitled to liberty? that he is the rightful owner of his own body? You have already declared it. Must I argue the wrongfulness of slavery? Is that a question for Republicans? Is it to be settled by the rules of logic and argumentation, as a matter beset with great difficulty, involving a doubtful application of the principle of justice, hard to be understood? How should I look to-day, in the presence of Americans, dividing, and subdividing a discourse, to show that men have a natural right to freedom? speaking of it relatively, and positively, negatively, and affirmatively. To do so, would be to make myself ridiculous, and to offer an insult to your understanding. There is not a man beneath the canopy of heaven, that does not know that slavery is wrong for him.

What, am I to argue that it is wrong to make men brutes, to rob them of their liberty, to work them without wages, to keep them ignorant of their relations to their fellow men, to beat them with sticks, to flay their flesh with the lash, to load their limbs with irons, to hunt them with dogs, to sell them at auction, to sunder their families, to knock out their teeth, to bum their flesh, to starve them into obedience and submission to their masters? Must I argue that a system thus marked with blood, and stained with pollution, is wrong? No! I will not. I have better employments for my time and strength than such arguments would imply.

What, then, remains to be argued? Is it that slavery is not divine; that God did not establish it; that our doctors of divinity are mistaken? There is blasphemy in the thought. That which is inhuman, cannot be divine! Who can reason on such a proposition? They that can, may; I cannot. The time for such argument is past.

At a time like this, scorching irony, not convincing argument, is needed. O! had I the ability, and could I reach the nation's ear, I would, to-day, pour out a fiery stream of biting ridicule, blasting reproach, withering sarcasm, and stern rebuke. For it is not light that is needed, but fire; it is not the gentle shower, but thunder. We need the storm, the whirlwind, and the earthquake. The feeling of the nation must be quickened; the conscience of the nation must be roused; the propriety of the nation must be startled; the hypocrisy of the nation must be exposed; and its crimes against God and man must be proclaimed and denounced.

45   What, to the American slave, is your 4th of July? I answer: a day that reveals to him, more than all other days in the year, the gross injustice and cruelly to which he is the constant victim. To him, your celebration is a sham; your boasted liberty, an unholy license; your national greatness, swelling vanity; your sounds of rejoicing are empty and heartless; your denunciations of tyrants, brass fronted impudence; your shouts of liberty and equality, hollow mockery; your prayers and hymns, your sermons and thanksgivings, with all your religious parade, and solemnity, are, to him, mere bombast, fraud,

deception, impiety, and hypocrisy—a thin veil to cover up crimes which would disgrace a nation of savages. There is not a nation on the earth guilty of practices, more shocking and bloody, than are the people of these United States, at this very hour.

Go where you may, search where you will, roam through all the monarchies and despotisms of the old world, travel through South America, search out every abuse, and when you have found the last, lay your facts by the side of the everyday practices of this nation, and you will say with me, that, for revolting barbarity and shameless hypocrisy, America reigns without a rival.

Take the American slave-trade, which, we are told by the papers, is especially prosperous just now. Ex-Senator Benton tells us that the price of men was never higher than now. He mentions the fact to show that slavery is in no danger. This trade is one of the peculiarities of American institutions. It is carried on in all the large towns and cities in one-half of this confederacy; and millions are pocketed every year, by dealers in this horrid traffic. In several states, this trade is a chief source of wealth. It is called (in contradistinction to the foreign slave-trade) "the internal slave trade." It is, probably, called so, too, in order to divert from it the horror with which the foreign slave-trade is contemplated. That trade has long since been denounced by this government, as piracy. It has been denounced with burning words, from the high places of the nation, as an execrable traffic. To arrest it, to put an end to it, this nation keeps a squadron, at immense cost, on the coast of Africa. Everywhere, in this country, it is safe to speak of this foreign slave-trade, as a most inhuman traffic, opposed alike to the laws of God and of man. The duty to extirpate and destroy it, is admitted even by our DOCTORS OF DIVINITY. In order to put an end to it, some of these last have consented that their colored brethren (nominally free) should leave this country, and establish themselves on the western coast of Africa! It is, however, a notable fact that, while so much execration is poured out by Americans upon those engaged in the foreign slave-trade, the men engaged in the slave-trade between the states pass without condemnation, and their business is deemed honorable.

Behold the practical operation of this internal slave-trade, the American slave-trade, sustained by American politics and America religion. Here you will see men and women reared like swine for the market. You know what is a swine-drover? I will show you a man-drover. They inhabit all our Southern States. They perambulate the country, and crowd the highways of the nation, with droves of human stock. You will see one of these human flesh-jobbers, armed with pistol, whip and bowie-knife, driving a company of a hundred men, women, and children, from the Potomac to the slave market at New Orleans. These wretched people are to be sold singly, or in lots, to suit purchasers. They are food for the cotton-field, and the deadly sugar-mill. Mark the sad procession, as it moves wearily along, and the inhuman wretch who drives them. Hear his savage yells and his blood-chilling oaths, as he hurries on his affrighted captives! There, see the old man, with locks thinned and gray. Cast one glance, if you please, upon that young mother, whose shoulders are bare to the scorching sun, her briny tears falling on the brow of the babe in her arms. See, too, that girl of thirteen, weeping, yes! weeping, as she thinks of the mother from whom she has been torn! The drove moves tardily. Heat and sorrow have nearly consumed their strength; suddenly you hear a quick snap, like the discharge of a rifle; the fetters clank, and the chain rattles simultaneously; your ears are saluted with a scream, that seems to have torn its way to the center of your soul! The crack you heard, was the sound of the slave-whip; the scream you heard, was from the woman you saw with the babe. Her speed had faltered under the weight of her child and her chains! that gash on her shoulder tells her to move on. Follow the drove to

New Orleans. Attend the auction; see men examined like horses; see the forms of women rudely and brutally exposed to the shocking gaze of American slave-buyers. See this drove sold and separated forever; and never forget the deep, sad sobs that arose from that scattered multitude. Tell me citizens, WHERE, under the sun, you can witness a spectacle more fiendish and shocking. Yet this is but a glance at the American slave-trade, as it exists, at this moment, in the ruling part of the United States.

I was born amid such sights and scenes. To me the American slave-trade is a terrible reality. When a child, my soul was often pierced with a sense of its horrors. I lived on Philpot Street, Fell's Point, Baltimore, and have watched from the wharves, the slave ships in the Basin, anchored from the shore, with their cargoes of human flesh, waiting for favorable winds to waft them down the Chesapeake. There was, at that time, a grand slave mart kept at the head of Pratt Street, by Austin Woldfolk. His agents were sent into every town and county in Maryland, announcing their arrival, through the papers, and on flaming "hand-bills," headed CASH FOR NEGROES. These men were generally well dressed men, and very captivating in their manners. Ever ready to drink, to treat, and to gamble. The fate of many a slave has depended upon the turn of a single card; and many a child has been snatched from the arms of its mother by bargains arranged in a state of brutal drunkenness.

50 The flesh-mongers gather up their victims by dozens, and drive them, chained, to the general depot at Baltimore. When a sufficient number have been collected here, a ship is chartered, for the purpose of conveying the forlorn crew to Mobile, or to New Orleans. From the slave prison to the ship, they are usually driven in the darkness of night; for since the antislavery agitation, a certain caution is observed.

In the deep still darkness of midnight, I have been often aroused by the dead heavy footsteps, and the piteous cries of the chained gangs that passed our door. The anguish of my boyish heart was intense; and I was often consoled, when speaking to my mistress in the morning, to hear her say that the custom was very wicked; that she hated to hear the rattle of the chains, and the heart-rending cries. I was glad to find one who sympathized with me in my horror.

Fellow-citizens, this murderous traffic is, to-day, in active operation in this boasted republic. In the solitude of my spirit, I see clouds of dust raised on the highways of the South; I see the bleeding footsteps; I hear the doleful wail of fettered humanity, on the way to the slave-markets, where the victims are to be sold like horses, sheep, and swine, knocked off to the highest bidder. There I see the tenderest ties ruthlessly broken, to gratify the lust, caprice and rapacity of the buyers and sellers of men. My soul sickens at the sight.

"Is this the land your Fathers loved,
The freedom which they toiled to win?
Is this the earth whereon they moved?
Are these the graves they slumber in?"

But a still more inhuman, disgraceful, and scandalous state of things remains to be presented.

By an act of the American Congress, not yet two years old, slavery has been nationalized in its most horrible and revolting form. By that act, Mason & Dixon's line has been obliterated; New York has become as Virginia; and the power to hold, hunt, and sell men, women, and children as slaves remains no longer a mere state institution, but is now an institution of the whole United States. The power is co-extensive with the Star-Spangled Banner and American Christianity. Where these go, may also go the merciless slave-hunter. Where these are, man is not sacred. He is a bird for the sportsman's gun. By that most foul and fiendish of all human decrees, the liberty and person of every man are put in peril. Your broad republican domain is hunting ground for men. Not for thieves and robbers, enemies of society, merely, but for men guilty of no crime. Your lawmakers have commanded all good citizens to engage in this hellish sport. Your President, your Secretary of State, your lords, nobles, and ecclesiastics, enforce, as a duty you owe to your free and glorious country, and to your God, that you do this accursed thing. Not fewer than forty Americans have, within the past two years, been hunted down and, without a moment's warning, hurried away in chains, and consigned to slavery and excruciating torture. Some of these have had wives and children, dependent on them for bread; but of this, no account was made. The right of the hunter to his prey stands superior to the right of marriage, and to all rights in this republic, the rights of God included! For black men there are neither law, justice, humanity, not religion. The Fugitive Slave Law makes MERCY TO THEM, A CRIME; and bribes the judge who tries them. An American JUDGE GETS TEN DOLLARS FOR EVERY VICTIM HE CONSIGNS to slavery, and five, when he fails to do so. The oath of any two villains is sufficient, under this hell-black enactment, to send the most pious and exemplary black man into the remorseless jaws of slavery! His own testimony is nothing. He can bring no witnesses for himself. The minister of American justice is bound by the law to hear but one side; and that side, is the side of the oppressor. Let this damning fact be perpetually told. Let it be thundered around the world, that, in tyrant-killing, king-hating, people-loving, democratic, Christian America, the seats of justice are filled with judges, who hold their offices under an open and palpable bribe, and are bound, in deciding in the case of a man's liberty, hear only his accusers!

55   In glaring violation of justice, in shameless disregard of the forms of administering law, in cunning arrangement to entrap the defenseless, and in diabolical intent, this Fugitive Slave Law stands alone in the annals of tyrannical legislation. I doubt if there be another nation on the globe, having the brass and the baseness to put such a law on the statute-book. If any man in this assembly thinks differently from me in this matter, and feels able to disprove my statements,

I will gladly confront him at any suitable time and place he may select.

I take this law to be one of the grossest infringements of Christian Liberty, and, if the churches and ministers of our country were not stupidly blind, or most wickedly indifferent, they, too, would so regard it.

At the very moment that they are thanking God for the enjoyment of civil and religious liberty, and for the right to worship God according to the dictates of their own consciences, they are utterly silent in respect to a law which robs religion of its chief significance, and makes it utterly worthless to a world lying in wickedness. Did this law concern the "mint, anise and cummin"— abridge the fight to sing psalms, to partake of the sacrament, or to engage in any of the ceremonies of religion, it would be smitten by the thunder of a thousand pulpits. A general shout would go up from the church, demanding repeal, repeal, instant repeal! And it would go hard with that politician who presumed to solicit the votes of the people without inscribing this motto on his banner. Further, if this demand were not complied with, another Scotland would be added to the history of religious liberty, and the stern old Covenanters would be thrown into the shade. A John Knox would be seen at every church door, and heard from every pulpit, and Fillmore would have no more quarter than was shown by Knox, to the beautiful, but treacherous queen Mary of Scotland. The fact that the church of our country, (with fractional exceptions), does not esteem "the Fugitive Slave Law" as a declaration of war against religious liberty, implies that that church regards religion simply as a form of worship, an empty ceremony, and not a vital principle, requiring active benevolence, justice, love and good will towards man. It esteems sacrifice above mercy; psalm-singing above right doing; solemn meetings above practical righteousness. A worship that can be conducted by persons who refuse to give shelter to the houseless, to give bread to the hungry, clothing to the naked, and who enjoin obedience to a law forbidding these acts of mercy, is a curse, not a blessing to mankind. The Bible addresses all such persons as "scribes, Pharisees, hypocrites, who pay tithe of mint, anise, and cummin, and have omitted the weightier matters of the law, judgment, mercy and faith."

But the church of this country is not only indifferent to the wrongs of die slave, it actually takes sides with the oppressors. It has made itself the bulwark of American slavery, and the shield of American slave-hunters. Many of its most eloquent Divines. who stand as the very lights of the church, have shamelessly given the sanction of religion and the Bible to the whole slave system. They have taught that man may, properly, be a slave; that the relation of master and slave is ordained of God; that to send back an escaped bondman to his master is clearly the duty of all the followers of the Lord Jesus Christ; and this horrible blasphemy is palmed off upon the world for Christianity.

For my part, I would say, welcome infidelity! welcome atheism! welcome anything! in preference to the gospel, as preached by those Divines! They convert the very name of religion into an engine of tyranny, and barbarous cruelty, and serve to confirm more infidels, in this age, than all the infidel writings of Thomas Paine, Voltaire, and Bolingbroke, put together, have done! These ministers make religion a cold and flinty-hearted thing, having neither principles of right action, nor bowels of compassion. They strip the love of God of its beauty, and leave the throng of religion a huge, horrible, repulsive form. It is a religion for oppressors, tyrants, man-stealers, and thugs. It is not that "pure and undefiled religion" which is from above, and which is "first pure, then peaceable, easy to be entreated, full of mercy and good fruits, without partiality, and without hypocrisy." But a religion which favors the rich against the poor; which exalts the proud above the humble; which divides mankind into two classes, tyrants and slaves; which says to the man in chains, stay there; and to the oppressor, oppress on; it is a religion which may be professed and enjoyed by

all the robbers and enslavers of mankind; it makes God a respecter of persons, denies his fatherhood of the race, and tramples in the dust the great truth of the brotherhood of man. All this we affirm to be true of the popular church, and the popular worship of our land and nation—a religion, a church, and a worship which, on the authority of inspired wisdom, we pronounce to be an abomination in the sight of God. In the language of Isaiah, the American church might be well addressed, "Bring no more vain ablations; incense is an abomination unto me: the new moons and Sabbaths, the calling of assemblies, I cannot away with; it is iniquity even the solemn meeting. Your new moons and your appointed feasts my soul hateth. They are a trouble to me; I am weary to bear them; and when ye spread forth your hands I will hide mine eyes from you. Yea! when ye make many prayers, I will not hear. YOUR HANDS ARE FULL OF BLOOD; cease to do evil, learn to do well; seek judgment; relieve the oppressed; judge for the fatherless; plead for the widow."

60   The American church is guilty, when viewed in connection with what it is doing to uphold slavery; but it is superlatively guilty when viewed in connection with its ability to abolish slavery. The sin of which it is guilty is one of omission as well as of commission. Albert Barnes but uttered what the common sense of every man at all observant of the actual state of the case will receive as truth, when he declared that "There is no power out of the church that could sustain slavery an hour, if it were not sustained in it."

Let the religious press, the pulpit, the Sunday school, the conference meeting, the great ecclesiastical, missionary, Bible and tract associations of the land array their immense powers against slavery and slave-holding; and the whole system of crime and blood would be scattered to the winds; and that they do not do this involves them in the most awful responsibility of which the mind can conceive.

In prosecuting the anti-slavery enterprise, we have been asked to spare the church, to spare the ministry; but how, we ask, could such a thing be done? We are met on the threshold of our efforts for the redemption of the slave, by the church and ministry of the country, in battle arrayed against us; and we are compelled to fight or flee. From what quarter, I beg to know, has proceeded a fire so deadly upon our ranks, during the last two years, as from the Northern pulpit? As the champions of oppressors, the chosen men of American theology have appeared—men, honored for their so-called piety, and their real learning. The LORDS of Buffalo, the SPRINGS of New York, the LATHROPS of Auburn, the COXES and SPENCERS of Brooklyn, the GANNETS and SHARPS of Boston, the DEWEYS of Washington, and other great religious lights of the land, have, in utter denial of the authority of Him, by whom the professed to he called to the ministry, deliberately taught us, against the example or the Hebrews and against the remonstrance of the Apostles, they teach "that we ought to obey man's law before the law of God."

My spirit wearies of such blasphemy; and how such men can be supported, as the "standing types and representatives of Jesus Christ," is a mystery which I leave others to penetrate. In speaking of the American church, however, let it be distinctly understood that I mean the great mass of the religious organizations of our land. There are exceptions, and I thank God that there are. Noble men may be found, scattered all over these Northern States, of whom Henry Ward Beecher of Brooklyn, Samuel J. May of Syracuse, and my esteemed friend on the platform, are shining examples; and let me say further, that upon these men lies the duty to inspire our ranks with high religious faith and zeal, and to cheer us on in the great mission of the slave's redemption from his chains.

One is struck with the difference between the attitude of the American church towards the anti-slavery movement, and that occupied by the churches in England towards a similar movement in that country. There, the church, true to its mission of ameliorating, elevating, and improving the condition of mankind, came forward promptly, bound up the wounds of the West Indian slave, and restored him to his liberty. There, the question of emancipation was a high[ly] religious question. It was demanded, in the name of humanity, and according to the law of the living God. The Sharps, the Clarksons, the Wilberforces, the Buxtons, and Burchells and the Knibbs, were alike famous for their piety, and for their philanthropy. The anti-slavery movement there was not an anti-church movement, for the reason that the church took its full share in prosecuting that movement: and the anti-slavery movement in this country will cease to be an anti-church movement, when the church of this country shall assume a favorable, instead or a hostile position towards that movement. Americans! your republican politics, not less than your republican religion, are flagrantly inconsistent. You boast of your love of liberty, your superior civilization, and your pure Christianity, while the whole political power of the nation (as embodied in the two great political parties), is solemnly pledged to support and perpetuate the enslavement of three millions of your countrymen. You hurl your anathemas at the crowned headed tyrants of Russia and Austria, and pride yourselves on your Democratic institutions, while you yourselves consent to be the mere tools and bodyguards of the tyrants of Virginia and Carolina. You invite to your shores fugitives of oppression from abroad, honor them with banquets, greet them with ovations, cheer them, toast them, salute them, protect them, and pour out your money to them like water; but the fugitives from your own land you advertise, hunt, arrest, shoot and kill. You glory in your refinement and your universal education yet you maintain a system as barbarous and dreadful as ever stained the character of a nation—a system begun in avarice, supported in pride, and perpetuated in cruelty. You shed tears over fallen Hungary, and make the sad story of her wrongs the theme of your poets, statesmen and orators, till your gallant sons are ready to fly to arms to vindicate her cause against her oppressors; but, in regard to the ten thousand wrongs of the American slave, you would enforce the strictest silence, and would hail him as an enemy of the nation who dares to make those wrongs the subject of public discourse! You are all on fire at the mention of liberty for France or for Ireland; but are as cold as an iceberg at the thought of liberty for the enslaved of America. You discourse eloquently on the dignity of labor; yet, you sustain a system which, in its very essence, casts a stigma upon labor. You can bare your bosom to the storm of British artillery to throw off a threepenny tax on tea; and yet wring the last hard-earned farthing from the grasp of the black laborers of your country. You profess to believe "that, of one blood, God made all nations of men to dwell on the face of all the earth," and hath commanded all men, everywhere to love one another; yet you notoriously hate, (and glory in your hatred), all men whose skins are not colored like your own. You declare, before the world, and are understood by the world to declare, that you "hotel these truths to be self evident, that all men are created equal; and are endowed by their Creator with certain inalienable rights; and that, among these are, life, liberty, and the pursuit of happiness;" and yet, you hold securely, in a bondage which, according to your own Thomas Jefferson, "is worse than ages of that which your fathers rose in rebellion to oppose," a seventh part of the inhabitants of your country.

65   Fellow-citizens! I will not enlarge further on your national inconsistencies. The existence of slavery in this country brands your republicanism as a sham, your humanity as a base pretence, and your Christianity as a lie. It destroys your moral power abroad; it corrupts your politicians at home. It saps the foundation of religion; it makes your name a hissing, and a by word to a mocking earth. It is the antagonistic force in your government, the only thing that seriously disturbs and endangers your Union. It fetters your progress; it is the enemy of improvement, the deadly foe of education; it fosters pride; it breeds insolence; it promotes vice; it shelters crime; it is a curse to the earth that supports it;

and yet, you cling to it, as if it were the sheet anchor of all your hopes. Oh! be warned! be warned! a horrible reptile is coiled up in your nation's bosom; the venomous creature is nursing at the tender breast of your youthful republic; for the love of God, tear away, and fling from you the hideous monster, and let the weight of twenty millions crush and destroy it forever!

[Section Three: Douglass refutes the idea that the U.S. Constitution is pro-slavery, reaffirms the ideals of the Declaration of Independence, and ends on a hopeful note that slavery will be defeated.]

But it is answered in reply to all this, that precisely what I have now denounced is, in fact, guaranteed and sanctioned by the Constitution of the United States; that the right to hold and to hunt slaves is a part of that Constitution framed by the illustrious Fathers of this Republic.

Then, I dare to affirm, notwithstanding all I have said before, your fathers stooped, basely stooped "To palter with us in a double sense: And keep the word of promise to the ear, But break it to the heart."

And instead of being the honest men I have before declared them to be, they were the veriest imposters that ever practiced on mankind. This is the inevitable conclusion, and from it there is no escape. But I differ from those who charge this baseness on the framers of the Constitution of the United States. It is a slander upon their memory, at least, so I believe. There is not time now to argue the constitutional question at length—nor have I the ability to discuss it as it ought to be discussed. The subject has been handled with masterly power by Lysander Spooner, Esq., by William Goodell, by Samuel E. Sewall, Esq., and last, though not least, by Gerritt Smith, Esq. These gentlemen have, as I think, fully and clearly vindicated the Constitution from any design to support slavery for an hour.

70   Fellow-citizens! there is no matter in respect to which, the people of the North have allowed themselves to be so ruinously imposed

upon, as that of the pro-slavery character of the Constitution. In that instrument I hold there is neither warrant, license, nor sanction of the hateful thing; but, interpreted as it ought to be interpreted, the Constitution is a GLORIOUS LIBERTY DOCUMENT. Read its preamble, consider its purposes. Is slavery among them? Is it at the gateway? or is it in the temple? It is neither. While I do not intend to argue this question on the present occasion, let me ask, if it be not somewhat singular that, if the Constitution were intended to be, by its framers and adopters, a slave-holding instrument, why neither slavery, slaveholding, nor slave can anywhere be found in it. What would be thought of an instrument, drawn up, legally drawn up, for the purpose of entitling the city of Rochester to a track of land, in which no mention of land was made? Now, there are certain rules of interpretation, for the proper understanding of all legal instruments. These rules are well established. They are plain, common-sense rules, such as you and I, and all of us, can understand and apply, without having passed years in the study of law. I scout the idea that the question of the constitutionality or unconstitutionality of slavery is not a question for the people. I hold that every American citizen has a fight to form an opinion of the Constitution, and to propagate that opinion, and to use all honorable means to make his opinion the prevailing one. Without this fight, the liberty of an American citizen would be as insecure as that of a Frenchman. Ex-Vice-President Dallas tells us that the Constitution is an object to which no American mind can be too attentive, and no American heart too devoted. He further says, the Constitution, in its words, is plain and intelligible, and is meant for the home-bred, unsophisticated understandings of our fellow-citizens. Senator Berrien tell us that the Constitution is the fundamental law, that which controls all others. The charter of our liberties, which every citizen has a personal interest in understanding

thoroughly. The testimony of Senator Breese, Lewis Cass, and many others that might be named, who are everywhere esteemed as sound lawyers, so regard the Constitution. I take it, therefore, that it is not presumption in a private citizen to form an opinion of that instrument.

Now, take the Constitution according to its plain reading, and I defy the presentation of a single pro-slavery clause in it. On the other hand it will be found to contain principles and purposes, entirely hostile to the existence of slavery.

I have detained my audience entirely too long already. At some future period I will gladly avail myself of an opportunity to give this subject a full and fair discussion.

Allow me to say, in conclusion, notwithstanding the dark picture I have this day presented of the state of the nation, I do not despair of this country. There are forces in operation, which must inevitably work the downfall of slavery. "The arm of the Lord is not shortened," and the doom of slavery is certain. I, therefore, leave off where I began, with hope. While drawing encouragement from the Declaration of Independence, the great principles it contains, and the genius of American Institutions, my spirit is also cheered by the obvious tendencies of the age. Nations do not now stand in the same relation to each other that they did ages ago. No nation can now shut itself up from the surrounding world, and trot round in the same old path of its fathers without interference. The time was when such could be done. Long established customs of hurtful character could formerly fence themselves in, and do their evil work with social impunity. Knowledge was then confined and enjoyed by the privileged few, and the multitude walked on in mental darkness. But a change has now come over the affairs of mankind. Walled cities and empires have become unfashionable. The arm of commerce has borne away the gates of the strong city. Intelligence is penetrating the darkest corners of the globe. It makes its pathway over and under the sea, as well as on the earth.

Wind, steam, and lightning are its chartered agents. Oceans no longer divide, but link nations together. From Boston to London is now a holiday excursion. Space is comparatively annihilated. Thoughts expressed on one side of the Atlantic are, distinctly heard on the other. The far off and almost fabulous Pacific rolls in grandeur at our feet. The Celestial Empire, the mystery of ages, is being solved. The fiat of the Almighty, "Let there be Light," has not yet spent its force. No abuse, no outrage whether in taste, sport or avarice, can now hide itself from the all-pervading light. The iron shoe, and crippled foot of China must be seen, in contrast with nature. Africa must rise and put on her yet unwoven garment. "Ethiopia shall stretch out her hand unto God." In the fervent aspirations of William Lloyd Garrison, I say, and let every heart join in saying it:

God speed the year of jubilee
The wide world o'er
When from their galling chains set free,
Th' oppress'd shall vilely bend the knee,
And wear the yoke of tyranny
Like brutes no more.
That year will come, and freedom's reign,
To man his plundered fights again
Restore.

God speed the day when human blood
Shall cease to flow!
In every clime be understood,
The claims of human brotherhood,
And each return for evil, good,
Not blow for blow;
That day will come all feuds to end.
And change into a faithful friend
Each foe.

God speed the hour, the glorious hour,
When none on earth
Shall exercise a lordly power,
Nor in a tyrant's presence cower;
But all to manhood's stature tower,
By equal birth!
THAT HOUR WILL, COME, to each, to all,
And from his prison-house, the thrall
Go forth.

Until that year, day, hour, arrive,
With head, and heart, and hand I'll strive,
To break the rod, and rend the gyve,
The spoiler of his prey deprive-
So witness Heaven!
And never from my chosen post,
Whate'er the peril or the cost,
Be driven.

EXPLORATORY WRITING

Toward the end of the opening section, Frederick Douglass says, "I need not enter further into the causes which led to this anniversary. Many of you understand them better than I do. That is a branch of knowledge in which you feel, perhaps, a deeper interest than your speaker. The causes which led to the separation of the colonies from the British crown have never lacked for a tongue. They have been taught in your common schools, narrated at your firesides, unfolded from your pulpits, and thundered from your legislative halls, and are as familiar to you as household words. They form the staple of your national poetry and eloquence." Explain how Douglass constructs his rhetorical stance by positioning himself in relation to the Fourth of July and to his predominantly white audience. Notice that Douglass addresses the audience as "fellow citizens" but uses the pronoun "your" instead of "our" in "your nation" and "your fathers." "The Fourth of July is yours, not mine. You may rejoice, I must mourn." How does the position he establishes answer the question that Douglass poses to his listeners, "Why am I called upon to speak here today?"

TALKING ABOUT THE READING

Work in a group with three or four other students. Consider the three main sections of Douglass's speech and how they work together. Describe the function of each section. What is Douglass doing in each of the sections; what rhetorical moves does he make? What role does each section perform in the speech overall? Notice how Douglass gives his listeners cues to where he is in the speech—for example, when he explains, near the beginning of the middle section, that his "subject" is "American slavery" or, near the end, when he says, "Allow me to say, in conclusion, notwithstanding the dark picture I have this day presented of the state of the nation, I do not despair of this country."

WRITING ASSIGNMENT

Write an essay that explains how Douglass constructs his rhetorical stance in relation to the occasion of his speech (the Fourth of July), his presentation of self, his audience, and the topic of slavery.

A MORE PERFECT UNION

▬— *Barack Obama*

During the 2008 presidential primary campaign, then Senator Barack Obama encountered controversy about sermons from his pastor at the Trinity United Church of Christ in Chicago, the Reverend Jeremiah Wright, that some commentators interpreted as "offensive" and "unpatriotic." The speech "A More Perfect Union," delivered in Philadelphia, Pennsylvania, was Obama's response to the situation and, as many observers have acknowledged, a major oration on the history of race and racism in the United States.

SUGGESTION FOR READING In the middle of "A More Perfect Union," Obama describes "a racial stalemate we've been stuck in for years." As you read his speech, consider how Obama draws on history to explain the causes and the dimensions of this stalemate.

"We the people, in order to form a more perfect union."

1 Two hundred and twenty-one years ago, in a hall that still stands across the street, a group of men gathered and, with these simple words, launched America's improbable experiment in democracy. Farmers and scholars, statesmen and patriots who had traveled across an ocean to escape tyranny and persecution finally made real their declaration of independence at a Philadelphia convention that lasted through the spring of 1787.

The document they produced was eventually signed but ultimately unfinished. It was stained by this nation's original sin of slavery, a question that divided the colonies and brought the convention to a stalemate until the founders chose to allow the slave trade to continue for at least twenty more years, and to leave any final resolution to future generations.

Of course, the answer to the slavery question was already embedded within our Constitution— a Constitution that had at its very core the ideal of equal citizenship under the law; a Constitution that promised its people liberty, and justice, and a union that could be and should be perfected over time.

And yet words on a parchment would not be enough to deliver slaves from bondage, or provide men and women of every color and creed their full rights and obligations as citizens of the United States. What would be needed were Americans in successive generations who were willing to do their part—through protests and struggle, on the streets and in the courts, through a civil war and civil disobedience and always at great risk—to narrow that gap between the promise of our ideals and the reality of their time.

5   This was one of the tasks we set forth at the beginning of this campaign—to continue the long march of those who came before us, a march for a more just, more equal, more free, more caring and more prosperous America. I chose to run for the presidency at this moment in history because I believe deeply that we cannot solve the challenges of our time unless we solve them together—unless we perfect our union by understanding that we may have different stories, but we hold common hopes; that we may not look the same and we may not have come from the same place, but we all want to move in the same direction—towards a better future for our children and our grandchildren.

This belief comes from my unyielding faith in the decency and generosity of the American people. But it also comes from my own American story.

I am the son of a black man from Kenya and a white woman from Kansas. I was raised with the help of a white grandfather who survived a Depression to serve in Patton's Army during World War II and a white grandmother who worked on a bomber assembly line at Fort Leavenworth while he was overseas. I've gone to some of the best schools in America and lived in one of the world's poorest nations. I am married to a black American who carries within her the blood of slaves and slaveowners—an inheritance we pass on to our two precious daughters. I have brothers, sisters, nieces, nephews, uncles and cousins, of every race and every hue, scattered across three continents, and for as long as I live, I will never forget that in no other country on Earth is my story even possible.

It's a story that hasn't made me the most conventional candidate. But it is a story that has seared into my genetic makeup the idea that this nation is more than the sum of its parts—that out of many, we are truly one.

Throughout the first year of this campaign, against all predictions to the contrary, we saw how hungry the American people were for this message of unity. Despite the temptation to view my candidacy through a purely racial lens, we won commanding victories in states with some of the whitest populations in the country. In South Carolina, where the Confederate Flag still flies, we built a powerful coalition of African Americans and white Americans.

10   This is not to say that race has not been an issue in the campaign. At various stages in the campaign, some commentators have deemed me either "too black" or "not black enough." We saw racial tensions bubble to the surface during the week before the South Carolina primary. The press has scoured every exit poll for the latest evidence of racial polarization, not just in terms of white and black, but black and brown as well.

And yet, it has only been in the last couple of weeks that the discussion of race in this campaign has taken a particularly divisive turn.

On one end of the spectrum, we've heard the implication that my candidacy is somehow an exercise in affirmative action; that it's based solely on the desire of wide-eyed liberals to purchase racial reconciliation on the cheap. On the other end, we've heard my former pastor, Reverend Jeremiah Wright, use incendiary language to express views that have the potential not only to widen the racial divide, but views that denigrate both the greatness and the goodness of our nation; that rightly offend white and black alike.

I have already condemned, in unequivocal terms, the statements of Reverend Wright that have caused such controversy. For some, nagging questions remain. Did I know him to be an occasionally fierce critic of American domestic and foreign policy? Of course. Did I ever hear him make remarks that could be considered controversial while I sat in church? Yes. Did I strongly disagree with many of his political views? Absolutely—just as I'm sure many of you have heard remarks from your pastors, priests, or rabbis with which you strongly disagreed.

But the remarks that have caused this recent firestorm weren't simply controversial. They weren't simply a religious leader's effort to speak out against perceived injustice. Instead, they expressed a profoundly distorted view of this country—a view that sees white racism as endemic, and that elevates what is wrong with America above all that we know is right with America; a view that sees the conflicts in the Middle East as rooted primarily in the actions of stalwart allies like Israel, instead of emanating from the perverse and hateful ideologies of radical Islam.

15   As such, Reverend Wright's comments were not only wrong but divisive, divisive at a time when we need unity; racially charged at a time when we need to come together to solve a set of monumental problems—two wars, a terrorist threat, a falling economy, a chronic health care crisis and potentially devastating climate change; problems that are neither black or white or Latino or Asian, but rather problems that confront us all.

Given my background, my politics, and my professed values and ideals, there will no doubt be those for whom my statements of condemnation are not enough. Why associate myself with Reverend Wright in the first place, they may ask? Why not join another church? And I confess that if all that I knew of Reverend Wright were the snippets of those sermons that have run in an endless loop on the television and You Tube, or if Trinity United Church of Christ conformed to the caricatures being peddled by some commentators, there is no doubt that I would react in much the same way.

But the truth is, that isn't all that I know of the man. The man I met more than twenty years ago is a man who helped introduce me to my Christian faith, a man who spoke to me about our obligations to love one another; to care for the sick and lift up the poor. He is a man who served his country as a U.S. Marine; who has studied and lectured at some of the finest universities and seminaries in the country, and who for over thirty years led a church that serves the community by doing God's work here on Earth— by housing the homeless, ministering to the needy, providing day care services and scholarships and prison ministries, and reaching out to those suffering from HIV/AIDS.

In my first book, *Dreams from My Father*, I described the experience of my first service at Trinity:

"People began to shout, to rise from their seats and clap and cry out, a forceful wind carrying the reverend's voice up into the rafters. . . . And in that single note—hope!—I heard something else; at the foot of that cross, inside the thousands of churches across the city, I imagined the stories of ordinary black people merging with the stories of David and Goliath, Moses and Pharaoh, the Christians in the lion's den, Ezekiel's field of dry bones. Those stories—of survival, and freedom, and hope—became our story, my story; the blood that had spilled was our blood, the tears our tears; until this black church, on this bright day, seemed once more a vessel carrying the story of a people into future generations and into a larger world. Our trials and triumphs became at once unique and universal, black and more than black; in chronicling our journey, the stories and songs gave us a means to reclaim memories that we didn't need to feel shame about . . . memories that all people might study and cherish—and with which we could start to rebuild."

That has been my experience at Trinity. Like other predominantly black churches across the country, Trinity embodies the black community in its entirety—the doctor and the welfare mom, the model student and the former gang-banger. Like other black churches, Trinity's services are full of raucous laughter and sometimes bawdy humor. They are full of dancing, clapping, screaming and shouting that may seem jarring to the untrained ear. The church contains in full the kindness and cruelty, the fierce intelligence and the shocking ignorance, the struggles and successes, the love and yes, the bitterness and bias that make up the black experience in America.

20   And this helps explain, perhaps, my relationship with Reverend Wright. As imperfect as he may be, he has been like family to me. He strengthened my faith, officiated my wedding, and baptized my children. Not once in my conversations with him have I heard him talk about any ethnic group in derogatory terms, or treat whites with whom he interacted with anything but courtesy and respect. He contains within him the contradictions—the good and the bad—of the community that he has served diligently for so many years.

I can no more disown him than I can disown the black community. I can no more disown him than I can my white grandmother—a woman who helped raise me, a woman who sacrificed again and again for me, a woman who loves me as much as she loves anything in this world, but a woman who once confessed her fear of black men who passed by her on the street, and who on more than one occasion has uttered racial or ethnic stereotypes that made me cringe.

These people are a part of me. And they are a part of America, this country that I love.

Some will see this as an attempt to justify or excuse comments that are simply inexcusable. I can assure you it is not. I suppose the politically safe thing would be to move on from this episode and just hope that it fades into the woodwork. We can dismiss Reverend Wright as a crank or a demagogue, just as some have dismissed Geraldine Ferraro, in the aftermath of her recent statements, as harboring some deep-seated racial bias.

But race is an issue that I believe this nation cannot afford to ignore right now. We would be making the same mistake that Reverend Wright made in his offending sermons about America— to simplify and stereotype and amplify the negative to the point that it distorts reality.

25   The fact is that the comments that have been made and the issues that have surfaced over the last few weeks reflect the complexities of race in this country that we've never really worked through—a part of our union that we have yet to perfect. And if we walk away now, if we simply retreat into our respective corners, we will never be able to come together and solve challenges like health care, or education, or the need to find good jobs for every American.

Understanding this reality requires a reminder of how we arrived at this point. As William Faulkner once wrote, "The past isn't dead and buried. In fact, it isn't even past." We do not need to recite here the history of racial injustice in this country. But we do need to remind ourselves that so many of the disparities that exist in the African-American community today can be directly traced to inequalities passed on from an earlier generation that suffered under the brutal legacy of slavery and Jim Crow.

Segregated schools were, and are, inferior schools; we still haven't fixed them, fifty years after *Brown v. Board of Education,* and the inferior education they provided, then and now, helps explain the pervasive achievement gap between today's black and white students.

Legalized discrimination—where blacks were prevented, often through violence, from owning property, or loans were not granted to African-American business owners, or black homeowners could not access FHA mortgages, or blacks were excluded from unions, or the police force, or fire departments—meant that black families could not amass any meaningful wealth to bequeath to future generations. That history helps explain the wealth and income gap between black and white, and the concentrated pockets of poverty that persist in so many of today's urban and rural communities.

A lack of economic opportunity among black men, and the shame and frustration that came from not being able to provide for one's family, contributed to the erosion of black families—a problem that welfare policies for many years may

Barack Obama   A More Perfect Union   **497**

have worsened. And the lack of basic services in so many urban black neighborhoods—parks for kids to play in, police walking the beat, regular garbage pick-up and building code enforcement—all helped create a cycle of violence, blight, and neglect that continue to haunt us.

30   This is the reality in which Reverend Wright and other African Americans of his generation grew up. They came of age in the late fifties and early sixties, a time when segregation was still the law of the land and opportunity was systematically constricted. What's remarkable is not how many failed in the face of discrimination, but rather how many men and women overcame the odds; how many were able to make a way out of no way for those like me who would come after them.

But for all those who scratched and clawed their way to get a piece of the American Dream, there were many who didn't make it—those who were ultimately defeated, in one way or another, by discrimination. That legacy of defeat was passed on to future generations—those young men and increasingly young women who we see standing on street corners or languishing in our prisons, without hope or prospects for the future. Even for those blacks who did make it, questions of race, and racism, continue to define their worldview in fundamental ways. For the men and women of Reverend Wright's generation, the memories of humiliation and doubt and fear have not gone away; nor has the anger and the bitterness of those years. That anger may not get expressed in public, in front of white coworkers or white friends. But it does find voice in the barbershop or around the kitchen table. At times, that anger is exploited by politicians, to gin up votes along racial lines, or to make up for a politician's own failings.

And occasionally it finds voice in the church on Sunday morning, in the pulpit and in the pews. The fact that so many people are surprised to hear that anger in some of Reverend Wright's sermons simply reminds us of the old truism that the most segregated hour in American life occurs on Sunday morning. That anger is not always productive; indeed, all too often it distracts attention from solving real problems; it keeps us from squarely facing our own complicity in our condition, and prevents the African-American community from forging the alliances it needs to bring about real change. But the anger is real; it is powerful; and to simply wish it away, to condemn it without understanding its roots, only serves to widen the chasm of misunderstanding that exists between the races.

In fact, a similar anger exists within segments of the white community. Most working- and middle-class white Americans don't feel that they have been particularly privileged by their race. Their experience is the immigrant experience—as far as they're concerned, no one's handed them anything, they've built it from scratch. They've worked hard all their lives, many times only to see their jobs shipped overseas or their pension dumped after a lifetime of labor. They are anxious about their futures, and feel their dreams slipping away; in an era of stagnant wages and global competition, opportunity comes to be seen as a zero sum game, in which your dreams come at my expense. So when they are told to bus their children to a school across town; when they hear that an African American is getting an advantage in landing a good job or a spot in a good college because of an injustice that they themselves never committed; when they're told that their fears about crime in urban neighborhoods are somehow prejudiced, resentment builds over time.

Like the anger within the black community, these resentments aren't always expressed in polite company. But they have helped shape the political landscape for at least a generation. Anger over welfare and affirmative action helped forge the Reagan Coalition. Politicians routinely exploited fears of crime for their own electoral ends. Talk show hosts and conservative commentators built entire careers unmasking bogus claims of racism while dismissing legitimate discussions of racial injustice and inequality as mere political correctness or reverse racism.

35   Just as black anger often proved counter-productive, so have these white resentments distracted attention from the real culprits of the middle-class squeeze—a corporate culture rife with inside dealing, questionable accounting practices, and short-term greed; a Washington dominated by lobbyists and special interests; economic policies that favor the few over the many. And yet, to wish away the resentments of white Americans, to label them as misguided or even racist, without recognizing they are grounded in legitimate concerns—this too widens the racial divide, and blocks the path to understanding.

This is where we are right now. It's a racial stalemate we've been stuck in for years. Contrary to the claims of some of my critics, black and white, I have never been so naive as to believe that we can get beyond our racial divisions in a single election cycle, or with a single candidacy—particularly a candidacy as imperfect as my own.

But I have asserted a firm conviction—a conviction rooted in my faith in God and my faith in the American people—that working together we can move beyond some of our old racial wounds, and that in fact we have no choice if we are to continue on the path of a more perfect union.

For the African-American community, that path means embracing the burdens of our past without becoming victims of our past. It means continuing to insist on a full measure of justice in every aspect of American life. But it also means binding our particular grievances—for better health care, and better schools, and better jobs—to the larger aspirations of all Americans—the white woman struggling to break the glass ceiling, the white man whose been laid off, the immigrant trying to feed his family. And it means taking full responsibility for our own lives—by demanding more from our fathers, and spending more time with our children, and reading to them, and teaching them that while they may face challenges and discrimination in their own lives, they must never succumb to despair or cynicism; they must always believe that they can write their own destiny.

Ironically, this quintessentially American—and yes, conservative—notion of self-help found frequent expression in Reverend Wright's sermons. But what my former pastor too often failed to understand is that embarking on a program of self-help also requires a belief that society can change.

40   The profound mistake of Reverend Wright's sermons is not that he spoke about racism in our society. It's that he spoke as if our society was static; as if no progress has been made; as if this country—a country that has made it possible for one of his own members to run for the highest office in the land and build a coalition of white and black, Latino and Asian, rich and poor, young and old—is still irrevocably bound to a tragic past. But what we know—what we have seen—is that America can change. That is the true genius of this nation. What we have already achieved gives us hope—the audacity to hope—for what we can and must achieve tomorrow.

In the white community, the path to a more perfect union means acknowledging that what ails the African-American community does not just exist in the minds of black people; that the legacy of discrimination and current incidents of discrimination, while less overt than in the past, are real and must be addressed. Not just with words, but with deeds—by investing in our schools and our communities; by enforcing our civil rights laws and ensuring fairness in our criminal justice system; by providing this generation with ladders of opportunity that were unavailable for previous generations. It requires all Americans to realize that your dreams do not have to come at the expense of my dreams; that investing in the health, welfare, and education of black and brown and white children will ultimately help all of America prosper.

In the end, then, what is called for is nothing more, and nothing less, than what all the world's great religions demand—that we do unto others as we would have them do unto us. Let us be our brother's keeper, scripture tells us. Let us be our sister's keeper. Let us find that common stake we all have in one another, and let our politics reflect that spirit as well.

For we have a choice in this country. We can accept a politics that breeds division, and conflict, and cynicism. We can tackle race only as spectacle—as we did in the OJ trial—or in the wake of tragedy, as we did in the aftermath of Katrina—or as fodder for the nightly news. We can play Reverend Wright's sermons on every channel, every day and talk about them from now until the election, and make the only question in this campaign whether or not the American people think that I somehow believe or sympathize with his most offensive words. We can pounce on some gaffe by a Hillary supporter as evidence that she's playing the race card, or we can speculate on whether white men will all flock to John McCain in the general election regardless of his policies.

We can do that. But if we do, I can tell you that in the next election, we'll be talking about some other distraction. And then another one. And then another one. And nothing will change.

45   That is one option. Or, at this moment, in this election, we can come together and say, "Not this time." This time we want to talk about the crumbling schools that are stealing the future of black children and white children and Asian children and Hispanic children and Native American children. This time we want to reject the cynicism that tells us that these kids can't learn; that those kids who don't look like us are somebody else's problem. The children of America are not those kids, they are our kids, and we will not let them fall behind in a 21st-century economy. Not this time.

This time we want to talk about how the lines in the Emergency Room are filled with whites and blacks and Hispanics who do not have health care; who don't have the power on their own to overcome the special interests in Washington, but who can take them on if we do it together.

This time we want to talk about the shuttered mills that once provided a decent life for men and women of every race, and the homes for sale that once belonged to Americans from every religion, every region, every walk of life. This time we want to talk about the fact that the real problem is not that someone who doesn't look like you might take your job; it's that the corporation you work for will ship it overseas for nothing more than a profit.

This time we want to talk about the men and women of every color and creed who serve together, and fight together, and bleed together under the same proud flag. We want to talk about how to bring them home from a war that never should've been authorized and never should've been waged, and we want to talk about how we'll show our patriotism by caring for them, and their families, and giving them the benefits they have earned.

I would not be running for president if I didn't believe with all my heart that this is what the vast majority of Americans want for this country. This union may never be perfect, but generation after generation has shown that it can always be perfected. And today, whenever I find myself feeling doubtful or cynical about this possibility, what gives me the most hope is the next generation—the young people whose attitudes and beliefs and openness to change have already made history in this election.

50   There is one story in particular that I'd like to leave you with today—a story I told when I had the great honor of speaking on Dr. King's birthday at his home church, Ebenezer Baptist, in Atlanta.

There is a young, twenty-three-year-old white woman named Ashley Baia who organized for our campaign in Florence, South Carolina. She had been working to organize a mostly African-American community since the beginning of this campaign, and one day she was at a roundtable discussion where everyone went around telling their story and why they were there.

And Ashley said that when she was nine years old, her mother got cancer. And because she had to miss days of work, she was let go and lost her health care. They had to file for bankruptcy, and that's when Ashley decided that she had to do something to help her mom. She knew that food was one of their most expensive costs, and so Ashley convinced her mother that what she really liked and really wanted to eat more than anything else was mustard and relish sandwiches. Because that was the cheapest way to eat. She did this for a year until her mom got better, and she told everyone at the roundtable that the reason she joined our campaign was so that she could help the millions of other children in the country who want and need to help their parents too.

Now Ashley might have made a different choice. Perhaps somebody told her along the way that the source of her mother's problems were blacks who were on welfare and too lazy to work, or Hispanics who were coming into the country illegally. But she didn't. She sought out allies in her fight against injustice.

Anyway, Ashley finishes her story and then goes around the room and asks everyone else why they're supporting the campaign. They all have different stories and reasons. Many bring up a specific issue. And finally they come to this elderly black man who's been sitting there quietly the entire time. And Ashley asks him why he's there. And he does not bring up a specific issue. He does not say health care or the economy. He does not say education or the war. He does not say that he was there because of Barack Obama. He simply says to everyone in the room, "I am here because of Ashley."

55 "I'm here because of Ashley." By itself, that single moment of recognition between that young white girl and that old black man is not enough. It is not enough to give health care to the sick, or jobs to the jobless, or education to our children.

But it is where we start. It is where our union grows stronger. And as so many generations have come to realize over the course of the two hundred and twenty-one years since a band of patriots signed that document in Philadelphia, that is where the perfection begins.

EXPLORATORY WRITING

Barack Obama quotes William Faulkner's famous line, "The past isn't dead and buried. In fact, it isn't even past." Use this sense of the past to explore how Obama invokes history to explain the racial situation in contemporary America. What is the weight of the past as it impinges on the present? How does this manifest itself among black and white Americans?

TALKING ABOUT THE READING

Work in a group with three or four other students. We have not divided Obama's speech into sections, as we did with Frederick Douglass's "What to the Slave Is the Fourth of July." Your task here is to divide Obama's speech into sections (there may be more than the three we marked in Douglass's speech). Label each section in two ways: according to what it says (paraphrase the content of the section), and according to what it does (identify the functions it performs in developing the overall argument of the oration). Compare your group's findings with those of other groups. The point is not to determine who's right or wrong but what the group's sense of what Obama is saying and doing brings to light or ignores.

WRITING ASSIGNMENT

Write an essay on Obama's rhetorical stance in "A More Perfect Union." Consider how he positions himself in relation to the occasion of the speech, his audience, and the topic of race relations in the United States.

WRITING SEQUENCE

1. Read the exploratory writing you've done so far on the rhetorical stances of Douglass and Obama. (If you haven't done any exploratory writing, respond to the Exploratory Writing topics at this point, for 10 minutes on each.) Review what you've written, then write another exploratory piece—this time to see what comes to light when you look at Douglass and Obama together, to see how they draw on the past to establish their positions in the present. Consider their differences and similarities.

2. Write a 2-page analysis of how Douglass and Obama establish their respective rhetorical stances in relation to the occasion of their speeches, their audiences, and the topic of race and racism in the United States. To what extent do they use similar and different rhetorical strategies? How would you explain these differences and similarities?

3. In the culminating assignment, write a longer finished essay (drafted, revised, and edited) that compares how the two speeches make the history of race and racism in the United States, in Alan Trachtenberg's words, "intelligible and usable." Reread the speeches and reread the writing you've done so far in preparation for the essay. Consider what you have noticed about the way Douglass and Obama use the past to establish their positions in the present and how they craft a rhetorical stance in relation to the occasion, their presentation of self, their audiences, and the topic at hand. The task now is to connect your ideas by examining how Douglass and Obama use the past to fashion a rhetorical stance in the present. Move back and forth between what you've written and the two speeches to develop your analysis, noticing where you can sharpen connections and where you need to expand or clarify or modify your thinking.

VISUAL CULTURE   Representations of War

This Visual Culture unit asks you to consider how past and present wars have been pictured in the United States and how technologies of representation have influenced the way people receive and understand information. T.H. O'Sullivan's "A Harvest of Death, Gettysburg, July 1863," for example, has an eerie stillness and an elegiac quality, due in part to the limits of photography at the time, when the size of cameras and long exposures made it impossible to shoot live action. The medium of circulation has changed as well. Joe Rosenthal's famous photo of the flag raising at Iwo Jima was distributed through a wire service to newspapers, which, along with radio and newsreels in movie theaters, were the primary means people relied on for information about World War II. Twenty years later, the Vietnam War became the first "living-room war" that people experienced by watching television. The startling image of Colonel Loan executing a Viet Cong suspect, for which AP photographer Eddie Adams won the Pulitzer Prize in 1969, appeared in both newspapers and film footage by NBC cameraman Vo Su, who was with Adams, shown on the nightly news. But as the media critic Marita Sturken notes, photographs and film shot in Vietnam were subject to the delay of developing, and it was only with the availability of satellite technology and portable video cameras that the world watched war live, as it happened, during the 1991 Persian Gulf War and the Iraq invasion in 2003.

— A Harvest of Death,
Gettysburg, July 1863.
Photographed by
T.H. O' Sullivan.

— Flag raising at Iwo
Jima. Photographed by Joe
Rosenthal.

Colonel Loan executing a Viet Cong suspect. Photographed by Eddie Adams.

SUGGESTION FOR DISCUSSION

Consider the three photographs—T.H. O'Sullivan's "A Harvest of Death" from the Civil War, Joe Rosenthal's "Flag-raising at Iwo Jima" from World War Two, and Eddie Adams' "Colonel Loan Executing a Viet Cong Suspect" from the Vietnam War. What is the dominant impression that each photo creates? How does the image shape our understanding and memory of the particular war represented?

VISUAL ESSAY   The Iraq Invasion and Occupation

The "struggle for meaning" that Alan Trachtenberg refers to in "Reading American Photographs" is strikingly evident in the photographs assembled here from the 2003 invasion of Iraq and the subsequent occupation. Alone, each captures a distinct moment that proposes to represent the Iraq War. Taken together, the images stand in an uneasy relationship to each other, bound by a common event but divided by what they depict and the meanings that they make available. Just as the meaning of the Iraq War remains volatile and contested in politics, historical interpretation, and popular culture, these images jostle against each other and call the viewer to different scenes and different ways of seeing the war.

SUGGESTIONS FOR DISCUSSION

Consider how you got your news about the Iraq War. Did you rely on newspapers, magazines, CNN, movies, blogs, Internet, *The Daily Show,* your older brother? What factors determine how you choose your sources—availability, entertainment value, reputation, political perspective, a combination of these factors, or other reasons? Compare the media that you and your classmates rely on. What do you see as their inherent capacities and limitations? How do these capacities and limitations influence their representations of the Iraq War and occupation?

2. Look closely at the photographs in the Visual Essay: The Iraq War and Occupation. First, consider each on its own terms as an icon of the Iraq War and occupation. How does each image shape an understanding and memory of events? Work with a group of three or four classmates. Write two captions for each photo—one that is informative, and one that is interpretive or argumentative. Exchange your photos and captions with those from another group. Ask members of the other group how the captions shape or slant their experience of each photo. In turn, respond to the other group's captions in the same way. What conclusions can you draw about the way captions influence viewers' understanding of photos.

SUGGESTED ASSIGNMENT

Design a photo essay of 5–7 photographs that represents your experience of the Iraq War. You can use any of the photos in the Visual Essay or others you find on the Internet or elsewhere. Notice that the images on pages 504–505 are arranged in chronological order. Consider how you want to sequence your photos and the effects of juxtaposing the images in various ways. Write a short (1–2 page) introduction to the photo essay and captions for the individual photos. Once you've finished, wait a day or two. Then reread the photo essay, imagining it is someone else's work. Write an analysis of the photo essay that examines its representation of the Iraq War and occupation. How does the designer of the photo essay seem to make sense of the war and occupation? How do the images assembled in the photo essay convey the designer's perspective? How does the photo essay seem to position the viewer/reader?

FILM CLIP   Film Genres: The Western

Films can be sorted into genres such as science fiction (the *Star Wars* series and *Space Odyssey 2000*), musicals (*West Side Story* and *Sound of Music),* horror (various Dracula and Frankenstein movies), romantic comedy (*My Best Friend's Wedding* and *Sleepless in Seattle*), and action adventure (*The Terminator* and *Raiders of the Lost Ark*), each of which has a predictable visual look and narrative formula. Of all the genres of Hollywood movies, the western is perhaps the most revered as a central part of American mythology. Hollywood is making few westerns today, but from the 1930s into the 1970s, it was a dominant form of filmmaking, with directors such as John Ford and Howard Hawks and stars such as John Wayne, Gary Cooper, Gregory Peck, and James Stewart in leading roles. The western relied on the relatively simple narrative formula that typically located a single heroic figure at the borderland between civilization and savagery, represented variously by Indians, outlaws, or unscrupulous entrepreneurs. The task of the western hero accordingly was to rescue an endangered community from the forces that threatened it. Some of the classic examples of this western formula are *Stagecoach, Red River, Shane,* and *High Noon.* With the political and moral crisis of the Vietnam War, however, the western was called into question, and a number of "revisionist" westerns telling a more complex story arrived in theaters—films such as *McCabe and Mrs. Miller, The Wild Bunch,* and *Little Big Man.*

Watch one or more of the classic westerns (there are many in addition to those mentioned here). What are the qualities that make a western hero? You may then want to watch one or more of the "revisionist" westerns. How do these films retell the story of the "opening of the West"?

FIELDWORK   Oral History

Oral histories offer the personal perspectives of people who are caught up in the history of their time. Oral history is a branch of historical studies that draws on the experience and memories of ordinary people to provide new insight into the meaning and texture of historical events. Sometimes referred to as "history from the bottom up," oral history is an organized effort to record the stories of ordinary people who traditionally have been ignored by historians. In this sense, oral histories are important correctives to older versions of history that focus on "great men," geopolitics, and institutions of power.

This does not mean, however, that oral histories are any more useful or authoritative than traditional historical work that is based on archives, government documents, or the correspondence of national leaders. Their value depends on how the oral historian handles the material once it is collected. "The Good War" by Studs Terkel is an example of the oral history form.

THE GOOD WAR

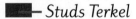— *Studs Terkel*

Studs Terkel acted in radio soap operas and movies and was a disk jockey and host of a daily radio show in Chicago, his hometown. He is best known, though, for his oral histories, which include *Division Street: America* (1967), *Working; People Talk About What They Do All Day and How They Feel About What They Do* (1974), and *Hard Times: An Oral History of the Great Depression* (1970). The following excerpts, which come from *"The Good War": An Oral History of World War Two* (1984), give a sense of how oral history can provide the perspectives of ordinary people on important historical events. As you will see, we have chosen selections that give very different viewpoints on World War II.

SUGGESTION   As you read, notice how each informant remembers the bombing of Pearl Harbor on
FOR READING   December 7, 1941, and the beginning of World War II. Consider how their various responses
call into question the notion that the United States reacted to the onset of World War II as a
unified nation.

YURIKO HOHRI

1   *She lives with her husband in Chicago. He is
national chair of the Council for Japanese
American Redress. She is active, too.*

The war became real for me when the two
FBI agents came to our home in Long Beach. It
was a few months after December 7. It was a
rainy Saturday morning. My three sisters, my
mother, and myself were at home doing the
chores. I was twelve.

A black car came right into the driveway. One
man went into the kitchen. As I watched, he
looked under the sink and he looked into the oven.
Then he went into the parlor and opened the glass
cases where our most treasured things were. There
were several stacks of *shakuhachi* sheet music. It's
a bamboo flute. My father played the *shakuhachi*
and my mother played the *koto*. At least once a
month on a Sunday afternoon, their friends would
come over and just enjoy themselves playing
music. The man took the music.

I followed the man into my mother and
father's bedroom. Strangers do not usually go into
our bedrooms when they first come. As I watched,
he went into the closet and brought out my
father's golf clubs. He turned the bag upside
down. I was only concerned about the golf balls,
because I played jacks with them. He opened the
tansu, a chest of drawers. My mother and sisters
were weeping.

5   My father was at work. He took care of the
vegetable and fruit sections for two grocery
stores. He was brought home by the agents. He
was taken to a camp in Tujunga Canyon. My
grandmother and I went to visit him. It was a different kind of visit. There was a tall barbed-wire
fence, so we were unable to touch each other.
The only thing we could do was see each other.
My father was weeping.

Our family moved to my grandmother's
house—my mother's mother. At least six of my
uncles were at home, so it was very crowded.
My next recollection is that my mother, my three
little sisters, and I were on this streetcar. My
mother had made a little knapsack for each of
us, with our names embroidered. We had a
washcloth, a towel, soap, a comb. Just enough
for us to carry. It was the first time we took a
streetcar. Because we always went by my
father's car.

We went to Santa Anita. We lived in a horse
stable. We filled a cheesecloth bag with straw—
our mattress. The sides of the room did not go up
to the ceiling, so there was no privacy at all. They
were horse stalls. We'd have fun climbing up. The
floors were asphalt. I do remember what we
called stinky bugs. They were crunchy, like cockroaches, large, black. Oh, it's really—(Laughs, as
she shakes her head.) We had apple butter. To this
day, I cannot taste apple butter.

PAUL PISICANO

*He is an architect, living in Manhattan. He is
fifty-two and "one hundred percent Sicilian."*

It was an Italian-speaking neighborhood in
New York. We were a whole bunch of people
who were just breaking into the system. We all
talked Italian at home. We talked a dialect we
thought was Italian, but was New York Italian.

10   Mussolini was a hero, a superhero. He made
us feel special, especially the southerners, Sicilian,
Calabrian. I remember the Abyssinian War, about
1935. I was five. It was talked about as a very positive thing. We had the equivalent of your pep rallies for football teams. To us it was a great victory.
We never really got down on Mussolini. He was
applauded. Then he went into Greece. He wasn't
doing too well (laughs) and had to be bailed out

by the Germans, remember? We were awfully disappointed by that.

It was us against the outside. One block against another block. We had less of a sense of nation than, say, the Israelis did. We were never comfortable with the northern Italians. We were Palestinians. (Laughs.)

It was very painful to live in America. You sorta wanted not to talk about it. Prior to Pearl Harbor, you tried not to talk about the Italian thing. We were very disappointed with their performance in the war. They weren't really heroes. They were brought up on this great macho crap. Our heroes were Joe DiMaggio and Phil Rizzuto. When the Yankees won the pennant in '41, they were our biggies. Crosetti was replaced by Rizzuto—I mean, it was an honorary Italian

position, shortstop. The Yankee Italians were our heroes. The Cubs ultimately got Cavarretta and Dallessandro, but they didn't count.

You go to movies once a week, right? All you see are Italian guys surrendering to the British. Remember Africa? (Laughs.) That was terrible. You grow up, you're gonna be King Kong. All of a sudden all the guys that look like you are running with their arms in the air. I was ten, eleven, and very impressionable. See, the Italians were chumps.

The surrendering happened early. Now the whole neighborhood was not for Mussolini and not really against him. But if he went away, it would be good. We were against Hitler and it was easy to be against the Japanese, but it was still hard to be against Italians.

SUGGESTIONS FOR DISCUSSION

1. Consider each of the reactions to the onset of World War II. How do these accounts compare what you have learned in school about World War II? How do Studs Terkel's informants provide a denser, richer view of the United States at this time?

2. Part of doing oral histories is to ask questions that get people talking. What questions can you imagine Terkel asked to get his informants to talk so eloquently?

3. Consider the point Michel-Rolph Trouillot makes about the difference between "what happened" and "that which is said to have happened." He is commenting on historians, but we can raise the same point about Terkel's informants. How would you apply the distinction to the oral histories presented here?

FIELDWORK PROJECT

This fieldwork project asks you to do an oral history. Follow these steps to get started.

1. *Choose a person and an event that will interest readers*—a Vietnam or Gulf War veteran; someone with experience in the antiwar movement or the counterculture of the 1960s; an older person who remembers the Great Depression, the bombing of Pearl Harbor, the end of World War II; a trade unionist involved in an important organizing drive or strike. The events listed here are largely on the national or international scene, but you may also find informants to talk about an important and interesting local event.

2. *Prepare for the interview by familiarizing yourself with the event in question.* Do some background reading. Develop a list of leading questions that will elicit detailed and in-depth responses from your informant (but don't be tied rigidly to them in the interview if it takes another, potentially fruitful direction). Set a time with your informant, bring a tape recorder, and conduct the interview.

3. *Type up a transcript from the interview that you can edit into an oral history.* Review "Writing the oral history," item 3, below, for advice on editing your interview.

Considerations in Doing an Oral History

1. **Selection.** Not every person will be a good interview subject, even if he or she was intimately involved in a historical event—some people just don't have interesting things to say. Therefore, oral historians usually select an informant who wants to share part of his or her past. Moreover, everyone's memory is selective in some sense. Oral historians expect to get one version of events, though it may be a perspective they didn't foresee.

2. **Interviewing.** The interview is not just a matter of turning on the tape recorder and allowing the informant to speak. The oral historian should let the informant know the purpose for the interview and encourage the informant to tell his or her history in detail. But in keeping the informant on track, the historian should be careful not to provide too much direction. The informant may skip over what might be key information or tailor his or her recitation to what the historian seems to want to hear.

   Once an interview begins, the historian faces many decisions—about, say, whether a rambling account is going somewhere or if it is time to intervene to redirect the informant, or if stopping an informant to clarify a point will risk interrupting the speaker's train of thought.

3. **Writing the oral history.** The transcript of an interview amounts to a kind of raw data that is likely to be filled with pauses, asides, fragmentary remarks, false starts, and undeveloped trains of thought. The oral historian's task is to fashion an account that is faithful to the informant as well as readable. There are several decisions that oral historians typically face at this point:

   ■ *How much of the original transcript should be used?* Oral historians rarely use all of the material in the transcript. In the introduction to *Portraits in Steel* (1993), a collection of photographs and oral histories of Buffalo steel workers, the oral historian Michael Frisch says he used as little as 20 percent of an original transcript and in no case more than 60 percent. When they decide to omit material from the transcript, oral historians are careful to make sure that their editing does not distort the informant's views or suppress important information.

   ■ *How should the material in the transcript be arranged?* Oral historians often decide to rearrange some of the material in the original transcript so that related points appear together. Thus the final version has a coherence that may be missing from the taped interview. The oral historian is by no means obliged to follow the chronological order of the transcript but needs to make sure that any restructuring is faithful to the informant.

   ■ *Should the interviewer's questions appear?* In some cases, oral historians craft the interview into a narrative that is told through the informant's voice. The oral historian stays out of the way, and readers get the sense that the informant is speaking directly to them. In other cases, however, the oral historian may decide to appear in the final text as an interviewer, and the question-and-answer format gives the oral history more of a conversational character, with a greater sense of dialogue and give-and-take.

   ■ *How much editing should be done at the sentence level?* Oral historians face the task of turning the transcript into readable prose that retains the distinctive qualities of the informant's voice. For example, in *"The Good War,"* Studs Terkel has edited the speech of his informants so that it appears for the most part in complete, grammatically correct sentences. But he does include some exceptions, along with slang and profanity, to suggest the vernacular speech patterns of his informants. Here is an example from Terkel's interview with Roger Tuttrup:

> I wanted to be in it. I was fifteen. I felt I wasn't doing anything constructive. I was spottin' pins in the bowling alley, besides goin' to high school. I figured I should be doin' something else. I guess it was a year later, I went to work in a war plant. Some of my friends started goin' into service. I figured: Why the hell don't I? I'm not dog, right?

MINING THE ARCHIVE   Local Museums and Historical Societies

Telling a story of change

The Mount Zion Albany Civil Rights Movement Museum will tell the story of the impact of the southwest Georgia movement on the rest of the world while focusing on the role of the African American church and the freedom music that emerged during this period.

The stories will be told through oral histories from those who were there—those who lived it, those who breathed it, those who walked it, those who went to jail and those who attended the mass meetings and sang about it.

The museum will restore much of Mount Zion Church as it was in the 1960s. The sanctuary will convey the sense of place as a church where visitors will be treated to stirring renditions of freedom songs and other public performances. Restored pews will seat 100.

A portion of the church will house the museum's artifacts. Educational exhibits will detail the civil rights struggle ranging from voter education and registration to nonviolent protest, song, economic boycott and legal action. The museum will also serve as a center for ongoing academic research and provide school tours and other programs and lectures. Through educational programming, the museum will preserve a part of the history of America and south Georgia and challenge today's and tomorrow's youth to learn more about themselves as citizens.

Promoters of the Mount Zion Albany Civil Rights Movement Museum have a vision beyond restoring the church into a museum. Long-range planning, in coordination with the Albany Dougherty Inner-City Authority and the Albany Convention and Visitors Bureau, includes a historic district and walking tours of restored buildings and residences in the Whitney Avenue neighborhood. These tours will depict life in the African American neighborhood before the end of segregation.

MOUNT ZION
ALBANY CIVIL RIGHTS MOVEMENT
MUSEUM INC.

Many towns and cities, as well as colleges and universities, have local museums or historical societies that collect and display historical materials, sponsor research, and put on public programs about local and regional history. There is likely to be one or more in the area near you. Your college library can help you find out where they are and what kind of archival materials they hold.

Visit a local museum or historical society. Sometimes this will require making specific arrangements with its staff. The purpose of your visit should be to acquire an overview of the archival materials and collections. How does the museum or historical society describe its function? What are the nature and scope of the holdings? How were they acquired? What historical periods are represented? What kind of research do they

A celebration of courage and freedom

The Mount Zion Albany Civil Rights Movement Museum is a celebration of courage and freedom of ordinary people and their leaders in the Albany and southwest Georgia movements who bore witness to equal rights and helped to spark the national Civil Rights Movement and international struggles for freedom.

"Woke up this morning with my mind stayed on freedom..."

Freedom Song

The eyes of the nation were on Albany in the early 1960s as thousands of people attended mass meetings and marched in the streets seeking freedom and justice. In December 1961, Dr. Martin Luther King Jr. joined local activists and further inspired overflowing crowds who gathered to hear him at Mount Zion and neighboring Shiloh Baptist Church.

The strength of the Albany Movement gave rise to campaigns in nearby communities: Americus, Moultrie, Dawson, Thomasville, Cordele, Leesburg, Cairo and Newton.

We have in Albany a symbol of that historic struggle in Mount Zion Church. Silent for decades, the boarded-up windows and dust-covered pews of this historic 1906 church, that once echoed with freedom songs and the call for nonviolent social change, soon will give voice to a key part of the 1960s history of Albany and southwest Georgia.

The Albany Movement sprang from the community's grass roots. Young and old, rich and poor—citizens of every class, color and occupation were involved in it.

Many of those who participated in the Movement are members of the community today—our neighbors, co-workers and family members. The museum offers us a chance to hear their stories.

do? Does the archive publish books, pamphlets, or journals? Does it issue an annual report, newsletter, or other informative materials about its holdings and activities? Who uses the collection?

Use your answers to these questions—and other information you picked up during your visit—to prepare a report (either written or oral) on the kinds of historical questions you could answer by drawing on the archive's collection.

CHAPTER TEN

Living in a Transnational World

Photo courtesy Sage Evans.

When we use the word "alien" it seems to stick rather unproblematically and unquestioningly to something or someone, and it is only by a conscious, critical act that we think of something different. Several years ago, in a public speech, Reverend Jesse Jackson seemed to be questioning the fixed and arbitrary assumptions in the dominant ideology when he reminded his audience that undocumented Mexicans were not aliens, they were *migrant* workers.

E.T., Jackson said emphatically, was an *alien*.

—Amitava Kumar

At the time the United States declared its independence from the British Empire, the breakaway colony was already deeply entangled with other countries and peoples, across borders and oceans. By 1776, the triangle slave trade across the Atlantic had been operating for over a century, linking the fortunes of American merchants and plantation owners—and, ultimately, the fate of the new nation—to Africa and the Caribbean.

From its inception, the United States has been part of a transnational circulation of people, wealth, and power. Starting with the earliest European settlers crossing the Atlantic to establish colonies along the eastern seaboard and the African diaspora to slave plantations throughout the Americas, the story has been one of border crossings that go in both directions: the inflow of people (whether African slaves or Chinese contract workers, the inhabitants of Louisiana and the Mexican territories annexed through purchase and conquest, the millions of Europeans who settled in the United States between 1840 and 1920, or recent migrants, documented and undocumented, from all corners of the world in the wake of war and globalization); and the outflow that sends American capital, products, media, outsourced jobs, and military interventions around the world.

As we saw on September 11, 2001, the United States is deeply enmeshed in a transnational world system that emerged in the late twentieth century and that people throughout the world are struggling to understand today. The decisive events of the last quarter-century—the fall of the Soviet Union, the global spread of free market capitalism, the compression of time and space through worldwide communication networks, and the intensified movement of people, languages, and cultures across national borders—have refigured, in literal and symbolic ways, the map of the world and how people locate themselves in it.

The transnational world system is often described as a core (the rich nations of the West) and a periphery (the poor and developing countries), held together by unequal relations of power and asymmetrical flows of wealth that were installed between the metropolitan centers and their colonies in the age of imperialism. It is important, certainly, to recognize how relations between colonizer and colonized brought a transnational world into existence and how colonial influences linger in the present. But we must also take into account the changes in perception and feeling that took place during the successful anti-imperialist and anti-colonial struggles of the twentieth century—in India, China, Egypt, Indonesia, Algeria, Cuba, Vietnam, Ghana, Senegal, Guinea Bissau, South Africa, and elsewhere—as people sought to decolonize themselves mentally as well as politically and to fashion postcolonial identities.

Transnational encounters, which were once described so confidently in terms of the "white man's burden" or the "civilizing mission" of the West, have become blurrier, and the line between core and periphery more permeable. Significant numbers of people from the periphery now live and work in the metropolis—Pakistanis and Jamaicans in London, Cubans and Haitians in Miami, Mexicans in Los Angeles and Chicago, Puerto Ricans and Dominicans in New York City, Hmong and Cambodians in Providence, Turks in Germany, North Africans in Paris, and so on. Accordingly, the metropolitan centers of the West have become more cosmopolitan, polyglot, and transcultural. At the same time, the American consumer culture of McDonald's, Coca-Cola, and Hollywood is being exported to the periphery, to Beijing and Shanghai, Singapore, Mumbai, Lagos, and Johannesburg.

In all cases, the interpenetration of cultures has been complicated, often conflictual, and absolutely crucial to understanding what life in a transnational world means. The purpose of this chapter is to investigate life in this newly emergent transnational world—to identify how social patterns and forms of consciousness span borders, how transnational networks connect people to multiple communities and identities, and how crossings in music, art, writing, visual style, and ordinary speech have created hybrid forms of expression and new social solidarities.

PASSPORT PHOTOS

— *Amitava Kumar*

Amitava Kumar teaches English at Vassar College. This reading is an excerpt from the opening chapter of *Passport Photos* (2000), a multigenre book that combines poetry and photography with literary and cultural analysis. As you can see, Kumar is concerned with the transnational movement of people, encounters at the border, and the condition of immigrants in the Western metropolis.

SUGGESTION   As you read, consider how the photograph Amitava Kumar took near the U.S.-Mexico bor-
FOR READING   der establishes the terms he is exploring—"caution" and "prohibido," "aliens" and "citizens," "home" and "migration," "English" and "Spanish."

1 I took this photograph very close to the U.S.–Mexico border, somewhere between San Diego and Tijuana. There was a tear in the fence; I climbed under it and came up close to the highway to get a better shot. When I went back to the place in the fence, I was startled out of my skin by a Border Patrol van that was very slowly driving past. The officer did not see me, however, and I was soon back in the bar next to my motel.

While sipping my beer, I imagined a conversation with the border patrol officer who had only narrowly missed catching me.

OFFICER: I saw you photographing that sign. That was good, an excellent idea. What do you think about the sign though?

ME: Mmm. I don't know. It's just that—this is the first time I saw that sign. In my country, we have family-planning signs with figures like that. Father, mother, kid. The Health Ministry has a slogan painted beneath it, One or Two Kids. Then Stop.

OFFICER: That's very interesting. This is what I like about multiculturalism. You get to learn about cultural difference.

ME: You really think so? Yes, that's great. What can I learn from *this* sign?

OFFICER: Well, you've gotta get into the semiotics of it, you know what I'm saying?

ME: Uh-huh.

OFFICER: I'll be damned if language is transparent. That's the bottom line here. Just look at that sign—in English it's Caution, but in Spanish, it's *Prohibido*. You don't think those two words mean the same thing, do you?

ME: I don't know. I don't know Spanish.

OFFICER: Okay, well, I'll be patient with you. The sign in English is for folks who drive. They're being cautioned. Now, the sign in Spanish—

ME: Yes, yes, I see what you're driving at! The *Prohibido* sign is for the Spanish speaker—

OFFICER: There you go! Bingo! Bull's eye! They don't have the word *Caución* there. It's plain Prohibited: pure and simple. The picture, the image—it splits, right before your eyes!

ME: The scales have fallen . . .

OFFICER: Well, but you gotta stay alert. 'Cause culture is a moving thing, meanings change. Or sometimes, just get plain run over. All the time.

ME: Yes, yes.

OFFICER: What work do you do?

ME: I teach English.

OFFICER: No kidding! See, this is America! You teaching *English* to our kids, I love it. Say, did you ever watch *Saturday Night Live* when it first came on?

ME: No, I don't think so.

OFFICER: Michael O'Donoghue played a language instructor. He was teaching this confused immigrant played by John Belushi. You know the sentence that O'Donoghue used to introduce the language?

ME: What was it?

OFFICER: I will feed your fingers to the wolverines.

We could have gone on, the officer and I. If we were swapping stories today, I'd have mentioned the news report that the telephone company Sprint, in its billing letter in Spanish, threatens customers with phone cutoff unless their check is received by the end of the month. According to the news report, the Anti-Defamation League and the National Council of La Raza have filed complaints. Why? Because the billing letter in English is somewhat differently worded: "As a customer you are Sprint's number one priority. We . . . look forward to serving your communication needs for many years to come."

And, if the officer had had more time, we might have arrived at an understanding that language, especially English, has been used as a racial weapon in immigration.

5   To cite a historical example: in 1896 a colonial official argued against the restrictions imposed on the entry of Indians in South Africa, adding that this would be "most painful" for Queen Victoria to approve. At the same time, he sanctioned a European literacy test that would automatically exclude Indians while preserving the facade of racial equality.

Almost a hundred years later a Texas judge ordered the mother of a five-year-old to stop speaking in Spanish to her child. Judge Samuel Kiser reminded the mother that her daughter was a "full-blooded American." "Now, get this straight. You start speaking English to this child because if she doesn't do good in school, then I can remove her because it's not in her best interest to be ignorant. The child will only hear English."

Who is permitted to proceed beyond the gates into the mansion of full citizenship? And on what terms? These are the questions that the episode in the Texas courthouse raises. Apart from the issue of gross paternalism and an entirely injudicious jingoism, what comes into play here is the class bias in North American society that promotes bilingualism in the upper class but frowns on it when it becomes an aspect of lower-class life.

More revealing of the ties between language and U.S. Immigration is the following newspaper

◼— California road sign near U.S.-Mexico border, 1994.

report: "School and city officials expressed outrage this week over the Border Patrol's arrest of three Hispanic students outside an English as Second Language class."

For the Chicano poet Alfred Arteaga, the above story about arrest and deportation has a double irony: "irony, not only that 'officials expressed outrage' at so typical an INS action, but irony also, that the story made it into print in the first place." Arteaga knows too well that what Chicanos say and do in their own language is rarely found worthy of printing.

10   I think it is equally significant to remark on the fact that the officers who conducted the arrest were patrolling the borders of the dominant language to pick up the illegals. They are ably assisted by the likes of the California state assemblyman William J. Knight, who distributed among his fellow legislators a poem, "I Love America." That poem begins with the words "I come for visit, get treated regal, / So I stay, who care illegal." This little ditty makes its way through the slime of a racist fantasy. Its landscape is filled with greedy swindlers and dishonest migrant workers. The breeding subhumans speak in a broken syntax and mispronounce the name Chevy, the heartbeat of America, as (call the National Guard, please!) Chebby. The poem ends with a call that emanates like a howl from the guts of the Ku Klux Klan:

We think America damn good place,
Too damn good for white man's race.
If they no like us, they can go,
Got lots of room in Mexico.

If the immigration officer were to ask me about my language, what would I say? That any precious life-giving sense of language loses all form in this arid landscape of Buchanan-speak? Perhaps. That any answer I could possibly give is nothing more defined than a blur moving on the infrared scopes of those guarding the borders of fixed identity.

Homi Bhabha writes: "The enchantment of art lies in looking in a glass darkly—a wall, stone, a screen, paper, canvas, steel—that turns suddenly into the almost unbearable lightness of being." But where is this buoyancy, the refulgence, the mix of new life and new art? As the case of Fauziya Kasinga reminds us—the young woman who fled Togo to avoid genital mutilation and was held for long in detention by the U.S. Immigration authorities—grim reality so often persists in its unenchanting rudeness.

In such conditions to speak is only to declare any speech a station of loss.

I brought two bags from home, but there was a
    third that I left behind. In this new country,
    apart from the struggles that made me a
    stranger, were your needs, of the ones who
    bid me goodbye, those I left behind. Among
    the papers I collected, you had put a small
    bag of sweets, I left behind.
There were divisions at home, there were other
    possibilities;
there were communities in my town, there were
    communities where I came;
I found a job, called it a struggle for survival,
    everything else I left behind. I didn't want to
    forget my traditions, the tradition of forgetting I
    left behind.
Bags, passport, my shoes crossed the yellow
    lines, something was left behind.
Here I am, a sum of different parts; travel agents
    everywhere are selling ads for the parts that
    were left behind.

And yet, while speaking of the patrolling of the borders of dominant identity, I must note the presence of one who is still eluding arrest: a border-artist/poet-performer/hoarder-of-hypehs/warrior-for-Gringostroika. Officer, meet Guillermo Gómez-Peña. You have been looking for him not only because Gómez-Peña declares "I speak in English therefore you listen / I speak in English therefore I hate you." But also because, like a "Pablo Neruda gone punk," this "border brujo" threatens mainstream America with the swaggering banditry of language, demanding as ransom a pure reality-reversal:

What if the U.S. was Mexico?
What if 200,000 Anglo-Saxicans
Were to cross the border each month
to work as gardeners, waiters

3rd chair musicians, movie extras
bouncers, babysitters, chauffeurs
syndicated cartoons, feather-weight boxers,
    fruit-pickers
and anonymous poets?
What if they were called Waspanos
Waspitos, Wasperos or Waspbacks?
What if literature was life, eh?

EXPLORATORY WRITING

Consider the imagined conversation between Amitava Kumar and the border patrol officer. What is Kumar trying to make us understand about the nature of the border between the United States and Mexico?

TALKING ABOUT THE READING

How can we read the photograph that Kumar took near the U.S.-Mexico border? To answer this question, take into account the three figures on the sign. What are they meant to represent? Think as well about the two words on the sign—one in English, "Caution," and the other in Spanish, "Prohibido." The meanings of the two words are different. What does this suggest about who is meant to read the sign and in what way?

WRITING ASSIGNMENTS

1. Write an essay that analyzes the sign Kumar photographed near the U.S.-Mexico border. Explain what the three iconic figures are meant to represent. What is the significance of the word "Caution" appearing in English and "Prohibido" in Spanish?

2. Kumar quotes Guillermo Gómez-Peña: "I speak in English therefore you listen / I speak in English therefore I hate you." What is Gómez-Peña getting at here? Write an essay that explains these two lines. Consider the "reality-reversal" in the poem by Gómez-Peña that closes this reading.

3. This excerpt from *Passport Photos* is concerned with the border between the United States and Mexico and the movement of people, documented and undocumented, across this border. Here is a passage from an essay by Richard Rodriguez, "Illegal Immigrants: Prophets of a Borderless World."

   Before professors in business schools were talking about global economics, illegals knew all about it. Before fax machines punctured the Iron Curtin, coyotes knew the most efficient ways to infiltrate southern California. Before businessmen flew into Mexico City to sign big deals, illegals were picking peaches in the fields of California or flipping pancakes at the roadside diner.
       We live in a world in which economies overlap, in which we no longer know where our automobiles are assembled. We are headed for a century in which the great question will be exactly this: What is a border?
       The illegal immigrant is the bravest among us. The most modern among us. The prophet. "The border, señor?" the illegal immigrant sighs. The border is an inconvenience surely. A danger in the dark. But the border does not hold. The peasant knows the reality of our world decades before the California suburbanites will ever get the point.

Write an essay that takes seriously Rodriguez's claim that the "great question" of the twenty-first century is, "What is a border?" Explain Rodriguez's and Kumar's perspectives on the question, noting similarities and differences. Use this discussion to set up your own commentary on what you see as the implications of the question, "What is a border?"

MAKING CONNECTIONS   Colonized and Colonizer

To understand the transnational world we are living in requires knowledge of its past and, in particular, of how transnational encounters in the age of colonialism shaped relations between the colonizing powers of the West and the people they colonized in Asia, Africa, and the Caribbean. By the end of the nineteenth century, the empires of Britain, France, Holland, Germany, Spain, and Portugal encompassed vast territories and controlled vast populations. In its westward expansion, the United States built an internal settler empire based on the annexation of land and people through purchase, conquest, and dispossession of native inhabitants; by the end of the nineteenth century, the United States had also acquired its own colonies, in Hawaii, Guam, the Philippines, and Puerto Rico.

The two readings in this sequence, the chapter "Columbus in Chains" from Jamaica Kincaid's novel *Annie John* and George Orwell's essay "Shooting an Elephant," offer telling insights into the complicated relations between colonized and colonizer and the legacy that colonialism has left. We catch glimpses, at the level of lived experience, of the loss of sovereignty, the subordination of the colonized, and their resentments and rebelliousness, as well as the "civilizing mission" of native education, the racial hierarchies, and the autocratic powers of the colonizer.

COLUMBUS IN CHAINS

■■— *Jamaica Kincaid*

Jamaica Kincaid is an award-winning novelist, short story writer, and essayist who grew up on the West Indian island of Antigua and now lives in Vermont. Her books include *At the Bottom of the River* (1983), *A Small Place* (1988), and *Autobiography of My Mother* (1996). "Columbus in Chains" was originally published as a short story in the *New Yorker* and then became a chapter in *Annie John* (1985).

SUGGESTION FOR READING   "Columbus in Chains" explores the interaction of two cultures in Antigua—the British culture of the schools and the local Antiguan culture. As you read, annotate passages where the narrator, Annie John, gives us clues about the two cultures and their relationship.

1   Outside, as usual, the sun shone, the trade winds blew; on her way to put some starched clothes on the line, my mother shooed some hens out of her garden; Miss Dewberry baked the buns, some of which my mother would buy for my father and me to eat with our afternoon tea; Miss

Henry brought the milk, a glass of which I would drink with my lunch, and another glass of which I would drink with the bun from Miss Dewberry; my mother prepared our lunch; my father noted some perfectly idiotic thing his partner in house-building, Mr. Oatie, had done, so that over lunch he and my mother could have a good laugh.

The Anglican church bell struck eleven o'clock—one hour to go before lunch. I was then sitting at my desk in my classroom. We were having a history lesson—the last lesson of the morning. For taking first place over all the other girls, I had been given a prize, a copy of a book called *Roman Britain,* and I was made prefect of my class. What a mistake the prefect part had been, for I was among the worst-behaved in my class and did not at all believe in setting myself up as a good example, the way a prefect was supposed to do. Now I had to sit in the prefect's seat—the first seat in the front row, the seat from which I could stand up and survey quite easily my classmates. From where I sat I could see out the window. Sometimes when I looked out, I could see the sexton going over to the minister's house. The sexton's daughter, Hilarene, a disgusting model of good behavior and keen attention to scholarship, sat next to me, since she took second place. The minister's daughter, Ruth, sat in the last row, the row reserved for all the dunce girls. Hilarene, of course, I could not stand. A girl that good would never do for me. I would probably not have cared so much for first place if I could be sure it would not go to her. Ruth I liked, because she was such a dunce and came from England and had yellow hair. When I first met her, I used to walk her home and sing bad songs to her just to see her turn pink, as if I had spilled hot water all over her.

Our books, *A History of the West Indies,* were open in front of us. Our day had begun with morning prayers, then a geometry lesson, then it was over to the science building for a lesson in "Introductory Physics" (not a subject we cared much for), taught by the most dingy-toothed Mr. Slacks, a teacher from Canada, then precious recess, and now this, our history lesson. Recess had the usual drama: this time, I coaxed Gwen out of her disappointment at not being allowed to join the junior choir. Her father—how many times had I wished he would become a leper and so be banished to a leper colony for the rest of my long and happy life with Gwen—had forbidden it, giving as his reason that she lived too far away from church, where choir rehearsals were conducted, and that it would be dangerous for her, a young girl, to walk home alone at night in the dark. Of course, all the streets had lamplight, but it was useless to point that out to him. Oh, how it would have pleased us to press and rub our knees together as we sat in our pew while pretending to pay close attention to Mr. Simmons, our choirmaster, as he waved his baton up and down and across, and how it would have pleased us even more to walk home together, alone in the "early dusk" (the way Gwen had phrased it, a ready phrase always on her tongue), stopping, if there was a full moon, to lie down in a pasture and expose our bosoms in the moonlight. We had heard that full moonlight would make our breasts grow to a size we would like. Poor Gwen! When I first heard from her that she was one of ten children, right on the spot I told her that I would love only her, since her mother already had so many other people to love.

Our teacher, Miss Edward, paced up and down in front of the class in her usual way. In front of her desk stood a small table, and on it stood the dunce cap. The dunce cap was in the shape of a coronet, with an adjustable opening in the back, so that it could fit any head. It was made of cardboard with a shiny gold paper covering and the word "DUNCE" in shiny red paper on the front. When the sun shone on it, the dunce cap was all aglitter, almost as if you were being tricked into thinking it a desirable thing to wear. As Miss Edward paced up and down, she would pass between us and the dunce cap like an eclipse. Each Friday morning, we were given a small test to see how well we had learned the things taught to us all week. The girl who scored lowest was made to wear the dunce cap all day the following Monday. On many Mondays, Ruth wore it—only, with her short yellow hair, when the dunce cap was sitting on her head she looked like a girl attending a birthday party in *The Schoolgirl's Own Annual*.

5   It was Miss Edward's way to ask one of us a question the answer to which she was sure the girl would not know and then put the same question to another girl who she was sure would know the answer. The girl who did not answer correctly would then have to repeat the correct answer in the exact words of the other girl. Many times, I had heard my exact words repeated over and over again, and I liked it especially when the girl doing the repeating was one I didn't care about very much. Pointing a finger at Ruth, Miss Edward asked a question the answer to which was "On the third of November 1493, a Sunday morning, Christopher Columbus discovered Dominica." Ruth, of course, did not know the answer, as she did not know the answer to many questions about the West Indies. I could hardly blame her. Ruth had come all the way from England. Perhaps she did not want to be in the West Indies at all. Perhaps she wanted to be in England, where no one would remind her constantly of the terrible things her ancestors had done; perhaps she had felt even worse when her father was a missionary in Africa. I could see how Ruth felt from looking at her face. Her ancestors had been the masters, while ours had been the slaves. She had such a lot to be ashamed of, and by being with us every day she was always being reminded. We could look everybody in the eye, for our ancestors had done nothing wrong except just sit somewhere, defenseless. Of course, sometimes, what with our teachers and our books, it was hard for us to tell on which side we really now belonged—with the masters or the slaves—for it was all history, it was all in the past, and everybody behaved differently now; all of us celebrated Queen Victoria's birthday, even though she had been dead a long time. But we, the descendants of the slaves, knew quite well what had really

happened, and I was sure that it the tables had been turned we would have acted differently; I was sure that if our ancestors had gone from Africa to Europe and come upon the people living there, they would have taken a proper interest in the Europeans on first seeing them, and said, "How nice," and then gone home to tell their friends about it.

I was sitting at my desk, having these thoughts to myself. I don't know how long it had been since I lost track of what was going on around me. I had not noticed that the girl who was asked the question after Ruth failed—a girl named Hyacinth—had only got a part of the answer correct. I had not noticed that after these two attempts Miss Edward had launched into a harangue about what a worthless bunch we were compared to girls of the past. In fact, I was no longer on the same chapter we were studying. I was way ahead, at the end of the chapter about Columbus's third voyage. In this chapter, there was a picture of Columbus that took up a whole page, and it was in color—one of only five color pictures in the book. In this picture, Columbus was seated in the bottom of a ship. He was wearing the usual three-quarter trousers and a shirt with enormous sleeves, both the trousers and shirt made of maroon-colored velvet. His hat, which was cocked up on one side of his head, had a gold feather in it, and his black shoes had huge gold buckles. His hands and feet were bound up in chains, and he was sitting there staring off into space, looking quite dejected and miserable. The picture had as a title "Columbus in Chains," printed at the bottom of the page. What had happened was that the usually quarrelsome Columbus had got into a disagreement with people who were even more quarrelsome, and a man named Bobadilla, representing King Ferdinand and Queen Isabella, had sent him back to Spain fettered in chains attached to the bottom of a ship. What just deserts, I thought, for I did not like Columbus. How I loved this picture—to see the usually triumphant Columbus, brought so low, seated at the bottom of a boat just watching things go by. Shortly after I first discovered it in my history book, I heard my mother read out loud to my father a letter she had received from her sister, who still lived with her mother and father in the very same Dominica, which is where my mother came from. Ma Chess was fine, wrote my aunt, but Pa Chess was not well. Pa Chess was having a bit of trouble with his limbs; he was not able to go about as he pleased; often he had to depend on someone else to do one thing or another for him. My mother read the letter in quite a state, her voice rising to a higher pitch with each sentence. After she read the part about Pa Chess's stiff limbs, she turned to my father and laughed as she said, "So the great man can no longer just get up and go. How I would love to see his face now!" When I next saw the picture of Columbus sitting there all locked up in his chains, I wrote under it the words "The Great Man Can No Longer Just Get Up and Go." I had written this out with my fountain pen, and in Old English lettering—a script I had recently mastered. As I sat there looking at the picture, I traced the words with my pen over and over, so that the letters grew big and you could read what I had written from not very far away. I don't know how long it was before I heard that my name, Annie John, was being said by this bellowing dragon in the form of Miss Edward bearing down on me.

I had never been a favorite of hers. Her favorite was Hilarene. It must have pained Miss Edward that I so often beat out Hilarene. Not that I liked Miss Edward and wanted her to like me back, but as the other teachers regarded me with much affection, would always tell my mother that I was the most charming student they had ever had, beamed at me when they saw me coming, and were very sorry when they had to write some version of this on my report card: "Annie is an unusually bright girl. She is well behaved in class, at least in the presence of her masters and mistresses, but behind their backs and outside the classroom quite the opposite is

true." When my mother read this or something like it, she would burst into tears. She had hoped to display, with a great flourish, my report card to her friends, along with whatever prize I had won. Instead, the report card would have to take a place at the bottom of the old trunk in which she kept any important thing that had to do with me. I became not a favorite of Miss Edward's in the following way: Each Friday afternoon, the girls in the lower forms were given, instead of a last lesson period, an extra-long recess. We were to use this in ladylike recreation—walks, chats about the novels and poems we were reading, showing each other the new embroidery stitches we had learned to master in home class, or something just as seemly. Instead, some of the girls would play a game of cricket or rounders or stones, but most of us would go to the far end of the school grounds and play band. In this game, of which teachers and parents disapproved and which was sometimes absolutely forbidden, we would place our arms around each other's waist or shoulders, forming lines of ten or so girls, and then we would dance from one end of the school grounds to the other. As we danced, we would sometimes chat these words: "Tee la la la, come go. Tee la la la, come go." At other times we would sing a popular calypso song which usually had lots of unladylike words to it. Up and down the schoolyard, away from our teachers, we would dance and sing. At the end of recess— forty-five minutes—we were missing ribbons and other ornaments from our hair, the pleats of our linen tunics became unset, the collars of our blouses were pulled out, and we were soaking wet all the way down to our bloomers. When the school bell rang, we would make a whooping sound, as if in a great panic, and then we would throw ourselves on top of each other as we laughed and shrieked. We would then run back to our classes, where we prepared to file into the auditorium for evening prayers. After that, it was home for the weekend. But how could we go straight home after all that excitement? No sooner were we on the street than we would form little groups, depending on the direction we were headed in. I was never keen on joining them on the way home, because I was sure I would run into my mother. Instead, my friends and I would go to our usual place near the back of the churchyard and sit on the tombstones of people who had been buried there way before slavery was abolished, in 1833. We would sit and sing bad songs, use forbidden words, and, of course, show each other various parts of our bodies. While some of us watched, the others would walk up and down on the large tombstones showing off their legs. It was immediately a popular idea; everybody soon wanted to do it. It wasn't long before many girls—the ones whose mothers didn't pay strict attention to what they were doing—started to come to school on Fridays wearing not bloomers under their uniforms but underpants trimmed with lace and satin frills. It also wasn't long before an end came to all that. One Friday afternoon, Miss Edward, on her way home from school, took a shortcut through the churchyard. She must have heard the commotion we were making, because there she suddenly was, saying, "What is the meaning of this?"—just the very thing someone like her would say if she came unexpectedly on something like us. It was obvious that I was the ringleader. Oh, how I wished the ground would open up and take her in, but it did not. We all, shamefacedly, slunk home, I with Miss Edward at my side. Tears came to my mother's eyes when she heard what I had done. It was apparently such a bad thing that my mother couldn't bring herself to repeat my misdeed to my father in my presence. I got the usual punishment of dinner alone, outside under the breadfruit tree, but added on to that, I was not allowed to go to the library on Saturday, and on Sunday, after Sunday school and dinner, I was not allowed to take a stroll in the botanical gardens, where Gwen was waiting for me in the bamboo grove.

That happened when I was in the first form. Now here Miss Edward stood. Her whole face was on fire. Her eyes were bulging out on her head. I was sure that at any minute they would land at my feet and roll away. The small pimples on her face, already looking as if they were constantly irritated, now ballooned into huge, on-the-verge-of-exploding boils. Her head shook from side to side. Her strange bottom, which she carried high in the air, seemed to rise up so high that it almost touched the ceiling. Why did I not pay attention, she said. My impertinence was beyond endurance. She then found a hundred words for the different forms my impertinence took. On she went. I was just getting used to this amazing bellowing when suddenly she was speechless. In fact, everything stopped. Her eyes stopped, her bottom stopped, her pimples stopped. Yes she had got close enough so that her eyes caught a glimpse of what I had done to my textbook. The glimpse soon led to closer inspection. It was bad enough that I had defaced my schoolbook by writing in it. That I should write under the picture of Columbus "The Great Man . . . " etc. was just too much. I had gone too far this time, defaming one of the great men in history, Christopher Columbus, discoverer of the island that was my home. And now look at me. I was not even hanging my head in remorse. Had my peers ever seen anyone so arrogant, so blasphemous?

I was sent to the headmistress, Miss. Moore. As punishment, I was removed from my position as prefect, and my place was taken by the odious Hilarene. As an added punishment, I was ordered to copy Books I and II of *Paradise Lost*, by John Milton, and to have it done a week from that day. I then couldn't wait to get home to lunch and the comfort of my mother's kisses and arms. I had nothing to worry about there yet: it would be a while before my mother and father heard of my bad deeds. What a terrible morning! Seeing my mother would be such a tonic—something to pick me up.

10   When I got home, my mother kissed me absentmindedly. My father had got home ahead of me, and they were already deep in conversation, my father regaling her with some unusually

outlandish thing the oaf Mr. Oatie had done. I washed my hands and took my place at table. My mother brought me my lunch. I took one smell of it, and I could tell that it was the much hated breadfruit. My mother said not at all, it was a new kind of rice imported from Belgium, and not breadfruit, mashed and forced through a ricer, as I thought. She went back to talking to my father. My father could hardly get a few words out of his mouth before she was a jellyfish of laughter. I sat there, putting my food in my mouth. I could not believe that she couldn't see how miserable I was and so reach out a hand to comfort me and caress my cheek, the way she usually did when she sensed that something was amiss with me. I could not believe how she laughed at everything he said,

and how bitter it made me feel to see how much she liked him. I ate my meal. The more I ate of it, the more I was sure that it was breadfruit. When I finished, my mother got up to remove my plate. As she started out the door, I said, "Tell me, really, the name of the thing I just ate."

My mother said, "You just ate some bread-fruit. I made it look like rice so that you would eat it. It's very good for you, filled with lots of vitamins." As she said this, she laughed. She was standing half inside the door, half outside. Her body was in the shade of our house, but her head was in the sun. When she laughed, her mouth opened to show off big, shiny, sharp white teeth. It was as if my mother had suddenly turned into a crocodile.

EXPLORATORY WRITING

Annie John says, "Of course, sometimes, what with our teachers and our books, it was hard for us to tell on which side we really belonged—with the masters or the slaves—for it was all history, it was all in the past, everybody behaved differently then." Then, however, a line later, Annie says, "we, the descendants of the slaves, knew quite well what had really happened." What is it that Annie knows quite well and why was she hesitant for a moment about "on which side we really belonged"? In what sense is this struggle over what happened in history and whose side she is on played out in Annie's "defacing" her textbook?

TALKING ABOUT THE READING

Explain Miss Edwards's reaction to Annie John's writing in her history book. It is, of course, a violation of school rules for students to write in their books, but Miss Edwards's reaction seems to go beyond the protection of school property. Rather she uses the terms "arrogant" and "blasphemous" to describe what Annie has done. What clues can you find in the chapter that help explain Miss Edwards's reaction? How can we read this episode as not just a matter of teacher and pupil but, more generally, as an instance of the relations between colonized and colonizer?

WRITING ASSIGNMENT

The key event in "Columbus in Chains" involves an act of writing—when Annie writes "The Great Man Can No Longer Get Up and Go" under the picture of Columbus. Write an essay on the role that reading and writing play in the short story. Consider, for example, how Annie uses writing to rewrite the textbook history of Columbus. Notice, too, other passages where reading and writing take place or where Annie mentions written materials of one kind or another. What roles, literally and symbolically, do reading and writing play in this story?

SHOOTING AN ELEPHANT

■■■— *George Orwell*

George Orwell is probably best known for two of his novels, *Animal Farm* (1945) and *Nineteen Eighty-Four* (1949). He was born in India and, as the essay "Shooting an Elephant" (1936) reveals, served for five years in the Indian Imperial Police in Burma, the setting of his novel *Burmese Days* (1934). Orwell also published accounts of his experience doing menial jobs and living among the poor in *Down and Out in Paris and London* (1933), his investigations of working-class life in Britain during the Great Depression in *The Road to Wigan Pier* (1937), and his participation on the Republican side in the Spanish Civil War in *Homage to Catalonia* (1938).

SUGGESTION FOR READING There are layers of conflict in Orwell's essay: between his personal beliefs about imperialism and his job as a police officer; between him as a European and a representative of the British Empire and the Burmese people; and between his reluctance to shoot the elephant and the crowd urging him on. As you read, notice how Orwell overlaps these conflicts. How do they take on greater significance in light of each other? What do they make visible about the nature of colonialism?

1   In Moulmein, in lower Burma, I was hated by large numbers of people—the only time in my life that I have been important enough for this to happen to me. I was sub-divisional police officer of the town, and in an aimless, petty kind of way anti-European feeling was very bitter. No one had the guts to raise a riot, but if a European woman went through the bazaars alone somebody would probably spit betel juice over her dress. As a police officer I was an obvious target and was baited whenever it seemed safe to do so. When a nimble Burman tripped me up on the football field and the referee (another Burman) looked the other way, the crowd yelled with hideous laughter. This happened more than once. In the end the sneering yellow faces of young men that met me everywhere, the insults hooted after me when I was at a safe distance, got badly on my nerves. The young Buddhist priests were the worst of all. There were several thousands of them in the town and none of them seemed to have anything to do except stand on street corners and jeer at Europeans.

All this was perplexing and upsetting. For at that time I had already made up my mind that imperialism was an evil thing and the sooner I chucked up my job and got out of it the better.

Theoretically—and secretly, of course—I was all for the Burmese and all against their oppressors, the British. As for the job I was doing, I hated it more bitterly than I can perhaps make clear. In a job like that you see the dirty work of Empire at close quarters. The wretched prisoners huddling in the stinking cages of the lock-ups, the grey, cowed faces of the long-term convicts, the scarred buttocks of the men who had been flogged with bamboos—all these oppressed me with an intolerable sense of guilt. But I could get nothing into perspective. I was young and ill-educated and I had had to think out my problems in the utter silence that is imposed on every Englishman in the East. I did not even know that the British Empire is dying, still less did I know that it is a great deal better than the younger empires that are going to supplant it. All I knew was that I was stuck between my hatred of the empire I served and my rage against the evil-spirited little beasts who tried to make my job impossible. With one part of my mind I thought of the British Raj as an unbreakable tyranny, as something clamped down, in *saecula saeculorum*, upon the will of prostrate peoples; with another part I thought that the greatest joy in the world would be to drive a bayonet into a Buddhist priest's guts. Feelings like these are the normal by-products of imperialism; ask any Anglo-Indian official, if you can catch him off duty.

One day something happened which in a roundabout way was enlightening. It was a tiny incident in itself, but it gave me a better glimpse than I had had before of the real nature of imperialism—the real motives for which despotic governments act. Early one morning the sub-inspector at a police station the other end of the town rang me up on the phone and said that an elephant was ravaging the bazaar. Would I please come and do something about it? I did not know what I could do, but I wanted to see what was happening and I got on to a pony and started out. I took my rifle, an old 44 Winchester and much too small to kill an elephant, but I thought the noise might be useful *in terrorem*. Various Burmans stopped me on the way and told me about the elephant's doings. It was not, of course, a wild elephant, but a tame one which had gone "must." It had been chained up, as tame elephants always are when their attack of "must" is due, but on the previous night it had broken its chain and escaped. Its mahout, the only person who could manage it when it was in that state, had set out in pursuit, but had taken the wrong direction and was now twelve hours' journey away, and in the morning the elephant had suddenly reappeared in the town. The Burmese population had no weapons and were quite helpless against it. It had already destroyed somebody's bamboo hut, killed a cow and raided some fruit-stalls and devoured the stock; also it had met the municipal rubbish van and, when the driver jumped out and took to his heels, had turned the van over and inflicted violences upon it.

The Burmese sub-inspector and some Indian constables were waiting for me in the quarter where the elephant had been seen. It was a very poor quarter, a labyrinth of squalid bamboo huts, thatched with palmleaf, winding all over a steep hillside. I remember that it was a cloudy, stuffy morning at the beginning of the rains. We began questioning the people as to where the elephant had gone and, as usual, failed to get any definite information. That is invariably the case in the East; a story always sounds clear enough at a distance, but the nearer you get to the scene of events the vaguer it becomes. Some of the people said that the elephant had gone in one direction, some said that he had gone in another, some professed not even to have heard of any elephant. I had almost made up my mind that the whole story was a pack of lies, when we heard yells a little distance away. There was a loud, scandalized cry of "Go away, child! Go away this instant!" and an old woman with a switch in her hand came round the corner of a hut, violently shooing away a crowd of naked children. Some more women followed, clicking their tongues and exclaiming; evidently there was something that the children ought not to have seen. I rounded the hut and saw a man's dead body sprawling in the mud. He was an Indian, a black Dravidian coolie, almost naked, and he could not have been dead many minutes. The people said that the elephant had come suddenly upon him round the corner of the hut, caught him with its trunk, put its foot on his back and ground him into the earth. This was the rainy season and the ground was soft, and his face had scored a trench a foot deep and a couple of yards long. He was lying on his belly with arms crucified and head sharply twisted to one side. His face was coated with mud, the eyes wide open, the teeth bared and grinning with an expression of unendurable agony. (Never tell me, by the way, that the dead look peaceful. Most of the corpses I have seen looked devilish.) The friction of the great beast's foot had stripped the skin from his back as neatly as one skins a rabbit. As soon as I saw the dead man I sent an orderly to a friend's house nearby to borrow an elephant rifle. I had already sent back the pony, not wanting it to go mad with fright and throw me if it smelt the elephant.

5   The orderly came back in a few minutes with a rifle and five cartridges, and meanwhile

some Burmans had arrived and told us that the elephant was in the paddy fields below, only a few hundred yards away. As I started forward practically the whole population of the quarter flocked out of the houses and followed me. They had seen the rifle and were all shouting excitedly that I was going to shoot the elephant. They had not shown much interest in the elephant when he was merely ravaging their homes, but it was different now that he was going to be shot. It was a bit of fun to them, as it would be to an English crowd; besides they wanted the meat. It made me vaguely uneasy. I had no intention of shooting the elephant—I had merely sent for the rifle to defend myself if necessary—and it is always unnerving to have a crowd following you. I marched down the hill, looking and feeling a fool, with the rifle over my shoulder and an ever-growing army of people jostling at my heels. At the bottom, when you got away from the huts, there was a metalled road and beyond that a miry waste of paddy fields a thousand yards across, not yet ploughed but soggy from the first rains and dotted with coarse grass. The elephant was standing eight yards from the road, his left side towards us. He took not the slightest notice of the crowd's approach. He was tearing up bunches of grass, beating them against his knees to clean them and stuffing them into his mouth.

I had halted on the road. As soon as I saw the elephant I knew with perfect certainty that I ought not to shoot him. It is a serious matter to shoot a working elephant—it is comparable to destroying a huge and costly piece of machinery—and obviously one ought not to do it if it can possibly be avoided. And at that distance, peacefully eating, the elephant looked no more dangerous than a cow. I thought then and I think now that his attack of "must" was already passing off; in which case he would merely wander harmlessly about until the mahout came back and caught him. Moreover, I did not in the least want to shoot him. I decided that I would watch him for a little while to make sure that he did not turn savage again, and then go home.

But at that moment I glanced round at the crowd that had followed me. It was an immense crowd, two thousand at the least and growing every minute. It blocked the road for a long distance on either side. I looked at the sea of yellow faces above the garish clothes-faces all happy and excited over this bit of fun, all certain that the elephant was going to be shot. They were watching me as they would watch a conjurer about to perform a trick. They did not like me, but with the magical rifle in my hands I was momentarily worth watching. And suddenly I realized that I should have to shoot the elephant after all. The people expected it of me and I had got to do it; I could feel their two thousand wills pressing me forward, irresistibly. And it was at this moment, as I stood there with the rifle in my hands, that I first grasped the hollowness, the futility of the white man's dominion in the East. Here was I, the white man with his gun, standing in front of the unarmed native crowd—seemingly the leading actor of the piece; but in reality I was only an absurd puppet pushed to and fro by the will of those yellow faces behind. I perceived in this moment that when the white man turns tyrant it is his own freedom that he destroys. He becomes a sort of hollow, posing dummy, the conventionalized figure of a sahib. For it is the condition of his rule that he shall spend his life in trying to impress the "natives," and so in every crisis he has got to do what the "natives" expect of him. He wears a mask, and his face grows to fit it. I had got to shoot the elephant. I had committed myself to doing it when I sent for the rifle. A sahib has got to act like a sahib; he has got to appear resolute, to know his own mind and do definite things. To come all that way, rifle in hand, with two thousand people marching at my heels, and then to trail feebly away, having done nothing—no, that was impossible. The crowd would laugh at me. And my whole life, every white man's life in the East, was one long struggle not to be laughed at.

But I did not want to shoot the elephant. I watched him beating his bunch of grass against his knees, with that preoccupied grandmotherly air that elephants have. It seemed to me that it would be murder to shoot him. At that age I was not squeamish about killing animals, but I had never shot an elephant and never wanted to. (Somehow it always seems worse to kill a large animal.) Besides, there was the beast's owner to be considered. Alive, the elephant was worth at least a hundred pounds; dead, he would only be worth the value of his tusks, five pounds, possibly. But I had got to act quickly. I turned to some experienced-looking Burmans who had been there when we arrived, and asked them how the elephant had been behaving. They all said the same thing: he took no notice of you if you left him alone, but he might charge if you went too close to him.

It was perfectly clear to me what I ought to do. I ought to walk up to within, say, twenty-five yards of the elephant and test his behavior. If he charged, I could shoot; if he took no notice of me, it would be safe to leave him until the mahout came back. But also I knew that I was going to do no such thing. I was a poor shot with a rifle and the ground was soft mud into which one would sink at every step. If the elephant charged and I missed him, I should have about as much chance as a toad under a steam-roller. But even then I was not thinking particularly of my own skin, only of the watchful yellow faces behind. For at that moment, with the crowd watching me, I was not afraid in the ordinary sense, as I would have been if I had been alone. A white man mustn't be frightened in front of "natives"; and so, in general, he isn't frightened. The sole thought in my mind was that if anything went wrong those two thousand Burmans would see me pursued, caught, trampled on and reduced to a grinning corpse like that Indian up the hill. And if that happened it was quite probable that some of them would laugh. That would never do.

10   There was only one alternative. I shoved the cartridges into the magazine and lay down on the road to get a better aim. The crowd grew very still, and a deep, low, happy sigh, as of people who see the theatre curtain go up at last, breathed from innumerable throats. They were going to have their bit of fun after all. The rifle was a beautiful German thing with cross-hair sights. I did not then know that in shooting an elephant one would shoot to cut an imaginary bar running from ear-hole to ear-hole. I ought, therefore, as the elephant was sideways on, to have aimed straight at his ear-hole, actually I aimed several inches in front of this, thinking the brain would be further forward.

When I pulled the trigger I did not hear the bang or feel the kick—one never does when a shot goes home—but I heard the devilish roar of glee that went up from the crowd. In that instant, in too short a time, one would have thought, even for the bullet to get there, a mysterious, terrible change had come over the elephant. He neither stirred nor fell, but every line of his body had altered. He looked suddenly stricken, shrunken, immensely old, as though the frightful impact of the bullet had paralysed him without knocking him down. At last, after what seemed a long time—it might have been five seconds, I dare say—he sagged flabbily to his knees. His mouth slobbered. An enormous senility seemed to have settled upon him. One could have imagined him thousands of years old. I fired again into the same spot. At the second shot he did not collapse but climbed with desperate slowness to his feet and stood weakly upright, with legs sagging and head drooping. I fired a third time. That was the shot that did for him. You could see the agony of it jolt his whole body and knock the last remnant of strength from his legs. But in falling he seemed for a moment to rise, for as his hind legs collapsed beneath him he seemed to tower upward like a huge rock toppling, his trunk reaching skyward like a tree. He trumpeted, for the first and only time. And then down he came, his belly towards me, with a crash that seemed to shake the ground even where I lay.

I got up. The Burmans were already racing past me across the mud. It was obvious that the elephant would never rise again, but he was not dead. He was breathing very rhythmically with long rattling gasps, his great mound of a side painfully rising and falling. His mouth was wide open—I could see far down into caverns of pale pink throat. I waited a long time for him to die, but his breathing did not weaken. Finally I fired my two remaining shots into the spot where I thought his heart must be. The thick blood welled out of him like red velvet, but still he did not die. His body did not even jerk when the shots hit him, the tortured breathing continued without a pause. He was dying, very slowly and in great agony, but in some world remote from me where not even a bullet could damage him further. I felt that I had got to put an end to that dreadful noise. It seemed dreadful to see the great beast lying there, powerless to move and yet powerless to die, and not even to be able to finish him. I sent back for my small rifle and poured shot after shot into his heart and down his throat. They seemed to make no impression. The tortured gasps continued as steadily as the ticking of a clock.

In the end I could not stand it any longer and went away. I heard later that it took him half an hour to die. Burmans were bringing dash and baskets even before I left, and I was told they had stripped his body almost to the bones by the afternoon.

Afterwards, of course, there were endless discussions about the shooting of the elephant. The owner was furious, but he was only an Indian and could do nothing. Besides, legally I had done the right thing, for a mad elephant has to be killed, like a mad dog, if its owner fails to control it. Among the Europeans opinion was divided. The older men said I was right, the younger men said it was a damn shame to shoot an elephant for killing a coolie, because an elephant was worth more than any damn Coringhee coolie. And afterwards I was very glad that the coolie had been killed; it put me legally in the right and it gave me a sufficient pretext for shooting the elephant. I often wondered whether any of the others grasped that I had done it solely to avoid looking a fool.

EXPLORATORY WRITING

Explain Orwell's decision to shoot the elephant. How does it grow out of the unequal relations of power between colonized and colonizer and the situation, as Orwell puts it, of a "white man's life in the East"?

TALKING ABOUT THE READING

Work in a group of three or four. What do you think Jamaica Kincaid's character Annie John would have to say about Orwell shooting the elephant? Compare what your group imagines Annie John might say to what other groups have come up with. Consider how they are different and similar and what they bring to light about the colonized's perspective on the British Empire. Finally, given his complicated position in the empire, how do you think Orwell would respond?

WRITING ASSIGNMENT

Orwell says that this incident made him realize "the hollowness, the futility of the white man's dominion in the East." Write an essay that explains his realization.

WRITING SEQUENCE

1. If you have done some exploratory writing, reread what you have written. (If you haven't, write for 10 minutes on each of the Kincaid and Orwell Exploratory Writing topics.) Consider that both Kincaid and Orwell, in important respects, deal with conflicts of

allegiances and knowing which side they are on. Write a page or two of exploratory writing that explains how the question of taking sides figures in each reading.

2. Orwell says, "my whole life, every white man's life in the East, was one long struggle not to be laughed at." In a certain sense, we can read Annie John's writing in her history book as a way of laughing at Columbus. Write a 2-page essay that explains the nature of laughter on the part of the colonized and why it is seen as so subversive to colonial authority.

3. For the culminating assignment, first write a one-paragraph account of what happens in each of the two readings, as though you're writing a newspaper report on Annie John defacing her textbook and on Orwell shooting the elephant. Try to keep your reporting as objective and disinterested as possible, to get the facts of the event down in plain language. Then in a longer, finished piece of writing (drafted, revised, and edited), analyze how the narrators in the two pieces of writing (the fictional Antiguan schoolgirl Annie John and the actual Burmese police officer George Orwell) add their own consciousness to the events that take place. Consider how they present themselves to readers and the relationship they seek to establish with their readers—to give them a way of relating to and interpreting the events you have described in as objective terms as you could summon. Begin the essay by presenting the two objective accounts and then devote the bulk of your essay to an explanation of how Annie John and George Orwell make sense of these events, for themselves and for their readers.

HOW TO TAME A WILD TONGUE

— Gloria Anzaldúa

Gloria Anzaldúa writes in a language that grows out of the multiple cultures in the American Southwest—a mosaic of English (both standard and slang), Spanish (both Castilian and Mexican), northern Mexican and Chicano Spanish dialects, Tex-Mex, *Pachuco* (the vernacular of urban zoot suiters), and the Aztec language Nahuatl. The following selection is a chapter from her book *Borderlands/La Frontera* (1987). As the title of her book indicates, Anzaldúa sees herself as a "border woman." "I grew up between two cultures," she says, "the Mexican (with a heavy Indian influence) and the Anglo (as a member of a colonized people in our own territory). I have been straddling that *tejas*-Mexican border, and others, all my life." Anzaldúa's "borderland" refers to those places "where two or more cultures edge each other, where people of different races occupy the same territory, where under, lower, middle, and upper classes touch, where the space between two individuals shrinks with intimacy."

SUGGESTION FOR READING   As you read, you will notice how Gloria Anzaldúa combines English and Spanish in a sentence or a paragraph. Consider the effects of her prose and how it locates you as a reader on the border where two cultures and languages touch.

1 "We're going to have to control your tongue," the dentist says, pulling out all the metal from my mouth. Silver bits plop and tinkle into the basin. My mouth is a motherlode. The dentist is cleaning out my roots. I get a whiff of the stench when I gasp. "I can't cap that tooth yet, you're still draining," he says.

"We're going to have to do something about your tongue," I hear the anger rising in his voice. My tongue keeps pushing out the wads of cotton, pushing back the drills, the long thin needles. "I've never seen anything as strong or as stubborn," he says. And I think, how do you tame a wild tongue, train it to be quiet, how do you bridle and saddle it? How do you make it lie down?

> Who is to say that robbing a people of its
> language is less violent than war?
>
> *Ray Gwyn Smith*[1]

I remember being caught speaking Spanish at recess—that was good for three licks on the knuckles with a sharp ruler. I remember being sent to the corner of the classroom for "talking back" to the Anglo teacher when all I was trying to do was tell her how to pronounce my name. "If you want to be American, speak 'American.' If you don't like it, go back to Mexico where you belong."

"I want you to speak English. *Pa' hallar buen trabajo tienes que saber hablar el inglés bien. Qué vale toda tu educatión si todavía hablas inglés con un* 'accent,'" my mother would say, mortified that I spoke English like a Mexican. At Pan American University, I and all Chicano students were required to take two speech classes. Their purpose: to get rid of our accents.

5   Attacks on one's form of expression with the intent to censor are a violation of the First Amendment. *El Anglo con care de inocente nos arrancó la lengua.* Wild tongues can't be tamed, they can only be cut out.

OVERCOMING THE TRADITION OF SILENCE

> *Ahogadas, escupimos el oscuro. Peleando con nuestra propia sombra el silencio nos sepulta.*

En boca cerrada no entran moscas. "Flies don't enter a closed mouth" is a saying I kept hearing when I was a child. *Ser habladora* was to be a gossip and a liar, to talk too much. *Muchachitas bien criadas,* well-bred girls don't answer back. *Es una falta de respeto* to talk back to one's mother or father. I remember one of the sins I'd recite to the priest in the confession box the few times I went to confession: talking back to my mother, *hablar pa' 'tras, repelar. Hocicona, repelona, chismosa,* having a big mouth, questioning, carrying tales are all signs of being *mal criada.* In my culture they are all words that are derogatory if applied to women—I've never heard them applied to men.

The first time I heard two women, a Puerto Rican and a Cuban, say the word "*nosotras,*" I was shocked. I had not known the word existed. Chicanas use *nosotros* whether we're male or female. We are robbed of our female being by the masculine plural. Language is a male discourse.

> And our tongues have become dry the
> wilderness has dried out our tongues and we
> have forgotten speech.
>
> *Irena Klepfisz*[2]

Even our own people, other Spanish speakers *nos quieren poner candados en la boca.* They would hold us back with their bag of *reglas de academia.*

OYÉ COMO LADRA: EL LENGUAJE DE LA FRONTERA

> *Quien tiene boca se equivoca.*
>
> *Mexican saying*

"*Pocho,* cultural traitor, you're speaking the oppressor's language by speaking English, you're ruining the Spanish language," I have been accused by various Latinos and Latinas. Chicano Spanish is considered by the purist and by most Latinos deficient, a mutilation of Spanish.

10   But Chicano Spanish is a border tongue which developed naturally. Change, *evolución, enriquecimiento de palabras nuevas por invención o adopción* have created variants of Chicano Spanish, *un nuevo lenguaje. Un lenguaje que corresponde a un modo de vivir.* Chicano Spanish is not incorrect, it is a living language.

For a people who are neither Spanish nor live in a country in which Spanish is the first language; for a people who live in a country in which English is the reigning tongue but who are not Anglo; for a people who cannot entirely identify with either standard (formal, Castilian) Spanish nor standard English, what recourse is left to them but to create their own language? A language which they can connect their identity to, one capable of communicating the realities and values true to themselves—a language with terms that are neither *español ni inglés*, but both. We speak a patois, a forked tongue, a variation of two languages.

Chicano Spanish sprang out of the Chicanos' need to identify ourselves as a distinct people. We need a language with which we could communicate with ourselves, a secret language. For some of us, language is a homeland closer than the Southwest—for many Chicanos today live in the Midwest and the East. And because we are a complex, heterogeneous people, we speak many languages. Some of the languages we speak are

1. Standard English

2. Working-class and slang English

3. Standard Spanish

4. Standard Mexican Spanish

5. North Mexican Spanish dialect

6. Chicano Spanish (Texas, New Mexico, Arizona, and California have regional variations)

7. Tex-Mex

8. *Pachuco* (called *caló*)

My "home" tongues are the languages I speak with my sister and brothers, with my friends. They are the last five listed, with 6 and 7 being closest to my heart. From school, the media, and job situations, I've picked up standard and working class English. From Mamagrande Locha and from reading Spanish and Mexican literature, I've picked up Standard Spanish and Standard Mexican Spanish. From *los recién llegados,* Mexican immigrants, and *braceros,* I learned the North Mexican dialect. With Mexicans I'll try to speak either Standard Mexican Spanish or the North Mexican dialect. From my parents and Chicanos living in the Valley, I picked up Chicano Texas Spanish, and I speak it with my mom, younger brother (who married a Mexican and who rarely mixes Spanish with English), aunts, and older relatives.

With Chicanas from *Nuevo México* or *Arizona* I will speak Chicano Spanish a little, but often they don't understand what I'm saying. With most California Chicanas I speak entirely in English (unless I forget). When I first moved to San Francisco, I'd rattle off something in Spanish, unintentionally embarrassing them. Often it is only with another Chicana *tejano* that I can talk freely.

15   Words distorted by English are known as anglicisms or *pochismos*. The *pocho* is an anglicized Mexican or American of Mexican origin who speaks Spanish with an accent characteristic of North Americans and who distorts and reconstructs the language according to the influence of English.[3] Tex-Mex, or Spanglish, comes most naturally to me. I may switch back and forth from English to Spanish in the same sentence or in the same word. With my sister and my brother Nune and with Chicano *tejano* contemporaries I speak in Tex-Mex.

From kids and people my own age I picked up *Pachuco*. *Pachuco* (the language of the zoot suiters) is a language of rebellion, both against Standard Spanish and Standard English. It is a secret language. Adults of the culture and outsiders cannot understand it. It is made up of slang words from both English and Spanish. *Ruca* means girl or woman, *vato* means guy or dude, *chale* means no, *simón* means yes, *churro* is sure, talk is *periquiar, pigionear* means petting, *que gacho* means how nerdy, *ponte águila* means watch out, death is called *la pelona*. Through lack of practice and not having others who can speak it, I've lost most of the *Pachuco* tongue.

CHICANO SPANISH

Chicanos, after 250 years of Spanish/Anglo colonization, have developed significant differences in the Spanish we speak. We collapse two adjacent vowels into a single syllable and sometimes shift the stress in certain words such as *maíz/maiz, cohete/cuete*. We leave out certain consonants when they appear between vowels: *lado/lao, mojado/mojao*. Chicanos from South Texas pronounce *f* as *j* as in *jue* (*fue*). Chicanos use "archaisms," words that are no longer in the Spanish language, words that have been evolved out. We say *semos, truje, haiga, ansina,* and *naiden*. We retain the "archaic" *j,* as in *jalar,* that derives from an earlier *h* (the French *halar* or the Germanic *halon* which was lost to standard Spanish in the sixteenth century), but which is still found in several regional dialects such as the one spoken in South Texas. (Due to geography, Chicanos from the Valley of South Texas were cut off linguistically from other Spanish speakers. We tend to use words that the Spaniards brought over from Medieval Spain. The majority of the Spanish colonizers in Mexico and the Southwest came from Extremadura—Hernán Cortés was one of them—and Andalucía. Andalucians pronounce *ll* like a *y,* and their *d*'s tend to be absorbed by adjacent vowels: *tirado* becomes *tirao*. They brought *el lenguaje popular, dialectos y regionalismos*.)[4]

Chicanos and other Spanish speakers also shift *ll* to *y* and *z* to *s*.[5] We leave out initial syllables, saying *tar* for *estar,* *toy* for *estoy,* *hora* for *ahora* (*cubanos* and *puertorriqueños* also leave out initial letters of some words). We also leave out the final syllable such as *pa* for *para*. The intervocalic *y,* the *ll* as in *tortilla, ella, botella,* gets replaced by *tortia* or *tortiya, ea, botea*. We add an additional syllable at the beginning of certain words: *atocar* for *tocar, agastar* for *gastar*. Sometimes we'll say *lavaste las vacijas,* other times *lavates* (substituting the *ates* verb endings for the *aste*).

We used anglicisms, words borrowed from English: *bola* from ball, *carpeta* from carpet, *máchina de lavar* (instead of *lavadora*) from washing machine. Tex-Mex argot, created by adding a Spanish sound at the beginning or end of an English word such as *cookiar* for cook, *watchar* for watch, *parkiar* for park, and *rapiar* for rape, is the result of the pressures on Spanish speakers to adapt to English.

20   We don't use the word *vosotros/as* or its accompanying verb form. We don't say *claro* (to mean yes), *imagínate,* or *me emociona,* unless we picked up Spanish from Latinas, out of a book, or in a classroom. Other Spanish-speaking groups are going through the same, or similar, development in their Spanish.

LINGUISTIC TERRORISM

Deslenguadas. Somos los del español deficiente. We are your linguistic nightmare, your linguistic aberration, your linguistic *mestizaje,* the subject of your *burla*. Because we speak with tongues of fire we are culturally crucified. Racially, culturally, and linguistically *somos huérfanos*— we speak an orphan tongue.

Chicanas who grew up speaking Chicano Spanish have internalized the belief that we speak poor Spanish. It is illegitimate, a bastard language. And because we internalize how our language has been used against us by the dominant culture, we use our language differences against each other.

Chicana feminists often skirt around each other with suspicion and hesitation. For the longest time I couldn't figure it out. Then it dawned on me. To be close to another Chicana is like looking into the mirror. We are afraid of what we'll see there. *Pena*. Shame. Low estimation of self. In childhood we are told that our language is wrong. Repeated attacks on our native tongue diminish our sense of self. The attacks continue throughout our lives.

Chicanas feel uncomfortable talking in Spanish to Latinas, afraid of their censure. Their language was not outlawed in their countries. They had a whole lifetime of being immersed in their native tongue; generations, centuries in which Spanish was a first language, taught in school, heard on radio and TV, and read in the newspaper.

If a person, Chicana or Latina, has a low estimation of my native tongue, she also has a low estimation of me. Often with *mexicanas y latinas* we'll speak English as a neutral language. Even among Chicanas we tend to speak English at parties or conferences. Yet, at the same time, we're afraid the other will think we're *agringadas* because we don't speak Chicano Spanish. We oppress each other trying to out-Chicano each other, vying to be the "real" Chicanas, to speak like Chicanos. There is no one Chicano language just as there is no one Chicano experience. A monolingual Chicana whose first language is English or Spanish is just as much a Chicana as one who speaks several variants of Spanish. A Chicana from Michigan or Chicago or Detroit is just as much a Chicana as one from the Southwest. Chicano Spanish is as diverse linguistically as it is regionally.

25   By the end of this century, Spanish speakers will comprise the biggest minority group in the United States, a country where students in high schools and colleges are encouraged to take French classes because French is considered more "cultured." But for a language to remain alive it must be used.[6] By the end of this century English, and not Spanish, will be the mother tongue of most Chicanos and Latinos.

So, if you want to really hurt me, talk badly about my language. Ethnic identity is twin skin to linguistic identity—I am my language. Until I can take pride in my language, I cannot take pride in myself. Until I can accept as legitimate Chicano Texas Spanish, Tex-Mex, and all the other languages I speak, I cannot accept the legitimacy of myself. Until I am free to write bilingually and to switch codes without having always to translate, while I still have to speak English or Spanish when I would rather speak Spanglish, and as long as I have to accommodate the English speakers rather than having them accommodate me, my tongue will be illegitimate.

I will no longer be made to feel ashamed of existing. I will have my voice: Indian, Spanish, white. I will have my serpent's tongue—my woman's voice, my sexual voice, my poet's voice. I will overcome the tradition of silence.

My fingers
move sly against your palm
Like women everywhere, we speak in code . . .

Melanie Kaye/Kantrowitz[7]

"VISTAS," CORRIDOS, Y COMIDA: MY NATIVE TONGUE

In the 1960s, I read my first Chicano novel. It was *City of Night* by John Rechy, a gay Texan, son of a Scottish father and a Mexican mother. For days I walked around in stunned amazement that a Chicano could write and could get published. When I read *I Am Joaquín*[8] I was surprised to see a bilingual book by a Chicano in print. When I saw poetry written in Tex-Mex for the first time, a feeling of pure joy flashed through me. I felt like we really existed as a people. In 1971, when I started teaching High School English to Chicano students, I tried to supplement the required texts with works by Chicanos, only to be reprimanded and forbidden to do so by the principal. He claimed that I was supposed to teach "American" and English literature. At the risk of being fired, I swore my students to secrecy and slipped in Chicano short stories, poems, a play. In graduate school, while working toward a Ph.D., I had to "argue" with one adviser after the other, semester after semester, before I was allowed to make Chicano literature an area of focus.

Even before I read books by Chicanos or Mexicans, it was the Mexican movies I saw at the drive-in—the Thursday night special of $1.00 a carload—that gave me a sense of belonging. "*Vámonos a las vistas,*" my mother would call out and we'd all—grandmother, brothers, sister, and cousins—squeeze into the car. We'd wolf down cheese and bologna white bread sandwiches while watching Pedro Infante in melodramatic tearjerkers like *Nosotros los pobres*, the first "real" Mexican movie (that was not an imitation of European movies). I remember seeing *Cuando los hijos se van* and surmising that all Mexican movies played up the love a mother has for her children and what ungrateful sons and daughters suffer when they are not devoted to their mothers. I remember the singing-type "westerns" of Jorge Negrete and Miquel Aceves Mejía. When watching Mexican movies, I felt a sense of homecoming as well as alienation. People who were to amount to something didn't go to Mexican movies, or bailes, or tune their radios to *bolero*, *rancherita*, and *corrido* music.

30   The whole time I was growing up, there was *norteño* music sometimes called North Mexican border music, or Tex-Mex music, or Chicano music, or *cantina* (bar) music. I grew up listening to *conjuntos*, three- or four-piece bands made up of folk musicians playing guitar, *bajo sexto*, drums, and button accordion, which Chicanos had borrowed from the German immigrants who had come to Central Texas and Mexico to farm and build breweries. In the Rio Grande Valley, Steve Jordan and Little Joe Hernández were popular, and Flaco Jiménez was the accordion king. The rhythms of Tex-Mex music are those of the polka, also adapted from the Germans, who in turn had borrowed the polka from the Czechs and Bohemians.

I remember the hot, sultry evenings when *corridos*—songs of love and death on the Texas-Mexican borderlands—reverberated out of cheap amplifiers from the local *cantinas* and wafted in through my bedroom window.

Corridos first became widely used along the South Texas/Mexican border during the early conflict between Chicanos and Anglos. The *corridos* are usually about Mexican heroes who do valiant deeds against the Anglo oppressors. Pancho Villa's song, "*La cucaracha*," is the most famous one. *Corridos* of John F. Kennedy and his death are still very popular in the Valley. Older Chicanos remember Lydia Mendoza, one of the great border *corrido* singers who was called *la Gloria de Tejas*. Her "*El tango negro*," sung during the Great Depression, made her a singer of the people. The ever-present *corridos* narrated one hundred years of border history, bringing news of events as well as entertaining. These folk musicians and folk songs are our chief cultural mythmakers, and they made our hard lives seem bearable.

I grew up feeling ambivalent about our music. Country-western and rock-and-roll had more status. In the fifties and sixties, for the slightly educated and *agringado* Chicanos, there existed a sense of shame at being caught listening to our music. Yet I couldn't stop my feet from thumping to the music, could not stop humming the words, nor hide from myself the exhilaration I felt when I heard it.

There are more subtle ways that we internalize identification, especially in the forms of images and emotions. For me food and certain smells are tied to my identity, to my homeland. Woodsmoke curling up to an immense blue sky; woodsmoke perfuming my grandmother's clothes, her skin. The stench of cow manure and the yellow patches on the ground; the crack of a .22 rifle and the reek of cordite. Homemade white cheese sizzling in a pan, melting inside a folded *tortilla*. My sister Hilda's hot, spicy *menudo*, *chile colorado* making it deep red, pieces of *panza* and hominy floating on top. My brother Carito barbequing *fajitas* in the backyard. Even now and 3,000 miles away, I can see my mother spicing the ground beef, pork, and venison with chile. My mouth salivates at the thought of the hot steaming *tamales* I would be eating if I were home.

SÍ LE PREGUNTAS A MI MAMÁ, "¿QUÉ ERES?"

> Identity is the essential core of who we are as individuals, the conscious experience of the self inside.
>
> *Gershen Kaufman*[9]

35   *Nosotros los* Chicanos straddle the borderlands. On one side of us, we are constantly exposed to the Spanish of the Mexicans, on the other side we hear the Anglos' incessant clamoring so that we forget our language. Among ourselves we don't say *nosotros los americanos, o nosotros los españoles, o nosotros los hispanos*. We say *nosotros los mexicanos* (by *mexicanos* we do not mean citizens of Mexico; we do not mean a

national identity, but a racial one). We distinguish between *mexicanos del otro lado* and *mexicanos de este lado*. Deep in our hearts we believe that being Mexican has nothing to do with which country one lives in. Being Mexican is a state of soul—not one of mind, not one of citizenship. Neither eagle nor serpent, but both. And like the ocean, neither animal respects borders.

Dime con quien andas y te diré quien eres.
(Tell me who your friends are and I'll tell you who you are.)

Mexican saying

Si le preguntas a mi mamá, "¿Qué eres?" te dirá, "Soy mexicana." My brothers and sister say the same. I sometimes will answer *"soy mexicana"* and at others will say *"soy Chicana" o "soy tejana."* But I identified as *"Raza"* before I ever identified as *"mexicana"* or *"Chicana."*

As a culture, we call ourselves Spanish when referring to ourselves as a linguistic group and when copping out. It is then that we forget our predominant Indian genes. We are 70–80 percent Indian.[10] We call ourselves Hispanic[11] or Spanish American or Latin American or Latin when linking ourselves to other Spanish-speaking peoples of the Western hemisphere and when copping out. We call ourselves Mexican American[12] to signify we are neither Mexican nor American, but more the noun "American" than the adjective "Mexican" (and when copping out).

Chicanos and other people of color suffer economically for not acculturating. This voluntary (yet forced) alienation makes for psychological conflict, a kind of dual identity—we don't identify with the Anglo-American cultural values and we don't totally identify with the Mexican cultural values. We are a synergy of two cultures with various degrees of Mexicanness or Angloness. I have so internalized the borderland conflict that sometimes I feel like one cancels out the other and we are zero, nothing, no one. *A veces no soy nada ni nadie. Pero hasta cuando no lo soy, lo soy.*

When not copping out, when we know we are more than nothing, we call ourselves Mexican,

referring to race and ancestry; *mestizo* when affirming both our Indian and Spanish (but we hardly ever own our Black) ancestry; Chicano when referring to a politically aware people born and/or raised in the United States; *Raza* when referring to Chicanos; *tejanos* when we are Chicanos from Texas.

40   Chicanos did not know we were a people until 1965 when César Chávez and the farmworkers united and *I Am Joaquín* was published and *la Raza Unida* party was formed in Texas. With that recognition, we became a distinct people. Something momentous happened to the Chicano soul—we became aware of our reality and acquired a name and a language (Chicano Spanish) that reflected that reality. Now that we had a name, some of the fragmented pieces began to fall together—who we were, what we were, how we had evolved. We began to get glimpses of what we might eventually become.

Yet the struggle of identities continues, the struggle of borders is our reality still. One day the inner struggle will cease and a true integration take place. In the meantime, *tenémos que hacer la lucha. ¿Quién está protegiendo los ranchos de mi gente? ¿Quién está tratando de cerrar la fisura entre la india y el blanco en nuestra sangre? El Chicano, si, el Chicano que anda como un ladrón en su propia casa.*

Los Chicanos, how patient we seem, how very patient. There is the quiet of the Indian about us.[13] We know how to survive. When other races have given up their tongue we've kept ours. We know what it is to live under the hammer blow of the dominant *norteamericano* culture. But more than we count the blows, we count the days the weeks the years the centuries the aeons until the white laws and commerce and customs will rot in the deserts they've created, lie bleached. *Humildes* yet proud, *quietos* yet wild, *nosotros los mexicanos-Chicanos* will walk by the crumbling ashes as we go about our business. Stubborn, persevering, impenetrable as stone, yet possessing a malleability that renders us unbreakable, we, the *mestizas* and *mestizos,* will remain.

NOTES

1. Ray Gwyn Smith, *Moorland Is Cold Country,* unpublished book.

2. Irena Klepfisz, *"Di rayze aheym/*The Journey Home," in *The Tribe of Dina: A Jewish Women's Anthology,* Melanie Kaye/Kantrowitz and Irena Klepfisz, eds. (Montpelier, VT: Sinister Wisdom Books, 1986), 49.

3. R. C. Ortega, *Dialectologia Del Barrio,* trans. Hortencia S. Alwan (Los Angeles, CA: R. C. Ortega Publisher & Bookseller, 1977), 132.

4. Eduardo Hernandéz-Chávez, Andrew D. Cohen, and Anthony F. Beltramo, *El Lenguaje de los Chicanos: Regional and Social Characteristics of Language Used by Mexican Americans* (Arlington, VA: Center for Applied Linguistics, 1975), 39.

5. Hernandéz-Chávez, xvii.

6. Irena Klepfisz, "Secular Jewish Identity: Yidishkayt in America," in *The Tribe of Dina,* Kaye/Kantrowitz and Klepfisz, eds., 43.

7. Melanie Kaye/Kantrowitz, "Sign," in *We Speak in Code: Poems and Other Writings* (Pittsburgh, PA: Motheroot Publications, Inc., 1980), 85.

8. Rodolfo Gonzales, *I Am Joaquín/Yo Soy Joaquín* (New York, NY: Bantam Books, 1972). It was first published in 1967.

9. Gershen Kaufman, *Shame: The Power of Caring* (Cambridge, MA: Schenkman Books, Inc., 1980), 68.

10. John R. Chávez, *The Lost Land: The Chicano Images of the Southwest* (Albuquerque, NM: University of New Mexico Press, 1984), 88–90.

11. "Hispanic" is derived from *Hispanis* (*España,* a name given to the Iberian Peninsula in ancient times when it was a part of the Roman Empire) and is a term designated by the U.S. government to make it easier to handle us on paper.

12. The Treaty of Guadalupe Hidalgo created the Mexican American in 1848.

`13. Anglos, in order to alleviate their guilt for dispossessing the Chicano, stressed the Spanish part of us and perpetrated the myth of the Spanish Southwest. We have accepted the fiction that we are Hispanic, that is Spanish, in order to accommodate ourselves to the dominant culture and its abhorrence of Indians. Chávez, 88–91.

EXPLORATORY WRITING

Anzaldúa has composed the chapter "How to Tame a Wild Tongue" like a mosaic, in which she juxtaposes seven separate sections without offering an overarching statement of purpose to unify the sections. At the same time, the sections seem to go together in an associative, non-linear way. Look back over the sections of the chapter to identify how (or whether) the separate parts work together to form a whole. What in your view is the principle of combination that links them together?

TALKING ABOUT THE READING

Compare your experience of reading Gloria Anzaldúa's polyglot prose with the experiences of others in your class. As suggested, the purpose of her mix of language is to recreate the conditions of the borderland, where the use of one language leaves out or excludes those who know only the other language. But what are readers to do with such prose? If you don't know Spanish, how did you try to make sense of the Spanish words and phrases Anzaldúa uses? Even if you do know Spanish, are you familiar with the terms that she draws from regional dialects? What does your experience of reading "How to Tame a Wild Tongue" reveal to you about the nature of cultural encounters at the borderlands?

WRITING ASSIGNMENTS

1. Write an essay describing and analyzing your experience of reading "How to Tame a Wild Tongue." How do the mix of languages and the fragmentary character of the text put special demands on you as a reader? How and in what sense is this reading

experience equivalent to what Anzaldúa calls the "borderland"? What does your position as a reader on the border reveal to you about the nature of encounters across cultures in multicultural America?

2. Write an essay that compares the representations of the border found in "How to Tame a Wild Tongue" and in "Passport Photos." How does Anzaldúa's representation of herself as a *mestiza* of the borderlands compare to Kumar's picture of the border? What does each reveal about the movement of people in a transnational world? What does each reveal about the position of the United States in a globalized world?

3. Use Anzaldúa's chapter as a model to write your own essay about the contradictory and conflicting meanings of language use and cultural expression in your life. This assignment is meant to be an experiment in writing that asks you to emulate Anzaldúa in incorporating multiple voices, dialects, slangs, and languages and in composing by way of a collage that juxtaposes fragments of thought and experience instead of developing a linear piece of writing with a main point and supporting evidence. To develop ideas for this essay, you might begin by thinking of the different voices, musics, foods, and other cultural forms that are part of your experience, the conflicting ways of life that you have lived, and the multiple identities that you inhabit.

ARTS OF THE CONTACT ZONE

— *Mary Louise Pratt*

Mary Louise Pratt is the Silver Professor in the Department of Spanish and Portuguese at New York University. Prior to that, she taught for nearly thirty years at Stanford, where she was involved in designing the freshman culture program that expanded the curriculum beyond the traditional Western civilization courses to include cultures, texts, and languages from around the world. Pratt is the author of such well-regarded works as *Toward a Speech Act Theory of Literary Discourse* (1977) and *Imperial Eyes: Studies in Travel Writing and Translation* (1992), in which a revised version of "Arts of the Contact Zone" appeared as the introduction. "Arts of the Contact Zone" was originally delivered as a keynote address at the Modern Language Association Literacy Conference in 1990, and then published in *Profession 91*.

SUGGESTION FOR READING   You will notice that Pratt's essay is a wide-ranging one that places considerable demands on readers to put its parts together. She ranges from talking about her children to discussing the letter New Chronicle and Good Government, written in 1613 by the Incan Guaman Poma to King Philip III of Spain, to recounting a brief history of European literacy to describing curriculum reform at Stanford. To help you follow the overall argument that spans the sections, keep in mind Pratt's aim of reconsidering the familiar notions of communities and cultures as homogeneous, unified, geographically separate, and monolingual—and to see instead the contact zones "where cultures meet, clash, and grapple with each other, often in contexts of highly asymmetrical relations of power, such as colonialism, slavery, or their aftermaths as they are lived out in many parts of the world today."

1 Whenever the subject of literacy comes up, what often pops first into my mind is a conversation I overheard eight years ago between my son Sam and his best friend, Willie, aged six and seven, respectively: "Why don't you trade me Many Trails for Carl Yats . . . Yesits . . . Ya-strum-scrum."

"That's not how you say it, dummy, it's Carl Yes . . . Yes . . . oh, I don't know." Sam and Willie had just discovered baseball cards. Many Trails was their decoding, with the help of first-grade English phonics, of the name Manny Trillo. The name they were quite rightly stumped on was Carl Yastrzemski. That was the first time I remembered seeing them put their incipient literacy to their own use, and I was of course thrilled.

Sam and Willie learned a lot about phonics that year by trying to decipher surnames on baseball cards, and a lot about cities, states, heights, weights, places of birth, stages of life. In the years that followed, I watched Sam apply his arithmetic skills to working out batting averages and subtracting retirement years from rookie years; I watched him develop senses of patterning and order by arranging and rearranging his cards for hours on end, and aesthetic judgment by comparing different photos, different series, layouts, and color schemes. American geography and history took shape in his mind through baseball cards. Much of his social life revolved around trading them, and he learned about exchange, fairness, trust, the importance of processes as opposed to results, what it means to get cheated, taken advantage of, even robbed. Baseball cards were the medium of his economic life too. Nowhere better to learn the power and arbitrariness of money, the absolute divorce between use value and exchange value, notions of long- and short-term investment, the possibility of personal values that are independent of market values.

Baseball cards meant baseball card shows, where there was much to be learned about adult worlds as well. And baseball cards opened the door to baseball books, shelves and shelves of encyclopedias, magazines, histories, biographies, novels, books of jokes, anecdotes, cartoons, even poems. Sam learned the history of American racism and the struggle against it through baseball; he saw the Depression and two world wars from behind home plate. He learned the meaning of commodified labor, what it means for one's body and talents to be owned and dispensed by another. He knows something about Japan, Taiwan, Cuba, and Central America and how men and boys do things there. Through the history and experience of baseball stadiums he thought about architecture, light, wind topography, meteorology, the dynamics of public space. He learned the meaning of expertise, of knowing about something well enough that you can start a conversation with a stranger and feel sure of holding your own. Even with an adult—especially with an adult. Throughout his preadolescent years, baseball history was Sam's luminous point of contact with grown-ups, his lifeline to caring. And, of course, all this time he was also playing baseball, struggling his way through the stages of the local Little League system, lucky enough to be a pretty good player, loving the game and coming to know deeply his strengths and weaknesses.

Literacy began for Sam with the newly pronounceable names on the picture cards and brought him what has been easily the broadest, most varied, most enduring, and most integrated experience of his thirteen-year life. Like many parents, I was delighted to see schooling give Sam the tools with which to find and open all these doors. At the same time I found it unforgivable that schooling itself gave him nothing remotely as meaningful to do, let alone anything that would actually take him beyond the referential, masculinist ethos of baseball and its lore.

5   However, I was not invited here to speak as a parent, nor as an expert on literacy. I was asked to speak as an MLA [Modern Language Association] member working in the elite academy. In that capacity my contribution is undoubtedly supposed to be abstract, irrelevant, and anchored outside the real world. I wouldn't dream of disappointing anyone. I propose immediately to head back several centuries to a text that has a few points in common with baseball cards and raises thoughts about what Tony Sarmiento, in his comments to the conference, called new visions

of literacy. In 1908 a Peruvianist named Richard Pietschmann was exploring in the Danish Royal Archive in Copenhagen and came across a manuscript. It was dated in the city of Cuzco in Peru, in the year 1613, some forty years after the final fall of the Inca empire to the Spanish and signed with an unmistakably Andean indigenous name: Felipe Guaman Poma de Ayala. Written in a mixture of Quechua and ungrammatical, expressive Spanish, the manuscript was a letter addressed by an unknown but apparently literate Andean to King Philip III of Spain. What stunned Pietschmann was that the letter was twelve hundred pages long. There were almost eight hundred pages of written text and four hundred of captioned line drawings. It was titled *The First New Chronicle and Good Government.* No one knew (or knows) how the manuscript got to the library in Copenhagen or how long it had been there. No one, it appeared, had ever bothered to read it or figured out how. Quechua was not thought of as a written language in 1908, nor Andean culture as a literate culture.

Pietschmann prepared a paper on his find, which he presented in London in 1912, a year after the rediscovery of Machu Picchu by Hiram Bingham. Reception, by an international congress of Americanists, was apparently confused. It took twenty-five years for a facsimile edition of the work to appear in Paris. It was not till the late 1970s, as positivist reading habits gave way to interpretive studies and colonial elitisms to post-colonial pluralisms, that Western scholars found ways of reading Guaman Poma's *New Chronicle and Good Government* as the extraordinary intercultural tour de force that it was. The letter got there, only 350 years too late, a miracle and a terrible tragedy.

I propose to say a few more words about this erstwhile unreadable text, in order to lay out some thoughts about writing and literacy in what I like to call the *contact zones.* I use this term to refer to social spaces where cultures meet, clash, and grapple with each other, often in contexts of highly asymmetrical relations of power, such as colonialism, slavery, or their aftermaths as they are lived out in many parts of the world today. Eventually I will use the term to reconsider the models of community that many of us rely on in teaching and theorizing and that are under challenge today. But first a little more about Guaman Poma's giant letter to Philip III.

Insofar as anything is known about him at all, Guaman Poma exemplified the sociocultural complexities produced by conquest and empire. He was an indigenous Andean who claimed noble Inca descent and who had adopted (at least in some sense) Christianity. He may have worked in the Spanish colonial administration as an interpreter, scribe, or assistant to a Spanish tax collector—as a mediator, in short. He says he learned to write from his half brother, a mestizo whose Spanish father had given him access to religious education.

Guaman Poma's letter to the king is written in two languages (Spanish and Quechua) and two parts. The first is called the *Nueva corónica,* "New Chronicle." The title is important. The chronicle of course was the main writing apparatus through which the Spanish presented their American conquests to themselves. It constituted one of the main official discourses. In writing a "new chronicle," Guaman Poma took over the official Spanish genre for his own ends. Those ends were, roughly, to construct a new picture of the world, a picture of a Christian world with Andean rather than European peoples at the center of it—Cuzco, not Jerusalem. In the *New Chronicle* Guaman Poma begins by rewriting the Christian history of the world from Adam and Eve (Fig. 1), incorporating the Amerindians into it as offspring of one of the sons of Noah. He identifies five ages of Christian history that he links in parallel with the five ages of canonical Andean history—separate but equal trajectories that diverge with Noah and reintersect not with Columbus but with Saint Bartholomew, claimed to have preceded Columbus in the Americas. In a couple of hundred pages, Guaman Poma constructs a veritable encyclopedia of Inca and

FIGURE 1.

Adam and Eve.

pre-Inca history, customs, laws, social forms, public offices, and dynastic leaders. The depictions resemble European manners and customs description, but also reproduce the meticulous detail with which knowledge in Inca society was stored on *quipus* and in the oral memories of elders.

10   Guaman Poma's *New Chronicle* is an instance of what I have proposed to call an *autoethnographic* text, by which I mean a text in which people undertake to describe themselves in ways that engage with representations others have made of them. Thus if ethnographic texts are those in which European metropolitan subjects represent to themselves their others (usually their conquered others), autoethnographic texts are representations that the so-defined others

construct *in response to* or in dialogue with those texts. Autoethnographic texts are not, then, what are usually thought of as autochthonous forms of expression or self-representation (as the Andean *quipus* were). Rather they involve a selective collaboration with and appropriation of idioms of the metropolis or the conqueror. These are merged or infiltrated to varying degrees with indigenous idioms to create self-representations intended to intervene in metropolitan modes of understanding. Autoethnographic works are often addressed to both metropolitan audiences and the speaker's own community. Their reception is thus highly indeterminate. Such texts often constitute a marginalized group's point of entry into the dominant circuits of print culture. It is interesting to think, for example, of American slave autobiography in its autoethnographic dimensions, which in some respects distinguish it from Euramerican autobiographical tradition. The concept might help explain why some of the earliest published writing by Chicanas took the form of folkloric manners and customs sketches written in English and published in English-language newspapers or folklore magazines (see Treviño). Autoethnographic representation often involves concrete collaborations between people, as between literate ex-slaves and abolitionist intellectuals, or between Guaman Poma and the Inca elders who were his informants. Often, as in Guaman Poma, it involves more than one language. In recent decades autoethnography, critique, and resistance have reconnected with writing in a contemporary creation of the contact zone, the *testimonio*.

Guaman Poma's *New Chronicle* ends with a revisionist account of the Spanish conquest, which, he argues, should have been a peaceful encounter of equals with the potential for benefiting both, but for the mindless greed of the Spanish. He parodies Spanish history. Following contact with the Incas, he writes, "In all Castille, there was a great commotion. All day and at night in their dreams the Spaniards were saying, 'Yndias, Yndias, oro, plata, oro, plata del Piru'"

FIGURE 2.
Conquista. Meeting of Spaniard and Inca.
The Inca says in Quechua, "You eat this gold?"
Spaniard replies in Spanish, "We eat this gold."

("Indies, Indies, gold, silver, gold, silver from Peru") (Fig. 2). The Spanish, he writes, brought nothing of value to share with the Andeans, nothing "but armor and guns con la codicia de oro, plata oro y plata, yndias, a las Yndias, Piru" ("with the lust for gold, silver, gold and silver, Indies, the Indies, Peru"). I quote these words as an example of a conquered subject using the conqueror's language to construct a parodic, oppositional representation of the conqueror's own speech. Guaman Poma mirrors back to the Spanish (in their language, which is alien to him) an image of themselves that they often suppress and will therefore surely recognize. Such are the dynamics of language, writing, and representation in contact zones.

The second half of the epistle continues the critique. It is titled *Buen gobierno y justicia,* "Good Government and Justice," and combines a description of colonial society in the Andean region with a passionate denunciation of Spanish exploitation and abuse. (These, at the time he was writing, were decimating the population of the Andes at a genocidal rate. In fact, the potential loss of the labor force became a main cause for reform of the system.) Guaman Poma's most implacable hostility is invoked by the clergy, followed by the dreaded *corregidores,* or colonial overseers (Fig. 3). He also praises good works, Christian habits, and just men where he finds them, and offers at length his views as to what constitutes "good government and justice." The Indies, he argues, should be administered through a collaboration of Inca and Spanish elites. The epistle ends with an imaginary question-and-answer session in which, in a reversal of hierarchy, the king is depicted asking Guaman Poma questions about how to reform the empire—a dialogue imagined across the many lines that divide the Andean scribe from the imperial monarch, and in which the subordinated subject single-handedly gives himself authority in the colonizer's language and verbal repertoire. In a way, it worked—this extraordinary text did get written—but in a way it did not, for the letter never reached its addressee.

To grasp the import of Guaman Poma's project, one needs to keep in mind that the Incas had no system of writing. Their huge empire is said to be the only known instance of a full-blown bureaucratic state society built and administered without writing. Guaman Poma constructs his text by appropriating and adapting pieces of the representational repertoire of the invaders. He does not simply imitate or reproduce it; he selects and adapts it along Andean lines to express (bilingually, mind you) Andean interests and aspirations. Ethnographers have used the term *transculturation* to describe processes whereby members of subordinated or marginal groups select and invent from materials transmitted by a dominant or metropolitan culture. The term, originally coined by Cuban sociologist Fernando Ortiz

FIGURE 3.
Corregidor de minas. Catalog of Spanish abuses
of indigenous labor force.

in the 1940s, aimed to replace overly reductive concepts of acculturation and assimilation used to characterize culture under conquest. While subordinate peoples do not usually control what emanates from the dominant culture, they do determine to varying extents what gets absorbed into their own and what it gets used for. Transculturation, like autoethnography, is a phenomenon of the contact zone.

As scholars have realized only relatively recently, the transcultural character of Guaman Poma's text is intricately apparent in its visual as well as its written component. The genre of the four hundred line drawings is European—there seems to have been no tradition of representational drawing among the Incas—but in their execution they deploy specifically Andean

systems of spatial symbolism that express Andean values and aspirations.[1]

15   In Figure 1, for instance, Adam is depicted on the left-hand side below the sun, while Eve is on the right-hand side below the moon, and slightly lower than Adam. The two are divided by the diagonal of Adam's digging stick. In Andean spatial symbolism, the diagonal descending from the sun marks the basic line of power and authority dividing upper from lower, male from female, dominant from subordinate. In Figure 2, the Inca appears in the same position as Adam, with the Spaniard opposite, and the two at the same height. In Figure 3, depicting Spanish abuses of power, the symbolic pattern is reversed. The Spaniard is in a high position indicating dominance, but on the "wrong" (right-hand) side. The

diagonals of his lance and that of the servant doing the flogging mark out a line of illegitimate, though real, power. The Andean figures continue to occupy the left-hand side of the picture, but clearly as victims. Guaman Poma wrote that the Spanish conquest had produced *"un mundo al reves,"* "a world in reverse."

In sum, Guaman Poma's text is truly a product of the contact zone. If one thinks of cultures, or literatures, as discrete, coherently structured, monolingual edifices, Guaman Poma's text, and indeed any autoethnographic work, appears anomalous or chaotic—as it apparently did to the European scholars Pietschmann spoke to in 1912. If one does not think of cultures this way, then Guaman Poma's text is simply heterogeneous, as the Andean region was itself and remains today. Such a text is heterogeneous on the reception end as well as the production end: it will read very differently to people in different positions in the contact zone. Because it deploys European and Andean systems of meaning making, the letter necessarily means differently to bilingual Spanish-Quechua speakers and to monolingual speakers in either language; the drawings mean differently to monocultural readers, Spanish or Andean, and to bicultural readers responding to the Andean symbolic structures embodied in European genres.

In the Andes in the early 1600s there existed a literate public with considerable intercultural competence and degrees of bilingualism. Unfortunately, such a community did not exist in the Spanish court with which Guaman Poma was trying to make contact. It is interesting to note that in the same year Guaman Poma sent off his letter, a text by another Peruvian was adopted in official circles in Spain as the canonical Christian mediation between the Spanish conquest and Inca history. It was another huge encyclopedic work, titled the *Royal Commentaries of the Incas,* written, tellingly, by a mestizo, Inca Garcilaso de la Vega. Like the mestizo half brother who taught Guaman Poma to read and write, Inca Garcilaso was the son of an Inca princess and a Spanish official, and had lived in Spain since he was seventeen. Though he too spoke Quechua, his book

is written in eloquent, standard Spanish, without illustrations. While Guaman Poma's life's work sat somewhere unread, the *Royal Commentaries* was edited and reedited in Spain and the New World, a mediation that coded the Andean past and present in ways thought unthreatening to colonial hierarchy.[2] The textual hierarchy persists; the *Royal Commentaries* today remains a staple item on Ph.D. reading lists in Spanish, while the *New Chronicle and Good Government,* despite the ready availability of several fine editions, is not. However, though Guaman Poma's text did not reach its destination, the transcultural currents of expression it exemplifies continued to evolve in the Andes, as they still do, less in writing than in storytelling, ritual, song, dance-drama, painting and sculpture, dress, textile art, forms of governance, religious belief, and many other vernacular art forms. All express the effects of long-term contact and intractable, unequal conflict.

Autoethnography, transculturation, critique, collaboration, bilingualism, mediation, parody, denunciation, imaginary dialogue, vernacular expression—these are some of the literate arts of the contact zone. Miscomprehension, incomprehension, dead letters, unread masterpieces, absolute heterogeneity of meaning—these are some of the perils of writing in the contact zone. They all live among us today in the transnationalized metropolis of the United States and are becoming more widely visible, more pressing, and, like Guaman Poma's text, more decipherable to those who once would have ignored them in defense of a stable, centered sense of knowledge and reality.

CONTACT AND COMMUNITY

The idea of the contact zone is intended in part to contrast with ideas of community that underlie much of the thinking about language, communication, and culture that gets done in the academy. A couple of years ago, thinking about the linguistic theories I knew, I tried to make sense of a utopian quality that often seemed to characterize social analyses of language by the academy. Languages were seen as living in "speech communities," and these tended to be theorized as discrete, self-defined, coherent entities, held together by a homogeneous competence or grammar shared identically and equally among all the members. This abstract idea of the speech community seemed to reflect, among other things, the utopian way modern nations conceive of themselves as what Benedict Anderson calls "imagined communities."[3] In a book of that title, Anderson observes that with the possible exception of what he calls "primordial villages," human communities exist as *imagined* entities in which people "will never know most of their fellow-members, meet them or even hear of them, yet in the mind of each lives the image of their communion." "Communities are distinguished," he goes on to say, "not by their falsity/genuineness, but by *the style in which they are imagined*" (15; emphasis mine). Anderson proposes three features that characterize the style in which the modern nation is imagined. First, it is imagined as *limited,* by "finite, if elastic, boundaries"; second, it is imagined as *sovereign*; and, third, it is imagined as *fraternal,* "a deep, horizontal comradeship" for which millions of people are prepared "not so much to kill as willingly to die" (15). As the image suggests, the nation-community is embodied metonymically in the finite, sovereign, fraternal figure of the citizen-soldier.

20   Anderson argues that European bourgeoisies were distinguished by their ability to "achieve solidarity on an essentially imagined basis" (74) on a scale far greater than that of elites of other times and places. Writing and literacy play a central role in this argument. Anderson maintains, as have others, that the main instrument that made bourgeois nation-building projects possible was print capitalism. The commercial circulation of books in the various European vernaculars, he argues, was what first created the invisible networks that would eventually constitute the literate elites and those they ruled as nations. (Estimates are that 180 million books were put into circulation in Europe between the years 1500 and 1600 alone.)

Now obviously this style of imagining of modern nations, as Anderson describes it, is strongly utopian, embodying values like equality, fraternity, liberty, which the societies often profess but systematically fail to realize. The prototype of the modern nation as imagined community was, it seemed to me, mirrored in ways people thought about language and the speech community. Many commentators have pointed out how modern views of language as code and competence assume a unified and homogeneous social world in which language exists as a shared patrimony—as a device, precisely, for imagining community. An image of a universally shared literacy is also part of the picture. The prototypical manifestation of language is generally taken to be the speech of individual adult native speakers face-to-face (as in Saussure's famous diagram) in monolingual, even monodialectal situations—in short, the most homogeneous case linguistically and socially. The same goes for written communication. Now one could certainly imagine a theory that assumed different things—that argued, for instance, that the most revealing speech situation for understanding language was one involving a gathering of people each of whom spoke two languages and understood a third and held only one language in common with any of the others. It depends on what workings of language you want to see or want to see first, on what you choose to define as normative.

In keeping with autonomous, fraternal models of community, analyses of language use commonly assume that principles of cooperation and shared understanding are normally in effect. Descriptions of interactions between people in conversation, classrooms, medical and bureaucratic settings, readily take it for granted that the situation is governed by a single set of rules or norms shared by all participants. The analysis focuses then on how those rules produce or fail to produce an orderly, coherent exchange. Models involving games and moves are often used to describe interactions. Despite whatever conflicts or systematic social differences might be in play, it is assumed that all participants are engaged in the same game and that the game is the same for all players. Often it is. But of course it often is not, as, for example, when speakers are from different classes or cultures, or one party is exercising authority and another is submitting to it or questioning it. Last year one of my children moved to a new elementary school that had more open classrooms and more flexible curricula than the conventional school he started out in. A few days into the term, we asked him what it was like at the new school. "Well," he said, "they're a lot nicer, and they have a lot less rules. But know *why* they're nicer?" "Why?" I asked. "So you'll obey all the rules they don't have," he replied. This is a very coherent analysis with considerable elegance and explanatory power, but probably not the one his teacher would have given.

When linguistic (or literate) interaction is described in terms of orderliness, games, moves, or scripts, usually only legitimate moves are actually named as part of the system, where legitimacy is defined from the point of view of the party in authority—regardless of what other parties might see themselves as doing. Teacher-pupil language, for example, tends to be described almost entirely from the point of view of the teacher and teaching, not from the point of view of pupils and pupiling (the word doesn't even exist, though the thing certainly does). If a classroom is analyzed as a social world unified and homogenized with respect to the teacher, whatever students do other than what the teacher specifies is invisible or anomalous to the analysis. This can be true in practice as well. On several occasions my fourth grader, the one busy obeying all the rules they didn't have, was given writing assignments that took the form of answering a series of questions to build up a paragraph. These questions often asked him to identify with the interests of those in power over him—parents, teachers, doctors, public authorities. He invariably sought ways to resist or subvert these assignments. One assignment, for instance, called for imagining "a helpful invention." The students were asked to write single-sentence responses to the following questions:

What kind of invention would help you?

How would it help you?

Why would you need it?

What would it look like?

Would other people be able to use it also?

What would be an invention to help your teacher?

What would be an invention to help your parents?

Manuel's reply read as follows:

A grate adventchin

Some inventchins are GRATE!!!!!!!!!!! My inventchin would be a shot that would put every thing you learn at school in your brain. It would help me by letting me graduate right now!! I would need it because it would let me play with my friends, go on vacachin and, do fun a lot more. It would look like a regular shot. Ather peaple would use to. This inventchin would help my teacher parents get away from a lot of work. I think a shot like this would be GRATE!

Despite the spelling, the assignment received the usual star to indicate the task had been fulfilled in an acceptable way. No recognition was available, however, of the humor, the attempt to be critical or contestatory, to parody the structures of authority. On that score, Manuel's luck was only slightly better than Guaman Poma's. What is the place of unsolicited oppositional discourse, parody, resistance, critique in the imagined classroom community? Are teachers supposed to feel that their teaching has been most successful when they have eliminated such things and unified the social world, probably in their own image? Who wins when we do that? Who loses?

25 Such questions may be hypothetical, because in the United States in the 1990s, many teachers find themselves less and less able to do that even if they want to. The composition of the national collectivity is changing and so are the styles, as Anderson put it, in which it is being imagined. In the 1980s in many nation-states, imagined

national syntheses that had retained hegemonic force began to dissolve. Internal social groups with histories and lifeways different from the official ones began insisting on those histories and lifeways *as part of their citizenship,* as the very mode of their membership in the national collectivity. In their dialogues with dominant institutions, many groups began asserting a rhetoric of belonging that made demands beyond those of representation and basic rights granted from above. In universities we started to hear, "I don't just want you to let me be here, I want to belong here; this institution should belong to me as much as it does to anyone else." Institutions have responded with, among other things, rhetorics of diversity and multiculturalism whose import at this moment is up for grabs across the ideological spectrum.

These shifts are being lived out by everyone working in education today, and everyone is challenged by them in one way or another. Those of us committed to educational democracy are particularly challenged as that notion finds itself besieged on the public agenda. Many of those who govern us display, openly, their interest in a quiescent, ignorant, manipulable electorate. Even as an ideal, the concept of an enlightened citizenry seems to have disappeared from the national imagination. A couple of years ago the university where I work went through an intense and wrenching debate over a narrowly defined Western-culture requirement that had been instituted there in 1980. It kept boiling down to a debate over the ideas of national patrimony, cultural citizenship, and imagined community. In the end, the requirement was transformed into a much more broadly defined course called Cultures, Ideas, Values.[4] In the context of the change, a new course was designed that centered on the Americas and the multiple cultural histories (including European ones) that have intersected here. As you can imagine, the course attracted a very diverse student body. The classroom functioned not like a homogeneous community or a horizontal alliance but like a contact zone. Every single text we read stood in specific historical relationships to the students in the class, but the range and variety of historical relationships in play were enormous. Everybody had a stake in nearly everything we read, but the range and kind of stakes varied widely.

It was the most exciting teaching we had ever done, and also the hardest. We were struck, for example, at how anomalous the formal lecture became in a contact zone (who can forget Atahuallpa throwing down the Bible because it would not speak to him?). The lecturer's traditional (imagined) task—unifying the world in the class's eyes by means of a monologue that rings equally coherent, revealing, and true for all, forging an ad hoc community, homogeneous with respect to one's own words—this task became not only impossible but anomalous and unimaginable. Instead, one had to work in the knowledge that whatever one said was going to be systematically received in radically heterogeneous ways that we were neither able nor entitled to prescribe.

The very nature of the course put ideas and identities on the line. All the students in the class had the experience, for example, of hearing their culture discussed and objectified in ways that horrified them; all the students saw their roots traced back to legacies of both glory and shame; all the students experienced face-to-face the ignorance and incomprehension, and occasionally the hostility, of others. In the absence of community values and the hope of synthesis, it was easy to forget the positives; the fact, for instance, that kinds of marginalization once taken for granted were gone. Virtually every student was having the experience of seeing the world described with him or her in it. Along with rage, incomprehension, and pain, there were exhilarating moments of wonder and revelation, mutual understanding, and new wisdom—the joys of the contact zone. The sufferings and revelations were, at different moments to be sure, experienced by every student. No one was excluded, and no one was safe.

The fact that no one was safe made all of us involved in the course appreciate the importance of what we came to call "safe houses." We used the term to refer to social and intellectual spaces where groups can constitute themselves as horizontal, homogeneous, sovereign communities with high degrees of trust, shared understandings, temporary protection from legacies of oppression. This is why, as we realized, multicultural curricula should not seek to replace ethnic or women's studies, for example. Where there are legacies of subordination, groups need places for healing and mutual recognition, safe houses in which to construct shared understandings, knowledges, claims on the world that they can then bring into the contact zone.

30　　Meanwhile, our job in the Americas course remains to figure out how to make that crossroads the best site for learning that it can be. We are looking for the pedagogical arts of the contact zone. These will include, we are sure, exercises in storytelling and in identifying with the ideas, interests, histories, and attitudes of others; experiments in transculturation and collaborative work and in the arts of critique, parody, and comparison (including unseemly comparisons between elite and vernacular cultural forms); the redemption of the oral; ways for people to engage with suppressed aspects of history (including their own histories), ways to move *into and out of* rhetorics of authenticity; ground rules for communication across lines of difference and hierarchy that go beyond politeness but maintain mutual respect; a systematic approach to the all-important concept of *cultural mediation*. These arts were in play in every room at the extraordinary Pittsburgh conference on literacy. I learned a lot about them there, and I am thankful.

NOTES

1. For an introduction in English to these and other aspects of Guaman Poma's work, see Rolena Adorno. Adorno and Mercedes Lopez-Baralt pioneered the study of Andean symbolic systems in Guaman Poma.

2. It is far from clear that the *Royal Commentaries* was as benign as the Spanish seemed to assume. The book certainly played a role in maintaining the identity and aspirations of indigenous elites in the Andes. In the mid-eighteenth century, a new edition of the *Royal Commentaries* was suppressed by Spanish authorities because its preface included a prophecy by Sir Walter Raleigh that the English would invade Peru and restore the Inca monarchy.

3. The discussion of community here is summarized from my essay "Linguistic Utopias."

4. For information about this program and the contents of courses taught in it, write Program in Cultures, Ideas, Values (CIV), Stanford Univ., Stanford, CA 94305.

WORKS CITED

Adorno, Rolena. *Guaman Poma de Ayala: Writing and Resistance in Colonial Peru.* Austin: U of Texas P, 1986.

Anderson, Benedict. *Imagined Communities: Reflections on the Origins and Spread of Nationalism.* London: Verso, 1984.

Garcilaso de la Vega, El Inca. *Royal Commentaries of the Incas.* 1613. Austin: U of Texas P, 1966.

Guaman Poma de Ayala, Felipe. *El primer nueva corónica y buen gobierno.* Manuscript. Ed. John Murra and Rolena Adorno. Mexico: Siglo XXI, 1980.

Pratt, Mary Louise. "Linguistic Utopias." *The Linguistics of Writing.* Ed. Nigel Fabb et al. Manchester: Manchester UP, 1987. 48–66.

Treviño, Gloria. "Cultural Ambivalence in Early Chicano Prose Fiction." Diss. Stanford U, 1985.

EXPLORATORY WRITING

Write a letter to a friend at another college who has not read Mary Louise Pratt's "Arts of the Contact Zone," but who is interested in new ways to describe and analyze culture. In the letter, explain Pratt's main line of thought and the approach to culture she presents. You will need to explain what Pratt means by reading Guaman Poma's letter as an "autoethnographic text" and "product of the contact zone." But since your friend has not read the essay, it will help to provide other examples of the "contact zone" and "autoethnographic texts" that are more familiar. And since this is a letter to a friend, you will also want to describe your own experience working through Pratt's essay and the value of her perspective.

TALKING ABOUT THE READING

Pratt's notion of the "arts of the contact zone" are not without its difficulties. At the end of her discussion of Guaman Poma's letter, she offers the following summary:

> Autoethnography, transculturation, critique, collaboration, bilingualism, mediation, parody, denunciation, imaginary dialogue, vernacular expression—these are some of the literate arts of the contact zone. Miscomprehension, incomprehension, dead letters, unread master-pieces, absolute heterogeneity of meaning—these are some of the perils of writing in the contact zone. They all live among us today in the transnationalized metropolis of the United States and are becoming more widely visible, . . . more discernible to those who once would have ignored them in defense of a stable, centered sense of knowledge and reality.

In class discussion, take your time deciphering this passage, for it is a complicated one. To help you clarify what Pratt means by the "literate arts of the contact zone" and their "perils," find examples in the "transnationalized metropolis of the United States" that illustrate her ideas.

WRITING ASSIGNMENTS

1. In many respects, Pratt's analysis of Guaman Poma's letter is the centerpiece of her essay, the occasion for her to develop the notion of the "literate arts of the contact zone." If her terms are useful, you should be able to apply them to more contemporary forms of cultural expression. Write an essay that works with the notion of the "contact zone" to analyze a form of cultural expression written, produced, or performed in the contact zone. The choice of material is up to you, but keep in mind how Guaman Poma's letter creates a self-representation of a subordinate culture that responds to unequal relations of power by combining indigenous material with appropriations from the dominant metropolitan culture.

2. Pratt's view of a transnationalized United States contrasts dramatically with conventional ideas about a common, unified national culture of communities that share a common way of life. Think of the various communities in which you have lived or been a part—the neighborhood, town, or region of the country where you grew up, or the community of your college, church, workplace, military service, and so forth. Write an essay that uses Pratt's notion of the contact zone to contrast the view that community holds of itself as a unified body with Pratt's sense that communities are invariably based on transcultural and transnational encounters as much as on the similarities of their members. Begin your essay by describing how the community you are writing about represents itself in terms of common values and beliefs. Then use Pratt's notion of the contact zone to redescribe that community as insiders and outsiders, in unequal relations of power, representing themselves and their differences to each other.

3. Write an essay that applies Pratt's notion of "autoethnography" to the three images presented on the next two pages: two from Coco Fusco and Guillermo Gómez-Peña's performance art project "Two Undiscovered Amerindians Visit the West," and Samuel Fosso's photographic self-portrait "Le chef qui a vendu l'Afrique aux colons" (The chief who sold Africa to the colonizers). To prepare for this essay, do some background research by visiting "Coco Fusco's Virtual Laboratory" at http://www.cocofusco.com and by Googling Samuel Fosso. Then, use what you've learned to explain how these images might be read as examples of autoethnography, where, in Pratt's words, "people undertake to describe themselves in ways that engage with representations others have made of them."

"Two Undiscovered Amerindians Visit the West." The cage performance pictured here, in which Fusco and Gómez-Peña are "undiscovered Amerindians" from an island in the Gulf of Mexico, is part of a larger interdisciplinary arts project including multimedia, installation, and experimental radio soundtrack that premiered at the Walker Art Center in Minneapolis in 1992 and subsequently appeared in Madrid, London, and Washington, D.C.

Courtesy of Coc Fusco. Photography by Peter Barker.

— Tati Auto portrait. *Le chef qui a vendu l'Afrique aux colons* by Samuel Fosso, 1997.

WORKS IN TRANSLATION: GHADA AMER'S HYBRID PLEASURES

— *Laura Auricchio*

Laura Auricchio teaches in the Critical Studies program at Parsons School of Design. In "Works in Translation: Ghada Amer's Hybrid Pleasures," which appeared in *Art Journal* in 2001, she offers an introdution to the installations and embroidery art of the Ghada Amer.

SUGGESTION FOR READING Laura Auricchio is introducing the artist Ghada Amer to an American audience. Notice how Auricchio opens by describing Ghada Amer's artwork as an "uneasy alliance among feminist, Islamic, and postcolonial ideologies." As you read, consider what makes this "alliance" so "uneasy."

1 Ghada Amer's elaborately embroidered paintings, sculptures, and installations add discomfiting overtones to the needlework that has played an important role in feminist art for the past thirty years. Her works forge uneasy alliances among feminist, Islamic, and postcolonial ideologies, yielding hybrids that settle in no one place, culture, or political position. For example, viewers of Amer's *Private Room* (1999) encounter hanging garment bags made of richly colored satin and embroidered with extensive texts culled from the Qur'an. By presenting the holy Arabic words in French translation, Amer creates a double obstacle that blocks English-speakers' access to the original meanings.

The unsatisfied desire to understand is transformed into material pleasure in Amer's more recent stitched canvases. In *Gray Lisa* (2000) pornographic images of women traced or copied from sex-industry magazines challenge us to rethink female sexuality, while unmotivated drips and tangles of brightly colored thread revel in their own excess, and in an embrace of bodily enjoyment. Amer is one in an emerging generation of artists working to reclaim female pleasure as a subject for feminist art.

A BRIEF HISTORY OF FEMINIST EMBROIDERY ART

Since the 1970s, feminist artists have been challenging the boundaries that divide art from craft, public from domestic, and masculine from feminine by incorporating embroidery into their work. By appropriating this traditionally feminine and domestic form of creativity, artists ranging from Kate Walker to Judy Chicago to Elaine Reichek have called attention to the complicated history of women's needlework. Their sewn objects, canvases, and samplers critique the tradition that has classified sewing as hobby, craft or ornament, in opposition to the rarefied professional arts of painting and sculpture.

In *The Subversive Stitch: Embroidery and the Making of the Feminine,* Rozsika Parker locates these artists in the context of English sewing practices from the Middle Ages through the twentieth century. "Embroidery," she points out, "has provided a source of pleasure and power for women, while being indissolubly linked to their powerlessness. . . . Paradoxically, while embroidery was employed to inculcate femininity in women, it also enabled them to negotiate the constraints of femininity."[1] Feminist artists who have incorporated embroidery into their work are operating within this paradox, using a traditionally feminine endeavor to forge new models of womanhood and claiming high-art identity for an activity usually relegated to the status of craft.

5 In the 1970s Kate Walker and Judy Chicago called on the domestic and communal connotations of women's needlework to foster a new model of collaborative art practice. At the

— *Private Rooms* by Ghada Amer, 1999.
Embroidery on satin garment bags, variable dimensions (fifteen elements).

Women's Art Alliance in London, Walker took part in a postal art project known as *Feministo* that questioned whether the categories of public and private, home and work, were separate, gendered, and incompatible spheres.[2] The artist members of *Feministo* were women dispersed throughout England who created works of art in their homes and sent them to one another by mail. Walker contributed a sewn work entitled *Sampler* (1978) that featured the embroidered text, "Wife is a four-letter word." One year later, Chicago first displayed her *Dinner Party,* for which more than four hundred men and women had created a table with thirty-nine place settings, each devoted to a woman from the past or to a mythological female figure.[3] Embroidery, used to decorate the place mats, was combined with other traditional crafts, including pottery and china painting.

Elaine Reichek's embroidered works from the 1990s follow in this vein. *When This You See . . . ,* Reichek's 1999 installation in the Museum of Modern Art, New York, consisted of twenty-five samplers that encourage viewers to consider embroidery in relation to both the history of women and the history of modernism. Speaking of her choice of materials, Reichek explained, "It is deliberate that for tools historically associated with 'male' art—paint, brush, canvas—I substitute media usually seen as related to 'female' activities."[4] In *Sampler (Andy Warhol)* (1997) she performs a double substitution: with its horizontal format, all-over composition, and intertwined "drips" of red, black, and yellow thread, the work appears to be a reduced and sewn version of a Jackson Pollock drip painting. Yet the title does not reference Pollock. Instead, Reichek directs our attention to Andy Warhol's 1983 *Yarn Painting,* which was itself a comment on Pollock's enormous, hyper-masculine paintings of the late 1940s.[5]

PROBLEMS OF HYBRIDITY

Although Amer shares some of her feminist predecessors' sensibilities, her works complicate both their Western focus and their gender ideologies.

Private Room (2000) introduces the main themes that course through her oeuvre. In addition to challenging received wisdom regarding both femininity and embroidery, this piece addresses problems of sensual pleasure and cultural hybridity. Installed at the Greater New York Exhibition at P.S. 1, the visually enticing *Private Room* presented fifteen satin garment bags suspended from a rod stretched between two walls. Dyed in rich saturated colors, set off against white walls, and shimmering with reflected light, these otherwise prosaic sacks became a field of visual pleasure. Their sheer beauty beckoned visitors closer; the curious were rewarded with embroidered texts stitched across the surface of each suspended object.

The physical presence of heavy, life-size garment bags evokes the figures of women concealed in chadors increasingly seen in Amer's native Egypt. Amer has expressed dismay at the religious conservatism that often circumscribes the sartorial, personal, and professional choices of Egyptian women. Recalling the less constrained lives of Egyptian women in the 1970s, when her family moved to France, she laments the impact of conservative Islamic law on women's attitudes toward their own bodies. In a recent interview, she described her own experience of this effect: "When I go home, I feel so conscious of my body, every time, conscious of the relationship to the body of everything I wear. Everything is so hidden that if you have a finger out, it becomes the focus of sexuality."[6] Amer has identified her work as "a vengeance against this."

The texts embroidered on the garment bags of *Private Room* present the multiplicity of Islamic attitudes toward women, countering the sometimes monolithic gender politics of religious conservatism. As Amer explains, she "took all the sentences that speak about women from the Qur'an and embroidered them in French." The words of the Qur'an are sacred when written in Arabic. Not wanting to give offense, Amer offers the text in the secular French. Although religious concerns may have loomed large for Amer, the translation nonetheless has a significant impact on viewers' experiences of the work.[7] The scale of the piece was partly determined by the Qur'an itself, as the number of embroidered bags was set by her wish to include every text in which women are mentioned. Setting all of the statements side by side, she highlights the diversity of viewpoints expressed in the holy book and takes issue with the narrow perspective on women promulgated by some Egyptian authorities today.

10 Turning our attention from content to form, we find that Amer's text functions like the Egyptian woman's exposed finger: it is the unattainable focus of the viewer's desire.[8] Written out in near rows of clear capital letters in a Western European language familiar to Amer's fellow residents of France, the words of the Qur'an promise to yield their meanings to the attentive reader. Even so, *Private Room* requires us to grapple with the problem of reading across languages and among cultures. First exhibited at ARCO in Madrid, and later in New York, the work addressed local audiences in a language native neither to them nor to the Qur'an's original readers. Spanish- or English-speaking audiences who encountered the Qur'an as mediated by Amer's French translation struggled, to a greater or lesser degree, to understand the foreign words. Amer insists that the linguistic and cultural distances between viewer and work cannot be fully bridged. Try as we may to capture the original meaning, satisfaction will always be denied us.

For instance, English-speaking readers may wrestle with the meaning of one passage that offers guidance in selecting a bride. Amer's translation reads: "Une esclave qui croit, a plus devaleur qu'une femme libre et polythéiste." (A slave who believes is more valuable than a free and polytheistic woman.) The original text is from the Qur'anic book Sura al-Baqarah 2:221 (The Cow). English translations struggle with the terms that Amer has rendered in French as *polythéiste* and *libre*. Three translations available on the Internet provide a sampling: "Wed not idolatresses till they believe; for lo! A believing bondwoman is better than an idolatress though she please you; and give not your daughters in marriage to idolaters till they believe, for lo! A believing slave is better than an idolater though he please you." Or, "Do not marry unbelieving women, until they believe: A slave woman who believes is better than an unbelieving woman, even though she allures you. Nor marry [your girls] to unbelievers until they believe: A man slave who believes is better than an unbeliever, even though he allures you." One also finds this rendering: "And do not marry the idolatresses until they believe, and certainly a believing maid is better than an idolatrous woman, even though she should please you; and do not give [believing women] in marriage to idolaters until they believe, and certainly a believing servant is better than an idolater, even though he should please you."[9] These fine distinctions will always escape us, confounding our attempts to pin down a meaning.

Just as the Qur'an, already uprooted from its native tongue in her art, will never fully settle into one language, Amer herself is almost always identified as a figure in exile. In the exhibition reviews that have introduced her to an international public her name, like Homer's "rosy-fingered" Dawn, is rarely seen without an epithet. Barry Schwab-sky tells of "the Egyptian-born, French-educated" artist.[10] Writing for the French magazine *L'Oeil*. Eric de Chassey discusses Amer, "born in Cairo . . . lives in New York, following a lengthy stay in Paris."[11] Amer's exhibiting venues have also high-lighted her condition of exile. At the 1999 Venice Biennale, her works were in the large *Aperto* section, devoted to an international mixture of artists rather than those selected to represent their homelands, housed in pavilions sponsored by their countries. Amer is always out of place. Her international past defies attempts to pin her to any one nation or culture. Whether in Paris or New York, Venice or Madrid, she appears in translation. Wherever she may be, her identity is inflected with the traces of other cultures, and she continually spills across local boundaries.

In interviews Amer both calls attention to and voices concerns about her identity as a "postcolonial subject," with claims to several cultures but fully embraced by none.[12] Recently, she described herself as feeling "a little French," having lived in Paris for twenty-one years.[13] Her feeling, though, was not sufficient for the French government, which has three times rejected her applications for citizenship. Speaking with Nigel Ryan in 1998, she granted that seeing her work as the product of "a woman from a Muslim society" can be "liberating" and can help to "command an audience."[14] Yet, acknowledging the potential pitfalls of that tag, she warned that such an exclusive focus could also serve "simply to stereotype, to restrict." "I cannot resent people's interest on this level," she said, "but I cannot embrace it fully."

Amer's concerns about the stultifying effect of a "postcolonial" label echo anxieties voiced by several contemporary theorists about the resurrection of the postcolonial "hybrid" as a figure of fascination. In a historical analysis of hybridity, now an important term in cultural criticism, Robert J. C. Young offers a deceptively simple definition of the term: "Hybridity implies a disruption and forcing together of any unlike living things."[15] Young reminds us that hybridity emerged from nineteenth-century investigations of botanical or biological cross-breeding. Indeed, apprehensions about hybridity gained currency within an anxious discourse on racial identity, as the fear of miscegenation found expression in debates over whether Africans belonged to the same human species as Europeans. Young suggests that a similar presupposition of clear and separate races, if not breeds, remains latent in the writings of some postcolonial thinkers who see and use cultural hybridity as a liberating strategy. The very concept of hybridity, he warns, runs the risk of reifying difference by positing a prior state of

unadulterated purity, when cultural identities were both distinct and intact.

15   A more optimistic perspective, however, might see the hybridity of Amer's *Private Room*—and, more generally, the hybridity of postcolonial societies—as revealing the essentially mixed and always unstable nature of language and social relations. Rather than presuming preexisting differences among cultures, the artist who makes hybridity visible highlights a constant state of interaction among all cultures and shatters illusions of cultural purity. The critic Yuri Lotman's notion of the "semiosphere" offers one such optimistic model. His semiosphere encompasses "the semiotic space necessary for the existence and functioning of languages," which are marked by asymmetry, heterogeneity, and interaction.[16] Not a simple "sum total of different languages," the semiosphere is intricately "transected by boundaries of different levels, boundaries of different languages and even of texts."[17]

Perhaps we can recast Amer's series of literal and implied translations as an ever-changing system. Rather than understanding the process of translation as an inevitably failed attempt at replication, Lotman sees translation as a crucial and on-going process that creates meaning. He calls translation "a primary mechanism of consciousness. To express something in another language is a way of understanding it."[18] Since two languages often do not possess exactly equivalent words, every translation generates information by introducing or uncovering additional meanings.

Problems of dialogue and translation take center stage once again in Amer's *Majnun* (1997). Similar in structure to *Private Room*, *Majnun* features a row of life-size storage closets formed from orange plastic stretched over internal rectangular frames. A French text translated from an older Arabic text is embroidered in red thread across the surface. The embroidered fragment is from a tragic Persian love story in which a young suitor named Majnun writes letter after letter to his beloved Leila, but receives no response. Devastated by the apparent rejection,

Majnun by Ghada Amer, 1997. Embroidery on plastic storage closets, 64 x 69¾ in. (163 x 176.9 cm).

Majnun dies of a broken heart, and the silent but desiring Leila follows him to the grave. Amer gives form to Leila's voicelessness by imagining her as an Arabian Echo, who can form no words of her own but only reproduce the words of Majnun, her Narcissus. It is these words that Amer embroiders. When written by Majnun, the text conveys desire and longing. Yet when mimicked by the powerless Leila, the words become travesties that block fulfillment. The impossibility of dialogue sounds the lovers' death knell.

By giving voice to Leila's silence, *Majnun* offers an equivocal answer to the questions posed by Gayatri Spivak in her seminal essay, "Can the Subaltern Speak?"[19] Spivak maintains that the logic of colonialism permits the colonized to attain representation only through the language and voice of the colonizer. Focusing on the conditions that relegate women from former European colonies to political and social silence, Spivak encourages these women to create their own voices by interrupting the colonist's monologue. Although Amer's Leila can speak only in the colonizer's language (French, in this case), and can voice only the words of the man who desires her, Amer herself performs the kind of intervention that Spivak advocates. Like generations of women before her, Amer uses the medium of embroidery for her text, employing a traditional realm of women's subordination to speak about and against that oppression.

NOTES

1. Rozsika Parker, *The Subversive Stitch: Embroidery and the Making of the Feminine* (London: The Women's Press, 1994), 11.

2. Ibid., 207–9.

3. Ibid., 209–10. On Chicago's more recent collaborative embroidery projects see Paula Harper, "The Chicago Resolutions," *Art in America* 88, no. 6 (June 2000): 112–5, 137–8.

4. Elaine Reichek and Laura Engel. "Commentary: Mother/Daughter Dresses," *Fiberarts* 20, no. 3 (November–December 1993): 9, and cited in Beth Handler, "Projects 67: Elaine Reichek," exhibition brochure (New York: Museum of Modern Art, 1999).

5. Handler, "Reichek."

6. Sarah Robbins, "Love in Threads," *Australian Style* 49 (March 2001): 66–70, esp. 69.

7. Marilu Knode, "Interview with Ghada Amer," *New Art Examiner* 27, no. 4 (December 1999–January 2000): 38–39, esp. 38.

8. On desire in Amer, see Candice Breitz, "Ghada Amer/The Modeling of Desire," *NKA Journal of Contemporary African Art*, no. 5 (Fall–Winter, 1996): 14–16.

9. M. M. Pickthall, *Meaning of the Glorious Quran* (London: Islamic Computing Centre); M. H. Shakir, *The Holy Qur'an* (Elmhurst, New York: Tahrike Tarsile Qur'an, Inc.); and A. Yusufali, *Meanings of the Glorious Quran* (London: Islamic Computing Centre).

10. Barry Schwabsky, "Ghada Amer: Deitch Projects, New York," *Artext*, no. 70 (August–October 2000): 84.

11. Eric de Chassey; "La peinture est vivante: Dix artistes de moins de 40 ans," *L'Oeil*, no. 489 (October 1997): 52–61, esp. 56.

12. Homi Bhabha, arguably one of the most influential figures in postcolonial criticism, has described "postcolonial perspectives" as emerging "from the colonial testimony of Third World countries. They formulate their critical revisions around issues of cultural difference, social authority, and political discrimination in order to reveal the antagonistic and ambivalent moments within the 'rationalizations' of modernity." Homi K. Bhabha, *The Location of Culture* (London: Routledge, 1994), 171.

13. Sarah Robbins, "Love in Threads," *Australian Style* 49 (March 2001): 66–70, esp. 66.

14. Nigel Ryan, "A Stitch in Time," *Medina* (April 1998): 80.

15. Robert J. C. Young, *Colonial Desire: Hybridity in Theory, Culture, and Race* (London: Routledge, 1995), 26.

16. Yuri Lotman, *Universe of the Mind: A Semiotic Theory of Culture* (Bloomington: Indiana University Press, 2000), 123. For a summary of approaches to this hybridity, see Nikos Papastergiadis, "Restless Hybrids," *Third Text*, no. 32 (Autumn 1995): 9–18.

17. Lotman, 138.

18. Ibid., 127.

19. Gayatri Spivak, "Can the Subaltern Speak?" in Patrick Williams and Laura Chrisman, eds., *Colonial Discourse and Post-Colonial Theory: A Reader* (London: Harvester Whatsheaf, 1993), 66–111.

EXPLORATORY WRITING

Laura Auricchio locates Ghada Amer's artwork in a tradition of feminist embroidery but then says Amer complicates "both their Western focus and their gender ideologies." What is Auricchio getting at here? What is the nature of this complication?

TALKING ABOUT THE READING

Auricchio titles one of the sections of this reading "Problems of Hybridity." In a class discussion, consider what the term "hybridity" means in this context. What is the "problem" Auricchio refers to? Take into account the two different perspectives on hybridity offered by Robert J. C. Young and Yuri Lotman. How would you link the term hybridity to life in a transnational world? How is it pertinent to Amer's art?

WRITING ASSIGNMENTS

1. As you can see from the title of this reading, translation is one of its main themes. Write an essay on what Auricchio sees at stake in the fact that Amer has translated the Arabic text of the Qur'an into French. Notice Auricchio offers a number of translations of the passage from the Qur'anic book Sura al-Baqarah (The Cow). What is the point of these multiple translations?

2. Auricchio says that Ghada Amer is "almost always identified as a figure in exile." Write an essay that examines whether this is a good identification of Amer. Consider here the

meaning of the term "exile," as someone who is forced to live in another country either for personal or political reasons. To what extent is the term "transnational," instead of exile, useful to capture the multiple identifications in Amer's work?

3. As Auricchio notes, "hybridity" is "an important term in cultural criticism." What makes this term so important? What does it reveal? Write an essay that works with the definition of hybridity presented in the reading. Explain what the "problem" of hybridity is, as Auricchio describes it. Then use this discussion to analyze an example of hybridity you have chosen to illustrate the concept.

TRAVELING BARBIE: INDIAN TRANSNATIONALITIES AND THE GLOBAL CONSUMER

— *Inderpal Gerwal*

Inderpal Gerwal teaches women's studies at the University of California, Irvine. In addition to *Transnational America: Feminisms, Diasporas, Neoliberalism* (2006), from which this reading is taken, Gerwal has also published *Home and Harem: Nation, Gender, Empire and the Cultures of Travel* (1996) and, with Caren Kaplan, *Scattered Hegemonies: Postmodernity and Transnational Feminist Practices* (1994).

SUGGESTION FOR READING This excerpt is part of a longer analysis in *Transnational America* in which Inderpal Gerwal seeks to understand the consumption of American products by middle-class Indian women. As you read, notice that Gerwal uses as sources both Mattel annual reports and cultural critiques by Ulf Hannerz, Lauren Berlant and Elizabeth Freeman, and Erica Rand.

1 In 1985 Mattel had affiliates and plants in South Korea, Japan, Hong Kong, the Philippines, Australia, Chile, Venezuela, Puerto Rico, the United Kingdom, France, Spain, Switzerland, and Canada. Through the 1980s and 1990s Mattel became a multinational with factories, offices, and affiliates in Tijuana, Monterrey, Guangdong (China), Jakarta, Japan, Berlin, Budapest, Prague, Kuala Lumpur, and Bombay. A new plant opened in Thailand in 1985 after Mattel applied for an eight-year tax "holiday," a common practice to stimulate investment from the United States and other countries. Mattel closed two plants in the Philippines in 1988 after conflicts with what the corporation called "militant labor unions." Most Barbies sold in the United States through the 1990s were made in China, Malaysia, and Indonesia, with plastics made in Taiwan from oil bought from Saudi Arabia, hair from Japan, and packaging from the

United States. Making Barbie is extremely labor-intensive work, requiring at least fifteen separate paint stations and thus an enormous supply of cheap labor. Labor costs were about 35 cents for a Barbie costing about $10 (out of which almost $8 went to shipping, marketing, and wholesale and retail profits; Mattel made about $1 of this amount). Using the services of Asian women paid low wages for assembly line work, Barbie's production was as gendered as its consumption and circulation.

After a period in the mid-1980s during which U.S. sales remained steady while international sales increased by almost 40 percent, sales declined in 1987, necessitating layoffs of 22 percent of the work force in the Mattel headquarters in Hawthorne, California, which meant almost five hundred jobs. The Bombay office opened in 1988, even though at that point sales had declined by 30 percent from their peak, a fact not surprising when the corporate view was, according to the CEO, that "the future of the toy industry lies in international markets." By 1992 Mattel had come out of its slump, with a net sales increase of 25 percent, and by the following year Barbie sales worldwide hit $1 billion. That year Mattel donated $1 million to children's health programs in the United States.

In Mattel's corporate annual reports, the whole world was represented as a market waiting to buy Mattel's products. The annual reports reveal a belief that every child somehow naturally wants these toys and that the desirability of the toys is universal and transparent. Yet, paradoxically, every country is seen as a market in which the conquest of children is the goal. To pursue this children's market, Mattel linked up with Disney, another iconic name in the U.S.-based multinational production of what I call "children's transnational culture," agreeing to manufacture all the Disney brand toys. Awareness of Disney as a nationalist signifier of Americanness has been well documented. After the deal with Disney, Mattel in 1992 called Barbie and Disney its "global power brands."

How did Mattel's annual reports explain what they represented as Barbie's continued power and fascination? Barbie's global marketing practices were linked to America as a symbol of freedom and rights, especially for women. The marketing strategies linked the product to discourses of powerful "Americanness" associated with race, class, and gendered hierarchies. Relying on discourses of American nationalism that linked "choice" to "freedom," Mattel used race, gender, and nationalist discourse to sell its product. This connection was borne out in many subtle and not-so-subtle ways, as in Mattel's claim that when the Berlin Wall fell, Mattel "was the first company to advertise." Yet even while clearly using America as a marketing tool, Mattel universalized the child. Thus the corporate reports claimed that Mattel understood all little girls' fantasies, which were seen as universal: "Mattel has long believed that children's play patterns are the same around the world and that a successful toy has no nationality. The validity of this tenet was proven in Japan last year, where in a test market and subsequent expansion, the traditional Barbie doll was embraced by Japanese girls."

5   This "embrace" of the "traditional" Barbie purportedly reinforced the company's claims that it could cross all borders, since play and the consumption of toys are universal. But there was no mention of how this universal play was marketed and consumed in various nations, nor of how Barbie as a symbol of Americanness was consumed in these specific sites. One method that Mattel used to produce effective transnational connectivities was to exploit the discourses of feminism, made neoliberal by its association with free trade, entrepreneurship, and capitalism. The complicated baggage of the "American" image of Barbie as white, straight, young, and blonde in the 1990s began to utilize the gendered discourses of freedom and women's rights to make itself relevant to the greater presence of liberal feminism within popular culture in the United States. Moreover, these discourses relied on cold war representations used by the United States to link neoliberal democracy to a "freedom" to consume, which was promoted as quintessentially American. The same discourses invoked feminist themes in supporting women's participation in capitalism, contrasting women in the United States with those from the "third world" and "Other" women, and emphasizing the centrality of "choice" as a goal for liberal feminism. In using these discourses, the universality of gendered divisions as produced by Mattel's discourses of toy consumption was established.

According to Mattel, just as boys needed high-tech action toys such as BraveStarr to develop, girls grew through "imagination" and play with dolls. I do not suggest that such play could never be subversive of gendered stereotypes. Yet the corporate focus on fantasy for girls and action for boys suggested that for Mattel, the imaginary of the play that girls enacted worked in tandem with the symbolic and virtual nature of consumer culture. In a global framework of consumption, as Arjun Appadurai's work suggests, fantasy linked translocal practices connected through the imagination. The transnational imaginary of new nationalism was most easily available through the phantasmic life produced by consumer culture through which the consumer citizen could be constructed. As Ulf Hannerz argues, fantasy and aspiration are constitutive of the "global ecumene" of advertising that is at once diverse and homogenizing. To produce this citizen subject, however, fantasy had to be linked to the nation. As Lauren Berlant and Elizabeth Freeman have pointed out, even for groups subversive of much hegemonic culture, such as Queer Nation, consumer pleasure has become part of activist reformulations of public culture, linking "the utopian pleasures of the commodity with those of the nation." Mattel's use of discourses of "freedom" and "choice" connected fantasy with the nation, Americanness with liberal and neoliberal democracy. Thus Erica Rand points out that Mattel modifies its products to "bring competing definitions of good role model and acceptable fantasy object within its own conception of Barbie and to present its offerings as precisely those that fulfill consumer 'needs.'" The focus on imagination and fantasy used terms and concepts similar to those used by Disney in its theme parks.

What were the consumer fantasies that were put into circulation by Mattel? A consumer feminism was one of these discourses, in which consumption within capitalist expansion could bring work to many across the globe, even if what it brought were classed, gendered, and racialized inequalities. What Rand calls a pop feminist notion of choice was used by Mattel by the late 1990s to sell multiple Barbies to each consumer-child. Mattel's CEO in 1997, Jill Barad, who started her career in fashion and cosmetic sales, deployed this pop feminism to sell Barbies. Under her leadership, the very successful slogan "We girls can do anything" was launched, with the new career-girl Barbie capable of moving up the corporate ladder or having any career she wanted, from doctor to astronaut. As Rand has argued, the fantasies that Mattel claims are universal were also hegemonic. According to Rand,

the language of "infinite possibility" that Mattel deployed was used to "camouflage what was actually being promoted: a very limited set of products, ideas, and actions." Rand suggests that even if subversive uses of Barbie were rampant, these did not change the ideological effects that Mattel promoted: compulsory heterosexuality, ageism, sexism, white superiority, capitalism, and the unequal distribution of resources.

This emphasis on American liberal feminism's discourse of "choice" as essential to women's struggles was understood by Mattel as a universal value that could be transmitted across the transnational connectivities and bring new consumers to buy the product in different parts of the world. In its annual reports, Mattel emphasized universality within claims of concern for the global welfare of children that were presented through organized events functioning as advertisements and also as public relations strategies. In 1990 Barbie hosted an international summit where forty children from twenty-eight countries discussed issues relevant to themselves. The annual report of that year described the event in the language of children's welfare and empowerment and concluded that the children "identified world peace as a principal concern." The summit's conclusions were similar to pronouncements by contestants at beauty pageants, where the most commonplace clichés are spoken to infuse the event with civic value. Although Erica Rand suggests that these clichés are "popular but largely uncontroversial forms of political consciousness" that Mattel used to reach more consumers, it is clear that the connection between consumption and politics, between support for Mattel and support for the concerns for welfare that Mattel expressed, was an important sign of the neoliberal context of its transnational consumption. Consumer subjects were thus produced not merely through class positions but also through discourses of good citizenship and liberal values of equality and progress combined with a neoliberal feminism, all of which were seen as international and universal.

EXPLORATORY WRITING

Inderpal Gerwal says that "even while clearly using America as a marketing tool, Mattel universalized the child." What is her point here? How does Mattel seek to put the Americanness and the universality of Barbie's appeal together in one package?

TALKING ABOUT THE READING

Gerwal raises the question, "What were the consumer fantasies that were put into circulation by Mattel"? In a class discussion, consider how she answers this question and the evidence she assembles to support her answer.

WRITING ASSIGNMENTS

1. Gerwal describes the "freedom" to consume as "quintessentially American." Write an essay that draws on Gerwal's to explain how the notion of consumer choice has crossed national borders—and what the consequences might be.

2. Mattel's marketing campaign to sell Barbies featured what Gerwal calls the pop feminist slogan "We girls can do anything." Consider Erica Rand's claim that the language of "infinite possibility" that Mattel used only served to "camouflage what was actually being promoted: a very limited set of products, ideas, and actions." Write an essay that explains what Rand means and what you see as the larger implications when American companies seek to sell their products in the world market.

3. Both the Mattel manufacturers of Barbie dolls and Ghada Amer, in the previous reading, draw on stereotypically feminine practices—playing with dolls and doing needlework. Write an essay that compares the two ways of representing typically feminine activities and what consequential differences they reveal. Take into account how both Mattel and Amer draw on feminist discourses.

FILM CLIP   Bollywood

The Indian film industry is the largest in the world, producing over 800 films a year (or more than two per day) for movie-goers in India, Pakistan, and South Asian communities in Europe, Africa, and North America. "Bollywood," the name often given to the Indian film industry, combines "Hollywood" and "Bombay." As is true of the movie industry in Hollywood, Bollywood has a long history of filmmaking that dates back to the silent film era of the early twentieth century and includes its own classics. And like Hollywood, Bollywood has a number of large studios and popular stars who are featured in extravagantly made commercial films, as well as independent filmmakers who make smaller art films. Although Bollywood productions can be wide-ranging in subject matter and style, there are nonetheless some central characteristics that have come to define Bollywood. Bollywood films are typically longer than Hollywood films, running up to three hours, and a single film often combines elements of romance, melodrama, and action adventure with lavish musical productions featuring singers and dancers in brightly colored costumes performing on elaborate studio sets.

To get a sense of what is unique about Bollywood, you will need, of course, to watch some Bollywood films. A few of the many Bollywood films are listed below, but you will find more by doing an Internet search.

Kuch Kuch Hota Hai	*Dil Chahta Hai*
Dil Se	*Zakhm*
Satya	*Lagaan*
Dilwale Dulhaniya Le Jayenge	*Satta*
1942: A Love Story	*Qayamat Se Qayamat Tak*

As you watch one or more Bollywood films, notice the role of the stars and their romantic relationships. Does the film combine romance with action or melodrama? Consider how the musical scenes are integrated. You may want to compare Bollywood films to classic Hollywood musicals such as *Singing in the Rain* or *My Fair Lady*.

VISUAL CULTURE   Transnational Solidarity

The idea of responsibility for the fate of others, across national borders, has long been an impetus to transnational solidarity campaigns. These campaigns have taken a variety of forms, from the agitations against slavery and opposition to atrocities in the Belgian Congo that galvanized individuals in Britain and the United States during the nineteenth and early twentieth centuries to the more recent work of Doctors Without Borders and Amnesty International. Other campaigns have emphasized the solidarity of Third World people against domination by the West, such as the gathering of anti-colonial organizations at the League Against Imperialism in 1927, the meeting of nonaligned nations at Bandung in 1955, and the Tricontinental Conference founded in Havana in 1966, with its images of Che Guevara and freedom fighters in Southeast Asia, Africa, and Palestine.

To consider how the terms of solidarity are visualized in campaign posters, we present here two examples. Eleana Serrano's poster of Che Guevara marks the "Day of the Heroic Guerrilla," a Cuban celebration of revolutionary struggle in 1968. Favianna Rodriguez's "Hermano Kyang Hae Lee" commemorates the Korean farmer who stabbed himself to death at a protest against the World Trade Organization in 2003, and it urges farmers worldwide to unite against globalization.

"Day of the Heroic Guerrilla" poster by Eleana Serrano.

Favianna Rodriguez / www.favianna.com.

"Hermano Kyang Hae Lee" poster by Favianna Rodriguez.

SUGGESTIONS FOR DISCUSSION

1. The "Day of the Heroic Guerrilla" poster was commissioned by the Cuban Organization in Solidarity with the People of Africa, Asia, and Latin America (OSPAAAL). Visit their archive at http://www.docspopuli.org/CubaWebCat/gallery-01.html to see other Cuban posters from the 1960s and 1970s. Get a sense of what "solidarity" meant to OSPAAAL and of the visual style Cuban graphic designers became famous for. Then consider the composition of the "Day of the Heroic Guerrilla" and how the iconic image of Che Guevara radiates in a series of expanding frames over a map of Latin America. What is being signified visually?

2. Favianna Rodriguez's poster "Hermano Kyang Hae Lee" comes out of the anti-globalization movement that formed in the 1990s. If you aren't familiar with the term, look up "anti-globalization" at Wikipedia for background on how globalization has affected farmers worldwide. Use this information to analyze the visual message of transnational solidarity in the poster.

3. Another approach can be found in the Keep a Child Alive's "I Am an African" campaign, which quickly became a controversial one, particularly for its use of African tribal makeup and celebrities such as Gwyneth Paltrow in ads that appeared initially in fashion magazines. Visit the organization's Web site at http://www.keepachildalive.org/i_am_african/i_am_african.html for an explanation of the campaign's concept, developed by the model and cosmetics entrepreneur Iman. How are we to read the images of Gwyneth Paltrow and other celebrities? As a statement of transnational solidarity? The appropriation of African style by Western fashion? A normal public relations move on the part of celebrities wishing to associate themselves with humanitarian causes? An unfortunate reminder of Europeans who think of themselves as the saviors of Africa? Something else, or some combination? For a somewhat different visual approach, see Milton Glaser's "We Are All Africans" at http://www.miltonglaser.com.

SUGGESTION FOR WRITING

In a group of three, decide on a movement, cause, campaign, or organization that, in one way or another, promotes transnational solidarity. It could be a human rights group, a charity, a part of the anti-globalization movement. Your task is to examine the group's materials, both written and visual, to identify the terms of solidarity it is proposing. How does it seek to link people across borders, based on what principles and relationships? How does the group's promotional materials project its identity and mission? Present a report to the class (using PowerPoint if it is useful). Given the variety of organizations, consider as a whole class the range of meanings for transnational solidarity that emerge from the reports. What patterns do you see? What implications might you draw about life in a transnational world?

MINING THE ARCHIVE   Nineteenth-Century Orientalism

The Snake Charmer by Jean-Leon Gérôme, c. 1880. Oil on canvas. Acc: 1955.51. Sterling and Francine Clark Art Institute, Williamstown, Massachusetts, USA.

Representations of the Arab world in North Africa and the Middle East were favorite subjects in nineteenth-century European art. Often called Orientalist, with its scenes of Turkish baths, snake charmers, slave markets, and harems, this style represented Arab culture as exotic and alien. As you can see from the two paintings reproduced here— "The Slave Market" and "The Snake Charmer" by Jean-Leon Gérôme, perhaps the most important nineteenth-century French painter of Orientalist subjects— Orientalist art offered European viewers the titillation of sexual power and forbidden pleasures while assuring them such unthinkable desires and practices belonged to an Oriental Other, not to "us."

Nineteenth-century Orientalist artwork forms an important archive for understanding how representations of Arab culture were quite literally fantastic figments of the European imagination. An art museum near you may have Orientalist paintings in its collection. There are also several excellent books that have plenty of examples of paintings, such as the exhibition catalogue *The Orientalists: Delacroix to Matisse: The Allure of North Africa and the Near East* (1984), edited by MaryAnne Stevens, and Web sites you can find by entering "orientalism" and "art" in your search engine. Look for definitions of "Orientalism" so that you understand how art historians and cultural critics use the term. As you look at the paintings, consider what they reveal about Western representations of the Arab world and how these representations continue to shape perceptions today. For example, compare images of the Arab world that appear in nineteenth-century paintings and in *National Geographic*. Linda Street's book *Veils and Daggers: A Century of National Geographic's Representation of the Arab World* (2000) is a good source for this project.

The Slave Market by Jean-Leon Gérôme, 1866. Oil on canvas. 1955.53. Sterling and Francine Clark Art Institute, Williamstown, Massachusetts, USA.

Credits

Text Credits

Introduction   Williams, Raymond. From "Culture is Ordinary" from *Resources of Hope, Culture, Democracy, Socialism* by Raymond Williams. Copyright © by the Estate of Raymond Williams.

Codrescu, Andrei. "What is Culture" by Andrei Codrescu. Copyright © Andrei Codrescu. Reprinted by permission.

Chapter 1   Scribner, Sylvia. From "Literacy in Three Metaphors" from *American Journal of Education* 93.1 (1984): 6–21. Reprinted by permission of University of Chicago Press.

Kress, Gunther. From *Literacy in the New Media Age*. Copyright © 2003 Gunther Kress. Reproduced by permission of Taylor & Francis Books UK.

Welty, Eudora. From "Listening," reprinted by permission of the publisher from *One Writer's Beginning* by Eudora Welty, Cambridge, Mass.: Harvard University Press, Copyright © 1983, 1984 by Eudora Welty.

Haley, Alex. From *The Autobiography of Malcolm X* by Malcolm X and Alex Haley, copyright © 1964 by Alex Haley and Malcolm X. Copyright © 1965 by Alex Haley and Betty Shabazz. Used by permission of Random House, Inc.

Boyland, Conor. "Confessions of an Instant Messenger" as appeared in *The Boston Globe*, February 11, 2005. Copyright © 2005 by Conor Boyland. Reprinted by permission.

Heath, Shirley Brice. from "Talk is the thing" in *Ways With Words: Life, Language, and Work in Communities and Classrooms* by Shirley Brice Heath. Copyright © Cambridge University Press 1983. Reprinted with the permission of Cambridge University Press.

Finders, Margaret J. Reprinted by permission of the Publisher. From Margaret J. Finders, *Just Girls: Hidden Literacies and Life in Junior High*, New York: Teachers College Press. Copyright © 1997 by Teachers College, Columbia University. All rights reserved.

Sheridan, Valery. "'Please, order whatever you want. I insist:' Ordering Meals at the Burning Spear Country Club as a Literacy Event." Reprinted by permission of the author.

Chapter 2   Hochschild, Arlie Russell. "Coming of Age, Seeking an Identity" by Arlie Russell Hochschild, from *The New York Times*, 3/8/00. Copyright © 2000 The New York Times. All rights reserved. Used by permission and protected by the Copyright Laws of the United States. The printing, copying redistribution, or retransmission of the Material without express written permission is prohibited.

Hine, Thomas. Excerpt from *Chapter 14*, "Goths in Tomorrowland" (pp. 274–96) from *The Rise and Fall of the American Teenager* by Thomas Hine. Copyright © 1999 by Thomas Hine. Reprinted by permission of HarperCollins Publishers.

Naylor, Gloria. "Kiswana Browne," from *The Women of Brewster Place* by Gloria Naylor, copyright © 1980, 1982 by Gloria Naylor. Used by permission of Viking Penguin, a division of Penguin Group (USA) Inc.

Gilbert, James. "Juvenile Delinquency Films" from *A Cycle of Outrage: America's Reaction to the Juvenile Delinquent in the 1950's* by James Gilbert, copyright © 1986 by Oxford University Press, Inc. Used by permission of Oxford University Press, Inc.

"A Portrait of 'Generation Next': How Young People View Their Lives, Futures and Politics," 1/9/2007, a survey of the Pew Research Center For the People & Press. Reprinted by permission.

Mason, Wyatt. "My Satirical Self: How Making Fun of Absolutely Everything is Defining a Generation" by Wyatt Mason, *The New York Times Sunday Magazine*, 9/17/06. Copyright © 2006 Wyatt Mason. Reprinted by permission.

White, E. B. "Once More to the Lake" from *One Man's Meat*, text copyright © 1941 by E. B. White. Copyright © renewed. Reprinted by permission of Tilbury House, Publishers, Gardiner, Maine.

Martin, Courtney E. Reprinted with permission from Courtney E. Martin. "The Problem with Youth Activism, The American Prospect Online," November 19, 2007. www.prospect.org. The American Prospect, 1710 Rhode Island Avenue NW, 12th Floor, Washington, DC 20036. All rights reserved.

Mead, Margaret, "We Are All Third Generation" from *And Keep Your Powder Dry* by Margaret Mead. Copyright © 1942. Reprinted courtesy of the Institute for Intercultural Studies, Inc. New York.

Crafts, Susan D. Excerpts from *My Music*, copyright © 1993 by Wesleyan University and reprinted by permission of Wesleyan University Press.

Chapter 3   Sizer, Theodore. "What High School Is" from *Horace's Compromise* by Theodore R. Sizer. Copyright © 1984 by Theodore R. Sizer. Reprinted by permission of Houghton Mifflin Harcourt Publishing Company. All rights reserved.

Anyon, Jean. From "Social Class and the Hidden Curriculum of Work" by Jean Anyon from *Journal of Education*, 162.1 (1980), 67–92. Reprinted by permission of the author.

Rodriguez, Richard. "The Achievement of Desire" from *Hunger of Memory*. Reprinted by permission of David R. Godine, Publisher, Inc. Copyright © 1982 by Richard Rodriguez.

Lu, Min-Zhan. "From Silence to Words: Writing as Struggle," by Min-Zhan Lu from *College English*, Vol. 49, No. 4, April 1987, pp. 437–477. Copyright © 1987 by the National Council of Teachers of English. Reprinted with permission.

Jacobs, Jane. "Credentialing vs. Educating" as appeared in *Virginia Quarterly Review: A National Journal of Literature and Discussion*, Spring, 2004, pp. 154–165.

Photo Credits

Chapter 2   Page 48: Big Cheese Photo/Index Stock Imagery, Inc. **Page 97:** Courtesy of U.S. English. **Page 105 (left):** Columbia/The Kobal Collection. **Page 105 (right):** Courtesy Everett Collection. **Page 106:** Warner Bros/The Kobal Collection. **Page 113:** Nina Leen/*Life* Magazine, Copyright © Time Inc./Time & Life Pictures/Getty Images.

Chapter 3   Page 114: "A New York Elementary Classroom, 1942" All The Children, Annual Report of the Superintendent of Schools, City of New York (1942-1943). #70, 217. Courtesy of Teachers College, Columbia University. **Page 136 (top left):** Courtesy of the University of Arizona. **Page 136 (bottom):** Courtesy Russell Sage, design by Rytter Design. **Page 137:** Courtesy Undergraduate Admissions and University Relations/Publication, Virginia Tech. **Page 182 (top):** Courtesy Hampton University Archives. **Page 183:** Jane Addams Memorial Collection (JAMC neg. 613), Special Collections, The University Library, University of Illinois at Chicago. **Page 184:** Copyright © 1956 SEPS: Licensed by Curtis Publishing, Indianapolis, IN. All Rights Reserved. www.curtispublishing.com, Copyright © 2001 The New York Times Company. Reprinted by permission. **Page 193:** Text and illustrations pp. 18-19 from *The New Fun With Dick And Jane* by William S. Gray, et al. illustrated by Keith Ward and Eleanor Campbell, Scott Foresman, 1956.

Chapter 4   Page 194: "Down & Out in Discount America Cover" by Nation Magazine. **Page 202:** Courtesy of Vertamae Grosvenor. **Page 209:** Louvre, Paris/Erich Lessing/Art Resource, NY. **Page 210 (left):** Kunsthistorisches, Vienna, Austria/Erich Lessing/Art Resource, NY. **Page 210 (right):** Chiddingstone Castle Collection. **Page 211 (left):** National Gallery, London/The Art Archive. **Page 211 (top right):** Louvre, Paris/RMN/Art Resource, NY. **Page 212 (left):** Kunsthistorisches, Vienna/RMN/Art Resource, NY. **Page 212 (right):** Private Collection/Erich Lessing/Art Resource, NY. **Page 213:** Hermitage, St. Petersburg, Russia/Scala/Art Resource, NY. **Page 214:** Kunsthistorisches, Vienna/Erich Lessing/Art Resource, NY. **Page 215 (top):** Uffizi, Florence Scala/Art Resource, NY. **Page 215 (bottom):** Musée d'Orsay, Paris/ RMN/Art Resource, NY. **Page 222 (top):** Supplied with permission by The Breast Cancer Research Foundation. **Page 222 (bottom):** newscom. **Page 223 (left):** newscom. **Page 223 (right):** Courtesy of National Fluid Milk Processor Promotion Board (Lowe World Wide). **Page 225:** The Candie's Foundation. **226 (top left):** Courtesy of National Archives. **Page 226 (bottom left):** RAJ Publications, Lakewood, CO. **Page 226 (right):** Courtesy of National Archives. **Page 231:** The Granger Collection. **Page 232 (left):** The Granger Collection. **Page 232 (right):** George Eastman House. **Page 233:** Ruth Orkin. **Page 234:** Bettmann/Corbis. **Page 238 (top left):** Mauritshuis/The Hague/Art Resource, NY. **Page 238 (bottom left):** Courtesy of the artist. **Page 238 (right):** L.H.O.O.Q. by Marcel Duchamp, 1930. Copyright © 2005 Artists Rights Society (ARS), New York/ADAGP, Paris/Succession Marcel Duchamp. Cameraphoto Arte, Venice/Art Resource, NY. **Page 239 (top):** *The Grand Odalisque* by Jean Auguste Dominique Ingres, 1814. Photograph by Herve Lewandoswki/Reunion des Musées Nationaux/Art Resource, NY. **Page 239 (bottom):** Courtesy of Guerrilla Girls. **Page 240:** Patrick McGovern II. **Page 245:** Private Collection.

Chapter 5   Page 246: Courtesy of Nirvana L.L.C. **Page 252 (right):** ultrastar.com. **Page 252 (top):** Isisgallery.org, Copyright © Jamie Reid, www.jamiereid.uk.net (ArcovA Publishing Ltd.). **Page 253:** © wolfgangsvault.com. **Page 254:** Design: Michael Szabo; Art Direction: DB + Scotto. Courtesy of Mike Szabo and N.A.S.A. **Page 256:** AP Images. **Page 270:** Courtesy Sam Potts Inc. **Page 275 (bottom):** benjaminsiegel, a creative commons license. **Page 275 (top):** Imagebroker/Alamy. **Page 276 (bottom):** ilian food and drink/Alamy. **Page 276 (bottom):** becomingsustainable@mac.com. **Page 279:** AP images.

Chapter 6   Page 280: "La Familia" detail from "Chicano Time Trip" by East Los Streetscapers (Wayne Alaniz Healy & David Rivas Botello) 1977. Copyright © SPARC www.sparcmurals.org. **Page 307 (top):** Dan De Kleined/Alamy. **Page 307 (bottom):** Zbigniew Tomaszewski/Alamy Images. **Page 308:** Stan Kujawa/Alamy. **Page 319:** Courtesy of the artist. **Page 320:** Courtesy of the artist. **Page 325-326:** Courtesy Georgetown Historical Society.

Chapter 7   Page 327: Tomine/*The New Yorker,* Copyright © Conde Nast Publications. **Page 371–377:** From *Persepolis: The Story of a Childhood* by Marjane Satrapi, translated by Mattias Ripa & Blake Ferris. **Page 384:** From "Superman" #1 Copyright © 1939 DC Comics. All Rights Reserved. Used with Permission.

Chapter 8   Page 385: *Betty Crocker's Picture Cook Book* by Betty Crocker (Revised and Enlarged) McGraw-Hill Book Company. **Page 400 (top):** Wonder Woman Maria Luisa Romero from the State of Puebla works in a Laundromat in Brooklyn New York. Photo courtesy of Dulce Pinzon, www.dulcepinzon.com. **Page 400 (bottom):** Bernabe Mendez from the State of Guerrero works as a professional window cleaner in New York. Photo courtesy Dulce Pinzon, www.dulcepinzon.com. **Page 401:** Superman Noe Reyes from the State of Puebla works as a delivery boy in Brooklyn New York. Photo courtesy of Dulce Pinzon, www.dulcepinzon.com. **Page 422:** Copyright © 1998, Julian Cardona, Courtesy of Julian Cardona. **Page 423 (top):** Copyright © 1997, Julian Cardona, Courtesy of Julian Cardona. **Page 423 (bottom):** Copyright © 1998, Julian Cardona, Courtesy of Julian Cardona. **Page 424:** Copyright © 1998, Julian Cardona, Courtesy of Julian Cardona. **Page 435:** Lewis W. Hine, Courtesy George Eastman House.

Chapter 9   Page 437: Alfred Stieglitz's "The Steerage," 1907, Library of Congress. **Page 453:** Museum of the City of New York/Getty Images. **Page 454:** AP Images. **Page 455:** Minnesota Historical Society. **Page 474 (top):** Courtesy of Warren Neidich. **Page 474 (bottom):** Courtesy of Warren Neidich. **Page 475 (top):** Courtesy of Warren Neidich. **Page 475 (bottom):** Courtesy of Warren Neidich. **Page 502 (top):** George Eastman House/Getty Images. **Page 502 (bottom):** AP Images. **Page 503:** AP Images. **Page 504 (top):** Goran Tomasevic/Reuters/Corbis. **Page 504 (bottom):** Larry Downing/Reuters/Corbis. **Page 505 (top):** AP Images. **Page 505 (bottom left):** AFP/Getty Images. **Page 505 (bottom right):** AP Images. **Page 511–512:** Mount Zion Museum.

Chapter 10   Page 513: Photo courtesy Sage Evans. **Page 516:** Photography by Amitava Kumar. **Page 541–542:** Archaeological Museum, Lima/Gianni Dagli Orti/The Art Archive. **Page 543:** The Granger Collection. **Page 550 (both):** Courtesy of Coc Fusco, Photography by Peter Barker. **Page 551:** Courtesy of Jack Shainman Gallery, New York. **Page 552:** Courtesy of the artist and of Deitch Projects. **Page 556:** Courtesy of the artist and of Deitch Projects. **Page 563:** International Institute of Social History, Amsterdam. **Page 564:** Favianna Rodriguez/www.favianna.com. **Page 566 (top):** *The Snake Charmer* by Jean-Leon Gerome, circa 1880. Oil on canvas. 1995.51. Sterling and Francine Clark Art Institute, Williamstown, Massachusetts, USA. **Page 566 (bottom):** *The Slave Market* by by Jean-Leon Gerome, circa 1866. Oil on canvas. 1955.53. Sterling and Francine Clark Art Institute, Williamstown, Massachusetts, USA.

Index

Note to reader: All titles (of text selections, books, magazines, newspapers, television shows, movies, and songs) are printed in italic type. Names of authors of text selections are printed in bold type. Names of images are printed in regular type.